FOUNDATIONS OF ACCOUNTING THEORY AND POLICY

A READER

FOUNDATIONS OF ACCOUNTING THEORY AND POLICY

A READER

Robert Bloom, Ph.D.
JOHN CARROLL UNIVERSITY

Pieter T. Elgers, D.B.A.,C.P.A.
UNIVERSITY OF MASSACHUSETTS

The Dryden Press
Harcourt Brace College Publishers

Fort Worth   Philadelphia   San Diego   New York   Orlando   Austin   San Antonio
Toronto   Montreal   London   Sydney   Tokyo

Acquisitions Editors	Elizabeth Storey, Bill Teague
Developmental Editor	Craig Avery
Project Editors	Emily Thompson, Matt Ball
Art Directors	Beverly Baker, Linda Miller
Production Manager	Ann Coburn
Photo & Permissions Editor	Elizabeth Banks
Product Manager	Annie Todd
Marketing Coordinator	Sam Stubblefield
Copy Editor	Katherine M. Morse
Composition	Thompson Type
Text Type	10/12 Bembo

Address for orders:
The Dryden Press
6277 Sea Harbor Drive
Orlando, FL 32887-6777
1-800-782-4479 or 1-800-433-0001 (in Florida)

Address for editorial correspondence:
The Dryden Press
301 Commerce Street, Suite 3700
Fort Worth, TX 76102

ISBN: 0-03-010422-X

Library of Congress Catalog Card Number: 94-71735

Printed in the United States of America

4 5 6 7 8 9 0 1 2 3 039 9 8 7 6 5 4 3 2 1

The Dryden Press
Harcourt Brace College Publishers

THE DRYDEN PRESS SERIES IN ACCOUNTING

AUDITING

Rittenberg and Schwieger
Auditing: Concepts for a Changing Environment

Guy, Alderman, and Winters
Auditing
Third Edition

THEORY

Bloom and Elgers
Foundations of Accounting Theory and Policy: A Reader

Bloom and Elgers
Issues in Accounting Theory and Policy: A Reader

Belkaoui
Accounting Theory
Third Edition

TAXATION

Everett, Raabe, and Fortin
1995 Income Tax Fundamentals

Duncan
Essentials of U.S. Taxation
Second Edition

REFERENCE

Williams and Miller
Miller Comprehensive GAAP Guide
College Edition

Miller and Bailey
Miller Comprehensive GAAS Guide
College Edition

GOVERNMENTAL AND NOT-FOR-PROFIT

Douglas
Governmental and Nonprofit Accounting: Theory and Practice
Second Edition

Ziebell and DeCoster
Management Control Systems in Nonprofit Organizations

THE HARCOURT BRACE COLLEGE OUTLINE SERIES

Campbell, Grierson, and Taylor
Principles of Accounting I
Revised Edition

Emery
Principles of Accounting II

Emery
Intermediate Accounting I
Second Edition

Emery
Intermediate Accounting II

Frigo
Cost Accounting

Poteau
Advanced Accounting

PREFACE

Foundations of Accounting Theory and Policy: A Reader is essentially a new book. Its predecessor, *Accounting Theory and Policy: A Reader* (both the first and second editions), has evolved into two new volumes, each directed to a different audience. The *Foundations* book, which emphasizes theory rather than issues, has been created to appeal to students enrolled in theory courses at any university, whether in the United States or abroad. The second volume, *Issues in Accounting Policy: A Reader,* which emphasizes contemporary issues rather than theory, is directed toward 150-hour schools, and to M.B.A. and M.S. programs, also in the United States and abroad. Both books draw upon articles from academic and professional journals, although the *Foundations* book consists largely of articles from mainstream academic journals. The *Foundations* and *Issues* volumes contain approximately thirty selections each. Because no article appears in both volumes, they may be used together in a single course that addresses both theory and issues.

The articles selected for *Foundations* emphasize the role of accounting theory in accounting policy decisions. Several articles provide discussions of the criteria by which competing theories might be validated or discarded. Among the topics examined in this book are the measurement of assets and liabilities, international problems in financial reporting, and not-for-profit accounting. The editors wish to emphasize that the articles included in this volume are intended to persuade the reader that, though necessary in the accounting policy decision process, accounting theory is not sufficient—new theories and pertinent findings in related fields such as economics, finance, and the behavioral sciences have implications for both the subject matter and methodology of accounting.

The book consists of two parts. Part I deals with the foundations of accounting theory, including the following six sections: (A) the nature of accounting policy decisions; (B) the nature of accounting theory and history; (C) selected normative theories; (D) positive accounting theory; (E) postulates, principles, and the conceptual framework; and (F) market efficiency and economic consequences. Part II, which examines basic issues in accounting policy, consists of five sections: (A) an overview of issues in financial reporting; (B) definitions and measurement of income; (C) measurement of assets and liabilities; (D) international issues in financial reporting; and (E) not-for-profit accounting.

We have selected articles primarily on the basis of how provocative and stimulating they are, not for their compatibility with our own views. Our intent is to provide a catalyst for discussion rather than to present, or lead the reader to, our own conclusions. For the same reason, our interstitial comments on individual articles are descriptive rather than evaluative.

The editors most gratefully acknowledge the invaluable suggestions and comments of the following professors on the original outlines for both the *Foundations* and the *Issues* books:

Jeffrey Cohen, Boston College (United States)

Haim Falk, McMaster University (Canada)

Jayne Fuglister, Cleveland State University (United States)

Michael J. R. Gaffikin, University of Wollongong (Australia)

Eugene Imhoff, University of Michigan (United States)

Ross G. Jennings, University of Texas at Austin (United States)

Mayh Lo, Western New England College (United States)

K. V. Peasnell, University of Lancaster (United Kingdom)

Etzmun S. Rozen, Cleveland State University (United States)

Daniel B. Thornton, University of Calgary (Canada)

CONTENTS

CONTENTS

FOUNDATIONS OF ACCOUNTING THEORY AND POLICY

A READER

FOUNDATIONS OF ACCOUNTING THEORY

Focusing on accounting theory and policy in a decision-making context, this book exposes readers to the dilemmas confronted by accounting policy makers such as the Financial Accounting Standards Board, the Accounting Standards Board of the Canadian Institute of Chartered Accountants, and the Accounting Standards Board in England and Wales. Accounting theory is not an end in itself. Theories reflect either descriptive or prescriptive behavior—the way individuals or firms do act or the way they should act. Accounting policy making consists of developing accounting standards guided by a basic theoretical framework of financial reporting. It is therefore important to understand accounting theory in order to examine accounting policy decisions, which have economic, political, and social consequences.

The papers included in Part I provide a frame of reference for evaluating the specific accounting theories and issues covered in Part II. Part I consists of six sections, A through F. In Section A, "Accounting Policy Decisions," there are three papers. The initial paper by Sunder (1988) considers the economics of accounting standardization along with particular criteria for selecting standards. He discusses various mechanisms for formulating standards such as common law, market, referendum, legislature, judiciary, and bureaucracy. The author offers ideas on future standard-setting practices, favoring a broadly representative standard-setting body, with a legislative structure as opposed to a bureaucracy. Regardless of this body's mechanism, Sunder observes that the ability to formulate socially optimal principles is limited.

May and Sundem (1976) provide a means of examining the accounting policy-setting process. They contend that the most auspicious benefit of accounting policy research is to assist in formulating theories for policy choices. Viewing such theories in a social context, May and Sundem point to the role of political organizations such as the Financial Accounting Standards Board (FASB) in affecting social welfare. According to the authors, in light of ignorance about individual and collective decision-making processes, a social ordering of accounting policies cannot be set forth. Nevertheless, May and Sundem discuss various research strategies that may help to enlighten the policy decision. These strategies include security price-based research, a priori research, sensitivity of accounting time-series, modeling individual and aggregate decision making, and behavioral research with regard to empirical studies on association of accounting data with security prices.

Walker (1988) provides an analysis of the literature on information economics and its principal implications for accounting. The paper deals with the social benefits of furnishing public information, including extending the range of trading opportunities, improving production and investment decisions, and reducing expenditures associated with the generation of private information. According to Walker, information economics has not provided an adequate theory of income measurement or commercially sensitive information, not to mention having failed to resolve the arguments for and against regulation.

Section B, "Nature of Accounting Theory and History," consists of five papers. Lee (1990) reviews the historical evolution of accounting, interpreting changes in accounting education, practice, and research from a social-systems perspective. The author begins with an analysis of "early times," up to 1000 A.D., and then considers the Renaissance, followed by modern industrialization and professionalization. Over time, accounting has changed in some respects in response to changing environmental circumstances. Key changes have included the "site" of accounting, from individuals to corporations, accompanied by a separation of ownership from management. Additionally, accounting has come to be used in modern times as a tool for evaluating human performance. Lee argues that the accounting education framework has been a major factor in establishing monopolistic control over accountants. The author also asserts that accountants have organized in an effort to wield control over their services.

Beaver, Kennelly, and Voss (1968) argue that alternative accounting measurements are similar to competing scientific hypotheses, and thus may be evaluated based upon their ability to predict events of interest to decision makers. The authors caution that this predictive ability criterion is not to be interpreted as an indiscriminate search for a method of accounting that maximizes some measure of statistical association. Accounting theory has an important role to play, because it explains why a given association exists and enables the researcher to generalize from the sample data to a new set of observations.

Staubus (1985) argues that there is no descriptive theory of accounting measurement. After examining accounting measurement practices, he focuses on the role of eight basic accounting measures. Such measures deal with aspects of the wealth, liquidity, and risks of the entity. These measures are characterized by such attributes as stability of the income item in question, conservatism, flexibility, and to a lesser extent economy, understandability, reliability, and comparability. According to Staubus, without observed market prices for particular assets and liabilities, accounting tends to simulate those prices.

Wells (1976) contends that accounting theories are similar to scientific theories, although the former deal with financial rather than physical phenomena. This leads Wells, drawing upon Kuhn, to interpret the apparent disarray in accounting theory as a war of competing paradigms, which is a prerequisite and a harbinger of theoretical progress. A priori research, in particular, constitutes an important step in the revolution in accounting thought.

Watts and Zimmerman (1979) assert that accounting theory is an economic good and, as such, is subject to the forces of supply and demand. The authors contend that the demand for accounting theories pertains to the demand for rationales or excuses. These rationales are couched in terms of the "public interest," but actually reflect the needs of particular parties who lobby for specific accounting standards. The function of accounting theories is to supply excuses which, in turn, satisfy the demand engendered by political processes. Watts and Zimmerman hypothesize that there are three functions of accounting theories: *pedagogic* demand, *information* demand, and *justification* demand. In a government-regulated economy, the most prominent demand, in their view, is the justification demand, because the government needs to justify its actions. The authors then provide historical evidence to corroborate their hypothesis that accounting theories are used to buttress governmental intervention, for example, railroad legislation, income tax acts, and the Securities Acts of 1933–1934. In all cases cited, relevant accounting theories appeared subsequent to governmental intervention. Watts and Zimmerman conclude that no one theory of accounting will ever be able to explain or justify accounting standards, due to the nature and diversity of the demand function.

Section C, "Selected Normative Theories," presents four papers. Sterling (1972) evaluates different accounting valuation models—historical cost, replacement cost, exit values, and discounted cash flows—and concludes that exit-value accounting is the best in terms of furnishing useful information for decision making. Exit values "are necessary to define market alternatives, they express the investment required to hold assets, and they are a component of a risk factor." Accordingly, Sterling concludes the balance sheet and income statement should reflect exit values.

The next selection is Chambers's (1975) paper on "continuously contemporary accounting," which constitutes an amalgam of exit values and constant-dollar "capital maintenance" adjustments. Chambers compares the constant-dollar, replacement-cost, and exit-value models, asserting that neither general price-level accounting nor current-value accounting is a complete method of accounting for changing prices. Continuously contemporary accounting is advocated to deal with both changes in particular prices and general price-level changes.

Revsine (1970) furnishes a comparative analysis of economic income and replacement-cost income. In perfect competition, both models provide the same income. Revsine reaches the conclusion from his a priori research that, under certain assumptions, replacement-cost income may be viewed as a surrogate of economic income, with a view toward providing data for predicting long-run, cost-flow changes.

Bradford (1974) is critical of the general price-level accounting model because it fails to consider anticipated inflation in interest rates and differences in return on different monetary assets and liabilities. Using the Fisher-Kessel-Alchian analysis of wealth redistribution, Bradford observes that if the interest rate on monetary items fully anticipates inflation, then the firm will neither lose nor gain from holding monetary items. Consequently, purchasing power gains and losses in the general price-level accounting model may well furnish misleading information.

Section D, "Positive Accounting Theory," offers two papers presenting opposite viewpoints. Watts and Zimmerman (1990) evaluate positive accounting literature, which attempts to describe accounting practice, by considering the factors and costs underlying choices in accounting policy decisions. To achieve particular objectives, choices are made with respect to particular accounting methods. Positive accounting studies have emphasized the importance of contracting costs (information, agency, bankruptcy, and lobbying). Tests of the theory have been stock-price oriented, examining changes in stock prices in response to accounting changes; or accounting-choice oriented, explaining the choice of a single accounting method. Watts and Zimmerman respond to criticism of research on positive accounting and suggest future research, calling for closer linkage between theory and empirical tests.

Chambers (1993) offers a scathing critique of positive accounting theory. Its proponents rely upon the efficient market hypothesis and the capital-asset pricing model, which Chambers argues are abstract notions about aggregate markets and thus cannot be used to explain individual investors' actions. Additionally, positive accounting is based on a misunderstanding of both the theory of the firm and the theory of government regulation. Chambers criticizes the "self-interest premise underlying positive accounting," asserting that "[this] affirmation is not independently testable, and can therefore yield no scientifically acceptable explanation of the observed behaviour, no generalization that is empirically supportable." Chambers observes the efforts made by positive accounting researchers to glorify their own set of propositions and denigrate other theories. He also maintains that the results of positive accounting research have been contradictory and inconclusive.

Section E, "Postulates, Principles, and the Conceptual Framework," contains four papers. Chambers (1963) asserts that accounting has not been developed in a systematic fashion with regard to general truths or postulates. He defines a postulate as "[a]ny proposition descriptive of the environment . . . fundamentally necessary to support a conclusion, a principle or a practice. . . ." A statement of postulates should furnish guidelines for resolving accounting problems. Every practice in accounting is implicitly based on postulates. One way of deriving postulates is from observing and describing practices followed and discovering ideas inherent in those practices. Another way is to set forth the postulates by logical reasoning and test them in the business environment. Accounting principles can be formulated from postulates by considering the usefulness and implications of the postulates.

Peasnell (1982) sets forth the rationale for a conceptual framework of financial reporting. In his view, the United States has a greater need than the United Kingdom for a conceptual framework because of differences in the standard-setting processes of these two countries. Setting accounting standards in Britain is more of a bargaining process than in the United States, where the Securities and Exchange Commission oversees this work. Peasnell argues that a conceptual framework is most appropriate where both the responsibility and power for establishing accounting standards are given to one specific body, which is the case in Canada. The author asserts that a conceptual framework should at least furnish "the basic principles of, and sources of authority which financial reports are intended to have (and to avoid); the trade-offs which have to be made." A conceptual framework cannot, however, eliminate conflicts over perceived differences about the consequences of accounting standards.

Dopuch and Sunder (1980) provide a critical review of FASB *Statement of Financial Accounting Concepts No. 1* (1978) and of the exposure draft on the elements of financial statements. The authors judge these documents, as well as their antecedents, to be failures because they are unlikely to help resolve the specific accounting issues. The authors suggest a set of modest objectives for the FASB itself, primarily directed toward achieving compromise solutions to accounting issues, based on consideration of the interests of affected groups in society.

Miller (1985) examines several myths associated with the FASB's conceptual framework. He asserts that such a framework serves to describe existing practice, prescribe future practice, and define terminology and issues. However, there are conflicts among these goals, due to a lack of consensus among concerned parties. Three of the eight myths that Miller criticizes follow:

1. A conceptual framework will lead to consistent standards.
2. A conceptual framework will eliminate the problem of standards overload.
3. The FASB's conceptual framework captures only the status quo of accounting practices.

The conceptual framework is a "political document" rather than "a purely conceptual effort." It is flexible rather than rigid. In Miller's view, it has served to assist the FASB in its deliberations and to improve communications with its constituents.

The final section of Part I, "Market Efficiency and Economic Consequences," includes three papers. Beaver (1973) develops a set of objectives for the FASB based upon a large body of empirical research suggesting that capital markets are reasonably "efficient," in the sense that security prices behave as if they reflect all publicly available information. Beaver's interpretation of this evidence suggests that many current controversies in accounting are "much ado about nothing." Many issues in financial reporting can be readily resolved through disclosure. Accordingly, the substantive questions concern what information should be publicly disclosed and whether accounting reports are the best medium for disclosing this information.

Lev (1988) argues that disclosure of financial information should be regulated owing to inequity in capital markets. This inequity causes social consequences, such as high transaction costs, thin markets, low liquidity, and reduced trading gains. The author adopts an "equity" perspective in terms of equality of opportunity, thereby providing accounting policy makers and researchers with a public-interest orientation. Lev contends that uninformed investors take defensive actions to guard against exploitation and that such actions have adverse social consequences. Therefore, the information advantage of informed investors must be reduced, if not eliminated.

Zeff (1978) suggests that the recent prominence of arguments based on the economic consequences of accounting standards reflects a veritable revolution in accounting thought. Individuals and groups have been criticizing proposed standards based on their own perceived self-interests. The FASB, among other standard-setting bodies, should be expected to research the possible negative economic consequences of its proposed actions, even though accounting principles and fair presentation should continue to be the foundations for accounting policy decisions. Zeff argues that the FASB would be replaced as the standard-setting body in the United States if it were to formulate accounting standards only in terms of economic consequences.

ACCOUNTING POLICY DECISIONS

I-A1

POLITICAL ECONOMY OF ACCOUNTING STANDARDS

Shyam Sunder

How do we set the accounting standards? The topic has received much attention during the past 50 years. Perhaps the first step toward a satisfactory resolution of the problem is to recognize that the problem of standardization is not unique to accounting. There are approximately five hundred standard-setting organizations in the United States alone and many more in other countries, setting standards for everything from ships to shoe laces. In addition, there are international bodies that set standards for things such as radio transmissions that are applicable across the national boundaries. An examination of the standardization of accounting in the larger context of standardization of a variety of products and services may help us appreciate the costs, benefits, limitations, and economics of standardization.

After a brief review of the economics of standardization, I discuss criteria for choosing standards and the problem of devising social mechanisms to set socially optimal standards. I shall review the basic characteristics of six mechanisms—common law, market, referendum, legislature, judiciary, and bureaucracy. This theoretical overview of the economics and mechanisms of standardization prepares the groundwork for a critical examination of some stylized facts of accounting standard setting in the United States and leads me to make a few suggestions on how we might set standards in the future.

Shyan Sunder, "Political Economy of Accounting Standards," *Journal of Accounting Literature,* November 1988, 31–41. Reprinted by permission of the Journal of Accounting Literature.

I. Economics of Standardization

It is costly to keep inventories, to gather information, and to negotiate contracts. Our inclination to cut these costs is one source of our desire to standardize.

Take, for example, the design of an electrical wall receptacle. There are many possible designs for this small fitting and in different parts of the world different designs are used. In North America the design of wall outlets for 110 volt house current has been standardized. It enables us to plug any of the numerous appliances and electrical devices into any outlet. Standardization of wall outlets and matching adapters leads to economy in the inventory of adapters and outlets. This is true of thousands of articles of daily use whose standardization we take for granted and without which modern life would be very cumbersome if not impossible.

Standardization is common not only for products but also for the language of communication. Air and maritime traffic and international mails are two obvious examples. English has been standardized as the international language of communication between aircraft pilots and ground control. A Soviet pilot approaching Paris airport must communicate with ground control in English. Cost of confusion due to miscommunication is simply too high in such circumstances.

We are familiar with the problems that arise from the absence of standardization. If only my Macintosh could talk to my IBM PC. A Soviet spaceship carried an experiment designed by a U.S. physicist, Professor Simpson, to measure the dust in the tail of Halley's comet. The professor discovered to his dismay that the Soviet computer systems and communications gear were designed using fundamentally different standards and months of additional work was necessary before the U.S.-designed equipment could work satisfactorily with the Soviet communication systems and transmit data to the Earth.

High cost, or infeasibility, of gathering information by some agents in society also induces creation of some standards as rules by which a social game is played. Standards that prevent many people from performing surgery, cutting hair, or teaching accounting are often justified on the grounds that they are meant for the protection of the uninformed patients, customers, or students who may find it costly or impossible to discriminate between the competents and the crooks. Such standards, the argument goes, protect the informationally weak and enhance social welfare by promoting mutual trust and reducing the need for private investment in gathering information. Since the argument often originates with the professionals who clearly benefit from its acceptance, its validity is suspect in specific instances but not in general.

In spite of these benefits of standardization and the costs and inconveniences caused by its absence, standardization is neither universal nor complete. We do have many different models of cars, many computer languages, many types of doctors, and even more than one type of electrical outlet. There are at least two reasons why standardization is rarely taken to the extreme. First, saving costs is not the only motivation an industry has to standardize; standardization can also be used as a mechanism to limit competition and restrain trade. Second, while standardization may save some costs, it may impose others. Anticompetitive effects of standards can be a major factor for many types of industrial products but this does not appear to be the case for accounting methods. The cost of standardization provides a satisfactory explanation for limitations on the extent of standardization, as far as accounting methods are concerned. Hence, we shall concentrate our attention on the cost motive.

The standard home or office electrical outlet is designed to safely carry a current of 15 amperes. Appliances that need less than 15 amperes of current could work satisfactorily with an outlet of a lighter design that need not use as much metal or insulation as provided in the standard device. A standardized device necessarily wastes resources by providing too much for some applications and too little for others. Hence the need for a few 220 volt outlets in some homes. No standardized product can be completely satisfactory for all purposes.

Standardization, by definition, raises the cost of deviant behavior and thus stifles initiative, experimentation, and innovation. Products or technologies that are standardized too early burden society with inefficient, costly, or less desirable systems. The system of weights and measures and the television broadcast technology in the United States are two good examples of this disadvantage of standardization.

One must also consider the cost of devising, disseminating, enforcing, and updating standards. Standardization requires the creation and operation of a centralized institution whose costs must be paid for by someone. These costs can be substantial. Moreover, many standards are public goods in the sense that it does not cost more to allow one more party to use a standard and it is difficult to keep the benefits of standardization from those who are unwilling to pay for them. Just because standardization to an extent is desirable in some areas, it does not follow that it is good in all areas or that it should be carried to the maximum possible extent. Nor is it always possible to devise effective mechanisms to collect the costs of standardization from its beneficiaries.

OPTIMALITY OF STANDARDS

The costs and benefits of standards are unevenly distributed across members of a community; some receive a large share of benefits while others may carry a large burden of the costs. What kind of standard is socially desirable? There is no obvious answer to this question. Consider two possibilities.

One may argue that we should implement standards whose total benefits to all members of the society exceed the total costs borne by all the members. In other words, standards that increase the *size* of the "social pie" are desirable. This criterion implies that if depriving the poor of one dollar allows us to add one more Rolls Royce to the fleet of the rich, such action is socially desirable. Such a social welfare criterion is ethically unacceptable to many of us in the twentieth century.

An alternative to the social cost benefit criterion is the Pareto criterion. It is based on the idea that a standard that hurts anyone in the society cannot be acceptable as an improvement over the status quo. The Pareto criterion pays attention not only to the size of the social pie but also to its distribution among individual members of the society. It is hard to dispute this criterion on ethical grounds. However, its application places an almost impossible burden on those who set the standards. It is not easy to think of a law, rule, or standard that hurts nobody.

As a practical matter, it is necessary to compromise and consider both the *total* costs and benefits as well as the *distribution* of the costs and benefits of a standard across individual members of society. In other words, we cannot completely ignore the size of the pie. Nor can we completely ignore who gets how large a piece of it. Some standards get implemented because of their distributional consequences even though their net benefit may be negative. Some are justified on the basis of large net benefit to society even though some individuals may be hurt by the action.

PROBLEMS OF IDENTIFYING THE SOCIAL OPTIMAL

Even if all agree upon a criterion for choosing standards, the practical task of identifying which one of the proposed alternatives best satisfies this criterion remains to be addressed. And it is a nontrivial task for several reasons.

First, standard setters do not know which standard is better and for whom. Data on preferences of people involved must be gathered or inferred by some means. We can do so by one of three ways: (1) ask people what they prefer; (2) infer what they prefer from what they do; or (3) logically derive the preferences from other things known about them. Each of the three approaches has its own shortcomings.

When we ask people what standard, if any, they prefer, they may not know or they may not be willing truthfully to reveal to us what they prefer. Suppose the practice or design proposed to be standardized is new and unfamiliar to them. People often do not know if they prefer the new proposal to the current practice. It takes use and familiarity for a person to find out if a new proposal is good or bad for him. Mere technical description is simply not enough. Few people buy cars on the basis of blueprints. Even if they know what they prefer, it may not be in their own best interest to tell us what they prefer or why they do so. Responses to public surveys can often become an exercise in public relations and posturing. Market research conducted before the introduction of "New Coke" is a good example. The story goes that people prefer sweeter soft drinks in blind tests but are unwilling to admit that they do so.

One can try to infer from the past actions of constituents what their preferences are or try logically to derive these preferences from some theory about their behavior. Both these techniques are only as good as the theories employed in the process. As often as not, they lead one to wrong conclusions about what other people may like.

Second, it is costly to participate in the process of standardization. Constituents who respond to the invitations from standard-setting bodies are likely to be those who foresee either large gains or large losses for themselves from the actions of such bodies. Constituents for whom these amounts are small at the individual level but large in aggregate may organize themselves into lobbying groups provided that the cost of organizing is not too large. Others for whom the costs of organizing dominate the cost/benefits of standardization will simply not find it worth their while to participate in the process even if the number of such individuals is very large and in aggregate the impact of standards on their welfare is large. Volunteered participation in standard setting therefore tends to be unbalanced.

Third, after gathering data on what various people like, the standard-setting body has to pull it all together and apply a social welfare criterion to determine which standard, if any, will best serve that society. The problem is that formal aggregation of data requires quantification of costs and benefits. This is rarely feasible, and almost never feasible for both costs and benefits with equal accuracy. For example, the cost of a standard may be quantifiable but the benefits may be so diffuse as to make it impossible to place a dollar figure on them. A concrete comparison of costs and benefits is often ruled out for this reason.

II. MECHANISMS FOR MAKING SOCIAL DECISIONS

The difficulties of choosing a social welfare criterion and of identifying the socially optimal standards are pervasive. We have had to devise, over the centuries, a variety of mechanisms to make social decisions. Roughly speaking we could classify such mechanisms into six categories, though as a practical matter, actual social decision mechanisms frequently combine elements of more than one of these systems. We shall call them common law, market, referendum, legislative, judicial, and bureaucratic mechanisms.

The common law or grass roots approach to making social decisions does not require a centralized mechanism; it is the ultimate in decentralization. It is also slow. It is ineffective in making highly technical choices that cannot be widely distinguished by laymen. Paciolo's accounting text could perhaps be seen as common law rules of accounting. Societies which do not have publicly owned enterprises seem to be reasonably well served by this system. However, introduction of more complex organization, such as publicly held enterprises, places demands on accounting systems that cannot easily be met by the common law approach.

Market mechanisms can provide efficient solutions for the problems of production and distribution of private goods. Standards for the traded goods define the rules of the game by which the markets are governed. As rules of the game, product standards themselves are public goods because once they are implemented all can share in their costs and benefits. One can conceive of a competition among alternative sets of rules of the market (e.g., the computerized stock exchange at Cincinnati vs. the New York Stock Exchange with a trading floor). These alternative sets are public goods and no exchange market can exist for them and the choice of rules or standards must be arrived at by some social choice mechanism. To the extent the form of exchange in the product market is left to be specified by the participants, they may be found to overwhelmingly prefer one form over another. In such cases, one may use the evidence from the product market to introduce a new rule limiting transactions to the preferred form. Current accounting standards leave many aspects of financial reporting to the discretion of those who prepare, audit, or read the results. If a standard-setting body used evidence about choices made by reporting entities as an input to their decisions, it might be said to have used the market mechanism.

In a referendum voters speak for themselves. Referenda as social decision mechanisms are effective when the formulation of alternatives is simple and readily understandable by the constituents. When the formulation stage itself becomes important or when the technical nature of the alternatives renders it difficult for a large number of individuals to comprehend their consequences, direct voting becomes ineffective as a mechanism for making social decisions.

In legislative systems, constituent groups select or elect their representatives to speak on their behalf. A legislature takes action only if it is feasible to do so within its rules of order. If, for example, such a body cannot find majority support for any of the proposals on the table and its rules of order require a majority support to pass a resolution, no resolution is passed. Debate in legislative bodies is frequently partisan because the representatives are expected to, and do, argue in favor of the interests of their respective constituents. Attempts to protect one's own turf are not stigmatized in legislative settings.

The judicial model stands in sharp contrast to the legislative model in the sense that the members of the bench are expected to be impartial judges who listen to the partisan arguments presented before them and then decide on the basis of law or equity. Unlike the legislators, the judges are not supposed to have a partisan interest in the issues at hand. Also, unlike the legislative system, they must decide one way or the other on the issues presented before them. They do not usually enjoy the luxury to "pass."

Judicial and legislative mechanisms rarely stand alone and are frequently accompanied by bureaucratic support. However, some standard-setting mechanisms are almost purely bureaucratic. I return later to some problems of bureaucratic mechanisms.

As we move from common law to bureaucratic mechanism, fewer and fewer people are directly involved in making decisions, more of the power of an organized state is brought to enforce the decisions, decisions can be made and enforced more expeditiously, and the chances of making serious errors increase. Historically, this has been the direction of change in the United States.

III. STANDARD SETTING IN THE UNITED STATES

An examination of accounting standard setting in the United States suggests use of a variety of social decision mechanisms during the past quarter century. The Accounting Principles Board (APB) followed a quasi-legislative model. Some twenty-one members of the Board served part-time on the Board while holding other full-time jobs. With the possible exception of some accounting professors, members had a defined constituency. As in other legislative settings, these members were often expected to, and even tried to, advance the interests of their firms or clients through their participation in the Board's activities. Advocacy of self-interest does not bear a stigma in the legislative setting. No "punishment" for such advocacy was built into the system. As in legislatures, the Board took no action unless sufficient support (two-thirds majority under its rules of order) could be garnered in favor.

A major feature of the APB, and arguably a major source of its problems as a legislative mechanism, was its lack of representativeness. The Board consisted entirely of the members of the American Institute of Certified Public Accountants (AICPA). Most of the members were from public accounting with token representation allowed for the securities industry and academia.

The Wheat Commission appointed by the AICPA in the wake of the investment tax credit fiasco blamed the dissatisfaction of some people with the performance of the APB on the lack of independence of its members. Since the lack of independence of the legislators from their constituents is the essence of the legislative process, the Commission in effect condemned the legislative process as a mechanism for setting accounting standards. Instead, the commission proposed its replacement by a quasi-judicial structure of the FASB. They failed to recognize that the APB's lack of representativeness was its major weakness. Accordingly, the FASB, born in 1973, retained the unrepresentativeness of the APB but not the inherent protective immunity of a quasi-legislative system. In fixing what they thought was a defect, the Wheat Commission had taken away a major strength of the accounting standard-setting system in the United States.

A second crucial change was made: the Board was burdened with the responsibility to find, pay for, and keep employed a large and more or less permanent bureaucracy. Though the individuals appointed to the Board have consistently met the highest standards of competence and commitment to public service, often at considerable personal sacrifice, the basic structural defects of the FASB continue to impede its effectiveness.

The quasi-judicial structure of the FASB placed on seven individuals the burden of having to make and defend difficult judgments on accounting standards. The judgments they make often damage the interests of at least some of their constituents who pay for the cost of maintaining the FASB's establishment. The members of the FASB have precious little armor to defend themselves except to say that they vote according to the best of their personal judgment.

Unlike the members of the FASB, the justices of the Supreme Court have the opportunity to rely on common, case, statutory, and constitutional law to support the positions they take. FASB has no such luxury available to it. Its attempt to develop a conceptual framework as the accounting equivalent of constitutional law foundered on the rocks of its refusal to recognize the fundamental distributional consequences (i.e., the political aspect) of its actions. Legislative bodies do not have to defend their actions; their representative character and the partisan attitudes of their members constitute a protective cover for them. The AICPA's insistence that a clear majority of the members of the FASB be drawn from the ranks of practicing CPAs deprived the FASB of this vital cover in its infancy.

The first eight years of the FASB were characterized by a runaway pace of standard setting, aggressiveness (i.e., the willingness of the Board to recommend previously untried methods of accounting as exclusive standards), and a decline in constituent support. All three features can be traced to the fundamental structural characteristics of the organization.

The quasi-judicial structure of the Board made it difficult to refuse to issue standards on accounting matters brought before them. The guaranteed support of the disciplinary mechanism of the AICPA made the Board less cautious about whether their standards would be broadly accepted by their constituencies. The size of a permanent establishment of some hundred to hundred and fifty people made it even more difficult for them to refuse to issue a standard. Those who pay for this establishment expect to see performance. How else can a standard-setting body show performance?

There is something fundamentally incongruous about a permanent rule-making bureaucracy. Once you set up such an organization, you have to live with its cumulative output of rules. No such bureaucracy can afford the luxury of appearing to sit idle. Imagine, if you can, a period of a few years over which no new accounting problems that deserve to have a new standard issued are brought before the Board. Can the Board afford not to issue any rulings for a period of several years and expect various donors to continue to support a ten million dollar budget and employment of a large staff? The point is not that the members of the Board or the staff knowingly and deliberately engage in make-work; the point is that there exist strong incentives in the structure of a full-time board supported by a permanent staff to keep itself busy dealing with issues brought to their attention. Until the money or staff run out, there are no incentives to ask hard questions about whether a given project needs attention and what its priority level ought to be.

Indeed, the annual report of the FASB (and its parent organization, Financial Accounting Foundation) is built around the statistics of how many discussion memoranda, exposure drafts, or standards were issued during the reporting period and how many letters were received or how many hearings were held. These data, along with Gantt charts of project completion targets and punctuality figures, replace the revenue and profit figures of corporate annual reports as measures of accomplishment. Once such statistics are compiled and reported, it is only a small step to the illusion that more and faster is better. After all, bureaucracies, too, need measures of performance. Performance data for a rule-making bureaucracy consist of the number, pages, frequency, or promptness of the rules issued.

Sale of the Board's publications at prices significantly above the marginal cost of printing and mailing makes things even worse. Approximately one-half of the Board's budget is earned from such sales. The origins of this system probably lie in a common sense equity criterion; those who benefit from the activities of the Board should be the ones to pay for its fixed cost. This fixed cost is allocated among the constituents in proportion to their demand for publications simply because this demand is conveniently measured through the requests received at the publications office. However, this convenient and apparently harmless system induces perverse incentives at the organizational level. Those who have to worry about the Board's payroll, rent, and utilities cannot help but keep a wary eye on the revenue from the sale of publications. At its worst, publish or perish in academia keeps a few photocopying machines busy and the professors out of mischief; in standardization of accounting (or of anything else) the damage is more extensive.

Such a system of performance measurement does not serve the basic function of standard-setting organizations well. Recall that standards themselves can have positive or negative net social benefit and can have extensive distributive consequences. Proclamation of a standard per se has no social value unless the standard has been carefully tailored to meet a specified social welfare criterion. Indeed, a bias for action on the part of a standard-setting bureaucracy can impose substantial costs of adjustment and confusion on the constituents. FASB's performance and annual reports (over the years) revealed a bias for action during the first eight years of its existence when a more neutral stance might have been a socially preferred policy.

The bias-for-action culture at the FAF and the FASB led to relaxation of the voting requirements to approve a standard in 1977. The five-out-of-seven votes needed to issue a standard in the original charter of the Board were reduced to a simple majority in the wake of the oil and gas exploration cost controversies. The change lowered the threshold of consensus needed for the Board to act. The economics of standard setting took the back seat in the heat of public controversy. If four members of the Board can not convince three of their own colleagues about the merits of the proposed standard, how can they be so sure that society would be better off with such a standard than without it?

The bias-for-action culture also brought with it the aggressive standards of accounting—standards in which the Board recommended broad application of complex new accounting methods which had not previously been tried out in the field. By the mid-seventies the Board seems to have become confident enough of its ability to divine which of the previously untried methods of accounting are socially preferable to those which had already been tried out. Given the basic difficulties of learning constituent preferences and of aggregating these preferences, this was a tall order indeed. If constituent preferences with respect to known accounting techniques are difficult to find out, it is almost impossible to do so for newly devised complex techniques. The Board's overconfidence in its own abilities to do so led to such debacles as *FAS 8* (foreign currency translation) and *FAS 19* (oil and gas exploration costs).

By the early eighties, the cumulative effect of FASB's activism, induced by its structural design, began to show in the form of weakening constituent support. AICPA, which made the early mistake of demanding a majority membership in the FASB, ended up having to take the blame for the dissatisfaction many felt with the Board's performance. In recent years more room has been made for industry in the FAF and the FASB. However, fundamental structural problems remain. What, if anything, needs to be done?

IV. FUTURE DIRECTIONS

We must pay attention both to the design of institutional arrangements and to setting our expectations of what we can reasonably accomplish through such an arrangement. Setting of the attitudes and expectations is important because the failures of the past have resulted just as much from unreasonable goals as from the structural weaknesses of the systems used.

Structurally, there is need for an incentive-compatible system for setting standards. Such a structure should have incentives to try to identify and implement accounting standards which can reasonably be expected to enhance the welfare of the society on some broad scale. The structure should be such that it does not encourage the Board to act unless they have a strong justification for thinking that the standard is socially desirable. Nor should it aggressively promulgate as standards those methods of accounting with which accountants and investors have little prior experience. Conflict among parties should be openly discussed. No party should have to wrap in a veil of public interest its arguments which are intended really to protect its self-interest.

A quasi-legislative system which consists of part-time members who represent all relevant constituencies is appropriate to meet these objectives. The members would be free to argue for the interests of their own constituency in this forum. Support of substantially more than a bare majority (say three-fourths of the members) would be needed to issue a new accounting standard. Standards that do get issued can be expected to enjoy broad community support and are less likely to be undermined. No standard is better than the constituent support it receives. It may help to remind the FASB of this by weakening the support its standards receive from Rule 203 of AICPA's Code of Ethics.

The membership of a quasi-legislative body has to be reasonably representative of various segments of the economy who are affected by its action. At the very least it will require equal representation for corporate managers, the investment community, and public accountants and a variety of regulatory bodies whose functions overlap with the standards issued by the FASB. Others may have to be invited to join to work on accounting standards of special interest to them. If such a broad representative body were to fail, the failure would not be blamed on one narrow group. The public accountants have carried that burden in the past. A broadly representative body will spread that burden.

Just because the butcher and the baker may not be able or willing to serve on a standard-setting body for accounting, the idea of representativeness need not be laughed at. It is still possible to put together a body of technically competent people who are reasonably representative of the broad interests who are affected by accounting standards with appropriate adjustments on an issue-by-issue basis.

This body need have no significant permanent bureaucracy beyond a skeletal staff. The body does not have to meet regularly; only when necessary to address the issues brought before it by its members or by others. It does not have to have a large budget; it needs money only to pay for travel and for the cost of maintaining a small support staff and office. It does not have to issue an annual report listing as its accomplishments the new standards set during the reporting period.

Fortunately, FASB's experience is already pushing it in this direction. In recent years, more and more of the action has shifted to the Emerging Issues Task Force, whose structure is essentially quasi-legislative. My proposal will only promote this evolution to a more advanced level and formally recognize the advantages of a quasi-legislative structure and the dangers of a permanent rule-making bureaucracy.

Important as the structural recommendations are, the setting of attitudes and expectations is equally important.

First, the setting of standards is not a mere technical matter. Technical expertise is of course important to setting of standards but it is not sufficient. Standards, in accounting as in other areas, involve consideration of social efficiency (which is a technical matter) and of distribution of wealth (which is a political matter). As in all political matters, people can differ without any one being wrong. The quasi-judicial structure of the FASB, combined with a large technical staff, has tended to give a technical flavor to its task and for many years the FASB remained reluctant to recognize the political (i.e., distributional) aspects of its charge. A quasi-legislative system will shift the emphasis toward the political part without damaging the technical part. The members of the new structure will still be required to have a high level of technical competence as in the past.

Appointment of disinterested parties (e.g., accounting professors), who presumably have no identifiable political interests as a class in setting of accounting standards, to a standard-setting body tends to detract from the political aspects of its task. They need not be voting members of such a quasi-legislative structure and could continue, as in the past, to provide valuable advisory and technical support as members of the staff.

Second, no standard is indispensable. People can and do live without standards of many types. Absence of a standard is rarely catastrophic; people adjust their behavior to the status quo. On the contrary, issuance of a standard can be a catastrophe. The performance of a standardization organization can no more be measured by the number of pages of standards issued than the success of a parliament can be judged by the number of laws passed. There is no connection, not even an approximate one, between the two. Is an active parliament a good parliament? Is an active standard setter a good standard setter? We must get rid of the habit of carrying the positive image of "proactive" behavior from the personal to this institutional domain.

Refusal of a standard-setting body to issue aggressive standards means delay in standardizing accounting for newer types of business transactions and phenomena. It is no more reasonable to expect that accountants can instantaneously come up with efficient standards for newer types of business transactions than that physicians can come up with a cure for AIDS or that engineers can fix the space shuttle overnight. The imperfection of our knowledge generates the necessity to conduct field testing of a variety of solutions to new problems. Forcibly speeding up the process imposes the large costs of making mistakes, changes, and resultant confusion in financial markets. Accountants who worry that the Securities and Exchange Commission may not accept a slower pace of response to new issues only need to remember, and remind the SEC of, the reserve recognition accounting.

Third, no matter what institutional mechanism we devise to set accounting standards, our ability to identify socially superior solutions is, and will remain, limited and imperfect due to several reasons I discussed earlier. We cannot observe other people's preferences; people's preferences depend on what they know and their past experience, which change continually. When new solutions or standards are implemented, people adjust their behavior to the new situation. Therefore, an understanding or observation of how people change their behavior in response to new standards is indispensable to devising socially efficient standards. The more aggressive a standard is, the less likely it is that we can completely understand its consequences. Perhaps the practice-based orientation of accounting standards widely used in Canada and in other countries of the world does make sense after all; a shift in emphasis from aggressive toward more practice-based standards should be considered. Given the fourteen-year experience of the FASB going out on a limb with aggressive standards, some modesty with respect to our ability to devise new accounting methods which are socially preferred standards may not be out of place.

RESEARCH FOR ACCOUNTING POLICY: AN OVERVIEW

Robert G. May and Gary L. Sundem

A significant amount of accounting research is devoted to questions of accounting (financial reporting) policy. Such research is addressed to the alternative models, measurement rules and disclosure requirements that are or might be applied in current financial reporting by business enterprises. Such research accounts for much of the combined research efforts sponsored or undertaken by institutions such as the AICPA and FASB as well as for much of the independent academic research in accounting.

The purpose of this paper is to offer a model for organizing one's thoughts and efforts directed toward the process of accounting policy making and related research strategies. The motivation for attempting such a task is a conviction that results from individual accounting research studies must be interpreted as interrelated building blocks for accounting policy decisions. As Gonedes and Dopuch [1974] showed, virtually no research strategy used by accounting researchers to date is capable of selecting the most socially desirable accounting alternative. However, because Gonedes and Dopuch applied such a demanding performance criterion to accounting research (i.e., achieving a social ranking of alternatives), they leave an impression of great pessimism. Yet, as will be evident later, the most promising use of any given research strategy (data source) in the area of financial reporting policy is not in selecting optimal alternatives; rather, it is in contributing, *along with all other available strategies,* to developing theories that then may be used by policy makers to settle specific issues.

The authors would like to thank the participants of the accounting colloquia at the University of Washington and Oklahoma State University for their helpful comments on earlier drafts.

Robert G. May and Gary L. Sundem, "Research for Accounting Policy: An Overview," *The Accounting Review,* October 1976, pp. 747–763. Reprinted by permission of the American Accounting Association.

The paper begins with a description of accounting policy making as a social choice process. This discussion contains a brief enumeration of certain implications of the social choice dimension of accounting policy making; the second section presents a model for interpretation of research for accounting policy making; and the third section discusses the potential contributions of various research strategies.

ACCOUNTING POLICY DECISIONS AS SOCIAL CHOICES

For nearly half a century, the accounting profession has been concerned with forming accounting policy, i.e., deciding which measurement and reporting alternatives are acceptable and which are not. From the time the first standard audit report in 1933 referred to "accepted principles of accounting" [Rosenfield, 1964], the profession has taken upon itself the task of deciding what is acceptable. The Committee on Accounting Procedure (1939–1950), The Accounting Principles Board (1959–1973) and the Financial Accounting Standards Board (1973–) have had major policy-making responsibility. Yet, after all of these years of policy making, the procedures for policy formulation are not always well understood.

Before proceeding to a detailed discussion of policy decisions, it is necessary to distinguish between accounting theories and accounting policy [Ijiri, 1975, pp. 9–11]. An accounting theory is a descriptive or predictive model whose validity is independent of the acceptance of any goal structure. Though *assumed* goals may be part of such a model, research relating to a theory or model of accounting does not require acceptance of the assumed goals as necessarily desirable or undesirable. On the other hand, accounting policy requires a commitment to goals and, therefore, requires a policy maker to make value judgments. Policy decisions presumably are based on *both* an understanding of accounting theories *and* acceptance of a set of goals. Research relating to accounting policy decisions must recognize and discern the aspect of the policy-making process at issue.

For the moment, we will discuss the unique aspect of accounting policy, namely, goal formulation. Several recent attempts have been made to delineate the goals or objectives of financial accounting [e.g., Arthur Anderson & Co., 1972; Study Group on the Objectives of Financial Statements, 1973; Defliese, 1973; and Accounting Standards Steering Committee, 1975]. Since the selection of a set of goals is inherently a value judgement, most debate about sets of goals is a debate about whose value judgments are best. This is an insoluable problem, as value judgments are neither right nor wrong, true nor false. The resolution of the problem of selection of goals must be solved by general agreement, not by proof of correctness. Therefore, the first step in a logical process of policy formulation is to obtain general agreement on the goal of financial accounting.

The statements of goals of financial accounting made to date suffer from two major problems: (1) they have not received general acceptance and (2) they do not provide a basis for selecting among alternative policies. For instance, a recent statement of goals asserts that "the basic objective of financial statements is to provide information useful for making economic decisions" [Study Group of the Objectives of Financial Statements, 1973, p. 13]. However, this is not a statement of a goal of financial statements, but merely a delineation of the domain of accounting policy decisions. That is, it states *what* accounting policy makers are to be concerned with, but it does not state *how* comparisons among alternative policies are to be made.

We suggest that an objective of maximization of social welfare (which may be implied, though not stated, in the above objective) is a necessary addition to the above goal statement.[1] While this is admittedly our value judgment, such a goal seems to provide a criterion for policy decisions and, to our knowledge, no one has expressed disagreement with it as an objective. In a letter to the AICPA, the SEC has expressed concern that accounting policy decisions be "consistent with the public interest" [Burton, 1973, p. 271]. Indeed, the Securities Acts clearly were motivated by a desire to prevent recurrence of the socially deleterious events surrounding the crash and ensuing Great Depression. Moreover, the U.S. Congress has intervened in accounting policy decisions at least once, in the investment tax credit decision, when it felt that an accounting policy decision was not in the public interest. Since accounting policy decisions that apparently are not consistent with the public interest can be reversed by a higher authority, it is apparent that either accounting policy makers (the SEC-FASB) at least must appear to pursue a social welfare criterion or have their power consistently preempted by the legislature, which presumably applies such a criterion. Thus, the political environment of accounting policy formulation implies acceptance of a social welfare criterion for accounting policy decisions as social choices.

It is possible for accounting policy decisions to be made by each individual or firm producing a financial statement, in the same way that policy decisions concerning any other economic commodity are made. A demand for accounting information exists because individuals wish to improve their investment decisions. This private demand would lead to production and sale of financial statements.

Although general public policy would apply (e.g., general antitrust policy would apply to the industry structures that evolved in the production and sale of private financial information about business enterprises), no special public accounting policy would be necessary to satisfy demand for financial information on the part of individuals. Research in financial accounting could contribute to such a laissez-faire environment by producing microeconomic information (e.g., predicting individual costs and benefits), similar to cost and market research relevant to the production and distribution of other goods and services.

But accounting information may have public value apart from its private value [Fama and Laffer, 1971; Hirshleifer, 1971; and Demski, 1974a]. Because accounting information may influence individual investor's assessments and, through these assessments, the structure of security prices, therefore the information may influence the distribution of costs of capital among firms and, through that distribution, the allocation of capital to various uses in the economy. The possibilities of both production and consumption externalities in information generation imply that regulation of accounting information production may lead to an allocation of resources that is pareto superior to that achieved by a free-market equilibrium allocation. Moreover, changes in information production induced by regulation may alter the value of securities portfolios and, through those values, the distribution of wealth among individuals. Either one or both of these potential influences adds a social value dimension to the regulation of financial accounting information.

A necessary (but not sufficient) condition for regulation to create a socially *better* allocation of resources and/or distribution of wealth is that it *at least* be capable of producing a

---

[1]See Committee on Concepts and Standards; External Financial Reports [1975, pp. 42–44] for more details.

different allocation and/or distribution than would be attained in a free market.[2] There are several reasons that this condition may be met. First, regulation can impose production of information on entities with comparative advantages in producing the information (usually perceived to be the business enterprise in the case of financial accounting information). However, these entities do not necessarily have a private incentive to do so. In this way, it may be possible to alter the information set employed privately by investors in forming their preferences for various securities by altering the distribution of costs of information [May and Sundem, 1973]. Such alterations may affect resource allocation and wealth distribution directly by changing the production opportunities of other (external) information suppliers, even though their effect on the security price structure is minimal. Second, since optimal investment strategies imply interfirm comparisons, some external economies in information processing may be achievable through imposition of certain uniformities in financial accounting information produced. This may mean lower costs of acquiring information for investors and other decision makers. Third, to the extent that a policy apparatus lessens the probability of major financial scandals, it may contribute to the general perception of risk *over a vast number of risky investments* and, therefore, the level of savings and investment in the economy as a whole.

Accounting information is like many other commodities produced in our economy today: the private market for such information is modified by explicit public policy (regulation) decisions. The decisions to produce and consume accounting information are influenced by the FASB, SEC and other regulatory bodies. As noted earlier, in practice as well as in theory, the social welfare impact of accounting reports apparently is recognized. Therefore it is no surprise that the FASB is a political body and, consequently, that the process of selecting acceptable accounting alternatives is a political process. If the social welfare impact of accounting policy decisions were ignored, the basis for the existence of a regulatory body would disappear. Therefore, the FASB must consider explicitly political (i.e., social welfare) aspects as well as accounting theory and research in its decisions.

In a democratic-capitalist society, it is virtually unassailable in principle that social policy should be sensitive to individual preferences.[3] However, Demski [1973] has shown that, in general, the characteristics of accounting information per se (e.g., relevance, objectivity) do not reflect the preferences of individuals affected by the use of the information. This implies that policy makers must go beyond comparing alternative policies regarding the degree to which their outputs conform to certain purely technical or aesthetic standards, e.g., "true economic value," "true income," relevance and objectivity. That is, accounting policy makers must employ a decision model that is sensitive to individual preferences. Such a decision model is called a collective choice rule.

---

[2]The social desirability of any piece of *regulation* will depend on the amount of and ownership of resources used to decide on and enforce the regulation as well as the reallocation of resources and redistribution of wealth brought about by the regulation. Henceforth, we will not be concerned about the desirability of any particular regulation, but we will accept the result that regulation is potentially desirable. The dilemma of comparing the social desirability of alternative *allocations* is discussed in Demski [1974a, pp. 227–228].

[3]This notion was expressed most succinctly by Quirk and Saposnik as follows: "In principle, one could conceive of a whole host of theories of welfare economics, based upon differing sets of value judgments concerning the manner in which the term "desirable" state of the economy or economic system should be defined; in practice, essentially all of modern welfare economics is based upon one fundamental ethical postulate. To borrow Samuelson's phrase: In evaluating states of the economy, *individuals' preferences are to count.*" [1968, p. 104].

Unfortunately, selection of a collective choice rule is complicated by two very formidable difficulties. First, it has been proven that it is impossible to construct a collective choice rule that satisfies even a minimal set of general conditions.[4] Second, notwithstanding the impossibility of constructing a completely satisfactory collective choice rule, it seems reasonable to assert further that it is extraordinarily costly, if not impossible, to construct a social decision-making system that could assess the consequences for and preferences of every individual who might be affected by a given accounting policy decision.[5]

Clearly, the above discussion presents a paradox. On the one hand, we would like to have a systematic way for accounting policy makers to choose among alternatives based on individual preferences. At the same time, no such systematic way exists that satisfies even a relatively few desirable properties. Moreover, as a practical matter only limited knowledge of individual preferences is feasible.

One way to face this challenge is to explore applications to accounting of the concepts of social choice that have evolved in welfare economics and decision theory. Some initial efforts in this direction were Demski [1974a and 1974b], Gonedes and Dopuch [1974] and May and Sundem [1976], but the issues are far too formidable to resolve here. Research into the selection of an appropriate collective choice rule for accounting policy decisions is one of the most difficult tasks facing accounting researchers. We will proceed on the assumption that no satisfactory resolution of the issues will abandon completely the ethical judgment that *individuals' preferences are to count* in accounting policy decisions.

A MODEL FOR ACCOUNTING POLICY DECISIONS

Our model of accounting policy decisions now has a goal—maximization of social welfare—and a social decision process employing some collective choice rule (currently, the FASB with their operating procedures) for selecting among accounting alternatives. This section completes the model by describing the framework for research in accounting theories to support the accounting policy decisions. This framework is shown in Figure 1; this figure provides the basis for the subsequent discussion of potentials for and limitations of accounting research.

Notice that Figure 1 is subdivided (by the dotted lines) into several sectors, including (1) business firms and auditors, (2) individuals, (3) markets and (4) accounting policy makers. These sectors are not meant to be mutually exclusive in the sense that no individual may be represented in more than one. Rather, they are intended to represent individuals in various distinguishable roles relevant to the discussion. Notice that there is a counterclockwise flow in the figure. This represents the general direction of impetus or influence in the accounting policy-making process, at least in principle, and necessarily abstracts from the many potential counter-currents and forces. We will discuss each of the four sectors individually, indicating briefly some of the kinds of research that are appropriate for that part of the policy process. Then we will discuss the overall framework of accounting research for policy decisions.

---

[4]Arrow's original proof, which applies to collective choice rules that represent orderings of social states, first appeared in Arrow [1951]. Arrow's theorem was first cited in the accounting literature by Demski [1974a]. The conditions, the proof and its implications are described in very readable style in the unstarred (non-mathematical) chapters of Sen [1970] and in Quirk and Saposnik [1968, Chapter 4].

[5]A social decision-making system, as the term is used here, is intended to include a collective choice rule plus the necessary institutional apparatus to implement the rule.

FIGURE 1

The Accounting Policy-Making Process

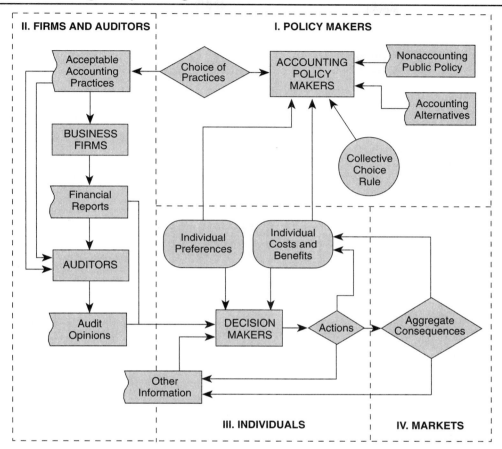

Sector I represents the formal accounting policy decision system. Accounting policy makers are shown explicitly, but there is no implication that they must exert an influence on the choice of accounting practices allowed. They could allow a laissez-faire environment to exist, with financial accounting statements treated as a nonregulated commodity. However, the potential social welfare impacts of these statements and the current institutional structure suggest that some regulation is likely, so the framework is more consistent with the existence of specific accounting policy makers with some power to enforce their policy decisions. It is also consistent with the current political environment within which the FASB and SEC operate— one in which accounting policy decisions must be acceptable to a broad set of individuals and not merely consistent with "accounting theory."

Accounting policy makers must specify the set of acceptable accounting practices, which depends on the collective choice rule and social decision system they use (which were discussed in the previous section). It also depends on the accounting alternatives available; development and refinement of these alternatives is an important area for research. Nonaccounting public policy is also an important input. An often neglected area of research is how accounting policy fits into an overall public policy framework. (See, e.g., Committee on Concepts and Standards: External Financial Reports [1975], p. 43.) Other inputs relate to feedback on the impacts of policy decisions on individuals which will be discussed in more detail later.

Section II of Figure 1 traces through the effect of policy decisions on financial statements, including auditors' opinions. A first step in predicting ultimate consequences of policy decisions is to predict their effect on financial statements. Therefore a priori research, which predicts the financial statement effects of alternative measurement and reporting rules, can be an important research contribution. And, where possible, empirical research confirming or describing actual financial statement effects is probably even more helpful.

Sector III consists of all individuals in society, each of whom makes consumption and investment decisions. We arbitrarily could divide these individuals into three categories: (1) those who produce and/or audit financial statements or other information, (2) those who use financial statement and other data in their decision making and (3) those who do not use any investment-relevant information. Most accounting research makes these divisions and concentrates only on *users* of financial statement data. This is a major simplification that is not necessarily desirable. Only if the extra cost of a complete analysis is greater than the benefit achieved is such simplification desirable. So, in our general framework we include *all* individuals whose welfare can conceivably be affected by accounting policy in this sector. Thus, this sector may include individuals who act in the capacities of enterprise management and independent auditors or, for that matter, public policy makers in the other sectors.

Individuals use information, including, but by no means limited to, financial statements and auditors' opinions, in making consumption and investment decisions. Tracing through the effect of financial reports on individual actions is an important area of accounting research. Such research may examine directly the influence of financial reports on actions. Or, it may assess the influence on predictions of the feasibility and consequences (costs and benefits) of various courses of action, and perhaps to a lesser extent, any influence on preferences. Further, the effects of financial reports cannot be restricted to their influence on only traditional investment decisions. For example, one effect of available financial reports may be to stimulate decision makers to produce other information, either for their own or others' consumption.

Direct effects of financial reports on individual actions may be assessed by examining the decisions of users of the data. But secondary effects, some due possibly to the presence of information or decision alternatives that would not exist in the absence of financial reports, may affect the action of nonusers as well.

Section IV, markets, highlights even more effects on nonusers of financial reports. Individual consumption and investment decisions in the aggregate generate equilibrium market prices. These, in turn, influence the allocation of resources and distribution of wealth in the economy. While virtually all investment decision makers may act rationally on the assumption that their individual transactions cannot affect prices, in the aggregate many such decision makers, taking similar actions, may change prices. Similarly, a decision by one individual to seek or produce information to supplement or complement what appears in financial reports supplied by firms may only affect that individual. On the other hand, many decision makers making similar conclusions may create sufficient demand to stimulate the emergence of a new firm or industry specializing in production of such information.

When such aggregate effects take place, not only are they not necessarily taken into account (predicted) by the many individual decision makers whose collective actions cause them, but also they may touch the lives of many individuals whose actions did not contribute in the least to their occurrence. For example, when the relative price of a security changes, the wealth levels of all holders of that security change, even though some holders chose to hold the security at both the former and the present prices.

Three primary areas of research are relevant in the market sector: (1) determine the method by which individual actions combine to yield equilibrium prices, (2) develop descriptive models of equilibrium prices with accounting numbers among the explanatory variables and (3) determine the effects of different sets of equilibrium prices on resource allocation and wealth distribution. Researchers in finance and economics probably have a competitive advantage over accounting researchers in areas 1 and 3, but it is still necessary for accountants to be aware of research in these areas and to apply that research to accounting problems. Moreover, area 2 may not stimulate much interest among researchers in finance and economics.

Combining the individuals and markets sectors, we can see the ultimate consequences of accounting policy decisions. If a social welfare criterion is accepted, these policy decisions ideally should be judged on (1) their aggregate consequences, (2) the effect on individual costs and benefits implied by these consequences and (3) the preferences of individuals for alternate possible consequences. Prediction of these elements is part of the policy-making process and completes the circle in Figure 1.

An overview of Figure 1 gives several insights into potential directions for accounting research. Most important is the fact that with our current state of knowledge about decision processes, markets and collective choice, it is impossible to derive a definitive social ordering (or partial ordering) of accounting alternatives. No one piece of research can do that, and none should claim to. Gonedes and Dopuch [1974] correctly criticize many studies for making such a claim. Yet, research studies do not have to provide a social ranking to be helpful to policy makers. Any research that increases our understanding of any of the relationships in Figure 1 can provide a benefit. We should not despair because accounting research cannot provide conclusive evidence about the optimal set of allowable accounting practices. Rather, we should focus our research effort on producing information that is useful to policy makers in their decision process, including information that may help them revise their process.

Given the present political and institutional structure (including an implied but not necessarily well-specified collective choice rule and sensitivity to non-accounting public policy), the two primary inputs to policy decisions are: (1) forecasts of the *consequences to individuals* of policy alternatives and (2) forecasts of *individual preferences* over those consequences. The role of research in support of actual policy decisions is *not one of selecting the best alternatives*. Rather, it is one of forecasting or producing information for forecasting consequences for and preferences of individuals. It is generally impossible to construct a social decision-making system that possesses all of even a minimal set of desirable characteristics: therefore, it is also impossible to construct *conclusive* accounting research strategies (methods) for determining optimum accounting policies—without first assuming away the collective choice dimension. (See Beaver and Demski, [1974], pp. 175–176; or Gonedes and Dopuch, [1974], pp. 78–80).

To forecast consequences and preferences, researchers must specify the level of analysis. Demski [1974a, pp. 222] has suggested use of a complete general equilibrium analysis of alternative accounting policies, specified in terms of the individual ". . . consumptions schedules to which they give rise." However, the suggestion would seem to apply only to the general theoretical level rather than the specific policy-decision (operational) level. Under present technology, it is clearly infeasible to consider the consequences and preferences over those consequences of each possible variation on accounting policy for each individual in society who is potentially affected. Moreover, it is doubtful that policy makers could comprehend the full set of tradeoffs of costs and benefits over all affected individuals. Yet, if it is generally accepted that a market (laissez-faire) system for accounting information is inadequate, policy decisions must be made. This implies that although a sensitivity to individual preferences may be desirable, it is one of the things that inevitably will be traded off to some degree in favor of tractability and efficiency in any practicable policy-making process.[6] Most likely, information (research) produced for accounting policy decisions will consist of evidence relevant to predictions of consequences of various policy alternatives for various groups of *similarly affected individuals,* along with evidence relevant to predictions of the preferences (or at least the direction of preferences) *of the same groups* for such consequences.

In considering the sources and methods of obtaining such data, another important implication of the accounting policy-making process (as depicted in Figure 1) should be emphasized. The introduction of aggregate effects of direct individual actions (sector IV of Figure 1) is a reminder that not all consequences can be predicted at the individual decision-maker level. Aggregate or market effects (e.g., price changes) are spillover effects of direct actions taken by individuals. Such spillover effects may have consequences for other individuals who have not contributed directly to their occurrence. Thus, for instance, the set of relevant expected consequences and preferences for a given accounting policy decision includes the expected consequences for and preferences of *non-users as well as users* of accounting information.[7]

RESEARCH STRATEGIES: SOME EXAMPLES

We have used the framework in Figure 1 to point out some potentially fruitful areas for accounting research. In this section we use the framework to examine some specific existing research strategies. The framework will allow us to assess both the potential and limitations of these strategies.

The inability of research strategies generally to provide conclusive evidence for significant policy problems takes us back to Figure 1 with the question: "What avenues are available to help policy makers predict consequences, particularly aggregate consequences, of major policy alternatives?" It is of considerable importance that Figure 1 depicts a *linked process* from the use of acceptable accounting alternatives in financial reporting (sector II) through the aggregate consequences of the use of the resulting information by individual decision makers (sector IV), finally leading to the individual costs and benefits associated with those aggregate consequences (upper right of sector III.).

In principle, policy makers should be able to trace the implications of any given policy alternative through each link in the process. In practice, of course, this is hardly possible to any satisfactory degree because of the lack of a comprehensive and cohesive theory or set of theories descriptive of the behavior of the process in each stage. Of particular significance are:

---

[6]Demski seems to agree implicitly with this implication in acknowledging the value of research efforts that may help ". . . simplify the consequence domain . . ." in Beaver and Demski [1974, p. 176].

[7]In essence, this is a rejection of the approach used, in part, in Study Group on the Objectives of Financial Statements [1973], pp. 17–20, where the objectives of financial statements are referenced to their presumed usefulness to typical investors and creditors.

(1) the absence of a theory of individual investment decision making, based, at least in part, on accounting information and (2) the absence of a theory which explains equilibrium market prices, at least in part, in terms of accounting variables and which is consistent with the theory of individual decision behavior. Mutually consistent theories of individual equilibria and market equilibria have been put forth in the finance literature in recent years (i.e., portfolio theory and capital asset pricing theory), but these theories are nonspecific as to how observable forms of information, such as available accounting information, influence individual decisions and the structure of market equilibrium prices.

The challenge of developing such accounting-specific theories of individual and market behavior is formidable. Moreover, the demands of the task probably cannot be met without employment of virtually all research tools and methods presently in use by accounting researchers (and, perhaps, some yet to be developed). This is the basic theme of the remainder of the paper.

Before reviewing several potentially productive research strategies, an additional comment is in order. Some people may argue that the individual investment decision level is irrelevant for accounting policy making since the latter inherently is oriented toward aggregate consequences. For instance, in a recent critique of various research strategies (vis-a-vis accounting policy decisions), Gonedes and Dopuch [1974, p. 106] made the following statement specifically aimed at lab/field research studies:

> Specifically, given an efficient capital market, studies of the behavior of particular types of investors (e.g., 'average' investors or 'financial analysts') are not likely to lead to reliable generalizations about the relationship between the production of accounting information and capital market equilibrium. To see this, recall that, within a competitive market, market behavior is a function of the interaction among rivalrous price takers. The attainment of equilibrium in such a market is induced by the workings of the system as a whole, or *aggregate* market behavior, and not by the actions of particular individuals.

We do not disagree with this description of how market equilibria obtain—which perhaps makes it appear paradoxical that previously we pinpointed as significant the absence of a theory of *individual* investment decision making incorporating accounting variables. Actually, we see no inherent conflict as long as theories of individual behavior are not themselves taken to be ideal predictors of market behavior. A predictive theory of capital market equilibria could, of course, be constructed without regard to individual decision making, but there is no intrinsic superiority to such an approach. Moreover, although individual actions are not necessarily one-for-one with competitive market phenomena, there is no inherent reason suggesting that theories predicting market phenomena *cannot* be constructed based on theories of individual "rivalrous price-taking" behavior. Indeed, precisely because market equilibria are established (at least as manifest by observable exchange prices) by the interactions of individuals, this approach would seem to be very promising a priori. Yet another reason to pursue a theory of individual decision making is that, as Figure 1 depicts, the consequences for individuals of altering accounting policy are jointly a function of individual action and aggregate or market actions.

A PRIORI RESEARCH

Before accounting policy makers can choose among alternatives in accounting, alternatives must exist from which to choose. So, an important precedent to accounting policy decisions is research that specifies alternative measurement and reporting possibilities. Included in this research is the development of accounting models such as price-level-adjusted models, replacement cost models and exit value models. Also included is research into methods of measurement and reporting that are potentially applicable within any of these models. While this research itself cannot provide evidence on the desirability of various models or measurement methods, it can direct empirical investigations into the most promising areas.

A priori research also may be useful in constructing potential models of behavior at all major points in Figure 1. Such a priori models will be especially helpful in developing testable hypotheses regarding the effects of accounting variables on individual decisions and on market equilibria.

PREDICTIVE-ABILITY RESEARCH

One specific potentially fruitful avenue for accounting research is investigation into the relationship between accounting signals and the distributional properties of future returns from investments in firms' securities to which decision makers' preferences are presumably sensitive. The types of investigations include such things as studies of the time-series properties of accounting numbers and tests of predictive ability.

Early in the history of empirical research in accounting, Beaver, Kennelly and Voss [1968] introduced the predictive ability criterion. Hakansson [1973, p. 160], among others, expressed a belief that the criterion was well suited to research problems in accounting—particularly as a building block in a decision theoretic approach.

However, the predictive-ability criterion is not without its faults. Greenball [1971] pointed out: (1) that studies of predictive ability are really joint tests of the outputs of alternative accounting methods and the particular prediction model(s) selected and (2) that such tests are irrelevant for assessing the potential of various accounting methods to serve nonprediction-oriented decisions (e.g., performance measurement). Similarly, Gonedes and Dopuch [1974, p. 109] observe that there ". . . remains the question about whether . . . predictive ability is a sufficient basis for selecting from alternative accounting techniques."

However, these limitations should not be taken as fatal flaws, since, as pointed out earlier, no research technique consistently will produce conclusions as to the relative social "desirability" of accounting alternatives. If the predictive-ability criterion and other criteria for examining the time-series properties of accounting alternatives are used and interpreted judiciously, they offer a potential contribution, albeit a limited one, to research for accounting policy making. This potential is present because, as is evident in Figure 1, all consequences of accounting policy (other than the direct production-related consequences of imposing the policy on firms and auditors) come through the use of the outputs in decisions—some of which inevitably will hinge on *predicted* values of relevant variables.

SENSITIVITY OF ACCOUNTING TIME-SERIES TO POLICY ALTERNATIVES

A largely neglected (in recent times), but potentially profitable, avenue of accounting research is investigating the degree to which actual accounting time series may be expected to differ under various accounting alternatives, given observable or even assumed or simulated environmental conditions under which firms operate. Although unappealing as a sole basis of choices among accounting alternatives, such investigations can make a potentially important, though perhaps prosaic, contribution—particularly when integrated with the predictive ability and basic time series approaches mentioned in the preceding section. In the linked sequence leading to predictions of consequences of policy alternatives depicted in Figure 1, every link contributes to the ultimate objective. Moreover, since predictions of the effects of alternatives on accounting outputs is the first substantive step in predicting consequences, it has special implications for the efficiency of the *applied policy-making process*. That is, considerable savings potentially may be realized if the prediction process stops at this point in those cases where the alternatives being considered show no potentially significant differences in accounting outputs. However, again we must emphasize the importance of a cohesive theory covering the entire chain. "Significance" must be gauged in terms of possible ultimate consequences of the alternatives at the end of the chain in order for a cutoff decision to be appropriate at the accounting output prediction stage.[8]

MODELING INDIVIDUAL DECISION MAKING

Upon reflection, the most serious limitation of studies of time-series properties and/or predictive ability is the lack of criteria within those research strategies for determining (1) what constitutes variables worthy of prediction and (2) what constitutes significantly different predictive ability (or other characteristic) of accounting outputs under different policy alternatives.[9] This again emphasizes the importance of employing such strategies within the fuller context depicted in Figure 1. The principal direct source of criteria for time-series and predictive-ability studies is a theory or model of individual investment decision making under uncertainty—specified, at least in part, in terms of accounting variables.

The central method in deriving such a model would be the application of decision theory similar to the way it has been applied in finance in recent years. However, there is an important distinction. Since the investment decision essentially boils down to a tradeoff between present and future consumption (usually in the form of claims to the intermediate good, cash), it is obvious that present and future consumption (cash) streams are the variables of interest to an investor—not historical accounting variables per se. Thus the challenge to accounting in modeling the investment decision is to specify how and which accounting variables that satisfy the constraints of a public reporting environment in which management and investor goals are potentially incongruent relate to the variables to which investor preferences are sensitive. Of course, this is precisely the problem implied by time-series and predictive-ability research—which brings out a virtually unavoidable interaction between model building and time-series and predictive-ability efforts.

BEHAVIORAL RESEARCH

To date, most behavioral research aimed at financial accounting has been oriented toward testing the so-called functional fixation hypothesis [Ijiri, Jaedicke and Knight, 1966] in lab or field environments controlled to various degrees, i.e., testing subjects' decision sensitivity to

---

[8]This is another way of saying that statistical significance and behavioral or economic significance are not the same.

[9]A third major limitation pointed out by Greenball [1971] is the dependence of predictive-ability tests on prediction models selected. However, this limitation can be ameliorated by fairly exhaustive replications over the set of plausible prediction models available under a given state of technology.

alternative accounting measurement rules, e.g., FIFO versus LIFO [see Gonedes and Dopuch, 1974, Exhibit 1, p. 107 for a list of such studies through 1973]. Such studies are in general highly susceptible to criticism, particularly for lack of external validity, i.e., failure to sufficiently simulate conditions under which actual investment decisions are made so that few, if any, valid generalizations can be drawn from the results [Gonedes and Dopuch, 1974, pp. 104–106]. Aside from such methodological problems, there are also the issues of whether the way individuals actually use information should influence financial reporting policy and, therefore, whether actual information processing is a fruitful subject for research aimed at policy making.

Clearly if research for accounting policy making were aimed strictly at constructing normative theory, the relevance of such studies could be questioned quite legitimately. However, if our earlier conclusion is accepted that the purpose of research for accounting policy is aimed at constructing theories enabling policy makers to predict consequences of policy alternatives, then studies concerned with how individuals process information, and, specifically, how they process accounting-type signals, take on considerable potential relevance. Of course, this potential relevance is also dependent upon acceptance of the relevance of a theory of individual, as opposed to purely aggregate, investment decision making for which we made a case earlier. Its importance is limited by the fact that nonusers as well as users of financial statements are affected by accounting policy decisions.

MODELING AGGREGATE MARKET BEHAVIOR

Moving to sector IV, the market sector, from sector III, the individual decision sector, in Figure 1 we can observe that general equilibrium analysis, or even more limited theoretical work into equilibrium in the capital markets, has a potential contribution to make. For even if a satisfactory theory of individual decision making based on accounting information can be developed, there remains the problem of predicting the aggregate effects of individual decisions, which are also conditional on accounting information.

Bearing in mind that presumably "individual preferences are to count" in accounting policy choices, general equilibrium analysis, in which aggregate phenomena, e.g., equilibrium prices and quantities traded, are derived from a model in which individuals and their preferences are represented, would seem to be a preferred methodology [Demski, 1974a]. However, due to the dimensionality problem noted earlier associated with representing each individual, firm, etc., in one model, as a practical matter traditional macroeconomic methods, which typically operate only on aggregate variables and, often, in a partial equilibrium mode, may be more promising.

SECURITY PRICE-BASED RESEARCH

Recently, much hope was placed in the security price structure as a source of direct evidence for determining optimum accounting policy, based on the apparent fair-game efficiency [Fama, 1970] of the market with respect to publicly available information. The basic objective of this research was to identify the set of accounting practices that would produce financial reports that were most highly associated with the security price structure. Most methods of measuring association may be described in general terms by (1), where R_{jt} is the observed rate of return for security j over time period t. R_{mt} is the corresponding rate of return on the market portfolio (usually represented by some broad-gauged index), A_{jt} is the cumulative record of accounting data about firm j as of time t and g' is the selected measure of association (e.g., the now-familiar API) between unexpected increments in firms' accounting records and unexpected changes (not explained by market changes) in firms' securities prices:

(1) $$R_{jt} - E(R_{jt}|R_{mt}) = g'[A_{jt} - E(A_{jt}|A_{jt-1})]$$

In terms of Figure 1, this measure of association relates the output of sector II, financial reports, with the aggregate consequences of sector IV. But Figure 1 highlights some potential problems with this research strategy.

First, this method can be applied only when the effect of accounting alternatives on financial reports is known (i.e., when A_{jt} is known for each alternative). Research identifying accounting alternatives and predicting the effects of these alternatives on financial reports is a necessary adjunct to security price-based research.

A second concern is the measurement problems caused by "leapfrogging" from accounting outputs to aggregate market consequences; this treats the territory between (i.e., individual decision making and the process or phenomenon of aggregation) as a "black box." Any alleged association is based on a chain of causation: (1) from unanticipated accounting signals (new information) through their impact on individual expectations, (2) from individual expectation changes through individual actions and (3) from individual actions to their impact on aggregate supply and demand for securities which would imply price changes. Confidence in the associations developed, especially predicting continuing associations of the same type, would be much greater if there were a well-developed theory describing at least some of these links. Research into opening up the black box in sector III of Figure 1 seems to be an important supporting factor for security price-based research.

A third class of problems, closely related to the black-box aspects of security price research to date, relates to the treatment and effects of "other information." The effect of nonaccounting information on prices is surrogated by R_{mt}, so that the effects of the data in individual firms' financial reports can be isolated. This created two potential problems: (1) other information may have an impact not adequately reflected by R_{mt} and (2) market-wide effects of accounting reporting practice may be reflected in R_{mt} and thus not identified as an effect of the accounting policy. In addition, accounting policy may affect the economic availability of other information; thus, the full impact of accounting policy cannot be reflected in the association between accounting outputs and security prices [May and Sundem, 1973]. This is especially true if data from a nonextant accounting policy is being associated with extant prices.

The fourth major problem with security price-based research is that it stops at aggregate consequences, not relating these consequences to individual costs and benefits or preferences. Gonedes and Dopuch [1974, pp. 48–75] show that only under various combinations of very limiting assumptions do the prices of firms' securities reflect the ex ante values to investors of information production decisions of management. Since it is hard to conceive of any real situations where these assumptions hold, security price-based research has little potential for assessing the desirability of accounting alternatives.

Despite these limitations, security price-based research does have some potential value by providing a measure of the relative effects on prices of alternative accounting policies (see Gonedes and Dopuch [1974, p. 76]). However, even to provide this benefit, security price-based research must overcome the several measurement problems mentioned earlier. Most important is the bias present in association measures when accounting policy decisions involve choices between the status quo and potentially costly alternatives [May and Sundem, 1973]. Unfortunately, the majority of nontrivial accounting policy decisions involve such choices. In those cases, the only way presently available to divine information about the potential relative effects on security prices of heretofore undisclosed-costly alternatives is to experiment—a strategy most policy makers would be loathe to attempt.

On a more positive note, not all accounting policy decisions involve highly costly but previously unreported alternatives. For instance, there may be questions of whether the status quo policy of requiring costly reporting under multiple alternatives by certain firms should be continued, e.g., whether firms should continue to be required to report fully diluted earnings per share as well as primary earnings per share figures. The apparent marginal contribution to market estimates of securities' expected returns and risks of one such alternative, given that extant reporting policy requires reporting of both alternatives, conceivably can be tested using security price data (see Sundem, Felix and Ramanathan [1975]). Similar strategies apply to alternatives that are not all included in current mandatory reporting requirements—*provided* excluded alternatives are known to be available to market participants at virtually zero acquisition costs (as in Beaver and Dukes [1972]).

On an additional positive note, it should be pointed out that measures of the effects of accounting changes have potential value in ex post evaluation of actual policy decisions. Since accounting policy decisions, like other decisions, involve uncertain future consequences, knowledge of errors in prediction in one case may lead to refinements of predictions in other cases. That is, if an alteration in accounting policy is adopted based on policy maker's predictions of expected changes in relative securities' prices, confirmation of whether such changes take place subsequently as expected is potentially valuable in refining policy makers' models for predicting consequences of policy alternatives. In effect, what holds for policy makers' predictions holds as well for theory verification, i.e., the security price structure is a potentially valuable source of data for verification of proposed theories of equilibrium prices, specified in terms of accounting variables.

In conclusion, security price-based research encompasses only part of the policy-making process. As such, it cannot provide a social ranking of alternatives. But it does make an important link in the process. If measurement problems can be overcome so that confidence can be placed in that link, this type of research potentially has a contribution to make.

CONCLUSION

We could continue with additional examples of research methods that by themselves will not yield results that directly bear on the desirability of accounting alternatives but can serve as building blocks in a complete view of accounting policy decisions. However, by now our main point should be clear. With our present state of technology in accounting research, there is no research method that will identify the most desirable accounting policy alternative. Nor is there any great likelihood that such a method will emerge, given the social choice dimension of accounting policy making. But there are many research methods that can provide data useful to accounting policy makers who must predict consequences of accounting alternatives and preferences over those consequences. The results of such research should not be put forth as conclusive support for any accounting alternative; neither should it be rejected because it is not able to provide such conclusive support.

This paper does not support the usefulness of any piece of accounting research that might be attempted. Such research still must be carefully designed and carried out. We do not propose any methods of judging the internal validity of research designs. But, given that a research study has internal validity, we propose a framework in which its external validity can be examined. By identifying the aspects of the accounting policy-making process in Figure 1 that are being examined, both the potential contributions and the limitations of research projects readily can be identified. We hope this provides an interpretative framework for accounting research, such that: (1) contributions are not ignored, (2) unwarranted generalizations are minimized because they are no longer perceived as necessary to justify the research effort and (3) accounting research will be more productive in general due to greater complementarity among individual research efforts.

REFERENCES

Accounting Standards Steering Committee. *The Corporate Report* (Accounting Standards Steering Committee, 1975).

Arrow, K. J., *Social Choice and Individual Values* 1st edition (John Wiley and Sons, 1951: 2nd edition Yale University Press, 1963).

Arthur Andersen & Co., *Objectives of Financial Statements for Business Enterprises* (Arthur Andersen & Co., 1972).

Beaver, W. H. and J. S. Demski, "The Nature of Financial Accounting Objectives: A Summary and Synthesis," *Studies on Financial Objectives 1974*. Supplement to Volume 12 of the *Journal of Accounting Research*.

———, and R. E. Dukes, "Interperiod Tax Allocation, Earnings and Expectations, and the Behavior of Security Prices," *The Accounting Review* (April 1972), pp. 320–332.

———, J. W. Kennelly and W. M. Voss, "Predictive Ability as a Criterion for the Evaluation of Accounting Data," *The Accounting Review* (October 1968), pp. 675–683.

Burton, J. C., "The SEC and the Accounting Profession: Responsibility, Authority, and Progress," in R. Sterling, *Institutional Issues in Public Accounting* (Scholars Book Co., 1973), pp. 265–275.

Committee on Concepts and Standards: External Financial Reports; "Objectives of Financial Statements: An Evaluation," Supplement to *The Accounting Review* (1975), pp. 41–49.

Defliese, P. L., *The Objectives of Financial Accounting* (Coopers and Lybrand, 1973).

Demski, J. S., "The General Impossibility of Normative Accounting Standards," *The Accounting Review* (October 1973), pp. 718–723.

———, "The Choice among Financial Reporting Alternatives," *The Accounting Review* (April 1974a), pp. 231–232.

———, "The Value of Financial Accounting" (Unpublished paper, Standford University, Graduate School of Business, 1974b).

Dopuch, N., and L. Revsine, eds., *Accounting Research 1960–1970: A Critical Evaluation* (University of Illinois, 1973).

Fama, E. F., "Efficient Capital Markets: A Review of Theory and Empirical Work," *Journal of Finance* (May 1970), pp. 383–417.

———, and L. Laffer, "Information and Capital Markets," *Journal of Business* (July 1971), pp. 289–298.

———, and M. H. Miller, *The Theory of Finance* (Holt, Rinehart and Winston, 1972).

Gonedes, N., and N. Dopuch, "Capital Market Equilibrium, Information Production, and Selecting Accounting Techniques: Theoretical Framework and Review of Empirical Work," *Studies on Financial Accounting Objectives: 1974*, Supplement to Volume 12 of the *Journal of Accounting Research*.

Greenball, M., "The Predictive Ability Criterion: Its Relevance in Evaluating Accounting Data," *Abacus* (June 1971), pp. 1–7.

Hirshleifer, H.: "The Private and Social Value of Information and the Reward to Inventive Activity," *American Economic Review* (September 1971), pp. 561–574.

Ijiri, Y., *Theory of Accounting Measurement* (American Accounting Association, 1975).

———, R. Jaedicke and Kenneth E. Knight, "The Effects of Accounting Alternatives on Management Decisions," in Jaedicke *et al.*, eds., *Research in Accounting Measurement* (American Accounting Association, 1966), pp. 186–199.

May, R. G. and G. L. Sundem, "Cost of Information and Security Prices: Market Association Tests and Accounting Policy Decisions," *The Accounting Review* (January 1973), pp. 80–94.

———, "Cost of Information and Security Prices: A Reply," *The Accounting Review* (October 1974), pp. 791–793.

————, "Accounting Policy Decisions as Social Choices" (Unpublished paper, University of Washington, Seattle, 1976).

Quirk, J. and R. Saposnik, *Introduction to General Equilibrium Theory and Welfare Economics* (McGraw-Hill, 1968).

Rosenfield, P. H., "The Auditors Standard Report Can Be Improved," *Journal of Accountancy* (October 1964), pp. 53–59.

Sen, A. K., *Collective Choice and Social Welfare* (Holden-Day, 1970).

Study Group on the Objectives of Financial Statements. *Objectives of Financial Statements* (AICPA, 1973).

Sundem, G. L., W. L. Felix and K. V. Ramanathan, "The Information Content of Earnings Per Share" (Unpublished paper, University of Washington, 1976).

THE INFORMATION ECONOMICS APPROACH TO FINANCIAL REPORTING

Martin Walker

INTRODUCTION

Since the late sixties, researchers in information economics have made a number of important contributions towards our understanding of the role and value of information in capitalist economies. This literature is of considerable potential importance for accounting policy decisions which influence the timing, quality and quantity of public financial information. Unfortunately the information economics literature is mathematically forbidding and, to outsiders at least, gives the appearance of being somewhat fragmented. The purpose of this paper is to provide a non-technical overview of the economics literature as it relates to financial reporting.

THE ANALYTICAL METHOD

Research in the information economics area to date has been primarily analytical, concerning itself with the value of information in hypothetical decision contexts. The analytical approach studies the behaviour of model economies under alternative information scenarios. For example, one might compare the behaviour of the economy in the absence of an information system with the behaviour of the economy in the presence of an information system. This kind

Martin Walter, "The Information Economics Approach to Financial Reporting," *Accounting and Business Research,* vol. 18, no. 70, 1988, 170–182. Reprinted by permission of Accounting and Business Research.

of work is analogous to the modelling work of, say, engineers. For example, to test the wind resistance of a new car shape they construct a computer model designed to predict the likely resistance factors under alternative body shapes. Of course such models cannot capture all the relevant features of reality. At best they can only take into account the main factors likely to affect the final outcome. Nevertheless such models are useful because they help to structure the thinking of the design effort and because they often produce a working 'prototype' to which minor modifications can be made to reflect the influence of the factors not taken into account by the model.

The key difference between engineering modelling and information systems modelling is the human element. The behaviour of inanimate objects like cars can be predicted on the basis of natural laws of wide validity. Unfortunately, from the modeller's point of view, the same cannot be said of the behaviour of human agents. Because of the human element the predictive success of economic models tends to be somewhat patchy at least when judged by the standards used to assess the validity of the models of natural science. Nevertheless, when used properly, economic theory can provide a useful tool. In particular, analytical economic models are useful conceptual devices which help one to organise one's thinking about a problem. Moreover even though the predictive ability of economic models is poor, this does not imply that society would be better off without them.

BASIC PRINCIPLES OF NEO-CLASSICAL INFORMATION ECONOMICS

The information economics approach to accounting is based on the view that the demand for and supply of accounting information can and should be explained in terms of the choice behaviour of individuals. It is a scientific approach to accounting in the sense that its prime objective is to understand accounting practices and procedures.

The information economics approach is essentially neo-classical in the following sense (Hahn, 1984):

1. First, it is individualist in that it attempts to locate explanations in the actions of individual agents.

2. Second, it imposes strong assumptions with regard to the rationality of individuals. In particular almost all the information economics literature assumes that individuals choose as if to maximise their own expected utility.

3. Third, to the extent that it is concerned with the results of bargaining behaviour between individuals the approach focuses entirely on equilibrium positions, i.e. positions in which the intended action choices of individuals are mutually consistent and can be implemented.

Some social scientists (e.g. Marxists) reject individualism. Most economists believe it to be the approach most likely to lead to fruitful results. Ultimately acceptance of individualism is a matter of personal conviction.

The assumption of expected utility maximisation is more difficult to justify. Its main advantage is that it provides a mathematically convenient characterisation of individual choice behaviour that is often consistent with observed choice behaviour. Its main limitation, for present purposes, stems from the fact that it rules out *a priori* any possibility of information overload. It simply assumes that individuals make full and correct use of all information available to them.

With regard to the rationality assumption it should also be stressed that the assumption of rationality is an assumption about individual behaviour. It says nothing about the rationality of society as a whole or of the rationality of collective actions such as the actions of a firm.

At first sight the restriction of focus to equilibrium positions seems somewhat limiting. Certainly this would be so if by 'equilibrium' was meant 'competitive equilibrium under market clearing conditions'. In fact there is a whole variety of equilibrium concepts which can be fruitfully applied to the analysis of bargaining under uncertainty. Most of these equilibrium concepts are derived from the theory of games rather than the somewhat narrow field of competitive equilibrium theory (see e.g. Harsanyi, 1977; Shubik, 1982; Stiglitz & Weiss, 1983).

From a policy point of view there are two possible arguments against the information economics approach: that the perfect rationality assumption renders the approach useless because it is unrealistic; and that the approach is of no practical value because it focuses only on equilibrium positions.

Against the first of these criticisms it is important to note that even though particular individuals may exhibit irrational behaviour, nevertheless the information economics approach may yield the best predictions on average if the deviations from rationality are unsystematic and unpredictable. Furthermore, the rationality assumption offers considerable advantages from a modelling point of view. As a practical matter, models based on rationality assumptions tend to be more tractable than models based on alternative behavioural assumptions. Against the second criticism one can argue that corporate reporting policy changes very slowly. Thus even though the predictions of information economics are valid only in the long run, this is not a practical weakness of the approach since the long run predictions of the theory are the ones most relevant for policy making.

Finally, we should note one other common feature of the information economics models reviewed below. All these models assume that most individuals exhibit a degree of risk aversion. This assumption motivates a demand for insurance and other forms of risk-sharing contracts.

SINGLE PERSON DECISION ANALYSIS

There are two novel features of the information economics approach which set it apart from earlier schools of thought. The first is that uncertainty is explicitly treated as a central feature of economic reality. This is in contrast to the more traditional schools of accounting thought which, at best, only treat uncertainty implicitly (*viz.* the prudence concept, extraordinary items, lower of cost or market value, etc.). The second is that information economics attempts to analyse the demand for and supply of information in a multi-person environment where conflicts of interest are prominent. Thus most recent information economics models are concerned with multi-person economies in an uncertain environment.

However, before examining these models, it will be helpful to begin by considering a simpler model involving just one individual in an uncertain environment. In this model uncertainty is represented by assuming that, at any point in time, the economy can be in one of several possible states of the world. Information is then represented as any device which helps one either to detect the current state of the world or to forecast its future state. For example consider the following decision problem of a farmer.

At the start of the year the farmer must decide whether to plant barley or potatoes. The profit he derives from his crop depends on whether the summer is wet or dry. The figures in the table show the farmer's profit under each weather/crop scenario. There are two alternative states of the world, 'wet' or 'dry'.

	Wet Summer	Dry Summer
Plant Barley	£10,000	£50,000
Plant Potatoes	£30,000	£20,000

Suppose the farmer believes that there is an equal probability of a wet or dry summer and that he wishes to maximise his expected profit, i.e. he is risk neutral. Then he will choose to plant barley since his expected profit from planting barley is £30,000 compared with only £25,000 if he plants potatoes.

Now suppose the farmer can purchase a perfect weather forecast before making his crop decision. In this case he will plant barley if the forecast is dry yielding a profit of £50,000 and potatoes if the forecast is wet yielding a profit of £30,000. His overall expected profit will be £40,000 which is £10,000 more than his expected profit in the absence of a perfect weather forecast.

The basic single person decision problem under uncertainty generalises the above example to allow for more than two states of the world and for forecasting systems which range between zero information and perfect information. To present this model formally, let $A = (a_1, \ldots, a_N)$ represent a set of alternative actions. Suppose the consequence of an action depends on the state of the world. Let C represent the set of possible consequences and S represent the set of possible states. Let C_{ij} stand for the consequence of action i if state j occurs. Thus, for example, the consequence of the farmer selecting the action 'plant barley' if the state is 'wet' is £10,000.

Under a plausible set of axioms with regard to the rationality of the individual's ranking of consequences and acts, it can be shown that an individual will choose his act as if to maximise his expected utility. The expected utility of an act is defined as follows

(1)
$$EU(a_i) = \sum p_i U(c_{ij})$$

where

$EU(a_i) = $ the expected utility of action i

$U(\cdot) = $ the utility function of the individual defined over consequences

$p_j = $ the subjective probability assigned by the individual to state j

In the absence of information the individual will choose the action yielding the highest value of $EU(a_i)$. Let EU (no information) stand for the expected utility of the optimum action choice.

Information is represented in the model as a mapping from the set of states to a set of possible signals $Y \equiv (Y_1, \ldots, Y_k)$. The signal is received by the individual before making his action choice. On receiving a particular signal the individual will first revise his prior subjective probabilities in the light of the information conveyed by the signal. Let p_{jk} stand for the revised probability of state j given signal k. Then the expected utility of action i given signal k is simply:

(2)
$$EU(a_i \,|\, \gamma_k) = \sum_j p_{jk} U(c_{ij})$$

The optimum action, given signal k, is the action with the highest value of $EU\,(a_i \,|\, \gamma_k)$. Let $EU(\gamma_k)$ be the expected utility of the optimum action, given signal k, that is:

$$EU(\gamma_k) = \underset{a,i\ A}{\mathrm{Max}}[EU(a_i \,|\, \gamma_j)]$$

If we let p_k stand for the probability of receiving signal k, then the overall expected utility of the individual with access to information can be expressed as follows:

$$EU(\text{under information}) = \sum_k EU(\gamma_k) \cdot p_k$$

An interesting feature of this model is that it can be used to assign a monetary value to information. In particular we can define the monetary value of information as the maximum amount of money that the individual with information would be able to pay in all states of the world and still remain as well off as he was without information. If we let EU (under information, F) stand for the expected utility under information if the individual has to pay F for the use of the information, then the individual's willingness to pay for information can be represented as the value of F such that:

$$EU(\text{under information, } F) = EU \text{ (without information)}$$

The model can also be used to examine how individuals rank alternative information systems. An important result in this respect is the fitness theorem which states that for any information systems (A and B) all individuals will prefer the finer of the two information systems if one system is finer than the other. On the other hand if A and B are not comparable as to fineness then the ranking of the two systems may differ from individual to individual according to the details of their preferences/prior beliefs. In particular if A and B are not comparable as to fineness then there will be some configurations of preferences and beliefs which rank A and B and some which rank B above A. Demski (1973) was the first to recognise the importance of the fineness theorem for financial reporting policy. Many financial reporting alternatives are not comparable as to fineness. For example current cost accounts contain information which is not contained in CPP accounts and vice versa. The importance of the fineness theorem is the implication that any ranking of such non-comparable alternatives is consistent with individual rationality. Thus any attempt to prove that all rational individuals necessarily exhibit the same ranking of two or more non-comparable alternatives is doomed to failure. For example it is impossible to prove that no rational individual would prefer CCA to CPP or vice versa.

A second general point to emerge from the single person model is recognition that the demand for information in this model relates only to a demand for state of the world forecasts. Conventional accounting statements such as balance sheets and income statements have no value in this context.

THE VALUE OF PUBLIC INFORMATION IN A SOCIAL CONTEXT

If the main purpose of corporate reporting is to provide public information to investors relevant for economic decision making and control then it is important to understand how public information affects the decisions and welfare of individuals and society as a whole. Ideally one would like to be able to perform a cost-benefit analysis of financial reporting alternatives but at present this seems to be an unattainable goal. More realistically it seems sensible to attempt to identify the potential sources of costs and benefits, and the possible distributional consequences of financial reporting alternatives. This will provide a kind of 'conceptual framework' within which rational debate can take place.

Information economics has made a number of important advances in understanding the potential benefits of public information. The purpose of this section is to review these advances.

Before analysing the social value of information it is important to define what it means to say that a public information system has social value. By analogy with the single person case reviewed in the previous section the definition of social value employed below involves a comparison of the expected utilities of all individuals in the economy without information with the expected utilities of all individuals in the economy with information. In particular, we will say that an information system is of potential social value if, in the economy with the information system, it is possible (perhaps following some lump sum redistribution) to increase the expected utility of at least one individual without reducing the expected utility of any other individual relative to the expected utilities that the individuals would have had in the economy without the information system. This is the Pareto Criterion, an idea which can be explained by reference to Figure 1 which assumes a two-person economy.

In Figure 1 the horizontal axis measures the expected utility of individual 1 and the vertical axis measures the expected utility of individual 2. The curve *fcg* represents the Pareto frontier of the economy in the absence of information. In other words every point on the curve *fcg* shows the maximum level of EU_2 that can be achieved for a given level of EU_1. For example if individual 1 achieves an expected utility of $0g$ the expected utility of individual 2 will be zero. The curve *dabe* represents the Pareto frontier of the economy in the presence of information. Here we have assumed that the introduction of information shifts the Pareto frontier of the economy outwards, i.e. information has social value.

Recent theoretical research on the economics of information has made important advances for our understanding of the social value of public information. The essential features of these advances can be explained by reference to a simple model economy with the following characteristics:

(i) there is a given set of I consumers,

(ii) there is a given set of J firms,

(iii) there is a single commodity,

(iv) the life of the economy is a single period,

(v) uncertainty is represented by assuming that the economy can be in one of S possible states of the world at the end of the period.

The following additional assumptions define a special case of this model which provides a useful starting point for our discussion of the social value of public information:

FIGURE 1

Pareto Criterion in a Two-Person Economy

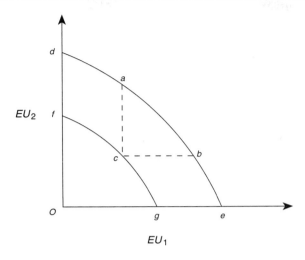

1. each consumer is a risk averse expected utility maximiser,
2. the utility function of each consumer is time additive,
3. consumers have homogeneous prior beliefs,
4. all economic agents have equal and costless access to information,
5. each firm has an exogenously given production plan,
6. the market for firm specific securities and claims to immediate consumption is both perfect and complete.

Implicit in assumption 6 is the idea that trade takes place only in firm–specific securities written against the end of period payoffs of the J firms. These securities can be traded against each other or against claims to immediate consumption. The assumption of a perfect market guarantees that all economic agents behave as price takers with respect to security prices and the risk-free rate of interest. The end-of-period production of each firm is an S-dimensional vector of state contingent payoffs. The S by J matrix formed by the J firm-specific production vectors will be referred to here as the end-of-period payoff matrix. The 'completeness' part of assumption 6 is equivalent to requiring the end-of-period payoff matrix to be of full row rank. This rank condition ensures that the J firm-specific production vectors span the entire S-dimensional space of end-of-period payoff patterns. Thus, within the limits of his wealth, each consumer can achieve any end-of-period consumption pattern he desires. Moreover, given price-taking behaviour on behalf of consumers, all consumers will prefer more wealth to less.

The concept of information in this model can be represented as any device which either helps economic agents to predict which state of the world is going to occur or which helps economic agents to determine which state has occurred. Beaver and Demski (1979) refer to the former type of information as pre-decision information and the latter type as post-decision information.

It is possible to prove the following propositions (see e.g. Ohlson and Buckman, 1981):

PROPOSITION 1

Given assumptions 1 to 6 inclusive, information has no social value in the sense that the Pareto efficient frontier of society is not affected by the introduction of information into any economy characterised by assumptions 1 to 6.

PROPOSITION 2

In an economy for which assumptions 1 to 6 hold, if pre-decision information is introduced *after* consumers have had a preliminary opportunity to trade, no consumer will wish to retrade following the release of information and there will be no effect on the welfare of any consumer.

PROPOSITION 3

The introduction of pre-decision information into an economy characterised by assumptions 1 to 6 before consumers have had any opportunity to trade can never result in a strict Pareto improvement and may result in every consumer being strictly worse off.

The intuition behind propositions 1 and 2 becomes clear when one recalls that the aggregate amounts of immediate consumption and state contingent end-of-period consumption are given exogenously. Thus information, at best, can only affect the distribution of claims between consumers. However assumption 6 guarantees that a Pareto efficient allocation of claims will be achieved in the absence of information whilst assumptions 2 and 3 ensure that there will be no demand to alter the distribution of claims following the release of new information.

Proposition 3 can be understood by considering a simple example involving two consumers, two states, and two firms with the following end-of-period payoff matrix:

	State 1	State 2
Firm 1	0	100
Firm 2	100	0

The example assumes that the two consumers have identical utility functions and identical endowments of immediate consumption. In addition both consumers believe the two states are equally likely. Consumer 1 owns the whole of firm 1 and consumer 2 owns the whole of firm 2. In the absence of pre-decision information the two consumers will agree to trade 50% of firm 1 against 50% of firm 2.

Now consider the effect of a perfect pre-decision information system with the signal being released before the consumers have had an opportunity to trade. If state 1 is signalled, consumer 2 will hold on to his endowment and consumer 1 will receive nothing. Similarly consumer 2 will end up receiving nothing if state 2 is signalled. Since state 1 and state 2 are equally likely, both consumers will have a lower expected utility than they would have had in the absence of information. This deleterious effect occurs because the release of information induces a revaluation in the initial endowments of the consumers before they have had an opportunity to insure themselves by trading to a less exposed position.

So far then we have identified no source of social benefit from public information and one potential source of social cost. We will, therefore, have to relax at least one of the assumptions 1 to 6 to produce a model economy in which information has social value. In fact, by relaxing any one of assumptions 1 to 6 it is possible to construct model economies in which the provision of public information leads to a strict Pareto improvement. Assumptions 1 to 6, therefore, are both necessary and sufficient for information to have no social value.

Now if we wish to conduct our analysis without the mainstream tradition of neo-classical financial economics we must retain the first assumption. Most of the published literature on the economics of information also retains the assumptions 2 and 3 (Hakansson, Ohlson and Kunkel 1982, present an analysis of an equilibrium model in which assumptions 2 and 3 are relaxed).

The remainder of this section, therefore, focuses on the implications of relaxing assumptions 4, 5 and 6 for our understanding of the social value of public information.

Within the class of models which retain assumptions 1 to 3 it is possible to show that public information has potential social value in model economies which relax any one of assumptions 4, 5 and 6. In model economies where market structures are incomplete (i.e. assumption 6 does not hold) public information may lead to improved social welfare if it facilitates the creation of new trading opportunities or new tradeable securities. We will refer to this possibility as the 'completion of markets' role of information. In model economies where production decisions are endogenous, public pre-decision information can lead to improved production investment decisions. Finally, in model economies in which assumption 4 is relaxed, social costs can arise when individuals have asymmetric access to information. The provision of public information, by removing or reducing such asymmetries, can serve to eliminate or reduce such costs. The remainder of this section examines these three possibilities in more detail.

To illustrate the 'completion of markets' role of information, consider a model economy involving just two identical individuals and three states with state contingent endowments as follows:

		S_1	S_2	S_3
Prior beliefs:		$\frac{1}{3}$	$\frac{1}{3}$	$\frac{1}{3}$
Endowments:	Individual 1	100	0	0
	Individual 2	0	100	0

Now if the state of the world is observable *ex post* by both parties they will be able to agree to share the aggregate payoff equally in state 1 and state 2. Their ability to enforce this agreement would vanish if the state of the world was not observable *ex post*. For example, if the individuals could only observe the information implicit in their own endowment no trade would be possible. Hence, we can see that information relating to the state of the world may be useful insofar as it increases the set of risk-sharing opportunities.

Recent research has shown that an increase in the set of risk-sharing opportunities can be achieved in two alternative ways. One possibility is to increase the fineness of the post-decision information system and to expand the set of state contingent contracts to take advantage of the improved post-decision information. Here by 'the post-decision information system' we refer to information relating to the state of the world released at time point 1. Four points should be noted about this post-decision role of information. First, only information which is available to all parties to the contract can satisfy this role. Second, this role does not involve prediction. It simply involves *validation* of the actual state occurrence. In this sense it is probably more akin to what most lay people would regard as the proper role of accounting, i.e. the reporting of the 'facts'. Third, even though state prediction is not involved, the parties to the contract must be able to rely on the information being released *ex post* otherwise they will not be able to base a contract upon it. Fourth, the observable effect of an improvement in the post-decision information system is an increase in the variety and complexity of risk sharing contracts. Amershi (1981 and 1985) and Strong and Walker (1987, chapters 3 and 4) contain detailed discussions on the 'completion of markets' role of post-decision information.

Ohlson and Buckman (1981) have focused on an alternative way of increasing the set of risk-sharing opportunities. This can be achieved by releasing additional pre-decision information (i.e. at time point zero) followed by an additional round of trading. Figure 2 illustrates the time line of the Ohlson/Buckman iterated market regime.

Under the Ohlson/Buckman approach the number of securities is held constant and the market is made more complete by allowing a further round of trading in the same set of securities following the release of pre-decision information. In comparison the post-decision information approach involves only a single round of trading but the set of tradeable securities is expanded as the fineness of the post-decision information system is increased.

Social benefits from the provision of public information may also arise where society has some control over the state contingent distribution of aggregate output, for example if society can trade output in one state against output in another, or if current output/leisure can be traded against future output/leisure. If, for example, society could forecast precisely which state was going to occur then resources could be moved into those activities which offered the greatest return in the light of the information received. (Kunkel, 1982, provides a formal demonstration of this possibility.) It is important to note that this type of benefit only arises to the extent that *real* production/investment decisions are affected by the information. To detect such influences one really needs to look at the effect of information on employment and real investment decisions. Changes in share prices and changes in the portfolios of individuals provide, at best, only indirect evidence with regard to these real effects. Finally, it should be noted that only pre-decision information is useful for this particular purpose.

The third major scenario under which public information can be of potential social value occurs when some individuals have access to private information or private information production opportunities. The economics of information has focused on two main types of information asymmetry, i.e. investor/investor asymmetry and outside investor/manager asymmetry.

The investor/investor case of information asymmetry refers to the possibility that some investors may have access to private information or private information production opportunities. This possibility was first examined rigorously by Hirshleifer (1971) and Fama and Laffer (1971). The main point to emerge from their analyses was that situations can arise when there are considerable private benefits to private information production even though the social benefits are zero. Marshall (1974) noted that this possibility provides yet another rationale for the public provision of information. If such information can be produced more cheaply than the aggregate amount spent on private information then public information will be beneficial to the extent that it leads to the attenuation of private information production. The precise details of these arguments have been criticised because they assumed that the relatively uninformed investors would simply react passively to price signals even though they would be aware that they were likely to be 'fleeced' by the informed investors. In recent years a number of models have been developed which assume a greater degree of sophistication on behalf of the uninformed investors. Relying heavily on the assumption of rational expectations, these models show that the uninformed may be able to infer some (and in some cases all) of the information available to informed investors from the behaviour of market prices (e.g. Grossman 1976 and 1981; Grossman and Stiglitz, 1980; Hellwig, 1980; Jordan and Radner, 1982; Radner, 1968 and 1979).

The question we now need to consider is whether there would be any social benefit to public information production where all individuals form their expectations rationally and take full advantage of the information reflected in market prices. Papers by Verrecchia (1982) and Diamond (1985) show that there will still be social benefits from the provision of public information so long as privately produced information is less than fully reflected in market prices, i.e. so long as the rational expectations equilibrium is a noisy one. As in the Marshall (1974) paper, the social benefit from public information production stems from the reduction of socially wasteful expenditure on private information production.

The case of outside investor/manager information asymmetry is an issue which has cropped up from time to time in the literature on the economic theory of the firm under the rubric of 'Separation of Ownership from Control'. The economics of information has focused on two main issues within this context. First there is a class of models known collectively as 'Agency Theory' which basically deals with the issue of how to motivate managers to take decisions consistent with the interests of outside investors. In all such models the manager has a number of decision variables under his control which are not directly observable by outside investors. In some models the manager also has access to additional private information at the time he makes his decision choice. An agency problem arises where the manager's preference ranking over alternative levels of the decision variables differs from that of the shareholders. The literature often refers to such quaint decision variables as the level of expenditure on perquisites or the manager's level of effort, but there are other, possibly more important, decision variables over which conflicts of interest can arise. For example, the manager and shareholders may disagree over what kinds of project risk are acceptable. From time to time the manager may find himself in a position where he would become a social leper by adopting the decision which maximises his shareholders' wealth (investment in South Africa for example).

The principal-agent literature has identified two major problems which arise in an agency context: the moral hazard problem and the adverse selection problem. A moral hazard problem arises when the action choice of the agent is unobservable and when the preference rankings of the principal and the agent over alternative actions diverge. As adverse selection problem arises when the agent has access to pre-decision information which is not observed by the principal. The agent uses his private information in making his action choice but the principal cannot verify whether the agent has used his information in the way that best serves the principal's interest. For example, a company manager might reject a project because of its high risk even though its acceptance would increase the market value of the firm. Outside shareholders would be unlikely to detect such a decision. Both the moral hazard problem and the adverse selection problem can be overcome by the provision of improved post-decision information. If the post-decision information system allows the principal to infer the agent's action choice then a 'forcing contract' can be used to force the agent to adopt the principal's desired action (a forcing contract is one that imposes a very high penalty on the agent if he deviates from the desired action). Similarly if the principal can infer both the agent's choice and the agent's pre-decision information a signal contingent forcing contract can be used to overcome the adverse selection problem. The asterisked articles in the bibliography will provide a useful basis for anyone wishing to pursue the topic in greater depth. For a useful introduction

FIGURE 2

Time Line of the Iterated Market Regime

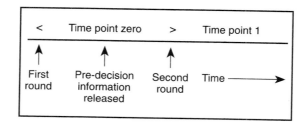

to the main ideas the reader should consult Pratt and Zeckhauser (1984) and chapter 8 of Strong and Walker (1987). Atkinson and Feltham (1982) and Watts and Zimmerman (1986) examine some of the implications of agency theory for financial accounting.

The second major class of issues that arise when managers have access to superior information is the question of whether managers will have an appropriate incentive to reveal truthfully their private information to outside investors and the related question of whether any costs will be incurred in communicating this information. The two main types of models used to examine these issues are known as 'signalling' and 'screening' models. Both types of models are game theoretic in nature and both involve two types of agents, i.e. informed insiders and uninformed outsiders. Stiglitz and Weiss (1983) have shown that the main differences between the two models stem from the fact that the informed have the first move in signalling models whilst the uninformed have the first move in screening models.

A paper by Leland and Pyle (1977) provides a useful illustrative example of a signalling model. In their model, inside owner managers observe private information about the future prospects for an investment project (the only project available to the firm). The owner managers decide whether or not to undertake the project and what proportion of their personal wealth to put into the project. If all owner managers were forced to hold the same proportion of their wealth in their own project there would be no way for them to communicate credibly their information to the market, since all the managers would have an incentive to claim that the prospect for their project was good to enhance the value of the company's shares. However, when managers are free to choose what proportion of their wealth to put into their own project their choice provides a credible signal to the market about their degree of confidence in the project's success. Assuming the manager is risk-averse, holding a large proportion of his wealth in his own firm is costly because it increases his risk. Only managers who are truly confident about the firm's prospects will be willing to accept such risks. However, whilst managers are able to communicate their information credibly (via their portfolio choice decision) there are real costs involved in signalling the information to outsiders. In particular, relative to a situation where all information is publicly available, the inside managers lose out to the extent that their portfolios are imperfectly diversified. These managers would, therefore, be willing to pay for any device which would allow them to communicate their private information credibly without a need to commit a large proportion of their wealth to a single project.

Articles on signalling and screening frequently draw a distinction between dissipative and non-dissipative signalling equilibrium. This distinction basically involves a comparison of the Pareto frontier of society when all individuals have cost-less access to all relevant information (the first-best frontier) with the Pareto frontier of society when there is unequal access to information and communication is achieved via market signalling/screening. In essence a signalling equilibrium is said to be non-dissipative if the vector of expected utilities of all individuals in that society is a point on the first-best frontier; otherwise the equilibrium is said to be dissipative. Public information has social value in a signalling context if it allows the replacement of a dissipative equilibrium by a non-dissipative equilibrium or if it allows the replacement of one dissipative equilibrium with another dissipative equilibrium with lower aggregate signalling costs. Again it is important to note that public post-decision information is capable of providing a non-dissipative solution to the signalling problem. In particular if the public post-decision information is at least as fine as the pre-decision information system of the insider manager, then a simple forcing contract can be used to induce the manager to reveal his information truthfully. More generally, provided there are no limits on the penalties one can impose on managers, one will always be able to design a contract to induce truth-telling behaviour provided there is a positive probability that any lie by the manager will be detected by the post-decision information system.

Spence (1976) provides a useful introduction to the basic ideas of signalling and screening theory. Ross (1977), in one of the earliest applications of signalling theory to financial theory, presents a non-dissipative signalling model of the capital structure decision. Bhattacharya (1980) presents a non-dissipative signalling model of the dividend decision. Miller and Rock's (1985) treatment of the dividend decision involves a dissipative signalling equilibrium. Stiglitz and Weiss (1981) use a screening model to explain the phenomena of credit rationing. Ross (1979) examines the implications of signalling theory for the debate on disclosure regulation and Bar-Yosef and Livnat (1984) use signalling theory to model the market for auditors.

In principle, the kind of forcing contracts that can be used to eliminate agency and signalling costs can also be used to overcome the problems arising from investor/investor information asymmetry. If the public post-decision information system can identify the pre-decision information of traders, then the less informed can protect themselves by insisting on an insurance contract which requires the other party to the trade to pay a penalty if the post-decision information system shows that the other party traded on the basis of insider information.

In summary there seem to be five main sources of social benefit from public information:

1. to extend the range of trading opportunities with a view to improved risk sharing,

2. to improve real production/investment decisions,

3. to reduce expenditure on private information production,

4. to improve control over management decisions,

5. to reduce the costs of signalling inside information to the market.

The surprise to emerge from this survey is recognition that four out of five (the exception being item 2) of these benefits can, at least in principle, be achieved on the basis of improved post-decision information linked to a sophisticated range of public information signal contingent claims contracts. This may be good news for those who believe that accounting is essentially about the reporting of 'facts' for stewardship purposes, especially if one interprets 'stewardship' broadly as the provision of information for 'contract enforcement'.

SOME UNRESOLVED ISSUES

Three issues remain unresolved by the information economics literature:

THE NATURE OF INCOME MEASUREMENT

The models reviewed in the previous sections all represented an information system as some kind of mapping from states of the world to a set of signals. The reader may well be wondering what this has to do with accounting. Accounting provides various kinds of statements to investors, such as earnings statements and balance sheets, but it is not obvious that any of these represent an information system in the sense defined above.

A paper by Beaver and Demski (1979) attempted to apply the insights of information economics to income measurement. Their paper established the following main points:

1. In a world of perfect and complete markets all shareholders will exhibit unanimous rankings over a firm's alternative production plans. This ranking will correspond to the ranking given by the market valuations of the alternative production plans.

2. Given the firm's production plan and a complete set of state contingent prices, one can construct an (*ex ante*) measure of economic income. The ranking of production plans induced by this income measure will be identical to the ranking given by the market valuation of the alternative production plans. Hence a fundamental income measure (in the sense that all shareholders prefer more income to less) will exist.

3. If markets are perfect and complete even though an income measure exists, its publication will be of no social value because investors have all the information they need for decision-making purposes if they know the firm's production plan and the set of state contingent prices.

4. If markets are incomplete, shareholders may differ in their rankings of alternative production plans in which case a fundamental income measure will not exist.

5. Whether or not income reporting is socially desirable depends on its ability to produce cost effective communications between the firm and its shareholders and not on its properties as a fundamental income measure.

In concluding their paper Beaver and Demski wrote:

> . . . the case for income rests on the assumption of aggregating more informative but also more costly data such that a cost effective communication is obtained. However this assumption is problematical and, in our view, one challenge to accounting theorists is to address the primitive question of the propriety of the accrual concept of income.

The idea that any attempt to explain financial reporting practices must be capable of demonstrating a willingness to pay on behalf of investors for financial reporting has been well received and never seriously challenged. Moreover their 'costly communications' perspective has exerted some influence on other income measurement scholars. For example, Parker *et al* (1986) included the Beaver and Demski paper in their influential book of readings and highlighted it as a major contribution to the theory of income measurement.

For income measurement theorists the most challenging feature of the Beaver and Demski article is their claim that the propriety of accruals-based income reporting as a cost effective communications device is yet to be demonstrated. In other words a cost/benefit rationale for accruals-based income reporting has never been established and, in particular, the search for a neo-classical equilibrium model which exhibits an endogenous demand for accruals-based earnings measures has so far, proved fruitless. The construction of a satisfactory response to this challenge stands out as a major unresolved item on the income measurement research agenda.

ON COMMERCIAL SENSITIVITY

Commercial sensitivity is often advanced by firms as a reason for resisting demands for increased financial disclosure. Given the importance of such arguments in the policy domain, it is unfortunate that commercial sensitivity has received little attention either from accounting theorists or from empirical researchers.

The limited amount of theoretical work that has been done suggests that some of the commercial sensitivity arguments are spurious, at least when viewed from the perspective of society as a whole.

Consider, for example, the case of financial disclosures to employees. Some scholars have suggested that information disclosure in a collective bargaining context may 'have adverse distributional effects from the management's point of view' (Foley and Maunders, 1977). Pope and Peel (1981) have questioned this argument. They argue that, if trade union representatives form their expectations rationally, any item of information not supplied by management will be replaced by their own unbiased estimate of that item. Sometimes the estimate will be too high and sometimes it will be too low but on average they will get it right. Hence if management does disclose the data item the only effect will be to reduce the variance of the union's forecast error. Pope and Peel argue that, in the absence of cost considerations, this reduction in variance can only be beneficial to the bargaining process.

Also from a policy point of view it is important to bear in mind that one firm's loss due to commercial sensitivity may well be offset by gains to other firms. For example, a firm may lose out to its competitors by obeying a requirement to disclose its profit margins but it will gain from the same disclosure requirement being imposed on its competitors. Moreover, even though individual firms may suffer a net loss as a result of increased disclosure, such losses may be acceptable to its shareholders if they also hold shares in the firms which benefit from these disclosures.

Finally, it is worth noting that situations can arise when all firms in an industry would unanimously prefer increased disclosure even though this would reduce the welfare of society as a whole. This logical possibility has been demonstrated in a recent paper by Fried (1984) in the context of a duopolistic industry where each firm has access to private information about its own cost conditions. He shows that each firm will be motivated to disclose this information publicly and that the industry as a whole will be more profitable as a result of the improved co-ordination of the two firms' output levels. In effect the industry is able to restrict aggregate output to lower levels than it would be in the absence of disclosure. The reduced output level yields higher profits for both firms at the expense of the hapless consumer.

REGULATION

A previous section of this paper identified the main potential sources of social benefit from the provision of public information. None of these arguments, however, in and of themselves, provide any justification for the regulation of financial reporting. The purpose of this section is to review the economic arguments for and against regulation.

There are two main lines of approach to establishing a case in favour of the regulation of financial reporting. One is to argue for regulation on equity grounds. For example, it might be argued that enhanced financial disclosure protects small investors (see e.g. the AICPA report on the objectives of financial statements). There is some scope for further research on such equity arguments. On the one hand it would be of interest to find out whether equity judgments have played a significant role in the determination of any accounting standards and, if so, to articulate the ethical judgements of standard setters. There may also be scope for normative research in this area. Rawl's Theory of Justice, Harsanyi's Utilitarian Theory of Ethics, and economic theories of fairness/superfairness, all offer interesting perspectives on the ethical issues faced by standard setters. However, at the end of the day one must always bear in mind that the government has plenty of other tools at its disposal for influencing the distribution of wealth. it may therefore be sensible for policy makers to focus on technical and efficiency arguments in their deliberations over financial disclosure alternatives under the assumption that the distributional effects can be taken care of by other policy instruments.

Several recent papers and monographs discuss the market failure arguments for regulation (see e.g. Gonedes and Dopuch, 1974; Leftwich, 1980; Beaver, 1981; Benston, 1983; Bromwich, 1985; Taylor and Turley, 1986). The argument most frequently advanced by this literature in favour of regulation is that information appears to exhibit the classic properties of a public good in the sense that it is costly to exclude non-purchasers from its use and the use of information by one user does not exclude its use by another. This argument has been questioned by Bird and Locke (1981) who noted that it may be possible to overcome the public good problem by divorcing the rights to receive information about a firm from the other ownership rights of its shareholders. Groups of investors would be allowed to form 'clubs' to purchase exclusive information from the firm. Similar arguments have been advanced by Gonedes *et al* (1974). The Bird and Locke argument, however, seems to ignore the possibility that individual club members will have an incentive to resell their information to non-members.

Another frequently cited rationale for regulation is that the public provision of information reduces the level of socially wasteful private information production. This has been demonstrated in the models of Diamond and Verrecchia mentioned above. However, the demonstration that public disclosure leads to the attenuation of private information production does not provide sufficient grounds for regulation. In the Diamond model, for example, investors unanimously agree on the optimum amount of public information production without the need for any form of regulation. In a recent review of this literature Watts and Zimmerman (1986) argue that all the currently published market failure arguments in favour of regulation reduce ultimately to unsubstantiated claims that government contracting costs are lower than private contracting costs. Watts and Zimmerman conclude that, in the absence of empirical evidence on the relative costs of private and government contracting, there is no clear justification for the regulation of financial reporting.

The ideas discussed in the previous section may ultimately lead to more sophisticated analyses of the regulation issue than those criticised by Watts and Zimmerman. In particular, recognition of the importance of reliable post-decision information as a pre-condition for the existence of sophisticated risk-sharing arrangements and incentive structures leads to a different conception of the purpose and effect of regulation in relation to market forces. Often advocates of regulation are portrayed as being unsympathetic to the market economy. The very word 'regulation' carries connotations of bureaucratic bumbling. The ideas discussed in the previous section, however, lead to an alternative conception of regulation oriented towards the creation of markets which otherwise would not exist. Thus, far from operating as a drag on the workings of the free market, regulation can serve to release the market's full potential.

CONCLUDING REMARKS

The economics of information has proved useful in refining our understanding of the social benefits of information and in highlighting the distinction between the private and social benefits of information. Furthermore, the possibility that many of the social benefits of information can be achieved by using post-decision information as a basis for improved risk-sharing is an important contribution which goes some way to narrowing the divide between information economists and accountants of the 'stewardship' school.

There are, however, a number of areas where the approach is, at best, inadequate. First, we have no satisfactory theory of commercially sensitive information. Further research on this topic is urgently required. Second, the theoretical arguments for (and against) regulation are woefully underdeveloped. Finally, and most worrying of all, the conceptual framework of information economics does not interface well with the accounting framework. As yet we have no rigorous model of as economic equilibrium in which rational individuals would be willing to pay for accruals-based earnings.

REFERENCES

AICPA (1973), *Report of the Study Group on the Objectives of Financial Statements.*

Amershi, A. H. (1981), 'Social value of information, spot-trading and rational expectations equilibria in informationally incomplete exchange markets'. Working Paper, *Graduate School of Business, Stanford University.*

Amershi, A. H. (1985), 'A complete analysis of full Pareto efficiency in financial markets for arbitrary preference, *Journal of Finance,* pp. 1235–43.

*Atkinson, A. A. and Feltham, G. (1982), 'Agency theory research and financial accounting standards', chapter in Basu, S. and Milburn, J. A. (eds), *Research to Support Standard Setting in Financial Accounting: A Canadian Perspective,* Clarkson Gordon Foundation.

*Baiman, S. (1982), 'Agency research in managerial accounting: A survey', *Journal of Accounting Literature,* Vol. I, pp. 154–213.

*Baiman, S. and Demski, J. (1980a), 'Variance analysis procedures as motivation devices', *Management Science,* August, pp. 840–8.

*Baiman, S. and Demski, J. (1980b), 'Economically optimal performance evaluation and control systems', *Journal of Accounting Research* (suppl) pp. 184–220.

*Baiman, S. and Evans, J. H. (1983), 'Decentralization and pre-decision information', *Journal of Accounting Research,* pp. 371–95.

Bar-Yosef, S. and Livnat, J. (1984), 'Auditor selection: an incentive signalling approach', *Accounting and Business Research,* pp. 301–9.

Beaver, W. H. (1981), *Financial Reporting: An Accounting Revolution,* Prentice-Hall.

Beaver, W. H. and Demski, J. (1979), 'The Nature of Income Measurement', *Accounting Review,* Vol. LIV, No. I, pp. 38–46.

Benston, G. J. (1983), 'An analysis of the role of accounting standards for enhancing corporate governance and social responsibility', in Bromwich, M. and Hopwood, A. (eds.), *Accounting Standards Setting: An International Perspective,* Pitman Books.

Bhattacharya, S. (1979), 'Imperfect information, dividend policy and the "bird in the hand" fallacy', *Bell Journal of Economics and Management Science,* pp. 259–70.

Bhattacharya, S. (1980), 'Nondissipative signalling structures and dividend policy', *Quarterly Journal of Economics,* pp. 1–24.

Bird, R. G. and Locke, S. M. (1981), 'Financial accounting reports: a market model of disclosure', *Journal of Business Finance and Accounting,* Vol. 8, No. 1, pp. 27–44.

Bromwich, M. (1985), *The Economics of Accounting Standard Setting*, Prentice-Hall.

*Christensen, J. (1981), 'Communication in agencies', *Bell Journal of Economics and Management Science*, pp. 661–74.

*Christensen, J. (1982), 'The determination of performance standards and participation', *Jornal of Accounting Research*, pp. 589–603.

Demski, J. S. (1973), 'The general impossibility of normative accounting standards', *Accounting Review*, pp. 718–23.

*Demski, J. S. and Feltham, G. (1978), 'Economic incentives and budgetary control systems', *Accounting Review*, pp. 336–59.

*Demski, J. S. and Sappington, D. (1984), 'Optimal incentives with multiple agents', *Journal of Economic Theory*, pp. 152–71.

Diamond, D. W. (1985), 'Optimal release of information by firms', *Journal of Finance*, Vol. 40, No. 4, pp. 1071–95.

*Dye, R. A. (1983), 'Communication and post-decision information', *Journal of Accounting Research*, pp. 514–33.

*Fama, E. F. (1980), 'Agency problems and the theory of the firm', *Journal of Political Economy*, pp. 288–307.

*Fama, E. F. and Jensen, M. C. (1983a), 'Separation of ownership and control', *Journal of Law and Economics*, pp. 301–26.

*Fama, E. F. and Jensen, M. C. (1983b), 'Agency problems and residual claims', *Journal of Law and Economics*, pp. 327–50.

*Fama, E. F. and Jensen, M. C. (1985), 'Organizational forms and investment decisions', *Journal of Financial Economics*, pp. 101–20.

Fama, E. F. and Laffer, A. (1971), 'Information and capital markets', *Journal of Business*, pp. 289–98.

*Fellingham, J. C., Kwon, Y. K. and Newman, D. P. (1984), 'Ex ante randomization in agency models', *Rand Journal of Economics*, pp. 290–301.

*Feltham, F. A. (1984), 'Financial accounting research: Contributions of information economics and agency theory', in Mattessich, R. (ed.), *Modern Accounting Research: Survey and Guide*.

Foley, B. R. and Maunders, K. T. (1977), *Accounting Information Disclosure and Collective Bargaining*, Macmillan.

Fried, D. (1984), 'Incentives for information production and disclosure in a duopolistic environment', *Quarterly Journal of Economics*, pp. 367–81.

*Gjesdal, F. (1981), 'Accounting for stewardship', *Journal of Accounting Research*, pp. 208–31.

*Gjesdal, F. (1982), 'Information and incentives: the agency information problem', *Review of Economic Studies*, pp. 373–90.

Gonedes, N. and Dopuch, N. (1974), 'Capital market equilibrium, information production and selecting accounting techniques', *Journal of Accounting Research* (supplement), pp. 48–169.

*Green, J. R. and Stokey, N. (1983), 'A comparison of tournaments and contracts', *Journal of Political Economy*, pp. 349–64.

Grossman, S. J. (1976), 'On the efficiency of competitive stock markets when investors have diverse information', *Journal of Finance*, pp. 573–85.

Grossman, S. J. (1981), 'An introduction to the theory of rational expectations under asymmetric information', *Review of Economic Studies*, pp. 541–59.

*Grossman, S. J. and Hart, O. D. (1983), 'An analysis of the principal agent problem', *Econometrica*, pp. 7–45.

Grossman, S. J. and Stiglitz, J. E. (1980), 'On the impossibility of informationally efficient markets', *American Economic Review*, pp. 393–408.

Hahn, F. H. (1984), *Equilibrium and Macroeconomics*, Basil Blackwell.

Hakansson, N. H., Ohlson, J. A. and Kunkel, G. (1982), 'Sufficient and necessary conditions for information to have social value in pure exchange', *Journal of Finance*, pp. 1169–81.

*Harris, M. and Raviv, A. (1970), 'Optimal incentive contracts with imperfect information', *Journal of Economic Theory*, pp. 231–59.

*Harris, M. and Raviv, A. (1978), 'Some results on incentive contracts with application to education and employment, health insurance and law enforcement', *American Economic Review*, pp. 20–30.

Harsanyi, J. C. (1977), *Rational Behaviour and Bargaining Behaviour in Games and Social Situations*, Cambridge University Press.

Hellwig, M. F. (1980), 'On the aggregation of information in competitive markets', *Journal of Economic Theory*, pp. 477–98.

Hirshleifer, J. (1971), 'The private and social value of information and the reward to incentive activity', *American Economic Review*, pp. 561–74.

*Holmstrom, B. (1979), 'Moral hazard and observability', *Bell Journal of Economics and Management Science*, pp. 74–91.

*Holmstrom, B. (1982), 'Moral hazard in teams', *Bell Journal of Economics and Management Science*, pp. 324–40.

*Jenson, M. C. and Meckling, W. (1976), 'Theory of the firm: managerial behavior, agency costs and ownership structure', *Journal of Financial Economics*, pp. 305–60.

*Jensen, M. C. and Smith, C. W. (1985b), 'Stockholder, manager and creditor interest: applications of agency theory', in Altman, E. I. and Subrahmanyam (eds), *Recent Advances in Corporate Finance*, Irwin.

*John, K. and Kalay, A. (1985), 'Informational content of optimal contracts', in Altman and Subrahmanyam, *Recent Advances in Corporate Finance*, Irwin.

Jordan, J. S. and Radner, R. (1982), 'Rational expectations in microeconomic models: an overview', *Journal of Economic Theory*, pp. 201–23.

Kanodia, C. (1985), 'Stochastic monitoring and moral hazard', *Journal of Accounting Research*, pp. 175–93.

Kunkel, J. G. (1982), 'Sufficient conditions for public information to have social value in a production and exchange economy', *Journal of Finance*, pp. 1005–73.

*Kunkel, J. G. and Magee, R. P. (1984), 'Relative performance evaluation: an examination of theory and some empirical results', working paper, Kellogg Graduate School of management.

*Lambert, R. A. (1983), 'Long term contracts and moral hazard', *Bell Journal of Economics and Management Science*, pp. 441–52.

*Lambert, R. A. (1984), 'Income smoothing as rational equilibrium behavior', *Accounting Review*, pp. 604–17.

*Lambert, R. A. (1985), 'Variance investigations in agency settings', *Journal of Accounting Research*, pp. 633–647.

*Lazear, E. P. and Rosen, S. (1981), 'Rank-order tournaments as optimum labor contracts', *Journal of Political Economy*, pp. 841–64.

Leland, H. and Pyle, D. H. (1977), 'Information asymmetries, financial structure, and financial intermediation', *Journal of Finance*, pp. 371–87.

Leftwich, R. (1980), 'Market failure fallacies and accounting information', *Journal of Accounting and Economics*, pp. 193–211.

Marshall, J. M. (1974), 'Private incentives and public information', *American Economic Review*, pp. 373–90.

Miller, M. H. and Rock, K. (1985), 'Dividend policy under asymmetric information', *Journal of Finance*, pp. 1031–51.

*Mirlees, J. (1975), *The Theory of Moral Hazard and Unobservable Behaviour Part I*, Mimeo, Nuffield College, Oxford.

*Mookherjee, A. (1984), 'Optimal incentive schemes with many agents', *Review of Economic Studies*, pp. 433–46.

*Myers, S. C. (1977), 'The determinants of corporate borrowing', *Journal of Financial Economics*, pp. 147–76.

*Myerson, R. B. (1979), 'Incentive compatibility and the bargaining problem', *Econometrica*, pp. 61–73.

*Nalebluff, B. and Stiglitz, J. (1983), 'Prizes and incentives: towards a general theory of compensation and competition', *Bell Journal of Economics and Management Science*, pp. 21–43.

Ohlson, J. A. and Buckman, G. (1981), 'Towards a theory of financial accounting: welfare and public information', *Journal of Accounting Research*, pp. 399–433.

Parker, R. H., Harcourt, G. C. and Whittington, G. (1986), *Readings in the Concept and Measurement of Income*, Philip Allan.

*Penno, M. (1984), 'Asymmetry of pre-decision information and managerial accounting', *Journal of Accounting Research*, Vol. 22, pp. 177–91.

Pope, D. A. and Pell, P. F. (1981), 'Information disclosures to employees and rational expectations', *Journal of Business Finance and Accounting*, pp. 139–46.

*Pratt, J. W. and Zeckhauser, J. (eds) (1984), *Principals and Agents: The Structure of Business*, Harvard Business School Press, Boston, Mass.

Radner, R. (1968), 'Competitive equilibrium under uncertainty', *Econometrica*, pp. 31–58.

Radner, R. (1979), 'Rational expectations equilibrium: generic existence and the information revealed by prices', *Econometrica*, pp. 655–78.

*Radner, R. (1980), *Does Decentralization Promote Wasteful Conflict?*, Bell Laboratories Economic Discussion Paper.

*Radner, R. (1981), 'Monitoring co-operative agreements in a repeated principal-agent relationship', *Econometrica*, pp. 1127–48.

*Ramakrishnan, R. T. S. and Thakor, A. V. (1984), 'The valuation of assets under moral hazard', *Journal of Finance*, pp. 229–38.

*Rogerson, W. P. (1985), 'The first-order approach to principal-agent problems', *Econometrica*, pp. 1357–67.

*Ross, S. A. (1973), 'The economic theory of agency: the principal's problem', *American Economic Review*, pp. 134–9.

Ross, S. A. (1977), 'The determination of financial, structure: the incentive signalling approach', *Bell Journal of Economics and Management Science*, pp. 373–90.

Ross, S. A. (1979), 'Disclosure regulation in financial markets; implications of modern finance theory and signalling theory', in Edwards, F. R. (ed), *Issues in Financial Regulation*, McGraw-Hill, New York.

*Rubinstein, A. and Yaari, M. (1983), 'Repeated insurance contracts and moral hazard', *Journal of Economic Theory*, pp. 74–97.

*Sappington, D. (1984), 'Incentive contracting with asymmetric and imperfect precontractual knowledge'. *Journal of Economic Theory*, pp. 52–70.

*Shavell, S. (1979), 'Risk sharing and incentives in the principal and agency relationship', *Bell Journal of Economics and Management Science*, pp. 53–73.

Shubik, M. (1982), *Game Theory in the Social Sciences*, Cambridge MIT Press.

*Smith, C. W. and Warner, J. B. (1979), 'On financial contracting: an analysis of bond convenants', *Journal of Financial Economics*, pp. 117–61.

Spence, A. M. (1976), 'Informational aspects of market structures: an introduction', *Quarterly Journal of Economics*, pp. 591–7.

*Stiglitz, J. E. (1975), 'Incentives, risk and information: notes toward a theory of hierarchy', *Bell Journal of Economics and Management Science,* pp. 552–79.

Stiglitz, J. E. and Weiss, A. (1981), 'Credit rationing in markets with imperfect information', *American Economic Review,* pp. 393–410.

Stiglitz, J. E. and Weiss, A. (1983), *Sorting out the Differences between Screening and Signalling Models,* Princeton University Working Paper, Princeton.

Strong, N. and Walker, M. (1987), *Information and Capital Markets,* Blackwell.

Taylor, P. and Turley, S. (1986), *The Regulation of Accounting,* Blackwell.

Verrecchia, R. E. (1982), 'The use of mathematical models in financial accounting', *Journal of Accounting Research,* pp. 1–42.

*Watts, R. L. and Zimmerman, J. L. (1986), *Positive Accounting Theory,* Prentice-Hall.

NATURE OF ACCOUNTING THEORY AND HISTORY

A SYSTEMATIC VIEW OF THE HISTORY OF THE WORLD OF ACCOUNTING

T. A. Lee

INTRODUCTION

A review of the current literature of accounting suggests there are a number of significant concerns about its present condition. For example:

- External financial reporting is increasingly characterized as a game of rules and rule compliance rather than as a function of principles and professional judgement (Gerboth, 1987; Lee, 1989b; Zeff, 1987). The main features observed include informational manipulation and creativity, inconsistent practices, rule avoidance and evasion, political lobbying, increasingly complex regulations and continuous recycling of issues.

- Serious complaints are made about the failures of management accounting to meet rapidly changing organizational, technological and managerial needs for relevant internal information (Behling and Dillard, 1987; Johnson and Kaplan, 1987; Staubus, 1987). A specific problem concerns the need for relevant performance indicators.

- The role of the auditor is the subject of constant scrutiny, particularly with respect to his duty of care in a climate of public expectation for expanding responsibilities

T. A. Lee, "A Systematic View of the History of the World of Accounting," *Accounting, Business and Financial History,* vol. 1, no. 1, 1990, 73–107. Reprinted by permission of the publisher, Routledge.

(Armstrong and Vincent, 1988; Connor, 1986; Mednick, 1987; Zeff, 1987). An example of this issue is the auditor's role with respect to fraud detection.

- The education function of the accounting profession is under increasing criticism for its orientation to short-term practice needs rather than longer-term requirements (Baxter, 1988; Lee, 1989a; Wells, 1987; Zeff, 1989). The rote learning of generally accepted accounting principles is an often-cited instance of this phenomenon, as is the failure of accounting research significantly to influence either accounting education or practice.

- The future prospects for accounting as a discipline have been seriously questioned in the context of its historical evolution (Cushing, 1989). Specifically, there is a concern about the effect of the rigidities of the accounting standards process and the more recent failures of accounting scholars to question and search for accounting principles.

The number and scope of these concerns, and the impression of turbulence or chaos associated with them, may not be unusual. Professions other than accounting may well have equivalent characteristics. Nevertheless, a natural curiosity suggests that there is at least a need to seek ways of providing some tentative explanation of these current issues prior to attempting to resolve them. One way is to search for an understanding of accounting in the context of the organizations and societies in which it is placed.

Such is the purpose of this paper—that is, to observe accounting contextually as a means of understanding its nature and role. Much is known of it as a specific technology in particular situations. But, arguably, too little is understood of its relationships with its environment. These views are compatible with similar but more detailed arguments by other accounting researchers. For example, Burchell et al. (1980) and Hopwood (1983, 1987) have suggested a general need for studies of the role of accounting with respect to organizations and society. In particular, their proposals are for such studies to be undertaken at least in part in historical terms. Hopwood (1987), for instance, advocates an archaeological approach, seeking evidence of accounting change in the layers of history. A decade earlier, Sterling (1977) hypothesized the current problems of accounting as a consequence of the stockpiling and reinforcing of ideas and practices by means of custom and habit through successive generations of accountants.

Thus, this paper has an apparently uncomplicated objective—to study accounting and accounting change in a historical context in order to better understand its nature and role and thereby provide means of attempting to explain issues which confront it and the potential that is associated with it.[1] In particular, the paper is concerned with observing accounting in the context of the

---

[1] An understanding of the utility of historical study with respect to this paper can be found by reading such sources as Carr (1987), Collingwood (1974), Lloyd (1986), Marwick (1981), Popper (1986), Toynbee and Somervell (1974) and Walsh (1974). In particular, a major emphasis is placed on history as the study of the life of the mind through time, transmitting ideas and skills through the generations. The role of the historian in relation to facts is also highlighted—specifically his problems with respect to discovering, reconstructing, selecting and interpreting these facts. In addition, the more specific role of accounting history is characterized by such writers as AAA (1970), Baladouni (1979, 1989), Goldberg (1974), Hopwood (1987), Hopwood and Johnson (1986), Lister (1984), Mills (1989), Napier (1989), Parker (1981) and Previts et al. (1990). These sources provide a means of evaluating the different approaches to the historical study of accounting and the problems associated with each such approach. In the context of this paper, the object for discovery by the accounting historian is accounting as it was in its specific context of time. Inevitably, interpretations of such observations will be required, thus introducing an element of speculation to the judgements made. However, such is the character of history generally and accounting history particularly (See Napier, 1989).

development of the occupation of accountant as it has gradually evolved to become the contemporary profession of accountancy.[2]

World of Accounting

The subject for study in the paper is the 'world of accounting'. The use of such a term demands that a definition be offered at this point. Its use is intended as a convenient means of broadly describing the social system which comprises the communicative acts of accountants. Thus, it should be interpreted as encompassing all actions which can be loosely termed 'accounting' and all individuals responsible for these actions who justify the broad label of 'accountant'. The purpose of this system can be stated to be the provision by human beings of accounting representations of observed or perceived phenomena for use in human activity. Such a system therefore comprises accounting acts associated with representations of economic or commercial activity, and involves both producers and verifiers of these representations; representational technologies; the various organizational functions and institutions associated with accounting education, practice, research, regulation and use; and the recipients of accounting representations.

Such breadth given to the term 'world of accounting' is necessary to be consistent with the nature of the historical analysis applied in this paper and is compatible with the recent plea for such a broad view of accounting history by Baladouni (1989). It is also compatible with the 'soft' systems approach to thinking about problems advocated by writers such as Checkland (1981) and Wilson (1984)—that is, in the context of their view that an understanding of issues can be obtained by thinking about them in terms of systems. With that in mind, it is important to explain in greater detail the meaning of systems as a background to observing the world of accounting as a social system within a historical context.[3]

One further point, however, is relevant at this stage. The defined world of accounting is essentially about accounting acts. But accounting acts cannot take place without human actors—in this case, accountants. Thus, the paper will review both acts and actors. In doing so, this does not signify that the primary emphasis is on the actor. What it does mean is that he is inseparable from his actions.

Nature of Systems

The world of accounting has been defined as associated with the now professionalized occupation of accountant and as comprising the actions and representations which result from such

---

[2] A general understanding of what is meant by occupations and professions may be obtained from such sources as Bledstein (1976), Carr-Saunders and Wilson (1933), Hall (1969), Johnson (1972), Krause (1971), Larson (1977) and Reader (1966).

[3] For a more detailed study of the nature and role of systems, the following sources are recommended—Beer (1979), Checkland (1981), Kast and Rosenzweig (1985), Selznick (1969), von Bertalanffy (1976) and Wilson (1984). In particular, these writers assist in explaining the process of systems thinking from the non-holistic approach of reductionism and mechanism, to the construction of a general systems theory involving common properties of systems, and then to the most recent approach of systems modelling to observe real-world problems (which is used in this paper).

an occupation. This description appears to fall within the generally accepted definition of a system as an organization of specific relationships constituting a coherent whole. In fact, it seems to be contained within the specific category of a social system—that is, the world of accounting comprising human actions of a communicative nature. Put more specifically, the world of accounting can be construed as involving the production, verification and dissemination of communications in the form of accounting representations of aspects of an observable economic or commercial activity. It is a system which requires human beings as resources, but is primarily constructed by their communicative actions in the specific functional contexts of education, practice, regulation, research and use.

The world of accounting can therefore be interpreted as a social system of educational, practice, regulatory, research and use acts of a communicative nature, existing in dynamic relationship over time and providing some coherent pattern for research analysis in a historical context. Of course such a system is a man-made construction—it is defined by a human being, dependent on human resources for energy and reflects human behaviour influenced by attitudes, beliefs, perceptions and motivations. In particular, its purpose is given by its observer. In this case, the world of accounting has been constructed with the enabling aim of providing a vehicle for observing the historical development of accounting actions—particularly with respect to the nature of accounting representations and the role of accountants in producing these representations.

In making these distinctions and definitions, the world of accounting is subject to the well-known characteristic of systems closure at two distinct levels—that is, the system is bounded and distinguished from its environment, first, by the initial definitional restrictions placed on it by its observer for purposes of research and discussion; and, second, by interpretations of perceived observations of its behaviour over time. Closure thus can be argued as the main topic of this paper in the sense that the history of the defined world of accounting is being observed as a system in order to identify aspects of its behaviour which can be interpreted as specific closures associated with such a system; that is, establishing its boundaries through time and stabilizing its relationships with its environment.

Essentially the social system which is described in this paper as the world of accounting is open to its environment and involves various relationships concerned with its adaptability, security and stability. Such a system is maintained in a viable condition by means of behaviour interpretable as closures which create a state of dynamic equilibrium.[4] The inherent tendency of all such systems, however, is to move to a state of internal disequilibrium or entropy created by excessive closure. Thus, in the process of transforming its inputs to outputs in a viable form, the world of accounting has to seek to achieve a state of dynamic equilibrium by operating closures while remaining sufficiently open to its environment to input energy from neighbouring systems—a stabilizing process described as negative entropy.

Systems closures for purposes of this paper can be taken to be the various processes by which the system loops back on itself and which can be evidenced in an observation of the history of the world of accounting. These instances of self-referencing are the means by which

.

---

[4]As explained in the body of the paper, such closures are means of describing in a general sense the behaviour of the system in maintaining a stable and viable state. They should be distinguished from a more specific use of the term in the context of social systems which refers to restrictions of entry to various social groupings such as professions—for example, in the context of this paper, see Macdonald (1985). As such, these closures represent a specific practical sub-set of the generic label of closure.

the system provides itself with a completeness and an identity. They assist in bounding it for its observer and provide it with a self-sufficiency. However, one further matter related to such closures needs to be explained briefly prior to the historical analysis. This concerns the potential systems condition of autopoiesis.

Scientists and social scientists have observed a tendency for systems to move towards maximum entropy or disequilibrium. Put differently, complex systems tend to become more complex, eventually reaching a state of chaos. However, within such chaos an order can be observed. Autopoietic systems are those which, by definition, emerge from chaos to order by becoming organizationally closed and self-producing—that is, their main function becomes self-organization, and their activity can be seen to be recursive in the sense of their components existing solely to create similar components. These components effectively become resources of the system in order to sustain its viability. They cannot control the system and are dedicated to reproduction. In other words, such a system controls itself; it is self-defining and autonomous.

The condition of autopoiesis has been argued in biology in relation to cell reproduction by Maturana and Varela (1980). Its recursive nature has also been claimed with respect to law—in the sense of legal norms creating rules which create norms (Teubner, 1988). And Robb (1989) has investigated the general applicability of autopoiesis to organizational systems. The historical analysis in this paper will also question briefly the possibility of systems closure in the world of accounting reaching a point at which a supra-human autopoietic system exists; and in which accounting acts achieve a state of stable chaos beyond the influence of human beings.

HISTORICAL ANALYSIS

The most substantial part of this paper is concerned with examining available historical contributions from the accounting literature for evidence of the world of accounting behaving as a social system since its origins, and, in particular, evidencing systems closures to the present day. The analysis is also concerned to introduce the possibility of such closures being sufficient to suggest the existence of autopoiesis, and this possibility will be examined in a later paper.

For the purposes of this paper, the historical analysis has been kept as broad as possible. The aim is to provide a wide review of the history of the world of accounting in order to detect very general tendencies in the system's behaviour. This is consistent with the broad observational systems approach to the history of accounting which has been advocated as a means of establishing a coherent theory of the subject (Baladouni, 1989). At a later stage of research, however, it may be necessary to reduce the span of observation to more concise periods in order to identify greater detail.

The broad sweep of the paper also brings the attendant problem of ignoring or omitting specific changes at particular points of time. However, the counter-argument to this is the need to focus on significant change. The problem is identifying what is significant.

The historical evidence examined in this paper is of a secondary or tertiary nature. The analysis thus relies on the observations and interpretations of a great many individual accounting historians. The comments made, however, are derived from careful syntheses of such evidence, concentrating solely on points over which there appears to be general agreement among the historians concerned. Such syntheses are subject to the selections and interpretations made of the available literature.

The analysis is divided into four necessarily overlapping sections of accounting history—from the earliest times, through the Renaissance, to the contemporary times of industrialisation and professionalisation. These periods of accounting activity are mainly related to the accounting which appears to have taken place in what has loosely come to be known as the Western World (particularly Europe). The reason for this analytical narrowing is the relative lack of historical studies of accounting in other countries and civilizations.

The above paragraphs have attempted to pinpoint some of the main limitations of this study. However, it is also argued that they are insufficient to prevent interesting insights being presented for debate about the history of the world of accounting and, consequently, about accounting itself.

EARLY ACCOUNTING AND ACCOUNTANTS

This first section of analysis relates to a period from approximately 8000 BC to AD 1000.[5] The most fundamental point to make about the world of accounting in this period is that, from its unknown origins, it appears to have been concerned with various forms of representing different aspects of economic or commercial activity and with the correspondence of these representations with such activity. Indeed, among accounting and non-accounting researchers of the period, there appears to be a widespread support for the thesis that counting and writing systems were developed in the first place as a consequence of existing accounting systems having to cope more efficiently with the complexities of economic or commercial activity.

The process of representational development in the world of accounting in the earliest civilizations appears to have been based on symbols with a designated meaning. These may well have originated in the form of physical objects (such as bone tallies and clay tokens) which represented physical goods and were given conventional definitions. Then, with physical objects of representation becoming cumbersome and inefficient, and with the introduction and development of writing systems, accounting representations appeared to move from pictograms (symbols for objects) to ideograms (symbols of concepts) to phonograms (symbols for word sounds). In addition, counting systems evolved from one-to-one correspondence to concrete counting and then to abstract counting.

Thus, the world of accounting developed from attempts to show economic or commercial activity by means of representing it in symbolic physical form, to describing such activity via a written message of abstract symbols with a generally accepted meaning. In other words, accounting representation in the earliest times seems to have become increasingly more abstract and decreasingly related to a one-to-one correspondence with the relevant aspects of economic or commercial activity.

Inevitably, as these changes took place, both the producer and the recipient of the coded accounting messages were dependent on a knowledge of the meanings of the symbols and symbolic relationships in the accounting representations—otherwise their production and use would have occurred without meaning, and the communicative characteristic of the accounting acts would have been missing. The world of accounting of thousands of years ago was exhibiting signs of potential systems closure—that is, exclusion from such a world by means of symbolic abstractions based on a coded system that required to be learnt; in the case of written

---

[5]Synthesized from writings such as Costouros and Stull (1989), Edwards (1989b), Garbutt (1981), Hain (1966), Keister (1963, 1970, 1986), Lee (1971), Mattessich (1987, 1989), Most (1979), Parker (1989), de Ste Croix (1956) and Stone (1969).

representations, presumably by a process of formal education. In other words, it has to be presumed that only individuals possessing such knowledge could have been an effective part of the world of accounting. Thus, even in its earliest stages, such a world appears to have developed the potential to require formal education as a necessary requirement for involvement in its affairs.

The accounting process of these earliest times appears to have been intuitive and purposive, particularly from the point of view of being part of a co-operative effort in the economic and commercial activities of the communities concerned. The accounting emphasis seems to have been on record-keeping for control and settlement purposes, and each accounting act (whether in symbolic physical or written form) appears to have had at least the potential to recur—that is, a recorded transaction leading to a recorded settlement leading to a further recorded transaction, and so on. Whether such continuity and recursion took place in this period on a large scale is debatable. Certainly, evidence of the listed records of transactions and possessions gives no indication of internal self-referencing—being limited to detailed, chronologically based representations of specific economic or commercial activities. Nevertheless, it has to be noted that the accounting which took place seemed to be, in individual circumstances, by accountants for accountants, the accountant being the owner and/or the manager concerned with the economic or commercial activity accounted for.

What is clearer, however, is that there appears to have been a perceived need formally to memorize commercial activity for various reasons (for example, settlements, tax, status, etc.). The real-world phenomena for purposes of accounting were possessions and obligations, and related monetary and non-monetary exchange flows. Any commercial or domestic matter appears to have had the potential to be the subject of recording. In many instances, as indicated above, the accountant was also the manager of the activity concerned and, consequently, was the object of the accounting. Changes which took place in the world of accounting appear to have been concerned mainly with the complexity and elaboration of the particular accounting system—for example, the detail and abstraction of the accounting representations; monetary summations and balances; single accounting lists developing into bilateral formats; uses of accounting data for administrative purposes; and the verification of accounting records by audit.

A further and seemingly continuous feature of early accounting systems was that the accounting representations were often subject to third-party verification (either by a specialist auditor or the owner). This process was sometimes based on a prior expectation: what was recorded being compared with what was believed ought to be there. On other occasions, the accounting recordings were checked with related documentation or authorizations. This seemed to introduce the idea of penalty in accounting—that is, the accountant being punished for differences, errors and shortfalls found during the audit. The overall impression of the audit of these earliest times, therefore, was of a function primarily concerned with the accuracy of both accounting entries and the stewardship of possessions.

Early accounting and accountants must be observed within the context of what was possible and needed at the time. For example, the tools of representation used for accounting purposes would have acted as determinants of the system—bone tallies and clay tokens and tablets, stone tablets and papyrus materials each bounded what and how economic and commercial phenomena could be represented in abstract accounting form. The structure of pre-Arabic number systems can be presumed to have made summations and balancing potentially less efficient than with the Arabic system. And the nature of organized economic activity may well have determined the specific demands placed on accounting and accountants—for example,

FIGURE 1

The Occupation of Accountant: Stage 1

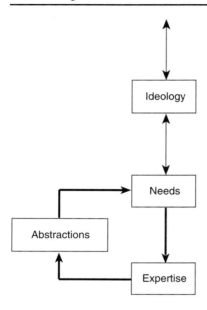

the use of cash rather than credit in transactions, the need for accountability by agents and managers, taxation based on possessions, ownership concerns with fraud and manipulation, and reliance on barter activity in given circumstances. However, despite these restrictions, the idea of accounting appears to have been capable of surviving, and was transported through different times and to different locations.

One reason for such continuity over many hundreds (indeed, thousands) of years appears to have been the scribe—the original accounting professional; highly valued in most but not all early civilizations; and the means by which accounting representations were recorded. Formally educated in temple and other schools, the literate scribe managed the early accounting systems. He had to be capable of translating economic and commercial activity into an abstract representational form. His selection for training was often made on the basis of intelligence rather than social position. The training was long, and involved rote learning, memorizing and copying. The emphasis tended to be on writing and counting in relation to commercial and domestic matters. Only in societies where literacy was high, or the class structure required it, was the office of scribe not a valued one. Thus, early accounting was informally professionalized in many circumstances, and the 'profession' appears to have exercised a form of occupational restriction of entry through maintenance of a tight loop between education and practice.

AN OVERVIEW

In order to assist in understanding the above review, the systems illustrations attempt to portray the world of accounting in these earliest times. They are, of course, abstract representa-

FIGURE 2

The Occupation of Accountant: Stage 2

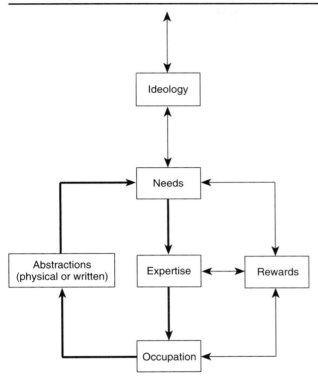

tions of that world in their own right—attempting to reflect the systems closures which have been argued to have taken place as accounting became more abstract than it was in its earliest three-dimensional physical form of representation, and as it relied increasingly on a formal knowledge of counting and writing systems—eventually depending on the services of the educated scribe.

The first stage is a general representation of the system in its earliest state, stimulated by a governing ideology in society such as a belief in the ownership of possessions and a desire to control and monitor economic and commercial exchanges, reflecting the basic need by owners and managers for accounting representations of these possessions and exchanges, and the satisfying of that need by the accounting provision of a physical or written abstraction of the possessions and exchanges. Within this system is a loop of self-reporting in circumstances where the accountant was also the owner and/or the manager.

The reader should note that, as in each of the following diagrams in the paper, the broad lines indicate the main relationships in the system which the accountants concerned appear to have had some means of controlling—that is, in the form of a closed loop. The narrow lines in and out of the system relate to other neighbouring systems with which the world of accounting interacted and from which came the potential to disturb or maintain its equilibrium state.

FIGURE 3

The Occupation of Accountant: Stage 3

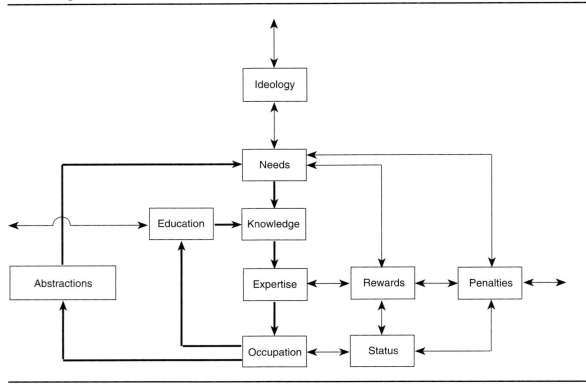

The second stage in the systems development of early accounting involved the formal creation of the occupation of accountant, and the rewarding of the accountant for the provision of his expertise in satisfying users' needs for records of economic exchanges and the possessions and obligations relating to these exchanges.

The third stage of this early development reveals the first major closure in the system beyond the initial needs-expertise-rewards closed loop. At this stage, the introduction of a formal education and training system for scribes provided the body of knowledge and expertise for the accountant serving users. It has to be speculated that the ability to maximize rewards and status, together with the emergence of a penalty system for failures, originated with this closure. It should be noted, however, that the overall system remained open to its environment—the education system was potentially open to new ideas and knowledge unless it was deliberately closed off by practitioners and teachers; and the penalties system was also subject to ideological and societal changes in attitude and practice. In other words, at this stage of its development, the social system defined as the world of accounting appears to have retained an openness despite the abstract nature of accounting representations, the self-reporting nature of many of the accounting acts and the need for a formal accounting education for scribes.

RENAISSANCE ACCOUNTING AND BEYOND

This section of the historical analysis will seek to demonstrate that, between approximately AD 1000 and AD 1800, the world of accounting can be observed as both changing and unchanged—that is, the system evidences aspects of stability and continuity with its early beginnings despite significant perturbations during the Renaissance.[6] Its earlier broad purpose of exchange and possession memory appears to have been unaffected by changes in specific accounting technologies. It appears to have survived the so-called Dark Ages, regained its social value during the Renaissance and maintained that position post-Renaissance. It also seems to have responded to the dominant ideologies of religion and capitalism, and existed in mutual dependence with organized economic and social activity.

Accounting can be evidenced in most of the formal private and public sector organizations of the period. And it assisted (or was advocated as assisting) in the specific relationships with which these organizations were involved (for example, agency and venture trading, cash and credit transactions, commercial disputations, tax collecting and partnerships). In addition, the specific accounting technologies in operation were increasingly systematized over time (for example, from unilateral to bilateral listings and from cash-based accounts charge and discharge to cash- and accruals-based double-entry bookkeeping records). Under these circumstances, it is not unreasonable to speculate that there must have been a corresponding change in the level of accounting expertise required to operate these technologies.

On the other hand, accounting continued through most of the period as an attempt to represent aspects of economic or commercial activity in wholly abstract and mainly written terms. Although physical abstract representations of economic or commercial activities continued in use (for example, tallies and checkerboards) and were not dependent on literacy, increasingly other forms of written representation depended on significant levels of literacy and numeracy (and, thus, on formal education). Whatever the situation, however, accounting remained purposive, and the main aim continued to be the recording of exchange-priced transactions and related possessions and obligations. Auditing continued in specific situations as the verification of actual representations against either a prescribed expectation or underlying documentation and other physical evidence.

The main accounting emphasis seems to have been to account for the honesty and integrity of individuals entrusted with entering into economic or commercial transactions, the care and/or use of possessions and the discharge of obligations. It was concerned mainly with evidencing economic actions rather than with constructing indicators for judging individual or organizational economic performance. Particularly before and often subsequent to the introduction of double-entry bookkeeping, the accountant was in effect the object of the accounting in many instances, being the manager of the recorded activity. Thus, as in earlier periods, the system contained a closed loop of self-reporting.

In addition to listed records and physical representations such as tallies and checkerboards, early forms of accounting technology in this period included accounts charge and discharge which conflated the detailed recording of exchange flows and resulting possessions and obligations with their reporting. Such reports were usually cash-based and avoided contemporary accounting abstractions and methodologies such as profit, capital, allocation and valuation.

---

[6]Synthesized from writings such as Baxter (1980, 1989), Cushing (1989), de Roover (1938), Edwards (1989a), Lee (1973), Mepham (1988), Noke (1981), Williams (1978), Winjum (1970) and Yamey (1947, 1949).

The later development of double-entry bookkeeping can be viewed as the introduction of an accounting technology which had the propensity to accelerate the abstract representation of commercial or economic activity by providing a convenient vehicle for profit and capital accounting, and consequential performance assessments, thereby further influencing the organizational and social environments of accounting. However, for much of the period under consideration, these highly developed man-made abstractions were the exception rather than the rule—presumably because the managerial requirement for accurate exchange, possession and obligation memories remained the primary accounting purpose. The organizational split between owner and manager was not a common situation—thus, self-reporting continued as the normal case. Nevertheless, double-entry bookkeeping eventually caused the accountant to become solely the recorder of activity rather than performing the dual role of both creator and object of the record, thus assisting to break down the previous self-reporting closed loop.

Transaction-based double-entry bookkeeping introduced accounting complexities which required considerable expertise. It was advocated in textbooks written by learned students of science and mathematics, and became a popular subject in schools and universities. This had two apparent systems effects—the first was a reinforcement of the restriction of accounting practice to a sufficiently educated elite; the second was the contrary opening up of accounting knowledge by means of a market in bookkeeping texts and teachers.

Bookkeeping texts and teachings also evidence the process of creating a demand for accounting services—that is, establishing client dependency by means of invoking tension concerning the need for organizational order through double-entry bookkeeping, and its specific use with respect to fraud prevention and detection, court actions, credit settlements and partnership arrangements. Considerable emphasis was given in these texts to the virtue of control through arithmetical balancing, as well as to accounting accuracy and commercial justice. As previously stated, such orderly systematizing of organizational information can be argued to have assisted in the splitting up of the owner-management function—enabling economic or commercial activity to be viewed indirectly by means of comprehensive and articulating double-entry records. Such a system can also be argued to have begun the process of separating the accountant from such activity. In other words, he became increasingly reliant on transaction-based documentation to prepare his representational abstractions in double entry form.

At this point in the analysis, some further essential features of double-entry bookkeeping introduced during the Renaissance should be noted. First, it was and is a completely self-referencing system—each accounting entry giving rise to a corresponding entry, and the total data recorded balancing to a net zero. Second, the prescriptive classification rules result in accounting states determining accounting flows and these flows, in turn, determining states. Third, it is a system which can be perpetuated so long as there are open balances within it—in essence, past data resulting in future data through an indefinite carrying forward by means of the process of allocation. And fourth, and following the second point, the rules which determine the data to be accounted for result in reported data which, if found useful, reinforce the need for the rules. Thus, double-entry bookkeeping, because of its inherent self-referencing and recursive nature, can be argued to have been a significant contribution to the development of the defined world of accounting.

Put more specifically, the above review suggests that the accounting technology of double-entry bookkeeping could well have provided a significant closure in the world of accounting—its prescribed orderliness but flexibility to cope with transactions creating a rule-dominated means of comprehensively observing and efficiently accounting for economic or commercial activity; its comprehensiveness and efficiency depending on prescribed rules; its articulating components providing a means of further abstracting such activity in representational form; and its complexity leaving accounting essentially in the hands of an educated elite.

Nevertheless, the dissemination of knowledge of double-entry bookkeeping by texts and teachers tended, to some extent, to counterbalance these systems closures by increasing the potential size of such an elite and by introducing competition in the market for accounting services. In addition, the separation of accounting from management and ownership could be argued to have tended partially to break the closed loop of self-reporting, although the essential feature of the latter remained, i.e. accounting being undertaken on behalf of the manager or owner-manager in order to assist him in providing a memory of the consequences of his managerial activities (in other words, information feedback, an essential aspect of systems behaviour).

The overall picture of accounting in this period, therefore, is of a social system which bounded itself firmly in terms of accounting acts to provide abstract representations of economic or commercial activity. The exercising of such closure was assisted by the use of a complex, prescriptive technology such as double-entry bookkeeping, the operation of which was reliant on individuals with sufficient skills acquired through formal education and training. This appears to continue the tradition of the scribe in earlier periods and to be the basis for professionalization in the next period.

AN OVERVIEW

It can be seen that the availability of the body of knowledge through texts tended to reinforce the closed loop between accounting education and practice, but also introduced the openness of competition through access to books. At this point, however, the threat of competition to the equilibrium of the overall system appears not to have been sufficient to destabilize the world of accounting. Literacy must have remained a principal means of closure at this point in the history of the world of accounting—partly because of the written nature of accounting and partly because of the increasing complexities of the technologies required to generate the communicative acts of accounting.

INDUSTRIALIZATION AND ACCOUNTING

The period covered in this section—the fourteenth to the twentieth centuries[7]—saw accounting developments largely as a result of a nineteenth century trend from merchanting to factory-based industry. The purpose of accounting altered from one of pure memory-aid to that of management tool; more specifically, from recording costs to controlling them and using accounting data to assess performance. Accounting can thus be seen in the period as appearing to respond to specific problems associated with organizational change—particularly the increasing use of man-made accounting abstractions such as profit and capital calculations with respect to efficiency assessment, individual achievement and the related importance, incidence and magnitude of

---

[7]Synthesized from writings such as Church (1910), Crossman (1953), Edwards (1989a, 1989b), Epstein (1978), Garner (1976), Johnson (1981), Kaplan (1984), Loft (1988), Mepham (1988), Parker (1968, 1980), Solomons (1968), Theiss (1937) and Wells (1977).

FIGURE 4

The Occupation of Accountant: Stage 4

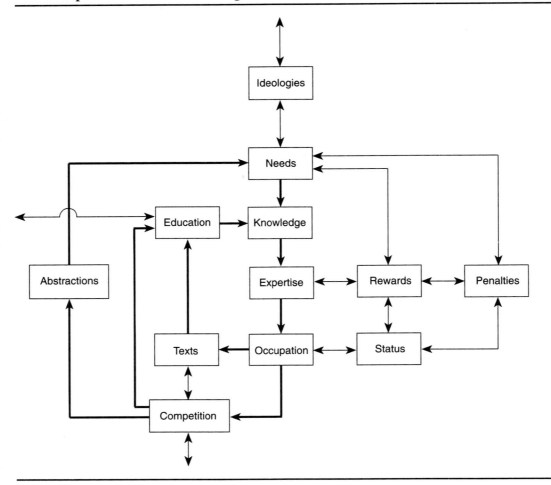

material, wage and overhead costs. These responses appear to have resulted in accountants becoming more divorced mentally if not physically from the economic or commercial activity they attempted to represent in accounting terms.

In other words, although many of the data used for accounting purposes were derived from observable economic or commercial activity, their derivatives (such as profit and capital), which were seemingly assuming increasing importance to managers, were representations of a bookkeeping rather than an economic reality. As a result, a further recursion can be evidenced in the system—the organizational importance of these pure accounting abstractions creating rules of calculation and the rules, in turn, creating the abstractions. At the same time, the potential power of accounting to control human behaviour was increased—specifically, pure accounting abstractions such as profit were available for purposes of assessing entity and, thus, managerial performance.

The history of the technical accounting function during this period reveals its origins in the twelfth to fourteenth centuries as a means of mercantile record-keeping which was capable of adapting to one of industrial bookkeeping (increasingly on a double-entry basis). It had an initial emphasis on entity costs but gradually switched to the recording of specific product or process costs. However, the introduction of factory-based systems of production reveals the problem of custom and habit in accounting—the traditional emphasis on entity costs did not appear to provide what was required managerially either in terms of cost control to maximize profits or with respect to producing data for purposes of pricing and competitive bidding. What seemed to be needed was a change in accounting from recording externally related transaction exchanges to providing internally orientated information on the cost effects of industrial processes which were controllable by management. The inability of the then existing financial record systems to provide this information created separate cost record and then cost accounting systems within industrial organizations.

Parallel with these structural changes in the world of accounting, brought about by organizational and managerial needs, were changes in the structure of costs—first, the increasing importance of wages due to production activities, and then a similar development in the incidence of overheads as a result of introducing the technologies of industrialization. These changes, in turn, appear to have created an opportunity for the further accounting abstraction of economic or commercial activity due to the increasing use of the complex process of cost allocation.

The idea of accounting representations corresponding faithfully with observable economic or commercial phenomena appears not to have been initially a major concern to accountants or managers. Indeed, the major influence in the development of costing can be seen as engineers responsible for production management. Unconcerned with, or perhaps unaware of the traditional stewardship responsibilities of the accountant, the engineer advocated and practised costing procedures very different from the accounting required for conventional record-keeping. Thus the main emphasis in such matters was on establishing methods of cost calculation for defined products and entities, and on deriving overhead allocation formulae which provided explainable connections between direct and indirect costs. Arbitrariness was recognized but appeared to be tolerated as a necessary part of accounting.

The use of cost data for management also appears to have caused a switch in attention by accountants from the past (records) to the future (budgets, predetermined cost rates and standards). Thus, a further recursion occurred in the world of accounting—past accounting data being used as a basis for producing forecasts of future data, and the latter being used as points of reference for the use of actual data once the related economic or commercial activity had taken place. In other words, the world of accounting appears to have been involved in a major attempt to 'capture' the future and bring it back into the present in the form of budgets, forecasts and other estimates, while at the same time pushing the past into the future by means of cost allocations.[8] The relationship or correspondence between the timing of economic or commercial activity and the timing of its representation in accounting terms thus became difficult to synchronize.

---

[8]This is not to suggest that such accountings had not occurred prior to this period in the history of the world of accounting. Budgeting may well have occurred at earlier times (Theiss, 1937). However, the advent of manufacturing and industrialization provided a managerial impetus for a more widespread use organizationally.

Perhaps because industrial accounting of the nineteenth century was so much in the hands of engineers, or perhaps because it was regarded as a commercially sensitive subject in relation to pricing and tendering, accountants were slow to respond to these new ideas of allocation. Gradually, however, they appeared to become convinced of their utility, and assisted directly in practice and through the literature in the further development of actual costings (based on arbitrary allocations) and estimated costings (based on predicted budgets and standards). They incorporated these data, where relevant, into cost-accounting systems using the double-entry bookkeeping technology, and were able (if required) to relate and reconcile the cost figures to their financial accounting records and statements. They appear also to have slowly absorbed ideas developed by economists, engineers and actuaries in relation to matters such as relevant costs, capital budgeting and performance indicators.

Several key findings can be drawn from the above brief analysis—that is, the constrictions to change caused by habits of thought passed on through the generations of accountants, with particular respect to developing beyond the original memory purpose of accounting; the ability of double-entry bookkeeping to handle sophisticated accounting practice changes; the increasing abstraction of accounting representations by non-accountants; the unwillingness of non-accountants to take indefinite responsibility for all accounting acts; the inheritance of an increasingly abstract accounting by accountants about to enter a period where reporting to external interests became a major function; the inheritance by accountants of the practice of basing accounting data on arbitrary estimates, formulae and judgement; and the continuing recursiveness of accounting acts, rules and representations.

However, arguably by far the most significant observation of the period was the explicit and separate internalizing of accounting actions—that is, as organizational changes caused accounting to be as (if not more) concerned with internal management of activity than with the specifics of monitoring external exchanges (for example, in relation to controlling production and manufacturing processes). The earlier development of double-entry bookkeeping to abstract external exchanges in a completely articulating and self-referencing system appeared to start a process of separating the accountant from the reality of these exchanges. The same process of separation can be argued to have continued in the development of cost and management accounting—not so much at the stage at which the engineering managers of economic or commercial activity were involved in accounting for it, but more when accountants inherited the allocation abstractions devised by these engineers.

Thus, the combination of a complete, self-referencing double-entry bookkeeping system with a large set of complex allocation procedures may well have caused a considerable mental if not physical separation of the accountant from the economic or commercial phenomena he was responsible for representing in accounting terms. What history may be revealing in this analysis is that accountants of this period were beginning to use accounting technologies which could represent such phenomena in abstract terms without direct involvement with that reality—unlike earlier systems where the accountant appears to have been part of the economic or commercial activity concerned. Nevertheless, despite this potential isolation of the accountant, the power of his representations was enhanced by means of their use in the context of individual and entity performance assessments.

The above comments should be coupled with those of the next section prior to making any changes to the systems diagram in Stage 4 of the history of the world of accounting. However, at this point, it is apparent that a fundamental inner stability had been created in the system—despite the increasing abstraction, presence of texts and expanding body of knowledge; and irrespective of the turbulence created by organizational and managerial changes caused by industrialization.

PROFESSIONALIZATION AND FINANCIAL REPORTING

This section also focuses on the period from the fourteenth to the twentieth centuries.[9] It deals with the specific inheritance by an organized and self-regulating accounting profession of the mutually compatible accounting technologies of double-entry bookkeeping and accounting allocations, together with their use in the context of attempting to report on economic or commercial activities to persons dislocated from these activities and therefore relying on a surrogate experience of them.

As mentioned in the previous section, the initial technical accounting emphasis of the period continued to be record-keeping, increasingly on a double-entry basis, but with the profit and loss account in the ledger used as a clearing house for all entries not specifically dealt with by other accounts. Faithful representation appears to have been perceived by accountants typically in terms of the accuracy of individual accounting entries. The main financial accounting statement was the balance sheet, a document that was for a considerable time nothing more than an abstract of ledger accounts. As with management accounting, the initial change in financial accounting of the period can be attributed to the growing complexity of economic or commercial activity. Industrialization caused organizational changes—first in the form of larger partnerships, and then gradually the splitting of ownership from managerial control, with owners often distant from corporate operations, and with the need for expert management on their behalf within legally defined corporate entities.

The emphasis in financial accounting thus changed from the proprietor to a purely legal abstraction—the entity. A need had been created for regular financial reporting to outside ownership interests and for the use of a profit-based justification of dividend returns to these interests. The focal point in accounting gradually switched from financial position (with a correspondence to certain empirical referents) to profitability (a pure accounting abstraction); and thus from balance sheet to profit statement. Accounting technologies moved away from valuation of economic phenomena to the matching of allocated data. Ideas from cost accounting with respect to allocations for matching purposes were available and slowly incorporated into accounting for external financial reporting. Gradually, with the development of an organized accounting profession, apparently poor and inconsistent allocation methods and rules were criticized and debated, and eventually standardized in the modern form by accountants and their professional bodies. Thus, the rules that determined accounting representations (which, in turn, created the rules) were institutionalized and legitimated by formal written standards of procedure which had general acceptance among accountants.

These processes of change suggest the culmination of a very long-term transition in the world of accounting from accounting for economic or commercial phenomena to accounting

---

[9]Synthesized from writings such as Anon (1954), Boys (1989), Brief (1976), Davidson and Anderson (1987), Edwards (1989b), Langenderfer (1987), Lee (1982, 1988), Nobes and Parker (1984), Parker (1978), Stewart (1975, 1986), Walker (1988) and Yamey (1977).

for bookkeeping phenomena. The contemporary emphasis on a man-made accounting construct such as profit, dependent on an articulating construct of aggregated financial position which reconciles to an abstract datum of capital, reveals the extent to which accounting had moved from observing and recording real-world empirical phenomena such as exchanges, possessions and obligations to representation of wholly artificial phenomena such as net worth or equity. The institutionalized standardizing of such accounting also warns of the problems associated with effecting changes to the basic principles underlying it.

The need for an organized accounting profession was first recognized by accountants in the mid-nineteenth century—industrialization, management information needs, company failures, court actions, regular reporting and auditing requirements and taxation each strengthening that need. The process of professionalization affected many occupations and, in the case of accounting, was strictly controlled by specific bodies—entry was largely restricted to the well-educated and well-off; qualification was dependent on a combination of training and examination under the auspices of existing members of the professional body concerned; and the separateness and legitimacy of the profession was determined by such means as the obtaining of royal charters, the use of prefixes such as CA or CPA, and restrictions on the type of work members of professional bodies could undertake. Control over the body of knowledge of accounting was achieved through a fusing of education and training, and the provision of examinations of practical competence.

The areas in which these professionals worked initially seem to have been influenced largely by custom and habit—that is, they related to record-keeping for ownership and management, and involved a secrecy with respect to the recorded information (largely as a result of the self-referential tradition of accounting—essentially reporting by accountants for accountants). This latter point can be evidenced in terms of such matters as the use of private ledgers; the apparently general acceptance by accountants of over- or understatement in accounting by managers and owners; the specific involvement of accountants in manipulation through secret reserve accounting; and consistently low levels of disclosure even within legally required financial statements. The record-keeping stewardship habit emphasized the use of historical costs as a basis for accounting. And this process may well have been consolidated by the conservative and long-lasting influence of legally based work by the early professional accountants with respect to activities such as arbitration and bankruptcies.

The owner-control split in organizations also resulted in the continuation of a specific audit need. The early audits of this period were bookkeeping audits—ensuring compatibility of the balance sheet with the underlying records and attempting, by retracing bookkeeping actions, to bring fraud and error to light. As in accounting, the work of auditors was legitimated by increasing legal or regulatory provisions for their services. The quality of the audited information and the audit report were expressed usually in particular but undefined legal terms (which, in most recent times, have tended to be interpreted by accountants and lawyers in the context of prescribed accounting standards; a self-referencing which has further solidified the body of knowledge of accounting).

The nature of accounting as a complex representational abstraction of economic or commercial activity appears to have been enhanced in part during the period by a combination of public criticism of financial reports, court actions and decisions, and a seeming fear by accountants and their professional bodies of government interference in accounting rule-making. The professional need to self-regulate was strong, and the urge to develop accounting standards of an increasingly authoritative nature became clear. The need to legitimate this process can be evidenced in relatively recent times by the continual reviewing of the standard-setting process and standards; the search for a conceptual framework to justify standards; and the gradual physical if not mental separation of the standard-setting process from the direct control of professional bodies. Perhaps unwitting concern by accountants to maintain the existing body of knowledge of accounting abstraction and representation is suggested by the continual ignoring or rejection of radical alternatives to it in the research field and by encouragement of the standardization process.

In auditing, changes can also be seen—the move away from pure bookkeeping audits to a wider and apparently more scientific auditing of accounting abstractions based on sample tests; the establishment of standards to govern such a process; coping and responding to criticisms of and actions against auditors; and the constant reviewing of public expectations of auditors and their duty of care. Observations of the overall audit process, however, reveal that auditors, as accountants, have tended to reinforce and legitimate the conventional accounting system of abstraction and representation.

The accounting profession has changed structurally over the last hundred or more years. There are fewer bodies, and fewer but larger public accountancy firms. This consolidation of control over accounting expertise, however, has been accompanied by a diffusion of accountants in employment outside such firms. In addition, the latter entities have expanded away from traditional high-risk work to areas with less public expectation and less well-defined responsibilities (such as consultancy). But a major and continuous focus for the accounting profession and its constituent bodies has been its control of education—matching the short-term needs of practice and increasingly accrediting the syllabus content of university and college courses. Legitimation of the process has been achieved through well-educated high school and then graduate entrants; the establishment of professional schools of accounting and accreditation boards mainly comprising accounting educators; and constant reviews of the education process in light of criticism.

Finally, this period witnessed the increasing use and importance of pure accounting abstractions such as profit and capital to assess the performance of human beings—thus enhancing the power potential of accounting (and accountants) and accentuating the interplay between human behaviour and accounting acts—accounting influencing and being influenced by human behaviour (for example, in relation to stock market activity, lending decisions, managerial compensation, taxation, etc.).

Several features of the above analysis of this period should be highlighted at this point. First, the apparent inheritance of a traditional view of financial accounting's purpose as record-keeping for memory, reporting for stewardship and the maintenance of a level of secrecy on behalf of owners and managers. Although the habit of accounting for stewardship must have been helpful when dealing with a similar reporting function to external interests, the other features appear contrary to the needs of the latter—particularly when these individuals are separated physically from the reporting entity. Second, the mutually supporting roles of the accountant and the auditor, initially through record-keeping and then through the twin processes of bookkeeping and cost allocation. In other words, the self-referencing nature of financial accounting is evident—rule-dependent accounting representations produced and verified by accountants using a mutually agreed set of representation-dependent rules for calculation and re-calculation. Third, the apparent inability of accountants to innovate significantly in accounting. Certain changes, such as consolidated financial statements, did take place but these tended to be extensions rather than radical departures from the existing body of knowledge. Fourth, the stipulation of education, training and qualification requirements to meet practice needs—a familiar process of professionalization in terms of control over the body of knowledge and creation of public confidence. Fifth, the legitimizing (and solidifying) of accounting through legislative and regulatory provisions, the standard-setting process, the siting of education in universities and the constant reviewing of education, practice and policy. Sixth, the further confirmation of the body of knowledge of accounting in terms of its basic adherence to complex bookkeeping abstractions of economic or commercial activity. Seventh, the growing importance of pure accounting abstractions as means of influencing or controlling human behaviour. And, finally, the concentration of the professional structure into a smaller, more powerful community of training firms and regulatory associations.

An Overview

Each of these features can be interpreted as signs of closure in a social system, and can be represented in the following expanded diagrams of such a system—The Accounting Profession: Stages 1 and 2.

The first diagram illustrates the original nature of professionalization in the world of accounting. It reveals the closures brought about by that process—particularly through regulation, training, registration and examination. It also suggests the formalization of the penalty structure through litigation and legislation, but the continuing openness of the system to other systems through ideologies, legislation, litigation, competition and education. In other words, the world of accounting at this stage appears to have further defined its boundaries through the closures brought about by professionalization. These closures, in turn, reinforced earlier closures relating to the abstract body of knowledge of accounting representations.

The second phase of professionalization is portrayed as a closing off with respect to education through accreditation and to practice through standardization. Further openness (actual and potential) is created by a research function—although, by ignoring or rejecting the results of research, or selecting those it requires to maintain its viability, the world of accounting can be argued to be exercising control through closure. The complete system has thus become a complex interrelationship of subsystems. The professional closures of the period are balanced by openness created by means of certain of these other systems such as education and research.

The broad lines on the left-hand side of the systems diagram, representing closed loops, indicate the ways in which the world of accounting has attempted to define its boundaries and control for purposes of viability. This appears to be done through the production and verification of abstract accounting representations which are difficult to understand, tight control over the professional process of regulation, training, education and examination, and the prescription of self-produced standards for accounting practice. It is now a matter of some interest to speculate whether further significant closures are or could be taking place on the right-hand side of the diagram—for example, with respect to the prescribing of standards and their incorporation into judgements in litigation and legislative provisions. Such speculations, however, are not the main purpose of this paper. The major point to be made is that there is evidence to argue that the world of accounting is a social system which, throughout its history, can be demonstrated to exhibit increasing closure.

EVIDENCE OF CLOSURE[10]

The purpose of this paper has been to pursue a natural curiosity by seeking possible explanations of the development of the world of accounting by referring to its history. By broadly observing and interpreting the social system through time, it was hoped that some explanation of accounting as a social system subject to systems closures would be possible. The evidence reviewed in this paper from the earliest times to the present day appears to imply a system reflecting both change and lack of change. This conclusion should not be surprising in the sense that, as mentioned earlier, complex systems have a tendency to become more complex and achieve higher levels of entropy through closures, until they reach a chaotic state—at which point an inner order may be possible to discern (Gleick, 1987). It is therefore relevant to examine the constants and changes in the system.

THE CONSTANTS

The most obvious constant to be found in the review is the existence of a body of knowledge of accounting. It has existed continuously from the very earliest of times as an apparently deliberate attempt by man to represent aspects of economic or commercial activity in the form of a series of symbolically based abstractions.

The second major constant is the literacy and numeracy dependence of accounting through time—its abstract representations have usually been 'written' and depended on the existence of number and writing systems (exceptions to this general rule concern physical representations at particular points of time). This, in turn, has meant that accounting has required the parallel existence of an education system (informal and then formal)—not only to teach the body of knowledge of accounting but also, in its earliest history, to instruct accountants in its necessary ingredients of counting and writing. Because of this educational requirement, accounting has appeared to maintain an elitist position in society for much of its existence—education creating an obvious and major boundary or closure to the system.

The self-referential and recursive nature of accounting is a further constant feature in the analysis—that is, the technical function of accounting has had a propensity for self-referencing and recursion. For example, at most times throughout the history of the world of accounting, accounting techniques have been the basis for communicative acts referencing the past to the present to the future, and vice versa. Recursion has been possible with past accounting actions

---

[10]The comments made in this section appear to be consistent with researched views and findings of other writers. For example, the constancy of ideas in accounting and the impact of habit and custom (Chambers, 1989; Sterling, 1977); the increasing abstraction of accounting and isolation of accountants (Sterling, 1988a, 1988b, 1989); accounting by accountants for accounts (Lee, 1984; Lee and Tweedie, 1977; Tweedie, 1977); the links between accounting, literacy, education and examination (Hoskin and Macve, 1986, 1988; Miller and O'Leary, 1987); and aspects of the professional monopoly (Dyckman, 1974; Macdonald, 1985; Montagna, 1974; Richardson, 1988; Walker, 1988; Zeff, 1987).

FIGURE 6

The Accounting Profession: Stage 1

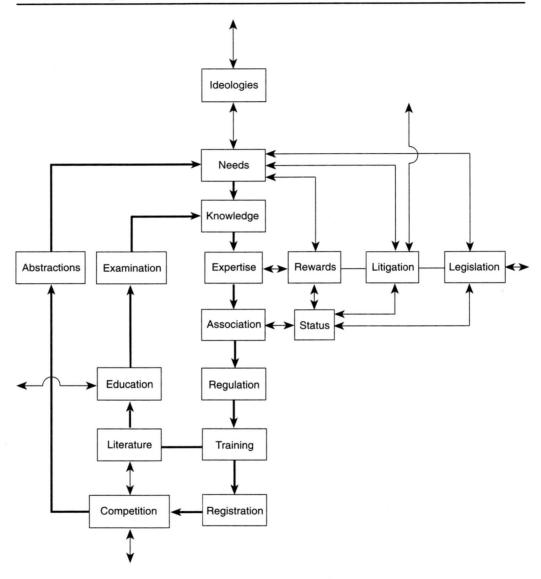

FIGURE 7

The Accounting Profession: Stage 2

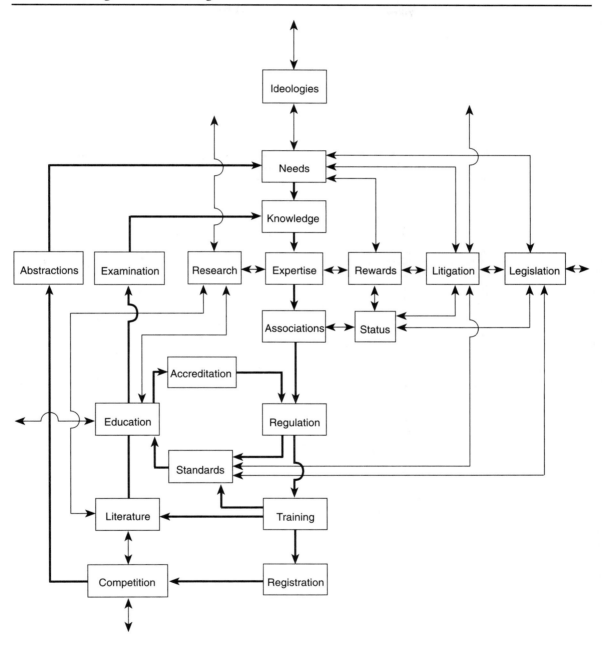

triggering an infinite chain of future accounting actions by means of continuous trading or regulatory activity. Recursion has also existed because of the process of custom and habit—successive generations of accountants perpetuating the basic principles of the body of knowledge of accounting (for example, in the form of double-entry bookkeeping and cost allocations).

The occupation of accountant in society represents the fourth major constant. The body of knowledge of abstractions, dependent on an underlying education system, has provided an occupational specialization which, with some exceptions, has given accountants status, prestige, rewards and penalties in society.

A consistent and major objective of accounting representations through time appears to have been stewardship in the broadest interpretation of that term. In this sense, a power-knowledge relationship has been persistent through time as accounting technologies have been used to record and control for the accountability of the individual for his actions in organizations and society. As such, this process can be explained relatively continuously through history as a 'management' tool for control purposes. Also relatively continuously through time, this process has been supported by a function of audit.

The broad nature of the accounting function also appears to have remained stable through time. The desire for a permanent memory of transaction exchanges, and resultant possessions and obligations, has been persistent. The need for owners to know what they own and owe has been recurrent and has sustained two characteristics of accounting—first, the output of the accounting process is regarded as largely secret and confidential to owners and/or managers; and, second, diversity of accounting practice in reporting is natural and tolerable as a consequence. This historical tendency has been most difficult to cope with in modern times when increased external disclosure is demanded.

A seventh constant has been the ability of the system defined as the world of accounting to adapt to a changing environment without fundamentally changing its purpose or its main characteristics. In particular, it has achieved this by 'improving' the efficiency and effectiveness of its technologies, and by using the processes of education and training associated with them (for example, the use of writing and counting; double-entry bookkeeping; cost allocations; and professionalization).

The final constant is the accountant's apparent lack of significant innovation but considerable talent and skills in developing the results of others' creativity. This can be evidenced in relation to such matters as double-entry bookkeeping, cost allocations and budgeting and standards.

The Changes

The first change concerns the site of accounting. This has evolved organizationally from the individual, to groups of individuals, to corporate bodies—inevitably resulting in a more complex environment for the world of accounting to exist in. In parallel with this development, the nature of economic activity to be accounted for has translated from individual exchanges, to continuous exchanges, to exchanges following processes of manufacture and production—again, an increasing complexity.

In turn, this has created separations which have affected and changed accounting and accountants. First, the separation of ownership from management—with changes in accounting emphasis from owner to entity and from valuation to matching in order to provide indicators of performance for accountability purposes. Second, the separation of the manager and the accountant, with the accountant becoming more the operator rather than the object of the accounting process. Each of these separations has had the propensity to isolate the accountant physically if not mentally from the economic or commercial activity he is expected to represent in abstract terms. And this appears to have caused that reality to change for reporting purposes from economic phenomena to bookkeeping data—seemingly accentuating the inherently abstract nature of accounting representations.

Coupled with the changes relating to the site of accounting has been the increasing use in recent times of pure accounting abstractions as a means of assessing human performance. This goes much beyond the constant mentioned above of accounting for stewardship by means of formal memory. Instead, it can be interpreted as accounting achieving a level of potential organizational and societal power much beyond that attained in earlier times. Indeed, it can be argued that assessment and related decisions associated with organized economic or commercial activity are largely dependent on accounting representations of a purely abstract nature. This, in turn, has created a significant situation of self-referencing—accounting being used to assess individual performance, and those individuals being assessed (in whatever way) attempting to use accounting to enhance the assessments.

In addition to the above separations and connections, accounting representations appear to have become increasingly abstract through the use of technological innovations such as double-entry bookkeeping and cost allocations. This can be argued to have reinforced the switch of emphasis to a bookkeeping reality, widened and deepened the body of knowledge of accounting abstraction and made its teaching an increasingly important element in the world of accounting. In particular, the accounting education system has become a crucial element of monopolistic control for accountants. This has also appeared to further separate accountants (as accountants) from the non-accounting world. However, it has opened up the world of accounting to potential competition through the influence of teachings in the accounting classroom and textbooks, and from research activity.

The above separations have been accompanied by an increasing demand for accounting services and caused accountants to organize formally to attempt to create a monopoly of service and control over the body of knowledge of accounting. This process of professionalization has resulted in issues concerning a balancing of such matters as self-interest and public interest; diversity of accounting practices, and standardization and codification; risk, reward and punishment; secrecy and disclosure; and education and practice needs and research.

Essentially what appears to have been happening in recent times is that earlier informal closures of the world of accounting caused by the need for literacy and man's intuitive secrecy in relation to economic or commercial activity have been accentuated by institutionalized closures which give power and authority to accounting and accountants, and by the increasingly legitimated uses to which accounting representations have been put. The accounting profession has been institutionalized through professional bodies controlling registration, training, examination, education and accreditation; and legitimated through legalized use of accounting, regulations, standards, literature and research. These processes in combination attempt to provide the control needed to maintain a professional monopoly over the body of knowledge of accounting and to give practice autonomy and social mobility. Such attempted control has been strengthened by the increasing size of the accounting profession, a reduction in the number of its practice and training units and regulatory bodies, and an apparently insatiable appetite for the services of its members.

CONCLUSIONS

What this historical analysis appears to suggest is that the defined world of accounting can be viewed as a social system which, in its contemporary form, controls a body of complex abstract accounting knowledge and rewards its practitioners so long as such knowledge is required for record-keeping and performance assessment, and concerns about it are responded to (but arguably not resolved) through codification of accounting rules of calculation.

Societal needs for accounting expertise are central to the system, and the satisfaction of these needs provides accountants with rewards and status in society. But maintaining rewards and status depends on use of the power-knowledge relationship. The objective appears to be to obtain a monopoly position in terms of power and knowledge, from which practice autonomy and social mobility for the accountant are natural consequences. However, in order to achieve this objective, the world of accounting as a social system open to its environment, and in terms of competition and potential conflicts of interest with other systems, closes in order to establish and then maintain a state of dynamic equilibrium.

The system now exercises closures in two main ways—formally, by having its actions in society legitimated by means of a variety of devices, and by institutionalizing its most significant functions; and informally, by operation of a written system of abstract accounting representations requiring an education-based expertise which is desired organizationally and societally. The combined effect of these closures in the world of accounting appears to provide it with the authority to exercise the power it has through its body of knowledge in satisfying societal needs for accounting representations of economic or commercial activity.

As the reviews and analyses in this paper have indicated, the history of the world of accounting evidences the increasing shaping of the system by means of closures at various points of time. It has also been subject to constant pressures from other systems in its environment. These pressures have required responses resulting in adaptations and changes which, in turn, have led to further pressures and closure responses. The increasing accreditation of education programmes to meet practice needs; the accelerating abstraction and manipulation of accounting representations; the incoherent structures of inconsistent standards, the stockpiling of practices and the recycling of issues; the consolidation and growth of practice entities and regulating bodies; and an uneasy relationship with the state—all appear to be contemporary signs of an increasingly complex system having to cope with attempting to obtain at least some form of dynamic equilibrium.

Whether this chaos or messiness in the system is potentially autopoietic is a matter offered finally and briefly for more extensive debate and discussion elsewhere. It is advanced as a logical extension of the argument that the world of accounting can be perceived in terms of systems thinking. It is also given as a means of thinking about the curious mixture evidenced in this paper of change and no change throughout the history of accounting—that is, of ordered chaos. In other words, it could be suggested that, if it has reached an autopoietic state in terms of its self-referential nature and recursiveness, the world of accounting as a social system is being selective with respect to change—accepting change which does not alter its state of equilibrium and rejecting change which has the potential to do so. In other words, it would have become self-organizing and concerned solely with the reproduction of its existing components such as accounting technologies, rules and representations. The major conundrum in this respect is that autopoietic systems define themselves. In other words, if the world of accounting is autopoietic, what is its shape, what are its boundaries and what is its purpose?

These are issues and questions which, perhaps fortunately, must be the subject of further papers. Meantime, it is hoped that this paper gives sufficient food for significant thought about the nature of accounting.

I am grateful for comments of colleagues at the Universities of Alabama and Edinburgh, Professor Richard Macve and participants in the 1990 BAA Conference at the University of Dundee, and for the detailed suggestions of two anonymous reviewers. Without this openness, the paper would have retained its closed loop. The paper is a condensation and greatly amended version of the author's book *The Closure of the Accounting Profession,* Garland Publishing, 1990, and is published with the kind permission of Garland.

REFERENCES

American Accounting Association (1970) 'Report of the Committee on Accounting History', *Supplement to The Accounting Review,* 53–64.

Anon. (1954) 'The origins of accountancy as a profession in Scotland', in *A History of The Chartered Accountants of Scotland From the Earliest Times to 1954,* Edinburgh: Institute of Chartered Accountants of Scotland, pp. 1–19.

Armstrong, M. B. and J. I. Vincent (1988) 'Public accounting: a profession at a crossroads', *Accounting Horizons,* March: 94–8.

Baladouni, V. (1979) 'The study of accounting history', in E. N. Coffman (ed) *Working Paper 19, Working Paper Series 1,* Alabama: The Academy of Accounting Historians, 318–28.

Baladouni, V. (1989) 'A paradigm for the analysis of accounting history', in R. H. Toudkar and E. N. Coffman (eds) *Working Paper 66, Working Paper Series 4,* Alabama: The Academy of Accounting Historians, pp. 95–109.

Baxter, W. T. (1980) 'The account charge and discharge', *The Accounting Historian's Journal,* Spring: 69–71.

Baxter, W. T. (1988) *Accounting Research—Academic Trends Versus Practical Needs,* Edinburgh: The Institute of Chartered Accountants of Scotland.

Baxter, W. T. (1989) 'Early accounting: the tally and checkerboard', *The Accounting Historian's Journal,* December: 43–83.

Beer, S. (1979) *The Heart of Enterprise,* Chichester: John Wiley.

Behling, O. and J. F. Dillard (1987) 'Accounting: the intuitive challenge', *Accounting Horizons,* June: 35–42.

Bledstein, B. J. (1976) *The Culture of Professionalism,* New York: Norton.

Boys, P. (1989) 'What's in a name', *Accountancy,* January: 100–2.

Brief, R. P. (1976) *Nineteenth Century Capital Accounting and Business Investment,* New York: Arno Press.

Burchell, S., C. Clubb, A. Hopwood, J. Hughes and J. Nahapiet (1980) 'The roles of accounting in organisations and society', *Accounting, Organisations and Society,* 5(1): 5–27.

Carr, E. H. (1987) *What is History?,* Harmondsworth: Penguin.

Carr-Saunders, A. and P. A. Wilson (1933) *The Professions,* Oxford: Oxford University Press.

Chambers, R. J. (1989) 'Time in accounting', *Abacus,* March: 7–21.

Checkland, P. B. (1981) *Systems Thinking, Systems Practice,* Chichester: John Wiley.

Church, A. H. (1910) *Production Factors in Cost Accounting and Works Management.* Reprinted (1976) New York: Arno Press, particularly pp. 36–59 and 113–37.

Collingwood, R. G. (1974) 'Human nature and human history', in P. Gardiner (ed.) *The Philosophy of History,* Oxford: Oxford University Press, pp. 17–40.

Connor, J. E. (1986) 'Enhancing public confidence in the accounting profession', *Journal of Accountancy,* July: 76–83.

Costouros, G. J. and J. B. Stull (1989) 'The development of letters and numbers as tools of accounting', in R. H. Toudkar and E. N. Coffman (eds) *Working Paper 71, Working Paper Series 4,* Alabama: The Academy of Accounting Historians, pp. 160–9.

Crossman, P. (1953) 'The genesis of cost control', *The Accounting Review,* October: 522–7.

Cushing, B. E. (1989) 'A Kuhnian interpretation of the historical evolution of accounting', *The Accounting Historian's Journal,* December: 1–41.

Davidson, S. and G. D. Anderson (1987) 'The development of accounting and auditing standards', *Journal of Accountancy,* May: 110–27.

de Roover, R. (1938) 'Characteristics of bookkeeping before Paciolo', *The Accounting Review,* June: 144–9.

de Ste Croix, G. E. M. (1956) 'Greek and Roman accounting', in A. C. Littleton and B. S. Yamey (eds) *Studies in the History of Accounting,* London: Sweet & Maxwell, pp. 21–50.

Dyckman, T. R. (1974) 'Public accounting: guild or profession?' in R. R. Sterling (ed.) *Institutional Issues in Public Accounting,* Lawrence, Kan.: Scholars Book Co., pp. 189–210.

Edwards, J. R. (1989a) 'Industrial cost accounting developments in Britain to 1930: a review article', *Accounting and Business Research,* Autumn: 305–17.

Edwards, J. R. (1989b) *A History of Financial Accounting,* London: Routledge.

Epstein, M. J. (1978) *The Effect of Scientific Management on the Development of the Standard Cost System,* New York: Arno Press, particularly pp. 155–65.

Garbutt, D. (1981) 'The origins of accounting and writing', *The Accounting Historian's Notebook,* Fall: 10–11.

Garner, S. P. (1976) *Evolution of Cost Accounting to 1925,* Alabama: University of Alabama Press, particularly pp. 341–9.

Gerboth, D. (1987) 'The accounting game', *Accounting Horizons,* December: 96–9.

Gleick, J. (1987) *Chaos: Making a New Science,* Harmondsworth: Penguin.

Goldberg, L. (1974) 'The future of the past in accounting', *The Accountant's Magazine,* October: 405–10.

Hain, H. P. (1966) 'Accounting control in the Zenon Papyri', *The Accounting Review,* October: 669–703.

Hall, R. H. (1969) *Occupations and the Social Culture,* Englewood Cliffs, NJ: Prentice-Hall.

Hopwood, A. G. (1983) 'On trying to study accounting in the contexts in which it operates', *Accounting, Organisations and Society,* 8(2/3): 207–34.

Hopwood, A. G. (1987) 'The archaeology of accounting systems', *Accounting, Organisations and Society,* 12(3): 207–34.

Hopwood, A. G. and H. T. Johnson (1986) 'Accounting history's claim to legitimacy', *International Journal of Accounting,* Spring: 37–46.

Hoskin, K. W. and R. H. Macve (1986) 'Accounting and the examination: a genealogy of disciplinary power', *Accounting, Organisations and Society,* 11(2): 105–36.

Hoskin, K. W. and R. H. Macve (1988) 'The genesis of accountability the West Point connections, *Accounting, Organisations and Society,* 13(1): 37–73.

Johnson, H. T. (1981) 'Toward a new understanding of nineteenth-century cost accounting', *The Accounting Review,* July: 510–18.

Johnson, H. T. and R. S. Kaplan (1987) *Relevance Lost: The Rise and Fall of Management Accounting,* Boston, Mass.: Harvard Business School Press.

Johnson, T. J. (1972) *Professions and Power,* London: Macmillan.

Kaplan, R. S. (1984) 'The evolution of management accounting', *The Accounting Review,* July: 390–418.

Kast, F. E. and J. E. Rosenzweig (1985) 'The modern view: systems and contingency concepts', *Organisations and Management: A Systems and Contingency Approach,* New York: McGraw-Hill, pp. 102–20.

Keister, O. R. (1963) 'Commercial record-keeping in ancient Mesopotamia', *The Accounting Review,* April: 371–6.

Keister, O. R. (1970) 'The influence of Mesopotamian record-keeping', *Abacus,* December: 169–81.

Keister, O. R. (1986) 'Accounting 101 four thousand years ago', *The Accounting Historian's Notebook,* Fall: 28–31.

Krause, E. A. (1971) *The Sociology of Occupations,* Boston, Mass.: Little, Brown & Co.

Langenderfer, H. Q. (1987) 'Accounting education's history: a 100-year search for identity', *Journal of Accountancy,* May: 302–31.

Larson, M. S. (1977) 'Monopolies of competence and bourgeois ideology', *The Rise of Professionalism: A Sociological Analysis,* Berkeley: University of California Press, pp. 208–44 and 291–5.

Lee, G. A. (1973) 'The development of Italian bookkeeping: 1211–1300', *Abacus,* December: 137–55.

Lee, T. A. (1971) 'The historical development of internal control from the earliest times to the end of the seventeenth century', *Journal of Accounting Research,* Spring: 150–7.

Lee, T. A. (1982) 'The early history and development of company financial reporting', in *Company Financial Reporting,* New York: Van Nostrand Reinhold, pp. 79–98.

Lee, T. A. (1984) 'Cash flows and net realisable values: further evidence of the intuitive concepts', *Abacus,* December: 125–37.

Lee, T. A. (1988) 'An essay on the history of auditing', in *The Evolution of Audit Thought and Practice,* New York: Garland Publishing, pp. xi–xxviii.

Lee, T. A. (1989a) 'Education, practice and research in accounting: gaps, closed loops, bridges and magic accounting', *Accounting and Business Research,* Summer: 237–53.

Lee, T. A. (1989b) 'The turbulent stability of corporate financial reporting: observations on current issues', *Proceedings of Scottish BAA Conference,* University of Edinburgh.

Lee, T. A. and D. P. Tweedie (1977) *The Private Shareholder and the Corporate Report,* Edinburgh: Institute of Chartered Accountants in England and Wales.

Lister, R. J. (1984) 'Accounting as history', *International Journal of Accounting,* Autumn: 49–68.

Lloyd, C. (1986) *Explanation in Social History,* Oxford: Basil Blackwell.

Loft, A. (1988) *Understanding Accounting in its Social and Historical Context (The Case of Cost Accounting in Britain, 1914–1925),* New York: Garland Publishing.

Macdonald, K. M. (1985) 'Social closure and occupational registration', *Sociology,* November: 541–56.

Marwick, A. (1981) *The Nature of History,* London: Macmillan.

Mattessich, R. (1987) 'Prehistoric accounting and the problem of representation: on recent archaeological evidence of the Middle-East from 8000 BC to 3000 BC', *The Accounting Historian's Journal*, Fall: 71–91.

Mattessich, R. (1989) 'Accounting and the input-output principle in the prehistoric and ancient world', *Abacus*, September: 74–84.

Maturana, H. R. and F. J. Varela (1980) *Autopoiesis: The Organisation of the Living*, Dordrecht: D. Reidel.

Mednick, R. (1987) 'Accountants' liability: coping with the stampede to the courtroom', *Journal of Accountancy*, September: 118–22.

Mepham, M. J. (1988) *Accounting in Eighteenth Century Scotland*, New York: Garland Publishing.

Miller, P. and T. O'Leary (1987) 'Accounting and the construction of the governable person', *Accounting, Organisations and Society*, 12(3): 235–65.

Mills, P. A. (1989) 'Words and the study of accounting history', *Accounting, Auditing and Accountability Journal*, 2(1): 21–35.

Montagna, P. D. (1974) 'Public accounting: the dynamics of occupational change', in R. R. Sterling (ed.) *Institutional Issues in Public Accounting*, Lawrence, Kan.: Scholars Book Co., pp. 3–24.

Most, K. (1979) 'The accounts of Ancient Rome', in E. N. Coffman (ed.) *Working Paper 3, Working Paper Series 1*, Alabama: The Academy of Accounting Historians, pp. 22–31.

Napier, C. J. (1989) 'Research directions in accounting history', *British Accounting Review*, September: 237–54.

Nobes, C. W. and R. H. Parker (1984) 'The development of company financial reporting in Great Britain 1844–1977', in T. A. Lee and R. H. Parker (eds) *The Evolution of Corporate Financial Reporting*, New York: Garland Publishing, pp. 197–207.

Noke, C. (1981) 'Accounting for bailiffship in thirteenth century England', *Accounting and Business Research*, Spring: 137–51.

Parker, R. H. (1968) 'Discounted cash flow in historical perspective', *Journal of Accounting Research*, Spring: 58–71.

Parker, R. H. (1978) 'British men of account', *Abacus*, June: 53–65.

Parker, R. H. (1980) 'History of accounting decisions', in J. Arnold, B. Carsberg and R. Scapens (eds) *Topics in Management Accounting*, Deddington: Philip Allan, pp. 262–76.

Parker, R. H. (1981) 'The study of accounting history', in M. Bromwich and A. Hopwood (eds) *Essays in British Accounting Research*, London: Pitman, pp. 279–93.

Parker, R. H. (1989) 'How accountants invented counting and writing', *The Accountant's Magazine*, January: 26–7.

Popper, K. (1986) *The Poverty of Historicism*, London: Ark Paperbacks.

Previts, G. J., L. D. Parker and E. N. Coffman (1990) 'Accounting history: definition and relevance', *Abacus*, March: 1–13.

Reader, W. J. (1966) *Professional Men*, London: Weidenfeld & Nicolson.

Richardson, A. J. (1988) 'Accounting knowledge and professional privilege', *Accounting, Organisations and Society*, 13(4): 381–96.

Robb, F. F. (1989) 'Cybernetics and suprahuman autopoietic systems', *Systems Practice*, 2(1): 47–74.

Selznick, P. (1969) 'Foundations of the theory of organisation', in F. E. Emery (ed.) *Systems Thinking*, Harmondsworth: Penguin, pp. 261–80.

Solomons, D. (1968) 'The historical development of costing', in D. Solomons (ed.) *Studies in Cost Analysis*, London: Sweet & Maxwell, pp. 3–49.

Staubus, G. J. (1987) 'The dark ages of cost accounting: the role of miscues in the literature', *The Accounting Historian's Journal*, Fall: 1–18.

Sterling, R. R. (1977) 'Accounting in the 1980s', in N. M. Bedford (ed.) *Accountancy in the 1980s—Same Issues*, Council of Arthur Young Professors, University of Illinois, pp. 1–44.

Sterling, R. R. (1988a) 'Confessions of a failed empiricist', *Advances in Accounting*, 6: 3–35.

Sterling, R. R. (1988b) 'The subject-matters of accounting', Unpublished Paper, University of Utah.

Sterling, R. R. (1989) 'Teaching the correspondence concept', *Issues in Accounting Education*, Spring: 82–93.

Stewart, J. C. (1975) 'The emergent professionals', *The Accountant's Magazine*, March: 113–16.

Stewart, J. C. (1986) *Pioneers of a Profession: Chartered Accountants to 1879*, New York: Garland Publishing.

Stone, W. E. (1969) 'Antecedents of the accounting profession', *The Accounting Review*, April: 284–91.

Teubner, G. (1988) *Autopoietic Law: A New Approach to Law and Society*, Berlin: de Gruyter.

Theiss, E. L. (1937) 'The beginnings of business budgeting', *The Accounting Review*, March: 43–55.

Toynbee, A. and D. C. Somervell (1974) *A Study of History*, Oxford: Oxford University Press.

Tweedie, D. P. (1977) 'Cash flows and realisable values: the intuitive concepts? an empirical test', *Accounting and Business Research*, Winter: 2–13.

von Bertalanffy, L. (1976) 'General systems theory—a critical review', in J. Beishon and G. Peters (eds) *Systems Behaviour*, London: Harper & Row for Open University Press, pp. 30–50.

Walker, S. P. (1988) *The Society of Accountants in Edinburgh, 1854–1914: A Study of Recruitment to a New Profession*, New York: Garland Publishing, particularly pp. 1–29.

Walsh, W. H. (1974) 'Colligatory concepts in history', in P. Gardiner (ed.) *The Philosophy of History*, Oxford: Oxford University Press, pp. 127–44.

Wells, M. C. (1977) 'Some influences on the development of cost accounting', *The Accounting Historian's Journal*, Fall: 47–61.

Wells, M. C. (1987) 'What is wrong with accounting education?', *Working Paper 22*, University of Sydney Accounting Research Centre.

Williams, J. J. (1978) 'A new perspective on the evolution of double-entry bookkeeping', *The Accounting Historian's Journal*, Spring: 29–39.

Wilson, B. (1984) *Systems: Concepts, Methodologies and Applications*, Chichester: John Wiley.

Winjum, J. (1970) 'Accounting and its age of stagnation', *The Accounting Review*, October: 743–61.

Yamey, B. S. (1947) 'Notes on the origin of double-entry bookkeeping', *The Accounting Review*, July: 263–72.

Yamey, B. S. (1949) 'Scientific bookkeeping and the rise of capitalism', *The Economic History Review*, 1(2/3): 99–113.

Yamey, B. S. (1977) 'Some topics in the history of financial accounting in England, 1500–1900', in W. T. Baxter and S. Davidson (eds) *Studies in Accounting*, London: The Institute of Chartered Accountants in England and Wales, pp. 11–29.

Zeff, S. A. (1987) 'Does the CPA belong to a profession?', *Accounting Horizons*, June: 65–8.

Zeff, S. A. (1989) 'Recent trends in accounting education and research in the USA: some implications for UK academics', *British Accounting Review*, June: 159–76.

PREDICTIVE ABILITY AS A CRITERION FOR THE EVALUATION OF ACCOUNTING DATA

William H. Beaver, John W. Kennelly, and William M. Voss

The evaluation of alternative accounting measurements is a problem of major concern to the accounting profession. With respect to this problem, Ijiri and Jaedicke have stated:

> Accounting is plagued by the existence of alternative measurement methods. For many years, accountants have been searching for criteria which can be used to choose the best measurement alternative.[1]

One criterion being employed by a growing body of empirical research is *predictive ability*. According to this criterion, alternative accounting measurements are evaluated in terms of their ability to predict events of interest to decision-makers. The measure with the greatest predictive power with respect to a given event is considered to be the "best" method for that particular purpose.

The criterion has already been applied in several different contexts. Brown has investigated the ability of models using alternative income measures (i.e., with and without tax deferral) to predict the market value of the firm. Green and Segall evaluated interim reports in terms of their usefulness in the prediction of future annual earnings. Horrigan has examined

---

William H. Beaver, John W. Kennelly, and William M. Voss, "Predictive Ability as a Criterion for the Evaluation of Accounting Data," *The Accounting Review,* October 1968, pp. 675–683. Reprinted with the permission of the American Accounting Association.

[1]Yuji Ijiri and Robert K. Jaedicke, "Reliability and Objectivity of Accounting Measurements," *The Accounting Review,* (July 1966), p. 474.

the predictive content of accounting data, in the form of financial ratios, with respect to bond rating changes and ratings on newly issued bonds. One of the authors has studied accounting measures as predictors of bankruptcy and bond default.[2]

Because the predictive ability criterion is currently being used and is likely to experience even greater use in the future, this paper examines its origin, its relationship to the facilitation of decision-making, and the potential difficulties associated with its implementation. In order to illustrate the issues under discussion, the paper will refer to a hypothetical research project. The project proposes to evaluate the merits of alternative methods of reporting financial leases in terms of the prediction of loan default.

Loan default was chosen as the dependent variable for two reasons. A large body of literature in financial statement analysis suggests loan default is an event of interest to decision-makers (e.g., bankers), and *a priori* arguments can be advanced that will relate accounting measurements to the prediction of loan default. A cash flow model of the firm, such as that developed by Walter, implies that the probability of loan default is a function of the ratio of total debt to total assets.[3] However the model does not specify how debt and assets are best operationally measured. The financial lease controversy provides two measurement alternatives—capitalization and noncapitalization.

A priori arguments have been advanced, supporting each alternative as the more meaningful.[4] Empirically testable implications can be drawn from these arguments if they are interpreted in the light of the cash flow model. If the capitalization of leases does provide a "more meaningful" measure of debt and assets, then a debt-asset ratio that includes the capitalized value of leases in its components ought to be a better predictor of loan default than a debt-asset ratio that ignores capitalization.

The empirical part of the hypothetical study would involve the collection of financial statement data for a sample of default and nondefault firms. The debt-asset ratio would be computed for each firm, under each of the two lease treatments. The object would be to see which debt-asset ratio was the better predictor. An index of predictive ability is provided by the dichotomous classification test, which classifies the firms as default or nondefault based solely on a knowledge of the debt-asset ratio. The classifications are compared to the actual default status of the firms to determine the percentage of incorrect predictions—the lower the error, the higher the predictive power. The lease assumption that resulted in a lower percentage error

[2]Philip Brown, "The Predictive Abilities of Alternative Income Concepts" (an unpublished manuscript presented to the Conference for Study of Security Prices, Graduate School of Business, University of Chicago, November 1966); David Green, Jr. and Joel Segall, "The Predictive Power of First-Quarter Earnings Reports: A Replication"; James Horrigan, "The Determination of Long-Term Credit Standing with Financial Ratios"; William H. Beaver, "Financial Ratios as Predictors of Failure," The last three papers appear in *Empirical Research in Accounting: Selected Studies, 1966* (Institute of Professional Accounting, Graduate School of Business, University of Chicago, 1967), pp. 21–36, 44–62, and 71–102, respectively.

[3]James E. Walter, "The Determination of Technical Solvency," *Journal of Business* (January 1957), pp. 30–43. Extension of the Walter model as applied to financial ratios appears in Beaver, *op. cit.* The lease study need not restrict itself to only the debt-asset ratio. Other ratios affected by capitalization could also be studied.

[4]Arguments for and against capitalization appear in John H. Myers, *Reporting of Leases in Financial Statements* (American Institute of Certified Public Accountants, 1962); and Donald C. Cook, "The Case Against Capitalizing Leases," *Harvard Business Review* (January–February 1963), pp. 145–155.

would tentatively be judged the better, the more meaningful, measurement alternative for the purpose of predicting loan default.[5]

THE ORIGIN OF THE PREDICTIVE ABILITY CRITERION

Knowing the origin of the predictive ability criterion is important in understanding what is meant by predictive ability and why it is being used in evaluating accounting data. The criterion is well established in the social and natural sciences as a method for choosing among competing hypotheses.[6] It is our belief that alternative accounting measures have the properties of competing hypotheses and can be evaluated in a similar manner. Consider the following common features of competing hypotheses and alternative accounting measures:

1. Both are abstractions, which disregard aspects of reality deemed to be irrelevant and retain only those few crucial elements that are essential for the purposes at hand. Because there are many ways to abstract from reality, an unlimited number of mutually exclusive alternatives can be generated. Hence there is a need for a set of criteria for choosing among them.

2. Tests of logical propriety are one basis for evaluation. Conformity to these tests is a necessary but insufficient condition for selecting the "best." Two or more alternatives may pass the tests, and in that event it is futile to argue which is the "more logical." Ultimately, the choice must be made on the basis of which abstraction better captures the relevant aspects of reality. There is a need for an additional criterion that evaluates the alternatives in terms of the *purpose* for which they are being generated.

3. A primary purpose is the prediction of events, and hence comparison of alternatives according to their relative predictive power is a meaningful basis for evaluation. Predictive power is defined as the ability to generate operational implications (i.e., predictions) and to have those predictions subsequently verified by empirical evidence. More precisely, a prediction is a statement about the probability distribution of the dependent variable (the event being predicted) conditional upon the value of the independent variable (the predictor). Typically, the prediction asserts there is an association between x and y such that the outcome of y is dependent upon the value of

---

[5]The sample design described here parallels that used in the Beaver study. A more complete description of the classification test is discussed in that study (pp. 83ff.). Another index of predictive power is provided by an analysis of Bayesian likelihood ratios. In many respects, the likelihood ratio analysis is superior to the classification test. However, the classification test was used because it can be more briefly stated and more easily understood. Also both indices ranked accounting measures virtually the same in the Beaver study.

[6]This section relies heavily upon the literature in scientific methodology, especially the following works: Morris R. Cohen and Ernest Nagel, *An Introduction to Logic and the Scientific Method* (Harcourt Brace, 1934); Ernest Nagel, *The Structure of Science* (Harcourt Brace, 1961); C. West Churchman, *Prediction and Optimal Decision* (Prentice-Hall, 1962); Abraham Kaplan, *The Conduct of Inquiry* (Chandler, 1964); and several articles appearing in Sherman Krupp's *The Structure of Economic Science* (Prentice-Hall, 1966). Additional bibliographic references appear in Carl Thomas Devine's "Research Methodology and Accounting Theory Formation," *The Accounting Review,* (July 1960), pp. 387–399.

x [i.e., $P(y/x) = f(x)$].[7] But merely asserting the prediction does not make it "true." It must be verified by investigating the empirical correspondence between what the prediction asserts and what is in fact observed. Thus the determination of predictive ability is inherently an empirical question.

4. The use of the predictive ability criterion presupposes that the alternatives under consideration have met the tests of logic and that each has a theory supporting it. The determination of predictive ability is not an indiscriminate search for that alternative which will maximize the R^2 (or any other index of predictive power). Theory provides an explanation why a given alternative is expected to be related to the dependent variable and permits the investigator to generalize from the findings of sample data to a new set of observations. Consequently, a complete evaluation involves both *a priori* and empirical considerations.

The lease study reflects each of the points listed above. Each measurement system (i.e., with and without capitalization) is an abstraction. One basis for choosing between them would be to subject the underlying *a priori* arguments to the tests of logical propriety, but in this case neither argument is inherently illogical. Hence it is impossible to resolve the controversy on solely *a priori* grounds. Note also it would be erroneous to prefer the capitalization of leases merely because noncapitalization abstracts from certain aspects of the lease event. To say one measurement system is more abstract than another is not an indictment of that system. The additional data provided by capitalizing leases may be irrelevant for the purposes at hand or may even be harmful in the sense of contributing only "noise" to the system. A choice can only be made by applying some purposive criterion. In the lease study, the purposive criterion chosen was predictive ability—in particular, the ability to predict loan default.

It is possible to generalize beyond the context of the lease controversy. Most, if not all, accounting controversies can be viewed as disputes over the relative merits of one measurement alternative versus another. The inadequacy of relying solely upon *a priori* arguments is generally recognized by the accounting profession. Several recent articles have drawn attention to this inadequacy and have called for more empirical research in accounting.[8] One factor that has impeded a movement in this direction is the inability to specify what the nature of the empirical research should be, although there is a consensus that the research ought to relate alternative measures to the purposes of accounting data. The predictive ability approach provides a method for drawing operational implications from the *a priori* arguments such that the measurement controversies become empirically testable according to a purposive criterion.

---

[7]Occasionally, a hypothesis may specify an independent relationship among the variables [i.e., $P(y/x) = P(y)$]. For example, the random walk theory of security price movements asserts that the probability distribution of the price change in a given time period is independent of the price change in any previous period. See Eugene F. Fama, "The Behavior of Stock Market Prices," *Journal of Business,* (January 1965), pp. 34–105. In comparing competing predictors, the relative strength of association with the dependent variable becomes the relevant consideration. Strength of association can be measured in many ways, which will vary with the nature of the data and the inferences to be drawn from the data. In the lease study, the percentage error in classification was chosen as the index of association.

[8]For example, R. J. Chambers, "Prospective Adventures in Accounting Ideas," *The Accounting Review,* (April 1967), p. 251.

RELATIONSHIP TO THE FACILITATION OF DECISION-MAKING

A key issue in accepting this approach is the contention that predictive ability is a purposive criterion. This section will examine that contention in more detail and will relate predictive ability to what is generally regarded as the purpose of accounting data—the facilitation of decision-making.

The idea that accounting data ought to be evaluated in terms of their purposes or uses is one of the earliest and most prevalent thoughts in accounting. In 1922 Paton concluded:

> Accounting is a highly purposive field and any assumption, principle, or procedure is accordingly justified if it adequately serves the end in view.[9]

Recently the American Accounting Association's *A Statement of Basic Accounting Theory* stated:

> In establishing these standards the all-inclusive criterion is the usefulness of the information.[10]

In spite of the obvious appeal to the idea that accounting data ought to be useful, the utilitarian approach has lacked operationality. Chambers has noted:

> For, if accounting is utilitarian there must have been some concept or some theory of the tests which must be applied in distinguishing utilitarian from nonutilitarian procedures. . . . It is largely because the tests of "utilitarianness" . . . have not been made explicit that the body of accounting practices now employed contains so many divergent and inconsistent rules.[11]

One reason for the inability to specify tests of usefulness is the manner in which usefulness is interpreted. Almost without exception, the literature has related usefulness to the facilitation of decision-making. The primacy of decision-making has been stressed by both Paton and *A Statement of Basic Accounting Theory:*

> The purpose of accounting may be said to be that of compiling and interpreting the financial data . . . to provide a sound guide to action by management, investor, and other interested parties.[12]

> The committee defines accounting as the process of identifying, measuring, and communicating economic information to permit informed judgments and decisions by users of the information.[13]

---

[9]William A. Paton, *Accounting Theory* (The Ronald Press, 1922), p. 472.

[10]American Accounting Association, *A Statement of Basic Accounting Theory* (American Accounting Association, 1966), p. 3.

[11]Raymond J. Chambers, "Why Bother with Postulates?" *Journal of Accounting Research,* (Spring 1963), p. 3.

[12]William A. Paton, *Essentials of Accounting* (The Macmillan Company, 1949), p. 2.

[13]American Accounting Association, *op. cit.,* p. 1.

However, the use of the decision-making criterion faces two problems. The first is to define the decision models (or processes) of potential users of accounting data. This problem has been noted by both Anton and Vatter.

> If we assume an operationalist view—that is, that information ought to be for decision-making purposes—the criteria [sic] is based upon an extension of significance, i.e., for what is the information significant. . . . While this is a purposive criterion it also gives us the dilemma noted above as to who will be the decision-maker and the uncertainty of his context.[14]

> Observation, analysis, and projection should be aimed at decision-making. This implies a view of the past and present that permits and facilitates decisions, without making them. How this fine line can be established depends upon what the decisions are, who makes them, and what data are relevant for those purposes. These questions still remain unanswered.[15]

Most business decisions currently are not made within the framework of a formally specified decision model. That is, in most decision-making situations, no model is available with which to evaluate alternative accounting measurements. Consider the lending decision faced by a loan officer in a bank. The specification of his decision model would require a knowledge of what the decision variables are, what weights are assigned to each decision variable, and what constraints, if any, are binding on the loan officer. It is unlikely that even the decision-maker would produce a formal model that would describe the process he went through in making lending decisions. Rules of thumb, such as "do not loan to any firm with a current ratio below 2," can be found, but it would be extremely difficult to determine the decision model implied by such rules. Specification of decision models, for the most part, is beyond the current state of knowledge. Although operations research and other quantitative techniques offer promise of greater specification in the future, it is not clear how soon, or to what extent, such specifications will be possible.[16]

The second problem is, even after the decision model is specified, it is not sufficient for determining which accounting measure produces the better decisions. Many, if not all, of the decision variables are capable of being measured in more than one way. For example, assume that a loan officer's objective function for the lending decision is a known function of promised return and probability of default on the loan. The lease controversy provides two operational measures for assessing the probability of loan default. The decision model can indicate whether different decisions are produced by using different definitions of the debt-asset ratio as a surrogate for the probability of default, but it cannot indicate which definition (i.e., with or without capitalization) will lead to the better decisions. Additional information is needed as to which ratio provides the better assessment of probability of default (i.e., which ratio is the better predictor of loan default).

---

[14]Hector R. Anton, "Some Aspects of Measurement and Accounting," *Journal of Accounting Research,* (Spring 1964), p. 6.

[15]William J. Vatter, "Postulates and Principles," *Journal of Accounting Research,* (Autumn 1963), p. 197.

[16]The difficulties encountered in attempting to specify the decision processes of loan officers are well documented in several articles appearing in the text by Kalman J. Cohen and Frederick S. Hammer, *Analytical Methods in Banking* (Irwin, 1966). Of special interest is the article by Kalman J. Cohen, Thomas C. Gilmore, and Frank A. Singer, "Bank Procedures for Analyzing Business Loan Applications," pp. 219–249.

At this point the relationship between predictive ability and decision-making becomes evident. Note the distinction between a prediction and a decision. In the context of the bank's lending decision, a prediction states the probability of loan default if the bank loans to a firm with a set of financial ratios. The decision is whether or not the bank should grant the loan, which also involves additional decision variables such as the promised return. The illustration points out an important relationship between predictions and decisions. A prediction can be made without making a decision, but a decision cannot be made without, at least implicitly, making a prediction.

In a world where little is known about the decision models, evaluating alternative accounting measures in terms of their predictive ability is an appealing idea, because it requires a lower level of specificity regarding the decision model. To evaluate alternative lease treatments in terms of their ability to predict loan default, we assume only that the probability of loan default is a parameter of the decision process, even though we may know little about how the bank's loan officers use the assessments of probability of default in reaching their decisions. Hence the predictive ability of accounting data can be explored without waiting for the further specification of the decision models.[17]

Because prediction is an inherent part of the decision process, knowledge of the predictive ability of alternative measures is a prerequisite to the use of the decision-making criterion. At the same time, it permits tentative conclusions regarding alternative measurements, subject to subsequent confirmation when the decision models eventually become specified. The use of predictive ability as a purposive criterion is more than merely consistent with accounting's decision-making orientation. It can provide a body of research that will bring accounting closer to its goal of evaluation in terms of a decision-making criterion.

DIFFICULTIES OF IMPLEMENTATION

The purpose of this paper is to present the difficulties as well as the benefits of the predictive ability approach. However, none of the potential problems to be discussed are inherent to this approach. They are merely "facts of life" that are likely to be encountered in any meaningful attempt to evaluate alternative accounting measures.

1. One difficulty of implementation will be the specification of what events constitute parameters of decision models and the specification of a theory that will link those events to the accounting measures in some sort of predictive relationship. The studies cited earlier suggest some of the events that could be predicted.[18] Also, portfolio theory appears to be a productive area for providing dependent variables, although as yet the relationships between the parameters of the portfolio models and the accounting data have not been explored.[19] However, a brief survey of the

---

[17]The relationship between predictions and the decision model is further discussed in the next section.

[18]See footnote 2 for the bibliographic references.

[19]Harry M. Markowitz, *Portfolio Selection: Efficient Diversification of Investments* (Wiley, 1959). William F. Sharpe, "Capital Asset Prices: A Theory of Market Equilibrium Under Conditions of Risk," *Journal of Finance* (September 1964), pp. 425–42.

disciplines from which the dependent variables and the predictive theory are likely to originate indicates that much remains to be accomplished. In large part then the evaluation of accounting data, using the predictive ability criterion, will occur in conjunction with development and testing of predictive relationships in related disciplines, such as economics and finance.

2. The findings of a predictive ability study are conditional on how the predictive model is specified. The construction of the prediction model involves a specification of the functional form of the relationships (e.g., linearity) and also how the variables are operationally defined. In the financial lease study, the findings would be conditional upon the rates used to discount the lease payments and the particular set of financial ratios used in the study. If no difference in predictive ability is found between the two sets of ratios (capitalized, noncapitalized), the finding may be attributed to (a) the particular discount rates chosen were not the appropriate rates, (b) the ratio form is not a meaningful way to express relationships among financial statement items, (c) the particular ratios chosen were not the optimal ratios for the prediction of default, or (d) capitalization does not enhance predictive ability. Additional research regarding the possibility of (a), (b) and (c) must be explored before inference (d) can be drawn. The accounting measure and the prediction model are being jointly tested. Positive results constitute a joint confirmation, while negative results may be due to a flaw in either or both factors. In practice it may be difficult to isolate the source of the negative results.

   Another problem arises when positive results are obtained (i.e., when a "significant" difference between alternative measures is observed). For example assume the debt-asset ratio computed under the capitalization assumption predicts better than the noncapitalized debt-asset ratio in a single ratio prediction model. If additional ratios were included in the prediction model, the noncapitalized form of the debt-asset ratio might contribute more to the predictive power of the multivariate model than the capitalized form. If different models suggest contrary conclusions regarding the relative predictive power of the two lease assumptions, additional research will be needed to explain the reason for the conflicting results. Even if consistent results are observed for all of the models tested, there is always the possibility of an untested model which possesses greater predictive power and yet suggests the opposite conclusion regarding the relative predictive power of the alternative measures under study.[20]

3. A third difficulty occurs because accounting data are currently being used as decision variables. There are two possible reasons for observing an association between the accounting measures and the event being predicted. (a) There is a "true" causal relationship between the measures and the event. (b) Decision-makers perceive there to be a causal relationship, and this perception is sufficient to produce an observed relationship. In the lease study a relationship between financial ratios and loan default may be observed because there is a causal relationship such that a "poor" ratio increases the probability of default. However, a relationship may also

---

[20]There are two other related qualifications regarding a predictive ability study. (1) The findings are conditional upon the population from which the sample is drawn. (2) The findings are conditional upon the alternative measures chosen for study. For example, a third unspecified and untested measure may be better than the two measures under consideration.

be observed merely because bankers believe there is causal relationship and use the ratios as decision variables. The bank may sever a line of credit because a firm fails to improve its ratios to a respectable level. The severing of the line of credit forces the firm into default. Similarly, the efficacy of capitalizing leases may be diminished or eliminated if loan officers do not incorporate the capitalization of leases into their credit analysis. Any observed relationship may be due to either (a) or (b) or both. It may be impossible to tell from the sample data the extent to which factor (b) is present.

If the objective is predictive ability, do we care what its source is? Yes, if source (b) is not expected to be permanent. Decision-makers' use of accounting data as decision variables may change over time. In fact, the findings of a predictive ability study may cause them to change, and this might change the predictive relationships observed in the future.

4. The evaluation of relative predictive power may require an assumption about the loss function associated with the prediction errors, which in turn involves additional knowledge of other variables in the decision model. Without this knowledge it may be impossible to conclude which measure is the better predictor.[21]

For example, suppose the capitalized debt-asset ratio predicts the default status of a sample of default and nondefault firms with a lower number of total misclassifications. Can we conclude that capitalization is preferable? Not necessarily. Suppose the noncapitalized debt-asset ratio has more total misclassifications of both default and nondefault firms but fewer errors with respect to the classification of default firms. Since the loss of misclassifying a default firm is likely to be greater than the loss associated with misclassifying a nondefault firm, the latter measure may be the better predictor in terms of minimizing expected loss. More would have to be known about the loss function before one measure could be chosen over the other.

Moreover, even if the capitalized debt-asset ratio performed better with respect to both type errors, additional analysis is needed before capitalization of leases could be recommended, because capitalization involves a greater cost to collecting additional data and making the necessary computations. Capitalization might lead to better predictions, but are they sufficiently better to warrant the additional cost? The answer involves a cost-benefit analysis, which requires a knowledge of the loss function and hence the other decision variables.

The amount of additional knowledge of the decision model that will be required can only be assessed within the context of the empirical results of each predictive ability study. The margin of superiority of one measure over another may be so great that it is obviously the better predictor regardless of the form of loss function. In other situations, perhaps only the general form of the loss function (e.g., linear or quadratic, symmetric or asymmetric) need be specified. In instances where a greater knowledge of the loss function is needed than is available, the role of the predictive ability study may be to present the distribution of prediction errors for each measure and let the reader apply his own loss function in choosing among

---

[21]Every index of predictive ability involves some assumption regarding the loss function of the prediction errors and/or the distribution of prediction errors. If different indices suggest different measures are better, the inability to select which index is appropriate implies the inability to select which accounting measure is the better predictor, until the loss function can be specified.

the measures. In any event the researcher must be constantly aware of this relationship to avoid drawing unwarranted inferences from the data.

5. The findings of a predictive ability study are conditional upon the event being predicted. Even if a measure is a better predictor of one event (e.g., loan default), it is not necessarily a better predictor of other events. Additional research would be needed to investigate the predictive power of the measure for other purposes. If different measures are best for different predictive purposes, the problem of satisfying competing user needs arises.[22] If this problem exists, it would be difficult to resolve, although the use of multidimensional and special purpose statements offers a tentative solution.[23]

Concluding Remarks

Two implications emerge from the previous discussion: (1) The preference for an accounting measure may apply only within the context of a specific predictive purpose or prediction model. It may be impossible to generalize about the "best" measurement alternative across different contexts. (2) Even within a specific context, the conclusions must be considered as tentative.

The inability to generalize is a possibility, but not an inevitability. We have cited only *potential* difficulties, whose relevance can only be assessed empirically, not by *a priori* speculation. What is important is to know to what extent we can generalize across purposes, and the only hope of acquiring this knowledge is to conduct the predictive studies. If we discover that different measures are best for different purposes, it would be erroneous to believe that the predictive studies are any less important because of that discovery. The inability to generalize, if it does exist, is not a flaw of the predictive ability methodology. It merely reflects the state of the world or the state of accounting theory, but in neither case is it an indictment of the methodology that exposes that fact.

Even within a specific context, the preference for one measure over another is tentative. A measure that performed poorly may not be permanently rejected in the sense that the researcher may refine the measure (and its theory) or redesign the study in the hope that future research will demonstrate that the measure is really better. Also there is always the possibility of an unknown or untested measure that performs even better than the best measure tested. Theory construction in other disciplines is an evolutionary process, where the hypotheses are continuously being revised, redefined, or overturned in the light of new theory and new evidence. There is no reason to believe that accounting theory will be different.

Although it is important that a general awareness of these factors exists, neither the potential inability to generalize nor the tentative nature of the conclusions should be regarded as a deterrent to conducting the predictive studies. Extension of research efforts into the predictive ability of accounting data is necessary for the fulfillment of accounting's decision-making orientation and for the meaningful evaluation of alternative accounting measures.

---

[22]The decision-making criterion also faces the same potential problem. See comments made by both Devine and Moonitz. Carl Thomas Devine, *op. cit.,* p. 397. Maurice Moonitz, *The Postulates of Accounting* (American Institute of Certified Public Accountants, 1961), p. 4.

[23]For suggestions regarding multidimensional reporting see American Accounting Association, *op. cit.*

AN INDUCED THEORY OF ACCOUNTING MEASUREMENT

George J. Staubus

The recent literature of accounting includes little on descriptive theories of accounting measurement. Voluminous descriptive materials on accounting measurement are available—in textbooks and publications of accounting standards-setting bodies, for example—but they do not offer coherent theories. On the other hand, theories of accounting measurement abound, but they tend to have a strong normative flavor. To my knowledge, no one has woven accounting measurement practices into a coherent, comprehensive theory.[1] This paper is designed to move in that direction.

If a scientist in a field far removed from accounting asked an accountant to tell him the central ideas of accounting measurement practices, what could the accountant say? Could he say that historical cost is the basis of accounting measurement? Surely he could not feel that he has conveyed the essence of the subject by reference to a principle that applies to a minority of balance sheet items. Could he hang accounting measurement on matching costs and revenues as the central pillar? As much as that idea says about the *timing* of expense recognition,

---

The author is indebted to the Institut Européen d'Administration des Affaires for hospitality during the period the first draft of this paper was written.

George J. Staubus, "An Induced Theory of Accounting Measurement," *The Accounting Review,* vol. 60, no. 1, January 1985, 53–75. Reprinted by permission of the American Accounting Association.

[1]Students of accounting theory are familiar with the work of several writers who have applied inductive reasoning in attempts to formulate generalizations that describe accounting practices, including Goldberg [1965], Ijiri [1975, 1967], Sterling [1966 and elsewhere], and Skinner [1972]. Writers in previous generations, such as Paton and Littleton [1940], Littleton [1953], Gilman [1939], and Hatfield [1927], also sought induced descriptions to some extent. None of these writers, however, induced a theory of accounting measurement from systematic observations of measurement practices.

the scientist would have great difficulty if he tried to use it in determining the *amounts* of costs, revenues, gains, losses, assets, and liabilities. Is conservatism the "most pervasive principle of accounting valuation"? [Sterling, 1967, p. 110]. Perhaps so, but it can hardly be identified as the centerpost for the entire structure of accounting measurement. To what document might the accountant refer the enquiring scientist? To the Financial Accounting Standards Board's *Accounting Standards* volumes? The entire set? If not, what part? To *Accounting Principles Board Statement No. 4* [1970] or Grady's *Inventory* [1965]? Surely no coherent theory could be gleaned from those documents without careful induction.

Of course, one must recognize the possibility of diverse views regarding the content of a coherent descriptive theory of accounting measurement. The view underlying this paper is that such a theory should:

1. Include an unambiguous statement of the subject matter of accounting measurement—of what is being measured. APB Statement No. 4, for example, states (p. 45): "The subject matter of financial accounting is economic activity and financial accounting therefore involves measuring and reporting on the creation, accumulation, and use of economic resources." That statement is exemplary in its conciseness, but does it hit the mark? In any event, the document does not build on that starting point in a logical manner. Part I of this paper is essentially a review of accounting practices that is aimed at discovering what accounting does measure.

2. Summarize the measurement methods that are used in accounting and the qualities of those measurements. In Part II, a broad sample consisting of 31 prominent categories of assets and liabilities is examined in an attempt to discover the measurement methods that are used, those that could be used but are not, and the qualities possessed by the accepted and rejected methods and the measurements they yield.

3. Focus on a central idea that serves as a basis for nearly all accounting measurement practices, or that describes the totality of accounting measurement. Modifying ideas that temper applications of the central idea might also be included. Part III develops such a central idea and relates the qualities of accounting measurements discovered in Part II to the central idea.

The authoritative literature of accounting has remarkably little to say on the above points, and none of that literature combines them in a coherent theory. The gap is wide.

A few comments regarding matters of methodology and style may help to set the stage. The reviews of practice included in Parts I and II cover much familiar ground. Experienced accountants may find it overly detailed and obvious; they may choose to skim those pages lightly. However, the evidence produced in those detailed reviews is the basis for the inductions that follow, so they are prerequisites to the conclusions. The underlying evidence examined in this research consists of accounting practices. Information about those practices comes from sources such as *Accounting Trends and Techniques* [AICPA, annually], accounting standards, annual reports, textbooks, and personal experience. Specific references are cited sparingly; the general authority for the practices reported here is generally accepted accounting principles.

The method for this descriptive research is empirical and inductive. The raw material consists of (direct and indirect) observations of measurement practices employed in accounting. Generalizations are produced by inductive reasoning. Because of the paucity of literature codifying and summarizing accounting measurement practices, my own interpretations play a large role in the association of specific measurement practices with a few general measurement methods, as well as in the comparison of measurement methods on the basis of the extent to which they possess certain qualities. There can be little doubt but that others would make different interpretations here and there. A substantial number of differences that tend to form a pattern could, of course, lead to different conclusions. I would be surprised, however, if many readers reached distinctly different conclusions.

Finally, I have found it convenient to personify accounting as capable of doing or saying this or that, sometimes as an alternative to referring to "the accountant" as doing this or that. The intent is to attribute choices of GAAP to accountants collectively.

THE SCOPE OF ACCOUNTING INFORMATION

A good starting point for a study of accounting measurement is a simple statement describing accounting in a general way. The development of such a statement could be approached as a major research project, but that may not be necessary to accomplish the present objective. The following brief definition may be acceptable to many as a basis for an investigation of the scope of accounting. *Accounting is a set of activities, focused on an economic entity, and concerned with information regarding the economic effects of events on the entity.*

ACCOUNTING ACTIVITIES

The "set of activities" included in accounting may be expressed accurately in more or less detail according to one's purpose. The entire range of activities engaged in by those viewed as accountants is much too broad to indicate the scope of accounting activities according to common usage. Thus, when accountants participate in the management of risk (insurance), personnel, purchasing, cash, credit, and inventories, in the direct planning of "line" activities, and in making decisions regarding investments, they are not accounting. When they provide financial information for making such decisions, they are accounting. A listing of accounting activities sufficient to provide a basis for the explication needed here includes: discovering, identifying, or recognizing; classifying, measuring, recording, summarizing, analyzing, interpreting, and reporting. The subject matter of all these activities is the effects of economic events on the entity.

THE ENTITY FOCUS

The focusing of accounting activities on one "entity" is occasionally suggested as the key difference between accounting and other activities dealing with economic information, such as economic analysis, and that usage appears to be generally accepted. Beyond that, little need be said about the entity concept in the present context. Whenever the question is raised as to what point of view is taken in accounting (e.g., the proprietary, "entity," or residual equity viewpoint) the definition of the entity is likely to be questioned, but these matters are well settled in practice. The "accounting entity" is generally viewed as an economic unit under one management, so the scope of the management's power determines, in a general way, the boundaries of the entity.

ECONOMIC EFFECTS OF EVENTS

The "events" and "economic effects" mentioned in the above definition of accounting are closely related. Millions of events occur every day, so accounting faces the task of screening out those to be ignored. Little is contributed by adding the adjective "economic" to events, not only because the economic character of accountable events is obvious, but also because any distinction between economic events and others is impractical, being a matter of degree. Some events, e.g., securities transactions, may generally be viewed as having a more distinctly economic character than others, e.g., a kiss, but who would dare to say that a kiss has no economic motivation or consequences? Surely most events have some economic effect on someone. The accounting screen is designed to separate those events having an economic effect on the entity from the total set of events. Thus, the economic effects of events on the entity is the subject matter of accounting.

Just as events span a wide range on the scale of how distinctly economic they are, so do the impacts of various economic effects on the entity differ widely. Different events, involving the same amount of money, may have great or small impact on the entity and that difference cannot be ignored by the accountant. The economic effects of some events, e.g., the issuance of securities by a corporation, are recognized by accountants; the economic effects of other events, e.g., the issuance of securities by competitors, are ignored; and the effects of still other events, e.g., making certain executory contracts, are recognized only enough to report them in notes. Why?

SELECTION OF EVENTS TO RECOGNIZE

The criteria on which accountants decide to account for, or ignore, events are not stated clearly in the authoritative literature of accounting.[2] Occasionally accountants are heard expressing preferences for "transaction-based" financial reporting, but those are normative statements, unless "transaction" is being given such a broad meaning as to make it virtually synonymous with event. Provisions for uncollectibles, depreciation, and various write-downs and write-ups are too common to permit acceptance of the statement that accountants limit their attention to transactions of the entity. Nor does an examination of accounting textbooks and the other descriptive literature of accounting reveal any other widely accepted "recognition criteria."

Perhaps an informal review of a wide range of events can yield a clue regarding recognition criteria. Certain types of events *usually are recognized* in an entity's double-entry accounting system:

1. Cash/other goods (commodities, services, money claims, etc.) exchanges between the entity and another entity.
2. Receipt or delivery of goods from or to another entity in accordance with a contract, i.e., partial or complete performance of a goods contract, including continuous performance, e.g., property rentals.
3. Synthesis of resources, as in manufacturing a product.

---

[2]In a recent exposure draft, "Recognition and Measurement in Financial Statements of Business Enterprises" [FASB, 1983b], the FASB proposes four broad criteria for recognizing specific elements of financial statements. The general impact of adoption of those criteria would be to add to the definitions of each element a clause to the effect that to be recognized, the element must have a relevant attribute that is measurable with acceptable reliability. Many definitions in the literature include such a clause.

Other types of events *sometimes are recognized* in accounting entries:

1. Changes in the economic significance of rights or obligations due to the passage of time.
   (a) Recognized: depreciation, amortization, accrual of implicit interest (discount) in many cases, and changes from long-term to current classification.
   (b) Not recognized: accrual of implicit interest (discount) in certain cases.
2. Physical changes in tangible property over time.
   (a) Recognized: depreciation and spoilage.
   (b) Not recognized: growth of timber and livestock.
3. Technological developments affecting the entity.
   (a) Recognized: Some of those impairing the value of plant or inventories.
   (b) Not recognized: Other cases of value impairment and technological advances through the entity's research and development activities.
4. Making wholly executory contracts.
   (a) Recognized: Capital leases.
   (b) Not recognized: Operating leases, employment contracts, etc.
5. Transactions between two other entities involving commodities or securities of interest to the entity.
   (a) Recognized: The effects of price decreases reflected in commodity and security transactions when the entity holds similar items classified as current assets.
   (b) Not recognized: Increases in prices of current assets and most changes in prices of noncurrent assets and the entity's outstanding debt.

Other events are *rarely recognized* in accounting entities:

1. Transactions between two other entities involving goods of a type not stocked by the entity. An exception is transactions reflecting lower prices of a commodity of a type for which the entity has made a purchase commitment.
2. Nontransaction, unpriced events directly involving other entities but not the accountant's entity.
3. The services of equity capital.

Many events are recognized by accountants but are *reported in supplementary materials* accompanying the primary financial statements as parts of financial reports, rather than being recognized by entries in the double-entry accounting system and reported in the primary financial statements. Examples are:

1. Making partly and wholly executory contracts that entail commitments to pay material sums of money in exchange for commodities or services.
2. Granting options to purchase the entity's securities.
3. Transactions of other entities establishing prices for certain securities or commodities of interest to the entity.

Significant generalizations based on the above observations are not readily formed, which means that principles for recognizing events in accounts—the first step in accounting measurement—are hard to find. However, if one augments the above review with a brief look at charts of accounts, "books," and financial statements of diverse entities, one finds that nearly all entries in the double-entry system have two common properties: they record changes in components of entity wealth,[3] and they record those changes in numbers. A third observation is that certain quantifiable changes in entity wealth items are not recorded as they occur. Thus, changes in wealth and quantifiability are necessary, but not sufficient, conditions for formally recording economic events. *Entries in double-entry systems record selected measurable changes in wealth items.*

Selection of Effects to Recognize

A simple type of accounting for the economic effects of events on an entity could be limited to measuring and reporting changes in entity wealth with neither omissions nor elaborations. Classes of wealth items and of events, causes of changes, and other circumstantial data could be ignored. All measurable changes in wealth could be included. In practice, however, accounting is neither so limited nor so inclusive. The omission of certain changes in amounts of wealth items will be dealt with, at least implicitly, later. The elaborative information reported by accounting is addressed here.

Accounting reports are not limited to a single number representing the amount of the entity's wealth. Much elaborative material typically is presented. An investigation into the scope of accounting information must not ignore that elaborative material. An important feature of accounting is the breakdown of entity wealth into classes. Accountants call the positive class assets and the negative class liabilities. The difference is described as owners' equity. The double-entry system is based on the residual claim of the owners; the balance of net assets is claimed by owners, so the net wealth items and owners' claims constitute an equation. Maintenance of the integrity of that equation requires that changes be made in at least two components at the same time. Double-entry does not, however, require accounts beyond balance sheet accounts. Nevertheless, we observe that accountants use temporary subdivisions of an owners' equity account to accumulate classified data on changes in owners' equity, and they report those classified changes in an "income statement." Other changes in owners' equity are also reported fully. Furthermore, classified changes in certain categories of wealth items are also reported, either generally or in certain cases, the most common category being one related to liquidity, viz., either cash or working capital. This is evidence of an interest in reporting on more than the amounts and changes in amounts of wealth items.

A review of the classification practices employed in financial statements might yield additional insights into the accountants' choices of which effects of economic events to report. Distinctions between short-term and long-term items, between monetary and nonmonetary items, the careful separation of positive and negative wealth items, the distinction between changes (in both owners' equity and cash or working capital) that tend to recur and those that do not, the disclosure of those operating costs that are determined by allocating long-term assets among periods, the disclosure of gross revenues and of various object classes of expenses—all of these provide indications of what accounting intends to report.

---

[3]A class of exceptions was noted by an anonymous reviewer: transactions with owners recorded entirely within the owners' equity section, such as stock dividends and conversion of preferred shares into common.

Finally, those parts of financial reports other than the financial statements that report account balances might be reviewed for evidence of the types of economic effects that accounting reports. Those parts include the statement of changes in financial position and various supplementary disclosures regarding contingencies; commitments made in executory contracts; tax, pension, and stock option information; quarterly, segment, and changing prices schedules; debt maturities; and many other subjects.

THE SCOPE OF ACCOUNTING INFORMATION: FINDINGS

The above review of the contents of financial reports leads to the following generalizations. The economic effects of events that are given the greatest emphasis in accounting practice are:

1. Measurable changes in specific components of entity *wealth* and in the owners' interest in the sum of entity wealth components. Evidence: the accounts included in the double-entry system.

2. Measurable and unmeasurable changes in the entity's *liquidity*. Evidence: the current/noncurrent and monetary/nonmonetary distinctions on the balance sheet; the statement of changes in financial position (focusing on cash or another category of net liquid assets); debt maturity schedules.

3. Effects on *risks* to which the entity and its constituents are exposed. Evidence: all of the information on liquidity, since the primary risk of concern to constituents is the risk of loss of liquidity; separation of items that tend to be nonrecurring and items that tend to recur and, to some extent, separation of costs that tend to be fixed and those that tend to vary directly with volume of revenue; notes on contingencies, commitments, etc.

Other economic effects of events are also included in financial reports, but they are not emphasized as much as the above three. Information on the distribution of "value added" among constituents—owners, creditors, employees, and government—may be given some attention in the United States, although much less than in the European Economic Community. Finally, a rather vague category, which might best be described as information to help readers understand the economics of the business, is also included in some financial reports, especially in "management's discussion and analysis."

In sum, the scope of accounting information is broad but clearly constrained. It includes quantified and unquantified information regarding entity wealth, information on entity liquidity and risk, information related to the distribution of value added among constituents, and a wide variety of information pertaining to the economics of the business. The focus is unquestionably on stocks and flows of entity wealth items, but the ways that accounting deals with the measurement of wealth items might well be affected by the inclusion of the other types of information. However, those other types of information—on liquidity, risk, distribution of value added, and economics of the business—may be viewed as elaborative information pertaining to entity wealth. For example, liquidity relates to the convertibility of a wealth item into a cash flow; risk includes variance in the distribution of cash flows from one, or a combination of, wealth items. *The heart of accounting is the measurement of aspects of wealth.*

MEASUREMENT OF THE EFFECTS OF ECONOMIC EVENTS ON ENTITY WEALTH

Accounting focuses on amounts of wealth items, including changes in those items. However, the review of the events recognized in the double-entry system showed that certain measurable changes in wealth are omitted from that system. Why? Does interest in reporting on liquidity, risk, and other matters affect the accountant's choice of which measurable changes in wealth items to report? Or are other factors involved? How do accountants measure wealth items? The objective of this section is to gain an understanding of accounting measurement practices. The first step is to make detailed observations of measurement practices. Then, generalizations in the forms of summaries and inferences will be attempted.

OBSERVATIONS OF MEASUREMENT PRACTICES

The review of the scope of accounting showed that accountants measure wealth items, i.e., assets and liabilities. The task at hand now is to discover how accountants measure wealth items and changes therein. This section focuses on measurement methods. The typical accountant is more likely to speak of alternative valuation bases than measurement methods. The latter term is used here to include both the particular valuation base that is the key feature of a measurement and the more specific procedures involved in applying that basis of valuation. For example, when the accountant speaks of accounting for machinery "on the historical cost basis of valuation," only the key feature of the measurement process is specified. The treatment of various "fringe acquisition costs," such as transportation, installation, and interest, as well as the question of how to assign the acquisition cost to periods and operations, is not specified in the term "historical cost basis of valuation." Here the term measurement method is used to include the specific procedures applied in measuring as well as the base value which the specific procedures modify.

MEASUREMENT METHODS

A representative selection of accounting's choices of measurement methods is presented in Exhibit 1. Those 31 cases are chosen on the basis of their prominence in textbooks and the attention they have received by standards-setting bodies. Most of the cases covered in the typical intermediate accounting course are included. The asset and liability items listed include items common in manufacturing, distribution, and service industries, as well as several found primarily in banks, securities firms, and extractive industries. Circumstances that accountants consider in choosing a measurement method are indicated, but the finer points of such circumstances are omitted in the interest of brevity. For example, the choice between the cost and equity methods for equity securities owned is based on circumstances affecting the investor's ability to exercise significant influence over the investee, not strictly on the 20-percent test.

The selection of "reasonably available" measurement methods is, as the term implies, a matter of judgment. Any method that actually is used is judged reasonably available, as are those methods which are used in other circumstances in which their application appears to be at least as difficult as in the case in question. For example, the original acquisition cost method is available for application to trade accounts receivable. The methods listed are limited to those found in practice, although current cost is extended to include proceeds for liabilities, and net realizable value includes the negative version for liabilities.

Choices of Accounting Measurement Methods in U.S. GAAP★

Net Asset Item and Circumstances	Measurement Methods Reasonably Available	Qualities on Which a Method Is Superior	Notes
Receivables:			
1. Trade Accounts	FCF, net (GAAP)		Discount may be immaterial
	PVFCF, current rate		
	FCF, gross	R, E, U	Direct write-off of losses
	OAC	Cn	Based on cost of goods sold
2. Notes, short-term trade, with accrued interest	PVFCF, net, old rate (GAAP)		
	PVFCF, current rate	Cp	
	FCF, gross	R, E	
	OAC	Cn	Interest not accrued
3. Long-term, miscellaneous	PVFCF, old rate (GAAP)	S	
	PVFCF, current rate	Cp	
	FCF, gross	R, E	
	OAC	E, Cn, U	
4. Banks' loans, with accrued interest	PVFCF, net, old rate (GAAP)	FC	
	PVFCF, current rate	CP	
	FCF, gross		
	OAC	R, E, Cn, U	
Newly restructured bank loans, modifications of terms:			
5. FCF > old PVFCF	PVFCF, old contract (GAAP)	E, S	
	PVFCF, new contract	Cn, Cp	
	FCF, gross	R, FC	
6. FCF < old PVFCF	FCF, gross (GAAP)	R, FC	
	PVFCF, new contract	Cn, Cp	
	PVFCF, old contract	E, S	
Debt securities owned:			
7. Current portfolio, market > cost	PVFCF, old rate (GAAP)	Cn, FC, S	Same as amortized OAC
	CMP	E, Cp, U	Same as PVFCF, current rate
	OAC	E, Cn, FC, S, U	No amortization
8. Current portfolio, market < cost	CMP (GAAP)	E, Cn, Cp	Practice is not uniform
	PVFCF, old rate	FC, S	
	OAC	E, FC, S	
9. Long-term or unclassified portfolio	PVFCF, old rate (GAAP)	FC, S	
	CMP	E, Cp, U	
	OAC	E, FC, S, U	
	Lower of PVFCF and CMP	Cn	
10. Securities firm's portfolio	CMP (GAAP)	E, Cp, U	Case includes investment company portfolios and trading portfolios
	OAC	E, FC, S, U	
	PVFCF, old rate	FC, S	
	Lower of PVFCF and CMP	Cn	
Equity securities owned:			Marketable shares only
11. Less than 20%, CMP > OAC	OAC (GAAP)	Cn, FC, S, U	OAC typically more conservative than EM. Both OAC and EM permit choice of date to realize gain or loss
	CMP	Cp, U	
	EM	FC	

(continued)

Exhibit 1

Choices of Accounting Measurement Methods in U.S. GAAP★ *(continued)*

Net Asset Item and Circumstances	Measurement Methods Reasonably Available	Qualities on Which a Method Is Superior	Notes
12. Less than 20%, current portfolio, CMP < OAC	CMP (GAAP)	Cn, Cp, U	A mixed method applies to shares in noncurrent portfolio
	OAC	FC, S, U	
	EM	FC	
13. 20–50%	EM (GAAP)	FC	
	CMP	Cp, U	
	OAC	FC, S, U	
14. Greater than 50%	Consolidation (GAAP)	FC	
	CMP	Cp, U	
	OAC	FC, S, U	
15. Securities firm's portfolio	CMP (GAAP)	Cp, U	
	OAC	FC, S, U	
	EM	FC	
Inventories:			
16. General case, "market" > OAC	OAC (GAAP)	R, E, Cn, FC, S	NRV not always available; also must reflect likely channel of disposition
	NRV (probable course)	Cp	
	CAC	Cp	
17. General case, "market" < OAC	CAC/NRV (GAAP)	Cn	NRV not always available; also must reflect likely channel of disposition
	NRV (probable course)	Cp	
	OAC	R, E, FC, S	
18. Joint products, majority case	OAC, allocated (GAAP)		
	NRV	Cp, U	
	CAC, allocated		
19. Joint products, minority case	NRV (GAAP)	Cp, U	
	OAC, allocated	FC, S	
	CAC, allocated		
Property, plant and equipment:			
20. General case	OAC, net (GAAP)	Cn, FC, S	
	OAC, gross	R, E, U	
	CAC, gross		
	CAC, net	Cp	
21. In discontinued segment	NRV (GAAP)	Cn, FC	
	OAC, net	R, E	Other methods could be listed
22. Natural resource reserves	OAC, net, full cost (GAAP)	S	Popular among small companies
	OAC, net, Suc. efforts (GAAP)	Cn, FC	Popular among large companies
	PVFCF	Cp	
Intangibles, other:			
23. Identifiable intangibles	OAC, net (GAAP)	S	
	OAC, gross		
	Immediate expense	R, E, Cn	
24. Goodwill, purchased	OAC, net (GAAP)	S	
	OAC, gross		
	Immediate expense	R, E, Cn	

EXHIBIT 1

Choices of Accounting Measurement Methods in U.S. GAAP* *(continued)*

Net Asset Item and Circumstances	Measurement Methods Reasonably Available	Qualities on Which a Method Is Superior	Notes
25. R and D benefits	Immediate expense (GAAP)	R, E, Cn	
	OAC, gross or net	S	
26. Tax allocation asset	OAC (GAAP)	S	Deferral method
	PVFCF, current rate	Cp	
	FCF		Liability method
	Flow through	R, E, Cn, U	
Liabilities:			
27. Tax allocation liability	OP (GAAP)	Cn, S	Deferral method
	PVFCF, current rate		
	FCF	Cn	Liability method
	Flow through	R, E, U	
28. Short-term payables	FCF (GAAP)	R, E, Cn, U	
	PVFCF	Cp	Discount may be immaterial
29. Borrowings, not publicly traded	PVFCF, old rate (GAAP)	FC, S	Amortized original proceeds
	PVFCF, current rate	Cp	
	OP	R, E, FC, U	
30. Borrowings publicly traded	PVFCF, old rate (GAAP)	FC, S	
	CMP	Cp	
	OP	R, E, FC, U	
31. Nonmonetary liabilities	OP (GAAP)	R, E, S, U	Revaluation is not common
	NRV	Cp	Negative value
	Current proceeds		

*The explanations in the text subsections on measurement methods and qualities of accounting measurements are integral parts of this Exhibit.

The practical literature on measurement methods is so fragmented that taking inventory of the methods in use is a challenge. Furthermore, the terminology of measurement methods is not well developed; some choices must be made to permit a condensed presentation. My search and terminology choices turned up eight basic measurement methods (plus variations) in current use. Their specifications, as the terms are applied in Exhibit 1, are as follows:

1. Current market price (CMP) applies only to those cases in which the entity buys and sells the item in the same market, e.g., an organized securities or commodity market. No fringe acquisition costs are added and no costs of disposition are deducted.

2. Future cash flows (FCF) are based on contractual evidence of the amounts to be transferred, without discounting for waiting. FCF could be net of estimated uncollectibles or gross—the amount specified in the agreement (oral or written). In the latter case, any losses due to a debtor's failure to pay are recorded on a direct write-off basis.

3. Present value of future cash flows (PVFCF) is based on contractual evidence of the amounts and times of future cash flows, less a discount for waiting. The discount rate is selected by more or less direct observation of market interest rates, so it usually includes a premium to cover uncollectibles. If an additional provision is made for uncollectibles (PVFCF, net), it is interpreted as a conservative form of double counting. The discount rate employed may be the rate observed at the date of origin of the claim or obligation (old rate) or it may be revised to the measurement date (current rate). PVFCF at the current rate is the same as current market price in the case of actively traded debt securities. In the case of restructured loans, the practice of ignoring modifications of terms is described as PVFCF, old contract, while a revision to recognize the revised terms is described as PVFCF, new contract. PVFCF differs from CMP in that the former entails observation of evidence of times and amounts of future cash flows and of a market discount rate. Those data are then processed by the accountant to obtain the result. When the accountant uses CMP he accepts the market's observations and processing of evidence.

4. Net realizable value (NRV) is the current price in the market in which the entity either expects to sell the asset or would sell it if required to do so to raise funds quickly, net of costs of disposition. Accounting practices regarding NRV vary. In some cases sale of the asset—for example, work in process or construction in progress—in its current condition (as–is) is assumed; in other cases sale in the ordinary course of business (completed cycle) is assumed. Furthermore, it is difficult to determine the accountants' limit with respect to the clarity of the evidence accepted. For example, determination of the NRV of business segments being discontinued or of manufacturing work in process may strain the accountant's reliability standard. Here the meaning of "reasonably available" is at its haziest. The application of negative NRV to an obligation to deliver goods or provide services is another unclear area.

5. "Original acquisition cost" (OAC) is used instead of "historical cost" because essentially all measurements in accounting are based on history. Accountants include fringe acquisition costs if they are material, including interest cost in accordance with the FASB's Statement No. 34. Measurement of notes receivable at OAC means interest is not accrued. OAC net means depreciation, depletion, or amortization is deducted. In the oil and gas industry, OAC may be determined on a full cost or successful efforts basis.

6. Current acquisition cost (CAC) is determined in the same manner as OAC except that current input prices are substituted for input prices at the original acquisition date. Current proceeds is the term adopted here for a symmetrical application to liabilities, i.e., the price the market offers now in exchange for similar promises.

7. Original proceeds (OP) is the amount of money received in exchange for the obligation in question at the date it was established.

8. The equity method (EM) of accounting for equity securities owned starts with OAC and adjusts for the investor's share of changes in the investee's owners' equity and for amortization of acquisition-date discrepancies between OAC and the book value of the equity interest acquired.

In addition to the above methods of measuring net asset items, the alternative of no measurement is listed in several cases where that has been recognized as a reasonable possibility. No measurement is called flow through in the cases of tax allocation items and immediate expense in the cases involving intangibles.

For each asset or liability item, two or more measurement methods are listed as reasonably available. The one required by U.S. GAAP is so labelled.

QUALITIES OF ACCOUNTING MEASUREMENTS

Alternative methods for measuring wealth items typically are available to accounting, although not to individual accountants.[4] Those alternative measurement methods vary in the degree to which they and the corresponding measurements possess various qualities. The major qualities that my observations show to be valued by accounting are:

1. Reliability (R), including verifiability, neutrality, and representational faithfulness, with respect to what the method purports to measure as described in SFAC No. 2 [FASB, 1980a].

2. Economy (E), or low cost of application.

3. Conservatism (Cn). (In assessing conservatism of methods, selling prices of goods are assumed to exceed cost.)

4. Flexibility and control of income measurement by management (FC), either currently or in the future. Measurement techniques that possess the flexibility/control quality are those that entail judgments, such as providing for uncollectibles or estimating net realizable value of a discontinued segment; those that permit some flexibility in timing, such as the timing of abandonment of a "dry hole" or of the decision to discontinue a segment or to restructure a debt; and methods that keep income determination options open, such as the reservoirs of instant earnings and/or instant losses made available by OAC measurements. The essence of this quality is choice, not variability over time.

5. Stability (S), or offering (if desired) a stabilizing influence on the series of income statement numbers associated with the net asset over its life. This quality characterizes several asset measurement techniques such as OAC in general (compared with CMP, CAC, or NRV), time-based calculations of depreciation and amortization, adhering to old discount rates or to old PV's of restructured loans, and full costing in extractive industries. Many recent popular statements of preference for this quality have included pejorative references to "yo-yo accounting."

6. Comparability (Cp), across entities and across like items within an entity. Any method that gives different measurements of things with similar economic significance as wealth items lacks comparability. Generally, abandoning varying old costs and discount rates in favor of uniform current prices contributes to comparability of measurements of similar items.

---

[4]The choices available to the individual accountant tend to be variations of one of the eight measurement methods listed above.

7. Understandability (U), from the point of view of both the accountant and the reader of financial reports.

These seven qualities are presented at this stage as a tentative list of qualities prized by accounting. Analysis of the 31 measurement cases in Exhibit 1 may eliminate one or more of the seven. Relevance is not listed because (1) it was not in the vocabulary of practical accounting until introduced by normative theorists, (2) clear observation of its presence or absence is difficult, and (3) it is easily confused with the more fundamental idea of measuring wealth items. Consistency is omitted because it is not a quality associated with any one measurement method.

The measurement methods listed for each net asset item were compared on each of the above seven qualities. When one (occasionally two) method(s) was judged to be substantially superior to the others on that quality, the symbol identifying that quality was entered in column three. When the quality was judged of minor importance in the circumstances of the case, it was not listed for any measurement method. Explanatory notes appear in column four.

MEASUREMENT PRACTICES: SUMMARIES

The detailed contents of Exhibit 1 are analyzed and summarized in Exhibits 2, 3, and 4. Exhibit 2 shows the frequency with which each of the eight methods of measuring net asset items is called for by GAAP in the 31 cases examined. In one case examined, no net asset item is recognized in the accounts, i.e., research and development costs are expensed as they are incurred, even though the overall results of a company's R and D efforts typically meet the tests of an asset as defined in SFAC No. 3 [FASB, 1980b]. The most important message in Exhibit 2 is that no one measurement method dominates accounting practice. Rather, accounting's measurement practices range across eight general methods.

Exhibit 3 summarizes the qualities characterizing GAAP measurement practices in the 31 cases examined. Column two tallies the number of cases in which the GAAP method is superior (or tied for superiority) to all other methods deemed reasonably available on the quality listed in column one. GAAP practices were found to be characterized by stability and conservatism more frequently than by the other qualities. In three cases the GAAP method was found to possess none of the seven qualities, thus raising a question regarding overlooked qualities.

The "trade-off matrix" in Exhibit 4 shows which quality(ies) was gained when the GAAP method was selected and which quality(ies) possessed by a nonGAAP method was sacrificed in choosing the GAAP method. To be listed here, a sacrificed quality had to be associated with a nonGAAP method and not associated with the GAAP method. A gained quality had to be associated with GAAP and not associated with any other available method. The cells with large numbers, such as the intersection of the comparability row and the stability column, show the more common consequences of the measurement method choices accounting has made. Large column totals draw attention to qualities frequently gained by the choices that have been made. Large row totals indicate qualities frequently sacrificed. Comparisons of numbers in the (S, Q_n) cells with those in the (Q_n, S) cells show that stability dominates every other quality and that conservatism and flexibility and control are also popular.

MEASUREMENT PRACTICES IN ACCOUNTING: GENERALIZATIONS

The observations, analyses and summaries of measurement practices found in U.S. GAAP justify the following generalizations:

EXHIBIT 2

Measurement Methods Identified in Exhibit 1 as the GAAP Method

Method	Number of Cases
Future cash flows	3
Present value of future cash flows	8
Current market price	4
Net realizable value	3
Current acquisition cost or current proceeds	1
Original acquisition cost	8
Original proceeds	2
Equity method or consolidation	2
Immediate expense	1
Total	32*

*There are 32 solutions to 31 cases because case 17 has two GAAP solutions.

EXHIBIT 3

Number of Cases in Which the GAAP Method is Superior to All Other Methods on Specified Qualities

Quality	Number of Cases
Reliability	5
Economy	5
Conservatism	10
Flexibility/Control	6
Stability	13
Comparability	5
Understandability	3
No superior quality	3

EXHIBIT 4

Trade-Offs Involved in 31 GAAP Measurement Choices

When This Quality is Sacrificed	Times Sacrificed	This Quality is Gained							
		R	E	Cn	F/C	S	Cp	U	None
Reliability	18	0	1	3	3	9	0	0	2
Economy	18	1	0	3	4	8	0	0	2
Conservatism	13	1	1	0	2	6	1	1	2
Flexibility/Control	12	0	1	3	0	2	5	3	0
Stability	16	2	1	5	2	0	5	2	0
Comparability	33	4	4	6	5	10	0	3	2
Understandability	11	0	0	1	2	6	0	0	2
Total sacrifices/gains	121	8	8	21	18	41	11	9	10

1. Eight general methods for measuring wealth items are used in accounting. No one method is dominant.

2. Stability of the related income statement line item, conservatism, and flexibility and control of income measurement by management are qualities frequently associated with the measurement methods chosen by accounting. Economy, understandability, reliability, and comparability appear less frequently.

3. The trade-offs made in choosing accounting measurement methods frequently have involved giving up methods that are superior on comparability, reliability, and economy and accepting methods superior on stability, conservatism, and flexibility and control.

A THEORY OF ACCOUNTING MEASUREMENT

The review displayed in Exhibit 1 discovered eight different methods (plus variations) of measuring entity wealth items. That review also showed that several qualities of measurements and measurement methods frequently characterize the application of those methods. A multiple-method, multiple-criteria picture of accounting measurement practices emerges. In view of these findings, is any central pillar of accounting measurement evident? Is there a single, coherent thread that ties accounting measurement practices together? What key idea can be presented (to students, practitioners, and others seeking an understanding of accounting measurement) that can contribute to that understanding? No answers are obvious.

MARKET PRICES AS RAW MATERIAL

Homogeneity of accounting subject matter has been found: wealth. Homogeneity of method is elusive. What does the accountant look for after he has recognized a wealth item? One feature of the accountant's method is obvious: quantification. The assignment of numbers to represent the significance of wealth items requires a source of numbers. In a markets-driven economy, that source is nearly always a market, rather than a government office or a manager's imagination. Most of the numbers accountants assign to wealth items are observed market prices or derivatives thereof.

The characteristics of the markets in which the raw material for the accountant's measurements are formed vary. We live in a world of incomplete markets, so prices for many net asset items are unobservable; no trading in the particular items owned or owed by the entity takes place. In other cases, markets are "thin," i.e., trading occurs infrequently. In still others, prices may be heavily influenced by one buyer or seller, thus casting doubt on those prices as predictions of future cash flows. Transaction costs and imperfect information add to the difficulties facing measurers of wealth items. In sum, incomplete and imperfect markets present many obstacles to one who would use market prices in measuring wealth items, so accounting seeks ways of overcoming those obstacles.

The dearth of market quotations mentioned above does not eliminate the necessity of choosing from among alternative prices. For example, prices of assets at their acquisition dates commonly are reported, but prices at the reporting date sometimes are substituted. Inventory cost flow assumptions involve alternative interpretations of acquisition dates. Another choice is that between entry prices and exit prices; accounting has chosen the former in most cases.

Prices established in market transactions are used in most accounting measurements, although the role of market prices in three of the common measurement methods is less obvious than it is in the other four. The equity method starts with an original acquisition price and is adjusted by changes in retained earnings, which are based largely on market prices used in measuring the investee's net asset items. Measurements based on future cash flows and present values of future cash flows often reflect market prices of nonmonetary items involved in the exchanges, and present value computations employ market prices for the use of money. The roles of market prices in the other measurement methods are obvious. Accounting measurements clearly are based largely on market prices.

PROCESSING PROCEDURES

Those who view accounting measurement as the selection and processing of evidence relating to the amounts of wealth items might view market prices as the dominant type of inputs to that process. In addition to obtaining various market price data and selecting specific prices to use in his measurements, the accountant performs additional procedures, including:

1. Combining prices, e.g., in adding fringe acquisition costs to a nominal purchase price, in product cost accounting, in discounting future cash flows, and in computing net realizable value.

2. Estimating or predicting, e.g., uncollectibles, lives of assets, future inputs of resources to complete a product or fulfill a warranty obligation, employee turnover and mortality related to pensions, matrix pricing of unquoted portfolio securities, and even prediction of prices such as salvage values of depreciable assets and prices of future inputs required to fulfill warranty obligations.

3. Allocating, especially splitting one value into parts in proportion to some base, as in allocation of indirect costs in product costing, allocation of process costs among joint products, and depreciation accounting.

4. Miscellaneous procedures such as indexing and tax allocation.

Experienced accountants can find many examples of similar processing procedures in the GAAP (and alternative) solutions to the 31 cases listed in Exhibit 1.

Why has accounting developed such a complex set of adaptations of primary market prices? The answer may follow from the interpretation of wealth items found in *Elements of Financial Statements of Business Enterprises* [FASB, 1980b, p. 9]. Assets are defined as probable future economic benefits obtained or controlled by a particular entity, not as physical commodities. Similarly, liabilities are defined as probable future sacrifices of economic benefits. Those definitions apply to assets and liabilities in general financial and economic usage, not to balance sheet categories. They include two subsets in each case: balance sheet assets (liabilities) and off-balance sheet assets (liabilities). I believe those definitions are close to the intuitive views of most economic actors, including accountants, except when they are making decisions regarding balance sheet content. Accounting measurement practices seem to be related to those views of assets and liabilities. The concepts of assets and liabilities may be described as *future-oriented* and *setting-specific,* because an item's significance derives from its *future* role in the *entity*—its contributions to future cash flows. No market prices for those setting-specific assets and liabilities are available. For example, prices established currently without the participation of the entity, even if the item being traded is essentially the same as an asset held by the entity, do not price the probable economic benefits the entity's asset will provide to the entity. Even a market price paid by the entity is not a market price for setting-specific benefits; it reflects the influence of two or more participants' views of benefits in a variety of settings. Market prices for the setting-specific benefits to be yielded by an entity's assets are not available. Accounting makes do with substitutes, including simple surrogates (i.e., a single price accepted as the value of a net asset item) and complex adaptations of observed prices. This combination can be called simulated market prices, because they are not observed prices of the setting-specific assets and liabilities that are of interest to those concerned with entity wealth.

ADAPTATIONS PER PRINCIPLES OF MARKET ECONOMICS

Another look at the measurement practices used in accounting can reveal the extent to which accounting relies on market simulation for its measurements. Exhibit 5 is a summary of such a review. Columns two and three show the generalizations that might be called principles of market economics that are related to the measurement practices—column two for those principles that are observed and column three for those ignored by accounting.

A few explanations may clarify certain of the rather cryptic statements in Exhibit 5:

1. Regarding FCF, while it is true that accounting fails to discount short-term trade receivables and payables, some may argue that lack of materiality, rather than disregard for market economics, is the explanation.

2. In the cases of entry price methods, one could say that accounting ignores the common belief that selling prices of entity products approximate future cash flows from those products more closely than the sums of entry prices of resources used in making the products approximate those flows. The interpretation here, however, is that in most applications of OAC and CAC, failure to use NRV does not indicate disregard for economic principles as much as it indicates the difficulties that would be involved in isolating portions of product selling prices attributable to a resource stock on hand. In other words, NRV is not practically available.

3. In the case of joint products, note that the failure of the relative sales value method of allocating costs to yield acceptable cost numbers does not indicate a departure from market simulation accounting. Taking the retrospective (input) view rather than the prospective (output) view is the departure from the market simulation notion.

4. When obligations to deliver goods are measured at original proceeds (the amount of money received when the obligation was created), that number might be interpreted as a surrogate for the sum of the costs of resources to be used in fulfilling the obligation, that is, a set of future costs. Both stability of price series over time and a strong tendency for costs to equal selling price are required if OP is to be a good predictor of future negative cash flows.

5. The effect of an asset's tax basis on the future cash flows it will yield is generally recognized. The deferral method of tax allocation says, in effect, that the tax saved or extra tax paid this period affects wealth by the same amount, without regard for delay in the reversal, changes in the tax rates, or the probability that reversal will never affect tax payments (or refunds). If assets were commonly traded with their

EXHIBIT 5

Market Simulation Accounting: The Association of Accounting Measurement Practices With Principles of Market Economics

Accounting Measurement Practices	Principles of Market Economics: Generalizations Based on Observations	
	Observed in Accounting	Ignored in Accounting
Future Cash Flows and PVFCF:		
Accrual accounting in general	Markets pay for prospective cash flows.	Markets discount for waiting. (Ignored in case of short-term trade items)
Deduct for uncollectibles	Markets recognize expected value.	
Discount when material, using risky, original rate	Markets discount for waiting and for risk.	Market discount rates fluctuate. (Old rates differ from current rates.)
Current market price	All.	None.
Matrix pricing of securities	Those specified in equation.	Omitted variables.
Net realizable value:		
Current exit price	Price series exhibit autocorrelation; current prices are predictors of future prices and cash flows.	
Deduct for future costs	Markets allow for both positive and negative components of expected value.	
Deferral accounting in general, including deferrals of cost and proceeds (e.g., capitalizing fringe acquisition costs, product cost accounting, deferring credits to revenue)	Firms tend to make productive uses of resources on hand; product prices (and future cash flows therefrom) are positively correlated with the sum of costs.	
Allocate common costs of joint products per relative net sales value	Price/cost correlation.	Markets pay for prospective cash flows, not for retrospective cash flows.
Depreciation, depletion and amortization accounting	Price/cost correlation. Markets tend to equalize the net unit costs of similar services available from alternative sources (so the market price of a bundle of services declines with the number and "quality" of units in the bundle.)	Markets discount for waiting; cost of capital is considered.
Original acquisition cost and original proceeds	Price series exhibit autocorrelation; old prices are related to current prices.	Autocorrelation in a price series is less than one. Markets pay for prospective cash flows.
Indexing to obtain current acquisition cost	Prices of goods constituting a homogeneous set (in use or production) are closely correlated (so a narrow index can be used to estimate a specific current price).	Price relationships vary over time.
Equity method for equity securities.	Book values and changes therein are correlated with market values and changes therein over long periods.	Markets pay for prospective cash flows.
Interperiod tax allocation per original proceeds or OAC	Markets value uncertain future cash flows.	Markets discount for waiting and for risk.

tax bases carried over to the buyer, markets presumably would take all of those factors into account in pricing those assets, just as bond markets distinguish between taxable future cash flows and nontaxable flows.

The evidence shows that every measurement method used in accounting incorporates one or more principles of market economics. Indeed, only two major principles have been widely—but not uniformly—neglected: (1) the cost of capital requires discounting of future cash flows, and (2) current market prices are closer surrogates for complete and perfect current market prices of setting-specific assets and liabilities than are old market prices. The trend towards rectifying the first case of neglect is apparent in many relatively recent standards that require recognition of interest, such as APB Opinions 8, 12, and 21 and FASB Statements 13, 34, and 35. Regarding the second case of neglect, decades of flirtation with and nibbling at current measurements in lieu of original acquisition cost suggest that the mainstream of accounting thought and the market simulation view of accounting measurement are not irreconcilable on the old-vs.-current-prices issue. (Neither case was as serious when prices were more stable.) Those exceptions clearly are big ones with material impacts on the results of the accounting measurement process, but they do not present a huge conceptual gap. A general pattern of respect for principles of market economics suggests that accounting measurement practices tend to simulate complete and perfect market prices. The entire fabric of accounting measurement now appears to be more tightly woven—more coherent—than was previously believed.

THE COMMON THREAD: MARKET SIMULATION ACCOUNTING

The search for a common thread in accounting measurement practices shows that:

1. Accounting uses market prices as the primary raw material going into the measurement process.

2. In a world of incomplete and imperfect markets, complete and perfect market prices for the setting-specific assets and liabilities that are of concern to users of financial statements cannot be observed.

3. Accounting applies a set of adaptive procedures to a set of basic market prices to fabricate the measurement methods listed in Part II of this paper. Applications of those methods to case-specific circumstances yield the measurements of entity wealth items reported in financial statements.

4. The adaptive procedures employed in accounting generally reflect familiar principles of market economics, subject to two important exceptions.

5. The choices of market prices and adaptive procedures reflected in GAAP yield measurements that can be labelled simulated market price.

The main conclusion of this review of accounting measurement practices is:

In the absence of observable current market prices for setting-specific assets and liabilities, accounting simulates such prices by selecting and blending pertinent observed market prices and other evidence in accordance with accepted principles of market economics.

OTHER EXPLANATIONS

The market simulation notion does not fully explain accounting measurement practices. Accounting deliberately ignores two important principles of market economics in many cases, as was pointed out in the preceding subsection. Any comprehensive, descriptive theory of accounting measurement must explain those deliberate anomalies in the application of market simulation accounting. Part II of this paper developed such an explanation. Accounting has been found so frequently to choose measurement methods with certain qualities that an observer might conclude that accounting values, even prizes, those qualities. The extent to which market simulation accounting is achieved in current GAAP measurements is constrained by respect for those qualities. The evidence reported in Part II suggests that stability of the related income statement line item, conservatism, and flexibility and control of income measurement by management are the qualities most valued by accounting. The market simulation concept combined with respect for those, and other, qualities explains most of the body of current measurement practices in accounting.

SUMMARY OF GENERALIZATIONS

All of the observations presented and discussed in this paper may be reduced to the following general statements:

1. Wealth is the fundamental subject matter of accounting measurement. Accounting identifies, measures, classifies, and reports stocks and flows of wealth so as to provide information on income, liquidity, risk, and other aspects of wealth.

2. Market prices of economic goods are the primary raw materials used in the eight general accounting measurement methods.

3. Accounting's choices from among alternative market prices invest the body of generally accepted accounting measurement methods and the resulting measurements with certain qualities, especially stability of the related income statement line item, conservatism, and flexibility and control of income measurement by management.

4. Prices for the setting-specific, future-oriented entity assets and liabilities with which the financial community is concerned are not observable. In their absence, accounting simulates such prices by selecting and blending pertinent observed market prices and other evidence in accordance with accepted principles of market economics, subject to a respect for certain "qualities" of measurement methods and measurements, such as those mentioned in no. 3 above.

CONCLUSION

The market simulation theory of accounting measurement, like any theory, might be viewed as a hypothesis that should be subjected to further testing and development. For example, the present research provides only crude evidence of the relative weights of the various explanations of measurement method choices. One auxiliary hypothesis that might be tested is that the qualities most frequently possessed by accounting measurements carry great weight in the selection of the basis of valuation, a matter of much concern to managements and other nonaccountants, but that the implementation choices that tend to be left to accountants are heavily influenced by the market simulation notion. Or perhaps certain qualities influence the selection of the basis of valuation and other qualities tend to influence the finer points.

Any reader who is dissatisfied with my interpretive assessments of the degrees to which specific measurement methods possess specific qualities in specific cases may wish to pursue such assessments by means of questionnaires. If such research resulted in refinements of the weights of the several explanations, the way might be paved for the use of the theory in predicting standards to be set in areas now on the FASB's agenda. A first step in that direction might be a study of the inputs received by the FASB in the last ten years in an effort to discover motivations behind the preferences expressed by respondents and by speakers at public hearings. Motivations of participants in the decision-making process could serve as the basis for a theory of accounting choice. The present research studiously avoids attributing motivations to anyone.

The market simulation notion is not represented as an excellent explanation of all accounting measurement practices. Current practice represents very crude market simulation accounting. The more important point is that the market simulation explanation fits present accounting measurement practices better than any other single explanation—better than historical cost, better than matching costs and revenues, better than exit values or current cost. Furthermore, GAAP is the best expression of the market simulation concept that is found in current accounting practice. GAAP is better market simulation accounting than is the cash basis, the income tax basis, or any known regulatory basis of accounting such as Interstate Commerce Commission or insurance commissioner requirements. GAAP is the best description of market simulation accounting that can be found in practice.

Finally, one might consider the parallel between the market simulation accounting hypothesis and the efficient market hypothesis. The latter can hold despite poor use of information by many individual investors and despite their refusal to accept the hypothesis. Market efficiency, to the extent that it occurs, is a collective phenomenon, not an individual one. Similarly, the collective impact of the views of those who have influenced GAAP over many decades may be a substantial degree of market simulation accounting, even if most individual accountants do not recognize it. Adam Smith might detect evidence of an invisible hand controlling not only the allocation of resources in a competitive economy and the pricing of securities in major world markets, but also the evolution of accounting measurement practices in the private sector.

REFERENCES

Accounting Principles Board, *Statement No. 4*, "Basic Concepts and Accounting Principles Underlying Financial Statements of Business Enterprises" (American Institute of Certified Public Accountants, 1970).

American Institute of Certified Public Accountants, *Accounting Trends and Techniques* (AICPA, annually).

Financial Accounting Standards Board, *Statement of Financial Accounting Concepts No. 2*, "Qualitative Characteristics of Accounting Information" (FASB, 1980a).

———, *Statement of Financial Accounting Concepts No. 3*, "Elements of Financial Statements of Business Enterprises" (FASB, 1980b).

———, *Accounting Standards* (McGraw-Hill, 1983a).

———, *Proposed Statement of Financial Accounting Concepts*, "Recognition and Measurement in Financial Statements of Business Enterprises" (FASB, 1983b).

Gilman, Stephen, *Accounting Concepts of Profit* (Ronald Press, 1939).

Goldberg, Louis, *An Inquiry into the Nature of Accounting* (American Accounting Association, 1965).

Grady, Paul, Accounting Research Study No. 7, *Inventory of Generally Accepted Accounting Principles for Business Enterprises* (AICPA, 1965).

Hatfield, Henry R., *Accounting, Its Principles and Problems* (D. Appleton and Co., 1927).

Ijiri, Yuji, *The Foundations of Accounting Measurement* (Prentice-Hall, 1967).

———, Studies in Accounting Research No. 10, *Theory of Accounting Measurement* (AAA, 1975).

Littleton, A. C., *Structure of Accounting Theory* (AAA, 1953).

Paton, W. A. and A. C. Littleton, *An Introduction to Corporate Accounting Standards* (AAA, 1940).

Skinner, R. M., *Accounting Principles: A Canadian Viewpoint* (The Canadian Institute of Chartered Accountants, 1972).

Sterling, Robert R., "An Operational Analysis of Traditional Accounting," *Abacus* (December 1966), pp. 119–136.

———, "Conservatism: The Fundamental Principle of Valuation in Traditional Accounting," *Abacus* (December 1967), pp. 109–132.

A REVOLUTION
IN ACCOUNTING THOUGHT?

M. C. Wells

Although the decade of the 1960s has been described by Carl Nelson as a "golden age in the history of a priori research in accounting" [Nelson, 1973, p. 4], the works cited as examples of that kind of research also have been severely criticized.[1] Nelson states that, "impressive as the scholarship is, we are not significantly advanced from where we were in 1960" [Nelson, 1973, p. 15]. He also is reported as having "contended that the existing a priori studies are of doubtful value" [Dopuch and Revsine, 1973, p. 32]. In similar vein, Gonedes and Dopuch are critical because, they allege, the same works are theoretically deficient, and it is possible "to declare the superiority of just about any set of accounting procedures, depending on the particular a priori model adopted" [Gonedes and Dopuch, 1974, pp. 49–50].

It will be argued here that those criticisms are based on a misunderstanding of the role of so-called *a priori research* in the overthrow of outdated ideas and practices. Far from being unproductive, the works referred to were a necessary step in the revolution currently underway in accounting thought. Far from being of doubtful value, those works have helped to place us in a significantly different position from that of 1960. Whether the works were theoretically deficient is, to some extent, irrelevant in this context, and the circularity implied by Gonedes and Dopuch's second criticism is a normal and healthy characteristic of theoretical works of that kind.

M. C. Wells, "A Revolution in Accounting Thought?" *The Accounting Review,* July 1976, pp. 471–482. Reprinted by permission of the American Accounting Association.

[1]The examples given were, "the writings of Chambers, Edwards and Bell, Sterling, and Ijiri" [Nelson, 1973, p. 3].

SCIENTIFIC REVOLUTIONS

The notion of a revolution in accounting is taken from Kuhn's *The Structure of Scientific Revolutions* [1970].[2] His thesis is that science does not progress through accumulation. Rather, a series of tradition-shattering revolutions occur in which one "time-honored scientific theory is rejected in favour of another incompatible with it" [Kuhn, 1970, p. 6]. The new theory, or set of ideas, is unique in that it is not derived from the previously accepted dogma. It is "seldom or never just an increment to what is already known" [Kuhn, 1970, p. 7], and in the process of moving from the old set of ideas to the new, the community of scientists follows a number of identifiable steps:

1. Recognition of anomalies
2. A period of insecurity
3. Development of alternative sets of ideas
4. Identification of schools of thought
5. Domination of the new practices or ideas

The first step is a precursor to the whole process; it initiates the period of crisis which follows. During that period, scientists became increasingly dissatisfied with the existing theoretical framework, and a search for alternatives begins. Therefore, the second and third steps are mutually interactive. As dissatisfaction grows, the search for alternatives gains impetus; as alternatives are discerned and discussed, the dissatisfaction is heightened. Schools of thought emerge, and one set of ideas gradually gains ascendency over the alternatives.

Because these steps involve such fundamental changes in the outlook and practices of the community of scholars, Kuhn applies the political metaphor of revolution to the process. He argues that the change takes place only after a serious malfunction has occurred in the sense that "existing institutions [or practices] have ceased adequately to meet the problems posed by an environment that they have in part created" [Kuhn, 1970, p. 92]. Just as political revolutions "aim to change political institutions in ways that those institutions themselves prohibit" [Kuhn, 1970, p. 93], so do scientific revolutions change previously held concepts of the field of enquiry in a way which is incompatible with those concepts. Such a fundamental change cannot take place within the existing institutional or conceptual framework. The challenger in incompatible with the incumbent. "The parties to a revolutionary conflict must resort to the techniques of mass persuasion" [Kuhn, 1970, p. 93], and, "like the choice between competing political institutions, that between competing paradigms proves to be a choice between incompatible modes of community life" [Kuhn, 1970, p. 94].

The process, or revolution, is unlikely to be completed quickly. The assimilation of new ideas will not be complete until previously accepted theories have been reconstructed and previously held facts have been re-evaluated. This is "an intrinsically revolutionary process that is seldom completed by a single man and never overnight" [Kuhn, 1970, p. 7].

---

[2]Kuhn's exposition has been subject to widespread criticism. See for example Shapere [1964] and Lakatos and Musgrave [1974]. However, references in this paper are to the enlarged edition of Kuhn's monograph. The postscript to that edition contains Kuhn's reply to his critics.

There is, of course, no necessary reason why the pattern of developments in science (and particularly the physical sciences from which Kuhn derives most of his examples) should be found also in accounting. Kuhn does consider the possibility of his thesis being applicable in other fields, despite some obvious differences [p. 208]. Nevertheless, just as scientific theories may both describe and prescribe physical phenomena, so may accounting theories describe and prescribe financial phenomena. Furthermore, if the pattern of events in accounting can be seen to be following the pattern of successful revolutions described by Kuhn, then we will be able to explain the reasons for and the importance of the "golden age of a priori research" referred to above. In doing that, we also will answer the criticisms made of the works which appeared during that golden age.

It should be emphasized that the analogy here is to accounting thought.[3] Given the political difficulties of initiating change in accounting practices, that may well be an evolutionary rather than a revolutionary process. But it will not, I suspect, take place until the revolution described here is complete.

However, to apply the analogy to accounting thought, one initial condition must be satisfied: a community of scholars must be identified. This was emphasized by Kuhn in his postscript. He pointed out that "scientific communities can and should be isolated without prior recourse to paradigms" [Kuhn, 1970, p. 176]. Accordingly, I will specify the community to which this paper relates as comprising the members of academic and research organizations such as the American Accounting Association, the Association of University Teachers of Accounting of the United Kingdom, the Accounting Association of Australia and New Zealand, the Research Division of the AICPA and the Australian Accountancy Research Foundation.

THE ACCOUNTING DISCIPLINARY MATRIX

The basic techniques used for keeping accounting records can be traced back more than 500 years, but the information conventionally stored within those records is largely a product of this century. Only within the last 75 years did the historical cost doctrine crystalize and come to dominate the literature and practices of accounting. More recently still, during the 1930s and the 1940s, attempts were made to formalize the framework underlying the rules for recording and reporting financial matters. The works of Gilman (1939), Sanders, Hatfield and Moore (1938), Paton and Littleton (1940)[4] and others[5] attempted to rationalize existing practices and to set the framework within which alternative ideas and procedures might be evaluated.

The framework of ideas which emerged during this period has characteristics of a paradigm. However, note that Kuhn used the term *paradigm* in a number of different ways. As this

---

[3]Other attempts to apply Kuhn's thesis to financial accounting may be seen in Chambers [1966, pp. 373–376] and to cost accounting in Wells [forthcoming].

[4]Paton and Littleton were also both members of the Executive Committee of American Accounting Association which in 1936 produced *A Tentative Statement of Accounting Principles Underlying Corporate Financial Statements*. This was "one of the first major attempts to develop a framework which might be regarded as representing a structure of the fundamental principles of accounting" [Bedford and Ziegler, 1975, p. 438].

[5]In their review of the influence of Littleton on accounting thought and practices, Bedford and Ziegler [1975] also identify the late 1930s as "the era to which the roots of much contemporary accounting practice may be traced" [p. 437]. Coincidentally, it was not until 1940 that the U.S. Securities and Exchange Commission brought together all of its various rules on the form and content of financial statements in one document—Regulation S-X [Zeff, 1972, p. 151].

was a cause of considerable confusion and a matter he dealt with at length in the postscript appended to the 1970 edition of his essay, we will avoid the use of the term here. Instead, substitute terms introduced in the postscript will be used as far as possible. For the general set of ideas that binds together a community of scientists, Kuhn uses the term *disciplinary matrix* [p. 182]. There are several features which distinguish a disciplinary matrix (disciplinary because it refers to the common possession by the members of a particular discipline; matrix because it comprises ordered elements of various sorts, each requiring further specification) [Kuhn, 1970, p. 182]. There are: (1) symbolic generalizations—readily understood and undisputed symbolic representations common to the discipline [p. 182]; (2) shared commitments—beliefs which help determine what will be accepted as explanations or solutions p. 184]; (3) values—the various qualities which members of the community expect in the work of their colleagues [pp. 184–186]; and (4) exemplars—the concrete problem—solutions which students entering the community encounter and which show by example how they are to go about seeking solutions [p. 187].

Following these descriptions, the disciplinary matrix of accountants which emerged during the 1940s may be described as follows: (1) The symbolic generalization included accepted notions and formulations such as the double entry equation, representations of income, current asset/fixed asset classifications and calculations of working capital, rate of return and debt/equity ratios. (2) The shared commitments included the so-called realization and matching principles, the notion of going concern and the cost basis of valuation. (3) The values included conservatism, consistency, materiality, etc.[6] (4) Finally, the exemplars were seen in the textbooks and expositions of the period. There was (and still is) a remarkable similarity in the contents of most texts—so much so that the content of academic courses and examinations had become almost completely predictable.

Once a student has absorbed the elements of a disciplinary matrix, he or she views all problem situations in the same way as other members of his or her specialist group. Writers and researchers have a common standard of practice, and problems tend to have common solutions, or shared examples [Kuhn, 1970, p. 187]. Thus, we have the commonality of training and outlook which helps to bind together a community of scholars.

However, the existence of a disciplinary matrix does not imply that a rigid, inviolable set of rules also exists. Rather, and because members of the community have been trained in problem-solutions (or as Kuhn expresses it "learning by finger exercises or by doing," p. 471), they do not need a full set of rules. Accounting was in this position prior to 1930. Writers took for granted, or simply explained, general principles.[7] Only after the criticisms of the 1920s and early 1930s were efforts made to formalize the framework of accounting ideas and were authoritative bodies set up for that purpose.[8] This development, too, is foreseen by Kuhn who suggests that only when accepted procedures come under attack, does consideration of the rules become important [p. 47].

---

[6]Notice the similarity of symbolic generalizations, shared commitments and values to the conventions, doctrines and standards described by Gilman [1939], especially pp. 4, 41–43; 254; and 186, respectively.

[7]"There is, it is believed, a corpus of principles of accounting which are generally accepted. It is true that they are not "written law", they have not been codified; they must be sought in accounts and financial statements," [Sanders, Hatfield and Moore, 1938, p. 5]. For this reason, "the search for rules [is] both more difficult and less satisfying than the search for paradigms" [Kuhn, 1970, p. 43].

[8]For examples of this kind of reaction, see Zeff [1972, pp. 119–140].

However, the formalization of rules did not eliminate all of the contradictions and conflicts that had plagued accounting expositions in the past. Neither accounting writers nor practitioners apparently saw any conflict in certain departures from a strict application of the historical cost rule, such as the valuation of inventory at the lower of cost or market or the deduction of depreciation charges from the cost of fixed assets.[9] Even this is to be expected, according to Kuhn. Because the rules are learned through their application in specific contexts, any diversity either is not apparent or may be explained away by the different facts of each case. Therefore, what the rules serve to do is to "limit both the nature of acceptable solutions and the steps by which they are obtained" [Kuhn, 1970, p. 38].

ANOMALIES AND PROFESSIONAL INSECURITY

Discovery commences with the awareness of anomaly, i.e., with the recognition that nature has somehow violated the paradigm-induced expectations that govern normal science [or conventional practice] (Kuhn, 1970, pp. 52–53).

There have long been critics of conventional accounting practices and of solutions to problems proposed within the conventional framework [Brief, 1975; and Chatfield, 1974, pp. 273–276]. Outstanding examples in the period before the historical cost disciplinary matrix crystallized were Paton [1922], Sweeney [1936] and MacNeal [1939]. However, their criticisms appear to have had little impact on the subsequent ascendancy of the historical cost model. Recognition was not given in the literature of accounting to the great number of anomalies which defied resolution and which brought the accounting profession into public opprobrium until the 1960s and early 1970s. During this period, and since, the fundamental defects in the historical cost model repeatedly were identified and criticized by scholars, by businesspersons and in the courts.[10] The criticisms culminated in the most simultaneous publication of Briloff's *Unaccountable Accounting* [1972] and Chambers' *Securities and Obscurities* [1973]. Leasco, Westec, Lockheed, Four Seasons, I.O.S., Rolls Royce, Reid Murray, Minsec and a host of other companies which were involved in cases which highlighted the "gap in GAAP" [Briloff, 1966, p. 484; 1972, pp. 31–33] became almost household names.

The reaction by theorists to the evidence thrust before them precisely follows that predicted by Kuhn; it corresponds to the period of *professional insecurity* [Kuhn, 1970, pp. 67–68] wherein the rules are subject to increasing scrutiny and occasional amendment. The disciplinary matrix is questioned, but not abandoned:

---

[9]The first writer to pay particular attention to these conflicts, without resolving them, was Gilman [1939, pp. 128–130, 174, 235].

[10]See, for example, the statement by the Inspectors of the Reid Murray Group of Companies, ". . . we believe that we are accustomed to the use of common sense, and common sense has compelled us to reject a number of accounting practices used in the group and, apparently regarded as acceptable by accountants," *Interim Report . . .* [1963, p. 107]. This case was commented upon by Stamp [1964]. This and similar comments by other inspectors provoked a Report by the General Council of the Australian Society of Accountants. See "Accounting Principles and Practices Discussed in Reports on Company Failures," *Members' Handbook,* Item 401 (January 1966). See also, Greer [1963]; "Unaccountable CPA's," [1966]; Louis [1968]; "Accounting—Profits Without Honor" [1970]; Raymon [1970]; Stamp and Marley [1970]; Birkett and Walker [1971]; Spacek [1969 and 1973]; de Jonquieres [1973]; and Bedford [1973].

when confronted by anomaly [scientists] will devise numerous articulations and *ad hoc* modifications of their theory in order to eliminate any apparent conflict [Kuhn, 1970, p. 78].

During the 1960s and 1970s, the Accounting Principles Board in the United States and equivalent committees in other countries and innumerable authors proposed amendments to the rules to cope with the anomalies and criticisms.[11] Pronouncements, monographs and journal articles on problem areas such as purchase versus poolings, equity accounting, tax effect accounting and materiality followed. There were even attempts to increase the solidarity of the practicing profession. Carey wrote disparagingly of CPAs who gave evidence against their professional brethren [Briloff, 1972, p. 351], and the professional bodies issued statements requiring stricter conformance with official pronouncements [Zeff, 1972, pp. 76, 180–182, 294–295; 1973, pp. 22–23].

The ad hoc solutions which emerge during a period of crisis have a far-reaching consequence; they make it possible to contemplate rules which previously would have been unacceptable. That is, ". . . by proliferating versions of the [disciplinary matrix], crisis loosens the rules of normal puzzle-solving in ways that ultimately permit a new [disciplinary matrix] to emerge" [Kuhn, 1970, p. 80]. For example, the purchase versus pooling debate provoked discussion of asset values which were not original costs; equity accounting involved revaluing investments in associated companies; tax effect accounting extended the acceptance of non-transaction-based debits and credits. If accounting follows the revolutionary sequence of events, the acceptance of the techniques adopted in response to these problems will have hastened the ultimate acceptance of an alternative disciplinary matrix.

However, there is one class of anomaly which has proved to be intractable. The historical-cost based system fails to take account of changes in asset prices and changes in the purchasing power of the monetary unit. That failure has been a source of criticism, particularly during periods of inflation. It is anomalous in that, despite the going concern values in the financial statements, those statements no longer represent the state of affairs of the corporation. There have been numerous instances of the abuse of privilege by people in possession of current price data which have been denied to others [Chambers, 1973, Chapter 10]. Yet, accounting for the effects of inflation requires a substantial revision of the conventional thought in accounting. Partial solutions, such as equity accounting or, in the U.K. and Australia, occasional revaluations, are only partially successful.[12] The specific price and price-level problems are the sorts of anomalies which lead, finally, to the overthrow of the existing set of rules. Their "characteristic feature is their stubborn refusal to be assimilated to existing paradigms. This type alone gives rise to new theories" [Kuhn, 1970, p. 97].

There is one further feature of the periods of crisis described by Kuhn for which we may find a parallel in accounting:

It is, I think, particularly in periods of acknowledged crisis that scientists have turned to philosophical analysis as a device for unlocking the riddles of their field. . . . To the extent that normal . . . work can be conducted by using the

---

[11]See Zeff [1972, pp. 173–224] and the Australian Society of Accountants' Item 401, referred to above.

[12]For further examples, including the switches to and from accelerated depreciation and to and from LIFO inventory values, see Chambers [1973, pp. 93–103].

paradigm as a model, rules and assumptions need not be made explicit. . . . But that is not to say that the search for assumptions (even for non-existent ones) cannot be an effective way to weaken the grip of tradition upon the mind and to suggest the basis for a new one [Kuhn, 1970, p. 88]:

Again, there has long been concern for the theoretical foundations of accounting practices [Chatfield, 1974, Chapter 16; Hendriksen, 1970, Chapter 2]. However, it is possible to discern two related developments like those referred to in the quotation above. The first is the search for assumptions. Of particular interest here are Littleton's *The Structure of Accounting Theory* [1953], Moonitz's *The Basic Postulates of Accounting* [1961], the American Accounting Association's *A Statement of Basic Accounting Theory* [1966], Ijiri's *The Foundations of Accounting Measurement* [1967] and various shorter contributions and comments.[13] These were, in varying degrees, attempts to define the underlying assumptions of accounting. Yet they did not lead to a widely recognized set of basic ideas. Rather, as Kuhn suggests, they served to highlight the defects of the disciplinary matrix and loosen the grip of tradition. Therefore, perhaps we should not be surprised to find that, despite the vast expenditure of time and money, the AICPA belatedly (in 1971) recognized a need for a statement of, and initiated a study of, the "objectives" of financial statements.[14] That the Trueblood Study fits the pattern of events is evident; the report includes discussion of both objectives and alternatives to generally accepted accounting principles. Those alternatives would have been rejected out of hand even 10 years previously.[15]

The other development which is particularly noticeable throughout this period is the concern with principles and theory construction generally. Commencing, perhaps, with Chambers' "Blueprint for a Theory of Accounting" [1955], notable contributions or comments by Mattessich [1957], Devine [1960], Chambers [1963], Vatter [1963] and Sterling [1970] followed. These philosophical discussions have served to increase the rigour of the discipline,[16] but hopefully, they also have helped to unlock the riddles of the field.

ALTERNATIVE PROPOSALS AND THEIR EVALUATION

One direct consequence of the philosophical discussions has been the emergence and refinement of alternatives to the disciplinary matrix of, e.g., asset values based on historical costs. There have been various attempts to derive logically consistent systems which overcome the defects of the historical cost system. Some of the authors proposing these systems which appeared during the golden age already have been identified—Edwards and Bell [1961] and Chambers [1966]; others include Sprouse and Moonitz [1962], Mattessich [1964] and Mathews [1965]. The works of these authors were debated throughout the 1960s, and that debate served to clar-

---

[13]For a useful summary and list of references, see [Hendriksen, 1970, Chapter 4].

[14]Report of the Study Group on the Objectives of Financial Statements [the Trueblood Study] (1973). The study was commissioned in May 1971.

[15]See the alternatives listed [Trueblood Study, 1973, p. 41]. Notice also Sterling's observation of the change in attitudes [1970, p. vii].

[16]See Nelson [1973, p. 15] for a comment on the contribution of logic and other philosophical techniques to the accounting problem.

ify and identify the alternatives. Without that identification, the next step of the revolutionary process could not proceed. It *has* proceeded, as shown by the published evaluations of the alternatives. The Trueblood Study report contained some discussion. More comprehensive evaluations have been undertaken by Chambers [1970], Macdonald [1974], McDonald [1972], Hanna [1974] and others, while the Price Waterhouse Study [Mueller, 1971] gives attention to the need for introducing consideration of the alternatives into regular teaching programmes.[17]

The fact that the evaluation process has taken place, and is continuing, is evidence of the importance of the so-called a priori works; hence, our disagreement with Nelson's comment that these works are of doubtful value. In the pattern of events described here, the works fulfill a critically important role; they are both a natural reaction to the recognition of anomalies and a vital step in the selection of a new disciplinary matrix. Furthermore, having those works to consider, and having the alternatives thus laid out, we are in a fundamentally different position from that of 1960. For while schools of thought embracing the various alternatives might now appear, that would not have been possible in 1960.

However, before discussing that possibility, there are some other characteristics of the evaluative stage which were described by Kuhn and which may be seen also in accounting. Kuhn drew attention to the similarities of the evaluative stage to the pre-paradigm period. It is the stage at which "frequent and deep debates over legitimate methods, problems, and standards of solution" take place, although "these tend to define schools rather than to produce agreement" [Kuhn, 1970, p. 48].[18] In accounting, this stage has been marked by debates about the admissability of data relating to events external to the firm and data based on managers' intentions; on the presentation of cash flow statements, earnings per share calculations, etc.; the raisings of problems, such as the translation of holdings of foreign currencies, the reporting for diversified companies, long-term contracts and land development projects; the legitimacy of cost allocations; and reconsideration of the standards which the solutions must meet such as objectivity, independence and freedom from bias.

It is also because of the importance of these debates, and the evaluative process generally, that we contended that the alleged theoretical defects in the works published in the 1960s were, in a sense, irrelevant. This is not to suggest that "anything goes." On the contrary, tightly reasoned and empirically valid theoretical prescriptions have a greater chance of being adopted than do loosely constructed sets of ideas. However, theoretical defects will, presumably, be discovered during the evaluation process, and their existence may even add to the extent and heat of the debate, thus aiding this part of the revolutionary process.

Yet another characteristic of this step in the process identified by Kuhn and found in accounting is the diversity of activity:

> In the absence of a paradigm or some candidate for a paradigm, all of the facts that could possibly pertain to the development of a given science are likely to seem equally relevant. As a result early fact-gathering is a far more random activity than the one that subsequent scientific activity makes familiar [Kuhn, 1970, p. 15].

---

[17]It is for the reason outlined here that Chambers was able to refer to Macdonald's book as a product of its time. See Chambers [1975]. The same comment might be made of May, Mueller and Williams [1975].

[18]Notice that Dopuch and Revsine saw a similar result emerge at the Conference on Accounting Research held at the University of Illinois in 1971: "As is true in the literature, many contributors were quite convinced that their approach was correct but were unable to persuade those who disagreed" [Dopuch and Revsine, 1973, p. 34].

This perhaps, is the reason why so many proposals have emerged in recent years. They include suggestions for publication of multicolumn financial statements and forecasts; the development of human resource accounting; and, on a different level, the far-ranging research into share price movements and their information theory and cost benefit analyses to the provision of financial information.

Schools of Thought

It may be possible to identify schools of thought in respect of some or all of the matters of interest just referred to. However, one example will suffice—asset measurement alternatives. Four schools may be identified:[19]

1. Price-Level Adjusted (or Current Purchasing Power) Accounting
2. Replacement Cost Accounting
3. Deprival Value Accounting
4. Continuously Contemporary (or Net Realizable Value) Accounting.

Strong or widespread support for these schools is not yet discernible,[20] which is understandable. For, as Kuhn points out:

> The man who embraces a new paradigm at an early stage must often do so in defiance of the evidence provided by problem solving. He must, that is, have faith that the new paradigm will succeed with the many large problems that confront it, knowing only that the older paradigm has failed with a few. A decision of that kind can only be made on faith [Kuhn, 1970, p. 158].

---

[19]A fifth proposal—present value accounting—is not listed here. Although it has been argued cogently by Hansen [1966], it does not appear to have won support as an operational alternative. It has been discussed rather as an ideal against which alternatives might be evaluated. See, for example, Solomons [1961] and Lemke [1966].

[20]The following is an example of one attempt at identifying members of schools of thought in relation to generalized theories of accounting based on alternative asset measurement systems. Some people undoubtedly will want finer distinctions; some will object to being linked with others with whom they disagree in some respects; some will object to having been omitted. Nevertheless, at the risk of offending some or all of the people concerned, I would identify the following on the basis of their published work:

1. Price-Level-Adjusted:	Jones [1956]
	Mason [1971]
2. Replacement Cost:	Edwards & Bell [1961]
	Mathews [1965]
	Gynther [1966]
	Revsine [1973]
3. Deprival Value:	Baxter [1970]
	Wright [1970]
	Stamp [1971]
	Whittington [1974]
4. Continuously Contemporary (Net realizable value)	Chambers [1966]
	Sterling [1970]
	McKeown [1971]

For a slightly different version of these schools, see Sterling [1970, pp. 7–19].

Accounting researchers are not likely to rely on faith or make that decision lightly. But there are sufficient examples of dispute in the literature for us to identify some of the characteristics of "paradigm debates" [Kuhn, 1970, p. 110]. For example, "each group uses its own paradigm to argue in that paradigm's defense" [Kuhn, 1970, p. 94]. The Provisional Statement of Accounting Practice, No. 7, issued by the I.C.A. in England & Wales, refers to the need for a method which shows the "effect of changes in the purchasing power of money on accounts prepared on the basis of existing conventions" [para. 3] in arguing for Constant Purchasing Power Accounting; the Replacement Price School relies on the notion of "maintenance of productive capacity" which implies the need to replace assets in kind, in support of replacement cost accounting [Edwards and Bell, 1961, p. 99]; Wright [1971, pp. 60–61] refers to the possible loss which a firm might suffer if deprived of an asset when arguing for deprival value (or value to the owner) accounting; and Chambers [1966, p. 190] stresses the importance of adaptive behaviour when arguing for a measure of assets which is indicative of the firm's capacity to adapt.

These examples of apparent circularity are not intended as criticisms. Obviously, different systems of ideas can be evaluated only in the context to which those systems apply[21]; hence, the comment at the beginning of this paper that the charge of circularity by Gonedes and Dopuch is misplaced. The point is that arguments of this sort are a necessary and inevitable part of the process of trying to win support for the competing points of view [Kuhn, 1970, p. 94]. Like Nelson, Gonedes and Dopuch's error lies in their failure to identify the place of a priori research works in the transition to a new disciplinary matrix.

These debates have other characteristics. Adoption of a new disciplinary matrix will, normally, require a fundamental shift in the view which theorists have of the world. Thus, in accounting there have been changes: the view that the value of the monetary unit is stable has changed to acceptance of the view that it is variable; the view that the point of realization should be the point of recognition of gains is giving way to the view that other evidence of gains is admissible; and the view that only actual transactions give rise to objective data is giving way to a less restricted notion of objectivity.

Similarly, members of competing schools will have different views of the phenomena which are the subject of their discipline:

> Practicing in different worlds, the two groups of scientists see different things when they look from the same point in the same direction. Again that is not to say that they can see anything they please. Both are looking at the world, and what they look at has not changed. But in some areas they see different things, and they see them in different relations one to the other. That is why a law cannot even be demonstrated to one group of scientists, and may occasionally seem intuitively obvious to another [Kuhn, 1970, p. 150].

Hence Gynther's view of firms is of ongoing nonadaptive organizations while Chambers sees organizations as being fluid and constantly adapting to environmental changes.[22] And, it seems, debate between them serves only to convince each of the validity of his own argument.

---

[21]Sterling and Harrison [1974, pp. 144] draw attention to the universality of this factor in their comments on the Gonedes and Dopuch paper.

[22]Compare Gynther [1966, pp. 46–48] and Penman [1970, p. 338]: "Companies . . . just do not adapt": with Chambers [1966, p. 190].

A NEW DISCIPLINARY MATRIX?

The analysis presented here suggests that financial accounting thought is undergoing a revolution. If that is so, then the criticisms of a priori research cited at the beginning of this paper are misplaced. The criticisms fail to recognize the importance of research which leads to the delineation of alternative sets of ideas. Those alternatives are candidates for a new disciplinary matrix; they are the basis of competing schools of thought.

If the analogy presented above is correct, i.e., if Kuhn's notion of a revolution can be applied to accounting, then it appears that accounting is emerging from a state of crisis [Kuhn, 1970, Chapter VIII]. Alternative sets of ideas have been proposed and debated, and schools of thought are beginning to emerge. Admittedly, the analysis does not enable us to identify neat periods of time which correspond with Kuhn's steps in the revolution. Yet, the characteristics of an accepted disciplinary matrix, the period of insecurity and the development of alternative sets of ideas appear to be well recognizable in accounting.

What will be the outcome? In accounting it is too soon to say. Researchers cannot be observed rushing to adopt any of the alternative sets of ideas. Continued debate, primarily amongst academics but increasingly involving the research organizations of the professional bodies is, however, serving to identify schools of thought. The next stage, according to Kuhn, will be "an increasing shift in allegiances" [p. 158] in favor of one of the alternatives. However, this is a process which takes time. After all, it involves the assimilation of a new theory, and that in turn involves a "reconstruction of prior theory and the reevaluation of prior fact"; i.e., "an intrinsically revolutionary process." But note, "it is seldom completed by a single man and never overnight" [Kuhn, 1970, p. 7].

REFERENCES

"Accounting: Profits Without Honor," *Time* (March 1970), p. 70.

American Accounting Association, "A Tentative Statement of Accounting Principles Affecting Corporate Reports," *The Accounting Review* (June 1936), pp. 87–91; reprinted as a Tentative Statement of Accounting Principles Underlying Corporate Financial Statements (1936).

Baxter, W.T., "Accounting Values: Sale Price Versus Replacement Cost," *Journal of Accounting Research* (Autumn 1967), pp. 208–214.

Bedford, Norton M., "The Need for an Evaluation of Accounting Research" in Dopuch and Revsine, eds., *Accounting Research 1960–1970: A Critical Evaluation*, Monograph 7 (Center for International Education and Research in Accounting, University of Illinois, 1973).

———, and Richard Ziegler, "The Contributions of A. C. Littleton to Accounting Thought and Practice, *The Accounting Review* (July 1975), pp. 435–443.

Birkett, W. P. and R. G. Walker, "Response of the Australian Accounting Profession to Company Failures in the 1960's," *Abacus* (December 1971), pp. 97–136.

Brief, Richard P., "The Accountants' Responsibility in Historical Perspective," *The Accounting Review* (April 1975), pp. 285–297.

Briloff, Abraham J., "Old Myths and New Realities in Accountancy," *The Accounting Review* (July 1966), pp. 485–495.

———, *Unaccountable Accounting* (Harper and Row, 1972).

Chambers, R. J., "Blueprint for a Theory of Accounting," *Accounting Research* (January 1955), pp. 17–25.

———, "Why Bother with Postulates?", *Journal of Accounting Research* (Spring 1963), pp. 3–15.

———, *Accounting, Evaluation and Economic Behavior* (Prentice-Hall, 1966).

———, "Methods of Accounting," Parts I–VI, *The Accountant* (February 1970), pp. 299–303; (March 1970), pp. 341–345; (March 1970), pp. 408–412; (April 1970), pp. 483–486; (April 1970), pp. 551–555; (April 1970), pp. 643–647.

———, *Securities and Obscurities: A Case for the Reform of the Law of Company Accounts* (Gower Press; 1973).

————, "Profit Measurement, Capital Maintenance and Service Potential: A Review Article," *Abacus* (June 1975), pp. 98–104.

Chatfield, Michael, *A History of Accounting Thought* (The Dryden Press, 1974).

de Jonquieres, Guy, "U.S. Firms Under Fire," *The Financial Times* (June 1973), p. 44.

Devine, Carl T., "Research Methodology and Accounting Theory Formation," *The Accounting Review* (July 1960), pp. 387–399.

Dopuch, Nicholas and Lawrence Revsine, eds., *Accounting Research 1960–1970: A Critical Evaluation,* Monograph 7 (Center for International Education and Research in Accounting, University of Illinois, 1973).

Edwards, Edgar O. and Philip W. Bell, *The Theory and Measurement of Business Income* (University of California Press, 1961).

Gilman, Stephen, *Accounting Concepts of Profit* (The Ronald Press, 1939; reprinted 1956).

Gonedes, Nicholas J. and Nicholas Dopuch, "Capital Market Equilibrium, Information Production and Selecting Accounting Techniques: Theoretical Framework and Review of Empirical Work," *Studies on Financial Accounting Objectives: 1974* (Supplement to Volume 12), *Journal of Accounting Research* (1974).

Greer, Howard C., "How to Succeed in Confusing People Without Really Trying," *The Journal of Accountancy* (March 1963), pp. 61–65.

Gynther, R. S., *Accounting for Price-Level Changes: Theory and Procedures* (Pergamon, 1966).

Hanna, John R., *Accounting Income Models: An Application and Evaluation* (The Society of Industrial Accounts of Canada, 1974).

Hansen, Palle, *The Accounting Concept of Profit* (North-Holland, 1966).

Hendriksen, Eldon S., *Accounting Theory* (Irwin, 1970).

Jones, Ralph Coughenour, *The Effects of Price Level Changes* (American Accounting Association, 1956).

Kuhn, Thomas S., *The Structure of Scientific Revolutions,* International Encyclopedia of Unified Science, 2nd enlarged edition (University of Chicago Press, 1970).

Lakatos, Imre and Alan Musgrave, eds., *Criticism and the Growth of Knowledge* (Cambridge University Press, 1974).

Lemke, Kenneth W., "Asset Valuation and Income Theory," *The Accounting Review* (January 1966), pp. 33–41.

Louis, Arthur M., "The Accountants are Changing the Rules," *Fortune* (June 1968), p. 177.

Macdonald, Graeme, *Profit Measurement: Alternatives to Historical Cost* (Accountancy Age, 1974).

MacNeal, Kenneth, *Truth in Accounting* (Ronald Press Co., 1939).

McDonald, Daniel L., *Comparative Accounting Theory* (Addison-Wesley, 1972).

McKeown, James C., "An Empirical Test of a Model Proposed by Chambers," *The Accounting Review* (January 1971), pp. 12–29.

Mason, Perry, *Price Level Changes and Financial Statements* (American Accounting Association, 1971).

Mattessich, Richard, "Toward a General and Axiomatic Foundation of Accountancy," *Accounting Research* (October 1957), pp. 328–356.

————, Richard, *Accounting and Analytical Methods* (Irwin, 1964).

Mathews, R. L., "Price-Level Accounting and Useless Information," *Journal of Accounting Research* (Spring 1965), pp. 133–155.

May, Robert G., Gerhard G. Mueller and Thomas H. Williams, *A New Introduction to Financial Accounting* (Prentice-Hall, 1975).

Mueller, Gerhard G., ed., *A New Introduction to Accounting* (The Price Waterhouse Foundation, July 1971).

Nelson, Carl L., "A Priori Research in Accounting" in Dopuch and Revsine, eds., *Accounting Research 1960–1970: A Critical Evaluation,* Monograph 7 (Center for International Education and Research in Accounting, University of Illinois, 1973).

Paton, W. A., *Accounting Theory—with Special Reference to the Corporate Enterprise* (Ronald Press Co., 1922; reprinted, Accounting Studies Press, 1962).

———— and A. C. Littleton, *An Introduction to Corporate Accounting Standards* (American Accounting Association, 1940, reprinted 1965).

Penman, Stephen H., "What Net Asset Value?—An Extension of a Familiar Debate," *The Accounting Review* (April 1970), pp. 333–346.

Raymon, R., "Is Conventional Accounting Obsolete?" *Accountancy* (June 1970), pp. 422–429.

Report of the Study Group on the Objectives of Financial Statements, *Objectives of Financial Statements* (American Institute of Certified Public Accountants, October 1973).

Revsine, Lawrence, *Replacement Cost Accounting* (Prentice-Hall, 1973).

Sanders, T. H., H. R. Hatfield, and U. Moore, *A Statement of Accounting Principles* (The American Institute of Accountants, 1938, reprinted 1959).

Shapere, Dudley, "The Structure of Scientific Revolutions," *Philosophical Review* (July 1964), pp. 383–394.

Solomons, David, "Economic and Accounting Concepts of Income," *The Accounting Review* (July 1961), pp. 374–383.

Spacek, Leonard, *A Search for Fairness* (Arthur Andersen & Co., 1969 and 1973).

Sprouse, Robert T. and Maurice Moonitz, *A Tentative Set of Broad Accounting Principles for Business Enterprises,* Accounting Research Study No. 3. (American Institute of Certified Public Accountants, 1962).

Stamp, Edward, "The Reid Murray Affair," *Accountancy* (August 1964), pp. 685–690.

————, "Income and Value Determination and Changing Price-Levels: An Essay Towards a Theory," *The Accountants' Magazine* (June 1971), pp. 277–292.

————, and Christopher Marley, *Accounting Principles and the City Code* (Butterworth, 1970).

Sterling, Robert R., "On Theory Construction and Verification," *The Accounting Review* (July 1970), pp. 444–457.

————, and William Harrison, "Discussion of Capital Market Equilibrium, Information Production, and Selecting Accounting Techniques: Theoretical Framework and Review of Empirical Work" in *Studies on Financial Objectives: 1974,* supplement to Vol. 12 of *Journal of Accounting Research,* pp. 142–157.

Sweeney, Henry W., *Stabilized Accounting* (Harper Bros., 1936; reprinted, Holt Rinehart & Winston, 1964).

"Unaccountable CPA's," *Forbes* (October 1966), p. 15.

Vatter, William J., "Postulates and Principles," *Journal of Accounting Research* (Autumn 1963), pp. 179–197.

Wells, M. C., *Accounting for Common Costs* (International Center for Education and Research in Accounting, University of Illinois, forthcoming).

Whittington, Geoffrey, "Asset Valuation, Income Measurement and Accounting Income," *Accounting and Business Research* (Spring 1974), pp. 96–101.

Wright, F. K., "A Theory of Financial Accounting," *Journal of Business Finance* (Autumn 1970), pp. 51–79.

————, "Value to the Owner: A Clarification," *Abacus* (June 1971), pp. 58–61.

Zeff, Stephen A., *Forging Accounting Principles in Five Countries* (Stipes Publishing Co., 1972).

————, *Forging Accounting Principles in Australia* (Australian Society of Accountants, March 1973).

THE DEMAND FOR AND SUPPLY OF ACCOUNTING THEORIES: THE MARKET FOR EXCUSES

Ross L. Watts and Jerold L. Zimmerman

I. INTRODUCTION

The literature we commonly call financial accounting theory is predominantly prescriptive.[1] Most writers are concerned with what the contents of published financial statements should be; that is, how firms should account. Yet, it is generally concluded that financial accounting theory has had little substantive, direct impact on accounting practice or policy formulation despite half a century of research. Often the lack of impact is attributed to basic methodological weaknesses in the research. Or, the prescriptions offered are based on explicit

---

This research was supported by the Center for Research in Government Policy and Business, Graduate School of Management, University of Rochester. The authors wish to acknowledge the suggestions of Ray Ball, George Benston, Richard Brief, Nicholas Dopuch, Nicholas Gonedes, David Henderson, Robert Holthausen, Michael Jensen, Melvin Krasney, Richard Leftwich, Janice Maquire, William Meckling, Philip Meyers, Katherine Schipper, William Schwert, Clifford Smith, and Jerold Warner. We also acknowledge the suggestions received on an earlier version of this paper presented at the Stanford Summer Research Colloquium, August 2, 1977, and the comments of the anonymous reviewers.

Ross L. Watts and Jerold L. Zimmerman, "The Demand for and Supply of Accounting Theories: The Market for Excuses" *The Accounting Review,* April 1979, pp. 273–304. Reprinted with the permission of the American Accounting Association.

[1]For example, see Canning [1929], Paton [1922], Edwards and Bell [1961], Sprouse and Moonitz [1962], Gordon [1964], Chambers [1966], and American Accounting Association [1966]. We would prefer to reserve the term "theory" for principles advanced to explain a set of phenomena, in particular for sets of hypotheses which have been confirmed. However, such a definition of theory would exclude much of the prescriptive literature and generate a semantic debate. To avoid that consequence, in this paper (unless qualified) we use the word "theory" as a generic term for the existing accounting literature.

or implicit objectives which frequently differ among writers.[2] Not only are the researchers unable to agree on the objectives of financial statements, but they also disagree over the methods of deriving the prescriptions from the objectives.[3]

One characteristic common to the prescriptions and proposed accounting methodologies, however, is their failure to satisfy all practicing accountants and to be accepted generally by accounting standard-setting bodies. A committee of the American Accounting Association recently concluded that "a single universally accepted basic accounting theory does not exist at this time."[4]

The preceding observations lead us to pose the following question: What is the role of accounting theory in determining accounting practice? Our objective in this paper is to begin building a theory of the determinants of accounting theory. This theory is intended to be a positive theory, that is, a theory capable of explaining the factors determining the extant accounting literature, predicting how research will change as the underlying factors change, and explaining the role of theories in the determination of accounting standards.[5] It is *not* normative or prescriptive.[6]

Other writers have examined the relationship between accounting theory and practice. For example, Zeff [1974, p. 177] examines the historical relationship and concludes:

> A study of the U.S. experience clearly shows that the academic literature has had remarkably little impact on the writings of practitioners and upon the accounting policies of the American Institute and the SEC. *Too often, accounting theory is invoked more as a tactic to buttress one's preconceived notions, rather than as a genuine arbiter of contending views* (emphasis added).

Horngren [1973, p. 61] goes further and suggests an explanation for accounting theory's limited impact on the setting of accounting standards:[7]

> My hypothesis is that the setting of accounting standards is as much a product of political action as of flawless logic or empirical findings.

---

[2]For example, Chambers [1966, Chapters 9–11] apparently adopts economic efficiency as an objective while the American Institute of Certified Public Accountants (AICPA) Study Group on the Objectives of Financial Statements [1973, p. 17] decided that "financial statements should meet the needs of those with the least ability to obtain information. . . ."

[3]Some writers (*e.g.,* Chambers [1966]) make assumptions about the world without regard to *formal* empirical evidence and derive their prescriptions using those assumptions. Others (*e.g.,* Gonedes and Dopuch [1974]) argue that prescriptions to achieve any given objective must be based on hypotheses which have been subjected to formal statistical tests and confirmed.

[4]American Accounting Association, [1977, p. 1]. This report also reviews the major accounting theories.

[5]The Committee on Concepts and Standards for External Reports, American Accounting Association [1977] examines many of these same questions, and the interested reader should refer to this committee report for an alternative explanation of these phenomena, specifically Chapter 4.

[6]The terms "normative" and "prescriptive" are used interchangeably. See Mautz and Gray [1970] for an example of prescriptions to "improve" accounting research and hence its impact on practice.

[7]See Sterling [1974, pp. 180–181] for Horngren's response to Zeff's initial remark.

Our tentative theory is consistent with both Zeff's and Horngren's observations. It predicts that accounting theory will be used to "buttress preconceived notions" and further, it explains why. Our contribution to Zeff's and Horngren's ideas is to give them more structure so that we can make additional predictions about accounting theory. The source of that structure is economics. We view accounting theory as an economic good and examine the nature of the demand for and the supply of that good.

Understanding why accounting theories are as they are requires a theory of the political process. We model that process as competition among individuals for the use of the coercive power of government to achieve wealth transfers. Because accounting procedures[8] are one means of effecting such transfers, individuals competing in the political process demand theories which prescribe the accounting procedures conducive to their desired wealth transfers. Further, because individual interests differ, a variety of accounting prescriptions, hence a variety of accounting theories, is demanded on any one issue. We argue that it is this diversity of interests which prevents general agreement on accounting theory.

While individuals want a theory which prescribes procedures conducive to their own interest, they do *not* want a normative theory which has their self-interest as its stated objective. The reason is that information is costly to obtain. Some voters will not obtain information on political issues personally. Those voters are not likely to support political actions which have as their stated objective the self-interest of others. The most useful theories for persuading uninformed voters are theories with stated objectives appealing to those voters, *e.g.*, the "public interest." As a result, individuals demand normative accounting theories which make prescriptions based on the "public interest." In other words, the demand is for rationales or excuses. Because it arises from the political process, the demand for normative, "public interest"-oriented accounting theories depends on the extent of the government's role in the economy.

Section II analyzes the demand for financial accounting and accounting theory first in an unregulated economy, in which the only role of government is to enforce contracts, and then in a regulated economy. In Section III, we examine the nature of the supply of accounting theories. Because of the diverse demands for prescriptions, we expect to observe a variety of normative theories. Further, we expect theories to change over time as government intervention changes. In Section IV we examine the effect of government intervention on extant accounting theory during the last century. Section V summarizes the issues and presents our conclusions.

II. THE DEMAND FOR ACCOUNTING THEORIES

This section analyzes the demand for accounting theories in an unregulated economy (Part A) and the additional demands generated by government intervention (Part B).

---

[8]Accounting "procedures," "techniques," and "practices" are defined as any computational algorithm used or suggested in the preparation of financial accounting statements. "Accounting standards" are those "procedures" sanctioned or recommended by an "authoritative" body such as the APB, FASB, SEC, ICC, *etc.*

A. The Demand for Accounting Theories in an Unregulated Economy

1. Accounting in an Unregulated Economy   Audited corporate financial statements were voluntarily produced prior to government mandate.[9] Watts [1977] concludes that the original promoters of corporations or, subsequently, corporate managers have incentives to contract to supply audited financial statements. Agreements to supply financial statements were included in articles of incorporation (or by-laws) and in private lending contracts between corporations and creditors.[10] These contracts increase the welfare of the promoter or manager (who is raising the new capital) because they reduce the *agency costs*[11] which he bears.

Agency costs arise because the manager's (the agent's) interests do not necessarily coincide with the interests of shareholders or bondholders (the principals). For example, the manager (if he owns shares) has incentives to convert assets of the corporation into dividends, thus leaving the bondholders with the "shell" of the corporation. Similarly, the manager has incentives to transfer wealth to himself at the expense of both the shareholders and bondholders (*e.g.,* via perquisites).

Bondholders and shareholders anticipate the manager's behavior and appropriately discount the price of the bonds or shares at the time of issue. Hence, the promoter (or manager) of a new corporation receives less for the shares and bonds he sells than he would if he could guarantee that he would continue to act as he did when he owned the firm (*i.e.,* when there were no outside shareholders or bondholders). This difference in the market value of the securities is part of the cost of an agency relationship, it is part of agency costs, and is borne by the promoter (or manager).[12] Jensen and Meckling [1976, p. 308] call it the "residual loss."

Because he bears the residual loss, the manager has incentives to make expenditures to guarantee that he will not take certain actions which harm the principal's interest or that he will compensate the principal if he does. These are "bonding" and "monitoring" expenditures and are additional elements of agency costs. Examples of such expenditures include contracting to restrict dividend payments and expenditures to monitor such dividend convenants.

The final element of agency costs is the utility of the increase in perquisites, wealth transfers, *etc.,* the manager receives because of his actions as an agent. An equilibrium occurs when the net costs of an agency relationship, the agency costs, are minimized by trading off the de-

---

[9]Benston [1969a] reports that as of 1926 all firms listed on the New York Stock Exchange published a balance sheet, 55 percent disclosed sales, 45 percent disclosed cost of goods sold, 71 percent disclosed depreciation, 100 percent disclosed net income, and 82 percent were audited by a CPA.

[10]In the period 1862–1900, many U.K. companies voluntarily adopted the optional articles included in Table A of the 1862 U.K. Companies Act. See Edey [1968], Edey and Panitpakdi [1956] and Watts [1977]. Examples of private contracts can be found today in any note or bond indenture agreement.

[11]Jensen and Meckling [1976, p. 308] define an agency relationship as "a contract under which one or more persons (the principal(s)) engage another person (the agent) to perform some service on their behalf which involves delegating some decision making authority to the agent." There are at least two agency relationships which cause corporate promoters and managers to bear agency costs. The first is the relationship between shareholders (the principals) and the manager (the agent) and the second is the relationship between the bondholders (the principals) and the manager (the agent).

[12]See Jensen and Meckling [1976] for a formal proof that he bears this cost.

creases in the promoter's (or manager's) utility due to the residual loss, the monitoring and bonding expenditures, and the increased utility due to increased perquisites. The promoter or manager will write contracts for monitoring and bonding as long as the marginal benefits of these contracts (*e.g.,* reduction of the residual loss) are greater than the marginal costs (*e.g.,* the costs of contracting and the utility of any perquisites foregone). Moreover, since he bears the agency costs, the manager or promoter will try to write the contracts and perform the bonding or monitoring at minimum cost. In fact, the Jensen and Meckling analysis suggests that the equilibrium set of contractual devices is the one which minimizes the agency costs associated with the separation of management and control and with the conflict of interests associated with the different classes of investors.

Promoters and managers voluntarily included bonding covenants in corporate articles and by-laws in the nineteenth century. Dividend covenants were voluntarily included in company charters as early as 1620.[13]

Watts's [1977] analysis of agency relationships suggests that the function of audited financial statements in an unregulated economy is to reduce agency costs. This theory predicts that accounting practices (*i.e.,* the form, content, frequency, *etc.,* of external reporting) would vary across corporations in an unregulated economy depending on the nature and magnitude of the agency costs. Agency costs, in turn, are, among other things, a function of the amount of corporate debt outstanding and of the relative share of equity owned by the manager.[14] These variables affect the manager's incentive to take actions which conflict with the interests of shareholders and bondholders. Agency costs also vary with the costs of monitoring managers, which, in turn depend on the physical size, dispersion, and complexity of the firm. Further, the practices underlying financial statements will vary across firms because an accounting practice which minimizes agency costs in one industry may not minimize those costs in another.

As an example of the association between agency costs and accounting procedures, consider management compensation schemes in the nineteenth century. Some management compensation schemes in the nineteenth century were included in corporate articles. Those schemes tied management compensation to the firms' "profits" [Matheson, 1893, pp. vii–viii] to reduce the divergence between the interests of the managers and shareholders.[15] At that time "profits" were effectively operating cash flows, since accrual accounting was not used. [Litherland, 1968, pp. 171–172]. However, a cash flow "profit" index is susceptible to short-run manager manipulation. The manager can reduce repairs and maintenance expenditures and increase cash flows and "profits,"[16] which would increase the manager's compensation.[17]

---

[13]See Kehl [1941, p. 4].

[14]Agency costs are also a function of the tastes of managers for non-pecuniary income, the extent of managerial competition, the degree to which the capital markets and the legal system are able to reduce agency costs, *etc.* See Jensen and Meckling [1976, pp. 328–330].

[15]The terms "shareholders" and "stockholders" are used interchangeably.

[16]See Matheson [1893, p. 5] for a report that managers did in fact adopt this tactic in the nineteenth century.

[17]See Matheson [1893, p. vii] for a statement that managers did in fact resist depreciation charges because of the effect on their compensation.

In addition, reduced maintenance increases the ability of the corporation to pay current dividends. Such dividends could reduce the value of the creditors' claims and increase the shareholders' wealth.[18]

To reduce these agency costs of equity and debt, several contractual devices were used to decrease the likelihood that managers and shareholders would run down the value of the capital stock.

i)   Dividends were restricted to a fixed proportion of profits, thereby creating a buffer.[19]

ii) Reserve funds of fixed amounts had to be maintained if dividends were to be paid.[20]

iii) Fixed assets were treated as merchandise accounts with changes in value (usually not called depreciation) closed to profits prior to dividend distributions.[21]

In the latter procedure, depreciation was treated as a valuation technique which had to be estimated only in profitable years, since dividends were paid only in these years. A typical company charter requiring depreciation is:

> The directors shall, before recommending any dividend, set aside out of the profits of the company, but subject to the sanction of the company in general meeting, such sum as they think proper as a reserve fund for maintenance, repairs, depreciation and renewals.[22]

The court interpreted this article and the term "proper reserve" as a mechanism to account for declines in the capital stock.[23] Thus, the existence of a depreciation covenant (and hence the presence of depreciation in the financial statement) or other restrictions on dividends was a function of the amount of fixed assets and the nature and magnitude of the agency costs of debt.

Capital market participants contract to supply capital. Managers and owners seeking capital have incentives to enter into contracts which limit the agency costs they incur. But these contracts must then be monitored and enforced since managers have incentives to circumvent the contracts. For example, the promoter or manager of a corporation may contract to restrict

---

[18]See Smith [1976, p. 42]. Also, we find labor managed firms in socialist countries faced with the same agency problem. Labor has less incentive to maintain physical capital than an owner-manager. Jensen and Meckling [1977].

[19]For example, the General Bank of India had a provision in its charter limiting dividends to not more than 2/3 of net (cash) profits [DuBois, 1938, p. 365].

[20]The Phoenix Insurance Company, 1781, required a reserve fund of £52,000 before any dividends could be paid. *Ibid.*

[21]See Littleton [1933, pp. 223–227].

[22]*Dent v. London Tramways Company,* 1880, in Brief [1976, p. 193].

[23]"Take the case of a warehouse: supposing a warehouse keeper, having a new warehouse, should find at the end of the year that he had no occasion to expend money in repairs, but thought that, by reason of the usual wear and tear of the warehouse, it was 1,000*l.* worse than it was at the beginning of the year, he would set aside 1,000*l.* for a repair or renewal or depreciation fund, before he estimated any profits; because, although that sum is not required to be paid in that year, it is still the sum of money which is lost, so to say, out of capital, and which must be replaced." *Ibid.*

dividends to, or base management compensation on, profits after a deduction for depreciation because such a covenant enables him to sell bonds and shares at a higher price. However, *after* the contract is written the manager has incentives to minimize that depreciation charge, thereby leading to increased profits (and potentially increased management compensation) and dividends which transfer wealth from bondholders to shareholders (including management). Thus, contracts will reduce agency costs only if they include provisions for monitoring. Since audited financial statements are useful devices to monitor these voluntary agreements between owners and managers, these statements serve a useful role in the capital markets and owner-managers will agree to provide them in advance.

2. THE FUNCTION OF ACCOUNTING THEORIES   The preceding analysis suggests that accounting theories will serve three overlapping functions in an unregulated economy.

i) Pedagogic Demand.   Accounting procedures are devised in order to reduce agency costs of contracts. Since these costs vary across firms, accounting procedures will vary, giving rise to diversity of techniques, formats, *etc.*[24] However, diversity in accounting procedures increases the difficulty of teaching the practice of accounting. Consequently, accounting teachers develop pedagogic devices (rules-of-thumb) to assist learning and to structure the variation found in practice. Theorists examine existing systems of accounts and summarize differences and similarities. These descriptions of practice highlight the tendencies of firms with particular attributes to follow certain accounting procedures.

Nineteenth century accounting texts and articles indicate that accounting theorists recognized the diversity of practice and attempted to distill general tendencies from the diversity. For example:

> No fixed rules, or rates of depreciation can be established for general use, because not only do trades and processes of manufacture differ, but numerous secondary circumstances have to be considered in determining the proper course. It may, however, be possible to lay down some general principles which will always apply, or which, at any rate, may with advantage be held in view in deciding particular cases. [Matheson, 1893, p.1]

Similarly, Dicksee and Tillyard's [1906] treatise describes current accounting practice for goodwill and the relevant court cases. Based on this description, the authors "enunciate general business principles and explain their practical application" [Dicksee and Tillyard, 1906, p. vii].

ii) Information Demand.   In an unregulated economy there is a demand for writers to do more than just describe variations in accounting practice. There is a demand for predictions of the effects of accounting procedures on both the manager's and auditor's welfare via

---

[24]Prior to the creation of the Securities and Exchange Commission (SEC) in 1934, much variation existed in accounting procedures. See Blough [1937, p. 7]. In an unregulated economy, the market itself regulates the amount of diversity of accounting procedures. There are economies associated with using existing practices and terminology. If the firm adopts previously unknown accounting practices, then the users of the statements (*i.e.,* creditors monitoring shareholders and shareholders monitoring management) will incur costs in learning the new accounting procedures. If creditors and shareholders have alternative uses of their capital (*i.e.,* capital markets are competitive) the costs of the new procedures are ultimately borne by the shareholders and managers. Hence, new procedures (and increased diversity) will be implemented only if their added benefits offset the added costs they impose.

exposure to law suits. The auditor contracts with the shareholders (and creditors) to monitor management, and he is legally liable if he fails to report breaches of covenants in the corporation's articles or by-laws.[25] Furthermore, the demand for a given auditor's services is a function of the auditor's efficiency in monitoring management.[26] Hence, the auditor again has an incentive to understand how management's choice of accounting procedures affects agency costs.

Auditors would value information in the form of theories predicting how agency costs vary with accounting procedures. In particular, auditors would like to know how managers' actions and hence agency costs would be affected by alternative accounting procedures.

iii) Justification Demand.

Early accounting textbooks warned that managers would use accounting to serve their own interests at the expense of shareholders. The second edition of Matheson [1893] contains examples of such warnings. Matheson provides illustrations of how managers can take advantage of deficiencies in the definition of depreciation, repairs, and maintenance charges to increase "profits" and their own compensation at the expense of shareholders and/or bondholders. For example, on page 5 he writes:

> The temptation to treat as Profit the Surplus of Income over Expenditure, without sufficient allowance for Deterioration, appears to be often irresistible. Thus, in the case of a Tramway undertaking in its first years of working, a dividend may be possible only by writing off little or nothing from the capital value of the cars, the harness, and the horses. This, of course, cannot last without the introduction of new capital, but in undertakings long established there yet may be epochs of fictitious profits due to various causes. For instance there may be neglect of repairs, which, when the necessity for them becomes evident, will involve a heavy outlay for renewals; or it may arise from actual fraud in postponing expenditure, so as to show large profits, which will raise the value of shares for stock-jobbing purposes. There are railways where the dividend income and the corresponding value of the shares have fluctuated considerably, not according to alterations in the real earnings, but according to alternate neglect and attention in regard to plant.

Accounting texts (and theories) which detail how managers seek to manipulate profits and the consequent effects of those manipulations on shareholders and bondholders not only improve the auditor's ability to monitor such behavior, but also provide the auditor with ready-made arguments to use against such practices in discussions with management. It is clear that Matheson's work fulfilled this role. William Jackson, a member of the Council of the Institute of Chartered Accountants in England and Wales, stated that he used Matheson's book in that fashion:

---

[25]See the *Leeds Estate Building Company* case in Edwards [1968b, p. 148].

[26]Share prices are unbiased estimates of the extent to which the auditor monitors management and reduces agency costs (see Fama [1970] and Gonedes and Dopuch [1974] for a review of the evidence on market efficiency). The larger the reduction in agency costs effected by an auditor (net of the auditor's fees), the higher the value of the corporation's shares and bonds and, *ceteris paribus,* the greater the demand for that auditor's services. If the market observes the auditor failing to monitor management, it will adjust downwards the share price of all firms who engage this auditor (to the extent to which the auditor does not reduce agency costs), and this will reduce the demand for his services.

To those who honestly and from conviction treat the subject on the only sound basis, it may seem superfluous to urge due consideration of the arguments so convincingly set out in these pages; but Auditors, and especially those who have to deal with joint-stock or other concerns where the remuneration of the management is made wholly or partly dependent upon declared Profits, know in what varied forms resistance to an adequate Charge against profits for Depreciation is presented.

The fallacies underlying these objections present themselves again and again with the modifications caused by the lack of apprehension in some, or the ingenuity of others. *Mr. Matheson's work provides the Auditor with true antidotes to these fallacies, and it has been in past times used by the writer with satisfactory effect, where his own less-reasoned arguments have failed to convince.*

He therefore recommends it afresh to the notice and for the support, where necessary, of members of his own profession, and of those who, untrained in the practice of Auditing, are confronted with unfamiliar and specious pretexts for avoiding the unwelcome charge against Profits [Matheson, 1893, pp. vii–viii] (emphasis added).

B. The Demand for Accounting Theories in a Regulated Economy

This section extends the previous analysis of the demand for theories to include the effects of government. We assume that private citizens, bureaucrats, and politicians have incentives to employ the powers of the state to make themselves better off and to coalesce for that purpose. One way by which coalitions of individuals are made better off is by legislation that redistributes (i.e., confiscates) wealth.

1. Accounting and the Political Process Farm subsidies, tariffs, welfare, social security, even regulatory commissions[27] are examples of special interest legislation which transfer wealth. The business sector is both the source (via taxes, anti-trust, affirmative action, *etc.*) and the recipient of many of these wealth transfers (via tax credits, tariffs, subsidies, *etc.*).

Financial accounting statements perform a central role in these wealth transfers and are affected both directly and indirectly by the political process. The Securities and Exchange Commission (SEC) regulates the contents of financial statements directly (upward asset revaluations are not allowed, statements of changes in financial position must be prepared, *etc.*). The Federal Revenue Acts also affect the contents of financial statements directly (*e.g.,* LIFO). In addition, regulatory commissions (*e.g.,* state public utility boards, various banking and insurance commissions, the Interstate Commerce Commission, the Federal Trade Commission) often affect the contents of financial statements.

Besides these more direct effects, there are indirect effects. Government commissions often use the contents of financial statements in the regulatory process (rate setting, antitrust, *etc.*). Further, Congress often bases legislative actions on these statements.[28] This, in turn, provides management with incentives to select accounting procedures which either reduce the

---

[27]See Stigler [1971], Posner [1974], and Peltzman [1976].

[28]The reported profits of U.S. oil companies during the Arab oil embargo were used to justify bills to break up these large firms.

costs they bear or increase the benefits they receive as a result of the actions of government regulators and legislators.[29]

Since public utilities have incentives to propose accounting procedures for rate making purposes which increase the market value of the firm, their arguments are assisted if accounting standard-setting bodies such as the Financial Accounting Standards Board (FASB) mandate the same accounting procedures for financial reporting.[30] Consequently, managers of utilities and other regulated industries (*e.g.,* insurance, bank and transportation) lobby on accounting standards not only with their regulatory commissions but also with the Accounting Principles Board (APB) and the FASB.

Moonitz [1974 a and b] and Horngren [1973 and 1977] document instances of regulated firms seeking or opposing accounting procedures which affect the value of the firm via direct and indirect wealth transfers. Examples of other firms lobbying on accounting standards exist. Most of the major U.S. oil companies made submissions regarding the FASB's Discussion Memorandum on General Price Level Adjustments [Watts and Zimmerman, 1978].

2. THE EFFECT OF GOVERNMENT INTERVENTION ON THE DEMAND FOR ACCOUNTING THEORIES

The rules and regulations which result from government regulation of business increase the pedagogic and information demands for accounting theories. Even beginning accounting textbooks report the income tax requirements of LIFO, depreciation, *etc.* Practitioners demand detailed texts explaining SEC requirements (*e.g.,* Rappaport [1972]), tax codes, and other government regulations.

The justification demand for theories also expands with regulation. The political process in the U.S. is characterized as an advocacy proceeding. Proponents and opponents of special interest legislation (or petitioners before regulatory and administrative committees) must give arguments for the positions they advocate. If these positions include changes in accounting procedures, accounting theories which serve as justifications (*i.e.,* excuses) are useful. These advocacy positions (including theories) will tend to be based on contentions that the political action is in the public interest,[31] that everyone is made better off, that most are made better off and no one is harmed, or that the action is "fair," since those contentions are likely to generate less opposition than arguments based on self-interest. Often, those public interest arguments rely upon the notion that the unregulated market solution is inefficient. The typical argument is that there is a market failure which can only be remedied by government intervention.

Politicians and bureaucrats charged with the responsibility for promoting the general welfare demand public interest testimony not only to inform them of the trade-offs but also for use in justifying their actions to the press and their constituencies. Consequently, when

---

[29]See Watts and Zimmerman [1978] for a test of this proposition. Also, see Prakash and Rappaport [1977] for further discussion of these feedback effects. See a bill introduced into the Senate by Senator Bayh (U.S. Congress, Senate, Subcommittee on Anti-trust and Monopoly [1975, pp. 5–13] and [1976, p. 1893]). Note that it is absolute size and profits which are used as a justification. On this point, see the "Curse of Bigness," *Barron's* [June 30, 1969, pp. 1 and 8]. Also see Alchian and Kessel [1962, p. 162].

[30]The Interstate Commerce Commission based its decision to allow tax deferral accounting on APB Opinion No. 11. See Interstate Commerce Commission, *Accounting for Federal Income Taxes,* 318 I.C.C. 803.

[31]Other writers have also recognized the tendency for advocates to use public interest arguments. For example, Pichler [1974, pp. 64–65] concludes that the accounting profession has increased its economic power via control over entry "through legislation justified as protecting the public interest" (p. 64). "In most cases, *public rather than professional interest was cited as the primary reason for* [the legislation]" (p. 65) (emphasis added).

politicians support (or oppose) legislation, they tend to adopt the public interest arguments advanced by the special interests who promote (oppose) the legislation.

i) Examples of Public Interest or Market Failure Justifications.   The reported objective of the Securities Exchange Act of 1934 and of required disclosure is stated by Mundheim [1964, p. 647]:

> The theory of the Securities Act is that if investors are provided with sufficient information to permit them to make a reasoned decision concerning the investment merits of securities offered to them, investor interests can be adequately protected without unduly restricting the ability of business ventures to raise capital.

This objective stresses economic efficiency. The statement suggests that required disclosure can increase investors' welfare at virtually zero cost (*i.e.,* that there is a market failure).

Examples of "public interest" justifications of accounting procedures are observed in rate-setting hearings for public utilities. For example, Public Systems, an organization that represents municipalities and rural electrification agencies, applied for a hearing on the Federal Power Commission's (FPC) Order 530 which allowed the use of income tax allocation in setting rates.[32] Order 530 increases the cash flow of electric utilities "at the expense of customers using electricity" and hence harms the interests of Public Systems. But, Public Systems did not argue that it is in its self-interest to oppose Order 530. Instead, it argued that "normalization [income tax allocation] represents an *inefficient* means of subsidizing the public utility industry" [U.S. Congress, Senate, 1976, p. 683] (emphasis added).

Bureaucrats also use public interest arguments to justify their actions.[33] For example, the former SEC Chief Accountant, John Burton, a bureaucrat, justified the disclosure regulations imposed during his term in office by arguing:

> In a broad sense we hope [that disclosure regulations] will contribute to a more efficient capital market. . . . The way in which we hope that will be achieved is first by giving investors more confidence that they are getting the whole story and second by encouraging the development of better tools of analysis and more responsibility on the part of the professional analyst to understand what's going on. We think that by giving them better data we can encourage them in the direction of doing a better job, thus leading, we hope, to more effective [sic] capital markets [Burton, 1975, p. 21].

Government regulation creates a demand for normative accounting theories employing public interest arguments, that is, for theories purporting to demonstrate that certain accounting procedures *should* be used because they lead to better decisions by investors, more efficient capital markets, *etc.* Further, the demand is not for *one* theory, but rather for diverse prescriptions. On any political issue such as utility rate determination, there will be at least two sides. In the FPC Order 530 example, Coopers & Lybrand, who opposed Public Systems, wanted a theory which prescribed income tax allocation, while Public Systems wanted a theory which did not. When we consider that accounting methods are relevant to taxes, antitrust cases,

---

[32]U.S. Congress, Senate [1976, p. 59]. "Metcalf Staff Report."

[33]McGraw [1975, p. 162]. Also, see U.S. Securities and Exchange Commission [1945, pp. 1–10].

union negotiations, disclosure regulations, *etc.,* as well as utility rate-setting, we expect a demand for a multitude of prescriptions.

With increased government intervention in business, the demand for theories which justify particular accounting procedures (proposed in the self-interest of various parties) has come to eclipse the demand for theories which fulfill the pedagogic and information roles. We present evidence to support this proposition in Section V.

ii) Rationality or "Theory Illusion."   Until recently, it had been popular in the economics literature to assume that politicians, elected officials, bureaucrats, *etc.,* acted in the "public interest" (the public interest assumption).[34] In order to determine which actions are in the public interest, politicians require theories which predict the consequences of alternative actions. "Rational," "public interest"-oriented politicians/bureaucrats would tend to use the theories which best predict (*i.e.,* the "best" theories)[35] and hence those theories would predominate. Leading articles in the accounting literature are implicitly based on the public interest premise (AAA [1966, p. 5], AICPA [1973, p. 17], Gonedes and Dopuch [1974, pp. 48–49 and pp. 114–118], Beaver and Demski [1974, p. 185]) that the "best" theories prevail.

In recent years, however, economists have questioned whether the public interest assumption is consistent with observed phenomena.[36] They have proposed an alternative assumption—that individuals involved in the political process act in their own interest (the self-interest assumption). This assumption yields implications which are more consistent with observed phenomena than those based on the public interest assumption.[37]

The costs and benefits to voters of becoming informed, of lobbying, of forming coalitions, and of monitoring their representatives' actions are of central importance in a self-interest model of the political process. Downs [1957] suggests that the expected effect of one individual's vote on the outcome of an election is trivial, and, hence, the individual voter has very little incentive to incur the costs of becoming informed on political issues. On the other hand, indivdual voters do have incentives to act as groups in the political process. Economies of scale in political action encourage group participation. When several voters have similar interests on particular issues (*e.g.,* members of a trade union), those voters can share the "fixed" costs of becoming informed and moreover can increase the likelihood of affecting the outcome of an election by voting as a bloc.[38]

The costs of political action also depend on the existing political institutions (*e.g.,* whether political decisions are made by referendum or a vote of elected representatives) [Leffler and Zimmerman, 1977]. If we call the sum of the costs of political action the "transactions costs" of political decisions, the crucial question is "what is the magnitude of these transactions costs?" If the transactions costs of political decisions are high, self-interest motivated gov-

---

[34]For a summary of this literature see Posner [1974] and McCraw [1975].

[35]By "best" theory, we mean the theory most consistent with observed phenomena. Such theories allow public officials to predict the outcomes of their actions, thereby helping them select actions which increase social welfare.

[36]See Posner [1974].

[37]For analyses of the political process based on this assumption see Downs [1957], Jensen [1976], Meckling [1976a and b], Mueller [1976], Niskanen [1971], Peltzman [1976], Stigler [1971], and Leffler and Zimmerman [1977].

[38]Stigler [1971] attempts to explain the regulation of an industry on the basis of variation of coalition costs, free-rider costs, *etc.,* with such variables as group size, homogeneity of interest, *etc.*

ernment servants will not always act in the public interest; if they are zero, they will.[39] Hence, if the transactions costs of the political process are high, government officials will not use the "best" theory available; if they are zero, they will.

As an example of the importance of positive political transactions costs, consider the manager of a utility advocating deferred tax accounting because of its effects on utility rates. The manager will argue that recognizing deferred taxes as current operating costs is in the public interest. The official responsible for allowing or not allowing this practice has a greater incentive to resist the lobbying efforts of the utility manager if other individuals (*e.g.,* consumer advocates) lobby against the procedure. Whether those individuals lobby depends on the costs of consumers being informed about the effects of the accounting procedures on their welfare (which requires human capital), the costs of forming groups to oppose the procedure, *etc.* The manager's public interest theory (which is an "excuse" to cover a self-interest motive and need not be valid) increases the costs of others being informed and will tend to be accepted by the public official *if* the transactions costs are large enough.

We assume that political transactions costs are large enough to cause the acceptance of "invalid" theories, that the competition among excuses does not always lead to acceptance of the "best" theory. The usefulness of the assumption depends on the empirical consistency of its implications. It is an empirical-question. The work by Posner [1974], Stigler [1971], and Peltzman [1976] supports the assumption.

The assumption that the transactions costs of the political process are non-zero is analogous to the assumption of non-zero transactions costs in capital markets.[40] In capital market theory it is typically assumed that transactions costs are zero despite the fact they obviously are not, because that assumption yields empirically confirmed hypotheses. Why then, should political transactions costs be sufficiently more important than capital market transactions costs to warrant their inclusion in a political theory?

We suggest that there is an important difference between capital markets and the political process which make transactions costs important in the latter case. There is, in the capital markets, a direct market for control. If the manager of a corporation is not maximizing the market value of the corporation's shares, then an individual can, by buying its shares, acquire control of the corporation in the capital markets and, therefore, obtain the right to make the decisions. That individual can change the corporation's decisions and reap for himself the capital gain from the increase in the value of the corporation's stock. If the Chairman of the Securities and Exchange Commission were not making decisions in the public interest, an individual could not directly buy the right to make those decisions and capture the benefits of the changed decision. Because direct payments to elected officials are illegal and payments in kind are generally more expensive, it is costlier to bribe Congressmen, Senators, *etc.,* than to purchase a controlling interest in a corporation. It is also costly to establish indirect ways of achieving the same result.[41]

---

[39]The social choice literature (see Mueller [1976]) discusses the conditions which guarantee Pareto-efficient decisions by regulators.

[40]See Fama [1976] for a review of capital market theory.

[41]See Zimmerman [1977] for further discussion of this issue. Essentially, the reason it is costlier to purchase "control" of the political system (via a system of bribes, payoffs, *etc.*) is that the legal system does not enforce these contracts to the same extent that the state enforces the property rights of residual claimants in corporations. Hence, more (costly) monitoring is required to enforce contracts between politicians/bureaucrats and other parties.

Notice that in our model of the political process everyone is rational. No one is being "fooled" by accounting theories; they are not "fooled" by "theory illusion."[42] If people do not investigate the validity of theories, it is because they do not expect such investigation to be worthwhile. If the expected benefits of investigation to an individual are small, he will make only a limited investigation.

Our assumption of high political costs is crucial to our theory. As we shall see in the next section, the assumption enables us to discriminate between the empirical implications of our theory and the implications of an alternative theory. This allows empirical testing. Ultimately, the test of the political cost assumption is whether the implications of the theory based on the assumption are confirmed or not by empirical tests. Thus, the merit of an assumption is judged by the predictions it generates. Those accounting researchers who build theories on the assumption that information is a pure public good (*e.g.*, Gonedes and Dopuch [1974] and Beaver [1976]) often assert that information is a pure public good. Yet, no tests of these theories have been provided. In Section IV we argue that implications of our theory are consistent with the evidence.

III. THE SUPPLY OF ACCOUNTING THEORIES

Accounting theorists often view themselves as expert critics or defenders of accounting prescriptions (*e.g.*, replacement cost, historical cost, *etc.*). They argue that accounting theory should be used to determine accounting practice and standards.[43] The ideal state of affairs to them is one in which theorists logically and objectively determine the merits of alternative procedures.[44] For example, Hendriksen [1977, p. 1] writes: ". . . the most important goal of accounting theory should be to provide a coherent set of logical principles that form the general frame of reference for the evaluation and development of sound accounting practices." Theorists tend to bemoan the fact that this ideal state does not exist and that corporate managers, auditors, and politicians do not allow them to determine accounting standards.[45]

Most theorists probably believe that an objective of their research and the reason they supply theories to provide knowledge which will ultimately improve accounting practice. They would not regard themselves as supplying "excuses." But we suggest that the predomi-

---

[42]Buchanan and Wagner [1977, pp. 128–130] introduce the concept of "fiscal illusion" as a systematic bias in individuals' perceptions of the differential effects of alternative taxing procedures. They hypothesize "that complex and indirect payment structures create a fiscal illusion that will systematically produce higher levels of public outlay than those that would be observed under simple-payment structures." (p. 129) It could be argued that individuals also suffer from "theory illusion" (*i.e.,* that more complex theories obscure political behavior). We do not subscribe to this phenomenon, but offer it as an alternative explanation.

[43]Mautz [1966, p. 6] and Sterling [1973, p. 49].

[44]Ijiri [1971, p. 26] states, "Accounting theorists are scientific observers of accounting practices and their surrounding environment. Their theories are required to have the highest degree of objectivity."

[45]Moonitz [1974b] does not believe that accounting research should be the sole source for setting practice, but that it should have a role, "Almost everyone agrees that research is an essential component of the process of establishing accounting standards" (p. 58). He goes on to suggest that "accountants must curb the power of the management" (p. 68).

nant contemporary demand for accounting theories (the demand for accounting in a regulated economy) is the demand for justifications—"excuses." If that empirical proposition is correct, the question is: How responsive is the supply side (accounting research) to changes in the nature and quantity of the economic good being demanded?

As long as there exists a large number of individuals who are able to supply a wide diversity of theories (*i.e.,* as long as numerous close substitutes exist) at relatively low cost, then supply will be very responsive to demand. Stigler's observation succinctly summarizes this point:

> . . . consumers generally determine what will be produced, and producers make profits by discovering more precisely what consumers want and producing it more cheaply. Some may entertain a tinge of doubt about this proposition, thanks to the energy and skill of Professor Galbraith, but even his large talents hardly raise a faint thought that I live in a house rather than a tent because of the comparative advertising outlays of the two industries. This Cambridge eccentricity aside, then, *it is useful to say that consumers direct production—and therefore, do they not direct the production of the words and ideas of intellectuals, rather than, as in the first view, vice-versa?* [Stigler, 1976, p. 347] (emphasis added).

The consumers ("vested interests") determine the production of accounting research through the incentives they provide for accounting theorists. The greater the prestige and articulation skills of an accounting researcher, the more likely practitioners, regulators and other academics will know his work and the greater the flow of both students and funds to his university. Researchers have non-pecuniary incentives to be well-known, and this reputation is rewarded by a higher salary and a plenitude of research funds.[46] Practitioners, regulators, and those teaching future practitioners are more likely to read or hear of the output of an accounting researcher if it bears on topics of current interest. As a result, the researcher who is motivated by pecuniary and non-pecuniary factors (*e.g.,* "free" trips to conferences) will tend to write on the current controversies in accounting. Therein lies the connection to the demands of vested interests. Controversies arise in accounting when vested interests disagree over accounting standards. For example, the LIFO controversy arose when the Supreme Court outlawed the base stock method of valuing inventory for tax purposes and the American Petroleum Institute recommended LIFO to replace it, thereby reducing the present value of its members' taxes. The Internal Revenue Service resisted because of the effect on revenues. The parties demanded pro and con LIFO theories which were eventually produced [Moonitz, 1974, pp. 33–34].

Accounting researchers often include a set of policy recommendations as part of their research project.[47] Those recommendations, made on the basis of some objective assumed by the researcher, may never have been intended to serve as an "excuse" for the corporate manager, practitioner or politician who prefers the recommended procedure for self-interest reasons. Nevertheless, the research findings will be favorably quoted by those with vested

---

[46]Even though we have argued the existence of close substitutes, all researchers will not be earning the same compensation. Higher compensation will accrue to the most prolific, articulate, and creative advocates—to those who are able to establish early property rights in a topic and thus must be cited by later theorists.

[47]See Beaver [1973] for an example of policy prescriptions based on accounting research.

interests.[48] The more readable the research, the more frequently it is quoted, the more the researcher's fame increases. Similarly, criticisms of alternative accounting practices will be quoted by vested interests and will also increase the researcher's reputation.

The link between suppliers of accounting theory and consumers goes further than mere quotation. Partners in accounting firms, bureaucrats in government agencies and corporate managers will seek out accounting researchers who have eloquently and consistently advocated a particular practice which happens to be in the practitioner's, bureaucrat's, or manager's self-interest and will appoint the researcher as a consultant, or expert witness, or commission him to conduct a study of that accounting problem. Consistency in the researcher's work allows the party commissioning the work to predict more accurately the ultimate conclusions. Thus, research and consulting funds will tend to flow to the most eloquent and consistent advocates of accounting practices where there are vested interests who benefit by the adoption or rejection of these accounting practices.

The tendency of vested interests to seek out researchers who support their position produces a survival bias.[49] The bias is introduced by the vested interests. We do not mean to impugn the motives of accounting researchers who advocate particular practices. In fact, the more consistent the positions of the researcher and the greater his integrity, the more support he lends to the vested interest's position.

Given the rewards for supply theories on controversial issues, we expect to observe competition in the supply of accounting theories related to those issues. The prescriptions for an issue are likely to be as diverse as the positions of vested interests. But despite this diversity, we do not necessarily expect accounting researchers to be inconsistent from issue to issue. Academic evaluation and criticism create incentives for each researcher to be consistent. However, the rationales given for observed accounting standards may well be inconsistent across issues and different sections of the same accounting standard.

Rationales differ (and are inconsistent) across accounting standards because a standard is the result of political action. The outcome depends on the relative costs which the various involved parties are willing to incur to achieve their goals. And these costs will vary with the expected benefits. The rationale given for a standard will be the successful party's rationale; and if it is a compromise, such as APB Opinion 16 on business combinations, mixtures of rationales will be used.[50] The same party is not successful in every issue; indeed many are not even involved in every issue. Further, vested interests (*e.g.,* an insurance company) are less

---

[48]An interesting case in point is the work of Ijiri [1967 and 1975]. Ijiri claims to be a positivist—". . . the purpose [of this book] is a better understanding of the foundations of accounting as it is and not as someone thinks it ought to be." [1967, p. x] He states that his work "is not intended to be pro-establishment or to promote the maintenance of the status quo. The purpose of such an exercise is to highlight where changes are most needed and where they are feasible." [1975, p. 28] But, then, in the same monograph (pp. 85–90), Ijiri presents a defense of historical costs, saying, "Our defense of historical cost should not, however, be interpreted to mean that historical cost is without any flaw" (p. 85). Ijiri concludes this defense with a statement, "We should in fact try to improve the accounting system based on historical cost not by abandoning it, but by modifying it (*e.g.,* through price level adjustments) and supplementing it with data based on other valuation methods" (p. 90). Despite being a professed positivist, Ijiri is making a strong normative statement. No wonder the AAA [1977, p. 10] committee when summarizing Ijiri [1975] concludes, "[he] defends historical cost against the criticisms of current-cost and current value. . . ." At least part of the "market" views Ijiri as a defender of the status quo.

[49]Just as in any market, those who produce what is demanded have a better chance of survival than those who do not.

[50]See Zeff [1972, pp. 212–216] for an account of this compromise.

constrained to give consistent rationales across issues. Hence, we observe a party supporting historical cost valuation in some cases and market valuation in others.[51]

If political transactions costs are high so that there is a demand for excuses which are useful weapons in the political arena, if the demand for accounting theory is dominated by that demand for excuses, and if demand determines production, accounting theories will be generated by, not generate, political debates. We will observe the nature of accounting theory changing as political issues change. Accounting theory will change *contemporaneously* with or *lag* political issues. We will *not* observe accounting theory generally *leading* political action.

Contrast the preceding predictions to what we would expect under alternative theories of accounting theory. The only alternative theory which we can even partially specify is that theories in the accounting literature are used to further the "public interest" (*i.e.,* they assist politicians or bureaucrats in producing regulations to further the "public interest"). In order for politicians or bureaucrats to use that literature we would have to observe the theories appearing in the literature before or, at best, at the same time as the relevant regulation. The appearance of the theories in the literature could not *lag* the regulation. Thus, we can discriminate between our theory and the alternative public interest theory if the appearance of theories in the literature tends to lead or lag regulation. If it tends to lead, the public interest hypothesis is supported. If it lags, our theory is supported. On the other hand, if the literature and regulation are contemporaneous we cannot discriminate between the two hypotheses.

It is important to remember that we are attempting to explain accounting theory as it is represented in the accounting literature (see footnote 1). It is conceivable that an accounting theory could be produced and used in the political process to institute a regulation, but not appear until later in the accounting literature. In other words, the "public interest" could, in fact, motivate the theory and the regulation, but the publication of the theory nonetheless, could, lag legislation. In that case, neither the public interest theory nor our theory could explain the accounting literature. In essence, we would be left without a theory of the literature. However, those who would argue such a scenario must then produce another explanation for, or theory of, the accounting literature.

In Section IV we compare the timing of general movements in the accounting literature to the timing of regulation to see if *a priori* the evidence supports our theory or the public interest theory. We do not present any formal tests which discriminate between the two theories, although we believe such tests could be performed (*e.g.,* by using citation tests). However, the serious problem in doing a formal test is that the public interest theory, like other alternative theories, is poorly specified. Hopefully, this paper will cause others to specify the public interest theory better or specify alternative theories of the accounting literature so that testing is facilitated.

One or two papers discussing a topic prior to the time the topic becomes politically active is not sufficient to reject our theory, just as one or two "heads" is not sufficient to reject the hypothesis that a given coin is "fair." It is important to remember that as in all empirical theories we are concerned with *general* trends. Our predictions are for the accounting literature in general. We are not purporting to have a theory that explains the behavior of all accounting researchers or the acceptance, or lack of acceptance, of every published paper. There are many interesting phenomena that this theory, at this stage of development, cannot yet explain. But this does not *ipso facto* destroy the value of the theory.

---

[51]Ernst & Ernst [1976] has proposed that replacement cost be used for depreciable assets while historical costs be continued for other assets.

Our analysis suggests that the accounting literature is not the simple accumulation of knowledge and consequent development of techniques. It is not a literature in which, as Littleton suggests,[52] concepts become better understood and consequently leads to "better" accounting practices. Instead it is a literature in which the concepts are altered to permit accounting practices to adapt to changes in political issues and institutions.

In this section, the existence of close substitute suppliers of theories was shown to make the supply of accounting "excuses" very responsive to the demand. In the next section we argue that the evidence we have gathered is consistent with the proposition that the market for accounting research is the market for "excuses" and suggests that the theory will be confirmed in formal testing.

IV. THE EMPIRICAL RELATIONSHIP BETWEEN GOVERNMENT INTERVENTION AND ACCOUNTING THEORY

If the demand for "excuses" is important in determining the output of accounting theorists, we expect to observe changes in accounting theory when a new law is passed which impinges on accounting practice. This section examines how accounting practice and theories were affected by several major types of legislation. We have selected three types of legislation which we believe have had a pronounced impact on accounting theory: the laws regulating railroads, the income tax laws, and the securities acts.

In this section we do not purport to present an exhaustive list of legislation which has created a demand for accounting "excuses" or to present a complete analysis of each type of legislation. Our objective is merely to present *prima facie* support for the hypothesis that accounting theory has changed *after* the introduction of government regulation.

When dealing with historical events such as government regulation, the "evidence" presented is always subject to interpretation and the *ex post* selection bias of the researchers. Critics can always charge that "strategic sampling" of references produced the results. In fact, much of the economic theory of regulation suffers from this *ex post* rationalization. However, at this early stage in the development of the theory, an *ex post* case study approach has yielded insights [Posner, 1974] and appears to be the logical and necessary precursor to a general theory of regulation. We are aware of these methodological problems. Even though the evidence we present is somewhat "casual," and not as "rigorous" as we would like, it is, nonetheless, evidence.[53] Furthermore, we have endeavored to choose the references from the standard, classical accounting literature. Undoubtedly, conflicting citations and references exist. Critics can, will, and should raise these conflicting citations, keeping in mind the statistical fallacies of

---

[52]"There is little evidence of fresh ideas regarding depreciation until the middle of the nineteenth century. The appearance of steam railroads at that time directed attention as never before to fixed assets and their associated problems of maintenance, renewal and improvement. Out of the discussion and experience which followed, new ideas about depreciation took form and the ground was prepared for a better comprehension of the real nature of depreciation itself" [Littleton 1933, p. 227].

[53]It is tempting to suggest citation tests of the theory (*i.e.,* the frequency of articles on a subject increases with regulation). Besides the obvious cost of such a test, it suffers from the interpretation bias of the researchers. Also, how should changes in terminology be controlled? We would welcome anyone who can overcome these methodological difficulties to perform the tests.

drawing inferences based on sample sizes of one. We do not contend that all issues are settled, but rather encourage others to pursue, correct, and extend our analysis.

A. RAILROAD LEGISLATION

The growth of railroads is considered by many accountants to have been very important in the development of accounting theory, Hendriksen [1977, p. 40] lists it as one of the main influences on accounting theory in the period from 1800 to 1930. Littleton [1933, pp. 239–241] is more specific; he ascribes the development of depreciation accounting and the concern with depreciation in the literature in the nineteenth century to the growth of railroads.

There is no doubt that the development of railroads both in the U.S. and the U.K. affected the accounting literature on the nature of depreciation, including the question of charging depreciation as an expense [Pollins, 1956; and Boockholdt, 1977]. Holmes [1975, p. 18] writes:

> Depreciation was a knotty problem for these early railroad accountants. They argued over it, scorned it, denied it, anatomized it, and misused their own concepts. But in the end it was from the very ashes of their disagreements that our modern concepts of depreciation rose Phoenix-like fifty years later.

This literature existed at least by 1841 in the U.K. [*The Railway Times,* October 30, 1841, quoted in Pollins, 1956] and by 1850 in the U.S. [Dionysius Lardner's book quoted in Pollins, 1956]. Although the debate did not result in depreciation being treated as an expense in either the U.S. or U.K.,[54] theories of depreciation were enunciated. Consequently, given our theory, we have to answer two questions: (1) why did this depreciation debate arise with the railroads (*i.e.,* was there some government regulation or political action present in the case of the railroads that was not present for earlier corporations); and if so, (2) did that government regulation or political action precede the literature?

(1) THE REASON FOR THE DEBATE   was investigated by Littleton [1933]. He asserts that two conditions were necessary to the development of depreciation accounting—corporations with limited liability and long-lived assets. He suggests that limited liability was a necessary condition, because it led to covenants restricting dividends to profits and thereby created the demand for financial statements which report profits (see Section II). Long-lived assets were important because, if they had not existed, there would have been no necessity to calculate depreciation to determine profits.

We think that Littleton's analysis is incomplete. *First,* agency costs of debt and equity exist whether or not a corporation has legally limited liability. Limited liability merely shifts some of the risk [Jensen and Meckling, 1976, pp. 331–332]. Given that the function of dividend covenants is to reduce the agency costs of debt, it is not surprising to observe them existing as early as 1620 for U.K. companies, long before limited liability was generally recognized for companies. We can easily amend Littleton's argument for this defect; for the first condition of limited liability, we substitute the existence of dividend covenants.

---

[54]The general practice in both countries came to be the writing-off of the value of fixed assets at the time of retirement of the asset.

Second, dividend covenants and long-lived assets would not necessarily lead to depreciation being treated as an *expense.* The dividend covenants put a lower bound on the equity participation of shareholders. As long as sufficient earnings have been retained in the past to cover the depreciation of fixed assets to the current time, there would be no necessity to deduct depreciation systematically each year. We do not observe depreciation being treated as an expense prior to this century. Instead it was treated as an allocation of profits.

This suggests that Littleton's analysis has not been supported empirically. Observation of his two conditions would not necessarily be accompanied by depreciation being treated as an expense. Littleton's two conditions existed in the seventeenth and eighteenth centuries (dividend covenants can be observed as early as 1620 and were included in company charters as a general practice in the eighteenth century). Limited liability for U.K. companies existed *de facto* at least by the 1730s and was explicitly recognized by 1784.[55] The U.K. trading companies of the seventeenth and eighteenth centuries certainly had long-lived assets—forts and ships. Yet, we do not observe any real concern with depreciation expense until the nineteenth century.

Littleton recognized that his analysis was inconsistent with observed phenomena and that some other variable was necessary to explain the absence of concern about depreciation expense in both accounting theory and practice. He eloquently expresses the inconsistency [Littleton, 1933, p. 240]:

> The simultaneous appearance of these two elements—active, long-lived assets and a special need for the careful calculation of net profit—seems to be essential to the recognition of the importance of depreciation. Before these two are joined depreciation is incidental to the profit calculation; afterward it becomes indispensable. First in the trading companies, later in the railroads, these two elements were united and the foundations for depreciation accounting were laid. But, so far as could be learned, the depreciation of ships and forts did not receive consideration in the trading companies' bookkeeping, while the railroads, as has been seen, did give considerable attention to the problem of wear and tear of roadway and equipment. *Apparently some third element was also needed, which was present in the case of the railroads* but not earlier (emphasis added).

Littleton [1933, p. 240] suggests that the missing variable is knowledge, that it took 200 years for the nature of the corporation to become known. We suggest that a more plausible explanation is that, in the case of railroads, fares and rates were regulated by government on the basis of "profits."

Both in the U.S. and the U.K., some transportation prices were regulated before the existence of railroads. For example, the rates of the Fort Point Ferry (U.S.), incorporated in 1807,

---

[55]See DuBois [1938, pp. 94–95] for a report on the incorporation proceedings of the Albion Flour Mill in 1784. In those proceedings, the Attorney General gave an opinion on limited liability which caused DuBois to conclude that, "for England at any rate, the fact of incorporation either by the Crown or by Parliament came to be the criterion for the extent of limited liability" (p. 96). Note, however, that it was theoretically possible for shareholders of insolvent companies to be made subject to calls. (See DuBois, pp. 98–103). DuBois (p. 95) recognized that *de facto* limited liability existed in the 1730s and 1740s: "it should be noted that through the financial tribulations of the Charitable Corporation, the York Buildings Company, and the Royal African Company, which in the thirties and forties were making life miserable for their creditors, there was no suggestion of any attempt to proceed against the personal estates of the members of the corporations."

were, according to its charter, to be fixed by the court. [Dodd, 1954, p. 258]. However, railroad rates came to be tied to profits. The early U.S. railroad charters often had provisions for the adjustment of their rates based on profits. For example, the charter of the Franklin Railroad Company, incorporated in Massachusetts in 1830, included the following provision:

> if at any time after the expiration of four years from the completion of the Road, the net income shall have amounted to more than ten percent per annum, from the date of the completion aforesaid, upon the actual cost of said Road, the Legislature may take measures to alter and reduce the rates of toll and income, in such manner as to take off the overplus for the next four years, calculating the amount of transportation and income to be the same as the four preceding years; and, at the expiration of every four years thereafter the same proceeding may be had [Dodd, 1954, p. 260].

The charters of three other railroads incorporated in Massachusetts in the same year included a similar provision. [Dodd, 1954, p. 261].

The private acts of Parliament incorporating the early U.K. railroads typically fixed the maximum rates explicitly; but, in one notable exception, the Liverpool and Manchester Railway Act in 1826 limited the company's dividends to ten percent of the capital and required that its rates be reduced by five percent for each one percent of dividend above ten percent [Pollins, 1956, pp. 337–338]. Parliament soon began regulating railroad profits. In 1836, James Morrison sought to have Parliament restrict the profits of all railways. Clauses in Gladstone's 1844 Bill,

> authorized the Board of Trade to consider the position and profits of any railway which had a charter for fifteen years and to decide whether to buy it up on prescribed terms or, alternatively, to revise all its charges if it had made a profit of more than ten percent on its capital for three consecutive years [Cooke, 1950, p. 135].

Though these clauses were weakened in the actual Railways Regulation Act of 1844, a principle was established. Cooke [1950, p. 136] explains,

> The Act therefore fell short of the designs of Gladstone's committee and it is notable not for any reform it accomplished but rather for the principle embodied in it, that railway companies were one example of a class of company which was formed under special Parliamentary sanction to carry on an undertaking of a special public nature. Since for this purpose it had special powers, it should therefore be subject to special scrutiny and (if necessary) control by the State on behalf of the public.

The question of railroad profits and the public interest was raised in the political process in both the U.S. and the U.K. in the nineteenth century. Hence, it is not surprising that questions of calculating profits and whether depreciation should be charged as an expense were raised. The accounting methods of treating capital additions, depreciation, repairs and renewals, *etc.*, could affect reported profits and hence the rates and market values of railroads. Thus, there was a demand for rationalizations of alternative procedures.

The political issue of railroad profits led several U.S. states (Virginia (1837), New Hampshire and Rhode Island (1841), New York (1855), Massachusetts (1869) and Illinois (1869)) to pass legislation which in some way regulated railroads, usually by "controlling extortionate rates." [Boockholdt, 1977, p. 13; Johnson, 1965, p. 218; and Nash, 1947, p. 2]. According to Nash [1947, p. 3], "Several of the early state laws called for statements of provision for depreciation in annual reports but without definition as to what such provisions should be." Arguments for depreciation are expected to follow such regulations. Finally, in 1887 federal legislation established the Interstate Commerce Commission to prohibit unreasonable rates and price discrimination, control mergers, and prescribe a uniform system of accounts. The Interstate Commerce Commission adopted an accounting policy of charging "repairs or renewals of ties, rails, roadway, locomotives and cars under the classification 'operating expenses' [which typically results in higher reported expenses than depreciation] but did not mention depreciation" [Littleton, 1933, p. 236].

Although railroads were the prime target of regulation, the rates of other public utilities were also regulated in the nineteenth century. A Gas Commission was established in Massachusetts in 1885 and two years later was expanded to regulate electric companies. Later, it was given control over capitalization and rates [Nash, 1947, p. 3]. Municipalities regulated water company rates (*Spring Valley Water Works v. Schottler* (1883)) [Clay, 1932, p. 33] and such regulation led to legal disputes over whether depreciation should be considered in determining rates (*San Diego Water Co. v. San Diego*) [Riggs, 1922, pp. 155–157]. In addition, states regulated the charges for grain elevators (*Munn v. Illinois* (1877)) [Clay, 1932, p. 30].

It is our hypothesis that rate regulation (primarily of the railroads) created a demand for theories rationalizing depreciation as an expense. Furthermore, we expect that the more popular of these theories would stress that it is in the "public interest" for depreciation to be treated as an expense. Without regulation there was no necessity for depreciation to be a charge, systematically deducted each year in determining net income. However, because rate regulation was justified in terms of restricting the economic profits of monopolists (or eliminating "ruinous" competition), regulation created a demand for justifications arguing for depreciation to be treated as an annual charge to profits. Furthermore, because regulatory legislation was often based on economic arguments, theories of depreciation came to be couched in terms of economic costs.

(2) THE TIMING OF THE DEBATE appears to confirm our hypothesis that political action generated accounting theory, not vice-versa. As we have seen, the early U.S. railroad charters in the 1830s included provisions for regulation of profits. Those charters *precede* the debates observed in the accounting literature. The move by Morrison to have Parliament regulate the profits of U.K. railroads also *precedes* the debates.

B. INCOME TAX ACTS

The influence of the income tax laws on financial reporting *practice* is well known and much lamented by academics.[56] That influence is very obvious in the practice of charging depreciation to net income, rather than treating it as an allocation of profit. Saliers [1939, pp. 17–18] describes the effect of the 1909 Excise Tax Law, the forerunner of the 1913 Income Tax Law:

---

[56]Hendriksen [1977, p. 49] states, "The effect on accounting theory of taxation of business incomes in the United States and in other countries has been considerable, but it has been primarily indirect in nature. . . . While the revenue acts did hasten the adoption of good accounting practices and thus brought about a more critical analysis of accepted accounting procedures and concepts, they have also been a deterrent to experimentation and the acceptance of good theory."

"Financial looseness" describes the accounting practices of industries in general at that time. The company bookkeepers, when closing their books, based the amount of the depreciation charge on the amount of profit earned in that year. A lean year caused the property to receive little or not charge for depreciation, while a prosperous year caused a liberal allowance to be made. The authorities had reason for either action at their fingertips, shifting one side to the other as conditions warranted. But after the year 1909 the shift was to the side of larger depreciation charges, for in that year the Corporation Excise Tax Law was enacted. This law levied a 1% tax on net income of corporations in excess of $5,000. This net income was said to be the figure resulting after deducting ordinary and necessary expenses and all losses, including an allowance for depreciation, from gross profit. Depreciation expense was made an allowable deduction and was universally deducted by those corporations affected by the act. The effect of this act on the growth of the use of the depreciation charge cannot be overemphasized. *It was the first instance in which the writing off of depreciation as expense was definitely advantageous. That fact alone insured its general application* (emphasis added).

The influence of tax laws on accounting theory appears to be as dramatic as Saliers' description of the U.S. tax laws' effect on accounting practice, particularly with respect to depreciation. Concern with depreciation as an expense existed only in the *railroad* accounting literature until the 1880s. In that decade we observe a spate of U.K. journal articles and textbooks on the question of depreciation for corporations in *general*. We do not observe the same concern in the U.S. at that time. This raises the question of why the sudden concern with depreciation in the U.K., not just for public utilities, but for all corporations. Further, why did such a concern with depreciation for all corporations not manifest itself in the U.S.?

Brief [1976, p. 737] suggests that the U.K. literature was motivated by a concern with "paying dividends out of capital" and that "accountants sought first of all to clarify theory, and second, to understand their responsibility in these matters. However, they were offered little assistance from judicial and statutory authority which failed to specify rules of accounting behavior." Although the accounting authors of the time may have suggested that was the problem, we think it is a very unsatisfactory answer to the question of what really motivated the literature for two reasons. First, we have already noted that the "profits available for dividends" question had existed for 260 years. Second, there was no uncertainty in the law as to when depreciation should or should not be deducted before determining "profits available for dividends." The legal decisions were consistent: if the corporate articles required a provision for depreciation, it had to be taken; if not it did not. As Litherland [1968, p. 171] states, "the question of depreciation was a matter of internal management with which the law had nothing to do. The Articles of the given company were to govern."

We suggest that the reason a general concern with the depreciation for all corporations (and not just railroads) appeared in the U.K. literature in the 1880s and not before is that, prior to 1878, the U.K. tax laws made no allowance for depreciation. "In 1878 the law was modified to permit the deduction of a reasonable amount for the diminished value of machinery and plant resulting from wear and tear. Depreciation was not mentioned in the law and no amount was permitted for obsolescence" [Saliers, 1939, p. 255]. Now there was an additional reason for arguing over the concept of annual depreciation and its level—taxes [Leake, 1912, p. 180].

The income tax explanation for the late nineteenth century depreciation debate also explains the absence of that debate in the U.S. Brief's hypothesis does not. The first effective U.S. corporate income tax law was the Excise Tax Act of 1909 (which went into effect before it was delared unconstitutional).[57] Thus, in 1880 there was no federal tax motivation driving a debate over depreciation. There was in the U.S. in 1880 the problem of determining "profits available for dividends."

The tax laws affected not only the timing of depreciation discussions, but also the resulting concepts of depreciation and of accounting income. In the legal cases on "dividends out of profits," depreciation was regarded as a valuation procedure (see p. 278). Whether the amount of depreciation taken was sufficient would be decided in the event of a dispute. Administering the tax laws is less costly if the periodic valuation is replaced by an arbitrary proportion of historical cost. This saving was recognized in the early literature [Matheson, 1893, p. 15] and was the likely reason that both U.S. and U.K. income tax allowances for depreciation were based on historical cost. The demand for a rationalization of this procedure and other accruals under the tax law eventually resulted in the concept of income based on matching and the realization concept. Storey [1959, p. 232] reports this effect of the tax law as follows:

> [The realization concept] probably did not exist at all before the First World War, and at least one writer states that the first official statement of the concept was made in 1932 in the correspondence between the Special Committee on Cooperation with Stock Exchanges of the American Institute of Accountants and the Stock List Committee of the New York Stock Exchange. The letter referred to rejects the method of determining income by the inventorying of assets as the beginning and end of each period in favor of the recognition of profit at the time of sale. This concept of profit was gradually taking form during the period after the First World War and had become dominant in the field of accounting determination of net income by the late 1930's. *That it was influenced by the concept of income laid down by the Supreme Court in early income tax litigation is obvious* (emphasis added).

The timing of the depreciation debates in the U.K. also appears to confirm our hypothesis that political action caused the observed change in accounting theory. The tax allowance of the depreciation deduction (1878) *precedes* the 1880s debates.

It might appear that the development of the profession could explain the difference in the timing of the concern with depreciation in the U.K. and U.S. The professional bodies did not really develop until the 1870s in the U.K. and until the 1890s in the U.S. [Edwards, 1968a, pp. 197–199]. Hence, we could not observe depreciation debates in either country until those times. However, this alternative hypothesis is unsatisfactory on several counts. *First,* while the first professional society was not formed in the U.K. until 1854, Littleton [1933, p. 265] reports evidence of individuals (primarily lawyers) practicing accounting in the U.K. in the eighteenth century and suggests it is highly likely that accounting was practiced by lawyers in earlier times also. Similarly, there were public accountants in the U.S. at least as early as 1866 [Edwards, 1968a, p. 198]. *Second,* the lack of a *formal* accounting profession did not prevent the

---

[57]An increase in the effective corporate tax rate from less than 1 percent in 1909 to over 7 percent in 1918 further stimulated the concern for depreciation in the U.S. (Source: *Historical Survey of the United States,* U.S. Department of Commerce [1975, p. 1109]).

appearance of the railroad depreciation literature in both the U.S. and U.K. in the 1840s and 1850s. *Third,* the formation of professional societies, itself, is likely to be due, at least partly, to political action. Accountants have incentives to lobby on government prescription of accounting practices. Given some economies of scale in lobbying, government intervention in accounting would be expected to produce professional bodies.

C. SECURITIES ACTS

There appear to be at least two major effects of the U.S. Securities Acts of 1933–34 on the accounting literature: they caused the objective of accounting to shift to what we call the "information objective"; and they stimulated a search for accounting principles. Both *follow* the Securities Acts.

(1) THE INFORMATION OBJECTIVE Prior to the Securities Acts accounting theorists tended to describe and base their prescriptions on the multiple objectives of accounting, and they listed the numerous users. Consistent with our analysis of accounting in an unregulated economy, the control, or stewardship role, was frequently stressed. For example, Leake [1912, pp. 1–2] includes as reasons for calculating profit and loss:

1. the stewardship role of management to "uphold the value of the capital investment and to ascertain and distribute the annual profits with due regard to the differential rights" of the various classes of capital;
2. profit sharing schemes between capital and labor;
3. income taxes; and
4. public utility regulation.

Daines [1929, p. 94] describes the "orthodox" or dominant objective of accounting as being "to reflect that income which is legally available for dividends." Sweeney [1936, p. 248] states that "the fundamental purpose of accounting should consist of an attempt to distinguish between capital and income."

In his book based on his doctoral dissertation, Sweeney adds other functions to the stewardship role:

> Business management guides the affairs of business. For its own guidance it depends heavily on reports submitted to it by its employees. Periodically it renders reports of its stewardship to the owners of the business. From time to time it also renders reports to bankers who have lent money to the business, to federal and state governments that tax or regulate business, and to the general financial public.
>
> The whole system of business, therefore, depends upon reports. Reports are made up largely of accounting statements [Sweeney, 1936, p. xi].

Managers were frequently cited as important users of accounting. Paton [1924, p. 1] defines accounting as a

> mechanism and body of principles by means of which the financial data of the particular concern are recorded, classified, and periodically presented and interpreted, with a view, thereby, to the *rational administration of the enterprise* (emphasis added).

After the Securities Acts the providing of information to investors and creditors in order to aid them in making rational investment choices became the dominant objective in the literature. We call this the information objective. One of the earliest documents which illustrates this new emphasis on the investor's decision is the AAA's 1936 "Tentative Statement on Accounting Principles." A number of "unsatisfactory" accounting procedures are discussed, including upward asset revaluations:

> Occasional uncoordinated "appraisals" produce in the average financial statement a hodgepodge of unrelated values of no explicable significance to *the ordinary investor,* if indeed they have any to the managements of the enterprises affected [American Accounting Association, 1936, p. 189] (emphasis added).

Notice the emphasis given to investors. Hendriksen [1977, p. 54] also supports our contention that the objective changed "from presenting financial information to management and creditors to that of providing financial information to investors and stockholders." In a more recent example, *A Statement of Basic Accounting Theory* [American Accounting Association, 1966, p. 4], the information objective is listed first among four objectives of accounting. The objectives are:

1. to provide information for decisions concerning limited resources by "individuals acting in their own behalf, such as the stockholders or creditors of a firm, by agents serving in fiduciary capacities, or by individuals or groups in business firms, in government, in not-for-profit organizations and elsewhere" [p. 4].

2. to effectively direct and control an organization's human and material resources,

3. to maintain and report on the custodianship of resources,

4. "to facilitate the operations of an organized society for the welfare of all" [p. 5].

Recent writers no longer even list management as a principal user of financial statements. The dichotomy of internal and external accounting has become complete. The recent statement on accounting objectives, the FASB's Conceptual Framework Study [1976], also excludes management:

> Financial statements of business enterprises should provide information, within the limits of financial accounting, that is useful to present and potential investors and creditors in making rational investment and credit decisions [FASB, 1976, p. 10].

The dominance of the information objective arose, we suspect, as a public interest justification consistent with and in support of the *raison d'être* of the Securities Acts. The SEC was justified in terms of, and charged with, maintaining the orderly functioning of the capital markets. In particular the SEC was to protect the public from another stock market crash. That crash was alleged to have been caused in part by inadequate corporate disclosure, although very little evidence exists to support this claim.[58]

Although the SEC delegated the power to determine accounting standards for corporate disclosure to the accounting profession, there is evidence that it still exercised control over that determination. According to Horngren [1973] and Zeff [1972, pp. 150–160] the SEC managed

---

[58]See Benston [1969a and b]. The U.S. Securities and Exchange Commission [1945, pp. 1–3 and Part X] makes this claim, although Sanders [1946, pp. 9–10] disputes much of their argument.

by exception, threatening to intervene, or actually intervening in the standard-setting process whenever the Committee on Accounting Procedure (CAP) or the APB proposed a standard of which it did not approve. Consequently, proponents advocating particular accounting procedures would justify those procedures in terms of the SEC's stated objective—the public interest (which "requires" the information objective).

The hypothesis that the dominance of the information objective was caused by the Securities Acts is supported not only by the tendency of modern writers to cite the public interest as an objective along with the information objective [*e.g.,* the fourth objective of *A Statement of Basic Accounting Theory* listed above], but by the tendency to argue that fulfillment of the information objective is necessary to the "public interest." An example of that latter tendency is provided by the FASB [1976, p. 3]:

> Financial accounting and reporting is an important source of information on which investment, lending, and related decisions are based. Confidence in financial information is vital not only to ensure that individual decisions result in an equitable allocation of capital but to ensure continuing public support of the free enterprise system as a whole.

The close relationship between the information objective and the "public interest" is exemplified by the argument recently raised in the literature that information provided in accounting reports is a public good and that as a consequence, there may be an underproduction of information from society's viewpoint (*i.e.,* there may be a market failure). If there is a market failure, the argument proceeds, the "public interest" may require disclosure laws requiring the provision of information to investors [Beaver, 1976, p. 66].

(2) The Search for Accounting Principles   Before the Securities Acts most of the accounting literature did not stray far from practice, and prescriptions were usually based on rationalizations of practice (*e.g.,* the matching concept). Even Sweeney's price-level accounting proposals of the 1920s were based on practice. According to the author [Sweeney, 1936, p. xii] the work "has its roots in methods that were developed in Germany and France during the late inflation periods in those countries." There was, with the notable exceptions of Paton [1922] and Canning [1929], little effort devoted to establishing a theory of accounting.[59] Indeed, Chambers [1955a, p. 18] claims that except for Paton [1922] the word theory was not attached to any work in the accounting literature until after World War II.

Taggart describes the general situation in 1922 as follows:

> Some of the writers on theory, notably Sprague and Hatfield, not satisfied merely to describe practice, had earnestly addressed themselves to exposition of pure theory; but the textbook writers, for the most part, had quite naturally concerned themselves primarily with practice and with not much more than an occasional nod toward theory, where it seemed to bolster practice. Paton's *Accounting Theory* is concerned only with theory; it touches on practice only for illustration or contrast; and it is quite the opposite of an apologia for practice, [Foreword in the 1962 re-issue of Paton, 1922, p. v.].

---

[59]The Federal Reserve Board published a 1917 bulletin (*Uniform Accounting*) written by Price, Waterhouse & Co. in response to the Federal Trade Commission threatening to establish a federal accountant's register, but the bulletin "consisted of mainly audit procedures" [Carey, 1969, pp. 1:129–135].

Canning [1929, p. 160] himself wrote, "accountants have no complete philosophical system of thought about income; *nor is there evidence that they have ever greatly felt the need for one*"[60] (emphasis added).

A potential explanation for the two famous departures from the orthodox accounting thought of the 1920s [Canning, 1929; and Paton, 1922] is that both were based on doctoral dissertations written in economics departments [Zeff, 1978, p. 16]. Undoubtedly, both authors were influenced heavily by economists as well as accountants. Canning himself writes, "I need not declare my obligation to Professor [Irving] Fisher for the influence of his writings upon my thought—that obligation appears throughout the whole book" [Canning, 1929, p. iv].

If Paton and Canning were harbingers of a change in accounting thought, we would expect to observe a shift in the orthodox accounting view during the 20s, following publication of their books. Alternatively, if Canning's and Paton's views were outliers or aberrations due to their economics training, we would expect to observe them modifying their views towards the orthodox position to ensure their survival as accounting academics.

Zeff [1978] presents evidence that Paton's views, at least, moved more towards the orthodox view during the 1920s and 1930s, than the orthodox view moved towards Paton's. Thus, it is difficult to argue that Paton and Canning were representative of a change in the accounting literature which influenced the passage of the Securities Acts. Instead, we suspect that much of the attention which Paton's and Canning's views received after the Securities Acts was a result of the Acts themselves.

The literature's concern with practice before the Securities Act is not surprising (given our theory). Prescriptions based on rationalizations of practice are to be expected in an economy in which corporate reporting is not regulated. Theorists would base their prescriptions for individual firms on the current institutional arrangements determining practice (*i.e.,* in the terms of the agency or stewardship relationships, utility regulation, taxes, *etc.*). Hence, theory would be very concerned with practice. Further, because the advantages are to the individual firms, the theorist would not *require* all firms to follow his prescriptions, but expect his prescriptions to be adopted because of self-interest. The theorist would not try to specify accounting principles which all firms *should* adopt.

As we have noted, the Securities Acts were based on the argument that required disclosure is necessary to the "public interest." The idea was that without required disclosure capital markets would be less efficient. We do not observe this theory being generally advanced in the accounting literature prior to the Securities Act.[61]

The justification for required disclosure is that the private incentives to adopt accounting prescriptions are insufficient. Hence, current accounting practice cannot serve as a basis for prescriptions. This justification sets accounting theory free from practice. It makes it possible to "build up a theory of accounting without reference to the practice of accounting" [Chambers, 1955a, p. 19]. Further, the justification caused the SEC to demand such theories. Because

---

[60]Canning's principal intentions were not to reform existing practice or to construct a general theory but rather to make "the work of the professional accountant more fully intelligible to those in other branches of learning" [1929, p. iii].

[61]The theory does appear in *The Journal of Accountancy* in October, 1930 (see Hoxsey [1930], but the author is not an accounting theorist; instead he is an employee of the New York Stock Exchange. The theory also appears in the writings of Ripley in the popular financial literature in the 1920s (*e.g.,* Ripley [1926]). However, Ripley is also not representative of the financial literature.

they were to reform existing accounting practice, the SEC commissioners could not base regulations on practice; they required a theory or a set of accounting principles to justify their rulings.

Zeff [1972, pp. 133–173] documents the AICPA's initial search for accounting principles and the SEC's passing the responsibility for the determination of principles to the profession in SEC Accounting Series Release No. 4 [U.S. SEC, ASR 4].[62] Zeff also documents the search for accounting principles (or standards) by the succession of standard-setting bodies established by the profession. As noted, the SEC exercised control over the standard-setting bodies' search for accounting principles. Thus, we expect these bodies (like the SEC) to search for or demand accounting principles which do *not* describe existing practice.

We expect accounting theorists, who are accustomed to developing rules based on practice, to be perplexed by a demand for accounting principles not based on practice. *After* the SEC's call (in ASR 4) for accounting principles for which there is substantial authoritative support [1938], the accounting literature begins to discuss the nature of principles [Scott, 1941; Wilcox and Hassler, 1941; and Kester, 1942].[63] Further, as theorists come to observe less emphasis being placed on the practicality of their approach, we observe philosophical works becoming far removed from practice such as Chambers [1955a, 1955b, 1966], Mattessich [1957] and Edwards and Bell [1961].

It is instructive to compare the search for accounting principles in the U.S. to that in the U.K. where there has not been a government regulatory body with the statutory power to prescribe accounting procedures [Benston, 1976, pp. 14–30; Zeff, 1972, pp. 1–69].[64] Until recently there has been considerably less "progress" in the U.K. in the search for accounting principles [Zeff, 1972, p. 310 and Shackleton, 1977, pp. 17–21] and further, "the English began late" [Zeff, 1972, p. 310]. The evidence suggests that the U.K. search for principles is also a response to government pressure which arose out of various financial crises [Zeff, 1972, pp. 39–40; Benston, 1976, pp. 15–17; and Shackleton, 1977, pp. 17–21].

The difference in the timing of the search for principles in the two countries is reminiscent of the 30-year difference in the timing of the general depreciation debates in the U.K. and the U.S. That 30-year difference also coincides with a difference in the timing of government regulation (*i.e.,* corporate income tax laws allowing depreciation as a deduction). The difference in timing cannot be explained *per se* by the fact that we are comparing two different countries. In the depreciation debates, the U.K. led, while the U.S. led in the search for principles.

The discussion in this section has suggested that much of accounting theory (*e.g.,* the concepts of depreciation, accrual accounting, the application of the concept of economic income, and the idea that the objective of financial statements is generally to provide information to investors rather than to control agency costs), *follows* government intervention. Thus,

---

[62]ASR 4 stated that "financial statements filed with this Commission . . . [which] are prepared in accordance with accounting principles for which there is *no substantial authoritative support*, . . . will be presumed to be misleading or inaccurate" (emphasis added). ASR 4 created a demand for some procedure or device to provide "substantial authoritative" support.

[63]Storey [1964, p. 3] supports our contention that the Securities Acts were "landmark events" and directly related to the search for accounting principles.

[64]See Sanders [1946] for an overview of the different prevailing attitudes in the U.S. and U.K. in the 1940s.

the evidence is consistent with our hypothesis that much of accounting theory is the product of government intervention and that accounting theory satisfies the demand for excuses. The evidence appears to be inconsistent with what we have called the "public interest" hypothesis. Undoubtedly there are alternative theories which can also explain the timing of the accounting literature. The challenge is to those who would support those alternative theories to specify them and show that they are more consistent with the evidence than ours.

V. CONCLUSIONS

In our view, accounting theories have had an important role in determining the content of financial statements—although it might not be the role envisioned by the theorists. Instead of providing "an underlying framework" for the promulgation of "sound" financial reporting practices by standard-setting boards, accounting theory has proven a useful "tactic to buttress one's preconceived notions" [Zeff, 1974, p. 177]. While accounting theories have always served a justification role in addition to information and pedagogic roles, government intervention has expanded the justification role. The predominant function of accounting theories is now to supply excuses which satisfy the demand created by the political process; consequently accounting theories have become increasingly normative.

We are not offering any judgments on the desirability of accounting theories fulfilling an excuse role. What we are arguing, however, is that *given* the existing economic and political institutions and the incentives of voters, politicians, managers, investors, *etc.* to become involved in the process by which accounting standards are determined, the only accounting theory that will provide a set of predictions that are consistent with observed phenomena is one based on self-interest. No other theory, *no normative theory currently in the accounting literature, (e.g., current value theories) can explain or will be used to justify all accounting standards,* because:

1. accounting standards are justified using the theory (excuse) of the vested interest group which is benefitted by the standard;
2. vested interest groups use different theories (excuses) for different issues; and
3. different vested interest groups prevail on different issues.

While a self-interest theory can explain accounting standards, such a theory will not be used to justify accounting standards because self-interest theories are politically unpalatable. As a consequence, *not only is there no generally accepted accounting theory to justify accounting standards, there will never be one.*

REFERENCES

Accounting Principles Board, *Opinion 16: Business Combinations,* American Institute of Certified Public Accountants, 1970).

Alchian, Armen and Reuben Kessel, "Competition, Monopoly and the Pursuit of Money," in *Aspects of Labor Economics,* (Princeton University Press: N.B.E.R., 1962), pp. 157–175.

American Accounting Association, "A Tentative Statement of Accounting Principles Affecting Corporate Reports," THE ACCOUNTING REVIEW, (June 1936), pp. 187–191.

———, Committee on Basic Accounting Theory, *A Statement of Basic Accounting Theory* (American Accounting Association, 1966).

————, Committee on Concepts and Standards for External Reports, *Statement on Accounting Theory and Theory Acceptance* (American Accounting Association, 1977).

American Institute of Certified Public Accountants, *Objectives of Financial Statements,* (Trueblood) Report of the Study Group on the Objectives of Financial Statements (American Institute of Certified Public Accountants, 1973).

Beaver, William H., "What Should Be the FASB's Objectives?", *Journal of Accountancy,* (August, 1973), pp. 49–56.

————, "The Implications of Security Price Research for Disclosure Policy and the Analyst Community," in A. R. Abdel-khalik and T. F. Keller (eds.), *Financial Information Requirements for Security Analysis,* Duke Second Accounting Symposium, Duke University (December 1976), pp. 65–81.

———— and Joel S. Demski, "The Nature of Financial Accounting Objectives: A Summary and Synthesis," *Studies on Financial Accounting Objectives,* supplement to the *Journal of Accounting Research* (1974), pp. 170–187.

Benston, George J., "The Value of the SEC's Accounting Disclosure Requirements," THE ACCOUNTING REVIEW, (July 1969a), pp. 515–532.

————, "The Effectiveness and Effects of the SEC's Accounting Disclosure Requirements," in Henry G. Manne (ed.), *Economic Policy and the Regulation of Corporate Securities,* (American Enterprise Institute, 1969b), pp. 23–79.

————, *Corporate Financial Disclosure in the UK and the USA* (Saxon House, 1976).

Blough, Carman G., "Some Accounting Problems of the Securities and Exchange Commission," *The New York Certified Public Accountant,* (April 1937), pp. 3–14.

Boockholdt, James L., "Influence of Nineteenth and Early Twentieth Century Railroad Accounting on Development of Modern Accounting Theory," unpublished working paper 31, University of Alabama (July 1977).

Brief, Richard P. (ed.), *The Late Nineteenth Century Debate Over Depreciation, Capital and Income* (Arno Press, 1976).

Buchanan, James M. and Richard E. Wagner, *Democracy in Deficit: The Political Legacy of Lord Keynes,* (Academic Press, 1977).

Burton, John C., "An Interview with John C. Burton," *Management Accounting,* (May 1975), pp. 19–23.

Canning, John B., *The Economics of Accountancy* (Ronald Press, 1929).

Carey, John L., *The Rise of the Accounting Profession,* Vols. 1 & 2 (American Institute of Certified Public Accountants, 1969–70).

Chambers, Raymond J., "Blueprint for a Theory of Accounting," *Accounting Research,* (January 1955a), pp. 17–25.

————, "A Scientific Pattern for Accounting Theory," *Australian Accountant* (October 1955b), pp. 428–434.

————, *Accounting, Evaluation and Economic Behavior* (Prentice-Hall, 1966).

Clay, Cassius M., *Regulation of Public Utilities,* (Henry Holt and Company, 1932).

Cooke, C. A., *Corporation, Trust and Company* (Manchester University Press, 1950).

"Curse of Bigness," *Barron's,* (June 30, 1969), pp. 1 and 8.

Daines, H. C., "The Changing Objectives of Accounting," THE ACCOUNTING REVIEW, (June 1929), pp. 94–110.

Dicksee, Lawrence, *Depreciation, Reserves and Reserve Funds* (1903), reprinted by Arno Press, 1976.

Dodd, Edwin M., *American Business Corporations Until 1860* (Harvard University Press, 1954).

Downs, Anthony, *An Economic Theory of Democracy* (Harper and Row, 1957).

DuBois, Armand B., *The English Business Company After the Bubble Act 1720–1800* (The Commonwealth Fund, 1938).

Edey, Harold C., "Company Accounting in the Nineteenth and Twentieth Centuries," reprinted in Michael Chatfield (ed.), *Contemporary Studies in the Evolution of Accounting Thought* (Dickenson Publishing Co. Inc., 1968), pp. 135–143.

———— and Prot Panitpakdi, "British Company Accounting and the Law 1844–1900," in A. C. Littleton and B. S. Yamey (eds.), *Studies in the History of Accounting* (Richard D. Irwin, Inc., 1956), pp. 356–379.

Edwards, Edgar O. and Philip W. Bell, *The Theory and Measurement of Business Income* (University of California Press, 1961).

Edwards, James D., "Some Significant Developments of Public Accounting in the United States," *Business History Review* (June 1956), reprinted in Michael Chatfield (ed.), *Contemporary Studies in the Evolution of Accounting Thought* (Dickenson Publishing Co., 1968a), pp. 196–209.

————, "The Antecedents of American Public Accounting," *Accounting Research* (January 1956), reprinted in Michael Chatfield (ed.), *Contemporary Studies in the Evolution of Accounting Thought* (Dickenson Publishing Co., 1968b), pp. 144–166.

Ernst & Ernst, *Accounting Under Inflationary Conditions,* (Ernst & Ernst, 1976).

Fama, Eugene F., "Efficient Capital Markets: A Review of Theory and Empirical Work," *Journal of Finance* (May 1970), pp. 381–417.

————, *Foundations of Finance* (Basic Books, Inc., 1976).

Financial Accounting Standards Board, *An Analysis of Issues Related to Conceptual Framework for Financial Accounting and Reporting: Elements of Financial Statements and Their Measurement* (FASB, 1976).

Gonedes, Nicholas and Nicholas Dopuch, "Capital Market Equilibrium, Information Production and Selecting Accounting Techniques: Theoretical Framework and Review of Empirical Work," *Studies on Financial Accounting Objectives,* supplement to the *Journal of Accounting Research* (1974), pp. 48–129.

Gordon, Myron J., "Postulates, Principles and Research in Accounting," THE ACCOUNTING REVIEW (April 1964), pp. 251–263.

Hendriksen, Eldon, *Accounting Theory,* 3rd Edition (Richard D. Irwin, Inc., 1977).

Holmes, William, "Accounting and Accountants in Massachusetts," *Massachusetts CPA Review* (May–June 1975), pp. 18–21.

Horngren, Charles T., "The Marketing of Accounting Standards," *Journal of Accountancy,* (October 1973), pp. 61–66.

———, "Setting Accounting Standards in the 1980's," in Norton Bedford (ed.), *Accountancy in the 1980's—Some Issues,* (The Council of Arthur Young Professors, 1977).

Hoxsey, J. M. B., "Accounting for Investors," *Journal of Accountancy* (October 1930), pp. 251–284.

Ijiri, Yuji, *The Foundations of Accounting Measurement* (Prentice-Hall Inc., 1967).

———, "Logic and Functions in Accounting," in Robert Sterling and William Bentz (eds.), *Accounting in Perspective,* (South-Western Publishing Co., 1971).

———, *Theory of Accounting Measurement* (American Accounting Association, 1975).

Interstate Commerce Commission, *Accounting for Federal Income Taxes,* 318 I.C.C. 803, U.S. Government Printing Office.

Jensen, Michael C., "Towards a Theory of the Press," unpublished paper, Graduate School of Management, University of Rochester, June 1976.

——— and William H. Meckling, "Theory of the Firm: Managerial Behavior, Agency Costs and Ownership Structure," *Journal of Financial Economics,* (October 1976), pp. 305–360.

——— and William H. Meckling, "On 'The Labor Managed' Firm and the Codetermination Movement," Public Policy Working Paper Series GPB 77-2, Center for Research in Government Policy and Business, Graduate School of Management, University of Rochester, February 1977.

Johnson, Arthur M., *Government-Business Relations* (Charles E. Merrill Books, 1965).

Kehl, Donald, *Corporate Dividends* (The Ronald Press Company, 1941).

Kester, Roy B., "Sources of Accounting Principles," *Journal of Accountancy,* (December 1942), pp. 531–535.

Leake, P. D., *Depreciation and Wasting Assets and Their Treatment in Assessing Annual Profit and Loss* (1912), reprinted by Arno Press, 1976.

Leffler, Keith and Jerold Zimmerman, "A Theory of Municipal Government Agency Costs, Organizational Form, and Scale," working paper, Graduate School of Management, University of Rochester (July 1977).

Litherland, D. A., "Fixed Asset Replacement a Half Century Ago," reprinted in Michael Chatfield (ed.), *Contemporary Studies in the Evolution of Accounting Thought* (Dickenson Publishing Co., Inc., 1968), pp. 167–175.

Littleton, A. C., *Accounting Evolution to 1900* (1933), reprinted by Russell & Russell, 1966.

Matheson, Ewing, *The Depreciation of Factories, Mines and Industrial Undertakings and Their Valuation* (1893), reprinted by Arno Press, 1976.

Mattessich, Richard, "Towards a General and Axiomatic Foundation of Accountancy; with an Introduction to the Matrix Formulation of Accounting Systems," *Accounting Research,* (October 1957), pp. 328–355.

Mautz, Robert K., "The Role of the American Accounting Association in Accounting Research," *Research in Accounting Measurement,* Robert Jaedicke, Yuji Ijiri and Oswald Nielsen (eds.) (American Accounting Association, 1966).

——— and Jack Gray, "Some Thoughts on Research Needs in Accounting," *The Journal of Accountancy,* (September 1970), pp. 54–62.

McCraw, Thomas K., "Regulation in America: A Review Article," *Business History Review,* (Summer 1975), pp. 159–183.

Meckling, William H., "Towards a Theory of Representative Government," presented at the Third Annual Conference on Analysis and Ideology, Interlaken, Switzerland, June 4, 1976 (1976a).

———, "Values and the Choice of the Model of the Individual in the Social Sciences," *Revue Suisse d' Economic Politique et de Statistique* (December 1976b), pp. 545–560.

Moonitz, Maurice, "Accounting Principles—How They are Developed," in Robert Sterling (ed.), *Institutional Issues in Public Accounting,* (Scholars Book Company, 1974a), pp. 143–171.

———, *Obtaining Agreement on Standards in the Accounting Profession* (American Accounting Association, 1974b).

Mueller, Dennis C., "Public Choice: A Survey," *The Journal of Economic Literature* (June 1976), pp. 395–433.

Mundheim, Robert H., "Foreword, Symposium on Securities Regulation," *Law and Contemporary Problems* (Summer 1964), pp. 647–652.

Nash, Luther R., *Anatomy of Depreciation* (Public Utilities Reports, Inc., 1947).

Niskanen, William A., *Bureaucracy and Representative Government* (Aldine-Atherton, 1971).

Paton, William A., *Accounting Theory—With Special Reference to the Corporate Enterprise* (New York: The Ronald Press Company, 1922). Re-issued in 1962 by A.S.P. Accounting Studies Press, Ltd. Reprinted by Scholars Book Co., 1973.

———, *Accounting* (Macmillan Company, 1924).

———— and A. C. Littleton, *An Introduction to Corporate Accounting Standards* (American Accounting Association, 1940).

Peltzman, Sam, "Towards a More General Theory of Regulation," *Journal of Law and Economics,* (August 1976), pp. 211–240.

Pichler, Joseph A., "An Economic Analysis of Accounting Power," in Robert Sterling (ed.), *Institutional Issues in Public Accounting* (Scholars Book Co., 1974), pp. 45–73.

Pollins, Harold, "Aspects of Railway Accounting Before 1868," reprinted in A. Littleton and B. Yamey (eds.), *Studies in the History of Accounting* (Richard D. Irwin, Inc., 1956), pp. 332–355.

Posner, Richard A., "Theories of Economic Regulation," *Bell Journal of Economics and Management Science* (Autumn 1974), pp. 335–358.

Prakash, Prem and Alfred Rappaport, "Information Inductance and Its Significance for Accounting," *Accounting Organizations and Society,* Vol. 2, No. 1, (1977), pp. 29–38.

Rappaport, Louis H., *SEC Accounting Practice and Procedure,* Third Edition (Ronald Press, 1972).

Riggs, Henry E., *Depreciation of Public Utility Properties* (McGraw Hill Book Co., 1922).

Ripley, William Z., "Stop, Look, Listen!", *The Atlantic Monthly* (September, 1926), pp. 380–399.

Saliers, Earl A., *Depreciation; Principles and Applications,* Third Edition (Ronald Press Company, 1939).

Sanders, Thomas H., "A Review of Reviews of Accounting Progress," *Journal of Accountancy* (January 1946), pp. 9–26.

————, Henry R. Hatfield, and Underhill Moore, *A Statement of Accounting Principles* (American Institute of Accountants, 1938).

Scott, DR, "The Basis for Accounting Principles," THE ACCOUNTING REVIEW (December 1941), pp. 341–349.

Shackleton, Ken, "Government Involvement in Developing Accounting Standards: The Framework," *Management Accounting* (U.K.), (January 1977), pp. 17–21.

Smith, Clifford, "On the Theory of Lending," unpublished paper, Working Paper Series No. 7635, Graduate School of Management, University of Rochester, 1976.

Sprouse, Robert T. and Maurice Moonitz, "A Tentative Set of Broad Accounting Principles for Business Enterprises," *Accounting Research Study No. 3* (American Institute of Certified Public Accountants, 1962).

Sterling, Robert R., "Accounting Research, Education and Practice," *Journal of Accountancy* (September 1973), pp. 44–52.

———— (ed.), *Institutional Issues in Public Accounting* (Scholars Book Co. 1974).

Stigler, George J., "The Theory of Economic Regulation," *Bell Journal of Economics and Management Science* (Spring 1971), pp. 3–21.

————, "Do Economists Matter?", *Southern Economic Journal* (January 1976), pp. 347–363.

SELECTIVE NORMATIVE THEORIES

DECISION-ORIENTED FINANCIAL ACCOUNTING

Robert R. Sterling

I. Introduction

The purpose of this paper is to consider the various measures (valuation methods) of wealth and income that have been proposed in the recent literature. A prerequisite to the consideration of that issue is the development of criteria by which the various measures are to be judged. I will review some of the major conflicts that have arisen about the criteria, state my reasons for selecting an overriding criterion and then attempt to show how that criterion can be applied.

II. Conflicting Objectives

There are conflicting viewpoints about the objective of accounting reports. This conflict is rather difficult to detect. One must look closely for it. Almost all the literature on accounting states that accounting reports must be 'useful' or that accounting is a 'utilitarian art'. It seems that we all agree that the objective of accounting is to provide useful information. However, we discover conflicts when we examine the remainder of the 'basic concepts' of accounting. Consider the requirement that accounting data be objective and verifiable. It is possible for a measure to be useful even though it is not objective and verifiable. Thus, a conflict arises: Should we accountants provide useful data even if it is not objective, or should we provide objective data even if it is not useful?

There are many other conflicts. The particular terms that are used depend upon the author that one is reading. In regard to income, many authors begin their discussion with a

Robert R. Sterling, "Decision Oriented Financial Accounting," *Accounting and Business Research,* Summer 1972, pp. 198–208. Reprinted by permission of Accounting and Business Research.

remark about the need for providing useful information, but then they switch their attention to the realisation convention. It is possible that realised income is not the most useful measure of income. Thus, there is a conflict between realisation and usefulness. Other authors speak of the need to be conservative, and since it is possible for the most useful measure to be liberal, there is a conflict between conservatism and usefulness. Other authors note that a particular measure would violate the going concern assumption and reject the measure on those grounds without regard to the usefulness of that measure. And so forth for most of the other concepts of accounting. Each one of them may be set off against the notion of usefulness and be seen to be in conflict with it at some point.

Given the conflicts, we must decide which of the concepts is to be the overriding criterion. If we simply pay lip service to the notion of usefulness by allowing it to be constrained by all of these other concepts, then we are in fact denying the criterion of usefulness. Of course, if we can have our measures meet all of these requirements, then we are in the happy position of having no conflicts. The unfortunate fact is that they often are conflicting and we must decide which is the overriding criterion.

I think the overriding criterion should be usefulness. The other concepts are important but they are secondary. If, in order to make a decision, someone needs a measure of a particular property, then a rough guess at the magnitude of that property is useful. Of course, a precise, objective measure of that property is *more* useful, but the converse does not hold. If one does not need to know the magnitude of a particular property, then a measure of that property is useless no matter how precise and objective it may be.

Thus, I view accounting as a measurement-communication activity with the objective of providing useful information. Once we have discovered which properties are useful, then we must devise methods of measuring those properties. Hopefully, we can devise measurement methods which fulfil the requirements of objectivity, verifiability, etc. However, these requirements are secondary. They are desirable, but usefulness is indispensable. Therefore, providing useful information must be the primary objective of accounting.

III. CONFLICTING DEFINITIONS OF USEFULNESS

Problems arise whenever we attempt to define the concept of usefulness. Like other hortatory concepts (e.g. truth, justice, fairness) everyone is in favour of usefulness in the abstract. All of us agree with Spacek's postulate of fairness. Who could speak out in favour of being unfair? The difficulty is in defining fairness. In the same way, the difficulty with 'usefulness' is in making its meaning precise enough to be applicable to a concrete situation. In an attempt to be more precise, I have in previous works[1] replaced 'usefulness' with 'relevance.'

The dictionary defines 'relevant' as 'bearing upon or relating to the matter in hand.' This is what I mean by 'relevant information', except that I substitute 'decision model' for 'matter in hand'. In the same way that one cannot determine what is relevant to the matter in hand without being aware of the matter in hand, I cannot determine what is relevant information without being aware of the decision model. One of the characteristics of a well defined decision model

---

[1]Robert R. Sterling, *Theory of the Measurement of Enterprise Income* (The University Press of Kansas, 1970), pp. 50, 132, 354, *et passim* and 'On Theory Construction and Verification', *The Accounting Review,* July 1970, p. 454.

is that it will specify the measurement (or estimation) of certain properties. This allows my definition of relevance to be simple and straight-forward:

> If a property is specified by a decision model, then a measure of that property is relevant (to that decision model). If a property is not specified by a decision model, then a measure of that property is irrelevant (to that decision model).

One conflict that has arisen is concerned with that definition. Several people have argued that we should focus on decision *makers* instead of decision *models*. They say that if decision makers want to know the measure of a particular property, then that property is relevant or useful. Some of them have run tests designed to determine whether or not people (decision makers) use certain kinds of accounting data. When they found a certain kind of data being *used,* they concluded that this data was *useful.* They argue that we should supply the decision makers with the kind of data that they want and that this is the end of the question of relevance.

At first glance this view is rather appealing. In the same way that we give the voter and consumer a free choice, so the argument goes, we should give the decision maker a free choice. Thus, the argument is stated in terms of democracy or consumer sovereignty, and it is difficult for anyone to be against democracy. At the risk of making you think that I am a dictator, let me briefly outline my reasons for being opposed to this view.

(1) In the present system, the decision maker can either use the accounting reports that we give him or make his decision in the absence of that information. His choice is to use or not use our data. There is no third alternative.[2] If we were to adopt my suggestions for changing the kind of data to be included in accounting reports, the decision maker would have the same choice. Therefore, the adoption of my suggestions would be equally as 'democratic' as the present system. The only difference would be in the kind of data being reported.

(2) Decision makers are a diverse lot. They make their decisions on a wide variety of different bases. We have all heard about people who trade the market on the basis of astrological signs or arthritic pain. 'Technical analysts' on Wall Street trade the market on the basis of the 'flags', 'heads and shoulders' and 'double bottoms' they see in their charts. Given this diversity, it is an economic, if not a physical, impossibility for us to supply *all* the information that *all* decision makers want. Therefore, we must select and in the process of selection, we will fail to satisfy the wants of some decision makers. What we are arguing about then is the *basis* for selection.[3]

(3) The basis for selection that I prefer is to supply information for rational decision models. The modifier 'rational' is defined to mean those decision models that are

---

[2]This is the basis for a technical criticism of the tests that have been run to see if decision makers use accounting data. Most experiments require a 'control' of some kind. The tests would have more force if the decision makers were offered a choice between using accounting data and using some kind of control data. To put it another way, suppose we ran a test in which decision makers could choose either (1) zero information or (2) x information. I suspect that the decision makers would choose x information. A more powerful test would be to offer them the choice between x and y information.

[3]Section II was, in effect, an argument about the basis for selection. That is, it was an argument against excluding data on grounds of objectivity, realisation, etc. Thus, accountants are *now* being selective in the kind of data that they report. Indeed, they must be selective since no information system can report everything. The pertinent grounds for argument then must be the basis for selection and it is impertinent—the commission of the fallacy of alleging a non-existent difference—to argue on the grounds that one information system is selective (dictatorial) and another is not.

most likely to allow decision makers to achieve their goals. Since I don't believe that astrology allows people to achieve their stated goals, I am not interested in supplying them with an astrology report even though they use that kind of information in trading the market. For the same reason, I am not interested in supplying decision makers with some of the kinds of data now being included in accounting reports even though they use that data.

The above is only a rough sketch of the conflict. I have gone into some other aspects of the problem elsewhere.[4] Although there are a good many scattered remarks in opposition to this view, insofar as I know, there is only one article devoted exclusively to the problem.[5] As I have said before,[6] I believe that the proponents of the decision maker view have overlooked the distinction between pragmatic and semantic information. Pragmatic information is defined by the receivers' reaction to the report. For example, if I yelled 'Fire' and all of you ran to the exits, my report would be said to contain pragmatic informational content. Semantic informational content is concerned with the connection of reports to objects and events. For example, if there were a fire, my report would be said to contain semantic informational content. If there were no fire, it is semantic misinformation, or in plain English, a lie. Note that the two kinds of information are separable and that one kind does not imply anything about the other. Of course, we accountants know this from harsh experience. Everybody agrees that decision makers used the McKesson-Robbins financial statements and therefore there was pragmatic informational content. The problem was the absence of the inventory and therefore the presence of semantic misinformation.

Although many of my critics agree in principle with the decision model approach, they throw up their hands in despair at the prospect of trying to apply it. There are a great many different kinds of decision models, e.g. EOQ. PERT, Linear Programming, Capital Budgeting, etc. Such decision models are applicable to only certain kinds of decisions, e.g. inventory ordering, scheduling, allocations, investments, etc. In addition, there are a great many choice criteria that are used in reaching decisions, e.g. minimax, maximin, Hurwicz, least regret, etc. Thus, we have a great variety of decision models applicable to a variety of decision situations with a variety of proposed criteria. It appears to be impossible to set up a general information system or to design a set of general purpose financial statements which would meet the requirements of all these models. An even more difficult problem arises whenever we encounter decision situations for which there is no well defined decision model.[7]

The trick is to generalise—to try to capture the elements that are common to all decisions. Although such a generalisation, like all other generalisations, leaves out many important details, it allows us to get a handle on the problem. Let me attempt such a generalisation. All decision models require information about:

1. Alternatives $= A = \{a_1, a_2, \ldots, a_n\}$

---

[4]Sterling, *Enterprise Income*, pp. 54–61.

[5]A. Rashad Abdel-khalik, 'User Preference Ordering Value: A Model', *The Accounting Review,* July 1971, pp. 457–71.

[6]Sterling, 'Theory Construction', p. 453.

[7]See Robert R. Sterling, 'A Statement of Basic Accounting Theory: A Review Article', *Journal of Accounting Research,* Spring 1967, p. 107.

2. Consequences $= C = \{c_1, c_2, \ldots, c_n\}$

3. Preferences $= P =$ a function for ordering consequences.

Alternatives (or possible courses of action) must be presently feasible. There is no point in choosing a course of action that is not feasible. One may plan what he will do if and when an alternative becomes feasible or he may ruminate about past alternatives, but the choice is always restricted to the alternatives that are feasible at the time of the decision—the present. The alternatives must be competing in the sense that the selection of one obviates the selection of the other, and hopefully, the list would completely specify all alternatives. If alternatives are not competing, then no decision is required. One need not choose between x and y if one can select both x and y. If the list is not complete, then one may not know about the existence of a preferred alternative. Thus, a decision maker is faced with a set of alternatives, the elements of which are mutually exclusive and exhaustive. The decision maker may contemplate a broad range of possible courses of action but he must select from 'alternatives'—those courses of action that are available to the decision makers at the moment of choice.

Consequences (or outcomes or payoffs) of the alternatives lie in the future. They must be predicted. The consequences may be stated in terms of certain uncontrollable events, and then probabilities assigned to the uncontrollable events. For example, one can predict that if a_i is selected the consequence will be c_i^1 if event x_1 occurs, c_i^2 if event x_2 occurs, etc. By assigning probabilities to events, x_1, x_2, . . . and aggregating c^1, c_i^2, . . . , one can speak of 'the' consequence, c_i, associated with a_i.

Preferences are personal. Even though different decision makers are faced with the same alternatives and they predict the same consequences, they may make different decisions. This may come about from different assignments of probabilities or different choice criteria of different utility functions or simply the inexplicable choice of the decision maker. I include such things under the category of 'preferences' and in the present state of the art they are 'matters of taste' that are personal to the decision maker. Given the one to one correspondence of alternatives and consequences, the preference for a given consequence uniquely determines the alternative to be selected.

A summary of the decision process is shown in Figure 1.

FIGURE 1

The Decision Process

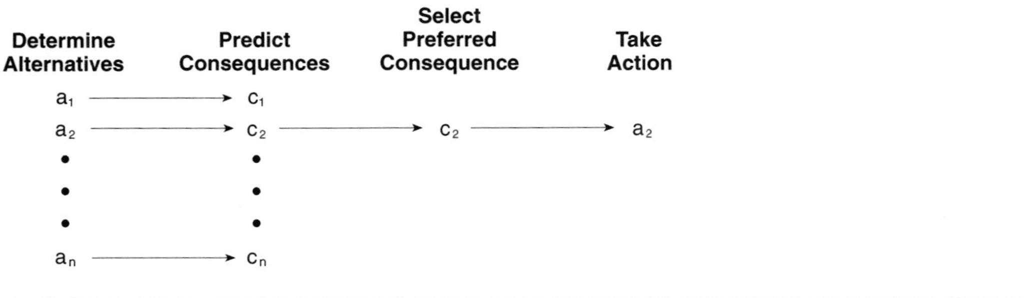

Determine Alternatives	Predict Consequences	Select Preferred Consequence	Take Action
a_1 ⟶	c_1		
a_2 ⟶	c_2 ⟶	c_2 ⟶	a_2
•	•		
•	•		
•	•		
a_n ⟶	c_n		

FIGURE 2

Information System

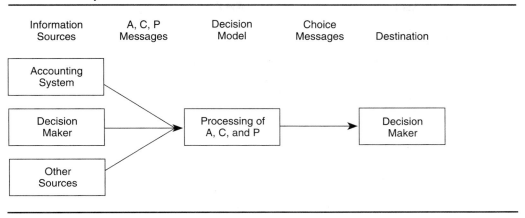

| Information Sources | A, C, P Messages | Decision Model | Choice Messages | Destination |

Decision models are abstractions which are separate and apart from decision makers. For example, the EOQ model is an idea which can be thought about separately from the persons who hold or use that idea. It is the decision *model* that requires information about alternatives, consequences and preferences. The decision maker can be thought of as a supplier of information to the decision model. Consider Figure 2.

The accounting system is also a supplier of information, but it is not necessary for it to supply all of the information required by the model. In non-feedback situations, such as providing financial statements to investors, it is impossible for the accounting system to provide information about the preferences of the decision makers. Since the decision makers already know their preferences, the point may seem to be unimportant. However, there are many accountants who have become bogged down in their efforts to design an information system because they were unable to specify the decision maker's utility function or because there were several different decision makers with different utility functions. If we view the decision maker as the supplier of this kind of information to the decision model, then this problem is bypassed, if not solved. The accounting system could then concentrate on supplying information which would aid in defining alternatives and predicting consequences.

In summary, an accounting system should be designed to provide relevant information to rational decision models. The accounting system cannot supply all the information desired by all decision makers and therefore, we must decide to exclude some kinds of information and to include other kinds. Restricting the decision models to rational ones permits the exclusion of a raft of data based upon the whims of decision makers. It permits us to concentrate on those models that have been demonstrated to be effective in achieving the decision makers' goals. Information specified by decision models may be classified as alternatives, consequences and preferences. Excluding information about preferences, on the grounds that the decision makers already possess this information, permits us to concentrate on supplying information concerning the definition of feasible alternatives and the prediction of consequences.

IV. CONFLICTING VALUATION METHODS

Although we sometimes attempt to separate the question of how to value assets from the question of how to measure income, the two are, in fact, inextricably entwined. This is indicated by the fact that we often say that our financial statements 'articulate'. It is even clearer whenever we consider the basic accounting equation.

(1) $$A = L + P$$

Almost every elementary accounting textbook has a problem which is concerned with the determination of income by utilising this equation. They assign a time index (t_i) and state the proprietorship as a residual.

(2) $$A(t_i) - L(t_i) = P(t_i)$$

Then the income (neglecting investment and disinvestment) for the period t_i to t_{i+1} is given by (3).

(3) $$P(t_{i+1}) - P(t_i) = Y$$

It is obvious that if the assets take on different values, then the income for the period will take on different values. For example, a switch from straight-line to accelerated depreciation or from FIFO to LIFO will affect both the reported asset values and the reported income. The same is true if we state the assets at their historical cost as opposed to, say, current market value. Thus, when one talks about different methods of valuation, and the conflicts between them, then one is also at the same time talking about conflicts in income measurement.

There are four major valuation methods that have been proposed in the literature:

(1) historical cost (HC),
(2) replacement cost (RC),
(3) exit values (EV), and
(4) discounted cash flows (DCF).

Some people have argued that price-level adjusted historical costs should be listed as a fifth valuation method. However, one could adjust each of the above methods for changes in price-levels and thereby add a total of four more methods. I am in favour of price-level adjustments, but I think that the selection of a valuation method is a separate problem. We must first select the valuation method(s) and *then* we can consider the necessary adjustment for price-level changes. Therefore, I will neglect the problems of price-level adjustments in this paper and concentrate on specific price changes.

The incomes that result from applying these valuation methods have been called

(1) realised income,
(2) business income
(3) realisable income, and
(4) economic income.

All of these names are somewhat inaccurate. Some economists would say that 'realisable income' is 'economic income' and therefore, they would object to the names that we have used. 'Historical cost' is somewhat inaccurate in that there are many assets on the balance sheet that are not valued at cost, e.g. cash and accounts receivable. 'Realised income' is somewhat inaccurate as, for example, when the percentage of completion method of revenue realisation is used. In addition, these methods sometimes borrow from one another. For example, HC sometimes uses DCF in accounting for bonds or notes. In the same way, some of the authors who propose, say, EV will occasionally revert to either RC or HC. Thus, none of the methods are pure. Finally, there are different procedures within each of the methods. Just as income may be calculated by using either LIFO or FIFO, and both of them referred to as 'realised income', there are different procedures within the other methods. I will not attempt to discuss all of these exceptions and differences; instead, I will concentrate on describing the major differences among the methods.

All four valuation methods use a price of some kind as the basis for valuing, but each method endorses a different price. The endorsed prices differ by their temporal location and by the market in which they are found. Both HC and RC use the prices found in the purchasing market. They differ only in the temporal location of those prices. A past (time of purchase) price is used in HC while a present (time of statement preparation) price is used in RC. Thus, except for the temporal location of the prices, RC is identical to HC. EV, by contrast, focuses on the present (time of statement preparation) prices in the selling market. EV is similar, but not identical, to the 'net realisable values' used in HC in applying the lower of cost or market rule to inventories.

DCF uses both purchase and selling prices, but it focuses on the future—the prices that will be in effect at the time of future exchanges. DCF is similar to the 'present value method' of accounting for bonds used in HC. In DCF the cash receipts from the future sale of the products and the cash expenditures for the future purchase of the factors of production are predicted and then discounted to get 'present value' or 'present worth'. Hereafter, I will substitute 'discounted value' for 'present worth' to avoid confusion.

These differences are summarised in the following matrix.

Market \ Time	Past (Purchase)	Present (Statement Preparation)	Future (Exchange)
Purchasing	HC	RC	DCF
Selling		EV	DCF

The differences in income may also be described in general terms. The revenues (asset inflows from sales) would be the same for all four methods, but the amount charged to expense would differ considerably. We all know how the allocations are made in HC. RC uses the same allocation techniques, but it costs out the quantities at their current purchase prices. The argument is that we should match current costs with current revenues and thus the line of reasoning is the same as that of many LIFO proponents. However, unlike LIFO, RC also uses current purchase prices on the balance sheet which results in including 'holding gains' (also called 'cost savings') in income. EV looks to the market to determine the expenses. Initially, the expense is the difference between the purchase price and the exit value at the date of statement preparation. Subsequently, it is the difference in the exit values at two statement preparation dates. Both

HC and RC are *allocations* (amortisations) of a purchase price on the basis of use or sale or passage of time. EV attempts to avoid the allocation problem by going to the market to determine how much the asset could be sold for. The decrease (increase) in the amount it could be sold for is the amount of the cost (gain) of using or holding that asset.

DCF recognises a gain at purchase equal to the difference between the discounted value of the products produced by the acquired asset and the face value of the cash sacrificed. The amount of the subsequent income is simply the interest earned (the interest rate times the discounted value) in exactly the same way that interest income is the yield rate times the discounted value of bonds receivable in HC. Adjustments are required in DCF whenever events are different from those predicted. These adjustments present problems similar to those encountered in HC when, say, the actual life of an asset is different from its predicted life.

There are many arguments in favour of and in opposition to all of these valuation methods. However, the proponents of the various schools rely most heavily on the usefulness or relevance criterion. Each school claims that its particular valuation method would be more useful than the others. For this reason, and also because I believe that usefulness should be the overriding criterion, I will ignore the other criteria and try to select the appropriate valuation method by applying the criterion of relevance.

V. APPLICATION OF RELEVANCE CRITERION TO MARKET DECISIONS

Although there are a good many decisions that do not involve a market exchange, in a market economy such as ours probably a majority of decisions are concerned with whether or not to make an exchange in the market. The market operates with prices, and since the conflicting valuation methods differ mainly in their endorsement of certain prices, a general consideration of prices and market decisions is pertinent to the conflict.

MARKET ALTERNATIVES

The market alternatives that are available to any person or any firm depend upon two factors:

(1) The funds that are currently available to invest in the contemplated project.

(2) The magnitude of the investment required to engage in the contemplated project.

Specifically, the funds available for a given project must be greater than or equal to the investment required for that project. Otherwise, that project is not a feasible market alternative.

Although this point is obvious, I wanted to make it explicit in order to demonstrate that 'profitability' is *not* the first nor the sole criterion for selecting projects. There are many projects which I think would be very profitable, but I cannot undertake them because my available funds are less than the required investment. For example, I would like to purchase General Motors, but since my available funds are less than the purchase price this is not a feasible alternative for me.

MARKET CONSEQUENCES

The market consequences of undertaking a given project are the future cash flows that result from that project. There may be non-market consequences which the decision maker should consider (e.g. one may be sent to jail for engaging in an illegal project or one may get satisfaction from beating the competition), but I will concentrate on the market consequences. Since these cash flows lie in the future, they must be predicted.

PREFERENCES

The decision maker is faced with an array of future cash flow magnitudes. He must select one of those magnitudes by applying his personal preference function. He may do this by converting the money magnitudes to utility magnitudes, assigning subjective probabilities to the flows under varying conditions, and utilising one of the various choice criteria. Such information is to be supplied to the decision model by the decision maker because it is a matter of personal preference.

In addition, the discount rate should be supplied by the decision maker because each decision maker is likely to have different needs for liquidity and different views on the time value of money. That is, people are likely to have different 'reservation rates' and these rates are likely to be different from the cost of capital rate of the firm. For this reason, I will distinguish 'future cash flows' (FCF) and 'discounted cash flows' (DCF) henceforth.

After appropriate adjustment for risk, I would select the project with the largest cash flows. That is, I am a maximiser. However, that is a personal preference and there may be some who have different preferences. The above discussion does *not* depend upon the assumption of profit or wealth maximisation for its validity. If one wants to minimise he can be a more efficient minimiser by following this general outline for decisions.[8]

The main point about preferences is that, as before, they are to be supplied to the decision model by the decision maker. Therefore, in the following discussion I will concentrate on supplying information about alternatives and consequences.

PRICE INTERPRETATION

The market alternatives and consequences have been defined and the preferences have been left to the decision makers. It is now necessary to give these alternatives and consequences a price interpretation. Recall that the market alternatives depend upon the available funds and the required investment. In turn, the available funds depend upon:

(1) The present selling prices of all assets held, including the 'selling price' of cash.

(2) The ability to borrow.

(3) The ability to raise equity capital.

I will consider (2) and (3) *infra*. In regard to (1), note that the present selling prices are the only prices relevant to defining the available funds. Past prices are irrelevant, because they are no

---

[8]This point should be underscored because several people have criticised my previous works for assuming profit maximisation or postulating an economic man. In the above classification scheme, the goal of the decision maker is included in the category of preferences. A maximiser's preferences will cause him to select a consequence different from the one selected by a minimiser. A satisficer will cease searching for additional alternatives whenever he has found a satisfactory consequence. Regardless of the goal, an accounting system which provided information about alternatives and consequences would aid the decision maker in achieving that goal. Of course, decision models are not usually designed to minimise, but that is simply an indication that few people are minimisers and that most minimisation problems are trivial. For example, a linear programming model could be used to search for the lowest profit-highest cost solution by simply altering the objective function, but a minimiser could more easily achieve his goal by considering the consequences of selling his product at a negative price or by burning his plant.

longer obtainable and future prices will be relevant to defining future alternatives, but they are irrelevant to defining the current alternatives. Purchase prices are obviously irrelevant if one is trying to determine how much cash he can get if he sells.

The required investment is given by:

(1) The present purchase price of assets *not* held.

(2) The present selling prices of assets held.

Obviously, if one is contemplating the purchase of an asset, then the present purchase price of that asset is relevant to the determination of whether or not the alternative is feasible. The investment required for maintaining the status quo, however, is given by the selling prices of the assets held. Since the individual or firm already holds the assets necessary to maintain the status quo, then there is no need to contemplate their purchase. Instead, the (implicit) required investment is the amount of cash that one could get if one sold those assets. That is, the decision not to disinvest is structurally identical to the decision to invest, and therefore, the required investment for continuing the status quo is the amount of cash that was not received by not disinvesting.

The future cash flows require a prediction of the future selling prices of the outputs of the project as well as the quantities that will be sold. The future selling prices of the inputs are also relevant. That is, the salvage values of productive assets at the termination or abandonment of a project are future cash inflows and are, therefore, relevant. If a project requires future replacement of productive assets or the purchase of the factors of production, then the future purchasing prices of the inputs are also relevant.

The decision requires the comparison of the future cash flows of each project. Other things equal, the decision maker can make his selection by scanning the array of future cash flows and applying his preference function. However, in this case other things are seldom equal. Usually, the required investments are not of equal magnitude. If the projects have unequal required investments, it is not possible to make a rational decision by considering only their future cash flows. One project may have large cash flows but an even larger required investment. A common method of overcoming this difficulty is to calculate the rate of return on the required investment and then compare the rates of return. Note that this method is a comparison of the required investment to the future cash flows, i.e. rate of return is the time adjusted quotient of the future cash flows and required investment. In general, whenever required investments are not equal one needs to compare the required investment to the future cash flows.

The above is simply a generalisation of the capital budgeting model, absent an explicit consideration of discounting. The capital budgeting model specifies the prediction of future cash inflows and outflows, and then the time adjusted net flows of the various projects are compared to one another or to the required investment. Since the capital budgeting model is usually applied to new projects, we tend to forget that it is also applicable to existing projects. Sometimes our predictions are wrong and sometimes we change our predictions after initiating a project. For this reason, existing projects should be re-evaluated periodically. In this re-evaluation, the decision model specifies a comparison of the *updated* prediction of cash flows to the *present* required investment. That required investment is given by the selling prices of assets held. Obviously, if one wishes to maximise, he should discontinue a project and sell the assets if the future cash flows are less than the sum of the selling prices. Just as in the case of a new project, a maximiser should not commit the required investment if it is greater than the predicted cash flows. In the case of an existing project, the required investment is the sum of the present selling prices of the assets.

In summary, a rational market decision model specifies the following prices:

(1) The present selling prices of all assets held because
    (a) when compared to (2), they define the feasible market alternatives, and
    (b) they completely define the investment required to maintain the status quo.

(2) The present purchase prices of all assets not held because
    (a) when compared to (1), they define the feasible market alternatives, and
    (b) they completely define the investment required for new projects.

(3) The future purchase and selling prices associated with a given alternative because when compared to the required investment [(1b) or (2b)], they permit a rational decision.

CREDITOR AND INVESTOR MARKET DECISION MODELS

The above analysis is general. In addition to managerial decision models it is also applicable to creditor and investor decision models. Each creditor and investor must determine the feasible alternatives by comparing the available funds to the required investments. The available funds are defined, as before, by the selling prices of the assets held (by the creditor-investor) and the ability to borrow or raise equity capital. That is, investors borrow and creditors issue equity shares, and therefore, the funds available to them are determined in exactly the same way as outlined above. The required investment for new projects is the amount of the loan application or the present purchase price of the stock. For existing projects, the required investment is the present selling price of the debt or equity instrument.

The creditor-investor decision model also calls for a comparison of the required investment to the future cash flows. In this case, the future 'selling prices' of the 'output' is the interest or dividends. The 'salvage value' is the maturity or liquidation value of the instrument. Since the project may be abandoned or aborted prior to the maturation of the debt or liquidation of the firm, the salvage value may be a future selling price of the instrument.

In short, the investor-creditor decision model specifies exactly the same prices as those given above. However, these prices refer to assets held *by the creditor-investor* and to the various prices *of the debt-equity instrument*. Strictly speaking, this is *all* that the creditor-investor needs to know. That is, after an investor has narrowed the stocks down to those that are feasible alternatives, the only thing he needs to know is their purchase prices and their future selling prices (including dividends) *in the stock market*. He can then compare and make his choice(s).

If the creditor-investor can predict these future prices without regard to the operations of the individual or firm to whom he is lending-investing, then we need go no further with this analysis. Many investors do not look beyond the securities market when they make such predictions. They act as if the price fluctuations in the stock market were completely independent of the economic fluctuations of the firms that issue the stock. If this is true, then the stock market is simply a lottery with no underlying economic meaning, and we accountants should quit wasting our time and paper by issuing financial statements. Instead, we should draw the income numbers out of a hat and thereby determine who has won and lost. However, I, personally, am not interested in the stock market qua lottery. I believe that stock prices (as well as dividends, interest and ability to repay loans) do in fact depend upon the economic conditions of the firms. Moreover, I believe that stock prices *ought* to depend upon the economic conditions of the firms and that if we accountants supplied better information about the firms, the stock prices would conform more closely to those conditions. In short, I believe that a well designed investor-creditor decision model should specify information about the states and operations of the firms. I am not trying to dictate to investors. If they want to trade the market by 'reading the tape', then that is their business. If they can be successful on that basis, then more power to them. However, I believe that information about the firms should be available to investors, whether they use it or not. For all these reasons, I will concentrate upon the information specified by a rational creditor-investor decision model and assume that other information about the market will be supplied from non-accounting sources.

FUTURE CASH FLOWS OF THE FIRM.   The ability of a firm to service a debt, pay dividends or simply to survive depend upon its future cash flows. Thus, the future cash flows of a debt-equity instrument depend upon the future cash flows of the firm. It follows that the future cash flows of the firm are relevant to the creditor-investor.[9] The creditor-investor may make his own predictions of the flows or be supplied those predictions by someone else. The predictor may assign probabilities to the completion of the project and the abandonment of the project and predict the cash flows under both conditions. Many other refinements of this kind could be listed. The only point that I want to make is that the future cash flows of the firm are relevant to the investor-creditor, because the future flows of debt-equity instruments depend upon them.

I would urge that the prediction of the future cash flows used by the creditor-investor be independent of the prediction made by the management. This is not to impugn the honesty of managements, but rather to note that managements are likely to be optimistic about their own projects. If they were not, they would not have proposed them. Thus, an independent prediction is called for. This means that, as a minimum, the creditor-investor needs to know *which* projects are planned by management. Then, the creditor-investor (or his agent) can independently assess the probability of success and independently predict the future purchase and selling prices of the project, as well as applying his personal discount rate.

SELLING PRICES OF FIRM ASSETS.   Whenever someone lends, invests or purchases, he is acquiring some value that exists now as well as some values that are predicted to exist in the near and distant future. The presently existing values can vary from zero to 100 per cent of the purchase price. For example, if I 'purchase' a ten dollar bill with two fives, then the presently existing value of the ten is 100 per cent of the purchase price. Moreover, the ten will not increase in value in the future. On the other hand, if I grubstake a miner in return for a share of his find, then the presently existing value is zero—*all* of the value that I have purchased lies in the future. That future value may be much greater than $10, or it may be zero. Obviously, grubstaking a miner is much riskier than purchasing a ten dollar bill. This risk relationship of the presently existing value to the purchase price is true in general. The smaller the presently existing value in relation to the purchase price, other things equal, the higher the risk.

This means that the present selling prices of the assets held (and the selling prices that will exist immediately after purchase) are relevant to the decision. Perhaps the point in regard

---

[9]Again, there are many other factors that are relevant, such as the 'character' of debtors and the 'resilience' and 'ingenuity' of management. However, I will focus on the more immediate market factors.

to an investor can be made clear by considering mutual funds. Suppose you have the option to purchase one share of either the L or the N fund for $100. Now the managers of both funds would promise you the moon if the SEC would let them get by with it. Therefore, you ought to make an independent prediction of the future 'performance' of both funds. Suppose you predict that the selling prices x years from now will be $140 and $120 for the shares of the L and N funds, respectively. Without further analysis, you can make your selection. If you are a maximiser, you will select the L fund. However, let me add two facts and then see if you agree that these facts should be specified by a well-designed decision model.

The L fund is a load fund and the amount of the load is $90. The N fund is a no-load fund. That is, the per share exit value[10] is $10 for the L fund and $100 for the N fund. Therefore, the value of the assets held by L must increase by 1,300 per cent to reach the predicted price while the increase required by N is only 20 per cent. Almost all of the value of L lies in the future while most of the value of N exists presently. Other things equal, L is a much riskier investment.

As many people have correctly pointed out, one should go ahead and buy a load fund if one thinks that it will out-perform a no-load fund by more than the amount of the load. However, the amount of the load is relevant to a well-designed decision model. This amount is determinable if the present selling prices of the assets held are disclosed.

There is also a 'load' or 'premium' on the price of the stock of industrial firms. The price of some stock is several hundred times its per share exit value. In such cases the purchased value lies almost wholly in the future. Other things equal, the greater the portion of the value that lies in the future the higher the risk. That is, if the firm does not perform in accordance with expectations the price of the stock is likely to drop drastically. By contrast, some stocks sell at a 'discount'—the price of the stock is less than its per share exit value. Closed-end funds, for example, often sell at a discount. The future price and dividends of discounted stock still depend upon the future cash flows of the firm, but, other things equal, it is much less risky. The value presently exists and therefore even if the firm liquidated immediately the investor would not lose. Indeed, he would profit.

Therefore, I conclude that the magnitude of the discount or premium is relevant to a well-designed decision model. That accountants know this is evidenced by their lower of cost or market rule. Although formally applicable only to inventories, it is also applied to a great many other assets. For example, I know of a case where the auditors insisted upon writing the value of land down to 'fair market value', even though they knew that this write-down would be likely to result in the liquidation of the firm. The land had been purchased at a price which reflected the expectation of mineral deposits which had failed to materialise. The auditors evidently thought that the 'fair market value' (exit value?) of this land was relevant to investors and creditors.

The problem is that this is a one-way rule. I know of another case where the stock of a retail chain is selling at about $10 per share. Based on its poor earnings, this is a reasonable price. That is, if it continues in the future as in the past, its future cash flows will be meagre and its reported income even less. However, this firm owns the land upon which its stores are built and the per share exit value of the land alone is conservatively estimated to be $40 per

---

[10]The sum of the present selling prices of the assets held by the fund less the liabilities divided by the number of shares outstanding.

share. This land is carried on the balance sheet at its ancient historical cost of about 20¢ per share. I believe that the exit value of that land is equally as relevant in this case as in the above case.[11] If the *Gerstle* v. *Gamble* case[12] is taken as evidence, it appears that the SEC also believes that exit values are relevant to investors.

Although these cases are extreme, they illustrate the fact that the price of stock ought to depend upon the presently existing exit values of the firm as well as depending upon the future cash flows of the firm.

I have spoken only of investors above because creditors have long recognised the relevance of the selling prices of assets. They are usually willing to loan only at a discount. That is, if a particular asset is pledged, they are willing to loan only a fraction of that asset's selling price. If they are general creditors, they are willing to loan only a fraction of the conservative (lower of cost or market) value of the total assets. Of course, creditors also look to the future cash flows of firms, if for no other reason than that they would prefer to avoid the expense of foreclosure. However, the selling prices are also relevant to them and they explicitly recognise the risk relationship when they speak of the amount of the discount or the amount of the net worth as providing a 'cushion of safety'.

VI. IMPLICATIONS FOR WEALTH AND INCOME MEASUREMENT

If the above analysis is correct and complete, then the implications are fairly straightforward. We noticed that

(*a*)   Present selling prices (EV) of assets held by the firm,

(*b*)   Present purchase prices (RC) of assets not held, and

(*c*)   Future cash flows (FCF) of the firm are relevant to well-designed market decision models of managers, investors and creditors.

Conspicuous by their absence from this list are past purchase prices (HC). I do not find them specified by any market decision model, and therefore, I conclude that they are irrelevant. This is a conclusion that I have held for many years and one that I have spoken about and written about many times. On one occasion, I challenged all readers to demonstrate just one case where historical costs were relevant to economic decisions.[13] It has now been five years since that challenge was made, and no one has published a direct reply. Since then, several people have argued for historical cost on the grounds of objectivity, feasibility, etc. This is the reason why I said in Section II that there were conflicting views on the objectives of accounting. Other people have argued for historical costs because managers, creditors and investors do, in fact, use the financial statements that we give them. However, the fact that they

---

[11]The only reason why I don't buy all the stock and liquidate the firm is that I lack the required investment of $10.00 per share for over two million shares.

[12]*Gerstle* v *Gamble-Skogmo,* 298 Federal Supplement 66 (1969).

[13]Sterling, *ASOBAT Review,* p. 111.

use HC does not indicate that they would use HC if other information were supplied or that they ought to use them, in the sense that other information may be more likely to allow them to achieve their goals. This is the reason why I discussed the conflict between decision makers and decision models in Section III. If we really mean it when we say that accounting data should be useful or relevant, then we should demonstrate the relevance of HC or the superiority of HC to other valuation methods, and if we cannot do that, then we should abandon HC as a valuation method.

I exclude present purchase prices (RC) for a different reason. Present purchase prices of the assets *not* held are relevant to market decisions models. The source of information about these prices is the market itself, and they are already being supplied to management by the purchasing department. Financial statements report on assets held, and since present purchase prices are not relevant to assets held, they should not be used as a basis for the valuation of assets on financial statements.[14]

Every decision requires a prediction of the future consequences of various alternatives. For this reason, if I thought it were possible, I would urge that accountants report future cash flows. Knowledge of the future is always the most valuable kind of information. The reason it is so valuable is that it is so scarce. We have no way of knowing what the future holds, and there are many conflicting views about it. The existence of these conflicting views of the future partially makes the market operate. Except for specialisation and liquidity requirements, there would be no market if buyers held the same view of the future as sellers. This is most obvious in the commodity markets, where there is a long for every short. The speculators hold diametrically opposed views of the future—the long (buyer) expects a price increase and the short (seller) expects a price decrease. One of them must be wrong. The same thing happens in varying degrees in other markets. Thus, differing predictions of the future are an inherent part of the operation of a market.

It is this difficulty which causes me to reject the notion that accountants ought to report FCF. First, we cannot report FCF, we can only report predictions of FCF. If we were perfect predictors, we would destroy the market, i.e. prices would be set equal to the discounted value of the future cash flows and, except for liquidity requirements and specialisation, no exchange would occur. For example, if we all had access to future issues of the *Wall Street Journal,* the price of every stock would be bid so as to equal the discounted value of the known future prices and dividends.[15]

---

[14]Future purchase prices of planned replacements and additions are also relevant since they are a component of FCF. Many people argue that income should be calculated on the basis of RC because it is a good predictor of FCF. This may or may not be true. It is an empirical question that cannot be settled here. It is important to note, however, that the claim of this argument is not that RC are relevant per se but rather that RC are good predictors of FCF. Note that this is my interpretation of the argument. It is usually stated that RC income is superior to other income concepts because it is a better predictor of future *RC income.* Using this reasoning, one could argue that straight-line depreciation is the superior depreciation concept because it is a perfect predictor of future straight-line depreciation. Obviously, this is not what the RC proponents mean. I think they mean that business income is the superior concept because it is a good predictor of a relevant property (FCF), not that it is superior because it is a good predictor of itself.

[15]*Supra* I said that the reason that knowledge of the future is so valuable is that it is so scarce. Note that in this case, it would not be valuable because it is not scarce. That is, the price of exclusive access to future issues of the *Wall Street Journal* would be extremely high. However, when everyone has equal access, the price would probably be about the same as the price of today's issue.

Of course, we really needn't worry about destroying the market because it is not very likely that we will be perfect predictors. That is, accountants are, in the present state of the art, about as prone to err in predicting FCF as are decision makers. Thus, we have the choice of (1) not predicting or (2) presenting erroneous predictions. Erroneous predictions are not relevant to decision models. Indeed, they are likely to be harmful and, given the attitude of the courts about accountants' legal liability, this harm is likely to redound to accountants. For these reasons, I don't think that accountants should at this time report their predictions of FCF.[16] Since DCF is simply FCF discounted by a rate and since different rates are appropriate for different decision makers, it follows *a fortiori* that DCF is not an acceptable method of measuring income and wealth.

We noted that selling prices (EV) were relevant to all three market decision models. They are necessary to define market alternatives, they express the investment required to hold assets and they are a component of a risk indicator. For all of these reasons, I conclude that the items on the balance sheet should be valued at their present selling prices. Since income is defined as the difference between wealth (net worth) at two points in time, it follows that the income statement would be an explanation of the changes in the exit values on two successive balance sheets.

---

[16]This leaves the predictions of FCF up to the decision makers. This presents no problem insofar as managements are concerned. A major part of managements' function is to try to peer into the future in order to select the preferred consequence. The problem is that the managements' decisions, based upon *their* predictions, affect the well being of the creditor-investor. Unless the creditor-investor is willing to rely solely upon the managements' predictions, he must make independent predictions. In order for the creditor-investor to make an independent prediction, he must know, at least in broad outline, the managements' plans. The budget is the most likely source of information about managerial plans. The creditor-investor can peruse this budget and then make (or have his agent make) a prediction of the future cash flows that will result. Therefore, I would urge that we include a partially audited management budget in our reports because it provides the basis for an independent prediction of the future cash flows.

Thus, I am not opposed to expanding the accounting function so that it includes information about expected futures. On the contrary, I think that we should provide all the relevant information that we can. However, I don't think that erroneous predictions are relevant. (This includes those erroneous predictions which are disguised as 'past' cost allocations in HC. Recall those costs capitalised because of the 'future benefits' expected from the Edsel, Cleopatra, TFX, supersonic transports, etc.) If we get to the point where our ability to predict is better than that of the decision makers, then I will argue that we ought to report our predictions. In the meantime, I think the best we can do is to supply information to decision makers which will aid them in making their predictions.

ACCOUNTING FOR INFLATION

R. J. Chambers

Conventional (historical cost based) accounting is almost universally recognized to be defective under inflationary conditions. Experience under these conditions has prompted the search for the dependable alternative.

There have been under consideration two major alternatives or supplements to conventional accounting: (1) current purchasing power (C.P.P.) accounting, and (2) replacement price accounting (R.P.A.) of which current cost accounting is a variety.

The first method deals with ways of taking account of some of the effects of changes in the purchasing power of money, but disregards the effects of changes in the prices of particular assets. The second proposes the use of the replacement prices of assets in financial statements, but disregards the general effects of changes in the purchasing power of money. As both types of change occur concurrently during inflationary periods, both of the above methods are partial or incomplete, and therefore potentially misleading.

This Exposure Draft deals with a method of accounting—continuously contemporary accounting—which takes into account both changes in particular prices and changes in the general level of prices. It is thus more comprehensive than the two methods previously mentioned. And the financial statements it yields are up-to-date, more realistic and more readily comprehensible.

R.J. Chambers, "Accounting for Inflation," Exposure Draft, University of Sydney, Australia, September 1975. Reprinted by permission of the author.

Part I—Accounting Generally

1. The Discussion and Conclusions to be Presented Will Have Reference to Business Firms Generally.

Any method of business accounting should be expected to be serviceable in substantially the same ways, no matter what the form of ownership of the business to which accounts relate. However, the most extensive array of uses of accounting information is exemplified by the relationships between companies and their shareholders, creditors and others. For this reason much of the discussion will relate to companies and company accounting. But, because the principles or rules which emerge are equally pertinent to companies and other types of business ownership, the general term "business firm" or simply "firm" will be commonly used. Also the terms "net profit" and "net income" will be used interchangeably, as synonyms.

2. Financial Statements Are Expected to Represent Fairly and in Up-to-Date Terms the Financial Characteristics of Firms.

The products of the accounting process are dated balance sheets and income (profit and loss) statements. These are expected, by the laws relating to companies, to give a true and fair view of the financial positions and of the result of companies as at the dates and for the periods to which they relate. They are put to use by a variety of parties; by actual and potential investors and creditors; by investment advisers and underwriters and trustees for creditors; by tribunals concerned with wages and prices; and by governmental authorities for fiscal and other regulatory purposes. The decisions and actions of all of these parties are taken in the light of what they know, at the time, of the past results and present financial positions of companies (or of firms generally). Unless the financial statements of companies correspond fairly well with their actual positions and results, actions based upon them may affect adversely, and quite unexpectedly, the interests of companies or of other parties related to them.

3. The Survival and Growth of Firms Depends on Their Command of Money and Money's Worth.

The actions of all the above mentioned parties are directly related to money receipts and payments of a company—receipts by way of sales income, loans or credits, subsidies or bounties, and the proceeds of new share issues; payments by way of purchases, wages, taxes, interest, and loan repayments. The capacity of a company to grow or to change its operations, on a small or large scale, as new opportunities arise and present operations become less attractive, depends on its command of money or money's worth. In the ordinary course of events, companies are expected to pay their debts to others when they fall due. In some circumstances they may find it worth while, or be forced, to repay debts before they fall due. Generally, then, the ability to meet debts owed is a condition of survival. For all these reasons, it is a matter of importance that the managers of companies, and that other parties having financial interests in companies, shall know from time to time the money and money's worth at the command of companies and their outstanding financial obligations.

4. FINANCIAL POSITION IS A DATED RELATIONSHIP BETWEEN ASSETS AND EQUITIES.

The money and money's worth at the command of a company at a point of time is given by the sum of its holdings of cash and receivables and the market (resale) prices of its other (non-monetary) assets. The resale price of an asset at a given date is its money equivalent at that date. Possession of the asset is financially equal to possession of the sum of money representing its resale price. It is therefore possible to add amounts of cash and receivables and the money equivalents of other assets to obtain a financially significant aggregate. The total amount of liabilities to short and long term creditors represents money claims against the aggregate money's worth of assets. The difference between total assets and total liabilities is a genuine money amount, since the amounts of total assets and total liabilities are genuine money amounts. This difference represents the residual interest of shareholders or owners in the total assets, or the total investment at risk in the business of the company. It also represents the amount of net assets, or assets financed otherwise than by credit.

5. THE AMOUNT OF INCOME IS DEDUCED FROM CHANGES IN DATED FINANCIAL POSITIONS.

A balance sheet in which assets are represented at their money equivalents gives to all users of it an up-to-date indication of the total wealth of a company at a point of time and total claims against or interests in that wealth. Given two such balance sheets, in the absence of inflation, the increment in the amount of net assets represents the retained profit of the intervening period (provided there has been no new share issue). The sum of retained profit and the dividends paid in the period is the net profit or net income of the period. Net income may be calculated by setting out the several classes of gain or loss of a company in a period. But the amount so obtained is necessarily equal to the difference between the opening and closing money amounts of net assets. It is a genuine increment in money's worth, since the net assets figures are genuine money amounts (para. 4).

6. FINANCIAL POSITIONS AND RESULTS ARE AGGREGATIVE; THEIR ELEMENTS MUST SATISFY THE RULES OF ADDITION AND RELATION.

Total wealth, total liabilities, the amount of net assets, the calculation of net profits, all entail addition and subtraction. Other calculations made by investors and creditors, such as rates of return and debt to equity ratios, are relations between aggregates. All particular elements of financial statements must therefore be capable of proper addition and relation. The money amounts and money equivalents referred to in the two previous paragraphs satisfy this condition. By contrast, no logical or financial significance can be assigned to the sum of an amount of money and the purchase price, past, present or future (including replacement price) of any good. No such sum can properly be related to any debt outstanding, or to any plan to purchase goods or services, or to pay taxes and dividends.

7. Financial Positions and Results Are Both the Consequences of Past Actions and the Cases of Future Actions.

The financial position of a firm is a consequence of past (historical) events up to the date for which it is ascertained. No future event or expectation of a future event has any bearing on it. But given an ascertained financial position (and other information and expectations), choices may be made among the courses of action available to the firm. If at a given date the liquidity of a firm is strained, action to restore its liquidity is necessary. If at a given date a firm is heavily in debt, liquidity cannot readily be restored by further borrowing. If the results of the immediately past period are unsatisfactory in any sense, action must be taken to improve the result in the following period. All deliberate actions having financial consequences must be considered in the light of the aggregative financial characteristics of the firm at the time of choice. And all estimations of the probable financial consequences of future actions must be based on the position of the firm at the time of choice of future courses of action. Financial position as described is the one common element in all calculations relating to choices of future actions.

8. The Money Equivalents of Assets, the Purchase Prices (Replacement Prices) of Assets and the User-Values of Assets Are Used in Conjunction; None Is a Substitute for the Other.

If a prospective course of action entails the "replacement" of an asset, it is necessary to know the money equivalent of the present asset and the purchase price of the new asset. If a prospective action entails the purchase of additional assets, their purchase prices must be known. Whether or not any such course is financially "feasible" can only be ascertained by comparison of those purchase prices with the money equivalents of present assets, or some selection of present assets. Which is to be preferred of the feasible courses of action is indicated, inter alia, by comparisons of the expected net proceeds of the alternative projects or investments in assets. Expected net proceeds, or present (discounted) values, are user-values. They are personal estimates based on expectations of the future; they are therefore subjective. They represent the expected outcomes of specific possible future actions. They cannot therefore be used in balance sheets as indicative of the financial feasibility of *any* course of action, even of those courses to which they relate. In short, the money equivalents of assets, the purchase prices of goods not presently held, and user-values of assets or projects are used when considering specific possible courses of action. But each is used for its own purpose and in its own way. None is a substitute for the other. None of them may properly be added together. Only the money equivalent of assets are properly useable for the representation of financial position at a given date.

Part II—The Effects of Inflation

9. Changes in the Structure and in the General Level of Prices Occur Concurrently but Not Equally.

In an inflationary period two things occur which affect the positions and results of companies. The prices of particular goods change relatively to one another. There is a change in the *struc-*

ture of prices. Such changes may occur at any time as the wants of consumers change, technology changes or the policies and outputs of companies change (collectively, supply and demand conditions). There is also a change in the general *level* of prices. "Inflation" is descriptive of a rise in the general level of prices, or of its counterpart, a fall in the general purchasing power of money. When inflation occurs all prices do not rise to the same extent or at the same time. Some may fall as rises in others force business firms and consumers to change their spending habits. Inflation may thus cause changes in the structure of prices, to the benefit of some firms and to the detriment of others. The beneficial or detrimental effects may arise from changes in the money equivalents of assets held, or from changes in the profit margins obtainable for goods and services sold.

10. THE EFFECTS ON A FIRM OF CHANGES IN THE STRUCTURE AND LEVEL OF PRICES CAN ONLY BE ASCERTAINED IN THE AGGREGATE.

When changes in the structure of prices and changes in the general level of prices occur in the same period, it is not possible to say that any particular price change is caused by inflation, or by the shift in the relation between the supply and demand conditions, or partly by the one and partly by the other. All that is known is that prices and the level of prices are different from those of an earlier date. Nevertheless, it is possible to calculate the aggregate effects of changes in prices and the general level of prices on the positions and results of firms. Because changes in particular prices and changes in the general level of prices influence one another, the effects of both should be brought into account. One cannot be considered as isolated from the other. Whatever the outcome, it cannot be said whether any part of the result is due solely to managerial judgements or solely to accidental or unforeseeable factors. Managers may be expected to use their best judgements at all times. Only the results in aggregate will indicate with what effect firms have been able to meet the conditions through which they have passed.

11. THE CONVENTIONAL MONEY UNIT, IN TERMS OF WHICH FINANCIAL POSITIONS ARE REPRESENTED, IS EQUALLY SERVICEABLE FOR THAT PURPOSE IN INFLATION.

Financial position has been described as the dated relationship between amounts of assets and equities (para. 4). The dating of a financial statement represents both (a) that the money unit used in it has reference to that date and (b) that the number of money units appearing beside any item is the appropriate money equivalent of that item at that date. To suppose otherwise would be anachronistic, and confusing. The money unit is by its nature the unit of general purchasing power and debt-paying power at any specified date whatever, and the unit in which the money equivalents (resale prices) of assets are expressed. That the same nominal money unit may have a different general purchasing power at some other date is of no consequence when determining a dated financial position.

12. THE INCREMENT IN THE NOMINAL AMOUNT OF NET ASSETS DURING A YEAR IS NOT SERVICEABLE AS INDICATING NET INCOME IN AN INFLATIONARY PERIOD.

Calculation of net income in the manner described in para 5 brings into account the effects of all changes in the money equivalents of assets, in the absence of inflation. If particular assets have risen or fallen in price during a year, for whatever reason, these changes in the structure of prices will be captured by taking the resale prices of assets at the opening and closing dates of the year. Since, in the absence of inflation, there is no change in the general purchasing power of money, the net income so calculated will represent a genuine increment in the general purchasing power or debt-paying power of the net assets of a firm. Part of it will be the resultant of trading costs and revenues, and part the resultant of rises and falls in the money equivalents of assets since the beginning of the period or since (the subsequent) date of purchase. The rises and falls during the year in the money equivalents of assets held at the end of a year may be described as *price variation adjustments*. But if the purchasing power of the money unit has changed during the year, the difference between the opening and closing amounts of net assets will not represent a genuine increment in general purchasing or debt-paying power.

13. Provision Must Be Made for the Loss of Purchasing Power in an Inflationary Period of the Amount of Net Assets (or Capital Employed) at the Beginning of the Accounting Period.

Money holdings and claims to fixed amounts of money may be described as monetary assets. Their money equivalents at any date may be discovered directly. All other assets are nonmonetary assets. Their money equivalents at any date must be discovered by reference to market resale prices at or near that date. Monetary assets held during an inflationary period lose general purchasing power. Likewise every dollar representing the money equivalent of nonmonetary assets at the beginning of a period loses general purchasing power. And likewise every dollar owed during an inflationary period loses general purchasing power; borrowings thus constitute a "hedge" against losses in the purchasing power of money. By subtraction, the amount at risk of loss in general purchasing power during inflation is the amount of net assets (total assets less liabilities) at the beginning of the accounting period. The amount of the loss thus sustained must be made good out of other surpluses before it can be said that a surplus in the nature of net income has arisen. This amount may be described as a *capital maintenance adjustment,* since its object is to secure that, in calculating net income, provision is made for the maintenance of the general purchasing power of the opening amount of net assets (or capital employed).

It may be noted that, across a whole community, the aggregate amount of price variation adjustments might be expected to correspond with the aggregate amount of capital maintenance adjustments, since the general price index is indicative of the average of changes in specific prices. But particular firms are affected differentially by changes in prices and in the price level. Rises in the prices of particular goods do not correspond with or offset falls in the general purchasing power of money. That is why the aggregates of both should be taken separately in the accounts of firms.

14. Net Income Is the Algebraic Sum of Trading Surpluses, Price Variation Adjustments and the Capital Maintenance Adjustment.

The amount of the capital maintenance adjustment is the opening amount of net assets multiplied by the proportionate change in the general level of prices. Thus, if a firm begins a period with net assets of $1,000 and an index of changes in the general level of prices rises from 130 to 143 in the period, the amount of the capital maintenance adjustment is $1,000 × 13/130, or $100. A general price index is used because the amount of net assets is a genuine dated money sum, irrespective of the composition of assets, and because the firm is considered to be free to lay out any part of its assets or the increment in its assets in any way it pleases. The index to be used would be chosen on the basis of competent statistical advice. From the two preceding paragraphs, net income will be the algebraic sum of trading surpluses, price variation adjustments and the capital maintenance adjustment. The amount charged as capital maintenance adjustment will be credited to a capital maintenance reserve. If any part of this reserve were appropriated as a dividend, it would impair the general purchasing power of the opening amount of net assets. (See also para 34).

Part III—General Principles of Continuously Contemporary Accounting

15. The Method of Accounting Described Is Called Continuously Contemporary Accounting (CoCoA).[1]

Asset valuations are brought up-to-date, at least at the end of each accounting period, by reference to independent sources of information. Those valuations are in terms of the purchasing power unit at the time. That the balance sheet is a dated statement implies that the amounts stated in it relate to that date and that the dollars in which those amounts are expressed are dollars of dated purchasing power (see para 11). CoCoA satisfies this requirement. Shareholders' equity amounts are augmented by the capital maintenance adjustment periodically and the balance of net income is a sum also expressed in dollars of the same dated purchasing power as other items in the balance sheet. All reported balances of a given date are therefore contemporary with that date. There are no prices of different dates nor purchasing power units of different dates in the balance sheet of any date. Hence the description "continuously contemporary accounting."

16. Accounts May Be Brought up to Date Periodically or More Frequently.

The price changes affecting a firm may be occasional or frequent, and individually large or small. As up-to-date information on a firm's assets and liabilities is the only dependable basis for managerial action, the accounts may be continually adjusted for changes in the prices of assets. In principle this is the most desirable mode of accounting. But for external reporting it is sufficient to bring the account balances to their money equivalents at the end of each reporting period. Accounts could be kept just as they are presently kept during the accounting

---

[1]The text of the original publication (1975) used "CCA" with reference to continuously contemporary accounting, an abbreviation used by the author since 1967. That abbreviation has since been widely used with reference to "current cost accounting." To avoid confusion, in this reprint "CoCoA" is used as an abbreviation for continuously contemporary accounting. Some minor changes have also been made in the prefatory note and the introductory material of Appendix B.

period. But at the end of the period all account balances are adjusted to their current money equivalents. The variations of money equivalents from book balances are summarized and charged or credited, as price variation adjustments, in the income account. And of course the capital maintenance adjustment is computed and charged. The method may be called "continuously contemporary" because, in principle, accounts can be kept continuously up-to-date, even though in practice adjustments may be made less frequently than price changes occur. Under either process the results will be exactly the same.

17. CoCoA Conforms with the Established Principle of Periodical, Independent Verification of Account Balances (the Objectivity Principle).

To verify the physical existence of, and legal title to, assets at balance date is a well established principle. Independent checking of cash balances and receivables balances has long been regarded as a necessary safeguard against misrepresentation. But the same process of verification is not applied under traditional historical cost accounting, to the money amounts assigned to other assets. The mere checking of physical existence and legal title is inconsistent with the fact that financial statements relate to the *financial* characteristics of firms, not to physical or purely legal characteristics. The financial characteristics of assets should be independently verified, no less than other characteristics. CoCoA applies this principle uniformly to all assets.

18. CoCoA Conforms with the Well-Established Accrual Principle.

The accrual principle entails accounting for changes in the financial characteristics of a firm independently of the conversion of assets and obligations to cash. Revenue is brought into account when customers are billed; earlier, that is, than cash is received from customers. Depreciation is brought into account periodically; that is, long before the diminution in value of an asset is discovered on its resale. Applications of the principle pervade current practice. Yet there are also numerous cases in traditional practice where the principle is not applied. Changes in the prices of assets are not accrued usually, unless they are downward changes. And quite generally the effects of advantageous changes are not accrued but the effects of disadvantageous changes are accrued; thus depreciation is charged, but appreciation is not brought into account. These inconsistencies cannot yield realistic and up-to-date statements of financial position and results. CoCoA avoids inconsistency by applying the accrual principle uniformly to all assets and liabilities, and hence also to shareholders' equity.

19. CoCoA Conforms with the Well-Established Going Concern Principle.

The going concern principle entails that the financial position as represented in a balance sheet shall be indicative of the position of a firm as a going concern. The significant financial characteristics of a going concern are its ability to pay its debts when due, to pay for its supplies of goods and labour service, to change the composition of its assets, liabilities and operations if the present composition hinders its survival or growth, and the ability to earn a rate of profit consistent with the risks of the business. The ability of a firm to pay its debts, to pay for its necessary inputs, to borrow on the security of its assets, and to change the composition of its assets and operations, is indicated only if assets are shown at their money equivalents, since all the matters mentioned entail receipts and payments of money. The ability of a firm to earn an adequate rate of profit may be judged only if the profit earned is a genuine increment in purchasing power and the amount of net assets (or shareholders' equity) to which it is related is a genuine money sum. The use of market (resale) prices in CoCoA has nothing to do with liquidation of a business; it is simply the only way to find the present money equivalents of non-monetary assets from time to time.

20. CoCoA Satisfies the Requirements of Stewardship Accounts.

As financial statements indicate in general terms the disposition of assets and increments in assets from time to time they are regarded as the basis upon which the performance of a company and its management may be judged. Such judgements must be supposed to be made periodically in respect of the year recently past; their formal expression lies in the resolutions of annual general meetings. It is necessary, therefore, to know the amount of the assets available for use and disposition by the management at the beginning of each year, if a satisfactory account is to be given of the use, disposition and increase of assets in that year. If the amounts of assets from time to time were stated on any basis other than their money equivalents, there would be no firm and satisfactory basis for determining the use and disposition of assets. Since all uses and dispositions in a period entail movements of money or money equivalents, financial statements based on the money equivalents of assets provide information on which periodical performance may fairly be judged.

21. CoCoA Adheres Closely to the Principle of Periodical Accounting.

Financial statements generally purport to represent dated positions and the results of defined periods. But the effects of events in one period are frequently allowed to influence what is reported of another. This occurs whenever some future event or outcome is anticipated (as in the usual calculation of depreciation charges), or whenever some actual effect on results or position is "deferred" for recognition in a later period. CoCoA makes no such concessions, on the ground that reports which do not represent the effects of events in a defined period cannot properly be interpreted, singly or in series, by reference to the dated context of business events and circumstances. It may be objected that to base accounts on a dated selling price could be misleading if the price were anomalous. But exactly the same can be said of dated purchase prices which are used in other forms of accounting. In any case the anomaly might be expected to be explained rather than concealed.

Part IV—The Determination of Money Equivalents

22. Any Asset for Which There Is Not a Present Resale Price Cannot Be Considered to Have a Present Financial Significance.

A company may have assets for which there is no present resale price. They may have a high user-value (see para 8), but they cannot be considered to have financial significance in the sense of purchasing or debt-paying power or as security for loans. Investors, creditors, suppliers and others would be misinformed of the financial capacity for action by balance sheets in which money amounts were assigned to assets having no current money equivalents. The assets to which this rule applies include some work in progress, and specialized plant and equipment for which there is no market in the ordinary course of business. The same rule applies to expenditures on exploratory or developmental work which has yielded no vendible product or asset. The notion of conservatism in traditional accounting would tend to have the same effect as the treatment suggested. But that notion is vague and loosely applied, whereas the principle here stated is definite and it yields information which is relevant to the judgements and decisions of parties financially interested in companies. If it is desired, on any ground, to indicate that a company has assets, or has incurred costs and outlays, having no present money equivalent, parenthetical or footnote information may be given.

23. THE DETERMINATION OF THE MONEY EQUIVALENTS OF ASSETS AT A STATED DATE IS NECESSARILY APPROXIMATE.

Prices may vary from place to place for the same goods on any given day. What is required is a fair approximation to the current money equivalent of each asset. This may require the exercise of judgement, but abuse of judgement is constrained by the necessity of approximating a definite characteristic of the asset and by the prices discovered at or about the balance date. In any case, no form of accounting escapes the use of dated prices; even historical cost accounting uses dated prices which may or may not have been the only prices, or representative prices, at dates of purchase. Any attempt to distort results and positions by the choice of prices which are not fair approximations to money equivalents is constrained by the independent inspection and judgement of auditors. It is also constrained by the fact that the whole of the asset balances of one year determine the amounts of the price variation adjustments, and hence the income, of the following year. There are no alternative permissible rules by resort to which this constraint may be avoided.

24. RESALE PRICES ARE ACCESSIBLE TO MOST FIRMS FOR MOST ASSETS.

All proposals considered in anticipation of purchases and the settlement of debts include at some point sums of money which are presently available, or which could shortly become available by the sale of assets (inventory or other assets), or which could be borrowed on the security of assets. In the latter two cases some approximation to the money equivalent or resale price of non-monetary assets is required. Changes in the prices of goods and services used and in the markets for a firm's products may at any time force its management to reconsider the costs of its present mode of operations. And if it is assumed that one of the functions of management is the pursuit of efficiency or economies, the possibility of changes in its operations and assets will be under examination from time to time. It follows that some person or persons will be acquainted with the approximate market prices of the assets the firm presently holds, and with changes in those prices from time to time. It is possible for any firm to draw on its purchasing officers, salesmen, engineers and project evaluation officers for information on the prices of assets; and to have recourse to prices published in trade journals and the general press as well as direct inquiry. A great deal of information of this kind is readily available without recourse to specialist valuers. But valuations by specialists on an asset resale basis may also be obtained, where necessary of themselves, or as a check on the information available otherwise.

25. Receivables: The Amount to Be Reported Will be the Amount Deemed, on the Evidence Available, to Be Recoverable from Debtors in the Ordinary Course of Business.

Generally this will be the face value or book value of debtors' accounts, for that is the amount of the claims against debtors at balance date. There is no need to speculate about the possibility that some debtors may take advantage of discounts offered for prompt settlement. Whether they do so or not, the consequence will lie in the following period and will be then reported. Where there is evidence that the full amount of a debt will not be recovered, the amount of the debt may be reduced or written off according to the evidence then available. The amount of receivables yielded by these rules will be the best approximation to the money equivalent of receivables in the light of the information then available, without speculative allowances for what may subsequently occur.

26. Inventories Will Be Valued Consistently on the Basis of Their Present Market Selling Prices in the Parcels or Quantities in Which They Are Customarily Sold by the Firm.

In the ordinary course of events, raw materials will have a somewhat lower money equivalent than their recent purchase prices, since the user is not a trader in those materials. Work in progress inventories may have a substantially lower money equivalent than their costs, for such work in progress may not be salable in its then state and condition. Finished goods inventories will generally have higher money equivalents (current selling prices) than their costs.

　　To report inventories at market resale prices is not novel. Nor is it novel that work in progress may appear at a low or zero value; for the traditional rule, "lower of cost and market," should produce the same result. By comparison with the recorded costs, the higher money equivalents of finished goods will to some extent "offset" the lower money equivalents of raw materials and work in progress. But whether the resulting aggregate differs much or little from a cost-based aggregate is less important than the fact that a uniform rule—market price—is used throughout, and that the aggregate has a definite, dated money significance which "cost" and the "lower of cost and market" do not have.

27. Plant and Equipment Will Be Valued at Market Resale Prices, in the Units or Combinations in Which, in the Ordinary Course of Business, They Are Bought, Sold, or Put out of Use.

The object of the traditional method of accounting for plant is to record its cost and to provide out of periodical revenues sufficient to reduce that cost to its market resale price, or scrap value, by the time it is put out of service. The method of CoCoA has exactly the same object; but it is attained by direct reference to market prices year by year, rather than by relying on an arithmetical formula and disregarding the actual changes, up or down, in market prices from time to time. Market resale prices may be estimated from information obtained by the methods mentioned in para 24. The prices sought are not prices obtainable on liquidation or under duress. They are to be the best approximations to the money equivalents of assets in the ordinary course of business. To determine the best approximation entails skill and judgement; but judgement is to be applied to the information obtainable on prices, not to construct imaginative valuations. Checks on the possibility of manipulation are (i) that auditors must be satisfied that the assigned market values are based on current price information, (ii) that excessive understatement reduces the profit of the year and the asset backing of shares and debt at the end of the year, and (iii) that excessive overstatement reduces the profit of a subsequent year and improperly boosts the asset backing of shares and debt. The use of market resale prices may entail heavy charges, due to the sharp drop from cost to money equivalent of some plant, in the early years of use. Some assets may have virtually no resale price, but high user-value. Such occurrences necessarily reduce the adaptive capacity of firms, their command of money and money's worth. The reduction is made explicit in the amounts by charges against revenues, or against other shareholders' equity accounts if the amounts are extraordinary. (See also para 22 above).

28. LAND AND BUILDINGS WILL BE VALUED AT MARKET RESALE PRICES, OR APPROXIMATIONS BASED ON OFFICIAL VALUATIONS, PRICES OF SIMILAR PROPERTY AND EXPERT VALUATIONS.

The same considerations apply to land and buildings as to plant and equipment. Local government valuations (for taxing or rating purposes) provide evidence additional to that from other sources. No single valuation or price need necessarily be taken as a proper approximation to money equivalent; but the chosen valuation must be justifiable in the circumstances. The checks mentioned in para 27 tend to limit arbitrary or unusual valuations.

29. INVESTMENTS IN THE SHARES OF OTHER COMPANIES WILL BE VALUED AT NET MARKET PRICES WHERE THE SHARES ARE PUBLICLY TRADED; OTHERWISE AT THE PROPORTIONATE INTEREST IN THE NET ASSETS OF THE INVESTEE COMPANY.

Holdings of listed shares are readily priced by reference to stock exchange quotations (i.e. "buyer"). Allowance may be made for commissions payable on sale, to obtain the net money equivalent of the investment. There is no readily available and dependable price for non-listed shares. An alternative is required which yields the best approximation to the money equivalent of the investment. If CoCoA is used uniformly, the proportionate interest in the net assets of the investee will provide an approximation; for the accounts of the investee will represent assets at money equivalents. Strictly the amount so calculated will not be the same as a share price; but it is a better approximation than the original cost, or a valuation related to user-value (e.g. based on capitalized prospective earnings).

30. LIABILITIES WILL BE REPRESENTED BY THE AMOUNTS OWED AND PAYABLE TO CREDITORS IN THE ORDINARY COURSE OF BUSINESS.

No amount shall be shown as a liability unless it represents an amount owed to and legally recoverable by a creditor. Whether the due date is near or distant is immaterial. Long-dated obligations may become due and payable if any circumstance threatens the security of creditors.

Part V—Owners' Equity Accounts

31. All Transactions of a Period Will Be Recorded at Their Actual Effective Prices, and So Charged or Credited in the Income (Profit and Loss) Account.

All transactions have determinate effects on balances of cash or receivables and payables. The general purchasing power of the cash receipts and payments during an inflationary period will change from time to time. But the aggregate effect of changes in the purchasing power of the money unit is brought into account by way of the capital maintenance adjustment at the end of the accounting period. By showing the actual amounts of receipts and payments, all such amounts are traceable, and identical with their counterparts elsewhere in the accounts.

32. Price Variation Accounts Will Be Credited with All Increases in the Book Values of Assets, and Debited with All Decreases, during the Period.

The book balances of accounts, other than monetary item accounts, may be adjusted for changes in asset prices during the year. The valuation of all assets at the end of the year at their resale prices gives effect to all variations in prices which have not previously been brought into account. The amounts by which the book values of assets are increased (decreased) during the year to correspond with market resale prices will be debited (credited) to the asset accounts and credited (debited) to the price variation accounts. There may be price variation accounts for as many separate asset classes as is deemed necessary. Under CoCoA, the depreciation account, representing a fall in the market resale price of an asset or class of assets, is a price variation account. The price variation accounts are closed by transfer of their balances to the income account.

33. The Capital Maintenance Adjustment Will Be Calculated by Applying to the Opening Amount of Net Assets the Proportionate Change in the Index of Changes in the General Level of Prices.

The net amount of price variations will tend to be (but will not necessarily be) positive during inflation. But these are gross increments, and the resulting asset balances are in units of year-end purchasing power. The full effect of the change in the purchasing power of money on the results of the year is given by the calculation of the capital maintenance adjustment. The calculation is a mathematically proper calculation, since under CoCoA the opening amount of net assets is a genuine, dated money sum to which a change in the index may legitimately be applied. The capital maintenance adjustment is debited in the income account (in inflationary years).

34. The Amount of the Capital Maintenance Adjustment Will Be Credited Proportionately to the Opening Balance of Undistributed Profits and to Other Opening Balances of Owners' Equity Accounts.

The amount of net assets at the beginning of a year is equal to the sum of the balances of the owners' equity accounts. The object of crediting the amount of the capital maintenance adjustment to owners' equity accounts is to restate the aggregate of the opening balances in units of purchasing power at the end of the year. Part of the capital maintenance adjustment may therefore be credited directly to the retained profits account, a part equal to the opening balance of retained profits multiplied by the proportionate change in the index of changes in the general level of prices. The remainder of the adjustment will be the appropriate amount to credit to a capital maintenance reserve. Where the amount subscribed by shareholders is required to be shown in balance sheets, this money amount may be carried indefinitely in the accounts. Following the above rules, the sum of the amount described and the balance of the capital maintenance reserve at the end of any year will be the purchasing power equivalent at that time of all sums deemed to have been subscribed by shareholders.

35. Where There Are Outstanding Issues of Preference Shares, These Shall Be Treated as Equivalent to Outstanding Debt, for the Purpose of Calculating the Capital Maintenance Adjustment.

Preference shares are, like debts, redeemable at fixed, contractual money amounts. Therefore, like debts, they provide a hedge against the effects of changes in the general purchasing power of money. The amount of outstanding preference shares will therefore be deducted (together with all other liabilities) from total assets to obtain the amount of net assets to be used in the calculation of the capital maintenance adjustment.

36. Net Income of a Year Will Be the Algebraic Sum of Transaction Surpluses (Para 31), Price Variation Adjustments (Para 32), and the Capital Maintenance Adjustment (Para 33).

The balance of the income account after incorporating the consequences of transactions and the price variation and capital maintenance adjustments will be the net income in units of year-end purchasing power. The whole of it may be paid out without impairing the purchasing power of the opening amount of net assets. Or if it or any part of it is transferred to a retained profits account, the whole of the balance of that account could be paid out (as dividends) without impairing the purchasing power of the amounts subscribed or deemed to have been subscribed by ordinary shareholders.

Part VI—Some Features of the System

37. All Original Entries Relate to the Amounts of Transactions; All Adjustments Are Based on Information from Sources External to the Firm.

These features ensure that all amounts represent actually experienced or accrued effects on a firm's position and results. Doubts about the magnitudes of accrued effects are resolved by recourse to external information, not to internal formulae. There are no arbitrary apportionments, no questionable assumptions about future events or uniformities, and no arbitrary demarcations between outcomes which are and which are not controllable, in some sense, by firms and their managements. The accounts and financial statements may be audited, therefore, with reference to independent sources of information; and the representations they make will be pertinent to the financial relations of the firm with the rest of the world.

38. CoCoA Applies a Single Valuation Rule Throughout, Avoiding the Addition of Different Kinds of Magnitudes in Balance Sheets.

There are no optional rules for asset valuation, as there are in all other systems. There is no possibility, therefore, that the significance of aggregates will be distorted by the addition of magnitudes of different kinds. Although the transactions figures and price variation adjustments are magnitudes expressed in money units of different purchasing powers, the combined effect of them and the capital maintenance adjustment is a net income in units of the same purchasing power as other items in a closing balance sheet.

39. CoCoA Entails Uniform Valuation Rules for All Companies, Making Possible Comparison of the Financial Features of Companies.

Under accounting systems which allow optional valuation rules, the financial significance of the resulting figures is always open to doubt, and strictly to direct comparison of financial magnitudes, rates and ratios is possible. Financial statements based on market resale prices, on the other hand, yield technically proper and practically significant indications of the composition of assets, of current ratios, debt to equity ratios, and rates of return—all of which may be directly compared with corresponding features of other companies and with corresponding features of the same company in prior years.

40. Some of the Figures Yielded by CoCoA May Seem Unusual by Contrast with Traditional Accounting; They Should Be Considered, Not Separately, but as Parts of the Whole System.

To value finished goods inventory at market price, when higher than cost, may seem unusual; and to value raw materials and work in progress at current market price, when lower than cost, may also seem unusual. It may appear that to calculate net income on such a footing is to "anticipate profits." But in the first place, the use of one valuation rule yields a comprehensible aggregate. Second, the "unusual" effects are to some extent offsetting. And third, the overriding charge for the capital maintenance adjustment is built-in protection against the overstatement of periodical net income. The same reasoning applies to the bringing to account of changes in the market prices of other non-monetary assets.

41. No Right or Advantage Which Arises Only on Disposal of the Company as a Whole Is Brought into the Accounts.

CoCoA is strictly concerned with a company as a going concern. No value is assigned to such things as developmental costs, goodwill and specialized plant having no resale value, which are realizable only on liquidation or disposal of part or whole of the company. Insofar as any amount has been paid out in respect of these items, it constitutes a sunk cost, and is not available as such for any financial purpose in the ordinary course of business. Such amounts may be charged against shareholders' equity directly, or treated in the manner of the "double account" system, above the balance sheet proper. This treatment is in accordance with the practice of financial analysis, and avoids the impression that the company has assets which are convertible to cash in the ordinary course of business. The mixing of subjective user-values with objective financial values has led, in many cases, to serious misdirection of investors and other financial supporters (see also para 8).

42. The Information Given by CoCoA Is Consistent with That Demanded by Lenders and Analysts of Business Affairs, and with the Sense of the Legislation Relating to Financial Disclosure.

Lenders on the security of property are concerned with the up-to-date market values of assets; they alone constitute effective cover for debt. Press discussion of company affairs has drawn attention repeatedly to the differences between "accounting values" and market values—both when specific prices have been rising and when they have been falling. The statutory requirements relating to financial disclosure have increasingly stipulated the publication (by footnote or otherwise) of market values, or have indicated that realizable value is important information to users of financial statements. Examples are the disclosure of the market values of listed securities, general provisions relating to the valuation of current assets, provisions relating to the valuation of property charged as security by borrowing companies, and the U.K. provision requiring directors to comment on differences between market values and book values of interests in property. CoCoA does systematically what all these practices, in piecemeal fashion, imply.

43. The Financial Statements Yielded by CoCoA Constitute, in Series, a Continuous History of the Financial Affairs of a Company.

Because the method of CoCoA embraces the consequences of actual transactions and of external changes which affect the wealth and results of companies, the statements for any period and at any date are all-inclusive. Taken in series, they represent a continuous record of shifts in wealth, solvency, gearing or leverage and achieved results. They are historical, avoiding the defects of dated speculation about the future; they are fully historical, avoiding the defects of partial representation of what has occurred up to any date or between any two dates.

Part VII—Summary

44. The Rules of Continuously Contemporary Accounting Are:

(a) All assets should be stated at the best approximation to their money equivalents, in their then state and condition, at the date of the balance sheet.

(b)   All transactions shall be accounted for in the amounts at which they occurred.

(c)   All variations from the costs of book values of assets, which are not already brought into account by the sale of assets in the period, shall be brought into the income account at the end of the period as price variation adjustments.

(d)   There shall be charged against total revenues, in calculating net income, the amount of a capital maintenance adjustment, so that the amount of net income is a surplus by reference to the maintenance of the general purchasing power of the opening amount of net assets.

(e)   Net income is the algebraic sum of the outcomes of transactions, price variation adjustments and the capital maintenance adjustment.

APPENDIX A

ILLUSTRATION OF METHOD OF CONTINUOUSLY CONTEMPORARY ACCOUNTING

The simplified example which follows traces the recording of transactions, the making of closing adjustments and the derivation of the final statements. All transactions are recorded at their cost throughout the year. The closing price adjustments convert closing book balances to their ascertained money equivalents, represented in the final two columns of the Work Sheet. The workings are shown fully in the Work Sheet. The transactions and adjustments are alphabetically keyed, in the following description and in the Work Sheet, so that the counterparts of all entries may be traced. The figures in the columns headed "Balances" are the money equivalents at the respective dates.

The paragraph numbers in the right hand column of the table of data are the paragraphs in the text of this Draft where the accounting treatment is described.

APPENDIX B

COMPARATIVE EVALUATION OF PRICE LEVEL ADJUSTED HISTORICAL COST ACCOUNTING [C.P.P.] REPLACEMENT PRICE ACCOUNTING [R.P.A.] AND CONTINUOUSLY CONTEMPORARY ACCOUNTING [CoCoA]

If a choice is to be made from the above alternatives to historical cost accounting, it must be based on the respective capacities of the systems to provide information which is unambiguous and significant for the purposes of investors, creditors, managers and others. There are many particular calculations and comparisons which these parties, and others concerned with the regulation and assistance of business, may make. The three systems may therefore be ranked according to their capacities to give reliable, significant and readily understandable figures. That system should be considered as the best which satisfies these tests.

The following assessment indicates whether or not each system satisfies the "test" points. For the purpose of making the assessment, the three systems have been analyzed in detail. The

Transactions of the Year		$	Para.
A	Credit sales	410	31
B	Receivables collected	390	31
C	Raw materials purchased (on credit)	160	31
D	Suppliers on credit paid	140	31
E	Wages and other costs (to Work in progress)	90	31
F	Raw materials to Work in Progress	145	
G	Work in progress to Finished Goods	225	
H	Cost of finished goods to Income Account	270	
J	Administrative and other cash costs	60	31
K	Interest paid	4	31
L	Taxes paid	20	31
M	Dividends paid	14	31
N	Dividends received	2	31
P	Plant purchased	25	31

Year-end Adjustments		$	Para.
Price variation adjustments (differences between book values and ascertained money equivalents at year-end)			
Q	—raw materials	10	32
R	—work in progress	15	32
S	—finished goods	−55	32
T	—plant and buildings	20	32
U	—land	−6	32
V	—shares	3	32
W	Provision for taxes	30	30
X	Provision for dividends	26	30
Capital maintenance adjustment (assuming the general price index rose by 10 per cent in the year). Apply this to the opening balance.			
Y	—undistributed profits (71 × 10/100)	7	34
Z	—capital maintenance reserve (150 × 10/100)	15	34
AA	Net profit transferred to Undistributed profits	39	36

WORKSHEET FOR YEAR ENDED 31 DECEMBER 19x4

Assets	Balances 31 Dec. 19x3 Dr	Cr	Transactions and Adjustments Dr	Cr	Balances 31 Dec. 19x4 Dr	Cr
Cash	20		390(B) 2(N)	140(D) 90(E) 60(J) 4(K) 20(L) 14(M) 25(P)	59	
Trade debtors (receivables)	40		410(A)	390(B)	60	
Inventories —raw materials	25		160(C)	145(F) 10(Q)	30	
—work in progress	30		145(F) 90(E)	225(G) 15(R)	25	
—finished goods	80		225(G) 55(S)	270(H)	90	

Investments in listed shares	15			3(V)	12	
Plant and buildings	80		25(P)	20(T)	85	
Land	40		6(U)		46	
Equities						
Trade creditors (payables)		30	140(D)	160(C)		50
Provision for taxes		20	20(L)	30(W)		30
Provision for dividends		14	14(M)	26(X)		26
Long-term creditors (10% p.a.)		25				25
Preferred shareholders (10% p.a.)		20				20
Ordinary shareholders						
—paid in		120				120
—capital maintenance						
reserve		30		15(Z)		45
—undistributed		71	26(X)	7(Y)		91
profits				39(AA)		
Income (profit and loss) items						
Sales				410(A)		
Finished goods sold—book value			270(H)			
Price variation adjustments						
—raw materials			10(Q)			
—work in progress			15(R)			
—finished goods				55(S)		
—plant and buildings			20(T)			
—land				6(U)		
—shares			3(V)			
Administrative and other cash costs			60(J)			
Interest paid			4(K)			
Dividends received				2(N)		
Provision for taxes			30(W)			
Capital maintenance adjustment						
—undistributed profits			7(Y)			
—capital maintenance reserve			15(Z)			
Net profit			39(AA)			
Totals	330	330	2,181	2,181	407	407

INCOME [PROFIT AND LOSS] ACCOUNT
FOR THE YEAR ENDED 31 DECEMBER 19x4

Sales			410
Dividends received			2
			412
Finished goods sold (book value)		270	
Inventory price variation adjustments (net)		(30)	
Depreciation, plant and buildings		20	
Price variation adjustment, land		(6)	
Price variation adjustment, shares		3	
Administrative costs		60	
Interest paid		4	
Capital maintenance adjustment			
—undistributed profits	7		
—capital maintenance reserve	15		343
Profit before tax			69
Provision for taxes			30
Net income			39

BALANCE SHEETS AT 31 DECEMBER

	19x3	19x4
Assets		
Cash	20	59
Trade debtors	40	60
Inventories	135	145
Investments in listed shares	15	12
Plant and buildings	80	85
Land	40	46
	330	407
Equities		
Trade creditors	30	50
Provision for taxes	20	30
Provision for dividends	14	26
Long term creditors (10%)	25	25
Preferred shareholders (10% p.a.)	20	20
Ordinary shareholders		
—paid in	120	120
—capital maintenance reserve	30	45
—undistributed profits	71	91
	330	407

Note: All assets are shown at the best available approximations to their money equivalents at the respective balance dates.

analyses are lengthy; they may be found in Chambers, *Price Variation and Inflation Accounting* (1980). For present purposes the three systems are described in terms of their salient features. The descriptions are brief and do not cope with the many variations of each "system-type" that occur in the literature. However, they are sufficient to identify the general elements of each of the types of system.

CURRENT PURCHASING POWER ACCOUNTING (C.P.P.)   The general basis of asset valuation is, for monetary assets their face values, for non-monetary assets, original cost "indexed" by changes in an index of the general level of prices. Discretionary variations from the rule for non-monetary assets are permissible. Periodical charges against gross revenues in respect of non-monetary assets are based on the "indexed" cost figures. Gains or losses of purchasing power in respect of monetary items are brought into account in income calculation.

CONTINUOUSLY CONTEMPORARY ACCOUNTING (COCOA)   The general basis of asset valuation is the money's worth, or money equivalents, of assets, which in the case of non-monetary assets means the best approximation to their resale prices at balance date. Charges against (or credits to) gross revenues are based on changes in the money equivalents of assets. Gains or losses of purchasing power are brought into account in respect of the whole of the opening amount for the year of net assets (or net owners' equity) by use of a readily calculated capital maintenance adjustment.

There are possible tests beside those listed below. There is, for example, the cost of doing the accounting. As C.P.P. and R.P.A. require numerous calculations to be made additional to the processing of original entries, and CoCoA requires only one additional calculation, the last is the least costly. There is the cost of getting the closing balance sheet valuations. Under C.P.P. (taking the historical cost accounts and supplementary C.P.P. accounts together), there are costs of getting several valuations and choosing between alternative valuation rules. Under R.P.A., there are the costs of getting replacement prices and choosing between alternative valuation rules. Under CoCoA, there are the costs of getting values according to only one valuation rule; and, as para 24 of the main text indicates, most of the valuations required are generally accessible. It could also be shown that CoCoA is superior in respect of most of the general "principles" of accounting; consistency of method, application of the accrual principle, representation of the facts of a company as a going concern, periodical matching of revenues and costs, and so on.

However, as financial statements are expected to be serviceable to their users, all the tests which follow relate to the usefulness of the products of the three systems.

EVALUATION

	CPP	RPA	CoCoA
1. Are assets shown at their money (or purchasing power) equivalents at each balance date?	No	No	Yes
2. Does net income, as calculated, represent a genuine increment in purchasing power up to balance date?	No	No	Yes
3. Can particular figures in balance sheets properly be added and related?	No	No	Yes

Monetary items are, in all systems, represented by money equivalents. It is logically improper and practically misleading to add to these figures any others which are not money equivalents. Hence the answer to (3). From (1), (2) and (3) flow the following consequences:

	CPP	RPA	CoCoA
4. Does the balance sheet yield a proper current ratio?	No	No	Yes
5. Does the balance sheet yield a proper debt to equity ratio?	No	No	Yes
6. Do the statements yield a proper rate of return?	No	No	Yes
7. Does the aggregate of asset values fairly represent gross wealth?	No	No	Yes

To make certain judgements or decisions it is necessary to compare the positions and results of different companies as at a given time and of the same company in successive years. Comparisons of the first kind are invalid unless all companies use the same valuation rules; comparisons of the second kind are invalid unless a given company uses the same rules from

year to year and those rules embrace all types of change in financial position and results.
Therefore:

	CPP	RPA	CoCoA
8. Is the rate of return technically comparable with the rate of return on other types of investment?	No	No	Yes
9. Are the aggregates and ratios yielded comparable from year to year and fair indicators of trends?	No	No	Yes
10. Are the main ratios comparable as between firms?	No	No	Yes

The information in financial statements is used by managers and by outsiders in a variety of
settings. The particulars and aggregates must be understandable by and useful to those parties.

	CPP	RPA	CoCoA
11. Are the figures free of ambiguity and equally interpretable by and useful to managers and others?	No	No	Yes
12. Do particular asset figures represent amounts of money accessible for alternative use?	No	No	Yes
13. Are the figures a firm basis from which to calculate prospective results and positions?	No	No	Yes
14. Does the net asset figure suggest a minimum acceptable takeover bid?	No	No	Yes
15. Are the statements fair and serviceable for negotiations and other relations with public and other bodies?	No	No	Yes
16. Are the statements complete as statements of results and position, needing no supplementary information or statements?	No	No	Yes
17. Are the statements a fair basis for periodical "stewardship" evaluation?	No	No	Yes
18. Do the statements give a true and fair view of financial results and position?	No	No	Yes
19. Are the amounts representing assets and liabilities verifiable independently of the company's internal calculations?	No	No	Yes

No specific reference has been made above to inflation or its effects, except by references to
purchasing power (1), (2), and to supplementary statements (16). There are several specific
tests, however, which should be satisfied.

	CPP	RPA	CoCoA
20. Are retrospective corrections or adjustments to previously reported figures avoided?	No	No	Yes
21. Are any adjustments made in respect of changes in the prices of particular assets?	No	Yes	Yes
22. Are any adjustments made in respect of changes in the purchasing power of money?	Yes	Yes	Yes
23. Are adjustments made for the gain or loss of purchasing power during each period in respect of all assets and liabilities?	No	No	Yes
24. Is the method of accounting a method of accounting for inflation?	No	No	Yes

Two further points might be made. Although C.P.P. accounting makes reference to current purchasing power, a C.P.P. balance sheet does *not* represent assets by amounts which are in fact their current purchasing power (or money) equivalents. The point is covered in (1) above; but it may escape notice because of the description of the system.

Secondly, although replacement price accounting purports to provide for the replacement of assets by charges against gross revenues, the figures it yields do *not* indicate whether or not a firm could in fact replace those assets; a replacement price valuation does not represent purchasing power at the command of the firm, yet purchasing power is the only means of buying a "replacement" asset.

These inconsistencies with their apparent or avowed aims score against the two systems mentioned.

The practical superiority of CoCoA is demonstrated.

ON THE CORRESPONDENCE BETWEEN REPLACEMENT COST INCOME AND ECONOMIC INCOME

Lawrence Revsine

Research is needed to establish the degree of correspondence between information generated by various measurement processes and the data needs of the users towards whom the resultant information is directed. Hopefully, knowledge about such linkages between detailed user decision processes and information required to satisfy the decision models will facilitate realization of a primary function of accounting—the provision of relevant information to decision-makers.

The accounting literature contains little decision-oriented research concerning the relevance of replacement cost income to a given, defined use. Nevertheless, it is possible to reconstruct from the literature a justification for the dissemination of replacement cost reports to investors.[1] This justification is based on the assumption that replacement cost income is a

The author is indebted to members of his doctoral committee at Northwestern University, particularly Professors John H. Myers (now of Indiana University), Thomas R. Prince, and Alfred Rappaport, for their counsel and guidance in the preparation of the dissertation upon which this study is based. Furthermore, the comments of Professor Nicholas Dopuch of the University of Chicago, and Professors Norton M. Bedford, James Wesley Deskins, James C. McKeown, and Frederick L. Neumann, colleagues at the University of Illinois, were particularly helpful. Financial assistance by the Ford Foundation, which supported the dissertation, is gratefully acknowledged.

Lawrence Revsine, "On the Correspondence between Replacement Cost Income and Economic Income," *The Accounting Review,* July 1970, 512–523. Reprinted by permission of the American Accounting Association.

[1]The term investor as used in this paper refers to parties divorced from management who buy or sell, or contemplate buying or selling, ownership interest in an enterprise. The designation "investor" undoubtedly encompasses many distinct subclassifications. That is, the decision model (and thus perhaps the data needs) of the speculative investor conceivably differs from that of "widowed and orphaned" investors. Although we will not specify a particular type of investor in this paper, whenever the term appears, a need for a relatively long-term time horizon for data will be assumed.

surrogate for economic income.[2,3] Economic income measurement embodies changes in the service potential of assets. Since the change in the service potential of assets is often regarded as an ideal income measure for investors,[4] the indirect approximation of this ideal by replacement cost income would explain its relevance to investors.

Beaver, Kennelly and Voss maintain that before we empirically test the predictive ability of a concept, the theory supporting such contentions must be developed.[5] However, the notion that replacement cost income represents an indirect measure of the results of economic income (hereafter referred to as the "indirect measurement hypothesis") has never been rigorously examined by its proponents. Therefore, in this paper we will develop an *a priori* model which will be used to assess the theoretical validity of the indirect measurement hypothesis.

THE INDIRECT MEASUREMENT HYPOTHESIS

REFERENCES IN THE LITERATURE

A brief examination of prior references to the indirect measurement hypothesis in the accounting literature accomplishes two objectives. First, it indicates that some accounting theorists have—at least implicitly—used the supposed relationship between replacement cost income and economic income as a rationale for replacement cost reporting. Second, these passing references should indicate that the basic nature of the assumed relationship between the two concepts remains to be explored.

Illustrative of the support given to the indirect measurement hypothesis in the literature is the statement by Zeff:

---

[2]Proponents of this surrogate relationship argument implicitly suggest that historical cost income is not as accurate an approximation of economic income as is replacement cost income. Since this issue has been treated elsewhere in the literature [see Sidney S. Alexander (revised by David Solomons), "Income Measurement in a Dynamic Economy," *Studies in Accounting Theory,* ed. W. T. Baxter and S. Davidson (Richard D. Irwin, Inc., 1962), pp. 174–188.], we need not dwell on it here.

The particular replacement cost income concept apparently implicit to these contentions of a surrogate relationship is essentially similar to the entry value concept of Edwards and Bell. [Edgar O. Edwards and Philip W. Bell. *The Theory and Measurement of Business Income,* (The University of California Press, 1961).] The specific economic income concept which this replacement cost concept supposedly approximates is measured as the difference between the beginning and end of the period net present value of future flows expected to be generated by owned assets.

In the remainder of this paper, whenever the term economic income is used, it should be understood to be a probabilistic expected value rather than a deterministic value. Furthermore, for ease of exposition, we will assume in the development which follows that no changes occur in prevailing interest rates; hence, changes in economic income can be attributed solely to underlying changes in the service potential of assets.

[3]An enumeration of the theorists who have posited this surrogate relationship is found in footnotes 6, 7, 8, and 9, *infra*.

[4]See, for example, John B. Canning, *The Economics of Accountancy* (Ronald Press Co., 1929), p. 184 ff.; The Committee on Accounting Concepts and Standards, "Accounting and Reporting Standards for Corporate Financial Statements 1957 Revision," *The Accounting Review,* XXXII (October 1957), p. 539; and Harold Bierman, Jr. and Sidney Davidson, "The Income Concept—Value Increment or Earnings Predictor," *The Accounting Review,* XLIV (April 1969), pp. 240–241.

[5]William H. Beaver, John W. Kennelly, and William M. Voss, "Predictive Ability as a Criterion for the Evaluation of Accounting Data," *The Accounting Review,* XLIII (October 1968), p. 677.

> But it can be argued that [Edwards and Bell's] "business profit" is not too bad an approximation of the current increment in the present value of future net receipts [economic income].[6]

Corbin advances a similar view:

> Given a satisfactory degree of competition, the prices of assets in the market place would then be based on estimates of their future income streams made by many independent individuals; market prices would serve as objective, indirect estimates of value. One could go to the stock exchanges to get present value estimates for stock and bonds, to the commodities markets or dealers' catalogues for inventories and equipment, to the real estate markets for land and buildings, etc. In this manner the values of all assets and liabilities, *except Goodwill,* could be determined indirectly each period, in order to calculate net income as the increase in an enterprise's net [present] value during the period.[7]

Other authors have made similar explicit contentions that replacement cost income represents an indirect measure of economic income.[8] In addition, the indirect measurement hypothesis is implicit in certain other replacement cost income studies.[9]

However, none of these references contain a detailed examination of the conceptual foundation for the indirect measurement hypothesis. Nor is such an examination found in other studies which are highly critical of the indirect measurement hypothesis.[10] Therefore, in the next section we will explore the basic nature of the relationship between replacement cost income and economic income.

THEORETICAL FOUNDATION

In this section, we will develop a model which provides the heretofore absent theoretical foundation for the indirect measurement hypothesis. We will see that in a perfectly competitive economy, the correspondence between replacement cost income and economic income is precise. Later, we will utilize the developed model to assess the validity of the indirect measurement hypothesis in an imperfect, but more realistic, competitive environment.

Before we develop this foundation for the indirect measurement hypothesis, we should isolate several characteristics of perfectly competitive economies which merit special empha-

---

[6]Stephen A. Zeff, "Replacement Cost: Member of the Family, Welcome Guest, or Intruder?" *The Accounting Review,* XXXVII (October 1962), p. 623. However, in a later article [Stephen A. Zeff and W. David Maxwell, "Holding Gains on Fixed Assets—A Demurer," *The Accounting Review,* XL (January 1965), p. 70], Professors Zeff and Maxwell seem to recant this earlier position.

[7]Donald A. Corbin, "The Revolution in Accounting," *The Accounting Review,* XXXVII (October 1962) p. 630.

[8]See, for example, Henry W. Sweeney, "Income," *The Accounting Review,* VIII (December, 1933), p. 325, and his earlier article, "Capital," *The Accounting Review,* VIII (September, 1933), pp. 189–191; and Joel Dean, "Measurement of Real Economic Earnings of a Machinery Manufacturer," *The Accounting Review,* XXIX (April 1954), p. 257.

[9]See, for example, Edwards and Bell, *Theory and Measurement,* p. 25; Norton M. Bedford, *Income Determination Theory: An Accounting Framework* (Addison-Wesley Publishing Company, Inc., 1965), p. 91; and George J. Staubus, "Current Cash Equivalent for Assets: A Dissent," *The Accounting Review,* XLII (October 1967), pp. 650–661. Professor Staubus explicitly refers to the asset valuation case. His comments extend to the income determination case by implication only.

[10]Robert L. Dickens and John O. Blackburn, "Holding Gains on Fixed Assets: An Element of Business Income?" *The Accounting Review,* XXXIX (April 1964), pp. 312–329; and Howard J. Snavely, "Current Cost for Long-Lived Assets: A Critical View," *The Accounting Review,* XLIV (April 1969), pp. 344–353.

sis. First, perfect competition implies the existence of perfect resource mobility. All firms are assumed able to adjust capital levels instantaneously in response to changed market conditions. Second, as a consequence of this resource mobility and other characteristics of a perfectly competitive economy,[11] the price of every asset at the beginning of the ith period (P_i) is equal to the discounted present value at the beginning of the ith period of the net cash flows expected to be generated by asset operations (V_i); i.e.,

$$(1) \qquad\qquad P_i = V_i$$

Finally, at any moment in time, all firms in a perfectly competitive economy have identical expectations regarding cash flows to be generated by owned assets.[12]

Economic income (as the term is used in this study) is measured as the change, over some period of time, in the value of a firm's assets. The total value of a firm's assets at any point in time can be determined by discounting, at some normal rate of return, the expected net cash flows from asset utilization. The total economic income figure which results from a comparison of beginning and ending period asset values can be fragmented into two components: (1) expected income, and (2) unexpected income.[13] The expected income (I_6) component of total

---

[11] These other characteristics of a perfectly competitive economy are: (1) each buyer and seller is so small in relation to the market in which he operates that he cannot influence the price of what is sold therein, and (2) there are no artificial constraints placed on prices, supply, or demand. See, for example, Kalman J. Cohen and Richard M. Cyert, *Theory of the Firm: Resource Allocation in a Market Economy*, (Prentice-Hall, Inc., 1965), pp. 49–51.

[12] This is a derivative of the familiar perfect knowledge assumption. Since this general characteristic of perfect competition is frequently misunderstood, amplification is warranted. In this regard Cohen and Cyert state (*ibid.*, p. 50);

"This [perfect knowledge] assumption should be interpreted as meaning that all buyers and sellers in the market are aware of all current opportunities. . . . *We do not assume perfect ability to forecast the future, but only perfect knowledge of current opportunities.*" [Emphasis supplied]

[13] J. R. Hicks, *Value and Capital*, 2d ed. (Clarendon Press, 1946), pp. 171–188; Alexander (revised by Solomons), "Income Measurement," pp. 174–188; and Bedford, *Income Determination Theory*, pp. 25–27. If for simplicity we assume that all cash flows occur on the last day of each period, these two components of economic income can be isolated symbolically in the following manner:

$$(Ye)_i = V_{i+1} - V_i$$

where $(Ye)_i$ represents the economic income for the ith period, V_i is the envisioned value of the firm's assets at the beginning of the ith period, and V_{i+1} is the envisioned value of the assets at the beginning of the $i+$ 1st period. Thus:

$$(a) \qquad V_i = \sum_{j=i}^{n} \frac{F_j(i)}{(1+r)^{j+1-i}} + L_i$$

where $F_j(i)$ represents the expected net cash flow in the jth period as envisioned at the beginning of the ith period, r equals the normal rate of return, n represents the terminal date of the planning horizon, and L_i is the value of the liquid assets at the beginning of the ith period. Similarly:

$$(b) \qquad V_{i+1} = \sum_{j=i+1}^{n} \frac{F_j(i) + \Delta F_j(i+1)}{(1+r)^{j-i}} + L_i(1+r) + R_{ij},$$

where $\Delta F_j(i+1)$ represents the change in the originally envisioned jth period cash flow now viewed from the beginning of the $i+$ 1st period, and R_i is the actually realized cash inflow of the ith period. Subtracting [a] from [b] and rearranging yields:

$$(c) \qquad (Ye)_i = \underbrace{\sum_{j=i+1}^{n} \frac{F_j(i)}{(1+r)^{j-i}} - \sum_{j=i}^{n} \frac{F_j(i)}{(1+r)^{j+1-i}} + L_i r + R_i}_{\text{expected income}} + \underbrace{\sum_{j=i+1}^{n} \frac{\Delta F_j(i+1)}{(1+r)^{j-i}}}_{\text{unexpected income}}$$

This particular dichotomization of the income components is appropriate only if it is assumed that R_i, the actually realized inflow of the ith period, equals $F_{i(i)}$, the expected ith period inflow as envisioned at the beginning of the ith period. However, if R_i diverges from $F_{i(i)}$, then equation (c) must be altered slightly.

economic income is the product of the normal rate of return (r) and the beginning of the period net present value of assets (V_i). Thus:

$$(2)^{14} \qquad\qquad\qquad\qquad I_6 = rV_i$$

The unexpected income component of economic income is equal to the sporadic increase in asset net present value which develops as a result of changes in expectations regarding the level of future net flows from operating assets.

      We will now demonstrate that, theoretically, replacement cost income is virtually identical to economic income in a perfectly competitive economy. Most replacement cost income concepts promulgated contain two general components: (1) an operating profit segment, and (2) a price change segment. In the terminology of Edwards and Bell these components are called current operating profit and realizable cost savings, respectively. Current operating profit is generally measured as the difference between revenues for the period and the replacement cost of those assets consumed in generating revenues. If an *economic* depreciation concept is used to measure the expiration of long-lived assets (i.e., a concept which measures the periodic decline in the discounted earning power of an asset[15]) the resulting actual rate of return from operations for a single-asset firm is given by:

$$(3) \qquad\qquad\qquad\qquad r_a = \frac{C_i}{P_i}$$

In (3), r_a represents the actual operating rate of return, C_i is the current operating profit, and P_i, as before, denotes the market price of assets. Given a perfectly competitive environment, the following relationship should hold in equilibrium:

$$(4) \qquad\qquad\qquad\qquad r_a = r$$

---

[14]From the preceding footnote we have, for expected income:

$$(c') \quad I_c = \sum_{j=i+1}^{n} \frac{F_j(i)}{(1+r)^{j-i}} - \sum_{j=i}^{n} \frac{F_j(i)}{(1+r)^{j+1-i}} + L_i r + R_i$$

which, after performing the indicated subtraction, yields:

$$(d') \quad I_c = \sum_{j=i+1}^{n} \frac{(1+r)F_j(i) - F_j(i)}{(1+r)^{j+1-i}} \frac{F_i(i)}{(1+r)} + L_i r + R_i$$

Since $F_i(i)$ equals Ri in this *ex ante* income conceptualization, we can substitute $F_i(i)$ for R_i in equation [d'] and simplify:

$$I_c = \sum_{j=i+1}^{n} \frac{rF_j(i)}{(1+r)^{j+1-i}} - \frac{F_i(i)}{(1+r)} + L_i r + F_i(i)$$

$$I_c = \sum_{j=i}^{n} \frac{rF_j(i)}{(1+r)^{j+1-i}} + L_i r$$

$$I_c = r\left[\sum_{j=i}^{n} \frac{F_j(i)}{(1+r)^{j+1-i}} + L_i \right]$$

$$I_c = r\, Vi$$

[15]See, for example, Eugene M. Lerner and Willard T. Carleton, *A Theory of Financial Analysis*, (Harcourt, Brace & World, Inc., 1966), pp. 50–51.

Substituting V_i for P_i and r for r_a in equation (3) and rearranging gives:

(5)
$$C_i = rV_i$$

A comparison of equations (5) and (2) indicates that:

(6)
$$C_i = I_6$$

Thus, in a perfectly competitive economy, the current operating profit component of replacement cost income is equal to the expected income component of economic income.[16]

In similar fashion the second component of replacement cost income—realizable cost savings—is a direct counterpart to the second component of economic income—unexpected income. Realizable cost savings are equal to the change in the market price of assets held during the period. Unexpected income consists of the discounted value of the change in the amount of future flows expected from operating owned assets. In a perfectly competitive economy, such changes in cash flow expectations are directly translated into changes in asset market value [equation (1)]; therefore, the realizable cost savings component of replacement cost income is equal to the unexpected income component of economic income.[17]

Given that each component of replacement cost income is equal to its counterpart component of economic income, *total* replacement cost income must also equal *total* economic income. While our analysis assumed a perfectly competitive environment in which all firms have homogeneous expectations, this correspondence between the two income concepts can also be demonstrated to exist when there is divergence among firms' expectations.[18]

THE INDIRECT MEASUREMENT HYPOTHESIS IN IMPERFECTLY COMPETITIVE ECONOMIES

Removing the conditions of perfect competition introduces imperfect resource mobility into the economy. This restricted mobility, or friction, changes the equalities in (1) and (4) to mere approximations. Then, performing substitutions similar to those in the perfect competition illustration, (5) becomes:

---

[16]Note that the conditions under which this relationship holds are rather limited. First, this relationship is valid only for economies in which all characteristics of perfect competition are satisfied and, because of equation (4), *only in equilibrium*. Second, equation (6) is valid only if the specific depreciation concept used in the replacement cost model is that of economic depreciation. However, Edwards and Bell (pp. 178–180) exclude economic depreciation from their model on both theoretical and practical grounds. Therefore, current operating profit as computed by Edwards and Bell need not equal expected income. Finally, a change in the composition or level of ending inventory of processed goods can destroy the equation (6) relationship. (See Edwards and Bell, pp. 105–108.) This is the case since the entry value replacement cost concept promulgated by Edwards and Bell specifically excludes value added by production.

[17]This correspondence between realizable cost savings and unexpected income is precise only if replacement cost depreciation is measured as the periodic decline in the earning power of an asset (economic depreciation). Only then will the difference between the book values of assets and ending market values correspond to the unexpected income component of economic income. If replacement cost depreciation is computed on a basis other than economic depreciation, realizable cost savings will vary from unexpected income by the amount of the divergence between economic depreciation and replacement cost depreciation as actually computed.

[18]For a development of the correspondence between replacement cost income and total economic income under conditions of divergent expectations, the interested reader is referred to a forthcoming article by author.

$$(5') \qquad\qquad\qquad C_i \cong rV_i$$

Thus, under conditions of imperfect competition, current operating profit is merely an approximation of expected income.

An approximate correspondence can also be attributed to the cost savings and unexpected income components. Even in imperfectly competitive economies asset prices approximate the average net present value of asset revenue generating potential. Theoretically, changes in asset revenue generating potential precipitate appropriate changes in asset price. Proponents of the indirect measurement hypothesis apparently would contend that just as market price is related to asset net present value, so too the *change* in asset market price is related to the *change* in asset net present value. Therefore, realizable cost savings, measured as the change in the market price of held assets, approximate unexpected income for a period, measured as the change in the net present value of asset revenue generating potential.

The basis for the indirect measurement hypothesis in "realistic" economies should now be evident. There are two distinct correspondences underlying this supposed relationship between total replacement cost income and total economic income: (1) that the current operating profit component of replacement cost income is an indirect measure of the expected income component of economic income, and (2) that the realizable cost savings component of replacement cost income is an indirect measure of the unexpected income component of economic income.

However, there are *a priori* grounds for questioning the validity of the posited relationship between changes in asset prices and changes in service potential in realistic economies. Therefore, below, we will examine the reasonableness of this assumption of positive covariance between asset prices and asset flows. Furthermore, we will explore the impact of this covariance assumption (and its possible invalidity) on the relationship between *total* replacement cost income and *total* economic income.[19]

MARKET PRICES AND CASH FLOW POTENTIAL

The relationship between replacement cost income and economic income rests, in part, on the assumption that changes in asset prices are in direct response to changes in the level of net cash flows expected to be generated by assets.

In an aggregate sense, this relationship between realizable cost savings and unexpected income is probably valid. Barring changes in the discount rate, etc., such a relationship between asset prices and asset cash flows must exist in the long-run for the economy as a whole. However, for any individual firm in the economy there is no *necessary* relationship between movements in asset prices and movements in cash flows. Actually, there are three possibilities regarding asset market price changes and changes in the service potential of assets to a firm. As an asset price changes:

---

[19]Heretofore, we have concentrated on the underlying correspondences between the subcomponents of each income concept. We did this in order to develop the theoretical foundation for the indirect measurement hypothesis in a comprehensible manner and to explain why this surrogate relationship has been extended to realistic economies by its proponents. When firms' expectations differ, however, we can demonstrate that these two underlying correspondences are not necessarily independent. (*Supra.*, footnote 18.) Since divergence of expectations is the norm in realistic economies, and since our concern centers on the *total* relationship between the two income concepts, in the remainder of the paper we shift our focus from the subcomponents to concentrate instead on the relationship between *total* replacement cost income and *total* economic income.

(A) Future cash flows resulting from asset operation could change in the same direction as the price change.

(B) Future cash flows could remain constant,

(C) Future cash flows could change in the opposite direction.

These three possibilities will be referred to as Type A, Type B, and Type C asset price changes respectively.[20]

If replacement cost income and economic income are indirectly related, there ought to be rather close correspondence between movements in each. This suggests that Type A price changes should predominate in order to validate the indirect measurement hypothesis.[21] However, if we can demonstrate that, theoretically, Type B and Type C price changes can be expected to occur with some frequency in realistic situations, and if we can further show that such price changes precipitate divergence between *total* replacement cost income and *total* economic income, then the essence of the indirect measurement hypothesis must be questioned.

This type of condition is illustrated in the following section.

AN ILLUSTRATIVE TYPE C PRICE CHANGE

Assume that the gamma industry manufactures a particular consumer good called a gamma. The industry is characterized by perfect competition and is initially earning an above normal rate of return at the beginning of 19x0.

Assume that the abnormal return induces capital movement into the gamma industry during 19x0 as new firms attempt to take advantage of inordinately high returns available therein. This movement will initially tend to raise asset prices to all firms in the gamma industry, including the established firms. Asset prices will rise because of the demand for fixed assets by entering firms; this demand is added to the replacement demand for productive equipment on the part of firms already producing gammas in the gamma industry. Unless perfect elasticity of supply in the capital goods industry is assumed, this increase in demand for gamma producing equipment will serve to raise the price of such equipment. However, the output of final goods, gamma, will not immediately increase since it is assumed that a certain lead time is necessary before the new firms entering the industry are able to utilize the new capacity for gamma production. Thus, in this initial stage, no change in the magnitude of established gamma firms' cash flows occurs, but asset prices are bid upward.

After the necessary lead-time passes, however, the gamma industry's new entrants begin production in 19x1. Utilization of this new capacity increases the supply of final output available. With demand constant (and not perfectly elastic), the increase in supply will tend to reduce the price obtained for each gamma unit sold; furthermore, the volume attained by new entrants is assumed to be garnered at the expense of established gamma industry firms. Each established firm, if we posit a constant demand for final output of the industry, will experience both a shrinking market and a decline in per unit gamma selling price. Furthermore, in an increasing cost industry, the increased output will trigger increases in the price of variable inputs

---

[20]It should be emphasized that for ease of exposition the general purchasing power of the monetary unit is assumed herein to be stable. Therefore, the influence on market prices of general inflation or deflation can be ignored.

[21]More specifically, not only must asset prices and cash flows move in the same direction, but also the magnitude of the price change must correspond to the magnitude of the change in the present value of expected cash flows.

used in production. The forces originally set into motion by the disparity in rates of return between the gamma industry and the remainder of the economy will eventually eliminate the disparity by: (1) raising the costs of factors of production, including fixed inputs, (2) lowering the average selling price of output, and (3) fragmenting the market into smaller individual shares.

The net effect of these events on the established firms in the industry will be: (1) a rise in the market price of capital assets used in production, and (2) a fall in expected future cash flows associated with operating the gamma producing equipment. Hence, a Type C price change (opposite movements in asset prices and future flows) is the likely result of this sequence of events. Thus, while it is apparently true that at the aggregate level changes in cash flow expectations translate directly into changes in asset prices, the possible existence of Type B and Type C price changes would indicate that this correspondence need not exist at the micro level. Furthermore, the quantification of this example in the Appendix demonstrates that this Type C price change precipitates opposite movements in *total* replacement cost income and *total* economic income.

It is not difficult to develop other examples of theoretical price movements of Type B or Type C. Since the conditions which give rise to these types of price changes (e.g., demand shifts in other industries, shifts in relative input prices, and technological changes[22]) appear to be representative of reasonable, real-world phenomena, the validity of the indirect measurement hypothesis must be viewed with some skepticism.

Empirical research is needed to determine the extent and frequency of such Type B and Type C price changes. Nevertheless, their possible existence, however infrequent, makes the relationship between replacement cost income and economic income uncertain and makes the indirect measurement hypothesis a potentially dangerous generalization.

SOME CONCLUDING COMMENTS

SUMMARY

This study had as its primary purpose an examination of the relationship between replacement cost income and economic income. Our basic concern centered on the ability of replacement cost income to approximate the results of economic income and thus provide statement users with information concerning changes in the cash flow potentialities confronting a firm.

Beaver, Kennelly and Voss have suggested that theoretical study must precede empirical analysis of the predictive ability of particular income concepts.[23] Since the presupposition of the indirect measurement hypothesis is that replacement cost income is a predictor of economic income, it seems appropriate to investigate the heretofore absent theoretical foundation for this contention.

---

[22]For a development of such examples see Lawrence Sherwin Revsine, "Replacement Cost Reports to Investors: A Relevance Analysis" (unpublished Ph.D. dissertation, Northwestern University, 1968), pp. 76–93.

[23]Beaver, Kennelly and Voss, "Evaluation of Accounting Data," (p. 677):

"The use of the predictive ability criterion presupposes that the alternatives under consideration have met the tests of logic and that each has a theory supporting it. . . . Theory provides an explanation why a given alternative is expected to be related to the dependent variable and permits the investigator to generalize from the findings of sample data to a new set of observations. Consequently, a complete evaluation involves both *a priori* and empirical considerations."

In the final section of this paper, as a means of emphasizing the practical importance of the indirect measurement hypothesis, we will illustrate a conceivable inferential error which replacement cost reports might precipitate if Type B and Type C price changes are incorporated.

CONSEQUENCES OF RELIANCE ON AN INVALID INDIRECT MEASUREMENT HYPOTHESIS

One rationalization for the dissemination of replacement cost reports to investors relies on the validity of the indirect measurement hypothesis. Investors are not primarily interested in the historical financial data provided to them in published financial statements, this argument goes. No rational investor purchases stock in a company because of its past profit performance; rather, it is the prospect of future profitability which induces investment.[24] Given this investor emphasis on the potentialities confronting the firm, indirect measurement hypothesis proponents have advocated the relevance of a replacement cost report to investors. They contend that since replacement cost income is supposedly an indirect measure of economic income, and since economic income incorporates the very potentialities of concern to investors, it follows that replacement cost reports should provide an indirect means of communicating potentialities to present and prospective investors.

However, a replacement cost report which contains Type B and/or Type C price changes could result in an investor making seriously misleading inferences regarding a company's prospects. For example, *if cash flow potentialities are indeed of paramount importance to the investor, the income concept reported to investors ideally should vary in the same direction and by the same magnitude that discounted cash flow expectations vary.* Thus, reported income should increase whenever the cash flow potential of the firm increases and should decrease whenever the cash flow potential decreases.[25] However, replacement cost income might not achieve this result whenever a Type B or Type C asset price change occurs. For example, in a type C price change situation, replacement cost income theory necessitates the recognition of a realizable cost saving in response to a rise in asset price. This realizable cost saving will be recognized in the year of the price rise despite the fact that future flows accruing to the firm already owning an asset whose price has risen are expected to fall. Such a firm is clearly in a deteriorated long-run cash flow position relative to its position before the price rise. Yet is must show "income" as a consequence of the price change. Clearly, following the indirect measurement hypothesis, the term "income" should be reserved for those instances in which an augmentation of cash flow potential has occurred. Such is not necessarily the case using the replacement cost income framework, however. An investor relying on total reported replacement cost income for a period could be led to a conclusion in direct *opposition* to the potentialities actually confronting

---

[24]See, for example, Robert T. Sprouse, "The Measurement of Financial Position and Income: Purpose and Procedure," *Research in Accounting Measurement,* ed. Robert K. Jaedicke, Yuji Ijiri and Oswald Nielsen (American Accounting Association, 1966), p. 106; George J. Staubus, *A Theory of Accounting to Investors* (The University of California Press, 1961), p. 50; The Committee to Prepare a Statement of Basic Accounting Theory, *A Statement of Basic Accounting Theory* (American Accounting Association, 1966), p. 23; and William J. Vatter, *The Fund Theory of Accounting and Its Implications for Financial Reports* (The University of Chicago Press, 1947), p. 72.

[25]Cf., Committee on Accounting Procedure, *Accounting Research and Terminology Bulletins,* Final Edition (American Institute of Certified Public Accountants, 1961), pp. 87–88; and Bierman and Davidson, "The Income Concept," p. 241.

the firm whenever the impact of a Type B or Type C price change is sufficiently large to cause a disparity between reported replacement cost income and the direction of change in cash flow potential.[26]

The possibility that replacement cost reports might convey misleading information regarding cash flow potentialities has serious repercussions. Empirical research is certainly needed to support or refute our *a priori* analysis. If this research does in fact indicate possible serious divergence between replacement cost income and economic income, the conditions under which such divergence is possible must be isolated. Then, in preparing replacement cost reports for a firm subject to these divergence conditions, a caveat to the user regarding such divergences would be necessary.

Since investors and other statement users are concerned with firms' cash flow potentialities, it is imperative that accountants develop some external reporting techniques which will satisfy these needs for anticipatory information. Replacement cost reports might, in certain circumstances, provide this information. It is hoped that this paper, by providing some theoretical background for the indirect measurement hypothesis, has isolated certain relationships deserving of further research attention concerning the predictive ability of replacement cost reports.

APPENDIX

Presented in this Appendix is a quantification of the Type C price change illustration which was developed in the body of the paper. Our objective herein is two-fold: 1) to illustrate in detail the effect of Type C price changes on the correspondence between the two income concepts, and 2) to demonstrate the potentially misleading inferences replacement cost reports might precipitate when Type C price changes are incorporated into the income determination process.

Using the basic facts presented in the gamma industry example above, let us assume that the industry in 19x0 is in temporary disequilibrium. Gamma producing equipment, which has a three year life, is expected to generate annual cash inflows of $110; given an economy wide normal rate of return of 5%, the equilibrium value of the asset would be:

Year	Net Inflow	Discount Factor (at 5%)	Present Value
1st	$110	.9524	$104.76
2nd	$110	.9070	99.77
3rd	$110	.8638	95.02
Equilibrium Market Price			$299.55

The actual market price of the asset, given the temporary disequilibrium, is $250.

Replacement cost income for 19x0 for an original firm in this industry which purchased a new gamma producing asset on January 1, 19x0 is:

---

[26]A numeric illustration of this phenomenon is presented in the Appendix to this paper.

ORIGINAL FIRM REPLACEMENT COST INCOME
FOR THE YEAR ENDED DECEMBER 31, 19x0

Current Operating Profit:
Net cash inflow $110.00
Depreciation:
Value of the asset at 1/1/x0 . . . . $299.55
Value at 12/31/x0:
19x1 flows ($110 × .9524) 104.76
19x2 flows ($110 × .9070 . . . . 99.77
204.53

Total Depreciation 95.02
Total current operating profit 14.98
Cost Savings:
Realizable Cost Savings. 0.00
Acquisition income:[27]
Value to the firm 299.55
Cost 250.00
49.55

Total replacement cost income. . . . . $ 64.53

Economic income for 19x0 is:

ORIGINAL FIRM ECONOMIC INCOME
FOR THE YEAR ENDED DECEMBER 31, 19x0

Expected Income:
From operations ($299.55 × 5%) . . . . $ 14.98
On acquisition 49.55
Total expected income . . . . $ 64.53
Unexpected Income: 0.00
Total economic income . . . . $ 64.53

Since the inordinately high economic rents in this industry have persisted, new entrants are attracted during 19x1. Assume that the entering firms cannot begin production until 19x2; however, it becomes apparent that, as a consequence of their entry, net cash flows generated each year by the gamma producing equipment will fall to $95 starting in 19x2. (For simplicity, we assume that this change in expectations is perceived instantaneously on January 1, 19x1.) The equilibrium price per capital unit will become:

---

[27]The replacement cost income concept of Edwards and Bell takes no cognizance of "bargain" purchases until they are validated by a market price change. By introducing an "acquisition income" segment into the replacement cost income determination model, we are utilizing Bedford's approach. (*Income Determination Theory*, p. 176).

Year	Net Inflow	Discount Factor (at 5%)	Present Value
1st	$95	.9524	$ 90.48
2nd	$95	.9070	86.17
3rd	$95	.8638	82.06
Equilibrium market price			$258.71

Let us compute 19x1 replacement cost income for the Original Firm whose statements for 19x0 were presented above.

ORIGINAL FIRM REPLACEMENT COST INCOME FOR THE YEAR ENDED DECEMBER 31, 19x1

Current Operating Profit:
Net cash inflow $110.00
Depreciation:
Value of the asset at 12/31/x0 . . . . $204.53
Value at 12/31/x1
19x2 flows ($95 × .9524) 90.48
Total Depreciation 114.05
Total Current Operating Profit . . . .   (4.05)
Cost Savings:
Realizable Cost Savings . . . .   6.21[28]
Total replacement cost income . . . . $ 2.16

Economic income for 19x1 would be:

ORIGINAL FIRM ECONOMIC INCOME FOR THE YEAR ENDED DECEMBER 31, 19x1

Expected income:
From operations ($204.53 × 5%) $10.23
Unexpected income:
Decline in 19x2 cash inflows ($15 × .9524) . . . .   (14.29)
Total economic income . . . . $(4.06)

---

[28]The realizable cost saving of $6.21 is computed as follows:

Equilibrium value of expected flows as of 1/1/x1:
19x1 ($95 × .9524) . . . . $ 90.48
19x2 ($95 × .9070) 86.17
New market price for 1 yr. old asset $176.65
Less: Market price of 1 yr. old asset at 12/31/x0 . . . .   170.44
Realizable cost saving . . . . $ 6.21

The old market price of $170.44 is determined by solving for x where:

$$\frac{x}{\$204.53} = \frac{\$250}{\$299.55}$$

The two income concepts provide the reader with quite dissimilar measures of the Original Firm's performance during 19x1. The negative economic income figure indicates that the market position of the firm has deteriorated during 19x1, due to the decline in expected future flows. Replacement cost income measurements, on the other hand, result in income being reported for 19x1. Income arises only because the Type C price change is included. Were this item to be omitted from the replacement cost calculation then (except for rounding errors) the resultant income measure would be identical to economic income.

Given the "functional fixation" users may have concerning definitions,[29] and given the overriding importance of cash flow potential in investors' decision models, the tendency might exist to identify income—irrespective of the measurement mode by which it was developed—with changes in cash flow potential. This fixation mechanism could cause investors to consider positive reported replacement cost income to be a reflection of increased profit potential when, in fact, the profit generating potential of the firm has actually diminished.

---

[29]Yuji Ijiri, Robert K. Jaedicke, and Kenneth E. Knight, "The Effects of Accounting Alternatives on Management Decisions," *Research in Accounting Measurement,* p. 194.

PRICE-LEVEL RESTATED ACCOUNTING AND THE MEASUREMENT OF INFLATION GAINS AND LOSSES

William D. Bradford

Accounting theory concerning the measurement of gains and losses to the firm during periods of changes in the general level of prices has had much discussion in recent literature.[1] One concern expressed has been that of specifying the gains or losses incurred by the firm as a result of holding monetary items during inflationary periods.

There is much justification for the use of price-level restated financial reporting. However, the conclusion of this paper is that the present method of restating for price-level changes ignores two things: (1) the effect of anticipated inflation on the degree of loss or gain on monetary items and (2) differences in return on monetary items.

As a result, gains and losses from holding monetary items as presently specified may give in fact incorrect information in terms of measuring (1) the effect of inflation on the wealth of the firm and (2) the efficiency with which monetary items have been managed by the firm.

Helpful comments were provided by Robert G. May. Errors are those of the author.

William D. Bradford, "Price-Level Restated Accounting and the Measurement of Inflation Gains and Losses," *The Accounting Review,* April 1974, 296–305. Reprinted by permission of the American Accounting Association.

[1]See Loyd C. Heath, "Distinguishing between Monetary and Nonmonetary Assets and Liabilities in General Price-level Accounting," *The Accounting Review* (July 1972), pp. 458–68; Paul Rosenfield, "Accounting for Inflation—A Field Test," *The Journal of Accountancy* (June 1969), pp. 45–51; Keith Schwayder, "Expected and Unexpected Price Level Changes," *The Accounting Review* (April 1971), pp. 306–19; Russell James Petersen, "Interindustry Estimation of General Price-level Impact on Financial Information," *The Accounting Review* (January 1973), pp. 34–43.

The next section examines the general methodology of specifying gains and losses from holding monetary items during an inflation. Then, the Fisher-Kessel-Alchian analysis of unanticipated inflation will be examined in terms of how their hypothesis affects the accuracy of general price-level accounting. Thereafter, this paper will consider the effect that different returns on monetary items has on the informational content of price-level accounting.

THEORY

We will express the method of defining gains and losses from holding monetary items as generally prescribed.[2] The residual equity or net worth of the firm can be expressed as

$$(1) \qquad\qquad E = R + M$$

where

E   is residual equity

R   is net real assets, equal to real assets minus real liabilities

M   is net monetary assets, equal to monetary assets minus monetary liabilities

Consider an inflationary period. The question which price-level accounting attempts to answer is: Given the magnitude and time duration of net monetary assets held by the firm during a period of a general price-level change, then what effect did the holding of these items have on the value of the firm's equity?

Assume that during the period prices increase such that the ratio of the end-of-period prices to the initial price-level, *a,* is greater than one. The value of equity at the end of the period, *E,* is

$$(2) \qquad\qquad E = aR + M = aE - M(a - 1)$$

The nominal value of net real assets increases based upon the inflation, whereas the nominal value of net monetary assets does not. The loss or gain from holding monetary items is

$$(3) \qquad\qquad -M(a - 1)$$

Expression 3 is the term used in general price-level restated accounting to define the gain or loss from holding monetary items. If M is positive (monetary assets are larger than monetary liabilities), the firm will lose $M(a - 1)$. If M is negative, the firm will gain $M(a - 1)$.

Accounting for gains or losses on monetary items is only one segment of the process of accounting for price-level changes, a process which if done accurately can increase the quality of economic decisions made by the firm and its owners. In this regard, the present analysis hopes to add to the accuracy of the process and its output.

---

[2]We will take the general methodology as described in Accounting Research Study No. 6, pp. 12–4. See *Reporting the Financial Effects of Price-level Changes* (New York: AICPA, 1963). Other analyses in this area have not differed materially, although the importance and timing of the restatement have found some disagreement. See R. S. Gynther, *Accounting for Price-level Changes—Theory and Procedures* (Pergamon Press, 1966), Chapter 11; and Edgar O. Edwards and Phillip W. Bell, *The Theory and Measurement of Business Income* (University of California Press, 1961), Chapter 7.

THE INCOME ADJUSTMENT

Economic theory has discussed the rate of income on monetary investments as affected by inflation since the initial investigation of Wicksell.[3] Fisher and Keynes subsequently examined the financial market relationships and concluded that the rate of income charged on monetary investments characteristically fails to compensate the investor for inflation—thus debtors gain and creditors lose during an inflation.[4] More recently, Kessel and Alchian corrected and extended Fisher's analysis by considering *net* monetary assets: fixed income claims on both the asset and liability sides of the balance sheet.[5] This section will discuss the hypothesis developed by Kessel and Alchian, summarize the results of empirical tests of the hypothesis, and relate the hypothesis and test results to price-level accounting theory.

Expression 3 defines the loss or gain to the firm from holding monetary items as defined by price-level accounting procedures. The wealth redistribution hypothesis, as formulated by Fisher, Kessel and Alchian, considers also the rate of interest on monetary items during a period of inflation, in the context of how an interest rate adjustment can compensate for an inflation.

Specifically, if a firm is a net creditor $(M > O)$, the firm will lose in real terms from holding monetary items *unless* the net monetary assets bear a high enough rate of interest to compensate for the increase in the price level.

As discussed in the previous section, and shown in expression 3, the loss in real wealth due to inflation is $M(a - 1)$ if the firm is a net creditor and the gain to the firm would be the same absolute amount if it were a net debtor. Given that p is the increase in the nominal interest rate, then pM would be the additional interest charges; and if $p = a - 1$, then the firm will be as well off before inflation as after inflation.

To symbolize this effect, let $h = (a - 1)$. Then

$$(4) \qquad\qquad B_1 = \frac{h - p}{h}$$

measures the degree of anticipation of inflation. $B_1 = 0$ means that inflation is anticipated correctly; $0 < B_1 < 1$ means that inflation is partially unanticipated; and $B_1 = 1$ means that inflation is completely unanticipated. The hypothesis that $0 < B_1 \leq 1$ implies that inflation is at least partially unanticipated and that a net monetary debtor (creditor) will gain (lose) during an inflation.

Empirical tests of the significance of B_1 have involved examining the relative change in common stock values of firms after classifying them into net debtor or net creditor position, and defining the degree of each firm in the two statuses. The model tested can be expressed as[6]

---

[3]Knut Wicksell, "Der Rankzins als Regulator der Warenpreise," *Jahrbücher für Nationalökonomie* (Band 58), 1897.

[4]See Irving Fisher, *Purchasing Power of Money* (Macmillan, 1911); *The Theory of Interest* (Macmillan, 1930); and J. M. Keynes, *Monetary Reform* (Harcourt, Brace, 1924).

[5]See Reuben A. Kessel, "Inflation-Caused Wealth Redistribution: A Test of a Hypothesis," *American Economic Review* (March 1956), pp. 128–41; and Armen Alchian and Reuben Kessel, "Redistribution of Wealth Through Inflation," *Science* (September 4, 1959), p. 535 f.

[6]See V. A. Broussalian, "Unanticipated Inflation: A Test of the Creditor-Debtor Hypothesis" (Unpublished Ph.D. Dissertation, University of California at Los Angeles, 1961); and Louis DeAlessi, "The Redistribution of Wealth by Inflation: An Empirical Test with United Kingdom Data," *Southern Economic Journal* (July 1963), pp. 113–23.

(5)
$$\frac{E_j}{E_j - a} = \frac{A_j - B_1(a-1)M_j'}{E_j' + U_j}$$

where e is the real rate of income for firm j; M' and E' are the estimates of M and E during the period; and U is the error term. Thus, if B_1 is significantly positive, then evidence is found that inflation is unanticipated, and holding of net monetary assets has a negative effect on the value of the firm.

Results of the tests of B_1 are inconclusive. Based upon their empirical tests, Bach and Ando, Bach and Stephenson, Bradford, and Broussalian concluded that B_1 is insignificant and/or the sign of B_1 is opposite of what is expected if inflation were unanticipated.[7] DeAlessi found weak support for the significance of B_1.[8] Kessel, Kessel and Alchian, and Gonzalez concluded that B_1 was significant and positive in their tests.[9] Examination of the methodology and data used in the studies shows that as a group they were plagued by measurement errors and large disturbance factors, such that theoretically sound conclusions concerning the empirical value of B_1 still cannot be made.[10]

The Fisher-Kessel-Alchian analysis of wealth redistribution is directly related to price-level accounting theory. If the interest rate on monetary items has been adjusted to compensate exactly for an inflation, then the firm will not lose or gain from holding monetary items. Therefore, holding net monetary assets would not be detrimental to the firm, and holding net monetary liabilities would not be advantageous to the firm, as suggested by the price-level restated accounting statements.

Therefore, the gain or loss from holding monetary items as calculated should be considered as only one part of the information needed to determine the effect on the firm of holding those items. Another set of information needed is the nature of any changes in return to monetary items to compensate for the price-level change.

ANALYSIS OF RETURN CHARACTERISTICS

Consider the components of M. The value of M is

(6)
$$M = A^* - L^*$$

where A^* is monetary assets and L^* is monetary liabilities. The monetary liabilities held by the firm will typically include both borrowings and the cost of borrowings. That is,

---

[7]George L. Bach and Albert Ando, "The Redistributional Effects of Inflation," *The Review of Economics and Statistics* (February 1957), pp. 2–13; George L. Bach and James B. Stephenson, "Inflation and the Redistribution of Wealth," Research Paper No. 124, Graduate School of Business, Stanford University (October 1972); William D. Bradford, "Inflation, the Value of the Firm, and the Cost of Capital" (Unpublished Ph.D. Dissertation, The Ohio State University, 1971); and Broussalian.

[8]Louis DeAlessi.

[9]Kessel; Alchian and Kessel; Nestor Gonzalez, "Inflation and Capital Asset Market Prices: Theory and Tests" (Unpublished Ph.D. dissertation, Stanford University, 1973).

[10]See William D. Bradford, "Inflation, the Kessel-Alchian Hypothesis, and the Value of the Firm," Research Paper No. 138, Graduate School of Business, Stanford University (February 1973).

(7)
$$L^* = L + cL$$

where c represents the average expense rate on L, and L represents the borrowed funds. Likewise, the monetary assets held by the firm during the year includes both investment in monetary assets (cash, securities, receivables, etc.) and the return to those monetary assets during the year. Therefore,

(8)
$$A^* = A + bA$$

where b represents the average return rate on monetary assets, and A represents the investment by the firm in monetary assets.[11] Given these considerations, the gain or loss to the firm from holding monetary items, when inflation is unexpected, is

(9)
$$-M(a-1) = -[(A + bA) - (L + cL)](a-1)$$

Expression 9 is another method of stating expression 3. Here the specific components of net monetary assets are considered. Also, expression 9 is true in the case where inflation is completely unanticipated, or where B_1 is 1. This is consistent with our analysis in the previous section. Implications when B_1 is not 1 will be discussed below.

However, expression 9 considers changes in the value of the firm caused only by changes in the price level. The loss or gain to the firm from holding monetary items includes not only a price-level effect, but *also* a nominal income effect. Specifically, although the firm *lost* $(A + bA)(a-1)$ on monetary assets because of the price level increase, it also *gained* the amount bA because of holding those assets. The firm had a loss because of the decreased real value of earnings and principle of monetary assets, but it also had a gain because of the absolute amount of earnings accruing to those assets. A similar analysis can be made for monetary liabilities. The point here is that price-level accounting explicitly considers only the gains of losses to the firm because of changes in the value of the monetary spending unit, whereas the total effect on the firm from holding monetary items includes the absolute return to those items.

Thus, two definitions will be expressed. The first type of losss or gain from holding monetary items is that due to changes in the price level. The *price-level increase gain or loss* is

(10)
$$[(A + bA) - (L + cL)](a-1)$$

Note that a loss will be incurred if $(1 + b)A > (1 + c)L$, and a gain if $(1 + b)A < (1 + c)L$. The *normal income gain or loss* represents the gain or loss based upon netted nominal income (expense) accruing to monetary items.[12] Symbolically, it is

(11)
$$bA - cL$$

---

[11]An important criticism of the Kessel-Alchian analysis of wealth redistribution, discussed in the previous section, is that it ignores the fact that the magnitude of return to monetary assets and liabilities can differ. See William D. Bradford, "Inflation, the Kessel-Alchian Hypothesis, and the Value of the Firm."

[12]For clarification, "normal" income or expense represents claims realized or given up in an accrual sense, measured in nominal money units.

Here, a gain will occur if $bA > cL$; a loss, if $bA < cL$. Therefore, although the firm may have lost or gained from holding monetary items if only price-level increase gains or losses were considered, the conclusion may be different if normal gains or losses were also considered.

The consideration of these relationships is important because normal income gains of losses will clearly magnify or minimize price-level increase gains of losses. Therefore, from an internal viewpoint, price-level gain or loss analysis is incomplete with respect to optimal decision making for the firm; and from an external viewpoint, price-level gain or loss analysis may not show the net effect of holding monetary items on changes in the value of the firm.

We can determine the requirements wherein a price-level increase gain or loss can be overcome by a normal income loss or gain, by expressing the relationships between total monetary losses and gains. If $(1 + b)A > (1 + c)L$ (the firm is a net creditor), then the nominal income relationship for price-level losses to be overcome by normal income gains is

$$(12) \qquad bA - cL \geq [(1 + b)A - (1 + c)L](a - 1)$$

If $(1 + b)A < (1 + c)L$ (the firm is a net debtor), then the relationship such that price-level increase gains would be overcome by normal income losses would be found by reversing the inequality signs of expression 12.

Two things should be noted at this point. First, costs of monetary liabilities are generally far more quantifiable than earnings on monetary assets. The cost of debt is generally based upon the contractual amount of interest, in relation to the principal received.[13] In comparison, the earnings on cash is a function of the opportunity costs if no cash were held. This would include earnings on discounts taken, transactions flexibility, and the subjective income from reducing illiquidity risks, in relation to earnings of invested cash. Earnings on marketable securities are easier to quantify, given their similarity to monetary liabilities on the other side of the balance sheet. The earnings on accounts and notes receivable represent gains (both now and in the future) of granting credit. Some positive aspects here are goodwill and increased sales; negative aspects are bad debt expenses and increased record keeping costs.

Second, this added specification of gains and losses does not change the overall sum of losses or gains to the firm during an inflation, as calculated under present methods. In general price-level accounting methodology, the normal income and expenses of monetary items are embedded in the income statement restated for price-level changes.[14] The price-level increase gains or losses of monetary items are included as a separate item in adjusting for price-level changes. The consideration here is that separating the normal income or costs accruing to monetary items misstates their total effect on changes in value of the firm when price-level changes occur. Thus, the recommended mode of reporting will not satisfy an analyst's interest in evaluating the management of net monetary assets during an inflation.

---

[13]However, in theory some of the cost of debt is the increase in the required rate of return of the equity holders because of the existence of debt in the capital structure of the firm. See Franco Modigliani and Merton Miller, "The Cost of Capital, Corporate Finance and the Theory of Investment," *American Economic Review* (September 1958), pp. 261–97. Nevertheless, from an accounting framework, this cost is not considered because it is a result of the external valuation processes of investors.

[14]Of course, income and costs of monetary items normally are not fully reported in the accounting statements (price-level restated or not) as mentioned above.

EXAMINATION OF THE RELATIONSHIPS

We have shown the relationships necessary for price-level increase losses (gains) to be overcome by normal income gains (losses). This section will define and examine these relationships more intensively. We will define the rate r to represent the normal income rate on monetary assets needed to equalize normal expenses on monetary liabilities plus or minus any price-level increase loss or gain. In defining r mathematically, it will be noted that expression 12 implicitly assumes that income or expense of monetary items is received or paid at the start of the period, so that the total amount of income, bA, for example, is held by the firm for the entire period. If that assumption were true, then the loss on income from monetary assets is $bA(a-1)$. It is more likely that bA is received periodically throughout the year, such that the average income or expense outstanding on monetary items is less than the total income or expense on those items.

If, for example, income on monetary assets is received evenly throughout the year, then the average amount of income from those items held by the firm is one-half of their total income. Thus, the average monetary assets held by the firm is $(1 + b/2)A$ instead of $(1 + b)A$. Likewise, the average monetary liabilities held by the firm is $(1 + c/2)L$ instead of $(1 + c)L$.[15] Given these considerations, the value of r is

(13)
$$r = \frac{2A(a-1) + L[2c - (a-1)(2 + c)]}{(3-a)A}$$

This rate is found algebraically by replacing b with r in expression 9, making the adjustments for average income and expenses as just noted, and solving for r.[16] Thus, if r is 0.05, then an annual earnings rate of 5% on monetary assets will result in any loss from netting the normal expenses of monetary items and any price-level gain or loss being exactly offset by the income from monetary assets. Hence, net holding losses (or gains) from holding monetary items would be zero.

The rate k represents the rate of income on monetary assets which will make an examination of price-level increase gain or loss the only one needed. That is, this rate represents that rate at which normal expenses of monetary liabilities are equal to normal income from monetary assets. This rate is found by setting $cL - kA$ equal to zero and solving for k. Symbolically, this rate is

(14)
$$k = \frac{cL}{A}$$

Thus, if k is 0.05, then normal earnings on monetary assets of 5% would result in normal income of monetary assets equaling normal expenses of monetary liabilities, and calculation of

---

[15]In practice, this is only one of the adjustments needed in making price-level restated statements. For simplicity, our discussion assumes a fixed amount of monetary assets and liabilities held during the year, and a one-time price-level increase immediately after the start of the year. In practice, specific consideration of the magnitude and timing of the monetary items held and the changes in the price level would be required for accurate measurement of monetary items and the inflation. The general use of the model developed and conclusions reached are not affected by the simplifications made here.

[16]The variables used in calculating r can be adjusted for the timing of the inflation and monetary items held. That is, A and L can be daily, monthly, etc., averages of monetary assets and liabilities held by the firm. The value of a can be adjusted to represent the average price level applicable to the timing of the measurement made for computing A and L.

EXHIBIT 1

I. $k < r$

Case:			Price-level Result	Net Holding Result
	(a)	$b > r$	Loss	Gain
	(b)	$k < b < r$	Loss*	Loss
	(c)	$b < k$	Loss	Loss*
	(d)	$b = k$	Loss**	Loss
	(e)	$b = r$	Loss	Neutral

II. $k > r$

Case:			Price-level Result	Net Holding Result
	(a)	$b > k$	Gain	Gain*
	(b)	$r < b < k$	Gain*	Gain
	(c)	$b < r$	Gain	Loss
	(d)	$b = k$	Gain**	Gain
	(e)	$b = r$	Gain	Neutral

*The loss or gain is larger in absolute size than the opposite column's loss or gain.
**The loss or gain is equal to the opposite column's loss or gain.

net holding gains or losses using only examination of price-level gains or losses during the period is correct.

Let b represent the firm's normal rate of return on its monetary assets. We can examine the effect on the value of the firm of any relationship between b, r and k, given two general situations: (1) $r > k$ and (2) $r < k$. An r-value greater than k results from the firm being in a net monetary creditor position, so that the return from monetary assets must compensate for the normal expenses of monetary liabilities and a price-level increase loss. Conversely, an r-value less than k results from the firm being in a net monetary debtor position, so that the required return from monetary assets to compensate for the normal expenses on monetary liabilities is decreased by the price-level increase gain.

Exhibit 1 summarizes the price-level and net holding results given different relationships between b, k, and r. It can be seen that the price-level analysis will give incomplete information on the effect of holding monetary items in most cases. Appendix A is a numerical example of the relationships shown in Exhibit 1.

Thus far in this section, we have discussed the net holding gains or losses for a firm, considering that inflation is completely unanticipated. If we consider that inflation is at least partially anticipated, then expression 12 becomes

$$(15) \qquad bA - cL \geq [(1 + b)B^*A - (1 + c)B^{**}L](a - 1)$$

where

$$B^* = [(a - 1) - p^*]/(a - 1)$$
$$B^{**} = [(a - 1) - p^{**}]/(a - 1)$$

$p^* =$ the amount of inflation anticipated by the firm, resulting in a corresponding adjustment to income from monetary assets

$p^{**} =$ the amount of inflation anticipated by the firm's creditors, resulting in a corresponding adjustment to expenses on monetary liabilities

EXHIBIT 2

Firm	Industry	Monetary Assets ($) Millions	Monetary Liabilities ($) Millions	r (%)	k (%)
Chock Full O'Nuts	Food Processing	14.5	10.1	1.2	1.3
Moore Corporation	Off. Equip. & Comptr.	94.4	81.1	1.6	1.3
Morse Shoe, Inc.	Footwear	17.8	19.3	2.8	3.0
Robertshaw Controls	Elect. Equip.	28.5	34.1	3.1	3.5
Gillette Corporation	Toiletries-Cosmetic	187.2	244.6	4.5	5.1
Systron-Donner	Precision Instr.	9.3	10.5	4.9	5.2
Manhattan Industries	Apparel	43.0	56.2	7.5	8.2
B. F. Goodrich	Tire & Rubber	329.9	722.1	9.7	12.0
General Motors	Auto & Truck	432.0	616.2	17.9	18.6
Uris Buildings	Real Estate	17.4	374.9	21.5	62.4
Central Telephone & Utilities	Telecommunications	34.6	517.5	56.4	83.8

Thus, expression 15 considers that inflation may be anticipated by the firm and/or its creditors. Suppose both the firm and its creditors properly anticipate inflation and initially adjust their rates accordingly. Then $B^* = B^{**} = 0$, and there is no price-level increase gain or loss. The net effect on the firm of holding monetary items will be based upon bA and cL. Conversely, if $B^* = B^{**} = 1$, which means that inflation were completely unanticipated, then the results of expression 13 will occur. Based upon expression 15, we can change expression 13 to

$$(16) \qquad r = \frac{2B^*A(a-1) + L\{c[2 - B^{**}(a-1)] - 2B^{**}(a-1)\}}{A[2 - B^*(a-1)]}$$

This expression shows the effect on r of an anticipation of inflation. If B^* and B^{**} are both zero, it can be seen that r is equal to k. An important consideration in expression 16 is that the firm and its creditors can anticipate inflation differently. This last consideration is important because equal percentage errors for the firm and its creditors in anticipated and actual inflation will affect the value of r differently.

Exhibit 2 shows a small sample of corporations' monetary assets and liabilities and their estimated r and k values for 1970–71.[17] The computations are based upon expressions 13 and 14 and thus assume that inflation is unanticipated. The exhibit demonstrates some variations that will occur between firms with respect to these variables. Central Telephone and Utilities has large r and k values because of the relatively small amount of monetary assets relative to monetary liabilities. Thus, the absolute costs of the firms' liabilities are so large that its price-level increase gain is dwarfed, and the firm had to earn 56.4% on monetary assets to offset the costs—net of price-level increase gains—of holding monetary liabilities.

Uris Buildings also demonstrates the potential effect on the firm of holding large monetary liabilities relative to monetary assets. Note that for both firms, if the return on monetary

---

[17]These firms, which were chosen arbitrarily, are not necessarily characteristic of their respective industries. Financial information was obtained from *Moody's* and company annual reports, referring to the 1970–71 fiscal year statements of the firms. An annual 4% rate of inflation was assumed.

assets (b) is larger than their k values, then the firms will gain from holding monetary items, but values of b less than r will mean that the firms will lose from holding monetary items. This result occurs although both firms have price-level increase gains.

At the other end of the continuum in this sample, Chock Full O'Nuts and Moore Corporation have relatively low r and k values. Thus, because of the relatively large monetary assets relative to monetary liabilities, Chock Full O'Nuts needed to earn only 1.2% on monetary assets to overcome the negative effect of a price-level increase loss and normal cost of monetary liabilities. A 1.6% earnings rate on monetary assets is required for Moore Corporation. Since both of these firms are net creditors, then they would suffer price-level increase losses, but the losses in relation to the investment in monetary assets is small. Note that for Moore Corporation the value of r is greater than k, so that different results from the other three firms will occur for the same size relationships among b, r, and k.

The remaining firms fall between the two extremes, and a wide variation may be seen between firms and their r and k values. Thus, this type of analysis will show different results when different industries and firms are examined. Characteristically, firms with large liabilities relative to monetary assets, such as utilities, will have large positive r and k values, which means that these firms will tend to lose on a net basis from holding monetary items, although they have price-level increase gains. Conversely, firms with large monetary assets relative to liabilities will have smaller r and k values, and thus many of those firms will gain on a net basis from holding monetary items, although they will have price-level increase losses.

The analysis made here can be used to specify more precisely the effect of holding monetary items on changes in the value of the firm during inflationary periods and can aid in specifying optimal working capital positions during those periods. Methodologically, the measurement of investment in monetary assets, the magnitude of monetary liabilities, and the cost rate of those liabilities can be easily specified for a firm. More problems can occur in defining the "return" from holding cash, marketable securities, accounts receivable, etc., as mentioned previously. However, relatively small (e.g., Moore Corporation) or relatively large (e.g., Uris Buildings) values of r and k can produce fairly reasonable conclusions about the direction of gains or losses from holding monetary items. Firms in between (e.g., Gillette and Manhattan) will need closer analyses to determine the gain or loss direction from holding monetary items.

CONCLUSION

The effect of inflation on the value of the firm, in the case of monetary items, can be analyzed at three levels. First, the price-level increase gain or loss measures the real losses to income and principal based upon the change in the general level of prices (expression 3). General price-level accounting methodology presently measures this effect, with exceptions as noted below. Second, the net holding gain or loss measures the net effect of holding monetary items, considering the price-level increase gain or loss *and* the absolute income or costs of the monetary items (expression 12). The possibilities of normal gains and losses offsetting or magnifying price-level increase gains and losses make this second consideration important. The third consideration, that of anticipated price-level increases, affects the accuracy of the conclusions reached in the first two levels of analysis (expression 15). The first two levels assume that inflation is unanticipated and thus ignore the fact that prior adjustments in return could compensate for the gains or losses as found in those analyses. For example, a price-level increase gain may not be a gain in a pure sense if the return to monetary liabilities has been increased beforehand to compensate creditors for losses in purchasing power. Likewise, the comparative position of the firm in terms of a pure net holding gain may be different if we consider prior adjustments to return to compensate for the inflation.[18] Therefore, the first two levels measure the occurrences during the period in terms of holding monetary items. Evaluation of the management of monetary items necessitates information considered in the third level of analysis, which considers the degree of adjustments in the return on monetary items, and the timing thereof.

With these relationships in mind, several implications will be stated.

I. Firms may insulate themselves from inflation not only by adjusting the amount of monetary assets and liabilities held, but also by adjusting the income and cost characteristics of their monetary assets and liabilities. By appropriate adjustment in any combination of these items, the firm can attain its desired balance sheet position during an inflation.

II. Accounting Research Study 6 states: " . . . Financial data adjusted for price-level effects provide a basis for a more intelligent, better informed allocation of resources . . . ," a goal which is easily justified. However, most present price-level restated statements are incomplete in expressing (a) the net effect on the equity of the firm of holding monetary items and (b) desirable or undesirable relationships between monetary assets and monetary liabilities. Holding positive (negative) net monetary assets may not mean losses (gains) for the firm on a net basis during an inflation. The effect on the firm depends upon the rates of income and costs of monetary items, as well as the magnitude of the separate items.

III. Accounting theorists and practitioners need to examine more closely the return of holding cash, demand deposits, accounts receivable, and the explicit and implicit costs involved. Although after a point this analysis becomes subjective and behavioral, the goals of wealth maximization and accurate measurement of wealth require this analysis.

---

[18] That is, we observe a price-level increase gain as $[(1 + c)L - (1 + b)A](a - 1)$, where $(1 + c)L > (1 + b)A$. The "pure" price-level increase gain is $[(1 + c)B^{**}L - (1 + b)BA](a - 1)$. If inflation is properly anticipated by the firm and its creditors, then $B^* = B^{**} + 0$, and there is no pure price level increase gain. Since the pure net holding gain is $[(1 + c)B^{**}L - (1 + b)B^*A](a - 1) + bA - cL$, then it is affected also.

APPENDIX A

Price-Level Increase and Net Holding Gains and Losses Hypothetical Example*

I. $r > 0$, $k < r$		Monetary Assets			$200,000		
		Monetary Liabilities			$ 80,000		

		Values (%)				Price-level Increase Gain (Loss)	Net Holding Gain (Loss)
Case	r	b	k	$a - 1$	c		
(a) $b > r$	3.42	5.00	2.00	3.00	4.00	($3,702)	$ 3,098
(b) $k < b < r$	3.42	3.00	2.00	3.00	4.00	($3,624)	($ 824)
(c) $b > k$							
1) $b > 0$	3.42	1.00	2.00	3.00	4.00	($3,612)	($ 4,812)
2) $b < 0$	3.42	−3.00	2.00	3.00	4.00	($3,462)	($12,622)
(d) $b = k$	3.42	2.00	2.00	3.00	4.00	($3,612)	($ 3,612)
(e) $b = r$	3.42	3.51	2.00	3.00	4.00	($3,655)	0

II. $r > 0$, $k > r$		Monetary Assets			$100,000		
		Monetary Liabilities			$200,000		

		Values (%)				Price-level Increase Gain (Loss)	Net Holding Gain (Loss)
Case	r	b	k	$a - 1$	c		
(a) $b > k$	4.96	10.00	8.00	3.00	4.00	$2,970	$4,970
(b) $r < b < k$	4.96	6.00	8.00	3.00	4.00	$3,030	$1,030
(c) $b > r$							
1) $b > 0$	4.96	4.00	8.00	3.00	4.00	$3,060	($ 940)
2) $b < 0$	4.96	−2.00	8.00	3.00	4.00	$3,150	($6,850)
(d) $b = k$	4.96	8.00	8.00	3.00	4.00	$3,000	$3,000
(e) $b = r$	4.96	4.96	8.00	3.00	4.00	$3,046	0

III. $r < 0$, $k > r$		Monetary Assets			$100,000		
		Monetary Liabilities			$300,000		

		Values (%)				Price-level Increase Gain (Loss)	Net Holding Gain (Loss)
Case	r	b	k	$a - 1$	c		
(a) $b > k$	−1.22	12.00	9.00	5.00	3.00	$ 9,925	$12,925
(b) $r < b < k$							
1) $b > 0$	−1.22	8.00	9.00	5.00	3.00	$10,025	$ 9,025
2) $b < 0$	−1.22	−0.05	9.00	5.00	3.00	$10,237	$ 987
(c) $b < r$	−1.22	−2.00	9.00	5.00	3.00	$10,275	$ 2,725
(d) $b = k$	−1.22	−9.00	9.00	5.00	3.00	$10,000	$10,000
(e) $b = r$	−1.22	−12.00	9.00	5.00	3.00	$10,256	0

*The terms are as defined in the text, and r was calculated using expression 13.

POSITIVE ACCOUNTING THEORY

POSITIVE ACCOUNTING THEORY: A TEN-YEAR PERSPECTIVE

Ross L. Watts and Jerold L. Zimmerman

It is more than a decade since our two papers, "Towards a Positive Theory of the Determination of Accounting Standards" and "The Demand for and Supply of Accounting Theories: The Market for Excuses" were published in *The Accounting Review*. The intervening time allows us to look back on these papers and the ensuing literature with some perspective.

The two papers were controversial ten years ago and remain so today. The papers (primarily Watts and Zimmerman 1978) contributed to a literature that has uncovered empirical regularities in accounting practice (Christie forthcoming; Holthausen and Leftwich 1983; Leftwich forthcoming; Watts and Zimmerman 1986). The empirical regularities have been replicated in different settings (Christie forthcoming) and it is clear there is a relation between firms' accounting choice and other firm variables, such as leverage and size and the signs of the relations are mostly consistent across studies. Positive accounting research guided the search for the empirical regularities and provided explanations for them. To date, there are no *systematic* alternative sets of *explanations* for those regularities articulated and tested in the

Financial support was provided by the John M. Olin Foundation and the Bradley Policy Research Center at the University of Rochester. The comments of Ray Ball, James Brickley, Andrew Christie, Linda DeAngelo, Robert Hagerman, S. P. Kothari, Richard Leftwich, Tom Lys, Clifford Smith, Jerold Warner, and Greg Whittred are gratefully acknowledged. We thank William Kinney for encouraging us to pursue this project. An earlier version of this paper was presented at the Accounting Association of Australia and New Zealand, July 4, 1989, Melbourne, Australia.

Ross L. Watts and Jerold L. Zimmerman, "Positive Accounting Theory: A Ten-Year Perspective," *The Accounting Review*, vol. 65, no. 1, January 1990, 131–156. Reprinted by permission of the American Accounting Association.

literature. Further, the literature has moved beyond the first simple exposition of the theory in the 1978 paper. The explanation for accounting choice is now richer and more sophisticated.

Our first objective in this paper is to convey our perspective on the evolution and current state of positive accounting theory and to summarize the evidence on systematic empirical regularities in accounting (Section I). The second objective is to evaluate the research methods and the methodology used to document the empirical regularities. We discuss criticisms of the original papers and of the subsequent positive accounting literature in Section II. While the positive accounting literature has explained some accounting practice, much remains unexplained. Our third objective is to provide our views about future directions for positive accounting literature (Section III).

I. Evolution and State of Positive Accounting Theory

Evolution

Modern positive accounting research began flourishing in the 1960s when Ball and Brown (1968), Beaver (1968), and others introduced empirical finance methods to financial accounting. The subsequent literature adopted the assumption that accounting numbers supply information for security market investment decisions and used this "information perspective" to investigate the relation between accounting numbers and stock prices.[1] The "information perspective" has taught us much about the market's use of accounting numbers. But, except for the choice of inventory methods, the "information perspective" has not provided hypotheses to predict and explain accounting choices. The "information perspective" has not provided hypotheses to explain why entire industries switch from accelerated to straight-line depreciation without changing their tax depreciation methods.

An important reason that the information perspective failed to generate hypotheses explaining and predicting accounting choice is that in the finance theory underlying the empirical studies, accounting choice *per se* could not affect firm value. Information is costless and there are no transaction costs in the Modigliani and Miller (1958) and capital asset pricing model frameworks. Hence, if accounting methods do not affect taxes they do not affect firm value. In that situation there is no basis for predicting and explaining accounting choice. Accounting is irrelevant.

To predict and explain accounting choice accounting researchers had to introduce information and/or transactions costs. The initial empirical studies in accounting choice used positive agency costs of debt and compensation contracts and positive information and lobbying

---

[1]The "information perspective" views accounting data (usually earnings, dividends, and cash flows) as providing information on inputs to valuation models (e.g., discounted cash flows) and tests for associations between accounting disclosures and stock prices or returns. In the contracting approach adopted in the literature and discussed in this paper, accounting methods are primarily determined by the use of accounting numbers in contracts between parties to the firm. Under this approach accounting disclosures directly affect parties' (including stockholders') contractual claims and, hence, the values of those claims (including stock prices). To the extent accounting disclosures are correlated with attributes investors use in valuing securities, these disclosures contain information and affect stock prices. Thus, under both an "information perspective" and a "contracting perspective," accounting disclosures have the potential to alter securities prices (Holthausen forthcoming).

costs in the political process to generate value effects for and, hence, hypotheses about accounting choice. Finance researchers had introduced costs of debt that increase with the debt/equity ratio (Jensen and Meckling 1976) to explain (in combination with differential taxes) how optimal capital structures could vary across industries. The debt costs first introduced were bankruptcy and agency costs. The agency costs were of particular interest to accountants because accounting appeared to play a role in minimizing them. Debt contracts apparently aimed at reducing dysfunctional behavior use accounting numbers (Smith and Warner 1979; Leftwich 1983). Accounting researchers recognized the implications for accounting choice and began using the accounting numbers in debt contracts to generate hypotheses about accounting choice (Watts 1977).[2]

Accounting numbers also are used in manager's compensation contracts and it is hypothesized that such use again minimizes agency costs (Smith and Watts 1982). This use of accounting numbers in bonus plans suggested the possibility that accounting choice could affect wealth and so accounting researchers began employing that use to explain accounting choice. Watts and Zimmerman (1978) is an early example of this approach.

Borrowing from the industrial organization literature in economics (Stigler 1971; Peltzman 1976) which assumes positive information costs and lobbying costs, accounting researchers postulated that the political process generated costs for firms. These political costs are a function of reported profits. Thus, incentives are created to manage reported accounting numbers. Information and lobbying costs are part of the costs of "contracting" in the political process. The extent and form of the wealth transfers created by the political process (such as the tax code) are affected by these contracting costs.

While the early literature concentrated on using debt and compensation contracts and the political process to explain and predict accounting choice, the theory underlying the empirical work was more general and had its foundation in an economic literature on the theory of the firm. Since the 1970s, economists have strived to develop a theory of the firm by attempting to explain the organizational structure of the firm (e.g., choice of corporate form, structure of contracts, management compensation, centralization-decentralization). The underlying notion (Alchian 1950) is that competition among different forms of institutions leads to the survival of those forms most cost-effective in supplying goods and services. Productive activity can occur via the marketplace or by the inclusion of several activities within a firm (Coase 1937; Alchian and Demsetz 1972). In the marketplace, direction of productive activity and cooperation is by market prices; within the firm alternative mechanisms such as standard costs are used (Ball 1989). Which productive activities are carried out by markets and which by firms depends on which arrangement is cost effective.[3] In competition among firms, those that organize themselves to minimize contracting costs are more likely to survive (Fama

---

[2]Prior to that time other studies investigate accounting choice without explicit recognition of contracting effects (e.g., Gordon 1964; Gordon et al. 1966; Sorter et al. 1966; Gagnon 1967).

[3]Coase (1937) suggests that economies of scale in long-term contracting are what cause activity to be organized in firms. Alchian and Demsetz (1972) point out that those economies are not sufficient since market arrangements could achieve the same economies (e.g., contracting consultants). What is necessary is some unique advantage of firm organization over market arrangements. Alchian and Demsetz suggest it is the advantage firms have in metering inputs to team production that generates firms. Monitors meter individual inputs and the monitors' incentive problem is solved by giving them the residual claim to the firm (hence, the firm structure). Klein et al. (1978) suggest firms emerge to solve post contractual opportunism associated with specialized assets. Meckling and Jensen (1986) suggest that firms have an advantage in generating information by aggregating data and using that information. Difficulties in capturing the information's benefits in the market result in the firm being the optimal form of organization.

and Jensen 1983a, 1983b). It was a short step to suggest that accounting methods affect the firm's organizational costs and so the accounting methods that survive are the result of a similar economic equilibrium (Watts 1974, 1977).[4] Accounting researchers have recently returned to using that notion of an efficient set of accounting methods to explain accounting choice (Zimmer 1986).

As noted above, the agency costs associated with debt and management compensation contracts and the agency, information, and other contracting costs associated with the political process provided the hypotheses tested in the early empirical accounting choice studies (bonus plan, debt/equity, and political cost hypotheses). However, the more general approach suggested agency and other costs associated with other contracts (e.g., sales contracts) could also affect accounting choice.[5] This potential for many contracts to play a role in explaining organizational choice (including accounting choice) and the fact that agency costs used to explain the contracts often arise in contractual scenarios that differ from those of the standard agency problem led researchers to start to use the term "contracting costs" instead of agency costs (Klein 1983; Smith 1980). The concept of contracting costs and the notion of accounting methods as part of efficient organizational technology play key roles in contemporaneous positive accounting theory.

CONTEMPORANEOUS POSITIVE ACCOUNTING THEORY

Contracting costs arise in (1) market transactions (e.g., selling new debt or equity requires legal fees and underwriting costs), (2) transactions internal to the firm (e.g., a cost-based transfer price scheme is costly to maintain and can produce dysfunctional decisions), and (3) transactions in the political process (e.g., securing government contracts or avoiding government regulation requires lobbying costs). Contracting costs consist of transaction costs (e.g., brokerage fees), agency costs (e.g., monitoring costs, bonding costs, and the residual loss from dysfunctional decisions), information costs (e.g., the costs of becoming informed), renegotiation costs (e.g., the costs of rewriting existing contracts because the extant contract is made obsolete by some unforeseen event), and bankruptcy costs (e.g., the legal costs of bankruptcy and the costs of dysfunctional decisions). Throughout this paper, we use the term "contracting costs" to incorporate this wide variety of costs. The term "contracting parties" is meant to include all parties to the firm including "internal" employees and managers and "external" parties, such as suppliers, claim holders, and customers.[6]

The existence of contracting costs is crucial to models of both the organization of the firm and accounting choice. Meckling and Jensen (1986) suggest that within the firm the lack of a market price is replaced by systems for allocating decisions among managers, and measuring, rewarding, and punishing managerial performance. Accounting plays a role in these systems and so appears to be part of the firm's efficient contracting technology. Trying to predict

---

[4]Watts adopted such a view in "Accounting Objectives" which he presented to the Annual Congress of the N.S.W. branch of the Institute of Chartered Accountants in Australia in 1974. The paper was later substantially revised given Jensen and Meckling (1976) and joint work with Zimmerman and published in Watts (1977).

[5]The influence of sales contracts on accounting choice is considered by Watts and Zimmerman (1986, 207) and by Zimmer (1986) and joint venture contracts by Zimmer (1986). Further, Ball (1989) suggests intrafirm transactions affect internal accounting choice (e.g., the basis for transfer prices).

[6]See Watts (1974) for an earlier and Ball (1989) for a later discussion of contacting parties other than capital suppliers and managers.

and explain the organization of the firm with zero contracting costs is pointless (Coase 1937; Ball 1989). How the firm is organized, its financial policy, and its accounting methods, are as much a part of the technology used to produce the firm's product as are its production methods. Hence, modelling accounting choice while assuming zero contracting costs is not productive.

The extent to which accounting choice affects the contracting parties' wealth depends on the relative magnitudes of the contracting costs. For example, *assume* accounting-based debt agreements have higher renegotiation costs than accounting-based bonus plans. Then, mandatory changes in accounting procedures by the FASB impose greater relative costs on firms with debt agreements than on firms with bonus plans, *ceteris paribus*. And, firms with debt agreements will conduct more lobbying and undertake more (costly) accounting, financing, and production changes to undo the effects of the mandatory change than firms with only bonus plans. Thus, developing a positive theory of accounting choice requires an understanding of the relative magnitudes of the various types of contracting costs.

Contracts that use accounting numbers are not effective in aligning managers' and contracting parties' interests if managers have complete discretion over the reported accounting numbers. If managers know (or can determine) which accounting methods best motivate subordinates, then the contracting parties want managers to have some discretion over the accounting numbers. Hence, we expect some restrictions on managers' discretion over accounting numbers, but some discretion will remain. When managers exercise this discretion it can be because (1) the exercised discretion increases the wealth of all contracting parties, or (2) the exercised discretion makes the manager better off at the expense of some other contracting party or parties. If managers elect to exercise discretion to their advantage *ex post, and* the discretion has wealth redistributive effects among the contracting parties, then we say the managers acted "opportunistically."

Ex ante, the set of accounting choices restricted by the contracting parties is determined by "efficiency" reasons (to maximize firm value). One cost of allowing managers more rather than less discretion is the increased likelihood of some *ex post* managerial "opportunism" (i.e., wealth transfers to managers) via accounting procedures. However, *ex ante* the contracting parties expect some redistributive effects and reduce the price they pay for their claims. *Ex post,* wealth is redistributed by managerial opportunism, but *ex ante* some redistribution was expected and the parties price protected themselves. Price protection does not eliminate the incentive to act opportunistically nor does price protection eliminate the dead weight costs of managers taking opportunistic actions. The extent to which contracts can be written *ex ante* to preclude such *ex post* behavior that causes dead weight costs increases the chance the firm will survive in a competitive environment (Klein 1983, fn. 2).

The set of accounting procedures within which managers have discretion is called the "accepted set." It is voluntarily determined by the contracting parties. Managerial discretion over accounting method choice (i.e., the "accepted set") is predicted to vary across firms with the variation in the costs and benefits of restrictions. These restrictions produce the "best" or "accepted" accounting principles even without mandated accounting standards by government. The restrictions are enforced by external auditors. Reacting to the incentive of managers to exercise accounting discretion opportunistically, the accepted set includes "conservative" (e.g., lower of cost or market) and "objective" (e.g., verifiable) accounting procedures (Watts and Zimmerman 1986, 205–206).

Figure 1 represents the concept of the "accepted set" of accounting methods as a Venn diagram. $A1$ denotes the accepted set of methods for firm 1. *Ex ante,* the accepted set is

FIGURE 1

Relation Between the Accepted Set of Accounting Methods and the Choice of Method from within the Accepted Set

$A1$ denotes the set of accepted methods for firm 1
$A2$ denotes the set of accepted methods for firm 2
$X1$ denotes the choice of method from within the accepted set by firm 1
$X2$ denotes the choice of method from within the accepted set by firm 2

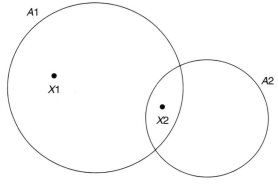

All Feasible Accounting Methods

determined jointly by the contracting parties to maximize the value of the firm (e.g., set $A1$ vs. $A2$ in Fig. 1). Managers have discretion to choose any method within the accepted set (e.g., $X1$). Also, managers in firm 2 are constrained *ex ante* to the set $A2$ and choose $X2$ *ex post*. For example, within the accepted set of procedures used for bonus plans managers might select the method that maximizes their utility, even if it comes at another contracting party's expense. Managers' *ex post* choice can either increase the wealth of all contracting parties or redistribute wealth among the parties. Empirically, it is difficult to separate *ex ante* from *ex post*. Contracts are continually being written, rewritten, and revised.

Variations across sets of accepted accounting procedures (e.g., $A1$ and $A2$ in Fig. 1) explain some cross-sectional variation in accounting choice (e.g., managers in firm 2 cannot choose method $X1$). For example, Zimmer (1986) argues Australian real estate development firms are restricted by accepted practice from capitalizing interest except for cost plus contracts that allow interest as a cost. His evidence is consistent with that hypothesis.

Most accounting choice studies assume managers choose accounting methods to transfer wealth to themselves at the expense of another party to the firm because they can take the firm's observed contracts as given and then determine managers' incentives for accounting choice. Some research studies assume accounting methods are chosen for efficiency reasons (i.e., they increase the pie available being shared among all parties to the firm (Watts 1974, 1977; Leftwich et al. 1981; Zimmer 1986; Whittred 1987; Ball 1989; Malmquist forthcoming; Mian and Smith forthcoming). However, no study to date has explained both the *ex ante* choice of the accepted set and the *ex post* choice of accounting method from within the accepted set. Most studies that assume opportunistic choice of accounting methods do not control for the fact that managers in different firms likely are choosing accounting methods from different constrained accepted sets.

The accepted set of accounting methods is one part of the firm's implicit and explicit contracts including the firm's capital structure, compensation plans, and ownership structure. All the contracting provisions (including the accounting policies) are endogenous. Capital structure choice is related to compensation policy and to accounting policy. But, the relation is not necessarily causal. Capital structure changes do not *cause* changes in the accepted set of accounting methods. Rather, some exogenous event, such as a new invention or government deregulation occurs and this causes changes in the contracting variables including accounting methods (Ball 1972; Smith and Watts 1986).

EVIDENCE ON THE THEORY

Two types of tests of the theory have been conducted: stock price tests and accounting choice tests. The stock price tests have been reviewed extensively elsewhere (Foster 1980; Ricks 1982; Holthausen and Leftwich 1983; Lev and Ohlson 1982; Watts and Zimmerman 1986; Bernard 1989). Stock price tests of the theory reveal some price reactions to mandatory accounting changes, especially involving oil and gas accounting (Lys 1984).[7] Stock price studies are probably relatively weak tests of the theory (Watts and Zimmerman 1986). The more promising ones are accounting choice studies.

Most accounting choice studies attempt to explain the choice of a single accounting method (e.g., the choice of depreciation) instead of the choice of combinations of accounting methods. Focusing on a single accounting method reduces the power of the tests since managers are concerned with how the combination of methods affects earnings instead of the effect on just one particular accounting method (Zmijewski and Hagerman 1981). Some studies seek to explain accounting accruals (the difference between operating cash flows and earnings). Accounting accruals aggregate into a single measure the net effect of all accounting choices (Healy 1985; DeAngelo 1986, 1988a; Liberty and Zimmerman 1986). But use of accruals as a summary measure of accounting choice suffers from a lack of control of what accruals would be without managerial accounting discretion.

Most accounting choice studies use combinations of three sets of variables: variables representing the manager's incentives to choose accounting methods under bonus plans, debt contracts, and the political process. Bonus plan and debt contract variables are used because they're observable. The three particular hypotheses most frequently tested are the bonus plan hypothesis, the debt/equity hypothesis, and the political cost hypothesis. The literature has

---

[7]Using Lys' own calculations, Frost and Bernard (1989, 20) and Bernard (1989, 14) conclude Lys' evidence is inconsistent with a link between stock price reactions to mandated oil and gas accounting and the violation of debt covenants. However, that conclusion is unwarranted. Lys estimates the average cost of violations as 2.5 percent of the stock value, the same order of magnitude as the stock price reactions observed. Frost and Bernard argue that given an average cost of violation of 2.5 percent, the average stock price reaction should be much less since according to Foster (1980) very few firms have a debt covenant violation as a result of the mandated accounting change. There are at least three problems with the Frost and Bernard argument. First, the Lys point estimates are likely to have large standard errors, Second, to obtain an estimate of the stock price reaction, the estimated cost of a violation has to be weighted not by the relative frequency of violation but by the change in the likelihood of violation. While few firms violated covenants, many firms' probability of violation likely increased substantially. Third, Malmquist (forthcoming) suggests Foster's description of oil and gas firms' covenants is incorrect. Frost and Bernard (1989) also use their own empirical study's results to argue that there is no link between the stock price reaction and debt covenants. Because of selection biases, however, their study provides little evidence on the issue (Begley forthcoming).

tended to state each of these hypotheses as managers behaving opportunistically. The bonus plan hypothesis is that managers of firms with bonus plans are more likely to use accounting methods that increase current period reported income. Such selection will presumably increase the present value of bonuses if the compensation committee of the board of directors does not adjust for the method chosen.

The choice studies to date find results generally consistent with the bonus plan hypothesis (Watts and Zimmerman 1986, chap. 11; Christie forthcoming). The early tests of the bonus hypothesis are not very powerful tests of the theory because they rely on simplifications of the theory that are not appropriate in many cases. For example, a bonus plan does not always give managers incentives to increase earnings. If, in the absence of accounting changes, earnings are below the minimum level required for payment of a bonus, managers have incentive to reduce earnings this year because no bonuses are likely paid. Taking such an "earnings bath" increases expected profits and bonuses in future years. By using bonus plan details to identify situations where managers are expected to reduce earnings, Healy's (1985) tests encompass more kinds of manipulation. His results are consistent with managers manipulating net accruals to affect their bonuses.

The debt/equity hypothesis predicts the higher the firm's debt/equity ratio, the more likely managers use accounting methods that increase income. The higher the debt/equity ratio, the closer (i.e., "tighter") the firm is to the constraints in the debt covenants (Kalay 1982). The tighter the covenant constraint, the greater the probability of a covenant violation and of incurring costs from technical default. Managers exercising discretion by choosing income increasing accounting methods relax debt constraints and reduce the costs of technical default.

The evidence is generally consistent with the debt/equity hypothesis.[8] The higher firms' debt/equity ratios, the more likely managers choose income increasing methods. Press and Weintrop (forthcoming) and Duke and Hunt (forthcoming) find that debt/equity ratios are correlated with closeness to bond covenants as assumed in the debt/equity hypothesis.[9] Some studies, however, have avoided using the debt/equity ratio as a proxy variable for closeness to the covenant constraint by using more direct tests. For example, Bowen et al. (1981) examine whether accounting choice varies with tightness of the dividend constraint as specified in the debt covenant and measured by "unrestricted retained earnings." The association between leverage and accounting method choice is an empirical regularity unknown prior to the positive accounting studies.

The political cost hypothesis predicts that large firms rather than small firms are more likely to use accounting choices that reduce reported profits. Size is a proxy variable for political attention. Underlying this hypothesis is the assumption that it is costly for individuals to become informed about whether accounting profits really represent monopoly profits and to "contract" with others in the political process to enact laws and regulations that enhance their welfare. Thus, rational individuals are less than fully informed. The political process is no different from the market process in that respect. Given the cost of information and monitoring, managers have incentive to exercise discretion over accounting profits and the parties in the political process settle for a rational amount of *ex post* opportunism.

---

[8]Holthausen (1981) and Healy (1985) fail to reject the null hypothesis of no association between leverage and accounting method choice (see Christie forthcoming, table 1).

[9]Researchers are beginning to distinguish between how close the firm is to a given covenant constraint versus the existence of the covenant. For example, Press and Weintrop (forthcoming) find the existence of a covenant has additional explanatory power in a model predicting accounting choice after including a leverage variable.

The evidence is consistent with the political cost hypothesis. However, the result only appears to hold for the largest firms (Zmijewski and Hagerman 1981) and is driven by the oil and gas industry (Zimmerman 1983). Difficulties with using firm size to proxy for political costs, including the likelihood that it can proxy for many other effects, such as industry membership, are discussed in Ball and Foster (1982). The interesting finding is the consistency of the sign of the relation between size and accounting choice across a variety of studies. The largest firms tend to use income decreasing accounting methods. Presently, there is no alternative theory for the empirical regularity between firm size and accounting choice other than the political cost hypothesis.

Bonus plan, debt contract, and political process variables other than bonus plan existence, leverage, and size have also been found to be associated with accounting choice. Christie (forthcoming) aggregates test statistics across the various studies and concludes ". . . six variables common to more than one study have explanatory power. These variables are managerial compensation, leverage, size, risk, and interest coverage and dividend constraints. Another conclusion is that the posterior probability that the theory taken as a whole has explanatory power is close to one."

While bonus, debt, and political process variables tend to be statistically significant (p-values smaller than .10), in many studies the explanatory power (R^2) of the models is low. In Zmijewski and Hagerman (1981), the model of cross-sectional choice of accounting methods is not significantly better than picking the most common combination, although Press and Weintrop (forthcoming) achieve slightly improved explanatory power. The alternative predictive model is that each firm uses the most common combination of accounting methods, a model with little explanatory appeal. The alternative model begs the question of what determines the majority accounting choice. Many accounting teachers would be uncomfortable with the explanation that managers choose their accounting procedures based on what most other firms are doing. The real issue is the lack of an alternative model with greater explanatory power, not the low explanatory power of the extant theory. Several problems with the existing research methods contribute to the low explanatory power. These are discussed next.

II. CRITICISMS OF POSITIVE ACCOUNTING RESEARCH

Table 1 lists most of the published papers with critical comments on our 1978 and 1979 papers. The second and third columns list the number of explicit references made by the authors to our 1978 and 1979 papers. These columns indicate which of the two papers is the primary focus of the article. The fourth column lists the general topic of the paper and the fifth column lists the major criticisms raised in the paper.

The criticisms in Table 1 can be dichotomized into two mutually exclusive sets: those concerning research methods (including the inferences drawn) and those concerning methodology (including the philosophy of science). For example, Ball and Foster (1982), Holthausen and Leftwich (1983), and McKee et al. (1984)[10] discuss research methods problems and not

---

[10]McKee et al. (1984) discuss problems of the tests in Watts and Zimmerman (1978), extend the tests to another sample of firms, and offer some statistical refinements. The only statistically significant explanatory variable in our 1978 paper was firm size. McKee et al. find that their refined measure of firm size, (SALES/MAXSALES)DTREND, is statistically significant in both our sample and their sample and remains statistically significant after various refinements are made. They do not discuss the importance of this finding.

TABLE 1

Summary of Papers Reviewing Watts and Zimmerman (1978 and 1979)

Authors	Number of References		Topic	Major Criticisms
	WZ (1978)	WZ (1979)		
Ball and Foster (1982)	13	1	Review of Empirical Accounting Research	• Firm size and bonus plans can proxy for omitted variables • Weak theoretical underpinning for size-political cost construct • Holdout sample not used
Tinker et al. (1982)	1	4	Positive versus normative theories	• Positive theories are value-laden and mask a conservative bias • Ignores underlying class struggles
Christenson (1983)	6	9	Methodology of Positive Accounting	• Logical Positivism is an obsolete methodological approach • Approach is a "sociology of accounting" instead of accounting theory • Tests introduce *ad hoc* arguments to excuse the exceptions to the theory • Inappropriate methods are used for constructing explanatory theories
Holthausen and Leftwich (1983)	7	0	Review of "Economic Consequences Literature"	Interpretation of results limited because: • Incomplete political and contracting theories • Specification problems in left-hand-side and right-hand-side variables
Lowe et al. (1983)	0	12	WZ (1979)	• Economic framework is unjustified • Positive approach open to dispute • Nature of proof is unscientific • Contrary evidence presented
McKee et al. (1984)	4	0	Replication of WZ (1978)	• Results do not hold in a new sample • Holdout sample not used • Foreknowledge of sample proportions biases parameter estimates
Whittington (1987)	0	7	Review of WZ (1986)	• Presentation of arguments and evidence is unbalanced • Extreme methodological stance • Positive theories are value-laden • Approach is a "sociology of accounting" instead of accounting theory
Hines (1988)	4	0	Christenson (1983) and Methodology	• Popper is not a practical evaluation guideline for empirical accounting research

philosophy of science issues. The remaining authors concentrate on philosophy of science issues to the near exclusion of problems with research methods. Except for Holthausen and Leftwich (1983), all the reviews of positive accounting ignore the accumulating body of evidence consistent with the theory. For example, Hines (1988) cites McKee et al. (1984) as contradictory evidence to Watts and Zimmerman (1978). Yet, she ignores 21 studies reviewed in Watts and Zimmerman (1986, chaps. 11, 12) and Christie (forthcoming) that present evidence generally consistent with the theory.

The research method issues are important and future research must attempt to address them. However, it is unlikely that the positive accounting literature or any other empirical literature will ever totally eliminate such issues. We do not agree with many of the philosophy of science issues raised and seek to eliminate the common misconceptions they reflect. Research method issues, some raised by others and some by us, are discussed first in this section and philosophy of science issues are discussed second.

RESEARCH METHOD ISSUES

The first research method issue involves the tests' lack of power. The second issue involves the possibility that the results obtained in the positive accounting literature are due to unrecognized alternative hypotheses, not the stated hypotheses.

REDUCTIONS IN THE TESTS' POWER   Tests of the theory lack power for several reasons: problems with model specification, problems specifying the left-hand-side and right-hand-side variables, and omitted variables. Each of these are discussed next.

MODEL SPECIFICATION   All the studies to date have assumed accounting choice results either from efficiency reasons or managerial opportunism. This produces two model specification errors. First, in probit type regressions where the choice of accounting method depends on the effect of the choice on the manager's wealth, the right-hand-side or explanatory variables reflect the wealth effects of the choice via compensation plans, debt agreements, and the political process. Implicitly researchers are holding constant the firm's investment opportunity set and contracts and interpret the compensation plan variable as managerial opportunism. But, the debt and political variables can represent both efficiency and opportunism. Thus, the model is misspecified. The second specification error results from ignoring the interaction effects among the right-hand-side variables. Higher earnings impose political costs and so reduce the size of the pie for the contracting parties and at the same time increase the manager's bonus compensation. The manager's increased share of the smaller pie might be larger than a smaller share of the larger pie. The bonus plan and political process effects interact. However, in the empirical models the right-hand-side variables are treated as additive and interaction effects are ignored. Solving these two specification problems requires researchers to specify the intertemporal interaction between opportunism (including managerial reputation incentives) and efficiency effects (see Christie 1987).

LEFT-HAND-SIDE VARIABLE   Problems specifying the accounting choice variable reduce the power of the tests. One such problem mentioned earlier is the use of single method choices as the left-hand-side variable. Zmijewski and Hagerman (1981) and Press and Weintrop (forthcoming) use sets of accounting methods and still achieve relatively low explanatory power. However, ranking the effects of various portfolios of accounting methods on earnings requires assumptions about the relative effects on earnings of the various accounting choices (e.g., the effect of depreciation choice vs. inventory choice). These assumptions induce error in the left-hand-side variable. Healy (1985) tries to overcome this problem by using net accruals as his left-hand-side variable. But, the variable "net accruals" is a noisy measure of the net accruals manipulated by managers. Some accounting decisions that affect accruals have been made earlier and are probably beyond the manager's discretion at the time of the measurement. Ideally, net accruals should be measured relative to what they would be without manipulation, so these variations are excluded from the left-hand-side variable. This requires a model of accruals that currently does not exist (Moyer 1988; McNichols and Wilson 1988; DeAngelo 1988b).

RIGHT-HAND-SIDE VARIABLES Some variables in accounting choice studies are mismeasured. For example, both the closeness to the covenant (i.e., the difference between the number specified in the covenant and the actual number) and the existence of the covenant are likely important determinants of accounting choice. But the debt/equity ratio by itself is an imprecise measure of both closeness to the constraint and the existence of a constraint. Also, the use of a zero-one variable to measure a bonus plan effect is simplistic. Ball and Foster (1982, 184) point out that other components of pay, such as salary, can depend on accounting earnings without a formal compensation plan and that even with a formal accounting-based plan the outside directors can adjust the incentive pay for accounting changes. However, finding an association between an indicator variable representing a bonus plan and choice of accounting methods is informative and suggests that further research with more refined measures based on the bonus plans' details will yield stronger results than the zero-one variable. Also, more direct measures of political sensitivity than firm size (Wong 1988; Jones 1988; Sutton 1988) provide more powerful tests of the political cost hypothesis.

OMITTED VARIABLES There are three different omitted variable problems in the current literature: omitting standard accounting-based contracts, omitting less standard contracts, and omitting variables representing the accepted set. First, contracting cost variables for standard contracts, such as bonus plans, occasionally are omitted because such variables are costly to collect. For example, Daley and Vigeland (1983) omit a variable representing accounting-based management compensation plans from their regression. Because leverage, compensation contracts, and accounting policy are part of the firm's efficient contracting technology, these variables covary and also vary with firm size. Omitting a right-hand-side variable correlated with included variables causes the existing right-hand-side variables to become surrogates for the omitted variables. This produces biased coefficients of the estimated right-hand-side variables and hampers their interpretation.

A second omitted variables problem is that to a large degree, the literature to date focuses only on debt and compensation contracts. Other contracts influence management's choice of accounting methods, but these are omitted in most tests. For example, the existence of a bonus plan is likely correlated with other organizational devices such as stock option plans. These other organizational structures might be driving the accounting choice rather than bonus plans (Ball and Foster 1982, 185). And, it is incorrect to ascribe all the explanatory effect of the bonus plan indicator variable results to the bonus plan. Corporate control issues also are often omitted as explanatory variables in seeking to explain accounting choices. DeAngelo (1988a) finds that net accruals are more positive (i.e., higher reported earnings) during proxy fights. Zimmerman (1979) and Ball (1989) argue that accounting numbers are part of the internal control process and, thus, affect manager's choice of accounting methods (e.g., cost allocations). Ignoring these, other less frequently researched informal contracts can produce biased coefficients.

Third, as discussed under specification problems above, the left-hand-side variable in most studies is the manager's choice of accounting methods. Even without a government regulatory defined set of accounting methods, this choice is made from within the "accepted set of methods" (see Fig. 1).[11] Yet, most studies do not control for differences across firms' accepted sets. Such control requires a theory of how the sets of accepted accounting methods vary and such a theory does not exist. Failure to control for differences in accepted sets induces another correlated omitted variables problem in the tests. The severity of this correlated omitted variables (and model specification) problem is likely to be larger in studies in which the sampled firms are drawn from several industries than in studies where the sampled firms are drawn from the same industry.

ALTERNATIVE HYPOTHESES   Alternative hypotheses can explain the bonus, debt/equity, and size results found in the positive accounting literature. Several scenarios illustrate how this problem might arise:

1. If the accounting system is part of the firm's efficient set of implicit and explicit contracts, accounting choice is endogenous. Contracting, investment, and production decisions are determined jointly. The type of contracts used (including the accounting methods) depends on the firm's investment opportunity set. Hence, the firm's investment opportunity set (e.g., whether it includes growth options or not) is correlated with the firm's financial, dividend, compensation, and accounting policies. Smith and Watts (1986) find significant cross-sectional correlations among firms' investment opportunity sets, financial policies, dividend policies, and compensation policies. The documented correlations between debt/equity and accounting choice and between bonus plans and accounting choice could be due to the correlation between financial and compensation policies and the optimal set of accounting procedures for contracting. Most researchers, however, interpret these associations as resulting from opportunistic actions by managers and have not considered efficiency-based hypotheses.

2. Accounting choice also is endogenous in the political process. The potential costs of a proposed accounting standard affect the standard before it is released. The correlation between financial and compensation policies and accounting policy is likely affected by the firm's tax accounting policies. While some financial accounting method choices do not affect taxes, reducing bookkeeping costs by keeping one set of books and the possibility that tax audits or future taxes might be levied using reported income induce a relation between financial accounting and tax accounting methods.[12]

---

[11]Mian and Smith (forthcoming) find that accounting policy decisions regarding consolidations vary by type of organization structure. Consumer finance subsidiaries are more prevalent where the parent is in the financial services industry and choice of consolidation is more homogeneous within like organization structures than in dissimilar structures. Also, operating interdependencies between the parent and subsidiary drive some accounting choices.

[12]The Corporate Alternative Minimum Tax under the Tax Reform Act of 1986 requires a portion of reported income be in the tax base. This act increases the tax incentives on financial reporting. Research to date has not documented the effect of 1986 tax reform on financial reporting incentives.

One cannot test claims that variables like debt/equity and size are surrogates for alternative explanations until those alternatives are identified and the relation specified. Given the investment opportunity set and taxes are identified as possible explanatory variables, future research can investigate their implications as alternative hypotheses to those currently advanced. For example, changing accounting methods can result from a change in the firm's investment opportunity set causing the efficient contracts and accounting methods to change. Or, some exogenous event occurs (such as reduced demand for the firm's products) and managers take opportunistic actions to undo the adverse compensation and debt contract effects of the exogenous event. Accounting changes likely are due to both efficiency reasons and managerial opportunism. Probing the relative importance of efficiency and opportunism for accounting method changes requires more refined theories and more linkage between the theory and the tests.

PHILOSOPHY OF SCIENCE ISSUES

POSITIVE THEORIES ARE VALUE-LADEN   Tinker et al. (1982, 167) argue that all research is value-laden and not socially neutral. Specifically, "Realism, operating in the clothes of positive theory, claims theoretical supremacy because it is born of fact, not values" (p. 172). We concede the importance of values in determining research; both the researcher's and user's preferences affect the process.

Competition among theories to meet users' demands constrains the extent to which researcher values influence research design. Positive theories are "If . . . then . . ." propositions that are both predictive and explanatory. Researchers choose the topics to investigate, the methods to use, and the assumptions to make. Researchers' preferences and expected payoffs (publications and citations) affect their choice of topics, methods, and assumptions. In this sense, all research, including positive research is "value-laden." The usefulness of positive theories depends on their predictive and explanatory power and on the user's preferences or objective function. To the extent that the researcher's values interfere with the theory's ability to predict and explain, the theory's usefulness is reduced.

APPROACH IS A "SOCIOLOGY OF ACCOUNTING" INSTEAD OF ACCOUNTING THEORY   Christenson (1983, 5) writes, "The program of the Rochester School is concerned with describing, predicting, and explaining the behavior of accountants and managers, not that of accounting entities." His definition of an "accounting entity" is "A business enterprise or other economic unit, or any subdivision thereof for which a system of accounts is maintained" (Kohler 1975, 14). Christenson (1983, 6) supports his criticism with an analogy from the physical sciences, "Chemical theory consists of propositions about the behavior of chemical entities (molecules and atoms) not about the behavior of chemists." In chemistry, chemical reactions exist without chemists and one can study reactions without studying chemists. But, there would be no accounting without accountants, managers, or preparers of the numbers; there would be no numbers or systems to investigate because people "*maintain*" the system (Lavoie 1989). Analogously, there would be no study of political science if politicians and voters were ignored.

The study of accounting (or political science) is a social science (Christenson 1983, fn. 5). An accounting theory that seeks to explain and predict accounting cannot divorce accounting research from the study of people. The contracting approach to studying accounting requires researchers to understand the incentives of the contracting parties.

INAPPROPRIATE METHODS ARE USED FOR CONSTRUCTING EXPLANATORY THE-ORIES   We apply traditional, generally accepted research methods and methodology from accounting, finance, and economics. Christenson (1983, 6) states, "The Rochester School has drawn its concept of 'positive theory' from that guru of the Chicago School of Economics, Milton Friedman."[13] Whittington (1987, 331) states, " . . . Watts and Zimmerman are not unique in owing intellectual allegiance to the Chicago view. . . . The majority of North American empirical accounting researchers would fall into this category, and their collective achievements are formidable."

The economic approach we and many others use applies a simple proposition: To predict and explain individual behavior, people (including accountants, regulators, and researchers) consider the private costs and benefits (broadly defined) of an action and choose the action if the benefits exceed the costs. This economics-based research methodology may be fundamentally flawed in ways we do not now understand. But, accounting research using this methodology has produced useful predictions of how the world works (e.g., association between earnings and stock prices, random walk model of earnings, contracting and size variables associated with accounting choice). A methodology that yields useful results should not be abandoned purely because it *may* not predict *all* human behavior. Do we discard something that works in some situations because it *may* not work in every circumstance? Despite what the critics think methodology *should be,* the methodologies that survive are the ones that produce useful theories. Competition in the marketplace of ideas will produce future research that uncover the errors of our present ways. Time will tell whether our approach is inappropriate.

CHOICE OF THE TERM "POSITIVE ACCOUNTING THEORY"   Positive accounting research existed long before the publication of our 1978 and 1979 papers. Early examples include Gordon (1964), Gordon et al. (1966), and Gagnon (1967). We applied the label "positive" to a set of existing research studies. The prime reason we attached this adjective in "Towards a Positive Theory of the Determination of Accounting Standards" was to emphasize that accounting theory's role is to provide explanations and predictions for accounting practice.

In Watts and Zimmerman (1986, 2) we state the objective of an accounting theory is to explain and predict accounting practice. Neither prediction nor explanation is preeminent. We adopted the label "positive" from economics where it was used to distinguish research aimed at explanation and prediction from research whose objective was prescription. Given the connotation already attached to the term in economics we thought it would be useful in distinguishing accounting research aimed at understanding accounting from research directed at generating prescriptions. In the 1960s researchers were still debating various normative theories of accounting (Chambers 1966; Sprouse and Moonitz 1962).

Our use of the term "positive" differentiated our and other people's (positive) research from traditional normative theories by emphasizing the importance of prediction and explanation. It helped place normative theories and their role in a clearer perspective. Our work was not directly related to the debate over alternative normative theories and we wanted to

---

[13]Christenson is referring to Milton Friedman's views on scientific methodology as expounded in Friedman (1953). In our opinion, Friedman places too much emphasis on prediction vis-à-vis explanation.

differentiate our work from that debate. The phrase "positive" created a trademark and like all trademarks it conveys information. "Coke," "Kodak," "Levis" convey information. A positive theory differs from a normative theory, though a positive theory can have normative implications once an objective function is specified (Jensen 1983).

In retrospect, the term "positive" generated more confusion than we anticipated. For example, some thought we meant logical positivism (Christenson 1983). We merely intended to distinguish positive propositions from the extant normative propositions in the literature. While the term "positive" avoided debates over normative uses of the work, the term "positive" generated considerable debate over philosophical issues.

Despite its problems, we prefer "positive accounting literature" to alternative terms that have arisen, particularly the term "economic consequences literature." This latter term suggests accounting standards are decided on some higher basis and that economic consequences are a secondary factor only considered after the initial decision is made on the higher basis.[14]

DEBATE OVER METHODOLOGY   Several papers listed in Table 1 involve a debate over what constitutes "proper" methodology (Tinker et al. 1982; Christenson 1983; Lowe et al. 1983; Whittington 1987; Hines 1988). For example, Christenson (1983, 1) concludes, ". . . [T]he standards advocated by the Rochester School for appraisal of their own theories are so weak that those theories fail to satisfy Popper's (1959) proposal for demarking science from metaphysics." Hines (1988) then criticizes Christenson for relying on Popper (1959) which later philosophers of science have questioned. Hines (1988, 658) argues these methodology issues are important and if ignored will "harmfully limit the nature and domain of accounting research."

The methodology criticisms have failed the market test because they have had little influence on accounting research. Researchers have not changed their approach. Referees and editors of journals have not asked researchers to alter their methodology based on these published critiques. There are at least three reasons these criticisms have had little effect on published research. First, the criticisms are written in an abstract fashion. Instead of just criticizing extant papers, if the critics would repeat studies without making the alleged errors, then users of the corrected research would demand such procedures be followed in the future. If the alleged errors are important to users, then other researchers, editors, and referees would adopt the suggestions. Second, critics who place unreasonable demands on studies cause other researchers to disregard their complaints. For example, Hines (1988, 661) argues that Watts and Zimmerman (1978) should have: (1) avoided crude proxies, (2) avoided unrealistic assumptions, (3) investigated the anomalies, (4) clarified their theories, and (5) rigorously tested their theories against competing hypotheses. All these standards are relevant, but if all were applied rigorously to individual papers (especially early papers in an area of thought), no research would be published. Third, to most researchers, debating methodology is a "no win" situation because each side argues from a different paradigm with different rules and no common ground. Our reason for replying here is that some have mistaken our lack of response as tacit acceptance of the criticisms.

---

[14]Some have suggested the term "contracting theory." While descriptive of most of the elements in the existing theory, it seems to preclude noncontractual variables that might be discovered later (e.g., taxes or information for the capital markets, Holthausen forthcoming).

III. SUMMARY AND CONCLUSIONS

Our prime objective in this paper is to provide a perspective on our 1978 and 1979 *Accounting Review* papers. The 1978 paper has proven more important than the "Excuses" paper. Based on citations, the 1978 paper has received over three times as many citations as the 1979 paper (Brown and Gardner 1985, 97). The 1978 paper was a catalyst for research into the choice of accounting methods. Except for generating debates over methodology, the 1979 "Excuses" paper has remained outside the mainstream of accounting research probably because of the more subjective type of evidence necessary to test theories of the effect of accounting research on policy.

The debate over methodology has been less useful than the discovery and explanation of empirical regularities. The positive accounting literature has discovered several empirical regularities in accounting choice and provided an explanation for them. Critics of the 1978 and 1979 papers raise issues involving research methods and philosophy of science. The methodology we and the subsequent literature use is the methodology of economics, finance, and science generally. This methodology has been successful in accounting and we feel no necessity to apologize for it. Under this methodology, a theory is not discarded merely because of some inconsistent observations. The best theory is determined in a competition to meet the demand from students and practitioners for theories that explain and predict accounting choice. It is unlikely an accounting or a social science theory with perfect predictions will ever exist. Researchers are influenced by their values. But, to the extent those researchers are competing to meet student and practitioners' demand for theories, they have incentives to reduce that influence. Further, the careful dichotomy between theory and prescription helps reduce that influence. Lastly, accounting is an activity carried out by people and one cannot generate a theory that predicts and explains accounting phenomena by ignoring the incentives of the individuals who account. In this final section we summarize the contributions made by this literature, our views on promising research directions, and some conclusions.

POSITIVE ACCOUNTING LITERATURE CONTRIBUTIONS

Discovering systematic patterns in accounting choice outlined in the preceding sections and providing specific explanations for the patterns are the literature's major contributions. However, we believe the literature has made other contributions: it provides an intuitively plausible framework for understanding accounting. A plausible framework is a useful pedagogy for teaching accounting. The literature also encourages researchers to address accounting issues and emphasizes the central role of contracting costs in accounting theory.

The literature explains why accounting is used and provides a framework for predicting accounting choices. Choices are not made in terms of "better measurement" of some accounting construct, such as earnings. Choices are made in terms of individual objectives and the effects of accounting methods on the achievement of those objectives. For example, some accounting instructors teach that certain accounting methods (e.g., current cost) are better than others (e.g., historical cost). But, no explanation is offered why these "better" measures are not adopted. The positive accounting literature takes as given the proposition that the accepted set maximizes the wealth of the contracting parties and then seeks to understand how wealth is affected by specific accounting methods.

The literature's emphasis on predicting and explaining accounting phenomena encourages research that is relevant to accounting. One of the first questions one pursuing this approach asks of a new model is whether it has any relevance to predicting and explaining accounting practice.

Another contribution of the literature is to highlight the importance of contracting costs (including information, agency, bankruptcy, and lobbying costs). Contracting costs have long been important in economics and date to Coase (1937). Positive accounting research has more recently recognized the importance of contracting costs to explain accounting. In the late 1960s and 1970s, financial economists derived pricing models (capital asset pricing models, option pricing models, arbitrage pricing models). These models were developed under assumptions of costless information and such models explain why different securities sell for different relative prices. Such models do not explain institutional differences, such as open- and closed-end mutual funds. To explain such institutional differences requires assumptions of costly information and contracting. Likewise, accounting would not exist without contracting costs and so it is difficult to produce a theory that predicts and explains accounting without making assumptions about the relative magnitudes of these costs. The central role of contracting costs highlighted by positive accounting research makes it difficult to ignore these costs in accounting theories. It directs researchers' attention to the appropriate issues.

FUTURE RESEARCH DIRECTIONS

Section II discussed two major research methods issues: the lack of power of the tests and alternative economic explanations for the empirical regularities. The following research suggestions focus on these two issues. We believe these suggestions will be more fruitful in advancing the understanding of accounting choice than "merely conducting more studies using existing formulations of the theory and existing ways of measuring variables" (Christie forthcoming) (also see Holthausen and Leftwich 1983, 109–114).

First, the single most important task facing positive accounting researchers is improving the linkage between the theory and empirical tests. The theory predicts that the magnitude of debt renegotiation costs will affect managers' choice of accounting methods and will set an upper bound on the magnitude of the default costs. To date, researchers have been unable to document the magnitude of the costs imposed by a technical violation of a debt covenant or the magnitude of renegotiation costs (Holthausen 1981; Leftwich 1981; Lys 1984; Leftwich forthcoming). Greater attention has to be placed on developing a unified theory that incorporates both the *ex ante* efficient restrictions on the managers' accepted set of accounting methods and the *ex post* exercise by managers of their discretion to choose accounting methods from within the accepted set. The empirical tests can no longer assume accounting choice is made for either efficiency or opportunistic reasons. Both must be incorporated into the tests. Also, estimates of the relative magnitudes of the various components of contracting costs can help to further refine the linkage between the theory and tests by identifying those costs most influential in driving accounting choice.

Developing and testing alternative hypotheses for the existing empirical regularities also will enhance the linkage between the theory and the tests. Hypotheses can be developed to predict new empirical regularities. Under the contracting approach, debt and compensation contracts are only some of the contracts that affect firms' cash flows. Other (explicit and implicit) contracts can be used to develop new predictions (DeAngelo 1988a). Particularly promising is the effect of accounting procedures for internal control on external reporting (Ball 1989). For example, Mian and Smith (forthcoming) find that the prevalence of consolidated reporting of financing subsidiaries depends on the extent to which the subsidiary is interdependent with the parent's main business. How the firm is organized internally (e.g., functionally or by product line), the type of internal compensation systems, and the investment opportunity set are likely associated with the type of internal accounting performance measurement systems. Internal contracting parties may well turn out to be as important a determinant of external financial reporting as the external contracting parties.

Finally, the political process can affect firms' cash flow other than via the simple political cost hypotheses. More detailed specification of government regulatory processes that rely on accounting numbers can be used to develop new hypotheses and a tighter linkage between the theory and tests by suggesting more precise proxy variables other than firm size (Sutton 1988; Wong 1988; Jones 1988).

Second, when accounting choice is cast as part of the efficient contracting technology, variables often used to explain and predict accounting choice are endogenous. For example, changes in accounting procedures occur simultaneously with changes in the firm's investment opportunity set, its financial and compensation contracts, its organizational structure, and even in its political environment. Managers choose packages of accounting policy, financial policy, and organizational structure (including performance evaluation and reward systems). Theoretical and empirical models have to be developed to sort out the endogeneity problems among the variables and, thereby, increase the power of the tests. While this is no easy task, it seems essential to significant advances in both the theories of the firm and of accounting.

Accounting numbers are used in different ways across industries. Besides the obvious regulatory uses of accounting numbers in financial institutions and public utilities, differences in industries' opportunity sets are likely to affect the accepted set of accounting methods. Two types of studies are likely to prove useful and again increase the tests' power. First, studies investigating differences in investment opportunity sets (e.g., the relative amount growth opportunities to assets in place, Myers 1977), accounting polices, organizational structures, and financial policies across industries are likely to produce information useful for the modelling suggested in the preceding paragraph. Second, intra-industry studies of accounting choice while requiring significant amount of industry-specific knowledge by the researcher, have the potential of generating useful insights about the magnitude of contracting costs.

Third, measurement errors in net accruals can be reduced to increase the tests' power. This requires a model of net accruals not subject to managerial accounting discretion (Kaplan 1985; McNichols and Wilson 1988; DeAngelo 1988b; Moyer 1988). Also, replacing the simple indicator variables used to represent a bonus plan or an accounting-based debt covenant with continuous variables that better measure the relative magnitudes of various contracting costs will probably increase the theory's predictive power.

CONCLUSIONS

While the positive accounting literature has yielded empirical regularities and explanations for these regularities, it is clear there are many research opportunities available beyond those currently exploited. The tests of the debt, bonus, and political cost hypotheses represent very limited exploration. Incorporating both *ex ante* contracting efficiency incentives with *ex post* redistributive effects is likely to prove useful. Likewise, investigating the implications of internal contracts and external contracts other than debt and bonus contracts is likely to be productive. The major breakthroughs are likely to come from viewing accounting as a choice that is endogenous with the choice of organization, contracting, and financial structures. Such a breakthrough will be difficult to achieve, but important foundations can be laid by stressing the linkage between the theory and the empirical tests and by investigating inter- and intra-industry variations in accounting methods and other organizational choices.

References

Alchian, A. A. 1950. Uncertainty, evolution and economic theory. *Journal of Political Economy.* (June): 211–221.

———, and H. Demsetz. 1972. Production, information costs and economic organization. *American Economic Review.* (December): 777–795.

Ball, R. 1972. Changes in accounting techniques and stock prices. *Journal of Accounting Research.* (Supplement): 1–38.

———. 1980. Discussion of accounting for research and development costs: The impact of research and development expenditures. *Journal of Accounting Research.* (Supplement): 27–37.

———. 1989. Accounting, auditing and the nature of the firm. Working paper, William E. Simon Graduate School of Business Administration, University of Rochester.

———, and P. Brown. 1968. An empirical evaluation of accounting income numbers. *Journal of Accounting Research.* (Autumn): 159–178.

———, and G. Foster. 1982. Corporate financial reporting: A methodological review of empirical research. *Journal of Accounting Research.* (Supplement): 161–234.

Beaver, W. 1968. The information content of annual earnings announcements. *Journal of Accounting Research.* (Supplement): 67–92.

Begley, J. 1990. Debt covenants and accounting choice. *Journal of Accounting & Economics.* (Forthcoming).

Bernard, V. 1989. Capital markets research in accounting during the 1980s: A critical review. Manuscript, University of Michigan.

Bowen, R. M., E. W. Noreen, and J. M. Lacey. 1981. Determinants of the corporate decision to capitalize interest. *Journal of Accounting & Economics.* (August): 151–179.

Brown, L. D., and J. C. Gardner. 1985. Using citation analysis to assess the impact of journals and articles on contemporary accounting research (CAR). *Journal of Accounting Research.* (Spring): 84–109.

Chambers, R. J. 1966. *Accounting, evaluation, and economic behavior.* Prentice-Hall.

Christie, A. A. 1987. On cross-sectional analysis in accounting research. *Journal of Accounting & Economics.* (December): 231–258.

———. 1990. Aggregation of test statistics: An evaluation of the evidence on contracting and size hypotheses. *Journal of Accounting & Economics.* (Forthcoming).

Christenson, C. 1983. The methodology of positive accounting. *The Accounting Review.* (January): 1–22.

Coase, R. H. 1937. The nature of the firm. *Economica.* (November): 386–405.

Daley, L. A., and R. L. Vigeland. 1983. The effects of debt covenants and political costs on the choice of accounting methods: The case of accounting for R&D costs. *Journal of Accounting & Economics.* (December): 195–211.

DeAngelo, L. E. 1986. Accounting numbers as market valuation substitutes: A study of management buyouts of public stockholders. *The Accounting Review.* (July): 400–420.

———. 1988a. Managerial competition, information costs, and corporate governance: The use of accounting performance measures in proxy contests. *Journal of Accounting & Economics.* (January): 3–36.

———. 1988b. Discussion of evidence of earnings management from the provision for bad debts. *Journal of Accounting Research.* (Supplement): 32–40.

Duke, J., and H. Hunt. 1990. An empirical examination of debt covenant restrictions and accounting-related debt proxies. *Journal of Accounting & Economics.* (Forthcoming).

Fama, E. F., and M. C. Jensen. 1983a. Separation of ownership and control. *Journal of Law and Economics.* (June): 301–325.

———, and ———. 1983b. Agency problems and residual claims. *Journal of Law and Economics.* (June): 327–349.

Foster, G. 1980. Accounting policy decisions and capital market research. *Journal of Accounting & Economics.* (March): 29–62.

Friedman, M. [1953] 1966. *The methodology of positive economics, essays in positive economics.* Reprint, Phoenix Books.

Frost, C., and V. Bernard. 1989. The role of debt covenants in assessing economic consequences of limiting capitalization of exploration costs. *The Accounting Review.* (October): 788–808.

Gagnon, J. M. 1967. Purchase versus pooling of interest: The search for a predictor. *Journal of Accounting Research.* (Supplement): 187–204.

Gordon, M. J. 1964. Postulates, principles and research in accounting. *The Accounting Review.* (April): 251–263.

———, B. N. Horwitz, and P. T. Meyers. 1966. Accounting measurements and normal growth of the firm. *Research in accounting measurement.* Eds. R. K. Jaedicke, Y. Ijiri, and O. Nielsen, 221–231. American Accounting Association.

Healy, P. M. 1985. The effect of bonus schemes on accounting decisions. *Journal of Accounting & Economics*. (April): 85–107.

Hines, R. D. 1988. Popper's methodology of falsificationism and accounting research. *The Accounting Review*. (October): 657–662.

Holthausen, R. W. 1981. Evidence on the effect of bond covenants and management compensation contracts on the choice of accounting techniques: The case of the depreciation switch-back. *Journal of Accounting & Economics*. (March): 73–109.

———. 1990. Accounting method choice: Opportunistic behavior, efficient contracting and information perspectives. *Journal of Accounting & Economics*. (Forthcoming).

———, and R. W. Leftwich. 1983. The economic consequences of accounting choice: Implications of costly contracting and monitoring. *Journal of Accounting & Economics*. (August): 77–117.

Jensen, M. C. 1983. Organization theory and methodology. *The Accounting Review*. (April): 319–339.

———, and W. H. Meckling. 1976. Theory of the firm: Managerial behavior, agency costs and ownership structure. *Journal of Financial Economics*. (October): 305–360.

Jones, J. 1988. The effect of foreign trade regulation on accounting choices, and production and investment decisions. Working paper, University of Michigan.

Kalay, A. 1982. Stockholder-bondholder conflict and dividend constraints. *Journal of Financial Economics*. (July): 211–233.

Kaplan, R. S. 1985. Comments on Paul Healy: Evidence on the effect of bonus schemes on accounting procedure and accrual decisions. *Journal of Accounting & Economics*. (April): 109–113.

Klein, B. 1983. Contracting costs and residual claims: The separation of ownership and control. *Journal of Law & Economics*. (June): 367–374.

———, R. Crawford, and A. Alchian. 1978. Vertical integration, appropriable rents, and the competitive contracting process. *Journal of Law & Economics*. (October): 297–326.

Kohler, E. L. 1975. *A dictionary for accountants*. 5th ed. Prentice-Hall.

Lavoie, D. 1989. The accounting of interpretations and the interpretation of accounts: The communicative function of "the language of business." *Methodology and accounting research: Does the past have a future*. Ed. O. Johnson, 107–149. Orace Johnson.

Leftwich, R. 1981. Evidence of the impact of mandatory changes in accounting principles on corporate loan agreements. *Journal of Accounting & Economics*. (March): 3–36.

———. 1983. Accounting information in private markets: Evidence from private lending agreements. *The Accounting Review*. (January): 23–42.

———. 1990. Aggregation of test statistics: Statistics vs economics. *Journal of Accounting & Economics*. (Forthcoming).

———, R. L. Watts, and J. L. Zimmerman. 1981. Voluntary corporate disclosure: The case of interim reporting. *Journal of Accounting Research*. (Supplement): 50–77.

Ler, B., and J. A. Ohlson. 1982. Market-based empirical research in accounting: A review, interpretation, and extension. *Journal of Accounting Research*. (Supplement): 249–322.

Liberty, S. E., and J. L. Zimmerman. 1986. Labor union contract negotiations and accounting choices. *The Accounting Review*. (October): 692–712.

Lowe, E. A., A. G. Puxty, and R. C. Laughlin. 1983. Simple theories for complex processes: Accounting policy and the market for myopia. *Journal of Accounting and Public Policy*. (Spring): 19–42.

Lys, T. 1984. Mandated accounting changes and debt covenants: The case of oil and gas accounting. *Journal of Accounting & Economics*. (April): 39–65.

Malmquist, D. 1990. Efficient contracting and the choice of accounting method in the oil and gas industry. *Journal of Accounting & Economics*. (Forthcoming).

McKee, A. J., Jr., T. B. Bell, and J. R. Boatsman. 1984. Management preferences over accounting standards: A replication and additional tests. *The Accounting Review*. (October): 647–659.

McNichols, M., and G. Wilson. 1988. Evidence of earnings management from the provision for bad debts. *Journal of Accounting Research*. (Supplement): 1–31.

Meckling, W., and M. Jensen. 1986. Knowledge, control and organizational structure. Working paper, University of Rochester.

Mian, S., and C. Smith. 1990. Incentives for unconsolidated financial reporting. *Journal of Accounting & Economics*. (Forthcoming).

Modigliani, F., and M. H. Miller. 1958. The cost of capital, corporation finance and the theory of investment. *American Economic Review*. (June): 261–297.

Moyer, S. 1988. Accounting choices in commercial banks. Dissertation, University of Rochester.

Myers, S. 1977. Determinants of corporate borrowing. *Journal of Financial Economics*. (November): 147–175.

Peltzman, S. 1976. Toward a more general theory of regulation. *Journal of Law and Economics*. (August): 211–240.

Popper, K. R. [1959] 1965. *The logic of scientific discovery*. Reprint, Harper & Row.

Press, E., and J. Weintrop. 1990. Accounting-based constraints in public and private debt agreements: Their association with leverage and impact on accounting choice. *Journal of Accounting & Economics*. (Forthcoming).

Ricks, W. 1982. Market assessment of alternative accounting methods: A review of the empirical evidence. *Journal of Accounting Literature*. (59–102).

Smith, C. W. 1980. On the theory of financial contracting: The personal loan market. *Journal of Monetary Economics*. (July): 333–357.

———, and J. B. Warner. 1979. On financial contracting: An analysis of bond covenants. *Journal of Financial Economics*. (June): 117–161.

———, and R. Watts. 1982. Incentive and tax effects of U.S. executive compensation plans. *Australian Journal of Management*. (December): 139–157.

———, and ———. 1986. Investment opportunity set and corporate policy choices. Working paper, University of Rochester.

Sorter, G. H., S. W. Becker, T. R. Archibald, and W. H. Beaver. 1966. Accounting and financial measures as indicators of corporate personality—some empirical findings. *Research in accounting measurement*. Eds. R. K. Jaedicke, Y. Ijiri, and O. Nielsen, 200–210. American Accounting Association.

Sprouse, R., and M. Moonitz. 1962. A tentative set of broad accounting principles for business enterprises. *Accounting Research Study No. 3*. American Institute of Certified Public Accountants.

Stigler, G. J. 1971. The theory of economic regulation. *Bell Journal of Economics and Management Science*. (Spring): 3–21.

Sutton, T. G. 1988. The proposed introduction of current cost accounting in the U.K.: Determinants of corporate preference. *Journal of Accounting & Economics*. (April): 127–149.

Tinker, T. A. M., B. D. Merino, and M. D. Neimark. 1982. The normative origins of positive theories: Ideology and accounting thought. *Accounting, Organizations and Society 2:* 167–200.

Watts, R. L. 1974. Accounting objectives. Working paper, University of Rochester.

———. 1977. Corporate financial statements, a product of the market and political processes. *Australian Journal of Management*. (April): 53–75.

———, and J. L. Zimmerman. 1978. Towards a positive theory of the determination of accounting standards. *The Accounting Review*. (January): 112–134.

———, and ———. 1979. The demand for and supply of accounting theories: The market for excuses. *The Accounting Review*. (April): 273–305.

———, and ———. 1986. *Positive accounting theory*. Prentice-Hall.

Whittington, G. 1987. Positive accounting: A review article. *Accounting and Business Research*. (Autumn): 327–336.

Whittred, G. 1987. The derived demand for consolidated financial reporting. *Journal of Acounting & Economics*. (December): 259–285.

Wong, J. 1988. Economic incentives for the voluntary disclosure of current cost financial statements. *Journal of Accounting & Economics*. (April): 151–167.

Zimmer, I. 1986. Accounting for interest by real estate developers. *Journal of Accounting & Economics*. (March): 37–51.

Zimmerman, J. L. 1979. The costs and benefits of cost allocations. *The Accounting Review*. (July): 504–521.

———. 1983. Taxes and firm size. *Journal of Accounting & Economics*. (August): 119–149.

Zmijewski, M., and R. Hagerman. 1981. An income strategy approach to the positive theory of accounting standard setting/choice. *Journal of Accounting & Economics*. (August): 129–149.

POSITIVE ACCOUNTING THEORY AND THE PA CULT

R. J. Chambers

So-called positive accounting theory, it has been claimed, has brought about a revolution in accounting thought and research. Full-bodied search, before the mid-1960s, for better modes of accounting has given way to virtual denial of the need or possibility of improvement. The survival of what is is taken to demonstrate that it is best. Typically, revolutions occur when a dominant body of ideas appears no longer to be serviceable in resolving problems, or fruitful of advances in knowledge or technique, and a more promising alternative is proposed in its place. It is, of course, notoriously difficult to foresee whether any innovation will live up to its promise. Ideas launched with zeal and promoted with passion may be found, only years later, to be genuine advances, or impediments—'fads, fashions and folderol', as a psychologist has described some work in his field (Dunnette, 1966, p. 343). A twenty-five year perspective may not be long enough, but the rate at which exotic organisms multiply in a predator-free environment suggests that it is ample.

Critics of the work of the positive accounting theorists have given varying degrees of attention to logical and methodological matters (e.g., Christenson, 1983; Schreuder, 1984; Whitley, 1988; Williams, 1989; Sterling, 1990). The present exercise touches those matters tangentially. It concerns itself principally with some features of the relationship of factual

An earlier draft of this paper (February 1990) was sent to the authors of the main works discussed; none has expressed comment or opinion.

R. J. Chambers, "Positive Accounting Theory and the PA Cult," *Abacus,* vol. 29, no. 1, 1993, 1–26.

financial knowledge to judgment and action, as they are portrayed or bypassed by positive accounting protagonists. It will be contended, among other things, that many of the claims made by or for leaders of the movement could be made, equally if not more properly, by or for others; that some such claims are unjustified; and that some ideas advanced as novel are longstanding ideas in new verbal garb. It is necessary therefore to distinguish the movement from the persons and the work of others. It, and as convenient shorthand its devotees, will be referred to as the PA cult.

The PA cult appears to have emerged from work in financial economics in the University of Chicago in the mid-1960s and from work on the nature of the firm in the University of Rochester about the same time. That these origins were beyond the mainstream of work in accounting is of more than passing interest. The study, teaching and practice of accounting had been passing through a period of external and internal criticism and self-doubt. The mood could perhaps be dispelled by a new look—a seemingly respectable verbiage, an apparently sophisticated research apparatus, a nodding familiarity with the concerns of scientists and economists. The verbal adornments of the cult—'positive', 'empirical', 'scientific', 'economics-based' and so on—its rituals, its congregations, its sanctions and its cohesion, drew a galaxy of followers into orbit about the Chicago–Rochester axis.

Attention can be given here only to a modest portion of the output of the cult, to what appear to be the key elements of its doctrines, hypotheses and procedures. The principal reference will be to Watts and Zimmerman (herinafter W&Z; 1986), which appears to be a compendious exposition of the work of the cult, but there will be modest references to other work of the same genre.

Origins

A paper of Ball and Brown (hereinafter B&B; 1968) was among the earliest indications of the direction that came to be taken. They purported to investigate, to evaluate, the usefulness of the products of conventional accounting. The paper began with some observations on criticisms of those products by Canning (1929) and others to Sterling (1970). B&B said: 'The limitations of a completely analytical approach to usefulness are illustrated by the argument that income numbers cannot be defined substantively, that they lack "meaning" and are therefore of doubtful utility' (p. 159). They thus challenged the findings of the critics. They purported to make an empirical evaluation of accounting income numbers.

They found that the change in the abnormal return on a given stock (calculated on the basis of stock prices and dividends paid) was generally of the same sign as the change in reported accounting earnings. They deduced that the published earnings numbers had information content and were useful. Recourse to directions of change, of course, bypasses altogether the question whether published earnings were demonstrably an approximation to an empirically determinate amount.

The exercise exemplifies the fundamental element of what may be called the PA twist, a switch from examining the processes and products of accounting to examining features of the stock market. No one had previously contested the proposition that the release of income information, and scores of other incidents, influence the course of judgments, and hence of stock prices. So the conclusion of B&B was commonplace. The underlying presumption of the argument, however, was that the firm, as a separate entity, is to be disregarded. What is then of interest is the incomes and rates of return of investors, and that has to do with changes in stock market prices and amounts of declared dividends. That is all; and that is the focus of attention of the project.

But the critics of conventional practice were concerned with differences between the disclosed income *of the firm* and the empirically determinate income *of the firm*. The firm was regarded by them as a distinct entity having assets (just as investors have as assets the shares they hold), the net amount of which is variable (just as the market value of an investor's shares is variable). The firm was deemed to have an income consisting of cash increments and accrued changes in the prices of assets (as in the case of investors; B&B, p. 162), and a rate of return, being the ratio of the income to the opening investment stated at market prices (as in the case of investors). Given the availability of such information on the rates of return to the firm *and* to investors, investors could compare the two rates, compare either or both of those rates with returns to other investors and to other firms, and draw inferences affecting their judgments, their willingness to buy or sell and the prices at which they might do so. This schema, it is apparent, gives investors a richer supply of information pertinent to their actions than the PA schema. And the premise that the firm is a distinct entity is empirically defensible, whereas the PA presumption is counterfactual.

If any attention had been given to the firm as such and to features of the released income information, several things might have been apparent. First, under conventional accounting firms do not calculate incomes and rates of return in the manner of the B&B calculation of the return on a given stock. The anomaly deserved attention, but received none. The amounts of declared dividends depend on the amounts represented from time to time as divisible surpluses. To be consistent with the B&B calculation, divisible surpluses should be represented by empirically determined incomes and prior surpluses; under conventional accounting they are not. Under conventional accounting for firms, there are made available to investors, not only income figures, but also balance sheets representing the dated amounts and compositions of assets and debts. That information provides inputs to judgments on the solvency and the financial flexibility of firms and on the riskiness of asset portfolios, all of which are potential modifiers of the prices at which rational investors may otherwise be willing to buy or sell. Of course, they would not be serviceable modifiers if calculated otherwise than by the B&B method for the dated amounts of the assets of investors; but under conventional accounting they are calculated by quite different methods. The B&B exercise disregards the whole of this, both the anomalies mentioned and the function of periodical information on dated financial positions. That is the inevitable consequence of taking no notice of accounting, and only notice of what momentarily hits the stock market in respect of each security considered severally.

To evaluate the conventional income numbers of firms by recourse to the incomes of investors is logically impossible, however sophisticated the procedure used may be; the two are not *in pari materia*. And to ignore the substantial differences in the modes of calculating those incomes is egregious oversight. Given these solecisms, notice may be taken of some subsidiary twists, for the PA literature is liberally supplied with examples of verbal legerdemain.

Note, first, the reference to income numbers. The products of accounting processes had long been described as measurements, improperly so described according to some of the critics. B&B seem to have acknowledged implicitly the impropriety of the description; but the reference to 'numbers' also implicitly severs the association of the products of accounting from the observables they are expected to depict. B&B did not deny that conventional income numbers 'lack substantive meaning', have no empirical referent to which the term 'income' can properly be applied. As has occurred so often in later work of the PA cult, such awkward contentions are just set aside—no proviso, no comment.

Second, what could be intended by 'further empirical testing'? The authors whose views B&B questioned were concerned with the failure to produce money amounts that corresponded with empirical phenomena, and were for that reason (a) unintelligible to recipients and (b) unserviceable as indicators of past and prospective real world relationships. 'Further empirical testing' would then mean further testing for correspondence and intelligibility. But 'further' was diversionary. B&B were altogether unconcerned with correspondence and intelligibility.

Third, 'useful' is clearly misused in the conclusion that disclosed earnings numbers are useful. It might be claimed that the published income numbers were *used*. Lacking a hammer, one might use the heel of a shoe, but it would be a gross overstatement to say that a shoe is *useful* as a hammer, and ludicrous to go to the shoe store when one wants a hammer. Lacking anything better, the market is (or, operators in it are) obliged to *use* whatever is called 'income' by those on whom they rely; but that does not mean that the number is *useful* as indicating or representing income. Whether the indifference of B&B to the distinction between used and useful is careless or tendentious the reader may judge.

Fourth, it is arguable that 'information content' is also misused. These are scores of events, or bits of information about events, that may influence the price of a stock at any point of time. The release of an income number is only one of them. At best, then, the release of such numbers is tenuously related to shifts in stock prices. To ascribe 'information content' to messages thus tenuously related is credulous in the extreme; and a misuse of a term having an entirely different and proper use. A message relates to some matter of which knowledge is available to the issuer. It can be said to have information content to the extent that it represents or corresponds with that matter, whether or not it brings about a response by any recipient. A response is the outcome of a complex evaluative process, of states and stimuli and needs and preferences, at a stated time. To ascribe information content to one of the inputs on the basis of an observed response is gross oversimplification. And it puts B&B on very slippery ground. Beaver on one occasion (1968) pointed out that the stock exchange trading volume statistics indicated that, on average, 'if corporation X has 10 million shares outstanding, during a normal week 50,000 shares will be traded, with an expected volume of 66,667 shares during the earnings report week' (p. 75). Thus the shares traded on any earnings announcement day would amount, on average, to less than 0.15 per cent of a company's outstanding shares. It seems precarious indeed to base the sweeping conclusion of B&B on reactions in respect of such tiny proportions of outstanding stock. At face value, the volume figures suggest that the earnings release had *no* information content in respect of holders of 99.85 per cent of an issue!

In any case, the method used biased the inquiry, and therefore the conclusions. It automatically excludes companies that were not among those listed over the full period of years examined. It thus excludes all companies that may have collapsed or been liquidated, during that period or at other times; and collapses and failures and the investigations that follow them are the richest source of evidence of deliberate, and inadvertent but no less objectionable, misrepresentation, in short, evidence of misleading information content. Where the methods used with that effect are used almost universally, their effects in any particular case are a matter of degree, not of kind.

B&B either overlooked or deliberately set aside the fact that statements that do not correspond with what they purport to represent can only have misinformation or disinformation content. They do not acquire meaning, in the sense of Canning and others, or in the sense pertinent in practical affairs, simply by being published. A falsification does not become a reality, a lie does not become a truth, a fiction does not become a fact, by its utterance.

The usefulness and information content conclusions must be regarded as overreaching, not proven. The inquiry was not, of course, an inquiry into any facet of accounting at all. It was not a further test of prior contentions. It was not a test or an evaluation of conventional income numbers. The paper's title misrepresents what the paper does. It could have been written, indeed, without any knowledge whatever of accounting. The exercise looks rather like the product of people who have newly learned a method of analysis looking for some way of applying it, rather than of people confronted with a problem looking for some appropriate means of solving it.

It is noteworthy that neither Ball nor Brown had contributed anything of substance on the particular rules and devices that have been advanced, analysed and criticized in the professional and academic literature. Nor did they pay any attention to the vast natural history of practice and its consequences that has provided practitioners and academics with empirical evidence of the anomalous nature of so much that was done and taught. Sufficient for them to hurl Jovian bolts from high Olympus on those menials who strove with such difficulties as vague and inapt terminology, inconsistent prescription, fallacious argument and the observable inequities associated with demonstrably false financial statements. An upsurge of concern with these very infelicities was the proximate spur to the emergence during the 1960s and 1970s of the APB and the FASB in the U.S. and of similar organizations elsewhere. But the contentions that conventional accounting, in spite of alleged flaws, was useful, provided information content and did not mislead the market cut right across the drift of the evidence and the urge for reform. All was right with the accounting world after all! Or, if there were flaws they were innocuous, for the market could, by some occult divination, 'see through' (W&Z, 1986, p. 99) the fictions and idiosyncrasies of accounting practice.

It was a short step to the position that all differences in precept or practice were justifiable, and that the business of inquiry in accounting was to discover what sets of conditions justified which sets of rules. If one obscures or suppresses the difference between knowledgeable reasoning and *ex post* rationalization, and describes the total package as theory, the ground is laid for the depiction of theory as excuse. Thus did W&Z (1979). Using theory 'as a generic term for the existing accounting literature' (p. 273) was a careless or a cunning way of bringing under one rubric work that was as different as the aprioristic and the empirical, or as rationalization and reasoning. The usage enabled them to lump all together under the summary description 'predominantly prescriptive'. The 'excuses' paper describes itself as '*not* normative or prescriptive', as if (since there is no other apparent reason for the remark) to distinguish it sharply from prior work. But the paper is not in the same vein or of the same kind as that prior work; it is concerned not with the substance of rules but with the role of theory in determining accounting practice or accounting standards. The setting is there laid for the subsequent use of 'positive theory of accounting' for what should properly be called some sort of theory of standard setting—for accounting and standard setting are quite different processes.

ACCOUNTING?

The B&B paper had been rejected by *The Accounting Review* on the ground that 'it was not an accounting manuscript' (Dyckman and Zeff, 1984, p. 242). Whether or not some set of ideas or rules falls, or should fall, within the domain of accounting may seem to be a pointless question. It is not. There is a basic similarity among methods of disciplined inquiry in all kinds of fields, but there are also critical differences. Arithmetic differs from bookkeeping; pathology from epidemiology; economics from administration; financial economics from accounting. Each item of these pairs has its own characteristic set of concerns, problems and problem-solving procedures. Each item may benefit from interchanges with its other. But its orderly development and practice are disciplined only to the extent that those expert in it keep its function and functioning under critical scrutiny. If no attempt is made to delimit the field, attention and effort are apt to be squandered on irrelevancies that masquerade as the proper business of accounting. That possibility lurks in the background of the PA doctrine.

Given the training in finance of the forerunners of the PA cult, said W&Z (1986), 'it was natural for them to concentrate on explaining and predicting security price behavior and not on explaining and predicting accounting practice' (p. 16). They made use of the efficient market hypothesis (EMH) and the capital asset pricing model (CAPM), knowledge of which is 'still crucial to current researchers and those wanting to understand and perform accounting research', according to W&Z (p. 16). The claim is unproven except for some special types of research in which the PA cult engages. But have these borrowed devices anything to do with accounting research?

As Ball (1972) saw the EMH: 'The efficiency of the market is defined as the speed with which equilibrium is reached after the release of some set of data' (p. 2). It's a matter of speed of ingestion, not of the quality of the information released. In the absence of anything to the contrary in the literature, it holds of data that are true and false, substantial and fabricated, financial and non-financial. It has nothing to do with explaining and predicting the specifics of accounting practice.

Neither has the CAPM. It is based on the assumptions—perfect markets; rational, risk-averse, maximizing investors; costless access by all to information; and homogeneous expectations (e.g., W&Z, 1986, p. 23). Given this roster of assumptions, 'in essence, under the multiperiod version of the CAPM, the market value of the firm is the discounted expected future cash flows' (p. 27). In the real world, in which none of the severe assumptions holds, to accept a calculated DCF as a market value would be plain error, and to use 'market value' of DCF in the passage cited is to confuse an imagined number with a number having, in principle, an empirical referent. So to confuse an imaginary with an observable is quite at odds with the view (which the PA cult claims to endorse) that reliable knowledge subsists in what can be shown to be the case. But, whatever it may have to do with the analysis of financial markets, the CAPM has not been shown to have anything to do with explaining and predicting accounting practices.

What, then, is to be taken as the domain of accounting and the subject matter of accounting theory? The quite general term 'positive accounting theory' implies that there is to be expounded a theory that deals with accounting generally. 'The objective of accounting theory is to explain and predict accounting practice' (W&Z, 1986, p. 2). W&Z affirmed that their concept of accounting theory is 'broader and has a different focus from that given in financial accounting texts' (p. 1). But broader does not mean narrower. It is to be expected, therefore, that the scope of positive accounting theory would embrace the substance, if not the particulars, of other expositions. In fact it does not.

In any developed community there may be hundreds of thousands of business firms that keep accounts. Of these suppose that 100,000 are corporations; and that of the corporations no more than 2 or 3 per cent have securities traded on stock exchanges. The studies of the PA cult cover only such corporations and only a select and much smaller proportion than that. In effect, the accounting of over 99 per cent of all firms is, by intent, excluded from notice and consideration. What, then, will serve to explain and predict accounting practice in their case? Certainly no inference from stock prices can do so. Further, there is not just a small number of varieties of accounting practice among the 1 per cent of firms noticed. Standard textbooks and manuals embrace a plurality of variously combinable rules for almost every item that appears in a set of accounts. Almost certainly the periodical accounts of every firm are *sui generis,* unique. The PA literature deals with only a very small part of all this diversity.

A large part of the textbook and discursive literature, and of practice, is concerned with balance sheets, their contents and the inferences that may or may not be drawn from them. Without a balance sheet it is impossible to derive for any firm indicators of solvency, the riskiness of asset and debt compositions and debt to equity relationships, financial flexibility, the financial feasibility of optional operations and the rate of return—all of which have some bearing on assessments of the firm's performance and prospects, and therefore on the market prices of its securities. Most of these crucial functions of the products of accounting, and what they imply, are completely disregarded.

Having found it necessary to explain at some length the nature of the firm (e.g., W&Z, 1986, p. 194), an occasion was introduced for considering accounting as a means of coordinating the internal use of resources with the object of maximizing profits and regulating liquidity and solvency. But the potential of accounting for service in this way has scarcely been noticed. Ball (1985, p. 7) has treated the products of conventional internal accounting as quasi-prices; but as they bear no relation to the prices which the firm must confront from time to time in external dealings, they can be of no value as coordinative or regulative devices.

The purview of Whittred & Zimmer (hereinafter WHZ; 1988) is likewise highly selective, limited to external financial reporting by companies having publicly traded securities. WHZ said they were 'more interested in the application [i.e., the selection] of accounting techniques than in the techniques *per se'* (p. xiii). They said they would investigate the perspective of shareholders and creditors on the choice of technique (though those parties have little effective say, and little understanding, in the matter), and the determinants of management's choice of techniques—why managers and others reveal strong preferences for one accounting method over another. To understand these things is to 'understand the fundamental nature of the accounting process' (p. xiv). But what fundamental proposition dictates or implies that there are or shall be options open to choice? How many options? In respect of what? May a given amount of money spent, or on hand, be represented by a variety of optional amounts? Is it the function of accounting to represent any observable event or object? If so, why, and how? And if not, why not? To have answers to such questions as these is preliminary, surely, to the offering of any grounds for managerial or other choice of techniques. But the PA literature asks no such questions.

In substance, then, the PA cult uses 'accounting' only of some phases of the accounting of firms having publicly traded securities. W&Z (1979, p. 300) advanced the hypothesis that 'much of accounting theory is the product of government intervention and that accounting theory satisfies the demand for excuses'. As noted already, they used 'theory' simply to describe the accounting literature. Even on that score a vast amount of the accounting literature was and is unrelated to government intervention. And, if 'theory' is used in a more exacting sense, a great deal of the discursive literature to which they alluded concerns itself with matters more fundamental and general than public reporting. The PA cult leaves the whole of that territory unnoticed and untouched.

Positive? Normative?

Inventing names, attaching labels, classifying and pigeonholing are all useful devices in their place. But too often they are made to stand in place of careful analysis and disciplined thought. The disputatious and the merely captious resort to them to advance or dismiss, to promote or put down, to set up or demolish argument, rather than to distinguish with care between what they consider meritorious and what objectionable. So it has been with 'positive' and 'normative'. 'Normative' has been widely used pejoratively, even though occasionally it is granted (e.g., W&Z, 1986, p. 9) that normative propositions are not unimportant. As positive research and positive theory are advanced as *the* proper way of going about the scientific study of accounting, it is necessary to be clear about the meanings of normative, positive and scientific.

Scientific inquiry does indeed make great use of propositions cast in the positive form: 'it is the case that A'. They are used as descriptions, as premises of reasoning and as the object of tests of the outcome of reasoning. However, that usage rests on underlying propositions that express ideals, judgments or values, or norms—propositions such as: observation is preferable to uninformed imagination or speculation as a basis of reliable knowledge; or, more reliable knowledge on any matter is preferable to less. The PA cult cannot object to such value-laden or normative propositions as these, for its avowed preference is an expression of such a proposition.

Next, scientific knowledge is simultaneously positive and normative, or descriptive and prescriptive. If it is true that gases and liquids expand on the application of heat or the reduction of pressure, it is true that one, anyone and everyone, must apply heat or reduce pressure to bring about an expansion of gases and liquids. The former proposition in positive form and the latter in prescriptive form are logically and practically equivalent. Scientists and others have never been queasy about affirming the intimate association between (positive) knowledge and the advancement of the ideals and aims of men. ' . . . only by a knowledge of what is can we make any practical programs of what ought to be' (Lundberg, 1942, p. 54). The theoretical and the experimental natural sciences 'both lead us to the formulation of practical technological rules stating what we cannot do' (Popper, 1972, p. 342). The greater part of the scientific enterprise is directed, not to the tolerance or preservation of inherited knowledge and devices, but to the improvement or supercession of both. Improvement, betterment, inevitably entails a departure from what is, or was previously believed to be, the case. Since the utterances of the PA cult (e.g., W&Z, 1986, p. 11) contemplate the possibility at any time of the emergence of better theories or better models, it cannot be supposed that positive accounting theory entails unswerving allegiance to what is at any time believed to be the case. But the PA cult does, implicitly and explicitly, champion conventional accounting against its critics, the so-called normatives.

There is, however, one class of normative propositions that is to be rejected, that class for which there can be adduced no greater support than the authority of the utterer. An instance may be the AAA (1948) dictum: there should be no departure from the cost basis to reflect the assets of an enterprise at amounts higher than unassigned costs. This dictum lies at the root of the conventional practice that the PA cult condones or endorses. But beneath some of the precepts of that style of practice, there do lie some propositions that are not essentially moral or authoritarian imperatives. The positive propositions and the reasoning underlying precepts may not always be apparent, or adjacent; but in many cases they are imaginable or discernible. The premises may be false or the reasoning fallacious, or both; a precept is then rejected, but for reasons other than its normative form. Thus, the AAA precept mentioned above is widely rejected. But, given that 'normative' is and has been used pejoratively, it is easier to use it of propositions from which one dissents than to try to discover the positive propositions on which the normative rests. That seems to have been the principal use of the term in the accounting literature of the past twenty years.

The object of the positive-normative distinction has not been to distinguish the 'good' from the 'bad', but to distinguish the testable from the untestable. ' . . . *is* and *ought* belong to different worlds, so that sentences which are constructed with *is* usually have a verifiable meaning, but sentences constructed with *ought* never have' (Bronowski, 1964, p. 61). The purport of such observations as this is that only empirically supportable (positive) propositions govern what men may confidently believe to be possible experiences, and grounds, therefore, for serviceable precepts.

The frenetic urge to distance themselves from their antecedents impelled the PA cult to shun prescription. ' . . . theory as we describe it yields no prescriptions for accounting practice . . . It is designed to explain and predict which firms will use a particular method of valuing assets, but it says nothing as to which method a firm should use' (W&Z, 1986, p. 7). This is curious. A theory is commonly understood to be a systematic body of propositions yielding an affirmation that, under all or stated conditions, certain phenomena are associated (as cause or antecedent) by specified means with other phenomena (as effect or consequent). An accounting theory, then, would affirm that, if a specified consequent is to be brought about, a specified antecedent is to be subjected to specified processes. However, W&Z (1986) held that the consequent, which they called the objective, cannot be specified in general terms; 'the decision on the objective is subjective' (p. 7). Which means that there can be no theory in the sense described above. If the consequent cannot be specified in general terms, there is no way of explaining or predicting, by recourse to the so-called theory, which firms will use which basis of valuation, or any other of a set of optional rules or procedures. Explanation and prediction turn on the possibility of applying to any given set of antecedents some generalization in the nature of laws or rules that leads to or entails a consequent. In the case of constructed devices such as accounts and accounting, the consequent is the performance of a specified function or functions. There can be no interest whatever in explaining and predicting if no such function can be specified.

The aversion to prescription, or anything that looks like it, may have stemmed from misunderstanding of constraints in the natural and physical sciences. In those fields it is of no consequence, and therefore improper, to describe any phenomenon as good or bad, preferable or not preferable. A phenomenon is simply what it is. But in human and social affairs that embargo does not hold. A chair, a rule, a theory may be good or bad, and therefore preferred or not, according as it performs well its intended function. The aversion may also have stemmed from the widespread misuse of 'objective' in the cited context. Devices have *functions; people* have objectives. Scientific generalizations and knowledge relate to functions, not to the personal and contingent aims and intentions of people who put that knowledge to use. By confusing the two terms, the quite proper rejection, as subjective, of the idiosyncratic objectives of people is improperly extended to debar the drawing of universal or general functional inferences.

EMPIRICAL?

In one sense, empirical means based on observation or experiment. Observation has two roles in the context of inquiry—to prompt generalizations that may serve as premises in deductive schemes, and to provide means of testing conclusions or inferences. Conclusions that are consistent with the wider range of observables are preferred, as having the greater explanatory or predictive power.

The critics of conventional accounting, mentioned in an earlier section, have taken as evidence of its misleading nature a wide range of observables. They included the widespread and frequently augmented and varied provisions of legislation and regulations enjoining the publication of true or fair representations of financial positions and incomes; like provisions proscribing the publication of misleading financial statements; writs and litigation alleging publication of false and misleading information; complaints by legislators, administrators, tribunals, analysts, financial reporters, accountants and academics, of the misleading nature of published accounts; long-concealed frauds and unexpected failures and bonanzas. These are overt manifestations of deceit or technical solecisms. As well, there is internal evidence, known or knowable among accountants, of the fictions and logical fallacies that underlie many common practices. The inference that investors and others are misled is thus well-supported. It could no doubt be shown that not a year passes without shareholders and creditors of some publicly noticeable companies suffering losses which, on the basis of published financial statements, they could not have expected to suffer.

The argument of at least some of the critics runs thus. Between successive dates of publication of corporate financial information, investors respond as they think fit to firm-specific, industry-wide and nationwide events and information on them. Only at and after those publication dates, however, is it possible to adjust their prior judgments in the light of the only source of potentially reliable firm-specific financial information. Prior guesswork and speculation are modified by observable, empirically determined magnitudes—ideally! In practice the correspondence between what is the case and what is represented to be the case may, and does by the very method of its derivation, fall far short of the ideal.

The PA cult takes no account of the above-mentioned observables. It is held on the contrary that managers, through the choice of accounting methods and of what shall be disclosed, 'cannot systematically mislead the stock market' (W&Z, 1986, p. 159). All the observables mentioned are thus, by implication, tokens only of costly and fruitless misapprehension! The complainants were all wrong; only the PA cult is right. The conclusion purports to rest on the EMH, the CAPM and observable stock price movements. However, the EMH and the CAPM are highly abstract constructs, devised for the abstract discussion of markets as wholes, not for the explanation or analysis of the actions of individual investors in a less than abstract world. In an efficient market, it is said (W&Z, 1986), the price of a stock 'is such that investors on average earn a risk-adjusted market rate of return . . . In other words in a semistrong efficient market, the market is not systematically misled by accounting earnings' (p. 21). This is no more than an assertion that things turn out to be how they turn out to be. And since, in the analyses of the PA cult, there is no input representing an empirically determinable net income, nothing can be deduced regarding the quality of reported accounting earnings. The contention of the PA cult is simply an example of that predilection for dealing with stock market prices rather than accounting practices which, as noted earlier, W&Z found so disarmingly excusable.

A note on observables of a different kind is perhaps apposite at this point. It is well known that we see (or perceive) what we are conditioned to see (or perceive). It takes a particular commitment to the eradication of error, a scientific commitment, to discriminate between what appears to be the case and what is the case. W&Z (1986) wrote of 'the natural desire of proponents of a new set of theories and methodology . . . to demolish the existing paradigm's theories' (p. 16). The natural desire puts special strains on scientific commitment; it may override that commitment altogether. If old theories must be demolished, so be it. But demolishing straw men in the guise of demolishing theories is something else.

The monopolistic hypothesis, attributed by Ball (1972) to the critics of conventional accounting, is such a straw man. Quoting some passages from Simpson, Spacek and Chambers, severally, Ball said: 'Presumably, accountants possess a monopolistic influence over the data used by the market, since it is assumed [by the parties cited] that either competing data sources do not exist or (if they exist) they are not used' (p. 3). The sources cited neither said nor implied any such thing. Their authors were dealing, not with 'data' in general, but with accounting information. In an earlier paragraph of this paper the market's access to non-accounting information was granted; all kinds of information may be taken as hints or clues to movements in a firm's income. In respect of such data, accountants have no monopoly. But in respect of firm-specific income information, firms and their accountants do have a monopoly. To give fabricated rather than empirically determinable information under cover of that monopoly is just as misleading as it would be to give fabricated stock prices in place of observed prices. Neither Ball nor anyone else has shown that there are sources of that information other than the income report. The switch by Ball from firm-specific income information to 'data' is either an instance of seeing in the sources quoted what was expected or wished to be seen, or carelessness of an equally indefensible kind.

In due course, the idea as enunciated by Ball came to be endorsed by W&Z (1986). They added a twist of their own, but of the same kind. 'It was asserted [by the critics] that earnings should measure changes in the value of the firm, so stock prices could be good signals for the allocation of resources' (p. 20). No source of the assertion was given. But the literature carries abundant expressions of the view that an earnings amount neither does nor should be supposed to measure changes in the value of a firm; earnings can only represent the change in the net assets of the firm. The W&Z twist is misconstruction or misrepresentation or careless imputation.

ECONOMICS-BASED?

Much of the work of the PA cult is described as 'the economics-based empirical literature in accounting' (W&Z, 1986, p. 1). Many have claimed to base their contributions to accounting discourse on economic ideas or doctrines. It is of some consequence to establish the sense in which PA theory is economics-based. The theory, we are told, is 'based on and is an outgrowth of two economic-based theories: the theory of the firm and the theory of (government) regulation' (W&Z, 1986, p. 353).

Use is made of a theory of the firm which regards it, not as an individual entity, but as a nexus of contracts between self-interested parties (p. 194). These contracts would specify limits to the powers of each participating contractor, and the manner in which the product (e.g., net income) of the firm is to be divided amongst them. Protection of self-interest would require that the manager, because of his unique position to influence the division of the product, would be subject to the monitoring of performance by or on behalf of each of the other classes of participant. The characteristic features of such a firm are thus contracting and monitoring. Therein lies a demand for accounting and auditing (W&Z, 1986, p. 196).

The participants in the firm thus postulated include managers themselves, debenture and stock holders, lessors, labour and trade creditors, and suppliers and customers. Since there is no single focal entity, every one of these classes, under the self-interest assumption, would have contracts with every other class, and each class would want to monitor performance under every contract against the possibility of collusive arrangements prejudicial to its own interest. A direct consequence of all this is that the terms of contracts and the elements of the monitoring device shall include a clear specification of the product in which the several parties are to share, and shall be equally intelligible to all parties. We are told that 'positive propositions are concerned with how the world works. They take the form "If A, then B", and are refutable' (W&Z, 1986, p. 8). The above consequence may then be set up thus: if the terms of contracts and the mode of accounting clearly specify the product that comes to be divided and are equally intelligible to all parties, then all parties have equal and equally fair means of judging the extent to which their interests are, or have been, served. Monitoring can only mean what it seems to mean if the monitoring device fairly represents what has been done and what has occurred under the direction of the manager as agent. A false account will not do.

This seems to be an incontestable consequence of the posited nature of the firm, and an unchallengeable basis of a practical precept. But the PA cult admits neither. Indeed, the description of some of the contracts belies the idea of contracting with monitored performance. WHZ (1988) said that the accounting method to be used may be specified in the contract, but in view of the expense of negotiation, 'contracting parties are more likely to leave the majority of such choices to management in full knowledge of the fact that management may act opportunistically, that is, choose a method that the parties would not have considered "reasonable" had it been on the negotiating agenda' (p. 22). If the latter step is the more likely, monitoring becomes fanciful, or rather, farcical; for then there is no contract covering the matter that would serve as grounds of a test of performance! The PA literature is, in fact, barren of a single example of a contract specifying fully the methods of accounting to be used. The exercise of Leftwich (1983), intended to show that methods are specified in debt contracts, illustrated very limited auxiliary provisions affecting only a fraction of the items that enter into the calculation of net assets and income. In effect, the PA cult does not push to any conclusion pertinent to accounting the assumptions made about the firm and its participants. And the whole contracting-monitoring edifice, as the PA cult sees it, collapses for lack or looseness of contracts.

It seems not unlikely that the PA cult has entirely misread Coase's (1937) theory of the emergence of firms. Coase observed that contracting between individual collaborators would be costly. Interposing a firm as an entity would reduce the costs of contracting, cross-contracting and monitoring. But given that firms exist, the postulated costly contracting is dispensed with. The costly contracting postulated by the PA cult has to do, it seems, either with the dismissal of the firm as an entity, or with the cost of negotiating contracts when a vast array of optional accounting methods gives every party an opportunity for demanding the use of his own choice of methods. But the former is inconsistent with what is observable, and the latter is a pseudo-problem, arising only because the PA cult grant the legitimacy of all possible rules in a circumstance that demands one set of commonly understandable rules. To imagine even a football game or a poker game in which the players may unilaterally make and change the scoring rules during play is impossible.

The nexus of contracts idea has been described by Fama (1980) as 'the striking insight of Alchian & Demsetz (1972) and Jensen & Meckling (1976)' (p. 289). But a similar idea, much closer to Coase's theory of the emergence of firms, was introduced to the accounting literature two decades earlier. From clues given in Barnard (1938) and Simon (1949), that idea was adumbrated in Chambers (1952) and amplified in Chambers (1967, p. 16). In the latter the firm was described as a temporary coalition of participants in unstable equilibrium.

There are some noteworthy differences between the PA nexus and the coalition hypotheses. Under coalition, the firm is regarded as a distinct entity, which it is at law in the case of corporations, and which it is for all practical purposes in commerce generally; under PA nexus, the firm is not an individual entity (Jensen and Meckling, 1976, p. 311; W&Z, 1986, p. 194). Under coalition, managers are regarded as agents of the firm, which they are in law in the case of corporations; under PA nexus, managers are treated as agents of the stockholders (Jensen and Meckling, p. 309; W&Z, Ch. 8). Under coalition, the firm through its agent is a party to all contracts and understandings with participants, including managers themselves as principal contractors; under PA nexus, there are no contracts with the firm, and no contracts with managers that cover separately their roles as independent contractor with the firm and as agent of the firm; there are contracts only between stockholders and managers as agents of stockholders. Under coalition, all parties can contract for, or otherwise discover, the pay-offs from the firm and from alternative engagements, and can from time to time renegotiate or sever association in the light of that discovery; under PA nexus, there is provision for monitoring within the firm, but scant attention to pay-offs in alternative employments, and no regard, therefore, for the uniformity or comparability of information on pay-offs which would secure informed choice between employment options.

On these and other grounds, the unstable coalition hypothesis is consistent with more observables (empirical features) of firms (and, incidentally, it is closer to the 1980 schema of Fama) than the PA nexus hypothesis. And it has been employed more fruitfully. The coalition hypothesis entails an accounting that would 'be neutral with respect to the wishes and claims of participants' (Chambers, 1952, p. 217) and equally comprehensible to all actual and prospective participants. These are countervailing features to the otherwise unconstrained use of the privileged information accessible to managers who play two conflicting roles. The PA nexus hypothesis justifies substantially the same inferences in respect of actual participants at any time, though the PA cult declines to draw them; but disregard of the comparative uses of information, especially where the mobility of factors is an element of the business system, robs the inference of its potential generality.

The second economics-based strand of argument on which the PA cult claims to rely is the 'economic theory of regulation [which] conceptualizes the political process as a competition among self-interested individuals for wealth transfers' (W&Z, 1986, pp. 224, 354). At best, this notion may serve as part explanation of some political behaviour at the margin of public tolerance. But, taking it as it is, the political process is made to appear to be substantially the same as the processes of competition in market economics. It's just a matter of comparative costs. The discussion of costs, however, is limited to inter-party costs under monitoring, and some generalizations on the relative costs of private and public determination of accounting rules. The unforeseeable and involuntary costs of losers under failures, liquidations and bankruptcies that have been associated with maladroit and venal accounting are passed off: 'On average, losses in bankruptcies do not cause a below market rate of return' (W&Z, 1986,

p. 21). And the enormous costs of private negotiation and of the common standard-setting apparatus under multi-optional accounting are unnoticed, though there is much publicly known and readily discoverable about their scale.

The adopted 'economic theory of regulation' overrides a serviceable distinction between economics and politics. In general, economics is concerned with wealth and politics with power. The two become linked when the power of some prejudices the interests in wealth of others. Hence the centuries-old laws on weights and measures and against misrepresentation of the quality of merchandise. The earliest steps in the regulation of published financial information (say, the U.K. Joint Stock Companies Act of 1844, and the U.S. Securities Act of 1933) arose out of experience of the losses of creditors and shareholders through the fraud and deceit of promoters and managers having privileged access to firm-specific financial information. Those steps were taken to curb the power (through knowledge) of those whose dual roles would enable them to benefit themselves and to defeat the reasonable expectations of others. That is a proper function of legislation in communities which prefer fair dealing among their members to the unrestrained pursuit of self-interest. The CAPM, by assuming equal access to costless information, implicitly acknowledges the possibility of privileged access, but the assumptions simply dismiss it from consideration. The PA cult 'has not pursued' the possibility of inequitable consequences 'because it is impossible to define an optimality criterion of "fairness" that is acceptable to everyone' (W&Z, 1986, p. 163).

What is thus set aside is not only the prime reason for legislative interest; it is also an intrinsic element of the contracting–monitoring schema. It is inconsistent with the rationality assumption to suppose that, in face-to-face negotiation, contracting parties would assent to non-factual representations of the product to be divided. They would insist on a fair game, a true, empirically determined account of the product. There is no ground for abandoning that expectation when contracting becomes institutionalized instead of face to face. It is said that competition for information underlies the EMH (W&Z, 1986, p. 20); it impels some to seek and others to supply information beyond what is contained in accounting reports. However, firm-specific information is not subject to and open to betterment under the force of competition. Its producers are natural monopolists, and its consumers are compulsory consumers. Competition as a discipline in that setting is a misapprehension, not even a myth.

The basic trouble with the second strand of the PA argument is that it begins with differences assumed to be inevitable. Six categories of parties are represented as having different interests in accounting reports (W&Z, 1986, p. 2), and the arguments, proposals and preferences aired in the press and in submissions to standard-setting bodies exemplify the variety and inconsistencies in what is demanded. But all of this ignores the *common* elements of interest to *all* parties—the aggregate available spending powers, the solvencies and the incomes of firms. As in personal affairs, only reliable and up-to-date information on these provides the ground for informed judgment, negotiation, and appraisal of performance and prospects, and regulates the behaviour of all but the wilfully improvident. No amount of politically engineered prescription can serve fairly the parties whose collaboration constitutes the firm unless it is of that kind.

It is widely overlooked (and not only by the PA cult) that there is a significant difference between regulation in accounting and in other fields. Regulation in other fields does not concern itself with technical knowledge and procedures; it presupposes the possession by practitioners of knowledge, based on scientific and practical grounds, of demonstrated and agreed merit. In accounting the greater part of what is considered as regulation deals with detailed procedures by fiat, a solution which accountants and their professional organizations have fostered, rather than rely on disciplined observation and reasoning. But, when science will serve, to depend on the waywardness of political processes is folly.

The extent to which the study of accounting is advanced by recourse to economics is, in any case, open to question. Accounting is concerned with the financial features of individual firms. Economics is concerned with the economic features of aggregative behaviour, disregarding many of the specific states and relationships which are of significance to individual firms. Accounting is concerned with the communication of constructed firm-specific information; economics is concerned almost exclusively with market mechanisms as generators and communicators of raw, unprocessed information. Accounting is concerned with the wealth and income of persons and firms; economics with the aggregate wealth and income of whole communities. The generic terms, wealth and income, have significantly different meanings in the two fields, except when economists make specific reference to firms as such. Accounting is concerned with the minutiae of experienced events; much of economics is concerned with the construction of analytical models which strip down to abstract form the complexity of real-world events. These differences make the literature of aggregative behaviour—economics and financial economics—an inapt source or model for the analysis of accounting, and provide some explanation of the infrequency (and the not uncommon inaccuracy) of references made to accounting in the literature of economics. Economics and accounting are arguably complementary (Chambers 1964–5), but they are certainly not the same in kind.

Accounting has long and widely been described as measurement and communication. Without limiting the 'fields' on which the analysis of accounting may draw, these appear to be the most fruitful of pertinent ideas. The Foreword of W&Z (1986) spoke of 'accounting, broadly conceived as the measurement and communication of economic information relevant to decision makers'; but the book deals with neither measurement nor communication; the two words do not even appear in the index.

THEORY?

Theory is valued for its capacity to explain recurrent or invariant relationships between phenomena. To theorize about objects, events or relationships that are occasional, accidental or dependent on personal taste is pointless; there is no accounting for tastes; there can be no serviceable generalizations about matters of taste. Self-interest is a matter of taste. The term is used of an unspecified but virtually unlimited package of preferences, of varying urgencies or intensities and changing composition. Those preferences, furthermore, may be egocentric or altruistic in a variety of senses. Such an amorphous package of preferences may be used by any person to justify or rationalize his behaviour, whether it is unique or commonplace, constant or variant. But no independent observer can affirm that an observed person acted in an observed manner out of self-interest; only the observed can make such an affirmation. The affirmation is not independently testable, and can therefore yield no scientifically acceptable explanation of the observed behaviour, no generalization that is empirically supportable. Yet the irrefutable premise, self-interest, is the basic and most commonly used 'explanation' of the behaviours noticed in the literature of the PA cult! As for prediction, it is impossible to predict behaviour that is 'explained' by recourse to idiosyncratic and unpredictably variable packages of self-interests.

Given a mass of data on observed accounting practices, one might ask why, for the valuation of inventories, some firms apply the lower of cost and market rule to items, some to inventory classes and some to aggregate inventories; why some use LIFO cost and some use FIFO cost; and why some use unmodified cost, replacement cost, net realizable value and so on. (Simply to ask why some firms use LIFO and some FIFO, as do W&Z, 1986, p. 2, leaves a vast range of observables unnoticed.) And beyond inventories, a host of other items are open to differential quantification. There can be no single general explanation that will account positively for these diverse usages. But there can be rationalizations. Some may claim that LIFO is 'income-reducing', and that that is a good thing. That may be a good excuse, but it is no explanation, for LIFO is 'income-increasing' when prices are falling. There must be a whole battery of such rationalizations to justify all the valuation rules mentioned. But a series of rationalizations relating severally to specific segments of a population is not a theory.

The general, and for that reason the more interesting, question is: why do so many different rules having different effects coexist? Or, alternatively: why do so many rules coexist which produce figures having no uniformly dated empirical referents? Or, again: why do so many rules coexist which quantify different properties of objects and events when those quantities are to be aggregated and otherwise related as if their components were qualitatively similar? Or, again: why are there so many rules that yield or are based on long out-of-date information, when contracting and monitoring are pointless unless the information is up-to-date? Each of these questions deals with a large class of observables, and each can be answered by recourse to one or more empirically supportable generalizations.

In choosing to deal with selected fragments of the observables, the PA cult has mistaken justification of particulars (i.e., excuses) for explanation by way of testable generalizations. It has not even attempted to do what theories are expected to do, namely, to explain large clusters of observables by economical recourse to testable general hypotheses. Some consequences of its aversion to setting up general hypotheses have been noticed. The nexus of contracts and rationality notions provide grounds for an up-to-date, reliable and generally intelligible accounting. But the consequence of articulating that hypothesis would look too much like a norm, and norms are taboo. So the hypothesis is not articulated; by default, a woolly and feckless monitoring, that tolerates the production of idiosyncratic, cryptographic and self-serving misinformation, is endorsed.

Anyone who attempts to establish good reasons for patently unrealistic and unreasonable processes and products is bound to find it difficult. And that is how it has turned out for the PA cult. Many of the empirical studies reported yield contradictory inferences; almost every one of them has had to be hedged about with *ad hoc* caveats or apologetics (W&Z, 1986, *passim*). That exploratory work may be like this is understandable. Of physics it has been said: 'The physics of undergraduate textbooks is 90% true; the contents of the primary research journals of physics is 90% false' (Ziman, 1978, p. 40). For even greater reason than for physics, that might hold of research papers in accounting. But it is odd that so much that is inconclusive should be included in a book that claims (p. 352) to represent the state of the art of the PA cult. Blame has been laid (e.g., W&Z, 1986, p. 357) on the lack of 'rich' theories in the fields on which it has relied; but no-one is obliged to use poor tools. The cult seems to be so enamoured of its own work and 'methodology' that it tirelessly boasts of its promise, disregards or denigrates the product and style of its precursors and takes scant, if any, notice of its own critics. It was the fate of Narcissus to perish from such devoted self-admiration. Or, if one disdains the lesson of the classical myth, perhaps an observation of a modern scientist deserves better: 'Beware of the man of one method or one instrument, either experimental or theoretical. He tends to become method oriented rather than problem oriented; the method oriented man is shackled' (Platt, 1964, p. 351).

EMPIRICALLY BASED THEORY BEFORE THE PA TWIST

As far back as Pacioli accounting has been, and it still is, represented as a means of keeping property and debt, and income and expenditure, under periodical and continuous observation for the informed management of the financial affairs of persons and firms. Whether or not a person or firm is able to pay debts, can maintain a given level of consumption or trade, is adding to a capital stock, and so on, are matters of perennial concern on which the products of accounting *may* shed light. But *will* shed light only if the figures correspond with discoverable facts from time to time. In a nutshell: informed action at any time depends on the correspondence of the information with dated facts. This proposition, a present indicative not a normative proposition, runs through the literature in various guises—some clear, some garbled, some in imperative form—as truth in accounting, realism, reliability, timeliness and like notions. It runs also through other literatures concerned with well-informed behaviour. In the form given it expresses one aspect of how the world works. Any such singular proposition may be an element in an empirically based theory. Any extended series of such propositions and legitimate inferences from them may properly be styled an empirically based accounting theory.

Much of the literature prior to the rise of the PA cult was not cast in the form of indicative (positive) propositions and inferences from them. Much was in the nature of precepts or prescriptions. That form had its origin in the modest bookkeeping manuals of long ago, and more recently in the recommendations, opinions and rules by which professional organizations sought to give guidance to bewildered practitioners. But underlying many of those precepts there are refutable but unrefuted empirical propositions. To dismiss all that preceded the PA twist as simply normative expresses either carelessness or contempt. There has long been a discursive literature which concerned itself with fundamentals expressible as positive propositions.

Take Canning, temporally the first on the B&B hit list. Canning observed (1929, p. 319) that many economists were grieved to find that the products of accounting arose from the aggregation of money amounts representing vastly dissimilar features of the phenomena under notice. The state of affairs under complaint, he said, does exist. It still exists. His condemnation of these 'statistical absurdities' was based on the proposition: 'If individual measures are to be merged by summation or otherwise, the individual things measured . . . must all be sensibly alike with respect to the property . . . under investigation' (p. 199). The 'must' is, of course, a logical imperative, not merely an opinion of Canning. To this as a major premise may be added the minor premise: 'In accounting, individual measures are merged by summation or otherwise', to yield the conclusion: 'In accounting, individual measures to be merged must be measures of the same property'. The appearance of the imperative may be circumvented, and what is analytical may be made empirical, by casting the major premise in the form: 'Sums of individual measures of different properties of things have no empirical counterpart' and varying the argument accordingly. A positive researcher, finding accounting practice universally at odds with this theorem, might seek to explain the anomaly. The PA cult takes no notice of it.

Sweeney (1936) likewise observed what he considered a serious flaw in practice, the assumed stability of the monetary unit. There was abundant evidence of its impropriety in the

Germany of 1923 and elsewhere at other times. Another of Canning's propositions dealt with it: 'If measures are to be merged, the unit of measure must either be uniform throughout the measuring, or all units must be convertible into the unit in terms of which the measures are to be merged'. Canning and Sweeney were, in the respects mentioned, clearly aware of how the world works, and of the inconsistency with it of the processes of conventional accounting.

By contrast with these elements of a theory, Sterling's *Theory and Measurement of Enterprise Income* (1970) was far more extensive. Sterling focused on measurement, valuation and communications problems pertinent to accounting. His conclusions were based on five measurement propositions and five valuation propositions cast in the present indicative (or positive) form, and certain information and communication propositions which are or may be cast in the same form. That is to say, all the propositions advanced are testable, and the whole exercise may quite properly be called an empirically based theory.

Chambers' *Accounting, Evaluation and Economic Behavior* (1966) was foreshadowed by certain testable propositions cast in the positive form in a paper of 1955. The intention was to avoid all precepts or imperatives that might conceal value-laden assumptions. The introduction to the 1966 work specified that there would be derived from the universe of experience a number of testable statements which, when arranged systematically, would 'enable us to specify the kind of accounting which will perform the functions required of it . . . within the universe of experience' (p. 7). That work enunciated scores of propositions cast in testable form. The major part of the work dealt with the products of accounting as contributories to informed action. But as the style of accounting that emerged from the analysis differed in material respects from practice, the final chapter, again by recourse to testable propositions, offered an explanation of how conventional accounting came to be what it was. The whole work was in substance an explanation of what is the case. It presupposed some familiarity on the part of the reader with the observable disputes, the demonstrable anomalies and the recurrent involuntary redistributions of wealth, of which the financial press gave (and still gives) abundant evidence. It carefully avoided recourse to all such general notions, functions or aims as economic efficiency, market efficiency and Pareto optimality, and all such theoretical constructs as perfect markets, perfect competition and their like, for every one of these is unrelated to the derivation of financial information of serviceable quality in the world as it is. Readers who failed to notice the dominant place of testable, refutable propositions in the work have erred in describing it as normative. The transactions, the firms, the markets and the relationships postulated are substantially consistent with the observables of ordinary commerce.

Sterling and Chambers found no special occasion to describe their work as positive, as distinct from the prescriptive style of other material. They were simply doing, and expected to be understood as doing, what investigators in the sciences and other technologies do in the ordinary course of events—observe widely, posit generalizations and draw operable and testable inferences. The hope that that way of proceeding might be more widely adopted, because those exercises demonstrated that what is done in disciplined inquiry elsewhere could be done in respect of accounting, has not been realized. But there has emerged evidence (e.g., Chambers *et al.,* 1987) to the effect that some 90 per cent of over 5,000 business-related respondents in six countries would determine wealth and financial position by references to resale prices of assets, a conclusion of Sterling and Chambers that, incidentally, is consistent with the method used by B&B in calculating rates of return. And there has continued to emerge evidence of the misleading nature of conventional information, in the unexpected collapses and bankruptcies of apparently flourishing firms.

REVOLUTION OR DEBACLE?

Of the present dominance of the work and *modus operandi* of the PA cult there can be no doubt. Its doctrines have, from the outset, been propagated with proselytizing zeal and beguiling rhetoric. Its products have attracted prestigious awards, engaging the emulation of others. It has spawned new journals only too willing to publish work of its kind. Its devotees, rising to editorial and referential posts, have shifted publication opportunities in its favour; it is the avowed policy of some journals and the implicit policy of others to disregard submissions not of its genre. Its products have captured the allegiance of whole schools in teaching institutions across the breadth of English-speaking communities, and perhaps elsewhere. As one may judge from journal acknowledgments, it is a most tightly knit and closely inbred brotherhood.

All of that is fine for the PA cult. But what of the advancement of knowledge and understanding? Peirce (1877/1958) had some apposite words on the fixing of belief:

> Let an institution be created which shall have for its object to keep current doctrines before the attention of the people, to reiterate them perpetually, and to teach them to the young; having at the same time power to prevent contrary doctrines from being taught, advocated or expressed. Let all possible causes of a change of mind be removed from men's apprehensions. Let them be kept ignorant . . . Let their passions be enlisted . . . Then, let all men who reject the established belief be terrified into silence. (p. 102)

This method of fixing belief he called the method of authority. One hundred years later, a physicist uttered a consequential caution: 'worldly wisdom teaches us to be a little suspicious of knowledge that emanates from a unique, compactly organized and self-regarding social institution, staffed by specially trained and thoroughly indoctrinated personnel using machinery of awesome size and complexity' (Ziman, 1978, p. 64).

Of course, power may be beneficent. Is there, then, at present or in the offing, a positive accounting theory that may be associated with the PA cult? Is there a specified set of assumptions or hypotheses, general in form and potential application, that can be shown to be consistent with much that is observable in the practice and context of accounting? It seems not. Having given a succinct description of 'a theory', it might have been expected that W&Z would show clearly in what respect PA theory corresponds with the description. There is no such demonstration. Rather, although there is much talk of 'the theory', the final sentence of W&Z (1986) expresses not an accomplishment, but a hope: 'we have *confidence* that the methodology . . . *will produce* a useful positive accounting theory' (emphasis added). Similarly, WHZ (1988, p. xiv) *hope* that their book *starts* to answer some of the questions *they* pose, though they brush aside a whole roster of questions and anomalous observables that a work of its kind might be expected to deal with. It is difficult to discern a single instance (if, indeed, there is one) of a finding of the PA cult that has added a proposition to the pre-existing corpus of accounting doctrine or knowledge. Monitoring is simply the old idea of stewardship under another name; the nexus of contracts and agency ideas are recycled notions of older vintage; not even 'positive' is novel in the field.

W&Z (1979), as noted earlier, set up the existing accounting theory (strictly literature) as ventures in the production of excuses. It now seems that the PA cult has produced the excuse to outdo all excuses. The self-interest hypothesis entails that every device that any person or firm chooses to employ is justified, excused. It follows that all the logical and practical flaws that have occupied the attention of practitioners, academics, lawyers, administrators and others are excusable, and objections to them otiose; 'no one is fooled by accounting' is the slogan forever (e.g., W&Z, 1986, pp. 21, 343). There can no longer be legitimate criticism of the utterances of professional bodies or standards boards or legislatures, for what they have done and do is done for good self-serving reasons. And perhaps the accounting curriculum should be reduced to a two-word program: 'Please yourself'.

As for the advancement of knowledge, it sometimes seems as if the clock has been set back a thousand years. WHZ (1988) averred that, where there are state-contingent pay-offs to individual productive factors (which is universally the case in respect of some parties in corporate business), 'these states are invariably defined in terms of the firm's financial position or performance'. Then: 'We argue that traditional accounting serves this role—that the historical cost system provides a basis for financial contracting . . . In this sense, accounting, rather than being a faithful representation of some underlying "true" (but unobservable) economic reality, becomes reality itself' (p. 84). Here is a pretty pass. We look back, with scorn or amusement, to primitive ages when men accepted figments of the imagination, myths and goblins as reliable knowledge. We suppose the scientific revolution to have disposed of that. But it is still with us. The foibles and fictions of conventional accounting become 'reality itself'. What is said to be, actually is, and the world must put up with it. Of such things Lerner (1960) wrote:

> Whereas the function of research is to test social theory by observation of reality, the function of agitprop [agitation and propaganda] is to make reality appear to conform to the Ideology. One does not consult the man who wears the shoe to learn where it pinches; one tells him that it must pinch to fit better later—or that it does not pinch at all. (p. 24)

The PA cult tirelessly counsels theorists and researchers to observe what is the case; but the practical world, in which what is the case is of urgent and ineluctable significance, is excused altogether from an equivalent admonition!

DOUBLE TALK AND PARADOX

The literature and practice of conventional accounting is a classic example of double think and double talk after the pattern described by Orwell (1955):

> Double think means the power of holding two contradictory beliefs in one's mind simultaneously, and accepting both of them . . . The process has to be conscious, or it will not be carried out with precision, but it also has to be unconscious, or it would bring with it a feeling of falsity and guilt . . . to forget any fact that has become inconvenient, and then, when it becomes necessary again, to draw it back from oblivion for just so long as it is needed, to deny the existence of objective reality and all the while to take account of the reality one denies— all this is indispensably necessary. (p. 171).

Conventional accounting, it is claimed, yields true and fair information on financial position and results; what it produces has neither of those features. It claims to be based on the accrual principle, but plays fast and loose with that principle as it pleases. It claims to yield information pertinent to decision making, but yields information of a kind that no reasonable person would use. It claims to be realistic, but liberally uses fictions that misrepresent reality. It claims to be historical, but at many significant points relies on conjectures about the future. And so on.

The work of the PA cult is essentially similar. PA theory sets up individual self-interest as the dominant explanations of accounting practice; it also sets up a contracting-monitoring model of the firm in which self-interest is necessarily constrained. It purports to deal with accounting, but ignores large tracts of the territory; the only applications it deals with at any length are compensation and debt contracting. When convenient it claims to be able to identify the impact of a single cause when there are joint causes; and when convenient it denies the possibility. It purports to be positive, descriptive; but it endorses conventional accounting which is observably and dominantly prescriptive. It claims to be scientific, but in many ways is non-scientific or anti-scientific; what could be more anti-scientific than the hubristic contention: 'not only is there no generally accepted accounting theory to justify accounting standards, there never will be one' (W&Z, 1979, p. 301)? It claims to be empirical, but the limited range of observables it notices are largely determined by the method used rather than the matter to be examined. The PA cult claims to present theory or a theory, but it actually presents an unsystematic set of propositions liberally buttressed by *ad hoc* addenda. Alluding to much work in psychology, Dunnette (1966) described it as

> folderol . . . tendencies to be fixated on theories, methods and points of view, conducting little studies with great precision, . . . asking unimportant or irrelevant questions . . . coining new names for old concepts, fixation on methods and apparatus, seeking to prove rather than test theories, and myriad other methodological ceremonies conducted in the name of rigorous research. (p. 343)

It's a caution deserving notice.

Conventional doctrine and the PA doctrine alike foster, not well-informed interaction in the practical and academic worlds respectively, but illusions. In moments of ease and relaxation the world is vastly entertained by illusionists; but no-one believes that the illusionist's assistant is really cut into halves, or disappears forever. In practical affairs, and in training for practical affairs, the world does not expect to be fed illusions when it needs facts. Unhappily, that is what it still must tolerate, and pay heavily for the privilege. For much of the PA literature provides, not a guide to the production of generally serviceable information, but a catalogue of the games people will play, and rationalize, when only they have power to make and change the rules.

Brown (1989) has claimed, with some pride: 'it is now hard to imagine any proposal to change U.S. accounting reporting requirements that will not have to run the gauntlet of a market-based test, as part of the routine evaluation of its economic consequences' (p. 207). But how well have generally accepted accounting principles fared, notwithstanding the test? 'The accounting standard setting process is in deep trouble, possibly in such deep trouble that our present structure is irretrievably lost to us. After seventeen years, the Financial Accounting Standards Board lies dead in the water beset by critics on all sides' (Burton and Sack, 1990, p. 117). 'The accounting profession is being battered again . . . the profession continues to be harried by litigation . . . public suspicion of its credibility, demands that the accounting standard setting process be reformed, and blame for every financial catastrophe' (Sommer, 1990, pp. 114–15)—this from the chairman of the Public Oversight Board of the SEC Practice Section of the American Institute of CPAs. These disastrous outcomes were all predictable from the contentions of the critics of generally accepted accounting principles twenty-five years ago.

But Brown still contends that the grounds of criticism were, and still are, 'insufficient grounds for rejecting reports prepared under generally accepted accounting principles' (p. 204).

The whole PA venture in fact constitutes a colossal paradox. Its founding fathers claimed to put under inquiry the *income numbers of firms;* they and their successors actually have had recourse to the *imputed income numbers of investors.* All inquiries using the procedures of B&B (1968) employ a rate of return consistent only with exit value or money equivalent accounting; notwithstanding that, the cult emerges as a champion of cost-based accounting. The cult professes to be averse to prescription; but it endorses, implicitly and explicitly, traditional cost-based accounting, the doctrines of which are full of unsupportable prescriptions. It lays the ground in the contracting–monitoring hypothesis for an up-to-date and intelligible accounting, but supports conventional accounting which has neither of those characteristics.

The greatest paradox of all is that such grossly paradoxical beliefs survive and flourish so luxuriantly in institutions dedicated to the cultivation of open inquiry and disciplined thought, and the elimination of the wayward paradox.

References

American Accounting Association, *Accounting Concepts and Standards Underlying Corporate Financial Statements,* AAA, 1948.

Ball, R., 'Changes in Accounting Techniques and Stock Prices', *Empirical Research in Accounting: Selected Studies 1972,* supplement to Vol. 2 of *Journal of Accounting Research,* 1972.

————, 'Accounting, Auditing and the Nature of the Firm', unpublished manuscript, University of New South Wales, July 1985.

Ball, R., and P. Brown, 'An Empirical Evaluation of Accounting Income Numbers', *Journal of Accounting Research,* Autumn 1968.

Barnard, C. I., *The Functions of the Executive,* Harvard University Press, 1938.

Beaver, W. H., 'The Information Content of Annual Earnings Announcements', *Empirical Research in Accounting: Selected Studies 1968,* supplement to Vol. 6 of *Journal of Accounting Research,* 1968.

Bronowski, J., *Science and Human Values,* Penguin, 1964.

Brown, P., 'Ball and Brown [1968]', *Journal of Accounting Research* (supplement), 1989.

Burton, J. R., and R. J. Sack, 'Standard Setting Process in Trouble (Again)', *Accounting Horizons,* December 1990.

Canning, J. B., *The Economics of Accountancy,* Ronald Press, 1929.

Chambers, R. J., 'Accounting and Business Finance', *Australian Accountant,* July, August 1952.

————, 'Blueprint for a Theory of Accounting', *Accounting Research,* January 1955.

————, 'The Complementarity of Accounting and Economics', *Calculator Annual,* Singapore Polytechnic Society of Commerce, 1964–5 (reprinted in R. J. Chambers and G. W. Dean (eds), *Chambers on Accounting,* Vol. III, Garland Publishing, 1986).

————, *Accounting, Evaluation and Economic Behavior,* Prentice-Hall, 1966.

————, *Financial Management,* Law Book Company, 1967.

Chambers, R. J., R. Ma, R. Hopkins, and N. Kasiraja, *Financial Information and Decision Making: A Singapore Survey,* Singapore Institute of Management and University of Sydney Accounting Research Centre, 1987.

Christenson, C., 'The Methodology of Positive Accounting', *The Accounting Review,* January 1983.

Coase, R. H., 'The Nature of the Firm', *Economica,* November 1937.

Dunnette, M. D., 'Fads, Fashions, and Folderol in Psychology', *American Psychologist,* April 1966.

Dyckman, T. R., and S. A. Zeff, 'Two Decades of the Journal of Accounting Research', *Journal of Accounting Research,* Spring 1984.

Fama, E. F., 'Agency Problems and the Theory of the Firm', *Journal of Political Economy,* April 1980.

Jensen, M. C., and W. H. Meckling, 'Theory of the Firm: Managerial Behavior, Agency Costs and Ownership Structure', *Journal of Financial Economics,* October 1976.

Leftwich, R., 'Accounting Information in Private Markets: Evidence from Private Lending Agreements', *The Accounting Review,* January 1983.

Lerner, D., *The Human Meaning of the Social Sciences,* Meridian Books, 1960.

Lundberg, G. A., *Social Research,* Longmans Green, 1942.

Orwell, G., *Nineteen Eighty-Four,* Penguin, 1955.

Peirce, C. S., *Values in a Universe of Chance* [1877], Doubleday, 1958.

Platt, J. R., 'Strong Inference', *Science,* October 1964.

Popper, K. R., *Conjectures and Refutations,* Routledge, 1972.

Schreuder, H., 'Positively Normative (Accounting) Theories', in A. Hopwood and H. Schreuder (eds), *European Contributions to Accounting Research,* Free University Press, 1984.

Simon, H. A., *Administrative Behavior,* Macmillan, 1949.

Sommer, A. A., Jr, 'Time for Another Commission', *Accounting Horizons,* December, 1990.

Sterling, R. R., *Theory of the Measurement of Enterprise Income,* University of Kansas Press, 1970.

————, 'Positive Accounting: An Assessment', *Abacus,* September 1990.

Sweeney, H. W., *Stabilized Accounting* [1936], reprint, Holt, Rinehart & Winston, 1964.

Watts, R. L., and J. L. Zimmerman, 'The Demand for and Supply of Accounting Theories: The Market for Excuses', *The Accounting Review,* April, 1979.

Watts, R. L., and J. L. Zimmerman, *Positive Accounting Theory,* Prentice-Hall, 1986.

Williams, P. F., 'The Logic of Positive Accounting Research', *Accounting, Organizations and Society,* Vol. 14, No. 5/6, 1989.

Whitley, R. D., 'The Possibility and Utility of Positive Accounting Theory', *Accounting, Organizations and Society,* Vol. 13, No. 6, 1988.

Whittred, G., and I. Zimmer, *Financial Accounting,* Holt, Rinehart & Winston, 1988.

Ziman, J., *Reliable Knowledge,* Cambridge University Press, 1978.

POSTULATES, PRINCIPLES, AND THE CONCEPTUAL FRAMEWORK

WHY BOTHER WITH POSTULATES?

R. J. Chambers

Accounting has frequently been described as a body of practices which have been developed in response to practical needs rather than by deliberate and systematic thinking. Thus: "In one important respect bookkeeping differs from other sciences, in that it is not in the least theoretical, but essentially and fundamentally practical. It is based upon expediency, and upon the actual needs and requirements of everyday life. It was invented because man wanted it, because he found that he could not get on without it. It is essentially utilitarian. It is not the result of the work of *dilletanti,* of men who conceived some theory and labored to prove the truth of it."[1] The view thus represented has persisted in various forms, such as: "Accounting is not formulated with reference to, nor does it stand on general truths or the operation of natural or general laws."[2]

In one sense such statements convey an idea of the way in which accounting rules and procedures have been developed. There has been little regard for an orderly and systematic formulation. Multiple solutions have been put forward and adopted for many specific accounting problems. In another sense such statements are confused and confusing. For, if accounting is utilitarian there must have been some concept or some theory of the tests which must be

---

R. J. Chambers, "Why Bother with Postulates?" *Journal of Accounting Research,* vol. 1, no. 1, 3–15. © 1963, Institute of Professional Accounting. Reprinted with permission.

[1]Woolf, Arthur H., *A Short History of Accountants and Accountancy* (London: Gee & Co., 1912), pp. xxix, xxx.

[2]C. A. Smith and J. G. Ashburne, *Financial and Administrative Accounting* (New York: McGraw Hill Book Company, Inc., 1955), p. 2.

applied in distinguishing utilitarian from nonutilitarian procedures. And, if rules are not formulated with reference to general laws or ideas of some kind then it is quite pointless to speak of rules and to write textbooks about them. It is largely because the tests of "utilitarian-ness" and the general ideas or laws which underlie accounting rules have not been made explicit that the body of accounting practices now employed contains so many divergent and inconsistent rules. Even rules which have been adopted, and recommendations which have been made, after considerable discussion over the past thirty years exhibit indeterminacies, divergencies and inconsistencies. The application of good intentions and long deliberations in an *ad hoc* setting cannot free practice of these features.

Recognition of this has given rise to the belief that some rigorous and extensive examination of accounting is necessary[3] and to demands that such an examination should be undertaken.[4] The response of the Special Committee on Research Program of the American Institute of Certified Public Accountants to all this is singular in that it envisaged a program in which attention would be directed initially to the "postulates" of accounting.[5] Reactions to the product of such an inquiry are likely to be extremely diverse, for an examination of basic assumptions is not the kind of thing which falls within the common and regular experience of practitioners or teachers. Although there are some important differences, there are also some important similarities between an inquiry of this nature and the solution of practical day-to-day problems. It is the present purpose to explore some of these for the light that may be thrown on the close link between what appears to be a quite theoretical pursuit and the exigencies of professional practice.

PRACTICE AND RESEARCH: SIMILARITIES AND DIFFERENCES

An everyday problem, no matter how extensive, is circumscribed by a host of details which lead or confine the efforts of a practitioner. These include the specific characteristics of the firm considered at the time, and its specific problem at that time; the general standards of practice or methods available for solving similar problems at that time; and the amount of time available and its cost to the client. It is a matter of experience that different practitioners confronted with the same problem will offer different solutions—not invariably, perhaps, but often enough to suggest that any given solution is no more than a hypothesis. In effect each says: "That is my best advice; try it that way and see how it works out." If the proposed solution works satisfactorily no one says: "That was a sound hypothesis," nor even, "That was a lucky guess." The matter is closed. If the proposed solution does not work satisfactorily, some other solution is tried—another hypothesis. In fact, by virtue of the first trial the situation may have changed, and when further advice is sought by the client, the practitioner has a slightly different problem to solve. The first piece of advice is not then seen as an unsound hypothesis, or even as a hypothesis at all. In any event, the constant modification of advice and adaptation of practices and policies are the means by which business behavior is geared to circumstances.

---

[3]Leonard Spacek, "The Need for an Accounting Court," *The Accounting Review,* July, 1958.

[4]Alvin R. Jennings, "Present-Day Challenges in Financial Reporting," *The Journal of Accountancy,* January, 1958.

[5]Report of the Special Committee, *The Journal of Accountancy,* December, 1958.

Every new set of circumstances creates a new problem in a new setting, providing the opportunity to choose new assumptions and avoiding the need for consistency in those assumptions from one situation to the next; for what is required is a practicable and acceptable solution to one problem at a time. When a practitioner has a number of clients or has any one client over a long period, he should (and most do) take steps to see that there is a measure of uniformity, or that there are no gross inconsistencies, in the advice he gives and the reports he gives on annual statements. But the range of clients of any practitioner is limited and every task he undertakes has a definite set of technical, temporal or institutional limits.

An inquiry into the postulates and principles of accounting has no such limits. From this, difficulties arise, both in carrying out the inquiry and in evaluating the products received. Ideally a statement of postulates or principles will be sufficiently comprehensive to provide the ground rules for solving problems in all specific situations in which people prepare or use accounting information. In other words, the person who seeks out postulates or principles is endeavouring to provide a general solution to the whole series of specific problems which may and do confront practitioners. To imagine or devise propositions which cover all conceivable situations is a difficult task because it is open-ended. It is possible to seek less comprehensive sets of postulates or principles, covering limited fields, such as, for example, corporate accounting, governmental accounting, fiduciary accounting. But even these are much more difficult to discover than is the framing of a solution to a particular problem. Once such a proposition has been put forward one or both of two things may befall it. It may be condemned "as a hypothesis" much more readily and by many more people than would condemn as a hypothesis a proposed solution to a practical problem. And it may be cause for considerable disappointment; for either it may appear to be so obvious that it is not worth stating, or it may appear to have no direct utility to the practitioner and give rise to irritation and impatience with the whole business.

These are natural reactions, even on the part of researchers, and more so on the part of practitioners. But a sense of history is some protection against disquiet. For all practical purposes, for over 2,000 years men accepted the postulates of three-dimensional geometry; but the practical utility of non-Euclidean multi-dimensional geometries now extends through to the latest and most sophisticated and practical of scientific and business calculations. For 1300 years it seemed reasonable to postulate that animal and human anatomies are the same; it required the insight of Vesalius to question this assumption of Galen and to lay the foundation for scientific study of human anatomy. The number system using the base ten has long been extolled for the economy it gives to calculation; but only by resort to the binary system has it been possible to do all the things which require the use of high-speed computers. There are literally thousands of examples of advances made in practically useful human knowledge by stating and questioning established hypotheses or their postulates, or by putting forward new hypotheses on the basis of postulates which appeared to be trivial or even ridiculous. There is no reason why accounting should be considered to be different in this respect from any other field of knowledge.

THE ANALYSIS OF PRACTICES

As the last paragraph suggests, there are two ways of examining the foundations of accounting. By one of these, a statement is made descriptive of an operation; the description being full and complete, it is analyzed to discover on what postulates the operation is based; finally these postulates are considered for the purpose of discovering whether they are reasonable by whatever criteria are deemed necessary to judge reasonableness. It will be useful to consider an example, say, the practice of setting down periodically the assets of a client or an employer, assigning dollar amounts derived by a diverse set of rules, and adding those amounts to arrive at a total. This is not all the accountant does periodically; but it is a full and complete description of one thing, one operation. The only objection that may be taken is in respect of the phrase "assigning dollar amounts derived by a diverse set of rules"; but a moment's thought will enable any accountant to recognize that different rules may be applied to different assets—to cash, the face amount; to receivables, the book value less a provision; to marketable securities, market value if less than cost; to inventories, cost on a LIFO basis; to fixed tangible assets other than land, cost less depreciation; to land, cost; to intangibles, a nominal sum—all these rules and many other variants of them are currently acceptable. Upon what postulates, then, is the above-mentioned operation based? There are at least two.

FIRST   The assignment of money amounts, *with the intention that they shall be added,* is based on the assumption that there is a common quality which all items in the list possess and which may be represented by a money sum. That this is a reasonable postulate cannot be denied. But it is not the postulate appropriate to the above operation; for it has been shown that for seven types of asset there are at least seven methods, all different and all acceptable, of assigning money amounts; and by the description given to each of these methods, it is clear that the amounts assigned do not represent a common quality of the assets. The postulate underlying the use of a diverse set of rules is that the subject items do *not* have a common quality; or alternatively, if they have a common quality, it is not a quality with which accounting is concerned. Both of these possibilities lead in curious directions. Take the former—that assets do not have a common quality. The fact that they are called by a generic name—assets—signifies that they have some quality in common. This fact stands out above all the different methods of assigning money sums; assets have some quality in common. The first alternative postulate is therefore invalid. Take, now, the second that, if assets have a common quality, it is not a quality with which accounting is concerned. It may be observed here that this is the only postulate which can justify the use of a diverse set of rules for assigning money sums; but clearly it makes nonsense of all the discussion in accounting about common denominators. This matter will crop up again when the other postulate underlying the described practice is considered.

SECOND   The practice of summing the several money amounts assigned to specific assets postulates that such an addition can be performed legitimately. Legitimately means that the set of magnitudes *can* be added, and that when added they will give a total which has a definable meaning, and in particular a meaning of the same kind as the meanings of the individual magnitudes added. Now it is unlikely that anyone would propose, if he were asked to find the combined weight of two men, to add the weight of one man at sea level to the weight of an astronaut in orbit. If he did he would reach the nonsensical conclusion that the weight of two men is equal to the weight of one man. The sum of two weights means nothing unless they are measured by the same rule. Similarly, an uninformed person might easily take equal distances on a map drawn on Mercator's projection to represent equal longitudinal distances on the spherical surface of the earth; if he were to add two such distances and convert them on the scale given for distances at the equator, he too would obtain a meaningless result, for it would imply that the circumference of *every* circle obtained by cutting a sphere is the same as that of the circle obtained by cutting the sphere through its center. What, then, about the procedure of adding the amount of cash held by a company today to the amount of cash paid twenty years ago for a piece of freehold land which the company still holds today? The practice is no less absurd than the other two examples. The two things can not be added because they have not been converted to common scale (unless a given amount of money *can* purchase the same amount of land as it could twenty years ago). And it follows that if they are added the result would be meaningless. As in the previous section the reasonable postulate stated at the outset is found to be inconsistent with the practice we are considering and we are forced to seek an alternative. The only alternative is this: that the process of addition can be applied to unlike things and that these may be added, regardless of their dissimilarity, to obtain a meaningful result. This, of course, is patently absurd.

In conclusion, of the only two postulates which are consistent with the described practice one makes nonsense of accounting and the other is absurd; therefore the practice is absurd; for there is no mental process by which two such propositions may yield a sensible result. It is quite useless to protest that this practice is "practical," or that it is time-honored, or that it is a generally accepted practice; it has only become these things because men have not asked: upon what postulates is the practice based?

One of the purposes of this exercise was to show that *every practice* has certain postulates. Postulates are not some theoretical nonsense. They are the hard core of which practice is merely an expression. Every time a practitioner acts, in whatever capacity, he is acting on some postulates. He may not even know them; he may never have thought of them, for he may have accepted the weight of opinion or authority in place of personal conviction; but he cannot escape them. It is the great difference between a technician and a skilled craftsman that the latter knows the powers and limitations of his art. And these he knows because he has sought out the postulates underlying his operations; he has sought to discover the qualities of the materials through which his art is expressed and of the communities in which or about which he uses that art. The example of the previous section was selected because it is a widespread everyday practice, not simply a novel or ephemeral problem. It was analyzed for the purpose of illustrating a method of inquiry into postulates or foundations which begins with known practices. It should not be supposed that every such analysis of a practice will reveal so starkly that there are flaws in the practice or its underlying ideas. But the consequence of proceeding this way is plain. No one likes his cherished habits to be lampooned, ridiculed or even criticized. What to one appears to be reasoned analysis appears to another to be an insolent, immoderate and irreverent attack on the establishment. A study which begins this way is likely to arouse animosity and resentment from the outset, and if it is more likely to be passionately rebuffed than dispassionately considered, the procedure is clearly impolitic. It will be dubbed "destructive criticism" and consigned to limbo or the waste basket.

But this procedure has also another flaw. If the inquirer is limited in his examination to practices which are already followed, the whole inquiry will be unnecessarily circumscribed. If "accounting" is the subject matter, the scope of the inquiry should not be limited by present circumstances—one particular country, one particular decade, one particular class of organization. Nor indeed should it be limited to the practices of all countries, all historical times, or all classes of organization. For if the practices of one organization in one country at one time are circumscribed by traditional, legal or accidental factors, so is the sum of all practices of all organizations in all countries at all times. The inquirer should also be free to imagine forms of accounting which have *not* been tried, in exactly the same way as does a practitioner confronted with an entirely novel problem; in exactly the same way as people have "imagined" freely moving, self-powered road transport, synthetic fibres, telephonic communication, color T.V., before these things were used in practice. The only requirements or constraints should be that the outcome of a line of inquiry should be reached by logical steps, and that no patently absurd assumptions should be made. This leads to the second method of inquiring into the foundations of accounting, a method which begins, not be describing practices but by discovering postulates which are useful.

Synthesis by Postulation and Reasoning

This method begins by selecting from the world of experience and reflection a set of ideas about things, which fall within the field of inquiry. If it is necessary these ideas are clarified by explicit definition, so that the correspondence between the ideas and the relevant aspects of the observable events and things they represent is established. Certain propositions are then set up which describe the relationships between the ideas or concepts thus derived, or rather the relationships which are postulated to exist. The implications of the ideas and the postulates are then worked out, the result being a set of theorems or conclusions about the events and things represented by the ideas and postulates. Postulates are thus propositions enunciated without proof—either because no proof can be given or because the assent of others to such propositions can be reasonably expected—and used in the derivation of other propositions. These latter propositions may culminate in a set of rules or prescriptions for doing something, such as keeping accounts and making summaries of results and position. If the set of rules and prescriptions is derived logically, reasonably, from the definitions and postulates, and if the result of applying those rules is something which is acknowledged to be useful, the postulates are confirmed, and the whole system of definitions, postulates, principles and rules will represent both a theory of and a method for producing the useful result. The proof of the pudding is in the eating, so to speak.

But what is a useful result? One may not judge the usefulness of a set of postulates, principles and rules by reference to the existing technical practices of practitioners or by generally accepted principles or procedures. Those practices themselves are the outcome of some judgments as to usefulness; but they may also be so hedged by conventions and expedients that usefulness has less than its share of influence. The existence of a practice is evidence that "it can be done"; it is not evidence of usefulness or of superiority over other possible practices, no matter how widely the practice may be found. The search for postulates is in the realm of the pursuit of useful knowledge, and, at every turn in the path to knowledge, history has proved generally accepted practices to be faulty, unreliable or incomplete and the ideas underlying them to be wrong, inadequate or inconsistent. That the earth is flat, that atoms are indivisible, that flying is only for the birds, that radio and television would reduce literacy, that pain is inevitable—all these are beliefs once widely held, beliefs which limited the practical pursuits of men until some individuals challenged their implicit assumptions and devised postulates which in due course gave men new knowledge and new practices.

The question of what is useful bedevils every inquiry, every science. And the typical answer of the scientist is: all knowledge is useful. By this he means that all propositions which put man in possession of more ideas about his environment or more ideas about his situation in that environment are useful. Now it may seem that the experimental sciences have the advantage of the social sciences here. For it is possible to test thoroughly the qualities of a new agricultural fertilizer, a new insecticide, a new paint, a new antibiotic, whereas it is not possible to test in any similar way the qualities of a new tax, a new form of city government or a new form of accounting. But the advantage is only an apparent advantage. Laboratory tests do not necessarily disclose all the consequences or even all the qualities of new products; they may have side effects which only become apparent over many years. Further, *all* knowledge, in the physical as well as the social sciences, is a matter of inference from statements put forward as descriptions of the phenomena under consideration, that is, from postulates.

Accounting, in common with other studies which relate to human behavior, has no recourse to experimental methods. Nevertheless there are two ways in which it is possible to determine whether any set of principles derived by logical processes from postulates are useful pieces of knowledge. It will appear that whichever of the two ways is adopted, practical experience and knowledge-of-acquaintance (i.e., knowledge of immediate perception and cognition as distinct from "book" knowledge) have much to do with any such determination.

The first way is to establish that the postulates are ample descriptions, for the purpose in hand, of the phenomena or events to which they relate. The process is simply an affirmation of the propriety of the postulates by skilled observers or by men of experience, preferably by both. It should be possible to reach agreement at this level. Given "the purpose in hand," the only room for difference of opinion arises from the word "ample." There is an enormous number of possible statements about the environment of accounting or about any aspect of it which can be affirmed. Not all of them will necessarily be useful in the sense that, taken together with others, they can be made to yield a conclusion. It is the particular problem of the researcher to ensure that he overlooks no possibly useful statement, and to select from all the statements about the environment those which will yield conclusions. Suppose one puts forward as a postulate the statement: Monetary calculation is concerned with market (or exchange) values. It should be possible to obtain agreement that this is or is not supported by observation and experience. If it is agreed that the statement is so supported, it is a potentially useful postulate. To give or withhold assent to such propositions is one of the functions of the voice of experience.

The next stage in deriving principles or rules is to draw out the implications of postulates, to link the bare statements in such a way that certain conclusions emerge. The process is the same, in kind, as men employ in the solution of any problem from a cross-word puzzle to the proof of an abstruse mathematical proposition. Given the same concern for care and rigor in reasoning, and the same level of skill, it should be possible for any person to assess the steps by which a conclusion is reached. Not necessarily the steps taken by the researcher in reaching the conclusion, because these involve initial insight, hesitation, subconscious reflection, re-examination of assumptions and eventual statement of the argument. By what personal processes is immaterial; at length he becomes able to state, step by step, an argument which can be assessed or tested by others. If it is agreed that the postulates are supported by observation and experience and if the steps in the argument are unobjectionable, the conclusion would appear to be unobjectionable.

The second point at which practical experience may bear on the whole process of deriving principles or methods from postulates is in testing the usefulness of the deduced result—in accounting this would mean testing the usefulness of the information flowing from a deduced method. This involves looking at the information from the point of view of all possible *users* for all possible purposes, but *not* from the point of view of the information-processor, the accountant. For example, in the field of business accounting, if the current rate of return on invested funds is important to users, the product of a deduced method must be such that the rate can be derived, and that this derived rate is both a logical relationship and a mathematically valid relationship. If the expected rate of cash flow is important to users, the product of a deduced method should enable users to derive a useful idea of expected cash flow. If both rate of return and rate of cash flow are important to users, the product of a deduced method should enable both to be derived. If different classes of users are envisaged, and if any person may at a given time be simultaneously a member of several such classes, the product of a deduced method should be such that it meets the needs of all classes simultaneously. It is on the hypothetical part of each of the preceding sentences—the "if" clause—that professional men should be able to pass judgment, and hopefully uniform judgment.

SOME PROBLEMS

In an examination of the propositions postulated by any person, or of the end-result of argument from postulates, it is important to keep in mind that the purpose of deriving general statements is to cover situations in general. If it is postulated that "all men act reasonably" (whatever "reasonably" may mean), it is no criticism to assert that sometimes men act foolishly or without reason. Some men appear to do so, sometimes; but accounting is not for them at those times. If it is postulated that "privately owned business firms and corporations are motivated by the expectation of profit," it is no criticism to assert that some companies do not make profits. If it is postulated that "monetary calculation is concerned with market (or exchange) values," it is no criticism to assert that generally accepted accounting principles do not uniformly indicate market or exchange values; for it will be found that, for any operation intended in the market for money or goods, one calculates in terms of market or exchange values regardless of what his accounting system tells him. Generally, then no criticism of postulates or principles can be accepted simply because there are some cases in which they do not apply. In this respect there may be a difference between the natural and the social sciences. One instance may give rise to doubt about a theory in the natural sciences; but because the social sciences are concerned with classes of people rather than individuals, their postulates and conclusions have only to meet the general test: does this postulate or that conclusion amply describe or relate to this or that class of people or this or that group of people?

Two methods of inquiry into postulates have been considered. By one, the procedure is to discover the ideas which are implicit in an established practice and to consider whether those ideas appear to be consistent with the "facts of life" or the requirements of reason. By the other, the "facts of life" and human reason are used to build systems of ideas which are examined in the light of observation and experience to establish whether they yield something useful. Both methods should yield answers of the same kind, for it is impossible for reason to contradict reason. And ideally both methods are used as checks on the possibility of errors or omissions or plain bad argument. It should also be clear that the mental processes involved are the same as any intelligent person adopts if he deliberately attempts to solve any practical problem intelligently rather than by tossing a coin.

There is one further point to make. The method of defining one's terms, stating one's postulates and deducing a system from them does not suffer from the same disability as the method of seeking postulates from observable practices and submitting them to analysis. The latter, as we have said, may readily be dubbed "destructive criticism." The former is essentially *constructive*. One may, of course, say in a disparaging way that this is all pure theory. But to do so is simply to deny the power of human reason, including the reason of those who disparage reason.

FROM POSTULATES TO PRINCIPLES

There is no such thing as a set of postulates which is independent of a set of conclusions or principles or hypotheses. Postulates are only postulated for the purpose of reaching some conclusion. It is necessary in short to consider a whole system of postulates and a conclusion together. One may set down five or fifty or five hundred potentially useful propositions as possible foundations for a conclusion; but if only three are necessary, all the rest are irrelevant to that specific conclusion; only three are postulates.

For any system of principles—say principles of accounting—there will be a series of separate sets of postulates, one set for each principle. Whether or not the system is internally consistent is of importance, for an internally inconsistent (i.e., contradictory) set of principles can not be a clear guide to practice, nor is it satisfying to the intelligence. The whole system of principles may entail quite a large number of postulates, but if it is to be an internally consistent system, the postulates, however large in number, will necessarily be consistent (this is the test used above when dealing with the listing of assets). To repeat, neither postulates nor principles can be considered *in vacuo*. They are inevitably linked and they may only be evaluated as part of a system.

As an illustration the following is offered. A principle is stated: certain postulates necessary to establish it are set out and certain definitions of the terms used are given; by relating the postulates step by step the conclusion stated at the outset is reached.

PRINCIPLE OF NEUTRALITY

The probability of optimal adaptation varies directly with the neutrality of accounting information.

1. Suppose a situation in which there is an actor and a processor of information on his behalf, so that acting and information processing are separate functions. (Postulate)

2. The state of satisfaction on the part of an actor, or action which procures it, will be called optimal adaptation. (Definition)

3. The independence of information with respect to any specific action will be called neutrality. (Definition)

4. Individuals have different systems of wants at any time. (Postulate)

5. The system of wants of any individual changes from time to time. (Postulate)

6. Satisfaction of an actor's system of wants at any time is the goal of and incentive to action. (Postulate)

7. The function of an information processor or processing system is to produce information relevant to action. (Postulate)

8. In the postulated situation 1 the processor will not know at any time what the present state of the actor's want-system is; or if he did know at some previous time, he will not know how far it has changed from that time to any other time.   (From 4 and 5)

9. The processor is thus not able to anticipate what the next action of the actor will be.   (From 8 and 6)

10. Therefore the greater the relevance of the information produced to all possible courses of action, the greater will be the possibility of optimal adaptation.   (From 2, 7, 9)

11. Accounting information is one class of information available to an actor.   (From 1)

12. From 8, 3 and 11 it follows that the probability of optimal adaptation on the part of an actor in the postulated situation 1 varies directly with the neutrality of accounting information.

Corollary: For even stronger reasons, the conclusion holds if the number of actors served by any financial statement is large and their interests are varied, for the information processor is removed from direct knowledge of the wants of any of them.

This principle is not to the writer's knowledge established at all in the literature of accounting; certainly not by the process adopted here. Yet it is an important and practical one. Apply for a moment the procedure of discovering the postulates underlying a stated operation, mentioned earlier in this paper. It is an established practice to publish one set of financial statements in respect of corporations in which it is known that the public and other institutions have equities, either as shareholders or as creditors. The only proposition which justifies this practice is: the information so published is equally useful to all parties in spite of their diverse interests. And this is simply a modified way of saying that the information is neutral with respect to the particular subsequent actions of all actors. The proposition is established from both directions! This should demolish the view, often asserted, but never found in practice, that companies should publish different financial statements for different classes of users (actors). The principle thus established in fact underlies a most important idea—the professional accountant's independence—an idea which has often been dogmatically stated, but the reason for which has never been proved by explicit argument. (It should be noted that the proposition discussed above has nothing whatever to say about the quality of the information contained in such statements; that is another matter altogether, requiring additional principles.)

WHAT IS A POSTULATE?

An attempt has been made to show by illustration what a postulate is. It will be seen on examination of all the statements described as postulates throughout this paper that none of them incorporates words or phrases which are peculiar to accounting. They are all descriptions of some thing, some event or some form of behavior found in the environment of accounting. Accounting has no justification whatever in itself. It has no rationale beyond the domain of men acting purposefully in monetary economies. All of its postulates must therefore be outside of it, must be descriptive of the world in which it plays a part. Of the thousands of statements it is possible to make about the environment in which we live, only those which deal with financial transactions or relationships or which have financial consequences or which deal with the problems of computation and communication can be related to accounting. That the same statements may at the same time be postulates or conclusions of other types of study is to be expected. In a sense it is to be welcomed, for it gives some assurance, if assurance be needed, that our concepts of the environment are not concepts we have invented for our own purposes. Those that are chosen as postulates are dictated by the function ascribed to accounting. Any proposition descriptive of the environment which is fundamentally necessary to support a conclusion, a principle or a practice in accounting is a postulate of accounting, however remote or trite it may appear to be.

Why Bother with Postulates?

Because every deliberate action of reasonable men, and every piece of advice proffered by practitioners, is based on some postulates, and reasonable men always want to be sure of their ground. Because it is common wisdom to re-examine the foundations of one's practices; practices may become so overlaid with habitual and conventional trappings that their avowed purposes are no longer well served. Because a man's postulates are the substance of his understanding of the world in which he acts; if his postulates are irrelevant or inconsistent, neither he nor his practices merit the esteem of his fellows. Because to examine one's postulates is the simplest and most effective way to discover the possibility and direction of improvements and innovations in practice. Because man's reasoned judgment is his only protection against self-delusion, cant and deceit.

THE FUNCTION OF A CONCEPTUAL FRAMEWORK FOR CORPORATE FINANCIAL REPORTING

K. V. Peasnell

INTRODUCTION

The purpose of the present article is to examine ways in which a statement of financial reporting objectives (hereinafter referred to as 'conceptual framework', or CF for short) can be expected to improve the quality of company financial reporting. It is argued here that there is considerable confusion surrounding the function of a CF, especially over the ways in which a CF can be expected to assist a financial accounting policy-making body such as the Accounting Standards Committee (ASC) or the Financial Accounting Standards Board (FASB); there seems little prospect of developing a CF of value to policy makers without first clarifying the powers and responsibilities of the policy makers themselves.

In the American literature in particular, there is a marked tendency to treat the problems of the development of a conceptual framework separately and independently of the determination of suitable institutional arrangements for standard setting; and yet they both have the same end in mind, namely the promulgation and improvement of accounting standards. More

I am greatly indebted to my Lancaster colleagues, Professor Edward Stamp and Mr. Simon Archer, for many hours of discussion on the subject matter of this paper. The contribution of Eddie Stamp, in particular, has been especially significant. Whilst I have not hesitated to plunder the ideas of both colleagues, it should not be supposed that either individual subscribes to the views contained in this paper. Embryonic versions of the paper were presented at the Universities of Glasgow and Manchester, and thanks are due to the participants in those seminars for their helpful comments.

K. V. Peasnell, "The Function of a Conceptual Framework for Corporate Financial Reporting," Accounting and Business Research, Autumn 1982, pp. 243–256. Reprinted with the permission of Accounting and Business Research.

to the point, it is the standard setters who have to make use of a CF, so it is important that their circumstances be considered first.

The plan of the paper is as follows. First the history of the search for a CF is briefly outlined and recent literature on the subject is summarised. Next, attention is directed to the standard-setting process currently in operation in the UK. Use is made here of a simple way of viewing social conflict resolution mechanisms devised by Boulding (1965). Section four develops the premise that whether or not a CF has anything major to contribute depends on the ways in which corporate financial reporting is organised and policed. Reference is made there to three different accounting environments—laissez-faire, state control, and delegation to the profession. The final section contains a summary and concluding comments.

The Quest for a Conceptual Framework

A Brief History of the Quest

Over the years, numerous attempts have been made to define the nature and purposes of corporate financial reporting—to develop a conceptual framework. Of course, most of these efforts are the works of individual scholars concerned to put the teaching of the subject on a sound theoretical footing; academic committees have also attempted to do the same, and for similar reasons in the main (e.g. see AAA, 1936, 1966, 1977). Only relatively recently have the professional accounting bodies shown any inclination to take part in this process. The concern in this subsection is with these officially commissioned studies; accounting theory development in the broad sense is of coincidental interest only. Attention is further restricted to developments in the USA, the UK and Canada.

The professional accounting bodies in these countries have taken the opportunity, from time to time, to issue statements about the nature, purposes and limitations of published financial statements of companies. No one has ever seriously suggested that any of these statements merited the title 'conceptual framework'. This is not to say that the statements were without influence or dealt with trivial matters—consider, for example, the English Institute's Recommendation N15, 'Accounting in Relation to Changes in the Purchasing Power of Money' (ICAEW, 1952)—merely that the objective in issuing them was much more limited.

Five attempts to develop a CF are worthy of special comment.[1] The first was a study commissioned by the American Institute of Certified Public Accountants (AICPA) some twenty years ago which saw the light of day as two interrelated monographs, one by the then AICPA Director of Accounting Research, Maurice Moonitz (1961), and the other by Sprouse and Moonitz (1962). The next study was explicitly charged by the AICPA with the development of a set of financial statement objectives intended to 'facilitate establishment of guidelines and criteria for improving accounting and financial reporting' and emerged as the Trueblood Report (AICPA, 1973). The third effort was commissioned in the UK in October 1974 by the (then styled) Accounting Standards Steering Committee; the report was eventually published as a discussion paper, *The Corporate Report* (ASC, 1975). The fourth and most extensive is that

---

[1] A sixth study is now completed. ASC commissioned Professor Richard Macve of the University of Wales to study the feasibility of developing a conceptual framework in Britain (published 1981).

by the FASB, which was charged with trying to make the Trueblood Report operational. Following a lengthy review process that started as long ago as 1974 with a public hearing, an exposure draft was issued in December 1977 (FASB, 1977). The first part of the exposure draft, dealing with the objectives of financial reporting, was issued as Statement of Financial Accounting Concepts No. 1 (SFAC1) a year later (FASB, 1978). The second part, outlining the elements of financial statements of business enterprises, was issued as SFAC3 in late 1980 (FASB, 1980b); SFAC2, 'Qualitative Characteristics of Accounting Information' (FASB, 1980a) was issued earlier in 1980.[2] The fifth study, also of very recent origin, was written by an academic, Edward Stamp, on behalf of the Canadian Institute of Chartered Accountants (CICA, 1980).

A common pattern can be seen both in the circumstances surrounding the commissioning of the first four of these five research studies and in the reactions of the accounting and business community to the proposals and arguments contained in the subsequent reports. First, they were established at a time when the standard-setting programme was running into trouble. Secondly, the reports were greeted with a mixture of cries of disappointment and anger.

All the AICPA's efforts at influencing the development of generally accepted accounting principles met with considerable criticism. The first really major effort in this direction was itself the result of mounting professional and legal criticisms both of the quality of corporate reporting practices and of the early attempts of the AICPA to remedy matters (Zeff, 1972, pp. 140–167). The Accounting Principles Board (APB) was established in 1959 as a direct result of these criticisms. The APB gave top priority to the launching of a study into the 'basic postulates' and 'broad principles' of accounting, the study which resulted in the Moonitz and Sprouse-Moonitz monographs.

The profession's reactions to the two monographs were most interesting. Moonitz's 1961 study of basic postulates caused almost no reaction. The reason seems to have been that it operated at too high a level of abstraction and generalisation; with hindsight, one can see that readers were holding fire, waiting for the follow-up study on principles (Zeff, 1972, pp. 174–175). When the second monograph was published all hell broke loose. Indeed, the Sprouse-Moonitz monograph itself contained 24 pages of comment and dissent by no less than 9 of the 12 members of the project advisory committee. Hardly an auspicious start! Needless to say, the study had little positive impact on the subsequent accounting practice pronouncements of the APB. The problem was that the 'broad principles' enunciated by Sprouse and Moonitz required that assets be shown at their current values, and the profession was not ready to endorse principles so at variance with then accepted practice.

How could this be? After all, the broad principles were deduced from the basic postulates identified in the first of the two monographs. There were few serious criticisms made of the soundness of the authors' deductions, and the publication of the basic postulates had passed largely without comment. The postulates were subjected to scrutiny and criticism only *after* it was realised what the postulates together logically entailed.

The critics won the day and the APB seemed to abandon hope that fundamental research might provide a logical foundation for pronouncements on accounting principles. But the Board's problems continued to grow. Several APB Opinions ran into difficulty during prepa-

---

[2]A fourth Statement, SFAC4 has also been issued by the FASB (1980c); but as it deals with the 'objectives of financial reporting by nonbusiness organisations', it falls outside the scope of the present article.

ration and in the period immediately following publication. Something had to be done. In 1965 a committee was established and charged with developing the fundamentals of financial reporting. Five years later, the Board approved APB Statement No. 4 (APBS4), 'Basic Concepts and Accounting Principles Underlying Financial Statements of Business enterprises' (AICPA, 1970). The charge was to produce a document which would serve two purposes: (a) to provide a rationale for currently accepted practices, one which would be useful in reducing alternative practices in accounting to those justified by substantial differences in factual circumstances; (b) to enhance understanding of the purposes, potential and limitations of financial statements in providing needed information. APBS4: (i) sets out a framework describing the environment in which accounting exists, the present objectives of financial accounting and financial statements and the basic features and elements of financial accounting and (ii) describes presently generally accepted accounting principles (Zeff, 1972, pp. 196–198).

Not surprisingly, APBS4 did little to quell criticism of the profession. Although a lengthy and impressive piece of work, APBS4 does not really amount to a Conceptual Framework. At best, it is essentially a defensive, descriptive document. It was widely criticised as an inadequate response to the problems facing the profession. There were those, including some of the members of the Board, who argued that a prescriptive statement was needed to complement APBS4's description of currently accepted practice. The idea of putting standard-setting on a sound footing by going back to first principles, looking at the basic issues of standard-setting, was revived.

The result was twofold: the establishment of FASB as recommended by the Wheat Report (AICPA, 1972) and the publication of the Trueblood Report (AICPA, 1973). It is noted that these reports were the work of two study groups, working independently. *It was assumed that one could 'refine' the objectives of financial statements without regard to the policy-making procedures.*

The Trueblood Report was, in effect, handed over to the newly-created FASB. The FASB acted quickly, putting the Report near the top of its agenda, issuing a discussion memorandum (FASB, 1974), inviting comments and arranging a public hearing. However progress from this point on was very slow, so slow that the standard-setting programme could not await finalisation of the objectives study. Thus the FASB was in a very similar position to that which the APB had found itself in, in that the FASB had to develop accounting standards without benefit of a formal framework.

Although the Trueblood Report received far greater support from within the profession than did the ill-fated Moonitz-Sprouse study, it was not without its critics. The public hearings arranged by the FASB showed that there was considerable opposition from industry to the Report's emphasis on user needs and to some of the forms of disclosure mentioned in the Report. In particular, criticism was directed at Objectives 10, 11, and 12 in the Report, dealing with financial forecasts, non-profit accounting and social accounting; SFAC1 omits any reference to these items.

The FASB has little to show for its four years of hard work on the CF project. As Dopuch and Sunder (1980, p. 3) point out:

> In wording and substance, little is new or different in SFAC1. Had the FASB pointed out the parts of the existing reports, such as APBS4 and the Trueblood Report, that it agreed with and emphasized its disagreements, its contribution would have been easier to discern. Without such aid, we are hard-pressed to discern the FASB's net contribution to these earlier efforts.

Of course, the proof of the pudding is in the eating: 'a basic test of the FASB's contribution is the extent to which SFAC1 may succeed where others have failed' (Dopuch and Sunder, 1980, p. 3). On this point, Dopuch and Sunder make two observations which are worth noting. First, they point out that the definitions of the main categories of accounts appearing in financial statements—assets, liabilities, owners' equity, revenues, expenses, gains, losses—depend on unspecified rules and conventions. 'How can a conceptual framework guide choices from among alternative principles and rules if the elements of the framework are defined in these very same terms?' (p. 4). They argue that the definitions 'provide only the necessary conditions for a resource or obligation to be included in the asset or liability categories, respectively, rather than both the necessary and sufficient conditions' (p. 4). The necessary conditions are conventional ones and as such are unlikely to be too restrictive.

Second, Dopuch and Sunder argue that nothing in the FASB's CF seems to be of much help in resolving contemporary disclosure issues. They support this assertion by selecting three issues—deferred tax credits, treatment of costs of exploration in the oil and gas industry, reports on current values of assets and liabilities—for detailed consideration. They conclude: (i) 'The FASB's definition of liabilities is so general that at this stage we cannot predict the Board's position on deferred taxes' (Dopuch and Sunder, 1980, p. 6). (ii) 'The fact that the framework supports two opposing principles of accounting [for oil and gas exploration costs—full costs and successful efforts] is preliminary evidence that the framework is unlikely to be a useful guide in resolving this issue' (p. 7). (iii) Neither SFAC1 nor the Exposure Draft addresses the problem of estimation; yet it is on the practical issue of reliability of estimates that past efforts to encourage publication of current costs have foundered (p. 8).

Not all commentators are as pessimistic as Dopuch and Sunder about the benefits that might flow from the FASB's CF programme. Scott and De Celles (1980) take the view that a *virtue* of SFAC1 is that it avoids establishing a definite association between accounting objectives and specific financial reports because it leaves room for future development. This appears to be the FASB's thinking on the matter.

The only UK attempt to date to develop a CF was the 1975 ASC discussion paper, *The Corporate Report*. The discussion paper was produced in a very short time. The working party began work in October 1974 and its report was published in July 1975—several weeks before the report of the government-appointed Inflation Accounting Committee (Sandilands, 1975) was presented to the Chancellor of the Exchequer and the Secretary of State for Trade. (For comparison purposes, the Sandilands Report took 17 months to complete, the Trueblood Report 30 months, and *The Corporate Report* some 9 months.) *The Corporate Report* caused great controversy within the business community and the accounting profession. In particular, the emphasis placed in the discussion paper on greater disclosure, including statements of 'future prospects' and 'corporate objectives', was the subject of much criticism. Also, the more or less simultaneous publication of the Sandilands Report drew attention away from *The Corporate Report*—a possibility that was in effect acknowledged by the (then) chairman of the ASSC, Sir Ronald Leach, in his Foreword to the discussion paper when he specifically drew attention to the contribution of both documents to 'the fundamental problem of measurement of profit'. The 'great inflation accounting debate' has occupied the centre of the stage ever since, and the far more fundamental issues concerning the scope and nature of financial reporting dealt with in *The Corporate Report* have received scant attention. The discussion paper has faded away into history—one suspects to the profession's great relief.

Meanwhile, the Accounting Standards Committee (ASC) has had to get on with its business without the benefit of a CF. Its difficulties are considerable, if the controversies surrounding its attempts to produce a generally acceptable inflation accounting standard, for example, are anything to go by.

The latest attempt to develop a CF comes from Canada (CICA, 1980). The contents of *Corporate Reporting* are similar to those of *The Corporate Report* in a number of respects—which is not particularly surprising bearing in mind that its sole author, Edward Stamp, was a member of the committee which produced the ASC discussion paper. Also, like *The Corporate Report* and unlike either the Trueblood Report or the FASB conceptual framework programme, *Corporate Reporting* was produced very quickly at negligible cost. Unlike either of its predecessors, *Corporate Reporting* attempts to deal with the subject of what a CF is for and how it is intended to assist standard setters; attention is devoted to the Canadian business and accounting environment. Stamp opts for an evolutionary approach, as distinct from the FASB's normative approach, and sees the function of a CF as providing objectives and criteria which CICA's Accounting Research Committee can use not in a strictly deductive fashion but as tools in developing standards in a manner analogous to common law.

It is too early to form a view on the profession's reactions to Stamp's proposals. Initial reactions have focussed, in the main, on the case made by Stamp that Canada needs a CF appropriate to its particular cultural and institutional needs; some commentators take the view that the most cost-effective line for the Canadian profession and business community to take is simply to adopt the FASB's standards except when clear and compelling local concerns dictate otherwise. This particular issue is peculiar to Canada and is beyond the scope of the present article.

A Brief Review of the Academic Literature

Academics have not neglected the subject of financial accounting standard setting and theory development. Perhaps the research most compatible with the type of programme being undertaken by the FASB, for example, is what is sometimes referred to as 'a priori theorising': the development and rationalisation, by means of deductive and inductive methods of reasoning, of systems of business accounting valuation and profit measurement. Certain types of empirical research can be and have been of direct and obvious value as well. The information economics approach, however, opens up a much wider perspective, one that brings the standard setting machinery and specific measurement and disclosure issues into one common framework.

Two consequences of the information economics approach to accounting theory development are worth noting. First, there is wider appreciation now in academic circles of the problems and pressures which quasi-official standard-setting bodies such as the FASB and the ASC have to deal with. This is the most positive result of the new approach. The tendency among academics to judge the output of the accounting policy-making process by some absolute standard of truth or private utility has greatly diminished as a result of this research. Second, there is a great deal of skepticism nowadays among academics about the worthwhileness of attempting to base accounting standard setting on a 'generally agreed' CF.

The information economics approach assumes that the various parties involved in standard setting (managers, the profession, users, etc.) are concerned with furthering their own interests and objectives, and not with ensuring that financial accounting standards meet the 'basic objectives of financial reporting'. Following this line of thought, Dopuch and Sunder (1980, p. 18) argue that

> There is little evidence that official statements of objectives of financial accounting have had any direct effect on the determination of financial accounting standards. Whenever the APB or the FASB has had to consider a financial accounting standard, various interest groups presented arguments to support the methods that each perceived to be in its own best interests. The standards issued had to be compromises among the contending interests.

Support for this pessimistic view is provided by Watts and Zimmerman (1978) who examined the corporate submissions made to the FASB concerning its Discussion Memorandum on 'Reporting the Effects of General Price-Level Changes in Financial Statements'.

It is not only managers, auditors and users whose views and submissions are subject to this sceptical evaluation; accounting theorists are given the same treatment. They are concerned with the pursuit of their own self-interest, in the sense of being active participants in the 'market for excuses'. Watts and Zimmerman (1979) argue that, in a regulated economy, financial accounting statements can have important and varying effects on the welfare of individuals and organisations affected by rate settings, anti-trust, labour negotiations, etc; therefore different parties want 'respectable' (in the sense of appealing to the 'public interest') accounting theories which will serve their cause.

Cushing (1977) suggests that the theorists who reject the possibility of finding an unobjectionable social welfare function (i.e. social goals which everyone is bound to accept) may be overstating the problem. In practice, society *is* able to reach decisions about the provision of 'collective' goods (which financial statements can be viewed as being) by the use of a partial, piecemeal approach. (This, in fact, is how accounting standard setters are proceeding—the continuing 'search' for a CF notwithstanding.) Cushing's suggestion, in effect, is that accounting policy makers should take a leaf out of the cost-benefit analyst's book and tackle problems one at a time, holding constant the welfare principles of concern in other areas of controversy.

Bromwich (1980) considers some of the conditions necessary for Cushing's partial standards approach to maximize the welfare of an individual using published financial reports for decision-making purposes. Bromwich shows that the individual's preferences (utility function) have to be somewhat unusual. This leads him to conclude that accounting policy makers, if they are to employ a partial standards approach in an unobjectionable manner, need to consider simultaneously accounting standards which display any significant element of interdependence. Although not despairing, Bromwich offers little comfort to those who would like to see standard setting put on a 'sound' basis secured upon a generally accepted CF.

A MODEL OF THE UK STANDARD-SETTING PROCESS

The above review of professional and academic developments hardly does justice to past and current thinking. However, it sketches out salient aspects of the present state-of-the-art and background developments. In this section an attempt will be made to put some flesh on the bones of the earlier arguments in such a way that the essentially political nature of the standard-setting process will be brought out.

FIGURE 1

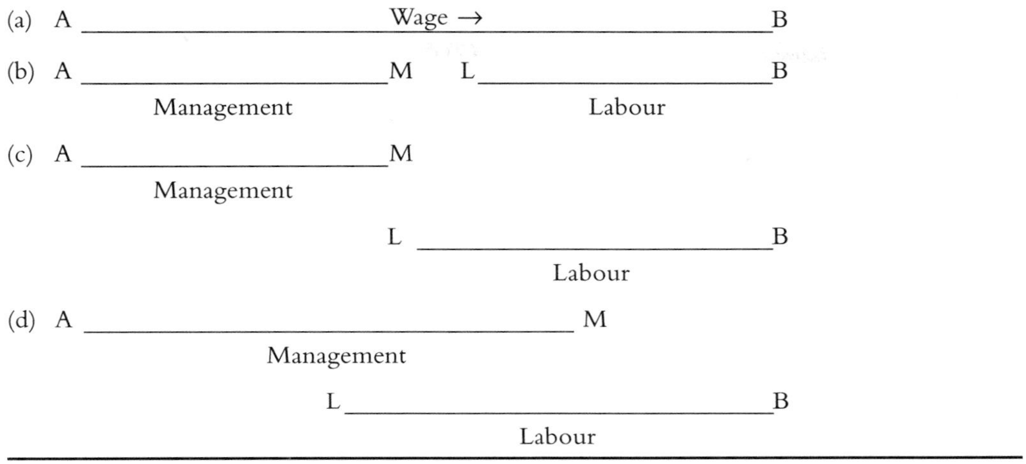

(a) A _____ Wage → _____ B

(b) A _____ M   L_____ B
           Management   Labour

(c) A _____ M
           Management

                        L _____ B
                                Labour

(d) A _____ M
                Management
                   L_____ B
                         Labour

Source: Boulding (1965), Figure 2, p. 331.

Standard-setting mechanisms such as the SEC, the FASB and the ASC have been brought into existence in order to deal with the conflicts of interest which exist in corporate reporting. The SEC, of course, is a government agency and, as such, has residual powers of enforcement denied to the FASB and the ASC. However, as the SEC has, by and large, delegated the setting of accounting standards to the FASB the distinction need not detain us. FASB and ASC have to deal with a variety of conflicts of interest and pressures, balancing one against the other. This is what is of interest here.

Use is made below of a model of conflict resolution devised by Kenneth Boulding (1965), an economist noted for his contributions to the literature on peace and conflict. The model is intended to throw light on the *dynamics* of bargaining and conflict such as in wage negotiations. It is helpful to go through the model with this application in mind and then to apply the model to standard setting.

Figure 1 concerns labour-management bargaining to fix a wage. A wage increases from A to B. In (b), labour will agree to any wage above L, and management will agree to any wage below M. But, as M is less than L, no agreement is possible. Negotiations will take place aimed at changing the positions of M and/or L. Management will try to persuade labour to lower L; labour will try to persuade management of the justice of L and that the firm can afford a greater wage, all in the hope of raising M. In the event of deadlock, there may be recourse to threats of strikes and lockouts. However, if such threats have to be carried out, both management and labour can be the losers. In the Figure, (c) represents a point where the gap between M and L has dropped to zero and a bargain can be struck. But, even where both parties recognise the dangers of conflict, there are difficulties in getting from (b) to (c). As Boulding (1965, p. 331) points out: 'Many of the difficulties in conflict situations arise out of the fact that in the actual division of the spoils of the bargaining process, victory tends to go to the recalcitrant.'

The parallels with management-labour negotiations are far from obvious but, nevertheless, often instructive. No longer is the conflict of the classical 'us' and 'them' variety. Instead, there are several parties involved; the mixture depends on the particular issue at stake, although corporate managements and the auditing profession are invariably interested in the outcome. Sometimes the unions, public interest pressure groups, government departments, and the investment community have an interest as well. On occasion, different corporate managements may be on opposite sides of the fence (e.g. over the proposal to include a monetary items adjustment in a current value accounting standard). In terms of Figure 1, 'management' remains as management (generally); 'labour' becomes the variety of parties with an interest in the particular accounting issue (e.g. investors and the Bank of England); for 'wage' now read 'the accounting issue in question' (e.g. 'accounting for foreign currency transactions', or 'current value accounting'). One can view the ASC as an arbitrator in a labour negotiation: the objective is somehow to bring M and L together.

To this point, the analogy between wage bargaining may seem uninteresting if not downright fanciful. After all, (b) in Figure 1 hardly represents most standard-setting disputes. The problem is usually not that different interest groups take up wholly incompatible positions, but that there is a variety of options open, each of which is acceptable to many (if not all) of the groups, the difficulty being to choose between the options. In other words the analogy is more often likely to be with the situation depicted in (d).

Figure 1(d) depicts what on first sight appears to be a non-conflict case: the minimum payoff required, L, is less than the opposition's maximum, M. In terms of the wage negotiation example, the minimum wage which labour will settle for is less than the maximum wage management is willing to pay. What could be better? The issue, though, is the whereabouts of the final settlement in the range of ambiguity, LM. If the wage is struck near L, management will obtain the bulk of the gains; conversely, if the wage bargain is struck near M, labour will take the lion's share. As Boulding (1965, p. 332) notes, 'a great deal depends upon the realism of the perception of the parties'. If labour appreciates the existence and extent of the LM overlap, but management does not, labour will have a very strong incentive to raise its L to near M, thereby securing gains that it previously could not have hoped for, and thus moving from (d) to (c). However, if management also comes to appreciate the extent of the LM overhang, it will be inclined to pull back M to near L. A consequence of *both* labour and management coming to appreciate the bargaining gains to be made can therefore be to change a situation full of opportunities for cooperation to one of conflict (b).

The same thing can happen in disputes over accounting standards. Different groups interested in a particular standard may start out with helpful attitudes, such as a strong desire to reach agreement, and with no very demanding or controversial requirements to be met. In this case they are likely to be in a situation like (d). Let us examine an hypothetical dispute over how best to take account of price changes in a period of rapid inflation. In particular, suppose that the business community is concerned about the destructive effects on business investment of taxation based on historical cost accounts and of wage claims based on 'inflated' profit figures. However, managers of businesses that are not capital-intensive are not greatly exercised over the subject and may well be sympathetic to the pleas of their less fortunate brethren. The unions are indifferent to the whole subject, regarding it as a 'technical' accounting matter of little relevance to wage negotiations. Furthermore, the government is concerned to maintain its tax revenue base but is mindful of the fact that punitive taxation that results in a rash of bankruptcies, falling investment and losses of industrial output is not likely to achieve this end in all but the very short run. A government Committee of Enquiry is set up and produces a set of Current Cost Accounting (CCA) proposals much like those contained in the Sandilands Report. All in all, the conditions of this hypothetical example might well be like (d) (with 'labour' representing the hardpressed industrial companies and 'management' signifying the government and managers of unaffected types of businesses such as banks). All seems to be set for the introduction of a CCA standard. Everything points to a solution very close to L in (d).

Matters do not rest there, however. Managers of the 'unaffected' financial institutions come to realise that all the benefits of this accounting standard are accruing to industrial companies and that the financial institutions gain nothing. Indeed, research studies suggest that, under the terms of the proposed CCA standard, the reported profits of industrial companies will be slashed; at the same time, inflation and accompanying high nominal interest rates have pushed up the profits of 'unaffected' financial institutions to record levels. Far from being unaffected by the new standard, banks, other financial institutions, retail stores, and the like now appear to be making huge profits relative to industrial companies. There is even a likelihood that the government will try to maintain its flow of-tax revenues from the corporate sector by shifting more of the burden to the financial institutions. It would be surprising in these circumstances if financial businesses did not clamour for some kind of 'relief' as well—perhaps by the inclusion of 'money items adjustments' in the standard. At the same time, industrial companies with large net money indebtedness can be expected to object to these departures from the 'pure' CCA system. The overall result might be that the situation changes from one like that depicted in (d) to that in (b).

Consider what happens when the parties are deadlocked as depicted in (b). The observations of Boulding (1965, p. 330) on how deadlock can be broken are of interest:

> An important principle which is often overlooked is that the parties that have reached a conflict set relevant to a state of the world defined by only a few variables can frequently break the impasse and open up opportunities for further trading and further benign moves by *widening the agenda,* that is, by introducing new variables into the relationship. We notice this phenomenon, for instance, in collective bargaining in industrial relations where *there is a strong tendency to proliferate clauses in the contract, partly at least because this opens up further opportunities for bargaining.* An impasse in bargaining about wages and hours may be broken if various other fringe benefits, job security, procedural relationships, and so forth are thrown into the bargaining process. (Emphasis added.)

In terms of Figure 1, a settlement is obtained such that (b) is changed to (c) by the parties doing business on something other than wages, i.e. on an aspect of their relationship not in dispute. Examples of such behaviour are commonplace in the wider political arena. In accounting, progress might be made by the parties involved in the dispute *obscuring the issues* at stake. To a 'negotiator' trying to find common ground, theoretical clarity need not be a virtue; logical consistency might be unattainable.

This brings us back to the search for a Conceptual Framework from which 'generally acceptable' accounting standards can be derived in a logical manner. If the analysis of this section is at all near the mark, it is difficult to avoid concluding that a CF is largely irrelevant to the needs of the ASC as presently constituted. *In a system highly dependent on the cooperation and goodwill of reporting companies, the ASC needs to preserve its freedom to bargain and hence to obfuscate points in dispute. Viewed from the ASC's perspective, a CF might be more of a hindrance than a help. Flexibility is all important; but flexibility seems to be what a CF is intended to eliminate.*

Accounting standards are produced in Britain by what is, in essence, a bargaining process. The ASC is the more or less private property of the professional accounting bodies and has little or no power which it can employ to enforce its standards. Therefore, the ASC has no choice but to try to obtain the cooperation of the companies affected by its pronouncements and the agreement of the bulk of practising accountants. The weakness of the ASC's position was illustrated in dramatic fashion by the revolt of the members of the ICAEW to ED18 (ASC, 1976). There is little that the ASC can do when faced by a determined opposition. Experience has shown that the ASC has no powerful friends to whom it can look for support in times of trouble.

The FASB is in a somewhat different position. It is true, of course, that the FASB lacks power and often seems to be without influential friends. But in the final analysis the FASB derives its authority from the power which the 1933 and 1934 Securities Acts confer on the SEC. Indeed, the American accounting profession's involvement in the setting of disclosure standards can be directly traced to political pressures. Prior to 1930, auditing procedures and terminology were the dominant concerns of the accounting profession (Zeff, 1972, p. 119). But the 1933 and 1934 Acts changed all that. The Acts are concerned with the issue and trading of company securities, and confer on the SEC broad authority to determine the accounting and auditing practices used by companies in the preparation of reports required under the Acts. Nowadays, the SEC largely delegates these powers to the FASB; the SEC exercises control on a 'management by exception' basis, there remaining the very real possibility that it would intervene whenever the FASB issues a standard which arouses opposition sufficient to muster political support of the kind likely to cause difficulties for the SEC itself or which contradicts a firmly-held SEC view.[3] (The SEC's introduction of a replacement cost disclosure requirement of 10-K registrants is a recent example.) The SEC has influence over the behaviour of registrant companies denied to the FASB. Therefore the FASB's freedom to bargain is somewhat circumscribed; it has the SEC (and sometimes *ad hoc* committees of the Senate) to contend with.

In Britain, government departments play a small part in standard setting. Of course, the government of the day is a force to be reckoned with, as the intervention of the Heath Administration over inflation accounting demonstrated. Nevertheless, government is just another of the parties that the ASC has to take account of and bargain with. In the United States, accounting policy making is an inherently political activity as a consequence of the SEC's involvement in and overseeing of corporate financial disclosure; in Britain, it is largely a matter of bargaining between interest groups.

Whether the differences in the circumstances of the FASB and the ASC are greater than the similarities is an interesting question; but it is not one on which we need dwell. For our purposes it is sufficient to note that the FASB seems to have a greater yearning for a CF than does the ASC: the FASB has accorded the highest priority to its 'Objectives and Elements' study, avowedly setting great store in the possibilities a CF will afford for putting its standards programme on a sound footing; whereas the ASC seems to be very sceptical about the possibilities of a substantial pay-off from such efforts (ASC, 1978). This difference of opinion may be due to variations in temperament, education, etc., between the two countries, or it might be due to the different needs and pressures faced by standard setters in a political regulatory environment versus those in a largely unregulated one. It is to this latter possibility that we now turn.

---

[3]Needless to say, the SEC often does accept standards of which it does not approve, e.g. the standard on capitalisation of interest. SEC disapproval is a necessary but not sufficient condition for its intervention in standard setting. Another necessary (perhaps sufficient) condition appears to be the build-up of political pressure of the kind we have tried to model above.

THE ALTERNATIVES

Whether or not a CF has anything major to contribute to corporate financial disclosure in general, and to accounting standard setting in particular, depends on the ways in which financial reporting is organised and policed. There are many different ways of organising and policing corporate disclosure. Three seem worthy of special attention:[4] (1) more or less complete *laissez-faire;* (2) state control and supervision; (3) delegation of power to the profession. These forms of organisation have been widely discussed in the literature. Each is considered briefly below.

LAISSEZ-FAIRE

One way of organising corporate disclosure is not to attempt to organise it at all. In the extreme, there would be no legal disclosure rules of any kind, not even rules governing disclosure to shareholders in general meeting of the kind set out in the British Companies Acts and in the corporation laws of most American states. A modified form of *laissez-faire* is where statutory provision is made for the disclosure of information (financial and otherwise) to clearly defined parties, such as shareholders of record and creditors, who have legal property rights in the enterprise; the information ('right to know') provisions are made part and parcel of the granting of limited liability.

It is likely that information will be provided to investors in excess of that demanded in law (assuming, of course, that the legal provisions are not particularly onerous). Promoters and managers of companies have financial incentives to contract to supply audited financial statements. If they do not incorporate, in the articles of association and in private lending contracts, provisions governing such supply then they will encounter great difficulty in raising finance at low cost (Jensen and Meckling, 1976). The various contracting parties (i.e. managers and owner-managers, outside investors, creditors, and union negotiators) will presumably weigh the costs and benefits of various alternative contractual arrangements in order to ascertain which disclosure and 'bonding' package has the best pay-off for each.

The purpose of disclosure agreements in an unregulated economy is to reduce *agency costs.* As Watts and Zimmerman (1979, p. 276) point out:

> Agency costs arise because the manager's (the agent's) interests do not necessarily coincide with the interests of shareholders or bondholders (the principals). For example, the manager (if he owns shares) has incentives to convert assets of the corporation into dividends, thus leaving the bond-holders with the "shell" of the corporation. Similarly, the manager has incentives to transfer wealth to himself at the expense of both the shareholders and bondholders (e.g., via perquisites).

---

[4]Perhaps a fourth could be added: where accounting is 'regulated' by setting up an Accounting Court to which dissatisfied parties could appeal against corporate accounting practices which offend them. As, strictly speaking, an Accounting Court does not provide an alternative regulatory means or environment but is an addition to one of the three models discussed above, it is not treated separately. The only country which seems to have anything resembling an Accounting Court is the Netherlands, where, in a largely unregulated environment similar in many (but not all) respects to the British one, there was established in 1971 the Enterprise Chamber which is a special section of the Court of Justice. The main role of the Enterprise Chamber seems to be that of providing some kind of lower bound to reporting standards and, in particular, to put pressure (via publicity) on the auditing profession. Klaassen (1980, p. 340) argues that the court cases he has examined 'demonstrate that a company court is not a proper institution to produce accounting standards'.

As agency costs may vary in amount and character from firm to firm, it follows that disclosure practices may vary between firms (and within a firm over time) *and with very good reason* (Watts, 1977). In fact, comparability may be desired by none of the parties involved. This is because what appears to be chaotic accounting practices or debenture-bonding arrangements may be, on the contrary, an equilibrium set of contractual devices which minimises the agency costs associated with the separation of management from control and with conflicts of interests between different classes of investors.

Auditing is an important activity in an unregulated economy. Indeed, it is one of the main ways of reducing agency costs: agency costs will not be reduced if the financial disclosures of management are not deemed credible and, as Stamp and Moonitz (1978, p. 23) point out, 'it can be said that the function of auditing is to lend credibility to financial statements.' Of course, there are those who view external auditing as a largely useless legal imposition which would (presumably) not come about (in present form) in an unregulated economy. Consider, for example, the views of Briston and Perks (1977, p. 48):

> We contend that neither the shareholder nor management derives obvious substantial benefit from the external audit process. The management of the company suffers disruption of its accounting and internal control systems as a result of the audit investigation and pressure upon its cash flow due to the monetary cost of the audit. . . . The auditor is not at all concerned that the published accounts are largely irrelevant to shareholders, whose information needs relate to future plans and forecasts of the company and assessments of its past and present efficiency.

There is no evidence known to the present author to support these assertions of Briston and Perks. On the contrary, auditing of much less impressive financial statements compiled on similar bases to those published nowadays was commonplace *before* statutory provision was made for mandatory audits (Watts and Zimmerman, 1979; Mumford, 1980). Moreover, agency theory suggests that published accounts are far from being 'largely irrelevant' to shareholders nor are audits of the same. Auditing is a 'contract compliance' cost (Demski and Feltham, 1976, p. 203).

Returning to the more general question of disclosure, even in an unregulated economy one can expect pressures to grow for professional accounting institutes to give some kind of 'guidance' or 'lead' in financial accounting matters. It is very difficult (if not impossible) to spell out, in the articles of association and in lending contracts, in sufficient detail the kinds of disclosures which will achieve the desired savings in agency costs. Recourse will almost certainly have to be had to poorly-specified terms such as 'profit' and 'financial position'; auditors will be asked to express a general 'opinion', such as whether or not the disclosures present a 'true and fair view'. It will, very probably, be cost-effective if the auditing profession pools its resources and sets up central agencies to provide guidance in these matters. There is a very great likelihood of a body along the lines of the ASC being set up even in an entirely unregulated economy. Indeed, the British standard-setting arrangements are largely the creation of the auditing profession and the business community, with the government playing a very minor role.

STATE CONTROL

It is instructive to pass to the opposite extreme, to consider what might happen in a totally regulated economy (i.e., totally regulated as far as the production and dissemination of corporate financial statements are concerned).

An unregulated economy does not necessarily produce economic 'goods' of the type, quantity and frequency which all—or even any—of the parties involved agree is optimal. With certain types of goods it can happen that the productive outcome brought about by all the parties bargaining and transacting on an individual basis is universally agreed to be inferior to the outcome that they collectively prefer. This can arise with a 'social good', that is good with the characteristic, *inter alia,* of being able to be consumed by more than one person and where other consumers cannot easily be excluded from consumption. In such a case, where free-riders are a problem, a collusive outcome can be superior for all or some and not worse for any if, but only if, it can be ensured that all the parties will cooperate. In general, a non-cooperative outcome involves less output of the good than does the collusive optimum (Van den Doel, 1979, ch. 2). Regulation of the output of social goods may be the only way of achieving the generally desired outcome. The difference between the non-cooperative and the collusive solutions corresponds to Rousseau's distinction between 'the will of all' and 'the general will' (Sen, 1967).

Published financial statements of companies can usefully be viewed as social goods. Of course, to managements interested in reducing agency costs and to actual and prospective investors they are private goods. But to the wider public which is interested, for example, in investing in rival companies or in assessing the extent of monopoly power, published accounting information is a social good.

Some would argue that published financial statements are social goods as far as the investing public is concerned, although the issue is the subject of great dispute (Benston, 1976). Certainly this line of thinking underlay the establishment of the SEC in the United States: 'full' disclosure is needed to reduce the incentives to insider trading the occurrence of which is a disincentive to external investment. Investment is important not only to the investors and firms directly involved but also to the public at large; the general will is involved.

State control and supervision of production is one frequently proffered solution to the social goods problem; another is to impose taxes and provide grants and other incentives to encourage the socially optimal level of output. In the case of accounting in Britain and America, the former solution has been adopted *in part.* Companies are compelled by law to make publicly available certain kinds of information. Legal provision is made for compulsory audit of the published data. In addition, in the USA, the SEC has a responsibility to ensure proper financial disclosure and has considerable powers (over 10-K filings) to this end. (State control in the sense of the state taking over the production of the social good is not really feasible in accounting.) But the amount of control over accounting exercised by government in Britain and America is not very great. In the USA the amount of control actually exercised by the SEC is rather small: the regulators take a watching brief, in the main, intervening very little, and effectively delegating day-to-day responsibility to the profession.

Another reason sometimes advanced for government regulation and control (of part or the whole) of the economy is to effect a change in the distribution of income and wealth in society. In a limited sense, the SEC's concern with protecting the 'lay' investor can be explained in these terms. As this is a concern of a strictly political nature, it is clear that responsibility and control must reside in the political arena. There seems to be no real role for professional accounting standard setters here, and hence no obvious reasons for incorporating such considerations into a CF.

Consider the hypothetical situation in which private sector corporate financial accounting is under the strict control of a state regulatory agency. Regulations and accounting standards are laid down in considerable detail by the agency's officials. There might well be a scale of penalties for non-compliance with the regulations and standards; at a minimum, auditors will be expected to express their opinion (as to whether a true and fair view is being shown) in terms of compliance with the regulations and standards. What role is there for a CF along the lines of say SFAC1? The answer must surely be: precious little. The situation described is very much like that in the government—particularly the local government—sector of the economy. Standards are developed internally by the government bureaucracy, modified on occasion as a consequence of external pressures made effective through the political process.

DELEGATION TO THE PROFESSION

Delegation can take one of three forms. There can be a delegation by the regulatory agency of responsibility to the accounting profession but with power being retained by the agency. This is the arrangement in the USA, the FASB and the AICPA together being charged with responsibility for the governance of corporate reporting standards, but real power residing in the hands of the SEC and the other government agencies. Alternatively, power can reside in the hands of the accounting profession and responsibility in those of a government agency. (This is a somewhat implausible alternative and is included here only for completeness.) A third alternative is for both responsibility and (*de facto* and *de jure*) power to be put in the hands of the profession. An example of this is to be found in Canada. Canadian Federal law requires that accounting standards, as laid down from time to time in the Canadian Institute's Handbook, *must* be used by Canadian corporations (incorporated under the Federal Act) in producing their published financial reports (Stamp, 1979, p. 23).

    The lot of the profession in America is not a happy one. The FASB and the AICPA are being urged more or less continually by the committees of the House and the Senate, sundry government agencies and interested politicians to 'do something'. There is the ever-present threat that, if the FASB does not improve the state of company reporting, then the SEC will take over the setting of accounting standards. The business community and constituent parts of the profession all agree that this would be undesirable—it would, after all, reduce their influence on and control of the standard-setting process. On the other hand, particular business corporations and audit firms individually have strong incentives, on occasion, to disregard their acknowledged common interests and pursue their private interests—especially as the FASB is without power to stop them doing so. In the absence of coercion, the will of all (consisting of the separate wills of autonomous, independent individuals) does not correspond to the general will. The FASB can, of course, appeal to the SEC for help in enforcing its standards; but the results of such an appeal are by no means certain to be in the FASB's favour.

    Companies and audit firms in conflict with the FASB can also appeal to the SEC both directly and via the wider political process. These other appellants may be able to muster powerful political support, say by 'log-rolling', i.e. conjoining the issue in question with another perhaps distant matter of considerable importance to the politicians (e.g. by offering financial and other support in a coming election). In such a case, the FASB might well find the SEC declining to help or even actively intervening against it. The result of such failure of the SEC to support the FASB is great damage to the prestige and hence the effectiveness of the FASB, thereby making the latter body reluctant to take on determined flouters of its accounting standards. An inevitable consequence of this kind of defeat is the public emphasis of the powerlessness of the standard-setting organisation. Thus, the FASB is in the worst of all worlds. Generally speaking, it is as dependent as is the ASC on the cooperation of business firms and their auditors, and hence has to do a great deal of wheeling and dealing; but it also has criticisms from the SEC and most other branches of government as well. All in all, the main beneficiary of the American responsibility-without-power form of delegation seems to be the SEC which can discharge its statutory obligations in a virtually risk-free manner.

It is not surprising that the FASB places so much emphasis on the importance of developing a CF; by doing so the FASB provides a (partial) answer to its critics: all will be well when the 'objectives and elements' of financial statements are determined. A cynic might argue that the CF programme is nothing more than a delaying tactic. Such cynicism is surely misplaced; if this had been the motive, the FASB would not have been so foolish as actually to *produce* (in parts) its conceptual framework. A more likely explanation for the FASB's professed faith in its CF programme is that, given its obvious lack of power (or powerful friends), it perceives a need to show that its heart and mind are in the right place: to demonstrate that it is trying by logical means to develop accounting standards based on principles of general appeal. More will be said on this point below.

The Canadian arrangement, whereby both responsibility and power are delegated to the profession, seems to have more to commend it as far as the profession and the business community in general are concerned. After all, the Canadian Institute is likely to be more responsive to the needs and concerns of those it exists to serve, and less whimsical and better informed on business matters than is the wider polity. Power is located where responsibility lies; hence accounting policy decisions are likely to take account of all the issues currently dealt with in divided fashion by the FASB and the SEC in the USA.

It could be argued, of course, that the Canadian Institute is likely to be too influenced by the narrow self-interest of accountants and auditors (and of the business community they serve); that the wider public interest is badly served by such an arrangement; that power rightly belongs in and only in the hands of the government and its agencies. May be this is so. However, sight should not be lost of the fact that the medical profession gets by with delegated powers of this kind without exciting too much hostility. As Stamp (1979, pp. 23–24) points out:

> Anyone who believes that such a system of legislative backing is objectionable, and who thinks that Parliament should be actively involved in the standard setting process, should reflect upon how he would feel if the same attitude were to be adopted by Parliament towards the setting of standards of medical practice.

Besides, the conjoining of power *and* responsibility in the hands of the profession leaves it wide open to public criticism if it is insensitive to the interests and needs of groups affected by its pronouncements. In any event disaffected parties still have access to the general political process: in the same way that legislation puts power in the hands of the Canadian Institute, disabling legislation can also be enacted at a future date.

The Canadian Institute would appear to have a great need of a CF. How can it show that its efforts at developing (and enforcing) accounting standards are proceeding in a fair, logical and highly professional manner other than by setting out the framework within which it is operating? As the main argument offered for delegating power to the profession is that accountants have essential technical skills denied to legislators and civil servants, it follows that the standard setters will have to produce standards which are seen not to conflict with this central assertion.

CONCLUDING REMARKS

The preceding sections can be summarised as follows:

1. There have been a number of attempts by the profession to develop a CF. All were undertaken at a time when the standard setting programme had run into trouble. None of them seems to have been of obvious value to the standard setters.

2. Academic researchers have tried in a variety of ways to throw some light on the issues and problems involved. Recently, considerable emphasis has been placed on what might be called the 'public choice' dimensions of financial accounting. Generally, the conclusions of such research have been discouraging to those in the profession interested in developing a CF that is capable of putting the accounting standards programme on a 'sound' footing.

3. British accounting has been analysed in terms of a bargaining model on the (not unrealistic) assumption that the ASC has little power and has to negotiate with groups whose interests may be in conflict. Little prospect is held out of a CF being of much direct help in such an environment.

4. Three different accounting 'environments' were examined. In only one did there appear to be an obvious role for a CF: where both responsibility and power is delegated to a body such as the ASC, as in Canada.

It has been assumed throughout that the purpose of developing a CF is to provide a basis for the creation of accounting standards. It has been tentatively concluded that only where both responsibility and power is delegated to the ASC is it likely that a CF has much to contribute. However, there is another way of viewing the role of a CF. Rather than providing a framework or platform for the standards programme, the CF could be intended to do no more than provide very broad general objectives for financial reporting to which no one could take serious objection; the aim would be to 'raise the moral tone' of the profession. The pressures and conflicts which the ASC has to handle would then cause no serious difficulty, as the CF would be expressed in sufficiently general terms as to avoid cramping the ASC's style. Indeed, to the extent that the documents which are currently in existence are statements of broad goals, they well serve this general purpose. Goals are achieved to a greater or lesser extent; they do not necessarily imply a moral or political imperative.

The role of such a tone-raising CF could be a valuable one. After all, much of the preceding analysis takes a somewhat dismal view of the motivations and interests of the people and organisations affected directly and indirectly by accounting standards. Conflicts of interest are seen to be a serious problem which the ASC has to deal with. One way of dealing with conflicts of interest is to try to encourage a feeling of common destiny and thereby reduce those conflicts (the siege syndrome). There is, after all, some evidence to suggest that accountants and businessmen do share beliefs about what is and is not good accounting. Perhaps these shared sentiments could be nurtured and strengthened. In which case, the purpose of a CF should be to encourage what might be called a 'professional' attitude.

Perhaps this is what the FASB's Conceptual Framework programme will yield. Needless to say, sceptics abound who suggest that, when enlightenment and self-interest are in conflict, enlightenment is the first to yield. There is more chance of success when self-interest is itself enlightened; i.e. when individuals are motivated by enlightened self-interest. This seems most likely to occur when there is a mechanism for ensuring that all parties keep to the (enlightened) bargain. The ASC needs power. For arguments on similar lines see Stamp (1979).

The problem of conflict has been stressed throughout. There are two main sources of conflict: conflict due to differences of opinion about consequences, and conflicts of interest. There is a need to distinguish between these two sources of conflict, wherever possible. This article has concentrated on the problem of conflicts of interest. However, many of the conflicts of opinion in accounting are due to lack of concrete knowledge about the consequences of various kinds of disclosures. A CF cannot eliminate consequence conflicts. Research is the only likely source of an answer.

It is appropriate to conclude by suggesting the appropriate structure for a 'real' CF designed to provide a base for the standards programme. If a CF is to serve as a guide to the standard setters then it should, in effect, provide them with a set of objectives and constraints. (Strictly speaking, accounting cannot have objectives; only people can (Chambers, 1976).) At a minimum, it seems essential to provide the elements of a 'constitution'. The framework should therefore set out: the basic principles of and sources of authority for 'accountability' and 'rights to know'; the consequences which financial reports are intended to have (and to avoid); the trade-offs which have to be made.

REFERENCES

Accounting Standards (Steering) Committee (1975), *The Corporate Report: A Discussion Paper.*

Accounting Standards Committee (1976), Exposure Draft 18, *Current Cost Accounting.*

Accounting Standards Committee (1978), *Setting Accounting Standards: A Consultative Document.*

American Accounting Association (1966), Committee to Prepare a Statement of Basic Accounting Theory. *A Statement of Basic Accounting Theory.*

American Accounting Association (1977), Committee on Concepts and Standards for External Financial Reports, *Statement on Accounting Theory and Theory Acceptance.*

American Institute of Certified Public Accountants (1970), Accounting Principles Board, APB Statement No. 4, *Basic Concepts and Accounting Principles Underlying Financial Statements of Business Enterprises.*

American Institute of Certified Public Accountants (1972), Report of the Study Group on Establishment of Accounting Principles, *Establishing Financial Accounting Standards.*

American Institute of Certified Public Accountants (1973), Report of the Accounting Objectives Study Group (chairman, R. M. Trueblood), *Objectives of Financial Statements.*

Benston, G. J. (1976), *Corporate Disclosure in the UK and the USA* (Saxon House).

Boulding, K. E. (1965), 'The Economics of Human Conflict', in E. B. McNeil (ed.), *The Nature of Human Conflict* (Prentice-Hall), pp. 172–191; reprinted in K. E. Boulding and F. R. Glake (eds), *Collected Papers. Volume Two: Economics* (Colorado Associated University Press, 1971), pp. 325–344.

Briston, R. and R. Perks, 'The External Auditor–His Role and Cost to Society', *Accountancy* (November 1977), pp. 48–52.

Bromwich, M. (1980), 'The Possibility of Partial Accounting Standards', *Accounting Review* (April 1980), pp. 288–300.

Canadian Institute of Chartered Accountants (1980), *Corporate Reporting: Its Future Evolution.*

Chambers, R. J. (1976), 'The Functions of Published Financial Statements', *Accounting and Business Research* (Spring 1976), pp. 83–94.

Cushing, B. E. (1977), 'On the Possibility of Optimal Accounting Principles', *Accounting Review* (April 1977), pp. 308–321.

Demski, J. S., and G. A. Feltham (1976), *Cost Determination: A Conceptual Approach* (Iowa State University Press).

Dopuch, N. and S. Sunder (1980), 'FASB's Statements on Objectives and Elements of Financial Accounting: A Review', *Accounting Review* (January 1980), pp. 1–21.

Financial Accounting Standards Board (1974), FASB Discussion Memorandum, *Conceptual Framework for Accounting and Reporting: Consideration of the Report of the Study Group on the Objectives of Financial Statements.*

Financial Accounting Standards Board (1977), Exposure Draft of Proposed Statement of Financial Accounting Concepts, *Objectives of Financial Reporting and Elements of Financial Statements of Business Enterprises.*

Financial Accounting Standards Board (1978), Statement of Financial Accounting Concepts No. 1, *Objectives of Financial Reporting by Business Enterprises.*

Financial Accounting Standards Board (1980a), Statement of Financial Accounting Concepts No. 1, *Qualitative Characteristics of Accounting Information.*

Financial Accounting Standards Board (1980c), *Objectives of Financial Reporting by Non Business Organizations.*

Her Majesty's Government (1977), Secretary of State for Trade, Cmnd. 6888, *The Future of Company Reports: A Consultative Document* (HMSO).

Institute of Chartered Accountants in England and Wales (1952), Recommendation on Accounting Principles No. 15, *Accounting in Relation to Changes in the Purchasing Power of Money.*

Jensen, M. C. and W. H. Meckling (1976), 'Theory of the Firm: Managerial Behavior, Agency Costs and Ownership Structure', *Journal of Financial Economics* (October 1976), pp. 305–360.

Klaassen, J. (1980). 'An Accounting Court: The Impact of the Enterprise Chamber on Financial Reporting in the Netherlands', *Accounting Review* (April 1980), pp. 327–341.

Moonitz, M. (1961), Accounting Research Study No. 1, *The Basic Postulates of Accounting* (AICPA).

Mumford, M. J. (1980), 'Accounting Information and Bargaining: An Historical Study of Some Early American Accounts' (unpublished working paper, University of Lancaster).

Sandilands, F. E. P., chairman (1975), Report of the Inflation Accounting Committee, Cmnd. 6225, *Inflation Accounting* (HMSO).

Scott, G. and M. Decelles (1980), 'United States: Objectives of Financial Reporting Revisited', *Accountant's Magazine* (February, 1980).

Sen, A. K. (1967), 'Isolation, Assurance and the Social Rate of Discount', *Quarterly Journal of Economics,* Vol. 81, pp. 112–24.

Sprouse, R. T. and M. Moonitz (1962), Accounting Research Study No 3, *A Tentative Set of Broad Accounting Principles for Business Enterprises* (AICPA).

Stamp, E. and M. Moonitz (1978), *International Auditing Standards* (Prentice-Hall).

Stamp, E. (1979), ICRA Occasional Paper No. 18, *The Future of Accounting and Auditing Standards* (International Centre for Research in Accounting, University of Lancaster).

Van den Doel, H. (1979), *Democracy and Welfare Economics* (Cambridge University Press).

Watts, R. L. (1977), 'Corporate Financial Statements: A Product of the Market and Political Processes', *Australian Journal of Management* (April 1977), pp. 53–75.

Watts, R. L. and J. L. Zimmerman (1978), 'Towards a Positive Theory of the Determination of Accounting Standards', *Accounting Review* (January 1978), pp. 112–134.

Watts, R. L. and J. L. Zimmerman (1979), 'The Demand for and Supply of Accounting Theories: The Market for Excuses', *Accounting Review* (April 1979), pp. 273–305.

Zeff, S. A. (1972), *Forging Accounting Principles in Five Countries: A History and Analysis of Trends* (Stipes Publishing Co.).

FASB'S STATEMENTS ON OBJECTIVES AND ELEMENTS OF FINANCIAL ACCOUNTING: A REVIEW

Nicholas Dopuch and Shyam Sunder

The Financial Accounting Standards Board (FASB) issued an exposure draft of the proposed statement on Objectives of Financial Reporting and Elements of Financial Statements of Business Enterprises on December 29, 1977. The first part of the Exposure Draft, dealing with the objectives of financial reporting, was issued in revised form a year later as the Statement of Financial Accounting Concepts No. 1 (SFAC 1) [FASB, 1978]. A final statement on the elements of financial statements has not yet been issued. In this paper we review the FASB's statement on objectives (as contained in SFAC 1) and on elements (as contained in the Exposure Draft). Though many of our comments could also be applied to other aspects of the project on the conceptual framework undertaken by the FASB, we shall limit our discussion to the two documents mentioned above.[1]

Few general criteria, other than internal consistency, have been proposed for evaluating conceptual frameworks. The approach taken in the reviews by Littleton [1962; 1963] of the Moonitz [1961] and the Sprouse and Moonitz [1962] monographs; by Ijiri [1971] of the APB *Statement No. 4* [AICPA, 1970]; by a subcommittee of the American Accounting Association (AAA) to respond to the FASB's Discussion Memorandum of the Conceptual Framework

We have benefited from many helpful comments, in particular those by Professors Raymond J. Chambers, William W. Cooper, Sidney Davidson, Rashad Abdel-khalik, William R. Scott, Stephen A. Zeff, and the anonymous reviewers.

Nicholas Dopuch and Shyam Sunder, "FASB's Statements on Objectives and Elements of Financial Accounting: A Review," *The Accounting Review,* January 1980, pp. 1–21. Reprinted with the permission of the American Accounting Association.

[1] These documents were preceded by two Discussion Memoranda [FASB 1974; 1976a]; the latter was accompanied by a statement of tentative conclusions on objectives of financial statements [FASB, 1976b].

[AAA, 1977b]; by Sterling [1967] of the AAA's *A Statement of Basic Accounting Theory* [1966]; by Vatter [1963], Hanson [1940], and Kester [1940]; and by Deinzer [1964] of various statements sponsored by the AAA [1936; 1941; 1948; 1957; 1964a; 1964b] seem too diverse to provide common criteria for evaluating a conceptual framework. We decided, therefore, to use two criteria in our review: (1) To what extent do these statements differ from previous attempts of this nature; and, regardless of the answer to (1), (2) to what extent will these statements, if adopted, yield the benefits expected by the FASB? Since we arrive at pessimistic answers to both questions, we are led to consider two further questions: (a) What are the fundamental difficulties in developing a set of objectives of financial accounting, and (b) why do authoritative bodies persist in trying to develop a conceptual framework? The final section of the paper contains the summary and concluding remarks.

COMPARISON WITH PREVIOUS ATTEMPTS TO DEVELOP A FRAMEWORK

OBJECTIVES

The SFAC 1 is divided into two parts: Introduction and Background, followed by Objectives of Financial Reporting. The introductory section includes subsections on: (a) financial statements and financial reporting, (b) the environmental context of objectives, (c) the characteristics and limitations of information provided, (d) potential users and their interests, and (e) general-purpose external financial reporting. Financial statements are defined to be a subset of financial reporting, but no limits are provided on the number of elements of financial reporting that one may include in financial statements. The discussion of the environmental context of accounting bears a resemblance to the discussion by Moonitz [1961, Chapter 2] and by the Accounting Principles Board in Statement No. 4 (APBS 4) [AICPA, 1970, Chapter 3]. A discussion of the major characteristics of the U.S. economy in the statement of objectives would be justified if it were accompanied by a theory which linked the characteristics of various economies to alternative financial accounting systems. Since no such theory is provided, it is not clear how a vague description of the U.S. economy is useful for determining or understanding objectives.[2]

    In the sections on potential users and general-purpose financial reporting it is stated that the specific objectives here refer to the general-purpose financial reports that serve the informational needs of external users who lack the authority to prescribe the financial information they want from an enterprise, a statement very similar to Objective No. 2 of the Trueblood Report [AICPA, 1973]. The FASB relies considerably on the Trueblood Report when it states that financial reporting "should provide information to help present and potential investors and creditors, and other users in assessing the amounts, timing, and uncertainty of prospective net cash receipts. . . ." [FASB, 1978, para. 37]. The need for information on cash flows leads

---

[2]For example, paragraph 13 refers to efficient allocations of resources within a market economy, but there are several definitions of allocation efficiency which might be employed. In the absence of an agreed-upon definition, inefficiencies cannot be identified.

to the need for information on "the economic resources of an enterprise, the claims to those resources (obligations of the enterprise to transfer resources to other entities and owners' equity), and the effects of transactions, events, and circumstances that change resources and claims to those resources" (para. 40). After more discussion, the Board arrives at the conclusion that the

> primary focus of financial reporting is information about an enterprise's performance provided by measures of earnings and its components. . . . Information about enterprise earnings and its components measured by accrual accounting generally provides a better indication of enterprise performance than information about current cash receipts and payments [FASB, 1978, para. 43–44].

This last statement is not an objective, but a means to an objective.

Although these paragraphs encompass many of the specific objectives of the Trueblood Report, the emphasis and order of presentation are different. Other departures from the Report are an omission of any reference to providing financial forecasts and to non-profit and social accounting (Objectives 10, 11, and 12, respectively, of the Trueblood Report).

In working and substance, little is new or different in SFAC 1. Had the FASB pointed out the parts of the existing reports,[3] such as APBS 4 and the Trueblood Report, that it agreed with and emphasized its disagreements, its contribution would have been easier to discern. Without such aid, we are hard-pressed to discern the FASB's net contribution to these earlier efforts. Given that previous authoritative efforts to write objectives are generally considered inadequate in helping to resolve accounting issues, a basic test of the FASB's contribution is the extent to which SFAC 1 may succeed where others have failed. We shall apply such a test after discussing the elements of financial statements and characteristics of financial information as provided in the FASB's Exposure Draft [FASB, 1977].

ELEMENTS OF FINANCIAL STATEMENTS

The second major section of the Exposure Draft [FASB, 1977], paragraphs 36 through 66, deals mainly with definitions of the main categories of accounts appearing in financial statements: assets, liabilities, owners' equity, revenues, expenses, gains, and losses. Supplementing these definitions are subsections containing discussions of the bases for definitions, the matching of efforts and accomplishments, and the need to provide financial statements which articulate with one another. The elements of financial statements are integrated—revenues and gains result in, or from, increases in assets, decreases in liabilities or combinations of the two; expenses and losses result in, or from, decreases in assets, increases in liabilities, *etc.*

A noteworthy feature of the FASB's definitions is their dependence on unspecified "accounting rules and conventions" [FASB, 1977, p. 19], again in the tradition of the definitions provided by two previous authoritative bodies, the American Institute of [Certified Public]

---

[3]Most and Winters [1977] analyzed the objectives promulgated by the Trueblood Study Group, APBS 4, several of the Big Eight firms, the AAA, the National Association of Accountants, *etc.* They found that of the ten main objectives issued by the Trueblood Study Group (Objectives 3 on cash flows, and 11 on non-profit accounting, were omitted), eight similar objectives could be found in APBS 4. Similarly, Objectives 1, 2, 4, 5, 6, 7, and 8 in the Trueblood Report had antecedents in from five to as many as eight other statements of objectives.

Accountants' Committee on Terminology and Accounting Principles Board.[4] This qualification appears to be inconsistent with the claim that conceptual frameworks can lead to the selection of appropriate principles and rules of measurement and recognition. How can a conceptual framework guide choices from among alternative principles and rules if the elements of the framework are defined in these very same terms?

The dependence of the FASB's definitions on unspecified rules and conventions leaves little basis on which to evaluate them, since a specific evaluation of these definitions would be speculative as long as we do not know what conventions will be adopted by the FASB at the subsequent stages of its project.

A second feature of the FASB's definitions is that they provide only the necessary conditions for a resource or obligation to be included in the asset or liability categories, respectively, rather than both the necessary and sufficient conditions. For example, a resource other than cash needs to have three characteristics to qualify as an asset:

> (a) the resource must . . . contribute directly or indirectly to future cash inflows (or to obviating future cash outflows), (b) the enterprise must be able to obtain the benefit from it, and (c) the transaction or event giving rise to the enterprise's right to or interest in the benefit must already have occurred [FASB, 1977; para. 47].

Similarly, three characteristics are also necessary for an obligation to qualify as a liability:

> (a) the obligation must involve future sacrifice of resources—a future transfer (or a foregoing of a future receipt) of cash, goods, or services, (b) it must be an obligation of the enterprise, and (c) the transaction or event giving rise to the enterprise's obligation must already have occurred [FASB, 1977, para. 49].

Since these are only necessary characteristics, their presence does not imply that an obligation will qualify as a liability or that a resource will qualify as an asset. All of these conditions may be satisfied and an obligation still may not qualify as an asset or, alternatively, as a liability. In the absence of sufficient conditions, these definitions will be of limited use to accountants.

The definitions of revenues and expenses given by the FASB follow the traditional practice of defining these as increases and decreases in assets or decreases and increases in liabilities, respectively, provided that the changes in assets and liabilities relate to the earning activities of the enterprise (broadly defined). Gains and losses are defined as increases and decreases in net assets, *other* than revenues and expenses or investments and withdrawals by owners.

The definitions of revenue and expense in APB Statement No 4 [AICPA, 1970] are similar to the above except that the definitions there do not explicitly distinguish between revenues and gains nor between expenses and losses. A distinction between revenues and gains is also made by Sprouse and Moonitz [1962, p. 50] and by Paton and Littleton [1940, p. 60]. But while a distinction between expense and loss is made by Sprouse and Moonitz, Paton and Littleton do not do so. Indeed, they do not even provide an explicit definition of expense, which is con-

---

[4]For example, the Committee on Terminology defined assets in Accounting Terminology Bulletin No. 1 [AICPA, 1953] as follows:

"Something represented by a debit balance that is or would be properly carried forward upon a closing of books of account according to the *rules or principles of accounting* . . . on the basis that it represents either a property right . . . or is properly applicable to the future" (para. 26, emphasis added).

The APB in its Statement No. 4 defined assets as "economic resources of an enterprise that are recognized and measured *in conformity with generally accepted accounting principles*. . . ." [AICPA, 1970, para. 132] (emphasis added).

sistent with their emphasis on *cost* rather than on the asset-expense distinction. It is not until their discussion of income that Paton and Littleton stress a distinction between costs matched against revenues (expenses) and those deferred to future periods (assets) [1940, Ch. V.].

On the whole, the differences between the FASB and the APB definitions are small and seem unimportant. An explicit discussion of the main sources of disagreement would have been more fruitful than a "new" set of definitions. Circular as they are, the conflict on definitions seems to us to be only a proxy debate whose principal, to which we return later, is the debate about the accounting rules themselves.

CHARACTERISTICS AND LIMITATIONS OF FINANCIAL INFORMATION

A part of the last major section of the Exposure Draft has been included in the introductory section of SFAC 1. There we find statements about: (a) the reliance of accounting on monetary transactions, (b) the emphasis of financial reports on individual enterprises and not on individual consumers or on society as a whole, (c) the role of estimation in accounting, (d) the fact that much of financial information reflects past events, (e) the coexistence of other sources of financial information, and (f) the costs of financial reporting.

The more well-known desirable "qualities" of accounting information, such as relevance, freedom from bias, comparability, consistency, understandability, verifiability, etc., are also referenced in the Exposure Draft, but are excluded from SFAC 1. The FASB acknowledges that trade-offs among these qualities are not easily accomplished in practice. The objectives and definitions of the elements of financial statements are expected to guide the Board in future phases of the conceptual framework project when these trade-off issues arise in more concrete form.

The characteristics and desirable "qualities" of accounting information discussed in the Exposure Draft are familiar to accountants and appear as "qualitative" objectives in APB Statement No. 4 and as components of accounting concepts or as postulates in other conceptual frameworks.

The above review of SFAC 1 and of certain parts of the Exposure Draft reveals little that is new on the objectives of financial reporting and definitions of the elements of financial statements. Lack of novelty, of course, does not imply worthlessness. It is quite possible that the FASB's effort may yet have the potential to yield some benefits. The FASB has suggested that the following benefits may manifest themselves as a result of achieving agreement on the conceptual framework [1976c, pp. 5–6]:

1. Guide the body responsible for establishing standards,
2. Provide a frame of reference for resolving accounting questions in the absence of a specific promulgated standard,
3. Determine bounds for judgments in preparing financial statements,
4. Increase financial statement users' understanding of and confidence in financial statements, and
5. Enhance comparability.

In reviewing this early part of the conceptual framework, it is probably fair to ask how reasonable it is to expect that the above-mentioned benefits will actually be realized. Of course, this evaluation may have to be changed when all the pieces of the conceptual project are in place. However, the evaluation of this part of the project, tentative as it is, should not await completion of the project.

In the following section we examine the degree to which the first two benefits stated by the FASB, *viz.*, guidance for establishing standards and resolution of accounting questions in the absence of standards, are likely to be attained on the basis of the given objectives and definitions. The effect of the project on users' understanding of, and confidence in, the financial statements is an empirical question and is beyond the scope of this review paper.[5] We are not sure what precisely is meant by (3), determination of the bounds of judgment in preparation of financial statements, and by (5), enhancement of comparability. Since the empirical or analytical contents of these benefits are not clear, it is difficult to evaluate, beyond purely subjective opinion, whether and to what extent these benefits will be derived from the FASB's objectives and definitions. We shall, therefore, confine ourselves to an evaluation of the first two benefits stated by the FASB.

RESOLUTION OF THREE ACCOUNTING ISSUES

As a means of evaluating the potential benefits the FASB's objectives and definitions may provide in resolving accounting issues, we selected three which have been debated for some time and which have received much attention from accountants and others. The issues are: (1) deferred credits, (2) treatment of costs of exploration in the oil and gas industry, and (3) reports on current values of assets and liabilities.

DEFERRED CREDITS

The FASB defines liabilities as "financial representations of obligations of a particular enterprise to transfer economic resources to other entities in the future as a result of a past transaction or event affecting the enterprise" [FASB, 1977, para. 49]. No specific reference to deferred credits appears in this section, although reference is made to liabilities arising from the collection of cash or other resources *before* providing goods or services, or from selling products subject to warranty. It is also stated that "legal enforceability of a claim is not a prerequisite to representing it as a liability" if future transfer is probable.

The APB, in Statement No. 4, is more direct:

> Liabilities—economic obligations of an enterprise that are recognized and measured in conformity with generally accepted accounting principles. Liabilities also include certain deferred credits *that are not obligations* but that are recognized and measured in conformity with generally accepted accounting principles [AICPA, 1970, Para. 132, emphasis added].

A footnote to the last sentence specifically singles out deferred taxes as an example of liabilities which are not obligations!

---

[5]The FASB may wish to commission such a study now, so that a preconceptual framework measure of confidence and understandability can be taken before this opportunity is lost.

Neither Paton and Littleton [1940] nor Sprouse and Moonitz [1962] refer to deferred credits arising from differences between financial and tax reporting, with both concentrating on the obligations of enterprises to convey assets or to perform services in the future.[6]

The FASB's definition of liabilities is so general that at this stage we cannot predict the Board's position on deferred taxes. However, those who favor the recognition of deferred taxes can adopt a somewhat broad interpretation of the FASB's definition of liabilities to justify the inclusion of deferred taxes as an element of financial statements, particularly at the individual asset level. In contrast, those who do not could take the FASB's statements literally and just as easily argue against the inclusion of deferred taxes. Hence, these broad definitions will not help resolve the issue.

ACCOUNTING FOR OIL AND GAS EXPLORATION COSTS

Bitter controversy still surrounds the issue of how to account for petroleum exploration costs. The issue surfaced in the petroleum industry some two decades ago when the full-cost method was introduced. But the essence of the issue has an earlier precedent.

Hatfield [1927, Chap. 2] considers the problem of whether the acquisition costs of successful experiments should be limited to the costs of the successful experiments themselves or whether they should also include the costs of unsuccessful experiments. Hence, the full-cost versus successful-efforts debate is part of a more general issue of what constitutes the costs of assets when the acquisition process is risky.

The issue reflects a difference of opinion regarding the level of aggregation at which the historical acquisition cost principle is applied to record assets for subsequent amortization. But there is no reference in the Exposure Draft to alternative levels of aggregation for asset recognition and measurement. The only explicit statement bearing on this problem is that "[i]nformation about enterprise earnings and its components measured by accrual accounting generally provides a better indication of enterprise performance than information about current cash receipts and payments" [FASB, 1978, para. 44]. However, both full-cost and successful-efforts accounting are forms of accrual accounting, so that proponents of the former (*e.g.*, the Federal Trade Commission) have the same support for their position as do proponents of the latter (*e.g.*, the FASB). The fact that the framework supports two opposing principles of accounting is preliminary evidence that the framework is unlikely to be a useful guide in resolving this issue.

SELECTING THE VALUATION BASIS FOR ASSETS AND LIABILITIES

Alternative theories of valuation and income were discussed in accounting texts published 50 years ago. For example, Hatfield [1927] states:

> Having accepted the principle that the original valuation of assets is normally their cost price, and having noticed the practical and theoretical difficulty in determining the exact cost price, there remains the more important question as to subsequent revaluations of assets. . . . Shall the accountant base revaluation on (1) the original cost . . . (2) on the estimated present cost of acquiring a similar asset . . . or (3) on what the asset might be expected to bring if thrown upon the market in the process of liquidation [p. 73]?

---

[6]The issue of deferred taxes did not appear in the accounting literature until about 1942. See AICPA [1942].

Similar discussions appear even earlier in Paton [1922], in Hatfield [1909], and in a much more detailed fashion in Canning [1929].

Liquidation values were generally ruled out in such discussions because they seemed inconsistent with the going-concern notion, and since discounted values had not yet achieved popularity then, the choice between alternative valuation bases was usually limited to historical or replacement costs.

With respect to these alternatives, it might be informative to quote some statements from Paton and Littleton [1940], who, some accountants believe, had no tolerance for valuation bases other than historical cost accounting. On pages 122–123, they state:

> With the passing of time, however, the value of the particular productive factor—as reflected in the current cost or market price of like units—is subject to change in either direction, and when a change occurs it becomes clear that the actual cost of the unit still in service or still attaching to operating activity is not fully acceptable as a measure of immediate economic significance.

Later, on page 123, they ask the question:

> [W]ould accounting meet more adequately the proper needs of the various parties concerned if, in the process of separating the charges to revenue from the unexpired balances, the estimated replacement costs or other evidence of current values were regularly substituted for recorded costs incurred? There seem to be no convincing reasons for an affirmative answer. Recorded costs are objectively determined data; estimated current values are largely matters of opinion and for some types of cost factors are conspicuously unreliable.

In the section on "Limitations of Estimated Replacement Cost," they comment: "In the first place continuous appraisals at the best are costly, and can be used only if the benefits to be derived clearly justify the additional cost incurred" (p. 132). They then suggest that in periods of price stability and situations involving complex enterprises, such benefits are unlikely to exceed the costs of implementation. Finally,

> The fair conclusion is that the cost standard of plant accounting holds up well, as compared with any alternative plan, when faced with typical business needs and conditions. . . . At the same time it would be going too far to hold that under no circumstances can any useful purpose be served by introducing into the accounts and reports, by appropriate methods, data designed to supplement the figures of actual cost [Paton and Littleton, p. 134].

The latter statement led them to recommend that alternative valuations be limited to supplementary schedules.

The above are practical, no theoretical, arguments and are probably representative of the views of many accountants who have expressed a reluctance to accept current costs in published financial statements. No conceptual framework, however logically conceived, can counter practical issues regarding the reliability of *estimates* of, say, replacement costs. The "true" replacement costs of assets are not observed until those assets are actually replaced (nor are "true" exit prices observed unless the assets are sold). So the issue is not whether current costs are useful "in making economic decisions"; rather, the issue is what criteria may be used to alternative estimates of unknown parameters. Unfortunately, neither SFAC 1 nor the Exposure Draft addresses this problem of estimation.

On the basis of the above analysis, we conclude that the results of the FASB's effort to write objectives and definitions are hardly different from previous attempts of this nature and, as such, are unlikely to help resolve major accounting issues or to set standards of financial reporting as the FASB had expected. Pessimistic as our conclusions are, they should not surprise those familiar with the standard-setting process during the past 30 years. The charge of the Trueblood Study Group was very similar to the first two benefits expected by the FASB:

> The main purpose of the [Trueblood] study is to refine the objectives of financial statements. Refined objectives should facilitate establishment of guidelines and criteria for improving accounting and financial reporting [AICPA, 1973, p. 67].

Both the supporters and the critics expressed doubts that this purpose of the study would be met. Bedford [1974, p. 16], while largely supporting the report, said, "I refer to the extremely difficult task of logically deriving accounting standards from objectives—not that I think it can be done but because I fear some will think it is appropriate." Miller [1974, p. 20], a critic of the report, stated, "The greatest shortcoming of the Trueblood Report is, it seems to me, that the accept/reject criteria are not sufficiently precise. I wish Professor Sorter and his associates had been less subtle." Sprouse stated, "I have no illusions about the use of such a document to prove that a particular accounting standard is 'right'" [1974, p. 28]. These doubts about the accomplishments of the Trueblood Report are very similar to our reservations about the fruits of the FASB's labors.

Since our conclusion about the potential value and effect of the FASB's objectives and definitions is pessimistic, we are led to inquire into the very nature of objectives of financial accounting and the fundamental difficulty of defining them in a social setting. The inability of different authoritative drafts of objectives produced in the last decade to achieve general acceptance on a conceptual framework is hardly due to the lack of diligence on the part of their authors; it may stem from addressing the wrong problem.

THE NATURE OF OBJECTIVES OF FINANCIAL ACCOUNTING

An objective is something toward which effort is directed, an aim or end of action, a goal [FASB, 1974, p. 13]. Financial accounting is a social or multiperson activity. Members of society engage in financial accounting or in other activities when they are motivated by their individual goals and objectives. We shall assume that the meaning of the terms "goal" and "objective," as they apply to individuals or homogeneous groups of individuals, is self-evident for the purpose of the present discussion. Given a clear definition of the objectives that motivate each individual to engage in an aspect of a social activity, what meaning can we assign to the term "objective" when it is applied not to individuals or groups, but to the activity itself? In what sense can a social activity be said to have an objective?

We suggest three different interpretations of the meaning of the objectives of a social activity: functional objectives, common objectives, and dominant group objectives. In this section we shall first explain the meaning and implications of each interpretation and then examine the nature of the objectives of financial accounting in light of these interpretations.

Functional Objectives

The union of individual objectives could be referred to as the objective of the social activity in a *functional sense*. A functional explanation of social phenomena assumes that the consequences of a social arrangement or behavior are essential elements of the *causes* of that behavior (see Stinchcombe [1968], esp. pp. 80–100). Objectives that motivate individuals to engage in an activity on a continuing basis must also be the consequences of the activity; otherwise the individuals will not continue to engage in it. Thus, the functional explanation implies that the union of individual objectives can be identified without probing into the motivations of individuals by simply observing the set of consequences of the social activity. These consequences themselves therefore can be regarded as the objectives of the social activity. Since the consequences are observable phenomena, they can be objectively determined. However, the set of consequences may be so large that a complex and lengthy description may be the result. Nevertheless, a statement of consequences is one possible interpretation of the objective of a social activity.

Common Objectives

A second possibility is to define the intersection of individual objectives, *i.e.*, the subset of objectives common to all individuals, as the objective of the social activity. By definition, common objectives are equal to or fewer in number than the functional objectives. If all individuals are motivated by an identical set of objectives, common objectives are the same as the functional objectives; if each individual is motivated by different objectives, the intersection is null and there are no common objectives.

Dominant Group Objectives

A third possible interpretation of the objectives of a social activity is the objectives of an individual or subset of all individuals in the society who are able, through whatever mechanism, to impose their will on all others involved in the activity. In the presence of such a dominant group, the objectives of individuals not included in the group become irrelevant, since the dominant group objectives become the objectives of the social activity. Obviously, this interpretation cannot be used if the dominant group does not have the power to impose its will on the society.

Accounting as a Social Activity

Accounting is a social activity engaged in by (1) corporate managers who perform in activities that are recorded by the accounting system; (2) corporate accountants who gather the data and compile the reports; (3) auditors who scrutinize and attest to the fairness of the reports; (4) outside government and private agencies, investors, employees, customers, *etc.*, who read these reports; and (5) college and university personnel who train their students in accounting. Each group of individuals engaged in financial accounting possesses its own private motives or objectives leading to this involvement. In the light of the three possible interpretations of the objectives of a social activity discussed above, what meaning can we assign to the objectives of financial accounting?

FUNCTIONAL INTERPRETATION OF ACCOUNTING OBJECTIVES

Since all consequences of accounting are included in the functional interpretation of objectives, consider the following sample of objectives that would qualify under this interpretation:

1. Increase employment of accountants, auditors, and teachers of accounting;
2. Help companies market their securities to creditors and investors;
3. Help outsiders monitor the performance of management;
4. Maximize the wealth of the present owners of the company;
5. Minimize income tax burdens of companies;
6. Aid in controlling inflation;
7. Disclose the impact of enterprise operations on the quality of the environment;
8. Help management avoid hostile takeover attempts;
9. Systematically record, classify, and report data on the business transactions of the enterprise;
10. Aid in enforcing anti-trust laws.

Each of the objectives listed above could be viewed as legitimate by one or more sets of individuals involved in financial accounting. Note that a complete description of the consequences of financial accounting will include not only "facts" but what is regarded as "fiction" by specific individuals. For example, a manager may regard the avoidance of hostile takeover attempts as a valid objective of financial statements while a shareholder may believe that the effect of financial accounting practices on avoidance of hostile takeovers is non-existent. In order to be included in the set, it is sufficient that someone involved in financial accounting believe in that consequence or use it as a personal objective. Note also that this step includes contradictory objectives and consequences. For example, management may believe that one accounting method for inventory accounting will help market the firm's securities, whereas shareholders may believe that an alternative inventory method is more revealing of management's competence. Similarly, the objective of accountants to increase the demand for their services may be in conflict with the objective of corporate managers to maximize their own or the shareholders' wealth.

Although probably not intended as such, the objectives stated by the FASB may be viewed as functional objectives. For example, the first objective given by the FASB is:

> Financial reporting should provide information that is useful to present and potential investors and creditors and others users in making rational investment, credit, and similar decisions. The information should be comprehensible to those who have a reasonable understanding of business and economic activities and are willing to study the information with reasonable diligence [FASB, 1978, para. 34].

If "should" is removed from each sentence, this objective is reduced to a mere statement of an empirically verified and a widely accepted consequence of financial accounting. Financial accounting does, indeed, provide information useful to investors and creditors, and it is comprehensible to those willing to study the reports with reasonable diligence. But, being purely descriptive, functional objectives themselves cannot serve as normative goals to guide policy making. Nevertheless, if they are reasonably complete, they can serve to improve the understanding of the role of financial accounting in society.

There is reason to believe that the FASB did not intend to offer its statement as one of functional objectives. First, the statement is far from complete, concentrating on a few facts and a few unverified theories about the consequences of financial accounting, without any effort to present, for example, the motivations behind the supply side of financial accounting services. And the normative tone of the statement precludes the possibility that the FASB has attempted to provide a statement of the union of individual objectives of all persons involved in financial accounting.

Common-Objectives Interpretation of Accounting Objectives

A second possible interpretation of the objectives of accounting is the subset of individual objectives which are common to all individuals involved in accounting. Cyert and Ijiri's [1974] model of heterogeneous interests can be modified to apply to the objectives. Cyert and Ijiri use a Venn diagram to illustrate their point. The elements of the sets considered by them are *pieces of information* which various interest groups—users, managers, and auditors—may be willing to use, provide, or attest, and the intersection of the three sets is the actual information provided by the financial statements. The choice problem posed by Cyert and Ijiri could be moved to a higher level of abstraction by considering the sets of *accounting principles* that each group would prefer to be used in the preparation of financial statements. A still higher level of abstraction would involve specific sets of objectives that each group would seek to fulfill through its involvement in financial accounting.

It is conceivable that the intersection of the three sets will become progressively smaller as we move to higher levels of abstraction from pieces of information to accounting principles to objectives, in which case the Venn diagrams at the three levels of abstraction might appear as in Figure 1.

We do not know whether the intersection of the sets grows larger or smaller as we move from items of information to principles to objectives and vice versa.[7] Generally, agreement on principles and objectives will be easier to obtain if such statements are sufficiently vague so as to allow room for various interest groups to adopt their own interpretations. But vagueness, while necessary to obtain initial agreement, will reduce the usefulness of a statement of objectives in setting accounting standards. The proposition is borne out by the statements of objectives we have seen thus far. The vagueness of statements of this nature is consistent with the level of generality at which agreement is sought. It allows enough room for each interested party to maneuver to protect its own interest when actual accounting standards and rules are written.

Some empirical evidence is available on the non-overlapping nature of accounting objectives. In 1976, when the FASB carried out a survey to determine how many people involved in various aspects of financial accounting agreed with the Trueblood objectives, the Board was surprised to learn that only 37 percent of the respondents believed that providing information useful for making economic decisions was an objective of financial accounting:

> Let me point this up for you. In our first discussion memorandum on the conceptual framework of accounting, . . . we sought an expression of opinion from respondents on the following as a basic objective of financial statements; it is taken directly from the Trueblood Report:

---

[7]The question is subject to debate; see, for example, the analysis of responses of various parties to the FASB's pronouncements by Coe and Sorter [1977–78] and Watts and Zimmerman [1978].

FIGURE 1

Accounting Information, Principles, and Objectives Preferred by Various Parties

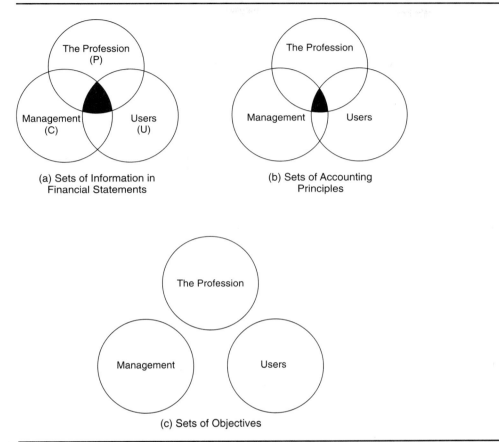

(a) Sets of Information in
Financial Statements

(b) Sets of Accounting
Principles

(c) Sets of Objectives

The basic objective of financial statements is to provide information useful for making economic decisions.

Could there be disagreement with a statement such as this? I am sure you will be astounded to learn that only 37 percent of our respondents were able to recommend the adoption of this objective. Twenty-two percent recommended that it be rejected out of hand; and 10 percent insisted that it needed further study. It is difficult to believe that only 37 percent can agree that the basic objective of financial statements is to provide information useful for making economic decisions. I think this suggests the problem quite clearly [Armstrong, 1977, p. 77].

We are puzzled at the Board's puzzlement. Why should we believe all groups of interested parties would adopt the provision of information useful for making economic decisions as their motivation for being involved in the financial reporting process? For example, we should not be surprised if auditors, like everyone else, seek to maximize their own wealth through participation in the accounting process. If the provision of economically useful information implies greater exposure to the risk of being sued without corresponding benefits of higher compensation, they will not see the provision of economically useful information (however defined) as *their* objective of the financial accounting process. Similar arguments could be made about any other interested party who might have been surveyed by the FASB. The members of each group probably stated what they believed were their objectives for being involved in the process.

At present, we do not have data to determine which, if any, objectives are actually common to all participants in accounting. Consequently we cannot yet determine whether the common objectives approach is a feasible interpretation of the objectives of accounting.

Dominant Group Interpretation of Accounting Objectives

Unlike the Trueblood Study Group, the FASB has not stated explicitly how it selected its subset of objectives from a much larger set of potential objectives. But from the objectives which the FASB did select, we can infer that it has followed the Trueblood Study Group in relying on the notion of user-primacy in financial accounting.[8] This notion represents the dominant-group approach to defining the objective of a social activity that we identified above.

Most of the discussion appearing in the literature on the objectives of financial accounting during the past ten years tends to rely on the notion of user-primacy. Beaver and Demski [1974], for example, concentrated their attention on the problems generated by the heterogeneity of tastes among the users of financial statements, on the assumption that this group would be the primary group whose interests would be reflected in the objectives of financial statements officially adopted by the authoritative agencies:

> There seems to be a consensus that the primary purpose of financial reporting is to provide information to financial statement users. Yet, the basic, fundamental role of objectives within this utilitarian, user-primacy framework remains obscure—largely we speculate because the problem of heterogeneous users has not been forcefully addressed. . . . A basic purpose of this summary and synthesis, then, is to offer a view of the nature and role of financial accounting objectives that explicitly rests on heterogeneous users [p. 170].

Cyert and Ijiri [1974] considered the heterogeneity of preferences for *information sets* among three diverse groups (assuming that the intragroup heterogeneity is unimportant) and analyzed the problem of determining accounting standards under the assumption that the user interest is primary. Referring to 1(a) of our Figure 1, they stated:

> This is a logical, if not a unique approach since in many user-corporate relationships the corporation is *accountable* to the users for its activities. If the users are in a position to demand information from the corporation based on a con-

---

[8]"While mindful of the importance of the audit function, the Study Group has been primarily concerned with the nature of information and not its attestability" [AICPA, 1973, p. 10]. The Trueblood Study Group left the problem of attestation and the interests of the management to "implementation" and did not consider these interests worthy of consideration within the set of objectives of financial reporting.

tractual or statutory relationship between them, it makes sense to define what Circle U is and then attempt to move Circle C toward it. Furthermore, in the interaction of the three groups, the profession's purpose is to help keep a smooth flow of information from the corporation to the users. Hence, Circle P is clearly subordinate to Circles C and U. Thus, it is perhaps the most practical way to state as objectives the need to move Circles C and P toward the goal of a newly defined Circle U [p. 32].

If the user group had the power to enforce its preferences at no cost to itself, the objectives of this group could be called the objectives of financial accounting. This would simplify the problem of setting objectives. Indeed, if the user group were homogeneous, the problem would be trivial. However, there is little evidence that the user group has the power to impose its preferences on financial accounting.

A considerable amount of confusion about the objectives of financial accounting has been generated by comparing them to the objectives of the firm. For example, Bedford [1974] notes, "The basic objective of financial statements is to provide information useful for making economic decisions. This statement is as direct as the statement that 'the basic objective of private enterprise is to make a profit' *and it is equally operational*" [p. 15; emphasis is added]. Few would dispute that, as stated, the profit-maximizing objective of the firm is merely a shorthand way of stating the objectives of the *shareholders* of the firm under the assumption of homogeneous shareholder preferences; it does not represent the specific objectives of the managers, employees, creditors or of any other parties inside or outside the firm. Besides, profit is a net concept in the sense that it is the difference between revenues and expenses, and its use as an objective implies that additional revenue should not be generated beyond the point at which the additional cost exceeds it. Provision of information for decision making, unlike profit, is a gross concept and cannot provide guidelines as to how far the firm should go in providing information for economic decisions.

The analogy to the theory of the firm is more apparent than real. In that theory, if the objective is to maximize the owners' wealth, production-investment variables can be chosen in view of the cost and revenue functions which serve as the environmental variables. What is the FASB (or any other agency entrusted with the task of writing accounting standards) supposed to maximize or optimize? When the FASB recommends that the objective of financial statements is to provide information useful for making rational credit and investment decisions, should we understand that the provision of such information should be maximized without regard to the cost and other consequences of making such information available? What are the variables over which to optimize, and what is the trade-off among these variables? Unless these trade-offs are defined, a statement of objectives that will be useful in arriving at the most satisfying accounting standards cannot be said to have been laid down, nor can there be a way of determining if the recommended objectives have been achieved by a given accounting standard.

The extraordinary emphasis of the recent pronouncements regarding objectives of financial accounting on user primacy can probably be traced to inappropriate applications of single-person decision theory in a multi-person context. In single-person decision theory, the generation of information is regarded as a more-or-less mechanical process which remains unaffected by its ultimate uses. The person making the choice of an information system out of the available alternatives calculates the expected present value of the benefits to be derived from the use of information produced by each system and makes the choice on the basis of the excess of these benefits over the respective costs. The same underlying event-generating mechanism is assumed to be common to all information systems, and it remains unaffected by the choice of information system made. This model, developed by the physical scientists and engineers for the control of mechanical or inanimate systems, is inappropriate for social systems, where the object of control is not an unchanging chemical process but a human being with learning capabilities. In control systems where human beings stand at both the sending and receiving end of the information channel, the flow of information affects behavior at both ends. We cannot choose an information line on the assumption of a constant behavior pattern of the persons at the other end. Indeed, the two-way effect of the information makes the designation of one party as user and the other as sender somewhat ambiguous. A user-primacy notion in the selection of objectives of financial accounting which ignores how firm managers are likely to adjust their behavior to the new information system (and how this adjustment in management behavior will affect the interests of the so-called users) represents a very short-sighted view of the whole problem. As such, solutions derived from this simplified approach will not work. A similar argument could be offered regarding the exclusion of the auditors from the "primary" groups whose interests must be explicitly considered in any realistic set of objectives of financial accounting.

To summarize, we have examined three possible interpretations of objectives of social activities in general and financial accounting in particular. We have concluded that the union of individual objectives, being too diverse and contradictory, cannot serve to guide policy; intersection of individual objectives may be null; the dominant-group objectives, assuming user primacy, do not reflect the economic reality of the power of suppliers in the accounting marketplace and are, therefore, unworkable. Fundamental to an understanding of the nature of financial accounting as they are, these difficulties in interpreting the objectives of financial accounting have received little attention in the literature. This lack of attention stands in sharp contrast to the repeated efforts to prepare a statement of objectives and definitions and leads us to examine the possible reasons that may stand behind the efforts to prepare an authoritative statement of objectives and definitions.

Why Search for a Conceptual Framework?

In the first section of the paper, we compared the SFAC 1 and Exposure Draft to the previous attempts of this nature and found little substantive difference. In the second section, we examined whether the first two of the five benefits claimed by the FASB may reasonably be expected to flow from these statements and reached a negative conclusion. Then we probed the very meaning of the term "objectives" as applied to financial accounting and found that term too ill-defined. These conclusions led us to inquire into reasons why authoritative bodies have continued to search for objectives and a conceptual framework of accounting. We consider several of these.

The first reason could be that our negative conclusions in section two regarding the usefulness of these statements in resolving accounting issues and standard-setting problems are wrong. If so, it should be easy for someone to illustrate, possibly using issues other than the three we selected, that these objectives and definitions will indeed help resolve the accounting issues. We are not aware of any such illustrations.

A second reason for the search for conceptual frameworks could be provided in terms of the three potential benefits claimed by the FASB and not examined in this paper. It may turn out that the issuance of the conceptual framework increases the users' confidence in, and understanding of, financial statements. Someone may also give workable definitions of "bounds for judgment" and comparability and show that the issuance of conceptual frameworks may have desirable consequences in these respects. Again, neither the theoretical arguments nor the empirical evidence that bears on these issues is available.

Two further reasons are possible: One lies in the form in which accounting problems are brought to the authoritative bodies, while the second lies in the attempts of the accounting profession to keep the rule-making power in its own hands.

Repeated efforts of authoritative bodies to define the conceptual framework of accounting in general and the elements of financial statements in particular may arise from the genuine belief that a determination of precise definitions of certain terms will somehow help resolve accounting controversies.[9] Such belief is reinforced each time an accounting controversy surfaces and the proponents of alternative methods present their arguments in the established terminology of accounting so as to convince the policy makers that the weight of tradition, so highly prized in accounting, is on their side. Given a strong motivation to have an accounting standard accepted which is favorable to one's interests, it is not difficult to devise an argument as to why a given transaction should be recorded in a certain way under the currently accepted definitions of accounting terms.[10] Since the views of various parties are presented to the policy-making bodies not in the form of conflicting private interests, but in the form of conflicting interpretations of accounting definitions, it may appear that a clearer definition of each accounting term will solve the problem. A frank discussion of the private interests of various contending groups may be tactically disadvantageous in open public discourse.[11] Hence, the overblown emphasis on authoritative definitions. However, definitions, no matter how carefully worded, cannot bear the burden of the struggle for economic advantage between various interest groups. Legal definitions survive in a similar environment only because their interpretations by the courts are backed by the power of the state to enforce them, a power not available to the FASB.

The conceptual framework-seeking behavior of the FASB and its predecessors can also be explained in terms of a self-interest perceived by the public accounting profession. The profession has long argued that its interests are best served if it can maintain control over prescription of accounting standards. This is revealed in its protests against any hint that the control of the profession over the standard-setting process may be weakened. Fear of governmental intervention has long been, and continues to be, the major reason for calls for action in the profession.[12] Consider, for example, the following:

---

[9]See Zeff [1978, pp. 57–58] for a typology of the arguments offered in accounting controversies.

[10]See Kitchen [1954] for a stimulating discussion of the problems of definition in accounting.

[11]Since everybody is assumed to be serving the interests of the information user, proponents of all accounting methods argue their case because it will benefit such user. Recall that in the heyday of the LIFO controversy, a major argument for LIFO was that it yields a better measure of income. Watts and Zimmerman [1979] have attempted to explain the existence of some normative theories in financial accounting, using a parallel argument.

[12]Of course, the auditors' fear of government intervention is asymmetric. Consistent with their self-interests, they do want the government to continue to require an audit of certain business firms to ensure demand for their services but want to keep the standard-setting process free of government control.

> If the practitioners, after sufficient time has elapsed, have not come to some substantial agreement as to what are or should be considered accepted accounting principles and practices, we may well expect the Commission's [SEC's] staff accountants to prepare, and the Commission to publish what it shall demand in the way of such practices . . . [Smith, 1935, p. 327].

Appropriate as it is today, note that the above statement appeared in an article published almost 45 years ago. Disagreements centering on diverse accounting standards continue to attract much of the criticism leveled at the accounting profession and are the source of the greatest threat to the profession's control over the standard-setting process. The presence of diverse accounting practices hurts the credibility of the standard-setting bodies in two ways. First, the existence of alternative accounting methods is taken as *prima facie* evidence that the accounting standard-setting body is not doing its work properly and is simply allowing firms to record transactions in an arbitrary fashion. Second, whenever the standard-setting body proscribes the use of all but one of the alternative accounting methods, the advocates of the methods were no longer permitted to criticize the agency for being arbitrary in not protecting their interests. No matter what it does, a body like the FASB can expect to find itself criticized by powerful interest groups. A good example is provided by the debate on accounting for oil and gas exploration costs. The FASB was instructed to develop a uniform accounting standard for the oil and gas industry or face the threat of having such a standard written by a government agency. When the FASB chose the successful-efforts over the full-cost method, it found, aligned against it, a powerful industry group as well as some government departments and agencies. Being largely an offspring of the accounting profession, the FASB has (as did the APB) little defense against the criticism that it does not have legitimate authority to make decisions which affect wealth transfer among members of society.

Thus, a body like the FASB needs a conceptual framework simply to boost its public standing.[13] A conceptual framework provides the basis for arguing that: (1) the objective of its activities is to serve the users of the financial statements (it is easier to use the public-interest argument for the user group than for any other group), and (2) it selects among accounting alternatives on the basis of broadly accepted objectives and not because of pressures applied by various interest groups seeking a favorable ruling from the Board. The ability, intelligence, ethical character, and past services, *etc.*, of the members of the FASB are not sufficient to convince the parties adversely affected by its rulings that it makes social choices through an impartial consideration of conflicting interests in society. Rather, a conceptual framework is needed to provide the rationalization for its choices.

If a more representative body were to take over the function of setting accounting standards, perhaps there would be less of a need for a conceptual framework. Indeed, the demand to develop a conceptual framework may be inversely related to the power of enforcement which the standard-setting agency can command. For example, the Securities and Exchange Commission, which has the legal power to enforce its Accounting Series Releases, has not been hampered by the fact that it has not yet enunciated a conceptual framework of accounting.

---

[13]A discussion of this public-interest argument appears in AAA[1977b].

CONCLUDING REMARKS

There is little evidence that official statements of objectives of financial accounting have had any direct effect on the determination of financial accounting standards. Whenever the APB or the FASB has had to consider a financial accounting standard, various interest groups presented arguments to support the methods that each perceived to be in its own best interests. The standards issued had to be compromises among the contending interests.[14] Whether the standard-setting process stays in the private sector or is transferred to some public agency, this feature is unlikely to change. What, then, will likely be the effect of the FASB's Conceptual Framework Project on the development of financial accounting standards in the future?

Our initial guess is that the objectives selected by the Board will be ignored in future rule-making activities, just as were those from previous authoritative attempts. Following the publication of these objectives, the Board will probably feel obliged to pay lip service to them in its future pronouncements, but these pronouncements will not be affected in any substantive way by what is contained in the present documents.

It might have been a more fruitful exercise for the FASB to develop a set of objectives for itself and not for the entire social activity called financial reporting. A few examples of such objectives are provided for consideration:

First, the Board could explicitly recognize the nature of financial accounting as a social activity which affects a varied set of interests, both of those who actively participate and those who do not.[15] As the interests of each group are affected by the actions of the Board, it must expect to hear arguments in support of, and against, its decisions. The representations made by these parties could be viewed in the context of their own private interests. In the past, accountants in public practice (*i.e.*, auditors) have tended to be more vocal in their reactions to the Board's actions than have other parties. But perhaps accountants in public practice should have less direct influence on the rule-making process in the future. In its statement of objectives, the Board could define mechanisms for arriving at a compromise ruling after a hearing has been given to all affected groups in society. The Board's primary objective would simply be to arrive at a compromise ruling after considering various points of view on each issue.

A second objective for the FASB might be to limit the detail and specificity of its accounting standards. The pressure to write increasingly detailed and specific accounting standards is great and, in recent years, the resistance of the Board to such pressures seems to be weakening. In this connection, we might note that one of three conditions laid down by the Council of the Institute of Chartered Accountants in England and Wales for approving recommendations on accounting principles to its members was simply that the document be reasonably concise in form (see Zeff [1972, p. 11]).[16] Judging from the length and detail of some of its recent pronouncements (*e.g.*, those dealing with leases and oil and gas exploration costs),

---

[14]See, for example, Horngren [1973, p. 61], "My hypothesis is that the setting of accounting standards is as much a product of political action as of flawless logic or empirical findings."

[15]An explicit objective along these lines was also proposed in AAA [1977b, pp. 10–11].

[16]Of course, there is no government agency in the UK which serves an enforcement role like that of the SEC in this country. This factor may allow broader statements in the UK.

the FASB seems to have abandoned an attempt to keep its Statement of Financial Accounting Standards concise.

A third objective of the Board could be to abstain from issuing an accounting standard unless the pronouncement could command a substantial majority. The recent move to lower the minimum voting requirement for issuing an FASB recommendation to a simple majority of seven members will probably increase the frequency of FASB pronouncements which are widely opposed by large segments of interested parties and therefore undermine the basis of its support.

In short, the FASB could assume that various functions of financial statements are well established and known generally by those who produce, audit, and use accounting information. Its task would be essentially one of trying to appease conflicting interests in the presence of disagreements over accounting rules, measurements, disclosures, *etc.* But once this role were recognized, what would be the advantages and disadvantages of allowing a private board like the FASB to make compromise decisions? Is this not a function essentially similar to that performed by the courts, and, if so, are we now back to the proposal for an accounting court?[17]

These questions appear to offer fruitful areas of research, more so than trying to deduce *the* objectives of financial accounting. Perhaps we can achieve more progress by developing and testing theories regarding why a major part of the responsibility for standard setting continues to lie with a private agency, and why members of the profession and corporate managers continue to contribute time and money to the process of developing a conceptual framework. It is unlikely that a general fear of government regulation alone can account for the latter. And, finally, to conclude with Baxter [1962, p. 427]:

> Recommendations by authority on matters of accounting theory may in the short run seem unmixed blessings. In the end, however, they will probably do harm. They are likely to yield little fresh knowledge. . . . They are likely to weaken the education of accountants; the conversion of the subject into cut-and-dried rules, approved by authority and not to be lightly questioned, threatens to reduce its value as a subject of liberal education almost to *nil.* They are likely to narrow the scope for individual thought and judgment; and a group of men who resign their hard problems to others must eventually give up all claim to be a learned profession.

REFERENCES

American Accounting Association (1936), Executive Committee, "A Tentative Statement of Accounting Principles Affecting Corporate Reports," *The Accounting Review* (June 1936), pp. 187–91.

_____, Executive Committee, "Accounting Principles Underlying Corporate Financial Statements," *The Accounting Review* (June 1941), pp. 133–39.

_____, Executive Committee, "Accounting Concepts and Standards Underlying Corporate Financial Statements, 1948 Revision," *The Accounting Review* (October 1948), pp. 339–44.

_____, Committee on Concepts and Standards Underlying Corporate Financial Statements, "Accounting and Reporting Standards for Corporate Financial Statements, 1957 Revision," *The Accounting Review* (October 1957), pp. 536–46.

_____, Committee on Concepts and Standards—Long-Lived Assets, "Accounting for Land, Buildings and Equipment," Supplementary Statement No. 1, *The Accounting Review* (July 1964a), pp. 693–99.

---

[17]First proposed by Littleton [1935].

_____, Committee on Concepts and Standards—Inventory Measurement, "A Discussion of Various Approaches to Inventory Measurement," Supplementary Statement No. 2, *The Accounting Review* (July 1964b), pp. 700–14.

_____, Committee to Prepare a Statement of Basic Accounting Theory, *A Statement of Basic Accounting Theory* (AAA, 1966).

_____, Committee on Concepts and Standards for External Financial Reports, *Statement on Accounting Theory and Theory Acceptance* (AAA, 1977a).

_____, Subcommittee on Conceptual Framework for Financial Accounting and Reporting, *Elements of Financial Statements and Their Measurement: Report to the Financial Accounting Standards Board* (AAA, June 1977b).

American Institute of [Certified Public] Accountants (1942), Committee on Accounting Procedure, *Unamortized Discount and Redemption Premium on Bonds Refunded (Supplement),* Accounting Research Bulletin No. 18, (AICPA, 1942).

_____, Committee on Accounting Terminology, *Accounting Terminology Bulletin,* No. 1 (AIA, 1953). Reprinted in FASB [1977b].

American Institute of Certified Public Accountants (1970), Accounting Principles Board, *Basic Concepts and Accounting Principles Underlying Financial Statements of Business Enterprises,* Statement No. 4 of the APB (AICPA, 1970).

_____, Study Group on the Objectives of Financial Statements, *Objectives of Financial Statements* (AICPA, 1973).

Armstrong, M. S., "The Politics of Establishing Accounting Standards," *Journal of Accountancy* (February 1977), pp. 76–79.

Baxter, W. T., "Recommendations on Accounting Theory," in W. T. Baxter and S. Davidson, eds., *Studies in Accounting Theory* (Sweet & Maxwell, 1962), pp. 414–27.

Beaver, W. H. and J. S. Demski, "The Nature of Financial Accounting Objectives: A Survey and Synthesis," *Studies on Financial Accounting Objectives, 1974,* supplement to the *Journal of Accounting Research* (1974).

Bedford, N. M., "Discussion of Opportunities and Implications of the Report on Objectives of Financial Statements," *Studies on Financial Accounting Objectives, 1974,* Supplement to the *Journal of Accounting Research* 12 (1974), p. 15.

Canning, J. B., *The Economics of Accountancy* (The Ronald Press, 1929).

Coe, T. L. and G. H. Sorter, "The FASB Has Been Using an Implicit Conceptual Framework," *The Accounting Journal* (Winter 1977–78), pp. 152–69.

Cyert, R. M. and Y. Ijiri, "Problems of Implementing the Trueblood Objectives Report," *Studies on Financial Accounting Objectives: 1974,* Supplement to the *Journal of Accounting Research* 12 (1974).

Deinzer, H. T., *The American Accounting Association-Sponsored Statements of Standards for Corporate Financial Reports: A Perspective* (Accounting Department, University of Florida, 1964).

Financial Accounting Standards Board, FASB Discussion Memorandum, *Conceptual Framework for Accounting and Reporting: Consideration of the Report of the Study Group on the Objectives of Financial Statements* (FASB, 1974).

_____, FASB Discussion Memorandum, *Conceptual Framework for Financial Accounting and Reporting: Elements of Financial Statements and Their Measurement* (FASB, 1976a).

_____, *Tentative Conclusions on Objectives of Financial Statements of Business Enterprises* (FASB, 1976b).

_____, *Scope and Implications of the Conceptual Framework Project* (FASB, 1976c).

_____, *Objectives of Financial Reporting and Elements of Financial Statements of Business Enterprises,* Exposure Draft of Proposed Statement of Financial Accounting Concepts (FASB, 1977).

_____, *Objectives of Financial Reporting by Business Enterprises,* Statement of Financial Accounting Concepts No. 1 (FASB, 1978).

Hanson, A. W., "Comments on 'An Introduction to Corporate Accounting Standards'," *Journal of Acountancy* (June 1940), pp. 440–42.

Hatfield, H. R., *Modern Accounting* (D. Appleton and Company, 1909).

_____, *Accounting: Its Principles and Problems* (D. Appleton-Century Company, 1927).

Horngren, C. T., "The Market of Accounting Standards," *Journal of Accountancy* (October 1973), pp. 61–66.

Ijiri, Y., "Critique of the APB Fundamentals Statement," *Journal of Accountancy* (November 1971), pp. 43–50.

Kester, R. B., "Comments on 'An Introduction to Corporate Accounting Standards'," *Journal of Accountancy* (June 1940), pp. 442–45.

Kitchen, J., "Costing Terminology, *Accounting Research* (February 1954). Reprinted in W. T. Baxter and S. Davidson, eds., *Studies in Accounting Theory* (Sweet & Maxwell, 1962), pp. 399–413.

Littleton, A. C., "Auditor Independence," *Journal of Accountancy* (April 1935), pp. 283–91.

_____, Review of Moonitz, *The Basic Postulates of Accounting, The Accounting Review* (July 1962), pp. 602–05.

_____, Review of R. T. Sprouse and M. Moonitz, *A Tentative Set of Broad Accounting Principles for Business Enterprises, The Accounting Review* (January 1963), pp. 220–22.

Miller, H. E., "Discussion of Opportunities and Implications of the Report on Objectives of Financial Statements," *Studies on Financial Accounting Objectives: 1974,* supplement to *Journal of Accounting Research* 12 (1974).

Moonitz, M., *The Basic Postulates of Accounting,* Accounting Research Study No. 1 (AICPA, 1961).

Most, K. S. and A. L. Winters, "Focus on Standard Setting: From Trueblood to the FASB," *Journal of Accountancy* (February 1977), pp. 67–75.

Paton, W. A., *Accounting Theory* (The Ronald Press, 1922).

Paton, W. A. and A. C. Littleton, *An Introduction to Corporate Accounting Standards,* Monograph No. 3 (AAA, 1940).

Smith, C. A., "Accounting Practice under the Securities and Exchange Commission," *The Accounting Review* (December 1935), pp. 325–332.

Sprouse, R. T., "Discussion of Opportunities and Implications of the Report on Objectives of Financial Statements," *Studies on Financial Accounting Objectives: 1974,* Supplement to the *Journal of Accounting Research* 12 (1974).

Sprouse, R. T. and M. Moonitz, *A Tentative Set of Broad Accounting Principles for Business Enterprises,* Accounting Research Study No. 3 (AICPA, 1962).

Sterling, R. R., "A Statement of Basic Accounting Theory: A Review Article," *Journal of Accounting Research* (Spring 1967), pp. 95–112.

Stinchcombe, A. L., *Constructing Social Theories* (Harcourt, Brace, and World, 1968).

Vatter, W. J., "$\sum_{i=1}^{i=22} (M_3)_i$—An Evaluation," *The Accounting Review* (July 1963), pp. 47–77.

Watts, R. L. and J. L. Zimmerman, "Towards a Positive Theory of Determination of Accounting Standards," *The Accounting Review 53* (January 1978), pp. 112–34.

_____, "The Demand for and Supply of Accounting Theories: The Market for Excuses," *The Accounting Review* (April 1979), pp. 273–305.

Zeff, S. A., *Forging Accounting Principles in Five Countries* (Stipes Publishing Co., 1972).

_____, "The Rise of 'Economic Consequences'," *Journal of Accountancy* (December 1978), pp. 56–63.

THE CONCEPTUAL FRAMEWORK: MYTHS AND REALITIES

Paul B. W. Miller

No endeavor in financial accounting has attracted more attention and criticism than the effort to create a comprehensive set of concepts for theory and practice. The attempts number in the dozens, beginning in the 1930s. The most recent and the most elaborate, of course, has been the work done on a conceptual framework by the Financial Accounting Standards Board, a project that had its inception in 1973, when the board was established.

With the issuing of FASB Concepts Statement no. 5, *Recognition and Measurement in Financial Statements of Business Enterprises*—the last originally scheduled building block of the framework—it seems worthwhile to explore the realities and the myths surrounding the endeavor.

Given the background and importance of the undertaking, it isn't surprising that several myths have sprung up about conceptual frameworks in general and about the FASB project in particular. This article, intended to lay to rest some of these misperceptions, explains what a conceptual framework might accomplish, sheds light on eight prevalent myths (see exhibit 1) and describes the real nature of the project.

GOALS OF A CONCEPTUAL FRAMEWORK

Much has been said and written about a conceptual framework for accounting, so the focus here will be on the three paramount reasons to establish one:

Paul B. W. Miller, "The Conceptual Framework: Myths and Realities," *Journal of Accountancy,* March 1985, pp. 62–71. Reprinted with permission from the Journal of Accountancy, Copyright © 1985 by American Institute of Certified Public Accountants, Inc. Opinions of the authors are their own and do not necessarily reflect policies of the AICPA.

1. To describe existing practice.
2. To prescribe future practice.
3. To define key terms and fundamental issues.

Conflicts among these goals, because they have contributed to the mythmaking, will also be explored.

Existing practice. One reason for bringing together accounting concepts is to provide an overview of what is done in practice. The basic objective of the description is to make understandable, in as cogent and simple a form as possible, what accounting is all about. A few broad principles generally are more comprehensible than a multitude of specific details.

Future practice. In the course of developing descriptive concepts, theorists generally become aware of inconsistencies and other deficiencies in practice. One result of these discoveries is the desire to develop another type of conceptual framework, one that goes beyond mere description and prescribes what ought to be done. These frameworks are often called normative because they reflect the values, or norms, of their compilers.

Key terms and fundamental issues. Another major purpose of a conceptual framework is to lay down broad definitions of basic terms to be used in debates about what ought to be done in practice. (In this limited sense a conceptual framework is like a constitution or other form of social contract that establishes basic principles.) These terms, moreover, help the profession and other interested parties identify the issues to be debated.

It is important to remember that having definitions doesn't eliminate the need for debates, nor does it predetermine an outcome. The need for discussion is continuous, and any given outcome depends on the powers of the participants at the time of the debate.

Conflicts among goals. No single framework, however, can satisfy more than one of these three objectives. In fact, there are barriers to setting up a framework that will meet even one of them.

First, it is difficult to establish a descriptive conceptual framework because not everyone agrees about what actually exists. Among accountants there is disagreement on, for example, the basic issue of whether the initial cost measurement of an asset is intended to be a description of the amount sacrificed to acquire it or a reliable estimate of its value at the date of acquisition. In most cases there is little difference between these two numbers; at other times, however, the difference is material, so the issue takes on importance.

Other limitations of a description of current practice are that it doesn't always help accountants cope with a new situation—say, a research and development partnership or an insubstance defeasance—or provide much help in improving existing practice.

Attempts to establish prescriptive frameworks have been unsuccessful, however, because of the near impossibility of reaching agreement between even two people, let alone among the seven members of the FASB or the hundreds of thousands of people who are involved in accounting. But even if a prescriptive conceptual framework could be achieved, practical impact would be unlikely if it lacked consensus and authoritative support. When, for example, the American Accounting Association published *A Statement of Basic Accounting Theory* in 1966, the document didn't influence practice because it didn't receive enough support from powerful interests.

EXHIBIT 1

Eight Myths about Conceptual Frameworks

1. The Accounting Principles Board failed because it didn't have a conceptual framework.
2. The Financial Accounting Standards Board can't succeed unless it has a conceptual framework.
3. A conceptual framework will lead to consistent standards.
4. A conceptual framework will eliminate the problem of standards overload.
5. The FASB's conceptual framework captures only the status quo of accounting practice.
6. The FASB's conceptual framework project has cost more than it should have.
7. The FASB will revise the existing standards to make them consistent with the conceptual framework.
8. The FASB has abandoned the conceptual framework project.

It's no easier to set up a framework that merely defines basic terms and issues because control of the definitions contributes to control of the debates and, eventually, of the selection of which practices are changed or left unchanged. Accordingly, a consensus on even seemingly obvious points may be elusive.

There can also be significant difficulty in interpreting the definitions and making them operational. Accountants are likely to thoroughly debate, for example, the meaning of the phrase *probable future economic benefits,* which is part of the definition of an asset in FASB Concepts Statement no. 3, *Elements of Financial Statements of Business Enterprises.* Finally, conflicts arise in developing this type of framework if the definitions don't describe existing practice or allow for flexibility in coping with new situations.

Because the task of creating a conceptual framework is so complex, it isn't surprising that accountants have encountered so much resistance to their efforts. Perhaps even more resistance has been directed toward the FASB because it plays a highly visible and central role in the process.

EIGHT MYTHS ABOUT CONCEPTUAL FRAMEWORKS

Those who have followed the recognition and measurement phase of the conceptual framework project know that there are many myths about such frameworks, especially the FASB's.

The eight most common myths, shown in exhibit 1, fall into four categories:

1. The political role of a conceptual framework (myths 1 and 2).

2. The technical role of a conceptual framework (myths 3 and 4).

3. The FASB's existing conceptual framework (myths 5 and 6).

4. The future of the FASB's conceptual framework (myths 7 and 8).

In each case, as is true of most myths, there is an element of truth, but there has been distortion over time, through telling and retelling.

MYTH NO. 1

One problem with the myth that the Accounting Principles Board failed because it didn't have a conceptual framework is its premise—that the APB did, indeed, fail. For the sake of argument, let's accept the definition of failure as the inability to stay in existence.

From the perspective of the 1980s, it seems more likely that the APB stopped operating because it had an apparent structural bias that favored the interests of auditors and their clients to the detriment of users of financial statements. Part of the problem arose from the fact that the APB was a committee of the American Institute of CPAs and thus was seen to be within the auditing profession. With one exception, there were no users among the members of the APB, and users generally weren't included directly in its procedures of due process.

Most important, the Securities and Exchange Commission didn't send a clear, unambiguous signal about its attitude toward the APB's pronouncements. As a result of all these factors, the APB's failure can more appropriately be attributed to its apparent neglect of users than to the absence of a conceptual framework.

MYTH NO. 2

The second myth is that the FASB can't succeed unless it has a conceptual framework. Again, it is easy to be sidetracked into a debate on what should be considered success. It can be argued, for example, that the FASB will succeed only if capital resources are allocated more efficiently as a result of its standards.

A more practical assumption can also be made, however—that mere continued existence constitutes success.

The FASB will survive if and only if it can maintain a mandate that reflects the interests of the beneficiaries of the capital market, who are, in effect, the participants in the national economy. To obtain this broad power base, the strong support of the SEC is essential. Specifically, some visible SEC action is needed to establish that the FASB has the best interests of the economy in mind, not just the interests of the preparers and auditors of financial statements.

By endorsing the FASB as the authoritative body for setting standards—in its Accounting Series Release no. 150, *Statement of Policy on the Establishment and Improvement of Accounting Principles and Standards*—the SEC has provide the needed visible support. Additional credibility is provided by the commission's continuing oversight activities.

From a political perspective, then, a conceptual framework isn't crucial to the FASB's viability, but the board may be able to operate more efficiently if some key terms and issues can be defined and identified.

MYTH NO. 3

The validity of the myth that a conceptual framework will lead to consistent standards hinges on the process by which standards are created. If standards were handed down by a higher authority strictly on the basis of their conceptual soundness, a conceptual framework would, of course, lead to consistency.

But standards don't descend. Rather, they emerge from a nested set of political processes that create inconsistencies as the search for a consensus continues.

The core process is the negotiating among the seven members of the FASB. Like everyone else, individual board members have different ideas and want to get their views incorporated into the final pronouncements. But to put together a majority, compromises must be made, with the result that some conceptual consistency is often lost. (Of course, inconsistency is also created as individual board members change their views or are replaced.)

Inconsistencies are also created through the board's highly visible procedures of due process. When common themes are heard in constituents' objections to proposed standards, it behooves the board to compromise and make some changes, with the result that consistency can be lost.

Broader political pressure, especially from the SEC, also plays a part in generating inconsistencies among standards. Because the commission has so much power, it is unlikely that the FASB can resist the pressure from Washington to produce compromise standards that meet the needs of the SEC and its constituents merely by arguing that the result isn't perfectly compatible with the published concepts.

Given the reasonably balanced powers that exist, then, it's clear that consensus can be reached only through compromise. In turn, these compromises are governed by the priorities different groups have for different issues. Many users of financial statements may not care much about accounting for futures contracts, for example, but they may be intensely interested in accounting for pensions. Thus, they may be willing to accept virtually any answer on futures but will hold the line on the pension issues.

MYTH NO. 4

To accept the myth that a conceptual framework will eliminate the problem of standards overload, one must first agree that there is an overload problem. This question won't be debated here.

Also implicit is the idea that the responsibility for decisions about accounting standards can be decentralized by shifting it to the auditor in the field. Doing so, it is argued, would mean that practitioners would be less burdened by detailed rules.

But it can also be argued that such decentralization isn't politically feasible because it would place power in the hands of one group (auditors) to the potential detriment of other groups (statement users and preparers). Giving so much control to auditors would be unacceptable to the other participants in the political processes by which standards are created.

Where, moreover, has the thrust for publishing more standards come from? It is likely that many auditors want them in order to have more leverage when facing down "creative" and perhaps stubborn clients who try to push the existing standards to their limits. As long as this situation exists, the FASB will be equally pressured to translate its broad concepts into authoritative and detailed standards rather than leave the interpretation to individual auditors, who are subject to client pressure.

MYTH NO. 5

Those who believe the myth that the FASB's conceptual framework captures only the status quo of accounting practice tend to want the framework to go further in prescribing future standards. In effect, they are complaining that its present structure makes change less likely to happen.

A variation on this myth is that the conceptual framework has captured only the obvious and left out the more difficult points. Who could disagree, for example, with the idea that useful information should be provided? Who would disagree with the notion that information must be both relevant and reliable to be useful?

In response to these criticisms, it can be pointed out that the results of the early phase of the framework project are useful for defining the terms used by the board members and their respondents. At the very least, the existing framework lays some groundwork that makes the deliberative process more efficient, even if it doesn't provide an exact description of current practice or a clear prescription for future practice.

In sharp contrast is an opposing myth—that the conceptual framework is revolutionary. It has been argued that the framework emphasizes the statement of financial position over the income statement. It must be acknowledged that the framework has, in fact, cast doubt on some of the long-standing practices associated with so-called good matching and in this sense may be considered revolutionary. FASB Concepts Statement no. 3, for example, points out that a credit balance in the deferred tax account created under APB Opinion no. 11, *Accounting for Income Taxes,* doesn't meet the definition of a liability or of any other of the FASB's elements.

But this tendency to evaluate practice in terms of its effects on the income statement and the statement of financial position isn't revolutionary in the light of long-standing trends. It is now considered inappropriate, for example, to capitalize operating losses of development stage companies, to recognize self-insurance reserves and not to capitalize leases that are in-substance purchases of assets. Each change was made with the idea of improving both financial statements.

Perhaps the proponents of this contrasting myth think that additional emphasis on the balance sheet demotes income reporting. If so, they are mistaken. Rather, as was suggested, the shift is better interpreted as an equalization of the importance of the two statements.

This conclusion is supported by the growing interest in reporting non articulated changes in owners' equity, as seen in accounting for long term investments in marketable securities (FASB Statement no. 12, *Accounting for Certain Marketable Securities*) and the foreign currency translation adjustment (FASB Statement no. 52, *Foreign Currency Translation*). (In its most basic form nonarticulation is the reporting of an income number that doesn't include all changes in owners' equity other than investments by owners and distributions to them.)

Nonarticulation of at least one income statement is clearly favored in FASB Concepts Statement no. 5, which proposes a statement of "earnings" (which wouldn't articulate with the statement of financial position) and a statement of "comprehensive income" (which would articulate).

MYTH NO. 6

The myth that the FASB's conceptual framework project has cost more than it should have is based on two premises: (1) the cost of the project is knowable; (2) the cost that should have been incurred is knowable. Both assumptions are questionable.

First, it's impossible to know precisely what the project has cost; there are simply too many joint costs. Any given board or staff member works on a number of projects at the same time. Further, the work on the framework has spilled over into other projects. There are also many hidden, hence unmeasurable, costs incurred by constituents in preparing responses to discussion documents.

To determine how much the project should have cost would require extraordinary insight, for no one has ever completed a conceptual framework under the circumstances that the FASB has faced. And any other method of estimating an appropriate cost would depend on individual evaluations of the goal of the project.

A parallel argument is that the costs have exceeded the benefits. One weakness of this view is, of course, the difficulty of measuring the costs and benefits. Another is the basic assumption that there are no further significant benefits to be derived from the framework. Although such an assertion may be true, it is premature at this point. Time and more evidence are needed.

Some have even contended that the project has produced no benefits. This view may be held by those who wanted the framework to be purely descriptive of existing practice or who preferred a purely prescriptive framework, one not bound by existing practice.

Of course, neither camp got what it wanted and thus may be unwilling to acknowledge that there are any positive elements in what the board has published.

MYTH NO. 7

Some subscribe to the myth that the FASB will revise the existing standards to make them consistent with the conceptual framework. This belief may have been encouraged by the FASB's sweeping generalizations early in the project and, later, by the board's specific declarations in certain standards that it would review and amend these standards, as needed, to make them conceptually sound.

But for most exciting standards there is insufficient interest in revising them to justify putting the issues back on the agenda. It is unlikely, for example, that anyone would want to reconsider the treatment of troubled debt restructurings or foreign currency translations solely to bring them into compliance with a conceptual framework.

Perhaps more significant is the fact that interactions among compromises on different issues make it unlikely that some of them can be overturned. That is, the board's ability to resolve future issues would be reduced by any action that would make it harder to generate a consensus among board members or the board's constituents.

If every hard-won consensus is to be thrown open for renegotiation because of the conceptual framework, a board member would be reluctant to compromise. The politics of the situation simply demand that a consensus be left intact as long as possible.

If, however, enough powerful people—including the board, the Financial Accounting Standards Advisory Council, the SEC and other constituent organizations—do want a standard to be changed, it will be changed; if they want it to be left alone, it will be.

MYTH NO. 8

The last widespread myth is that the FASB has abandoned the conceptual framework project. The nature of FASB Concepts Statement no. 5, issued in December 1984 after more than three years of effort, is one basis for this belief.

The overall strategy adopted was to draft and issue a less prescriptive and more descriptive statement. In effect, the board could claim a victory because the members did, at last, reach a consensus. Because this "victory" came about only because the board retreated from the unresolved substantive issues, the strategy has often been called the "Vietnam solution."

The statement reflects this strategy because it doesn't go far beyond earlier concepts statements and certainly doesn't tackle the measurement issue, on which the board was so deeply divided.

In particular, paragraph 66 of the statement says: "Items currently reported in financial statements are measured by different attributes, depending on the nature of the item and the relevance and reliability of the attribute measured. The Board expects the use of different attributes to continue." The question of which factors should be considered in making the choice among these attributes was, of course, the issue that the board members couldn't resolve.

The board's adoption of this strategy may indeed be an abandonment of the conceptual framework project. On the other hand, it may simply be an expedient action to allow other, more immediate issues (such as accounting for pension costs) to be addressed. Inevitably, the delay also provides an opportunity for power to shift in such a way that the previously intractable conceptual issues might be tackled and resolved more definitely in the future.

But it is also probably accurate to say that the board has indeed abandoned some of the original goals of the project, a step far different from abandoning the project itself.

REALITIES OF THE CONCEPTUAL FRAMEWORK

The conceptual framework is better understood as a political document than as a purely conceptual effort. The concepts statements have emerged from the same political processes—with the same need to compromise—that are used for setting standards. Inevitably, then, the framework lacks the conciseness of some other conceptual structures. But this potential shortcoming must be considered in light of the fact that the framework enjoys much more authoritative support and potential for affecting practice than any of its predecessors.

Another reality about the framework is that it is neither a complete description of existing practice nor a highly specific prescription for future practice. Yet it does broadly define a number of key terms and concepts that can be used in identifying and debating the issues.

Now for a warning of a lurking danger: the profession shouldn't consider the framework as the ultimate authority for resolving issues. The definitions are nonauthoritative enough to allow the board to work around them when seeking a consensus.

Further, the definitions aren't sufficiently precise to preclude debates about their meanings and applications. The framework isn't going to stop arguments—witness the pension project—but it may determine the ground rules for these arguments and the shape of the debates.

Finally, it must be remembered that the framework is still in its infancy. The profession is just starting to use it, and difficulties are inevitable. There are many more conceptual issues to tackle in the future, of course, and there are also many more benefits to be reaped from the existing concepts statements.

THE FRAMEWORK AND THE PROFESSION

At the very least, the framework seems to have helped the board itself. Now that the members and their constituents are using the definitions, clearer communication is a likely result. And this improved communication will benefit the profession and the financial world in general as the effects of the framework make themselves felt.

The most prudent strategy for the profession to adopt is to try to work with the conceptual framework. Accountants can use it, try to change it—and certainly criticize it. But no one is well served by perpetuating the myths that have arisen around it.

MARKET EFFICIENCY AND ECONOMIC CONSEQUENCES

I-F1

WHAT SHOULD BE THE FASB'S OBJECTIVES?

William H. Beaver

Was the acrimony out of the investment tax credit much ado about nothing? Does it matter whether special gains and losses are reported in the ordinary income or in the extraordinary item section? When firms switch from accelerated to straight-line depreciation, what is the effect upon investors? Did the Accounting Principles Board allocate its resources in an appropriate manner? If its priorities needed reordering, where should the emphasis have been shifted? What objectives should be adopted for financial accounting standards?

To answer such questions, the Financial Accounting Standards Board plans to sponsor a sizable research program.[1] For this reason, now is an appropriate time to take stock of the current body of knowledge and assess its implications for the setting of financial accounting standards. This article summarizes the results of recent research that has explored several facets of the relationship between financial statement data and security prices. The findings have a direct bearing on the questions raised at the outset and suggest that our traditional views of the role of policy-making bodies, such as the APB, SEC and FASB, may have to be substantially altered.

The author wishes to acknowledge financial assistance provided by the Dean Witter Foundation. The conclusions expressed here are those of the author and do not necessarily reflect those of the foundation or any of its members.

[1]"Recommendations of the Study on Establishment of Accounting Principles," *Journal of Accountancy,* May 72, pp. 66–71.

Currently we have far too little evidence on important issues in accounting. However, given this paucity of knowledge, it would be unfortunate if we ignored the evidence that we do have. Aspects of this research have already had a considerable effect on the professional investment community. Yet there has been no awareness of this research in accounting at the practical level or in the setting of past standards, as reflected in the APB Opinions. If the hopes for success of the FASB are to be realized, it is imperative that we lead, no lag, in incorporating the current state of knowledge into the setting of standards. Regulating financial accounting standards in ignorance of this evidence makes the prospect for success dim.

THE EVIDENCE

The behavior of security prices with respect to financial statement data is a widely discussed and hotly debated topic. The financial press is replete with articles of alleged effects of financial statement data on prices. In most cases, such allegations are not supported by any evidence. In a few cases, evidence of an anecdotal nature is offered. For example, the price of the stock of the ABC Company changed dramatically at approximately the same time the firm changed its method of depreciation to straight-line. Therefore, the cause was the change in accounting method. Such stories, while often entertaining, hardly constitute convincing evidence for several reasons. First, such an approach may select only those cases which are favorable to the hypothesis of the author while ignoring those instances that would refute it. For example, an examination of the price changes of only one firm or a few hand-picked firms that changed depreciation methods is insufficient. An examination must be made for all firms that changed depreciation methods or at least a large, randomly selected sample. Second, the analysis explains price changes after-the-fact on the basis of a single factor. There may be many factors that cause a price change. Usually, little or no care is taken to account for these other factors.

Unfortunately, until recently such evidence was the only type available. However, the issue is far too serious to be left to casual empiricism. Security prices are of obvious importance because of their impact upon the wealth, and hence the welfare, of investors. This importance is formally recognized in SEC legislation. Recent cases arising out of Section 10b-5 testify to the fact that accounting practices are evaluated in terms of their effect on security prices.[2] Moreover, it is inconceivable that the FASB could set optimal financial accounting standards without assessing the impact of their actions on security prices.

The prevailing opinion in the accounting profession is that the market reacts naïvely to financial statement information. This view is reinforced by the anecdotal data of the sort described earlier, and by the obvious fact that the market is populated with several million uninformed, naïve investors, whose knowledge or concern for the subtleties of accounting matters is nil. However, in spite of this obvious fact, the formal research in this area is remarkably consistent in finding that the market, at least as manifested in the way in which security prices react, is quite sophisticated in dealing with financial statement data. One rationale for the ob-

---

[2]For example, litigation is currently under way in the cases of *Memorex* and *Occidental Petroleum Corp.*, pursuant to SEC action under Section 10b-5. Brief summaries of issues appear in the June 25, 1971, and March 5, 1971, issues of *The Wall Street Journal,* respectively. In both cases, measures of damages being discussed are directly related to the effect of the firms' accounting practices on security prices.

served sophistication of security prices is that the professional investors "make the market" and competitive bidding among one another for securities effectively makes the prices behave in such a manner that they reflect a considerable amount of sophistication. In any event, regardless of what the actual causal mechanism may be, there is considerable evidence that security prices do in fact behave in a sophisticated fashion. In the terminology of this literature, the securities market is said to be "efficient" with respect to financial statement data.[3]

A market is said to be efficient if security prices act as if they "fully reflect" publicly available information, including financial statement data. In other words, in an efficient market the investor is playing a "fair game" with respect to published information. Specifically, this means no investor can expect to use published information in such a way as to earn abnormal returns on his securities. Each investor can expect to earn a return on a security commensurate with its risk.[4] All securities of the same degree of riskiness will offer the same expected return, regardless of what accounting methods are used and no matter how much time is spent gleaning the secrets of the financial statements hidden in the footnotes. Hence, no amount of security analysis, based on published financial statement data, will lead to abnormal returns. There are obvious implications for the community of professional investors, among others. However, there are also equally dramatic implications for the accounting profession. For this reason, the evidence, which has examined several aspects of market efficiency with respect to financial statement data, is summarized below.[5]

One aspect of efficiency is the speed with which security prices react to public information when it is announced. Empirical evidence indicates that prices react quickly and in an unbiased fashion to a variety of events, including announcements of stock splits, stock dividends, secondary offerings and rights issues, as well as both annual and interim earnings announcements. This finding is exactly what one would expect in a market where the security prices at any point in time fully reflect the information released. Moreover, the studies of earnings

---

[3]Three forms of efficiency have been delineated: (1) the weak form, which deals with efficiency with respect to the past sequence of security prices (e.g., the random-walk hypothesis), (2) the semistrong form, which concerns efficiency with respect to published information, and (3) the strong form, which involves all information including inside information. This article deals with efficiency in the semistrong form. There is also considerable evidence with respect to the weak form of efficiency, but it is beyond the scope of this article. For a summary of this literature, see W. Beaver, "Reporting Rules for Marketable Equity Securities," *Journal of Accountancy,* Oct. 71, pp. 57–61.

[4]A detailed discussion of security risk and how it relates to expected returns is beyond the scope of the article. However, there has been a substantial amount of research in the portfolio theory and capital asset pricing literature dealing with this relationship. Briefly, the literature suggests that expected return must be commensurate with the risk incurred, in that securities with greater risk must offer higher expected return. Of course, the actual return in a given period may differ from expected return. For a more complete discussion of this issue in a nontechnical manner, see C. Welles, "The Beta Revolution: Learning to Live With Risk," *The Institutional Investor,* September 1971, pp. 21–64; W. Sharpe, "Risk, Market Sensitivity and Diversification," *Financial Analysts Journal,* January-February 1972, pp. 74–79.

[5]A more detailed summary of the literature is provided in the article by Eugene Fama, "Efficient Capital Markets: A Review of Theory and Empirical Work," *Journal of Finance,* May 1970, pp. 383–417. The implications of this literature for accounting also have been discussed in the following articles: W. Beaver, "The Behavior of Security Prices and Its Implications for Accounting Research Methods," *The Accounting Review* (Supplement, 1972), pp. 407–37; R. Ball, "Changes in Accounting Techniques and Stock Prices" (unpublished paper, University of Chicago, 1972); and N. Gonedes, "Efficient Capital Markets and External Accounting," *The Accounting Review,* January 1972, pp. 11–21.

announcements find security prices anticipate earnings for several months prior to the announcement.[6]

Another aspect is this: Does the market look behind accounting numbers or is it fooled by them? Does the market act only on reported accounting numbers or does it adjust for other information, such as the accounting method used to calculate those numbers? In other words, does the market use a broader information set than merely the reported accounting numbers? In this respect, there have been several studies of changes in accounting methods and the subsequent behavior of security prices.[7] All of these studies show essentially the same result. There is no increase in price by changing to an accounting method that reports higher earnings than would have been reported had no change been made. The market, as reflected in price behavior, is not so naïve as many people claim. Instead, it acts as if it looks beyond accounting numbers and takes into account the fact that earnings are being generated by a different method.

Further evidence compared the price-earnings ratios of firms that use accelerated methods of depreciation for both tax and reporting purposes (A/A group) with the price-earnings ratios of firms that use accelerated methods for tax purposes but straight-line for reporting purposes (A/S group).[8] The price-earnings ratio for the A/A group was larger than the price-earnings ratio for the A/S group. This finding is consistent with a market which recognizes that firms will report lower earnings under accelerated methods of depreciation than they would have under straight-line methods. Further analysis suggested that risk and growth could not explain the difference in the price-earnings ratios. In fact, the average riskiness and average growth rates were the same for both depreciation groups. However, when the earnings of the A/S group were converted to the earnings that would have been reported had they used an accelerated method for reporting, the price-earnings ratios of the two depreciation groups were essentially equal. In other words, when the firms were placed on a uniform accounting method, the price-earnings differences disappeared. Thus, the market appears to adjust for differences in depreciation methods among firms and, in effect, looks behind reported accounting data. Moreover, further testing found that changes in security prices more closely follow changes in certain nonreported forms of earnings than they do changes in reported earnings.

---

[6]The studies referred to here are E. Fama, L. Fisher, M. Jensen and R. Roll, "The Adjustment of Stock Prices to New Information," *International Economic Review,* February 1969, pp. 1–21; M. Scholes, "The Market for Securities: Substitution Versus Price Pressure and the Effects of Information on Share Prices," *Journal of Business,* April 1972, pp. 179–211; R. Ball and P. Brown, "An Empirical Evaluation of Accounting Income Numbers," *Journal of Accounting Research,* Autumn 1968, pp. 159–78; P. Brown and J. Kennelly, "The Informational Content of Quarterly Earnings: An Extension and Some Further Evidence," *Journal of Business,* July 1972, pp. 403–21; G. Benston, "Published Corporate Accounting Data and Stock Prices," *Empirical Research in Accounting: Selected Studies, 1967, Journal of Accounting Research* (Supplement, 1967), pp. 1–54; and W. Beaver, "The Information Content of Annual Earnings Announcements," *Empirical Research in Accounting: Selected Studies, 1968, Journal of Accounting Research* (Supplement, 1968), pp. 67–92.

[7]The empirical studies referred to here include R. Kaplan and R. Roll, "Investor Evaluation of Accounting Information: Some Empirical Evidence," *Journal of Business,* April 1972, pp. 225–57; R. Ball, *op. cit.*; T. R. Archibald, "Stock Market Reaction to Depreciation Switchback," *The Accounting Review,* January 1972, pp. 22–30; and E. Comiskey, "Market Response to Changes in Depreciation Accounting," *The Accounting Review,* April 1971, pp. 279–85.

[8]W. Beaver and R. E. Dukes, "Interperiod Tax Allocation and Depreciation Methods: Some Empirical Results," *The Accounting Review,* July 1973.

This finding is consistent with a market where a broad information set is used in assessing price changes in contrast to one where there is sole, unquestioning reliance upon reported earnings.

In sum then, the evidence, across a variety of contexts, supports the contention that the market is efficient with respect to published information.

IMPLICATIONS

This evidence, together with the evidence on the performance of mutual funds, has led to changes in the investment community.[9]

Many portfolio managers and their clients have moved away from a "beat-the-market," high-turnover philosophy to one where the emphasis is placed upon risk management and the minimization of operating costs. The Samsonite pension fund contract is but one recent example. Wells Fargo Bank has agreed to manage the Samsonite pension fund where the agreement stipulates the maintenance of a given level of risk within prespecified limits, a lid on the maximum amount of turnover that can occur and a restriction on the minimum number of securities comprising the fund.[10]

Given the practical impact that this research has had on the investment community, one might suspect that there are implications for the practice of accounting as well. In fact, there are several important implications for accounting in general and for the FASB in particular. However, there has been virtually no reaction on the part of the accounting profession. One reason is a general lack of awareness of this research, because its dissemination has essentially been restricted to academic journals. Another reason is that the anecdotal form of evidence discussed earlier continues to carry considerable weight among many members of the accounting profession. As a result, many readers may refuse to accept the evidence in support of market efficiency. But what if the mounting evidence in support of an efficient market finally becomes so overwhelming and compelling that it is accepted by all seven members of the FASB, all SEC Commissioners and staff, and all congressmen? What are the implications for the FASB? There are at least four major implications.

First. Many reporting issues are trivial and do not warrant an expenditure of FASB resources. The properties of such issues are twofold: (1) There is essentially no difference in cost to the firm of reporting either method. (2) There is essentially no cost to statement users in adjusting from one method to the other. In such cases, there is a simple solution. Report one

---

[9]The empirical evidence finds that mutual fund returns fail to cover even research costs and brokerage commissions (let alone loading charges). After deducting these expenses, the net return to the mutual fund shareholder is below the return that could have been obtained from a simple strategy of buying and holding a portfolio of the same degree of riskiness. In fact, only after all such costs were added back in computing the return is the average mutual fund performance approximately equal to (but not greater than) the return from random portfolios of the same degree of riskiness. Moreover, these results not only apply to the average performance of all mutual funds but additional tests also indicate that no individual funds were able to produce superior returns consistently. For example, past performance by a fund appeared to be of no value in predicting superior performance in the future. See M. Jensen, "Risk, the Pricing of Capital Assets, and the Evaluation of Investment Portfolios," *Journal of Business,* April 1969, pp. 167–247. See also M. Zweig, "Darts, Anyone? As Market Pickers, Market Seers, the Pros Fall Short," *Barron's,* February 19, 1973, pp. 11–25.

[10]C. Welles, *op. cit.*

method, with sufficient footnote disclosure to permit adjustment to the other, and let the market interpret implications of the data for security prices.

Unfortunately, too much of the resources of the APB and others has been devoted to issues that warrant this straightforward resolution. For example, the investment credit controversy belongs in this category, as do the issues regarding the definition of extraordinary items, interperiod tax allocation, earnings per share computations involving convertible securities, and accounting for marketable equity securities. By contrast, the FASB should shift its resources to those controversies where there is nontrivial additional cost to the firms or to investors in order to obtain certain types of information (for example, replacement cost accounting for depreciable assets). Whether such information should be a required part of reporting standards is a substantive issue.

Second. The role of financial statement data is essentially a preemptive one—that is, to prevent abnormal returns accruing to individuals by trading upon inside information. This purpose leads to the following disclosure policy: If there are no additional costs to disclosure to the firm, there is prima facie evidence that the item in question ought to be disclosed.

This relatively simple policy could greatly enhance the usefulness of financial statements. Many forms of information are currently being generated internally by the firm and could be reported with essentially no additional cost (e.g., the current market value of marketable equity securities). Such information, if not publicly reported, may constitute inside information. Merely because prices reflect publicly available information in no way implies that they also fully reflect inside information. One information cost that investors may be incurring currently is abnormal returns earned by those who have monopolistic access to inside information. Opponents of greater disclosure bear the burden of proof of showing that individuals can be prevented from earning excess returns with the undisclosed information or that the cost of disclosure exceeds the excess returns. Given the private incentives to trade on inside information, such a condition is very difficult to ensure.

Incidentally, efficient securities markets also have some important implications regarding the accountants' growing concern over legal liability. Accountants can be held legitimately responsible for insufficient disclosure. However, they should not be held responsible for using a "wrong" method (e.g., flow-through v. deferral) as long as they disclose the method that was used and sufficient data to permit adjustment to the nonreported method.

Third. The FASB must reconsider the nature of its traditional concern for the naïve investor. If the investor, no matter how naïve, is in effect facing a fair game, can he still get harmed? If so, how? The naïve investor can still get harmed, but not in the ways traditionally thought. For example, the potential harm is not likely to occur because firms use flow-through v. deferral for accounting for the investment credit. Rather, the harm is more likely to occur because firms are following policies of less than full disclosure and insiders are potentially earning monopoly returns from access to inside information. Harm is also likely to occur when investors assume speculative positions with excessive transactions costs, improper diversification and improper risk levels in the erroneous belief that they will be able to "beat the market" with published accounting information.

This implies that the FASB should actively discourage investors' beliefs that accounting data can be used to detect overvalued or undervalued securities. This also implies that the FASB must not attempt to reduce the complex events of multimillion dollar corporations to the level of understanding of the naïve, or, perhaps more appropriately labeled, ignorant investor. We must stop acting as if all—or even most—individual investors are literally involved in the process of interpreting the impact of accounting information upon the security prices of firms.

An argument often advanced against fuller disclosure is that the increased disclosure will befuddle and confuse the naïve investor. A specific manifestation of this argument is that earnings under market value rules are more volatile and hence may lead to more volatile security prices. For example, the insurance industry currently opposes the inclusion of such information on marketable securities in the income statement, even though market values are already reported on the balance sheet. Given that market values on the balance sheet are already part of public information, it is absurd to think that there is going to be any further effect on security prices because of the income statement disclosure. Yet considerable resources of the APB, the insurance industry and others have been wasted on an attempt to resolve this issue. In the more general case where there is no reporting of market values, the efficient market evidence implies that the market is not reacting naïvely to the currently reported numbers but, rather, is forming "unbiased" assessments of the market values and their effects on prices. Since the market is currently being forced to assess the effects of market values indirectly, they are probably estimating the values with error. Hence, if anything, reporting the actual numbers may eliminate the estimation errors which may be one source of volatility in security prices.

Moreover, one message comes through loud and clear from finance theory. The investor is concerned with assessing risk as well as expected return. In this context, one role of financial statement data is to aid the investor in assessing the risk of the security. But presenting less volatile numbers, we may be doing him a disservice by obscuring the underlying riskiness of his investment. Hence, it is impossible to argue that less volatile numbers per se are better than more volatile numbers. Taken together with the evidence in the efficient market, this suggests that the market can decide for itself how it wishes to interpret a given piece of information. The same sort of reasoning should be applied to the currently hot topic of reporting and attesting to forecasts. In an efficient market, a paternalistic attitude is unwarranted; furthermore, operationally, if it is used to rationalize lesser disclosure, it is much more likely to result in the protection of management than in the protection of investors, which is its ostensible purpose.

Fourth. Accountants must stop acting as if they are the only suppliers of information about the firm. Instead, the FASB should strive to minimize the total cost of providing information to investors. In an efficient market, security prices may be essentially the same under a variety of financial accounting standards, because, if an item is not reported in the financial statements, it may be provided by alternative sources. Under this view, which is consistent with the evidence cited earlier, the market uses a broad information set, and the accountant is one—and only one—supplier of information. One objective is to provide the information to investors by the most economical means. In order to accomplish this objective, several questions must be addressed: What are the alternative sources of information to financial statements? What are the costs of providing a given piece of information via the alternative source vis-à-vis the financial statements? Most importantly, do financial statement data have a comparative advantage in providing any portion of the total information used by the market, and, if so, what portion?

The nature of the costs has already been alluded to. One set of costs is the "cost" of abnormal returns being earned by insiders because of monopolistic access to information. A second set of costs is excessive information costs. They can occur in two situations:

1. When the accountant fails to report an item that must be conveyed to the investing public through some other, more expensive source.

2. When the FASB requires firms to report an item that has a "value" less than its cost or items that could have been reported through other, less expensive sources of information. A third set of costs is incurred when investors erroneously believe that they can "beat the market" using published financial statement information. This set includes excessive transaction costs stemming from churning their accounts, improper diversification because of disproportionately large investment in "underpriced" securities and the selection of improper risk levels.[11]

NATURE OF FUTURE RESEARCH

One of the objectives the FASB must face is the establishment of a research program. Several areas should be explored:

1. Although the evidence in favor of market efficiency with respect to published information is considerable, the issue is by no means closed and further work on the particular types of accounting information items is needed.

2. Much more research is needed regarding market efficiency with respect to inside information. Such research will help to specify what the costs of nondisclosure are.

3. Evidence is needed on how individual investors, as opposed to the aggregate prices, react to information. Specifically, what is the process or mechanism by which information reaches individuals and is subsequently impounded in prices? What evidence is there of excessive transactions costs' being incurred by investors who act on information that already has been impounded in prices? Research into volume activity, as opposed to price activity, may be particularly insightful here. What evidence is there that individuals incur improper selection of risk levels by taking speculative positions based on accounting data? There are currently research methods available in finance that can provide at least a partial answer to these questions. The application of behavioral science also offers promise here.

4. More research is needed regarding the association between certain specific financial statement items and security prices. For example, are there certain items that are now being reported which do not seem to be used by the market as reflected in security prices? Conversely, are there certain types of information which are not currently reported but, in spite of that fact, are reflected in security prices? In the former instance, such items are candidates for being considered for possible exclusion from currently reported items. With respect to the latter, such items are candidates for being considered part of currently reported items.

---

[11]The costs of holding erroneous beliefs regarding market efficiency extend beyond investors. For example, consider the recent decision by Chrysler to change inventory methods because of alleged inefficiencies in the capital markets (both debt and equity markets). Even though Chrysler had reported supplemental statements in its previous annual reports, this was judged to be inadequate to overcome the inability of the capital market to look behind the reported numbers. The initial effect of a switch in inventory methods for both book and tax purposes was an incremental tax bill of approximately $50 million spread over a 20-year period. The efficient market evidence suggests that such a decision was a serious misallocation of resources. In fact, if anything, Chrysler is in worse economic position now because it is paying higher tax bills. For a summary of facts, see "Chrysler Posts $7.6 Million Loss for the Year," *The Wall Street Journal*, February 10, 1971.

5. Further research is needed to examine to what extent financial statement data are helpful to individual investors assessing the risk of a security. In an efficient market, the usefulness of financial statement data to individual investors is not to find mispriced securities, since they are nonexistent. What then is the value, if any? The value lies in the ability of financial statement data to aid in risk prediction. Some recent findings in the area by Beaver, Kettler and Scholes are encouraging, but much more research is needed.[12]

ERRONEOUS INTERPRETATIONS

The implications of market efficiency for accounting are frequently misunderstood. There are at least two common misinterpretations.

The first belief is that, in an efficient market world, there are no reporting issues of substance because of the "all-knowing" efficient market. Taken to its extreme, this error takes the form of asserting that accounting data have no value and hence the certification process is of no value.[13] The efficient market in no way leads to such implications. It may very well be that the publishing of financial statements data is precisely what makes the market as efficient as it is. As I was careful to point out earlier, merely because the market is efficient with respect to published data does not imply that market prices are also efficient with respect to nonpublished information. Disclosure is a substantive issue.

A second erroneous implication is simply to find out what method is most highly associated with security prices and report that method in the financial statements. As it stands, it is incorrect for several reasons. One major reason is that such a simplified decision rule fails to consider the costs of providing information. For example, a nonreported method may be less associated with security prices than the reported method because the cost of obtaining the nonreported numbers via alternative sources is too high. Yet such information may be provided via financial statements at substantially lower costs. In another context, suppose the nonreported method showed the higher association with security prices; does it follow that the nonreported method should be reported? No, not necessarily. Perhaps the market is obtaining the information at lower cost via the alternative sources.[14]

---

[12]W. Beaver, R. Kettler and M. Scholes, "The Association Between Market Determined and Accounting Determined Risk Measures," *The Accounting Review,* October 1970, pp. 654–82.

[13]In this regard it is imperative to distinguish between two important aspects of information: (1) The first is to aid the market in arriving at a given set of security prices. One aspect of this role is to provide a market where the investors are playing a fair game with respect to some given information set (e.g., accounting data). (2) The second is to aid individual investors, who face a given set of prices, to select the optimal portfolio. One aspect of this role is the use of financial statement data in risk prediction. It is entirely possible that future research will discover that financial statement data have no role to play at the individual investor level and that the sole role is a social one. In any event, the social level is of paramount concern to a policy-making body such as the FASB. The distinction is made particularly clear in E. Fama and A. Laffer, "Information and Capital Markets," *Journal of Business,* July 1971, pp. 289–98; and J. Hirshleifer, "The Private and Social Value of Information and Reward to Inventive Activity," *American Economic Review,* September 1971, pp. 561–74; see also, W. Beaver, *op. cit.,* pp. 424–25.

[14]These issues are discussed at greater length in R. May and G. Sundem, "Cost of Information and Security Prices: Market Association Tests for Accounting Policy Decision," *The Accounting Review,* January 1973, pp. 80–94.

Moreover, the choice among different accounting methods involves choosing among differing consequences, as reflected in the incidence of costs and security prices which affect individuals differently. Hence, some individuals may be better off under one method, while others may be better off under an alternative method. In this situation, how is the optimal method to be selected? The issue is one of social choice, which in general is an unresolvable problem because of the difficulty (impossibility) of making interpersonal welfare comparisons.[15]

There are certain specific issues (e.g., similar to those discussed in this article) which closely suggest a policy decision, if one is willing to accept the mild ethical assumption of Pareto-optimality.[16] However, such situations must meet a fairly specific set of conditions.

Regardless of the final resolution by the policymaker, it is still possible to specify the types of evidence that are relevant to choosing among alternatives. In simplest terms, although evidence cannot indicate what choice to make, it can provide information on the potential consequences of the various choices. Without a knowledge of consequences (e.g., as reflected in security prices), it is inconceivable that a policy-making body such as the FASB will be able to select optimal financial accounting standards. In spite of the importance of a knowledge of consequences, currently too little is known about price behavior and virtually nothing is known about the magnitude of the three types of costs outlined earlier.

CONCLUSION

Financial statement information is inherently a social commodity. However, it is clear that decisions regarding its generation and dissemination are of a much different nature than we have traditionally thought them to be. This change in the way we view the FASB is conditioned upon the assumption of market efficiency. While there is need for further research in this area, there is sufficient credibility in the evidence to date that we should be prepared to face its implications:

1. Many reporting issues are capable of a simple disclosure solution and do not warrant an expenditure of FASB time and resources in attempting to resolve them.

2. The role of accounting data is to prevent superior returns' accruing from inside information and can be achieved by a policy of much fuller disclosure than is currently required.

3. Financial statements should not be reduced to the level of understanding of the naïve investor.

4. The FASB should strive for policies that will eliminate excessive costs of information.

5. The FASB should sponsor a full-scale research program in the areas indicated, so that it may have some evidence of the consequences of their choices among different sets of financial accounting standards.

---

[15]K. Arrow, *Social Choice and Individual Values* (Yale University Press, 1968). The issue has been discussed in an accounting context in J. Demski, "Choice Among Financial Accounting Alternatives" (unpublished, Stanford University, 1972).

[16]The concept of Pareto-optimality states that a society prefers one alternative to another, if at least some people are better off and no one is worse off.

TOWARD A THEORY OF EQUITABLE AND EFFICIENT ACCOUNTING POLICY

Baruch Lev

Despite extensive research effort in recent decades, satisfactory answers to the fundamental questions concerning the operations and social consequences of accounting regulation still elude us.[1] Particularly intriguing is the question of "why regulation?" What justifies the strict prescriptions regarding the production and dissemination of corporate financial information in the U.S., and to varying degrees in practically all free-market economies? The absence of a compelling justification is manifested, for example, by repeated arguments that such regulation is redundant, since managers have sufficient incentives to disclose voluntarily financial information, or that the existing regulation is ineffective in achieving socially desired goals (e.g., Ross [1979], Grossman and Hart [1980], Benston [1976 and 1979], and Watts and Zimmerman [1979]). Particularly noteworthy is the fact that accounting regulatory institutions

Helpful comments and suggestions were obtained in particular from James Ohlson, and also from Yakov Amihud, William Baumol, Sidney Davidson, Avner Kalay, William Kinney, Haim Mendelson, Artur Raviv, Bret Trueman, and participants of the Stanford Summer Accounting Workshop and Workshops at Columbia and Tel Aviv Universities. I am deeply indebted to all.

Baruch Lev, "Toward a Theory of Equitable and Efficient Accounting Policy," *The Accounting Review,* January 1988, 1–22. Reprinted by permission of the American Accounting Association.

[1]The term "accounting regulation" refers throughout this study to the existing laws, rules, and generally accepted accounting principles concerning the timing, content, and form of periodic (e.g., quarterly and annual) corporate financial reports; other kinds of required filings (e.g., prospectuses and S-8 disclosures); and to the regulations regarding the verification of disclosed information, namely public accounting (auditing).

rarely address in their deliberations and pronouncements, the issue of justifying regulation. A typical example is the FASB's effort to outline the basic concepts and objectives of accounting—the "conceptual framework" project [FASB, 1974, 1976a and b, 1978]. The question of "Why regulation?" was not even raised in the various discussion memoranda, exposure drafts, and statements emanating from this project.

Statements on accounting objectives and procedures generally start from the premise that investors and lenders *use* financial information to make economic decisions, and go on to assume that the mandated provision of such information will improve the allocation of resources. However, even if the usefulness of information is taken for granted, this does not necessarily imply that its disclosure should be *mandated*. Bread, housing, art, books, and, in many countries, higher education satisfy important needs of wide groups of "users," yet the quantities provided and the timing of provision of such goods and services are not mandated by public institutions in the strict manner that financial information is.[2] It might be that the characteristics of information are inherently different from those of other goods and services, creating the need for stricter regulation of the former. Yet, even in the context of widely needed information, the regulation of financial disclosure is unique; why, for example, is such important information as the performance record of doctors, lawyers, and stockbrokers not required to be publicly disclosed and certified in the manner that corporate records are? Thus, a logical link is missing between assuming that financial information is useful and calling for mandated and closely regulated disclosure; usefulness is a necessary but not a sufficient condition for disclosure regulation.[3]

The "why regulation?" question is not the only intriguing one; additional policy questions abound. For example, the FASB repeatedly contends (e.g., [1976b, p. 163]) that the choice of the basic principles and detailed practices governing the disclosure of financial information should be guided by "a standard that specifies the public interest." But, what is this standard? Usefulness of information, a frequently mentioned criterion, is clearly an inadequate standard in a "multi-person" setting of many users with varied preferences and objectives, since usefulness depends on the characteristics of the specific users of information and on their decision environments. What is highly useful information for some investors might be irrelevant or even damaging (e.g., proprietary information) for others. So, what public interest criterion *does* and/or *should* determine the choices made by accounting regulators? Or, yet an-

---

[2]Laws regulating the *quality* of products (e.g., housing codes) are, of course, prevalent. But such regulations do not, in general, stipulate the *quantities* of goods to be produced and the *timing* of deliveries. The Securities laws, on the other hand, stipulate both the quality (e.g., the audit requirement) and the quantity (scope of disclosure and timing) of information to be released by firms. In this sense the regulation of financial information is much stricter and more comprehensive than regulations pertaining to other goods and services.

Moreover, several recent regulations by the SEC appear to have been aimed at affecting the *conduct of firms,* and not only to assure proper disclosure. Such a use of disclosure power to achieve substantive results is evident, for example, in the required disclosures bearing on the independence of corporate board members and management compensation. Such disclosure requirements probably had substantive effects on the compositions of boards (e.g., increasing the number of outside members), and on the structure of management compensation systems. For elaboration on these substantive aims of disclosure regulations, see Cohen [1981].

[3]To be sure, various attempts have been made to justify disclosure regulation on the basis of alleged "market failures," or to ascribe its existence to regulators' selfish motives or to "historical accidents." I will elaborate in Section III on these regulatory explanations and why I find them unsatisfactory.

other largely unanswered policy question—how should the social consequences of accounting regulation be evaluated and the effectiveness of these policies determined? Even within the empirical stock market-based research paradigm so widely used by researchers, implications for social desirability can be drawn only under very strong assumptions (see Lev and Ohlson [1982, section 3.1]). It is not clear whether other research methods (e.g., laboratory experiments) will be more successful in evaluating accounting regulation consequences.

One must conclude, therefore, that despite increased awareness of the issues involved, little progress has thus far been made in addressing the basic accounting policy issues. In fairness, similar criticism can be levelled at most other (non-accounting) forms of regulation and government interventions for which the justification and social consequences are not well established. Indeed, it might be the case that some of the obstacles preventing a clearer understanding of the above policy issues are not unique to accounting regulation. Nevertheless, this does not diminish the relevance of these issues for accountants, particularly given the major impact of disclosure regulation on the development of accounting research and practice.

I argue below that progress in addressing the fundamental accounting policy issues can be achieved by expanding the scope of analysis to include an explicit concern of policymakers—*equity* in capital markets:

> Persons who design public policy are, typically, at least as concerned with issues of equity as with allocative efficiency. The economist's influence is therefore impeded by his inability to deal with issues of fairness in applied problems. [Baumol, 1982, p. 639]

Equity is defined in this study (Section I) as equality of opportunity—an equal access to information relevant for asset valuation. Or, in the more familiar parlance—a state of symmetric distribution of information across investors. Equity considerations obviously extend beyond the Pareto concepts which traditionally guide economic and accounting researchers in the study of policy issues.[4] It will be argued (Section II) that *in*equity in capital markets resulting from information asymmetry can and does occur, and that its social consequences in the form of high transaction costs, thin markets, low liquidity and, in general—decreased gains from trade, are indeed very undesirable. This will lead to the formulation of an equity-oriented accounting policy which will provide the justification for mandating the disclosure of financial information (Section III). Furthermore, this equity objective appears to provide policymakers with a clearer, more operational "public interest" choice criterion than currently exists (Section IV), and opens to researchers an agenda for the study of policy effectiveness and the evaluation of social consequences (Section V).

It should be pointed out at the outset that the equity orientation presented here is not a traditional call for fairness or for defending the "small investors" against fraud and exploitation by insiders. Unconvincing motivations for regulation, such as falsely portraying individual investors as defenseless, effectively dampened the interest of most researchers in equity issues. In contrast, the equity concerns presented here are linked directly to recent, important finance

---

[4]A characteristic example is Watts [1980, p. 153], who defines the "public interest" objective of accounting regulation in terms of Pareto efficiency: "I shall define public interest in the manner long used by economists and some politicians, namely, as Pareto optimality or economic efficiency."

and economic theoretical developments, and as such, provide a rich foundation for equity-oriented research.

I. EQUITY AND INFORMATION DISTRIBUTION

There is a vast literature exploring equity, fairness, and justice concepts generated primarily by philosophers (for surveys, e.g., Sen [1970, ch. 9] and Rawls [1971]). Recently, various concepts of equity have been discussed in the economics literature and analytically integrated into models and theories. Notable among these are the justice principles of Rawls [1971] and Foley's [1967] equity-as-no-envy concept. These concepts have been applied to a wide array of economic issues, such as policy choices involving natural resources and commodity rationing [Baumol, 1980, 1982, 1986]; labor arbitration devices [Crawford, 1977, 1979, 1980]; fair wage structures [Svensson, 1980]; just allocation of rights [Austinsmith, 1979]; and income distribution and taxation [Allingham, 1976; Archibald and Donaldson, 1979; and Howe and Roemer, 1981]. There is thus an increasing awareness among economists that policy decisions are at least partially motivated by equity considerations.

At this preliminary stage in the application of the concept of equity to accounting it seems appropriate to use a relatively broad definition of equity—equality of opportunity. This definition is attractive because it is widely accepted as a goal of public policy and is proclaimed as such in public debate, party platforms, political speeches, and tracts on educational and social reform. It is even argued that equality of opportunity, as opposed to equality of actual outcomes, should be the sole principle of justice guiding government decisions (e.g., Joseph and Sumption [1979]).

A major characteristic of equality of opportunity is that it is an *ex ante* concept of equity, as opposed to the more familiar *ex post* concepts of justice that call for equality of actual outcomes. The two are not independent, of course. Intuitively, increasing equality of opportunity will contribute significantly to equality of outcomes [Okun, 1975]. The main attraction of the *ex ante* equality of opportunity concept is that it conflicts less with efficiency incentives than do the egalitarian *ex post* concepts of equity. Equalizing opportunities allows for more incentives to work and invest than does equalizing actual income or wealth. Thus, the equity-efficiency conflicts that frequently concern policymakers are mitigated when equality of opportunity is chosen as the guiding concept of equity.

When application to capital markets and information disclosure is considered, the superiority of an *ex ante*-based definition of equity is clear. Any mechanism that leads to equalization of actual outcomes across investors in capital markets will not only eliminate all incentives (e.g., to search for information) but also strip the stock market of its main attraction—the provision of a wide variety of risk-return alternatives to investors. No rewards for risk-taking are possible when differences in realized outcomes are redressed, *ex post,* in an egalitarian way.

It is postulated here that in the context of capital markets, inequality of opportunity is present when investors are endowed with different information about securities or market mechanisms, a situation known as differential, or asymmetric, information. This follows the path taken by information economic models, which show that the existence of information asymmetries is the major reason for systematic, *ex ante* risk-adjusted return differentials across investors.[5] That is, equality of opportunity is obtained when all investors are equally endowed with information, since in this case risk-adjusted expected returns would be identical across investors.[6]

The proposed definition of equity as equality of opportunity or symmetric information is appealing for accounting research since it lends itself to both theoretical analysis and empirical quantification. The extent of equality of opportunity can be defined and measured by the differences in expected, risk-adjusted excess returns across investor classes. Obviously, when market prices are fully informative—a special case of equality of opportunity—this measure will be zero. Furthermore, the effects of changes in the information environment (e.g., a new disclosure rule) on equality of opportunity can be evaluated on the basis of changes in such inequality measures as the disparity of expected returns. An equity-based accounting policy can thus be rigorously defined and its social consequences assessed quantitatively in terms of decreases in information asymmetries, or changes in observable variables affected by information asymmetries, such as bid-ask spreads and volumes of trade. Sections IV and V elaborate on the measurement and applications of the above concept of equity.

It is sometimes argued that since any investor could become informed if he chose to (e.g., analyze financial statements, subscribe to analysts' reports), differential information across investors could not be regarded as inequitable. Following the classical paradigm, each investor will acquire information until his or her marginal cost equals the marginal benefit of information. However, this laissez faire/perfect competition type of argument ignores an important characteristic of information—increasing returns to scale—which might endow some investors with monopolistic rents and effectively bar others from becoming informed. This characteristic was noted by Arrow [1974, pp. 38–39]:

> The main remark that can be ventured on now is the familiar one that there are increasing returns to the *uses* of information. The same body of technological information, for example, can be used in production on any scale and therefore

---

[5]For example, Grossman and Stiglitz [1976, p. 248, emphasis added] comment:

> Prices do not fully reflect all available information, in particular, that of the informed; the informed *do a better job* in allocating their portfolio than the uninformed.

This "better job," reflected in excess returns (above the competitive level), is thus ascribed to information asymmetries. Or:

> the effect of knowing more than others, *ceteris paribus,* in this case as well as in general, is to be able to improve upon one's welfare at the expense of those who know less. [Hakansson, 1981, p. 15]

While information asymmetries are obviously the major reason for differential expected returns, there might be additional reasons, such as transaction costs.

[6]Note that I define equality of opportunity as equal expected returns, while economic analysis is generally couched in terms of *utilities* of returns. This is a known inconsistency resulting from the need in equity analysis to compare situations across individuals; utilities, of course, cannot be cross-sectionally compared. Rawls [1971, p. 155] notes:

> The essential point though is that in justice as fairness the parties do not know their conception of the good and cannot estimate their utility in the ordinary sense. In any case, we want to go behind *de facto* preferences generated by given conditions. Therefore, expectations are based upon an index of primary goods and the parties make their choice accordingly. The entries in the example are in terms of money and not utility to indicate this aspect of the contract doctrine.

For elaboration of this issue in an economic context, see Howe and Roemer [1981].

towards productive enterprises with some degree of monopoly power, in accordance with familiar principles.

This applies where the value of information is independent of the choice of scale, or investment, and it seems to be the case for persons investing in human capital (e.g., learning and experience in the analysis of corporate financial statements), or in the development of analytical tools and techniques that can be applied repetitively to many investments (e.g., a bankruptcy prediction model, an earnings forecast model, a systematic risk estimation technique, or a "program trading" mechanism). Following Arrow's intuition, Wilson [1975] proved that there are indeed *increasing returns to scale* in the production of information: the cost of information per unit of scale declines as the scale increases, whereas the value of information per unit scale does not change—"The net result is ever-increasing expected returns to scale" [Wilson, 1975, p. 189]. Consequently, the possibility of monopolistic behavior by large-scale information producers and users arises. Accordingly, at relatively low levels of investment, acquisition of information may not be economically justifiable, whereas larger investment operations will justify becoming informed and will be associated with excess (at the limit—unbounded) returns. Thus, well-endowed investors operating on a large scale can be expected to earn a higher return on their investments than less endowed investors, given that the former have access to certain kinds of information which are characterized by increasing returns to scale. Indeed, Feldstein and Yitzhaki [1982] recently reported that wealthy investors earn a substantially higher return on their investments than do low-income investors.

Thus, classical equity concerns, resulting from the possibility of high-income investors gaining monopoly rents, and low-income investors facing barriers-to-entry into the information market, cannot be *a priori* ruled out. However, as argued in the next section, the equity orientation presented here is of a broader scope and applies even to cases where information yields competitive returns.

II. The Social Consequences of Inequity in Capital Markets

The traditional view, often espoused by policymakers and accountants, that there is a need to protect the "small" (presumably uninformed) investor was probably derived from genuine concerns about inequities in capital markets. However, the call for regulation to redress such inequities was generally phrased in vague, naive and somewhat paternalistic terms suggesting that uninformed investors were at the mercy of market insiders. This rather unconvincing plea for regulation, emphasizing *fraud* as the major hazard to investors, effectively dampened the interest of modern accounting and economic researchers in equity issues. A typical example is Ross [1979, p. 190], who dismisses equity considerations in disclosure regulation because they are based on such "defenseless investor" arguments:

> The equity benefits of [*disclosure*] legislation—as between insiders and outsiders—are more difficult to identify. The case for such benefits seems to rest on the traditional view that outsiders are at the mercy of insiders, and need to be protected from them.[7]

---

[7]See, also, Beaver [1981, ch. 7] for criticism of the traditional equity motivation of disclosure regulation.

The equity concern that underlies the thesis of this study stems from an entirely different perspective. The core idea, in contrast to the traditional view, is that uninformed investors are far from defenseless. Indeed, they have at their disposal a wide array of measures capable of protecting them against exploitation by the informed.

The uninformed can defend themselves by minimizing trade with the informed, that is by buying and holding well-diversified portfolios for the long run. Alternatively, the uninformed can identify specific groups of insiders, such as managers, and prohibit them, by legal or contractual arrangements, from trading in the securities of their own firms. At the extreme, suspecting gross information asymmetries, uninformed investors may quite rationally withdraw from trading in specific securities or from the stock market altogether.[8] Note that each of these protective measures is costly to both the informed *and* uninformed investors, as well as to the economy as a whole. Thus, holding securities for the long run denies investors the benefits of portfolio rearrangements as economic circumstances change. Prohibiting managers from trading in the securities of their firms decreases the benefits from owning such stocks, which, in turn, limits the usefulness of managerial stock ownership in aligning the interests of owners and managers (reduction of agency costs). A massive withdrawal of uninformed investors from the market will strip the informed of the benefits of their costly-acquired information (thereby decreasing incentive for information production), and will deprive the economy of the allocational and risk sharing benefits of large and efficient capital markets. Herein, therefore, should lie our concern with inequity in capital markets. It stems from the adverse social effects brought about by the defensive measures taken by uninformed investors who perceive significant inequity.

The economic consequences of the protective measures taken by less informed investors when facing informed ones are demonstrated rigorously by recent models of the capital market microstructure. These models establish a direct link between information asymmetries (inequity, in our context) and such market characteristics as bid-ask spreads, transaction costs, volume of trade, and social gains from trade. Consider, for example, the recent Glosten and Milgrom [1985] model in which the behavior of the "specialist" (market maker), who matches buyers and sellers, is investigated. The specialist faces two groups of traders: the "informed investors," who know more than he or she does about the specific firm (e.g., knowledge of an impending takeover bid), and the "liquidity traders"—those who either know less than the specialist or those who must trade because of pressing liquidity needs. The basic idea is that the specialist, like any other market participant, will lose, on the average, on trades with the more informed investors, because they will not trade with the specialist unless his or her quoted prices are favorable relative to their information.[9] The specialist must, therefore,

---

[8]For example:

> Concern about asymmetric information among investors could be an important reason why some institutional and individual investors do not invest at all in certain securities, such as shares in relatively small firms with few stockholders. [Merton, 1987, p. 488]

In many stock markets around the world (e.g., in Brazil, Chile, Spain, and Israel) the participation of individual investors is very limited. A frequent explanation provided for this phenomenon is that individuals shy away because these markets are dominated by a few, highly informed investors, rendering investment by individuals an unfair game.

[9]For example, Stoll [1976] reported that NASDAQ dealers tend to acquire shares when prices fall and sell when prices rise. Also, dealers' inventories tend to increase on days prior to price declines and decrease prior to price rises. This evidence is consistent with the prediction that dealers lose, on the average, on trades with informed investors.

recoup these losses by gains in trade with the liquidity traders, who incur a "fee" for immediate liquidity. This loss/gain balance is achieved by setting an appropriate bid-ask spread. The bid-ask spread thus serves as a *defensive mechanism* against the specialist's expected losses to more informed investors.[10]

Glosten and Milgrom show that "ask" prices (for the sale of securities by the specialist) will increase and "bid" prices decrease when: (a) the quality of information possessed by the informed investors improves (e.g., becomes less uncertain), and/or (b) the number of informed investors increases relative to liquidity traders. Significant information asymmetries lead the specialist to set the spread so wide as to render the trade in the stock very thin until it might cease to exist altogether:

> One of the interesting features of our model is that there can be occasions on which the market shuts down. Indeed, if the insiders are too numerous or their information is too good, . . . there will be no bid and ask prices at which trading can occur and the specialist can break even. Then, the equilibrium bid price is set so low and the ask price so high as to preclude any trade. . . . A market once closed, will stay closed until the insiders go away or their information is at least partly disseminated to market participants from some other information source. [Glosten and Milgrom, 1985, p. 74]

This specter of a market becoming thinner and eventually being shut down illustrates our earlier statement that uninformed investors suspecting gross inequity will not participate in the market. Note also that Glosten and Milgrom's solution to opening a "closed market" is to publicly disseminate some of the insiders' information. This plays an important role in the following section.

Information asymmetries, or inequity in capital markets, will thus be reflected in relatively wide bid-ask spreads, and the more severe the inequity (due to the number of insiders and/or the extent of their informational advantage), the larger the spreads. The size of spread, in turn, determines the effective transaction costs involved in trading the securities. Therefore, large informational asymmetries will be associated with large transaction costs (Demsetz [1968]; Epps [1976]; Amihud and Mendelson [1980]; and Copeland and Galai [1983]).[11] Furthermore, large spreads and transaction costs will also be associated with low volumes of trade and a lower number of traders (e.g., Glosten and Milgrom [1985]; Hamilton [1978]; Stoll [1985]; and Karpoff [1986]).[12] Recently, Mendelson [1985] has shown that increasing the

---

[10]Another hypothesized motive for maintaining a bid-ask spread is inventory holding costs (see, Garman [1976], and Amihud and Mendelson [1980]). The origins of the informational asymmetry motive for the spread can be traced to Bagehot [1971]. See, also, Copeland and Galai [1983], and Benston and Hagerman [1974].

[11]It is important to note that the effect of information asymmetries on fundamental market characteristics, such as transaction costs and gains from trade, is not limited to securities with large bid-ask spreads. The specialist model outlined above is merely a convenient way of demonstrating this link. Even with heavily traded securities having narrow spreads, investors suspecting serious informational disadvantages will protect themselves by either not trading at the current market price, or by giving "limit orders" that effectively restrict trade. In a limit order, the investor in fact operates as a specialist.

[12]The socially adverse effects of low volumes, reflecting decreased opportunities for risk sharing and withdrawal of investors from the market, can be shown even in cases of homogeneous information. Ohlson and Buckman [1981] show that in such cases information serves the role of markets, namely increases risk sharing by effectively enlarging (enriching) exchange opportunities.

number of traders always increases the expected average gains from trade, that is, the aggregate gain accruing to a community of traders as a result of the market operation. Furthermore, he showed that increasing the number of traders increases the liquidity of the market and decreases the variability of prices.

Thus, based on the above theoretical analysis and empirical evidence, increased information asymmetry, or inequity, is associated with a lower number of investors, higher transaction costs, lower liquidity of securities, thinner volumes of trade and it leads, in general, to decreased social gains from trade. Disclosure regulation, it is argued below, is aimed at mitigating these adverse effects resulting from capital market inequity.

III. THE POLICY QUESTIONS REVISITED

Equipped with an operational concept of equity and with appreciation of the adverse private and social consequences of inequity in capital markets, I now reexamine the largely unanswered policy questions raised in the introduction and consider whether equity analysis can provide insight into:

- Why is the public disclosure of financial information mandated?
- What "public interest" standard should guide regulators?
- How can the social consequences of regulation be evaluated?[13]

WHY DISCLOSURE REGULATION?

How can the adverse consequences of inequity in capital markets be alleviated? The most effective remedy would be to remove the major source of inequity—the informational advantage held by informed investors. This advantage could be decreased by instituting a policy mandating regular and timely public disclosure of information pertinent to the valuation of securities. This, then, provides a justification for disclosure regulation. Reemphasizing, such a public policy is not assumed here to be motivated by an altruistic or politically-oriented desire to assist some persons (e.g., uninformed investors) *at the expense* of others, in a zero-sum sense.[14] Rather, the proposed motivation for disclosure is based on the more economically

---

[13]This is not an exhaustive list of relevant policy issues. Another interesting issue, for example, is the division of regulatory responsibilities between the private and the public sectors, federal and state governments, etc. Currently, disclosure regulation is promulgated by the SEC, the FASB, and, to a lesser extent, by various state laws (e.g., the "blue sky" laws) and by the stock exchanges. Although the pros and cons of the various institutional settings are often discussed (e.g., Chatov [1977], and Easterbrook and Fischel [1984]), the issue of the socially optimal regulatory setting is still an open one. It is not clear at this stage whether equity analysis can contribute to this debate.

[14]Such a zero-sum motivation appears to underlie the well-known objective of information disclosure suggested by the Study Group on the Objectives of Financial Statements [AICPA, 1973, p. 17]:

An objective of financial statements is to serve primarily those users who have limited authority, ability, or resources to obtain information and who rely on financial statements as their principal source of information about an enterprise's economic activities.

The absence of a substantive, theoretically-founded motivation for this objective in the Study Group's report may have contributed to its abandonment by the FASB.

palatable notion that by removing the source of inequity, one lessens the generally harmful effects of the defensive measures that are naturally taken by the uninformed, thereby improving *overall* welfare. This is a well-known principle in public policy:

> It is possible in our society to argue for a government program to help the poor. But, the argument is not that the poor, being part of the winning coalition, should benefit at the expense of others. The argument is that by helping the poor we can make everyone better off, that helping the poor is not merely a means to make the poor happier but a means to reduce crime, make us all feel less guilty, make the cities livable, etc. What may, from the standpoint of wealth, be a (small) redistribution is defended as, from the standpoint of utility, a Pareto improvement. [Friedman, 1980, p. 231]

The complete equity-efficiency consequences of disclosure regulation have yet to be analyzed in detail. Under some circumstances, the transfer of information from the informed to the uninformed via a public disclosure rule will be Pareto preferable, namely will result in some investors being better off while none are worse off, due to the generally increased opportunities for trade and risk-sharing (e.g., through the increased investor base and/or higher liquidity brought about by decreased information asymmetries). Under different circumstances, such a disclosure policy might lead to weaker requirements of improved efficiency, in the sense that a suitable (hypothetical) redistribution of *endowments* will make everyone better off. It is, of course, also possible that some disclosure rules might result in "pure welfare redistribution," namely, in some investors benefitting at the expense of others. It should be emphasized, however, that even if such redistribution cases exist, the possibility of capital markets breaking down due to severe information asymmetries (recall Glosten and Milgrom's scenario, above) justifies disclosure regulation. Such regulation, it is argued here, is intended to shore up markets, and the possibility of a market breakdown is generally more harmful than some wealth redistribution.[15]

More efficient, nonregulatory (decentralized) means of achieving the desired decrease in informational asymmetries are not self-evident. Hypothetically, one can envisage the informed investors, who stand to lose as a group from the existence of significant information asymmetries, colluding to lessen these asymmetries. This could be done, for example, by a voluntary release of financial information by professional organizations such as the Financial Analysts Federation (a case of industry self-regulation).[16] However, such a collusive action by a large number of participants is highly impracticable. Incentives to break away from an arrangement

---

[15]Note that the current discussion is mainly concerned with disclosure policy. There are, of course, additional accounting issues of importance, such as the choice of specific measurement techniques from a given set of alternatives. Such "measurement" issues clearly have considerable impact on various uses of accounting numbers, such as for contracting purposes (e.g., in management compensation systems or loan covenants). However, to the extent that these measurement issues do not affect the extent of information asymmetry in capital markets, they appear to be unrelated to an equity-oriented accounting policy, and hence will not be pursued here.

[16]An interesting example of a voluntary release of information is found in racetrack betting. The programs of many racetracks (listing the horses, trainers, jockeys, etc.) include a prediction of the order of finish provided by the track's official handicapper. This prediction, sometimes known as the "selection," is based on a plethora of information about the past performance of the horses, jockey, and trainer standings, etc. The voluntary provision of such summary information is probably aimed at increasing the participation in betting by uninformed persons, by decreasing the informational advantage of the experts.

of this sort abound, since the *private* gains to some informed investors from exploitation of information will probably outweigh their loss from informational asymmetries.[17] As for the oft-mentioned argument that firms, motivated by self-interest, will voluntarily release financial information (the "disclosure principle" in, e.g., Ross [1979]), it seems highly likely that such private incentives may leave disclosure at a suboptimal level. Theory suggests that impediments to such voluntary release of information abound; for example, unless investors know that managers have the required information, there will be no incentives for the latter to release it (e.g., Dye [1985], Easterbrook and Fischel [1984]). Furthermore, empirical evidence also appears to be inconsistent with such voluntary release of information (Lev and Penman [1987]). Therefore, it seems fair to conclude that decentralized, self-regulatory alternatives to disclosure regulation, aimed at enhancing equity in capital markets, are not readily available.

The equity-oriented justification for disclosure regulation does not, of course, preclude the existence of other regulatory motives. However, the equity motive seems to be more compelling than others, mainly because it is not country- or period-specific as most other explanations are, and therefore applies well to a world-wide, persistent phenomenon such as disclosure regulation. Consider, for example, the argument that regulators are not really concerned with economic efficiency or with equity, rather their primary goals are: (a) to serve the needs of organized interest groups (e.g., security analysts, or public accountants), (b) to expand the scope of their own operations and power base, or (c) to avoid public scandals. These "political process" arguments view bureaucrats as seeking to transfer wealth among competing interest groups, where they themselves constitute one such group (for elaboration, see Watts and Zimmerman [1986, ch. 10]). While there is some general validity in these arguments, they do not provide, in my opinion, a convincing explanation for the prolonged existence and continuous expansion of disclosure regulation in virtually all free market economies.

Consider, for example, the "interest-groups" (or the "capture theory") argument which suggests that regulation is intended to benefit specific groups of market participants. Such groups vary considerably across countries in their power and structure (e.g., in many countries such as Israel, financial analysts and brokers are few and poorly organized, and public accountants do not enjoy strong political influence), yet extensive and quite uniform disclosure regulation is almost universal. Furthermore, the preliminary empirical evidence that exists on this issue in a non-accounting context does not support the "interest-groups" argument (e.g., Schwert [1977], and Kalt and Zupan [1984]).[18] As to the "power-base increasing" argument, how can one explain the fact that since 1934 the SEC has largely relinquished its all-important

---

[17]An analogy with agency theory suggests itself here. This theory postulates that it is often in the interest of agents (managers) to alleviate the concern of principals (owners) regarding the excessive appropriation of perquisites, by such means as a voluntary provision of information, bonding devices, or independent audits. Here, we argue, it is sometimes in the interest of informed investors to increase equity in capital markets in order to attract uninformed investors. The analogy stops here, however; whereas top management is a small, cohesive group that can easily collude in order to decrease agency costs, informed investors cannot effectively collude to decrease information asymmetries.

[18]Easterbrook and Fischel [1984, p. 672] note:

> The interest group explanation that might account for securities legislation also could explain airline and trucking regulation. Yet these systems have been almost obliterated. Perhaps securities laws have survived because they are not predominantly interest-group legislation. . . . We are less confident, however, that interest-group support is the sole explanation for securities regulation. We think it appropriate, therefore, to search for the "public interest" justification of those laws.

and powerful authority to set accounting standards to private-sector organizations, such as the APB and the FASB? What is more "power-base increasing" in the capital market context than the power to set accounting standards?[19] Also, changes in the political environment cannot be ignored. Both the current and previous administrations have significantly curtailed the scope of several regulatory agencies, such as the Civil Aeronautics Board and the Federal Trade Commission, despite the strongly vested interests and the "power base" motives involved.[20] Even the securities laws were curtailed, such as the 1975 deregulation of exchange services (brokers' price-fixing). Disclosure regulation, on the other hand, appears to withstand political changes. Thus, despite the possible validity of the politically-motivated arguments in other contexts, they do not appear to provide a satisfactory explanation for the pervasiveness of disclosure regulation across time, different cultures, economic regimes, and capital market structures.

Similar reservations apply to the "historical accident" explanation for regulation, namely that the securities acts arose as a response to the Depression-era financial crisis. While the timing of the securities acts in the U.S. was undoubtedly affected by the financial crisis of the 1930s, it is hard to attribute the unique persistence and continued expansion of this regulation to an event that occurred over 50 years ago, particularly as so many other Depression-related regulations fell by the wayside:

> The Securities Act of 1933 and the Securities Exchange Act of 1934 have escaped the fate of many other early New Deal programs. Some of their companions, such as the National Industrial Recovery Act, were declared unconstitutional; others, such as the Robinson-Patman Act, have fallen into desuetude; still others, such as Social Security, have been so changed that they would be unrecognizable to their creators. Many of the New Deal programs of regulation lost their political support and were replaced by deregulation; communications and transportation are prime examples. The securities laws, however, have retained not only their support but also their structure. [Easterbrook and Fischel, 1984, p. 669]

Moreover, the universality of similar disclosure regulations across practically all free market economies—a phenomenon of major importance which is emphasized throughout this study—is inconsistent with the "historical accident" argument. Historical accidents are usually country- and period-specific, making it difficult to argue that they explain persistent, worldwide phenomena. On the other hand, the above-proposed equity justification for disclosure regulation appears consistent with such phenomena.

---

[19]This statement is not generally accepted. William Kinney, for example, commented in private communication:

> The SEC may have "relinquished" its accounting rule making authority because it did not believe it was important, thought it was too costly or thought that it would expose the Commission to complaints *ex ante* and risk of being held responsible for disclosure-based scandals *ex post*.

[20]Note, for example, a recent statement in the *Wall Street Journal* (February 24, 1986, p. 6): "The Reagan Administration sent the U.S. Congress the biggest liberalization ever of the country's antitrust laws last week, widely thought of as America's guarantee against monopolization and predation in the marketplace. The package will make it harder for the Justice Department to ban mergers. . . . Douglas Ginzberg, the administration's assistant attorney general for antitrust, said that in the coming congressional scrutiny of the package, 'I think that what will emerge, and perhaps surprise some, will be the nonemotional character of the debate.'"

IV. AN OPERATIONAL PUBLIC-INTEREST CRITERION

Given that the enhancement of equity in financial markets is (or should be) a major public-interest objective of accounting policymakers, how can such an objective be operationalized? What equity criteria or guidelines should direct regulators in their choice of accounting disclosure rules? First, consider briefly the criteria that guide policymakers, particularly the FASB, at present. The basic premise underlying the FASB's activities is that:

> the principal role of financial reporting [is] to furnish the investor and lender with information useful to assess the prospective risks and returns associated with an investment. [FASB, 1976b, pp. 3–4]

However, given our limited knowledge of the specific information modes that are useful in assessing prospective risks and returns (e.g., are accrual earnings superior to cash flows?), it is not surprising that a general objective such as the aforementioned can hardly guide accounting policymakers in specific information choices.[21] The attempt to fall back on *qualities* of useful financial information, such as relevance, measurability and reliability, has also not been very successful. Not only are there fundamental conflicts among various desired qualities (e.g., the more relevant the information, say earnings forecasts, the lower in general its verifiability), but sole reliance on such qualities ignores a basic characteristic of information: the value (relevance) of an information item cannot be determined outside a specific decision context. There is no such thing as universally superior, or relevant information.

We thus reach the well-known impasse: given our limited knowledge of valuation-relevant information and the existence of diverse users of financial information (having diverse endowments, preferences, and information), it is not clear what criteria should guide policymakers in their disclosure choices, except for the rare situations in which *everybody* can be made better off (no conflict situation). The following statement by the FASB [1976b, p. 157; see, also, Arthur Andersen, 1960] appears to recognize this problem:

> Financial statements are used by various parties with often opposed interests, and information in those statements should not favor one interest to the detriment of another.

However, such "evenhandedness," or fairness of information is obviously impossible to achieve in most situations.[22] This led the FASB to recognize the need for a social desirability criterion:

> Since the arguments on both sides [*for and against a proposed accounting change*] are often biased by self-interest or preconceptions about the public interest, it is necessary to air those differences of opinion and the arguments for and against them. But no objective solution is possible in the absence of a standard that specifies the

---

[21]The situation is even more complicated, since even if the specific information modes needed for "assessing prospective risks and returns" were known, the welfare implications of a mandated public disclosure of this information would be very difficult to ascertain in a Pareto-efficiency context.

[22]See Ball [1987] for a different interpretation of fairness in a contracting context.

public interest or the most desirable effect on the economy or society. [FASB, 1976b, p. 163]

But, what is this elusive standard that "specifies the public interest"?
The equity objective seems to provide such a standard:

The interests of the less informed investors should, in general, be favored over those of the more informed investors.

Such a public policy, consistently applied, will contribute to equality of opportunity in financial markets through the decrease of information asymmetries and the increase in the degree of informativeness of prices, thereby alleviating the socially harmful effects of inequity discussed in Section II. Can this equity criterion of continuously decreasing information asymmetries be operationalized to provide plausible standards for accounting policymakers? Is it more operational than the current goal of searching for information that will be "useful in making investment decisions"? I believe it is, since identifying specific information items that are, at a given point in time, at the disposal of some investors while not of others seems a more manageable task than establishing whether and what information is in some sense useful (the current goal). The former is a matter of fact while the latter is, for the time being at least, a matter of judgment or, worse yet, speculation.

Consider a specific example—the public disclosure in financial statements of management's forecasts of earnings. The issue is obviously complex: the predictive quality of such forecasts, the legal liability of managers and auditors, the associated "moral hazard" of managers, and the possible compromise of company secrets, are examples of the potential problems associated with mandating the disclosure of earnings forecast. Accordingly, determining the social usefulness of such information from an allocative efficiency point of view seems, at present, an insurmountable task. However, from an equity perspective, this choice is more tractable. Two facts, potentially leading to inequality of opportunity in financial markets, seem indisputable: (a) information on management's perceptions of future earnings is asymmetrically distributed (probably known to the firm's bankers and major investors, in addition to corporate insiders), and (b) the use of such forecasts in investment decisions leads to excess returns. Evidence from voluntary releases suggests that many of these earnings forecasts are of high quality, relative to extrapolative forecasts (e.g., Brown and Rozeff [1978]), and that timely access to them yields abnormal rates of return (e.g., Patell [1976] and Penman [1980]). Therefore, from an equity perspective of decreasing information asymmetries, these facts seem sufficient to justify mandating the disclosure of earnings forecasts in financial statements, or preferably in more timely public releases.

How can an equity-oriented accounting policy aimed at identifying information items which are not in the public domain and could lead to excess returns, be operationally pursued? One approach is to investigate the operations of analysts or institutional investors who presumably are privy to inside information. For example, Leftwich [1983], in a different context, identified the typical information items used in lending decisions. Some of these items are not publicly disclosed, and tests can be conducted to determine whether the use of such information in, say, stock valuation models, leads to excess returns. Collins [1975] used a similar method in the context of lines-of-business reporting, showing that investors with private access to lines-of-business information prior to 1970 (when the release of such information became mandatory) could have gained excess returns. A similar, market-based methodology can identify items which are not currently disclosed in financial statements and that can possibly lead to excess returns. The set of candidates for such disclosures should extend beyond conventional financial data. For example, unfilled orders of manufacturers of durable goods—a leading indicator of future performance, or data on seat occupancy (load factor) of airlines, are potentially value-relevant information items which are known to some individuals outside the firm. It would, therefore, be instructive to examine empirically whether the use of such information is associated with excess returns.

The search for asymmetrically distributed information items, possibly leading to excess returns, can be aided by stock valuation and other economic models. For example, Bulow and Shoven [1978] developed a model in which the timing of corporate bankruptcy and the extent of creditors' losses depend, among other things, on the liquidation value of the firm's assets. Data on liquidation values might therefore be of importance to some investors, particularly unsecured creditors. Another example, is the extension of the Capital Asset Pricing Model to multi-product firms (Rubinstein [1973] and Collins and Simonds [1979]) where the firm's risk is shown to depend on the proportions of the total resources committed to the production of each product-line. This suggests the desirability of disclosing assets by product-lines, in addition to the currently required disclosure of sales and profits. Thus, the search for asymmetrically distributed information possibly leading to excess returns is an obvious area in which both theoretical and empirical research can be of direct usefulness to equity-oriented policymakers.

Finally, the policy of decreasing information asymmetries advocated here treats the informed investors as one group; in particular, it appears to make no distinction between a *costly* acquisition of information by the informed (say, financial analysts) and other means of getting informed. However, it is sometimes argued that there is no inequity involved in gains derived from the use of costly acquired information. On the contrary, goes the argument, such an endeavor should be encouraged since it increases market efficiency. On a closer examination, however, the distinction between costly and "non-costly" acquired information seems nonexistent; *any* acquisition of information is costly, in a direct or indirect way. Suppose, for example, that managers have a monopolistic access to information about their firms and that such information could be used by them to yield excess returns. Clearly, even such inside information will not be costless to managers, since competition in managerial labor markets will cause the expected rents from using the information to be reflected in lower managerial compensation. It is not clear, therefore, that there is a meaningful distinction between costly (presumably equitable) and costless acquisition of information. (There is, clearly, an important distinction between information benefits—competitive or monopolistic rents, discussed in Section I.)

Moreover, it is important to note that the adverse effects of information asymmetries, discussed in Section II, apply equally to cases where the "informed" acquired their information through research and analysis as well as to other means of information acquisition. Irrespective of the sources and costs of information, significant information asymmetries will result in socially adverse effects. Accordingly, it would be socially beneficial to reduce *to a certain extent* significant information asymmetries, even if they were obtained "legitimately," by research and analysis. Such a reduction of information asymmetries, through a mandated disclosure policy, will in general benefit even the active information searchers, as it will increase the number of investors in the market, improve liquidity and reduce transaction costs. Therefore, and contrary to widespread beliefs, incentives for information search will not necessarily be reduced by disclosure regulation.[23] In any case, the challenge to accounting researchers and policymakers is to design such information disclosure policies that will minimize the equity-efficiency conflicts.

V. Evaluation of Regulation Consequences

The evaluation of social consequences is an integral part of any public policy; it provides the basic input for the continuing process of assessment and restructuring of such policies. In recent years, the evaluation of accounting policy has focused on examining the impact of regulatory changes on the characteristics of stock prices.

Although such impact is of considerable interest, it does not directly address the issue of policy desirability, unless one makes strong assumptions (see Lev and Ohlson [1982]). Even a regulation change that leads to a rise in the stock prices of the affected firms cannot be unambiguously labelled socially desirable. Moreover, the preoccupation of current research with *average* beliefs and stock price reactions to informational events precludes the consideration of important equity issues, such as who gains and who loses from the informational change, and by how much. Additional lines of research should, therefore, be pursued in order to assess the social consequences of accounting policy. Several suggestions follow.

Bid-Ask Spreads and Volume Effects

The theory discussed in Section II suggests that the extent of information asymmetries will be reflected in the size of bid-ask spreads and in the level of volume of trade. Indeed, empirical evidence (e.g., Benston and Hagerman [1974], Morse and Ushman [1983], and Venkatesh and Chiang [1986]) supports the relation between information asymmetries and bid-ask spreads. Accordingly, the effectiveness of disclosure regulations, aimed at increasing capital market equity (i.e., lessening information asymmetries), can be determined by examining whether changes in average bid-ask spreads and trade volumes of the affected securities occurred subsequent to the regulation enactment. Or, by searching for the existence of cross-sectional differences in these variables between securities impacted by specific regulations (e.g., oil and gas) and those not affected by the regulation. The social-desirability implications of trade-volume studies [Lev and Ohlson, 1982, sec. 3.1] are still not fully appreciated by accounting re-

---

[23]This important point, which also plays a role in the current debate about the SEC's enforcement of insider-trading rules, appears to be lost on the debaters. Witness, for example, the following argument:

> On the one hand of the spectrum [*of the definition of insider trading*] are the advocates of the equity-based definition of inside activity, sometimes known as the "equal-information" theory. In this view anyone making a trade based on superior information is in effect "stealing" from other market participants by acting before all other stockholders. . . . Economists have questioned—indeed fought against—the equal information theory from its inception. They have argued that superior information, legally obtained, is fundamental to trading activity and efficiency in the stock market. [Jarrell and Pound, 1987, p. 38]

Here again, the equity ("equal information") approach is phrased in moralistic terms—"stealing from other market participants"—and is pitted against the economic/market efficiency approach. The important point missed here and so often elsewhere is that the "two approaches" are essentially one and the same: As argued in this study, it is not the "stealing" of information that is of major social concern, but that significant inequality (asymmetry) of information will lead to adverse economic consequences which will ultimately result in reduced market efficiency.

searchers. Welfare analysis essentially deals with *actions* of individuals rather than with changes in beliefs. The former are most clearly picked up by trading volume while the latter are indicated by price changes, which is generally the variable examined by accounting researchers. Note that the use of a trade-volume variable (e.g., Beaver [1968], Morse [1981], and Bamber [1986]) was aimed at inferring the information content of specific releases, such as earnings, from volume changes *at* disclosure date. On the other hand, the research approach suggested here is aimed at examining longer-term changes in average volumes, before and after significant regulation changes. As to the use of bid-ask spreads, the effects of regulatory changes on such spreads to infer equity changes have not been investigated so far, although it seems rather straightforward to extend current market-based research in this direction.

CHANGES IN PRICE INFORMATIVENESS

Ceteris paribus, the more informative security prices, the less, on the average, the potential gain in excess returns to informed investors. Thus, an increase in the degree of price informativeness (due, say, to mandated information disclosure) will enhance equity by decreasing, on the average, the expected returns to inside information. Empirical tests examining whether changes in price informativeness are associated with specific regulations can therefore be regarded as tests of the equity consequences of accounting policy. The degree of informativeness of prices can be inferred from the extent of price variability around the disclosure date of an information item, such as quarterly earnings. Ohlson [1979] showed that the more informative prices are, the lower their variance (response) will be at the time of the information disclosure. This was empirically supported, for example, by McNichols and Manegold [1983] who found that the variability of prices upon the release of annual earnings that were not preceded by quarterly disclosures were higher than those where annual earnings disclosures were preceded by quarterly earnings disclosures. Prices in the former cases were evidently less informative than in the latter. Similarly, Atiase [1985] and Grant [1980] reported that price variability on the earnings release date of small OTC firms was higher than for large NYSE firms. This differential reaction of prices to earnings disclosure can be attributed to the smaller amount of information available (or demanded) about small firms than about larger ones (or, to some extent, to differential stock exchange regulations).

The aforementioned method can be applied, for example, to determine the equity consequences of the 1933–34 securities regulations, by comparing the extent of price reaction (variability) to specific information disclosure prior and subsequent to 1933–34.[24] Of course, care should be taken to control for "other variables," such as changes over time in the average variability of prices, in the degree of unexpectedness of the information disclosed, or in the amount of voluntary information available to investors (see Barry and Brown [1984] for proxies for such information). If the post-1933–34 price variability *at disclosure date* is found to be smaller than the pre-1933–34 variability, it could be concluded that the post-1933–34 prices became, on the average, more informative, probably due to the securities regulations. Such a result would be consistent with the equity objective of these statutes. Similar "before and after" studies pertaining to other major accounting regulations could be conducted.

---

[24]Note that the suggested method is different from the one used by Benston [1973]. We are concerned here with variability at a specific date—disclosure time—and not with long-term variability, pre- and post-1933–34 (Benston's test).

Inside Information—Monopoly Rents

Regulation consequences can also be evaluated by examining directly whether specific regulations have decreased information asymmetries. Some methods within the context of "market-based accounting research" address this issue. Consider, for example, the SEC's lines-of-business disclosure requirement. Beginning with fiscal year 1970, multi-product firms were required to disclose revenues and profits by product lines for 1970 and for each of the preceding four years. Thus, before 1970, product-line data were available to a restricted number of persons only (e.g., managers, the firm's major bankers, and perhaps a few closely connected financial analysts). From an equity perspective, the question is whether the use of such data prior to its public disclosure could have yielded excess returns. Collins [1975] addressed this question: the 1967–1970 product-line data (first disclosed publicly in 1970), used as an input to a specific trading rule for investing in securities, yielded statistically significant excess returns for the years 1968 and 1969. Thus, investors with private access to product-line information prior to 1970 could have gained abnormal returns, relative to uninformed investors. From an equity perspective, therefore, the SEC's product-line disclosure requirements seem desirable in decreasing information asymmetries. A similar method can be applied to evaluate the social consequences of other accounting regulations, such as lease and inflation-adjusted disclosures.

Differential Expected Returns

Recall from Section I that the most fundamental equity issue in financial disclosure regulation is the extent of disparity in expected, risk-adjusted returns across investors, namely the extent of equality of opportunity. Obviously, if improvement in the equality of expected returns can be ascribed to a certain disclosure policy, its social desirability, from an equity point of view, would be established. This suggests an examination of the disparity of expected returns across classes of investors, and of changes in such disparities over time as a result of disclosure regulation. It is, of course, impossible to observe expected returns directly, but as is customary in finance and economic research, inferences about expected returns can be drawn from observed, systematic differences in realized returns.

A recent example of this line of research was provided by Feldstein and Yitzhaki [1982] who reported that stocks owned by high-income investors appreciated substantially faster than stocks owned by lower-income investors. An examination of a large sample of individual 1973 Federal income tax returns suggested a substantial return differential—a 3.0 percent average annual return in the lowest income group vs. a 10.0 percent return in the highest income group. Similar evidence was reported in an earlier study by the Internal Revenue Service for the year 1962 (IRS [1966]). To some extent such differential returns might be due to higher risk-taking by wealthy investors, and/or to more complete ("honest") reporting of capital gains by high-income investors (perhaps motivated by a tax audit threat). Nevertheless, Feldstein and Yitzhaki argue that the observed return differentials are large enough to suggest that wealthy investors enjoy systematic excess returns even within the current regulatory environment.

A related, more direct research approach regarding the consequences of disclosure policy would be the comparison of return differentials before and after major disclosure changes. For example, did return differentials across classes of investors decrease subsequent to the extensive disclosure mandated by the Securities Act of 1934? Or, was the change in the information environment following the intensive regulation implemented by the FASB during the last decade associated with a significant return differential decrease? A natural extension of this line of research would be a comparison of the extent of investor return differentials across countries having different disclosure regulations. Of course, systematic cross-country differences in economic conditions, in addition to the extent of financial disclosure, would have to be taken into account.

It should be noted that these lines of research differ markedly from current "market-based accounting research," which generally focuses on the *average* belief revisions through observations of price or volume reaction to the release of information. Direct equity analysis requires the classification of investors into several income or wealth categories or other categories, such as institutional vs. individual investors and the consideration of the impact of regulation on each category. This is similar to the analysis of other public policies (e.g., taxation, health, and education programs) which cannot be adequately evaluated by observing the impact of policies on the average person (or the average impact).

VI. SUMMARY

Inequity in capital markets, in the form of systematic and significant information asymmetries, leads to adverse private and social consequences: high transaction costs, thin markets, lower liquidity of securities, and in general—lower gains from trade. In the absence of efficient, decentralized solutions to these problems, a public policy of information disclosure aimed at mitigating the adverse effects of inequity seems warranted. This is not a policy aimed at favoring or defending a specific group of investors at the expense of others (a zero-sum situation). Rather, it is aimed at benefitting all, though not necessarily to the same extent. This is the equity-orientation of accounting public policy developed in this study.

The relevance of this equity orientation lies in its potential to improve the effectiveness of accounting regulatory bodies (e.g., the SEC and the FASB) and to enrich the accounting policy research agenda. In particular, the equity orientation provides a justification for the regulation of information disclosure; it offers policymakers an operational "public interest" criterion for disclosure choices—the systematic decrease of information asymmetries; and it opens up to researchers a rich agenda for suggesting ways to implement this public interest criterion and for an *ex post* evaluation of regulation consequences.

REFERENCES

AICPA (American Institute of Certified Public Accountants), "Objectives of Financial Statements" (New York: AICPA, October 1973).

Allingham, M., "Fairness and Utility," *Economie Appliquee* 29(2), (1976), pp. 257–266.

Amihud, Y., and H. Mendelson, "Dealership Market: Market-Making with Inventory," *Journal of Financial Economics* (March 1980), pp. 31–53.

Archibald, G. C., and D. Donaldson, "Notes on Economic Equality," *Journal of Public Economics* (October 1979), pp. 205–214.

Arrow, K. J., *The Limits of Organization* (New York: W. W. Norton & Co., 1974).

Arthur Andersen & Co., *The Postulate of Accounting—What It Is, How It Is Determined, How It Should Be Used* (September 1960).

Atiase, R., "Predisclosure Information, Firm Capitalization, and Security Price Behavior Around Earnings Announcements," *Journal of Accounting Research* (Spring 1985), pp. 21–36.

Austinsmith, D., "Fair Rights," *Economic Letters* 4(I), (1979), pp. 29–32.

Bagehot, W., "The Only Game in Town," *Financial Analysts Journal* (March–April 1971), pp. 12–14.

Ball, R., "Accounting, Auditing, and the Nature of the Firm," Unpublished working paper (Graduate School of Business Administration, University of Rochester, June 1987).

Bamber, L., "The Information Content of Annual Earnings Releases: A Trading Volume Approach," *Journal of Accounting Research* (Spring 1986), pp. 40–56.

Barry, C., and S. Brown, "Differential Information and the Small Firm Effect," *Journal of Financial Economics* (June 1984), pp. 283–294.

Baumol, W. J., "Theory of Equity in Pricing for Resource Conservation," *Journal of Environmental Economics and Management* (December 1980), pp. 308–320.

———, "Applied Fairness Theory and Rationing Policy," *American Economic Review* (September 1982), pp. 639–651.

———, *Superfairness* (The MIT Press, 1986).

Beaver, W., "The Information Content of Annual Earnings Announcements," Supplement to *Journal of Accounting Research* (1968), pp. 67–92.

———, *Financial Reporting: An Accounting Revolution* (Prentice-Hall, 1981).

Benston, G. J., "Required Disclosure and the Stock Market: An Evaluation of the Securities Exchange Act of 1934," *American Economic Review* (March 1973), pp. 132–155.

———, *Corporate Financial Disclosure in the U.K. and the U.S.A.* (Saxon House, 1976).

———, "Required Periodic Disclosure Under the Securities Acts and the Proposed Federal Securities Code," *University of Miami Law Review* (September 1979), pp. 1471–1484.

———, and R. Hagerman, "Determinants of Bid-Ask Spreads in the Over-the-Counter Market," *Journal of Financial Economics* (January–February 1974), pp. 353–364.

Brown, L. D., and M. S. Rozeff, "The Superiority of Analyst Forecasts as Measures of Expectations: Evidence from Earnings," *Journal of Finance* (March 1978), pp. 1–28.

Bulow, J. I., and J. B. Shoven, "The Bankruptcy Decision," *Bell Journal of Economics* (Autumn 1978), pp. 437–456.

Chatov, R., "Should the Public Sector Take Over the Function of Determining Generally Accepted Accounting Principles," *The Accounting Journal* (Spring 1977), pp. 117–123.

Cohen, M., "Regulation Through Disclosure," *Journal of Accountancy* (December 1981), pp. 52–62.

Collins, D. W., and R. R. Simonds, "SEC Line-of-Business Disclosure and Market Risk Adjustments," *Journal of Accounting Research* (Autumn 1979), pp. 352–383.

Collins, D., "SEC Product-Line Reporting and Market Efficiency," *Journal of Financial Economics* (June 1975), pp. 125–164.

Copeland, T., and D. Galai, "Information Effects on the Bid-Ask Spread," *Journal of Finance* (December 1983), pp. 1457–1469.

Crawford, V., "A Game of Fair Division," *Review of Economic Studies* (June 1977), pp. 235–247.

———, "A Procedure for Generating Pareto-Efficient Egalitarian-Equivalent Allocations," *Econometrica* (January 1979), pp. 49–60.

———, "A Self-Administered Solution of the Bargaining Problem," *Review of Economic Studies* (January 1980), pp. 385–392.

Demsetz, H., "The Cost of Transacting," *Quarterly Journal of Economics* (February 1968), pp. 33–53.

Dye, R. A., "Disclosure of Nonproprietary Information," *Journal of Accounting Research* (Spring 1985), pp. 123–145.

Easterbrook, F., and D. Fischel, "Mandatory Disclosure and the Protection of Investors," *Virginia Law Review* (May 1984), pp. 669–715.

Epps, T., "The Demand for Brokers' Services: The Relation Between Security Trading Volume and Transaction Cost," *Bell Journal of Economics* (Spring 1976), pp. 163–194.

Feldstein, M., and S. Yitzhaki, "Are High Income Individuals Better Stock Market Investors?", Working paper No. 948 (National Bureau of Economic Research, July 1982).

Financial Accounting Standards Board, "Conceptual Framework for Accounting and Reporting: Consideration of the Report of the Study Group on the Objectives of Financial Statements," Discussion memorandum (FASB, June 6, 1974).

———, "Tentative Conclusions on Objectives of Financial Statements of Business Enterprises," (FASB, December 2, 1976a).

———, "Conceptual Framework for Financial Accounting and Reporting: Elements of Financial Statements and their Measurement," Discussion memorandum (FASB, December 2, 1976b).

———, "Objectives of Financial Reporting by Business Enterprises," Statement of Financial Accounting Concepts No. 1 (FASB, November 1978).

Foley, D., "Resource Allocation and the Public Sector," *Yale Economic Essays* (Spring 1967), pp. 45–98.

Friedman, D., "Many, Few, One: Social Harmony and the Shrunken Choice Set," *American Economic Review* (March 1980), pp. 225–232.

Garman, M. B., "Market Microstructure," *Journal of Financial Economics* (June 1976), pp. 257–275.

Glosten, L. R., and P. R. Milgrom, "Bid, Ask, and Transaction Prices in a Specialist Market with Heterogeneously Informed Traders," *Journal of Financial Economics* (March 1985), pp. 71–100.

Grant, E. B., "Market Implications of Differential Amounts of Interim Information," *Journal of Accounting Research* (Spring 1980), pp. 255–268.

Grossman, S. J., and J. E. Stiglitz, "Information and Competitive Price Systems," *American Economic Review* (May 1976), pp. 246–253.

———, and O. D. Hart, "Disclosure Laws and Takeover Bids," *Journal of Finance* (May 1980), pp. 323–334.

Hakansson, N. H., "On the Politics of Accounting Disclosure and Measurement: An Analysis of Economic Incentives," Supplement to *Journal of Accounting Research* (1981), pp. 1–35.

Hamilton, J., "Marketplace Organization and Marketability: NASDAQ, the Stock Exchange, and the National Market System," *Journal of Finance* (May 1978), pp. 487–503.

Howe, R. E., and J. E. Roemer, "Rawlsian Justice as the Core of a Game," *American Economic Review* (December 1981), pp. 880–895.

IRS (Internal Revenue Service), Statistics of Income, Supplemental Report: Sales of Capital Assets Reported on Individual Tax Returns, Publication No. 458 (1966), pp. 10–66.

Jarrell, G., and J. Pound, "SEC Now Is On Target," *The Wall Street Journal* (March 26, 1987).

Joseph, K., and J. Sumptions, *Equality* (London: 1979).

Kalt, J. P., and M. A. Zupan, "Capture and Ideology in the Economic Theory of Politics," *American Economic Review* (June 1984), pp. 279–300.

Karpoff, J., "A Theory of Trading Volume," *Journal of Finance* (December 1986), pp. 1069–1087.

Leftwich, R., "Accounting Information in Private Markets: Evidence from Private Lending Agreements," THE ACCOUNTING REVIEW (January 1983), pp. 23–42.

Lev, B., "On the Adequacy of Publicly Available Financial Information for Security Analysis," in Abdelkhalik and Keller, Eds., *Financial Information Requirements for Security Analysis* (Duke University, 1978).

———, and J. A. Ohlson, "Market-Based Empirical Research in Accounting: A Review, Interpretation, and Extension," Supplement to *Journal of Accounting Research* (1982), pp. 249–322.

———, and S. H. Penman, "Voluntary Forecast Disclosure, Non-Disclosure, and Stock Prices," Unpublished working paper (University of California-Berkeley, March 1987).

McNichols, M., and J. G. Manegold, "The Effect of the Information Environment on the Relationship Between Financial Disclosure and Security Price Variability," *Journal of Accounting and Economics* (April 1983), pp. 49–74.

Mendelson, H., "Random Competitive Exchange: Price Distributions and Gains from Trade," *Journal of Economic Theory* (December 1985), pp. 254–280.

Merton, R. C., "A Simple Model of Capital Market Equilibrium with Incomplete Information," *Journal of Finance* (July 1987), pp. 483–510.

Morse, D., "Price and Trading Volume Reaction Surrounding Earnings Announcements: A Closer Examination," *Journal of Accounting Research* (Autumn 1981), pp. 374–383.

———, and N. Ushman, "The Effect of Information Announcements on the Market Microstructure," THE ACCOUNTING REVIEW (April 1983), pp. 247–258.

Ohlson, J., "On Financial Disclosure and the Behavior of Security Prices," *Journal of Accounting and Economics* (December 1979), pp. 211–232.

———, and A. Buckman, "Toward a Theory of Financial Accounting: Welfare and Public Information," *Journal of Accounting Research* (Autumn 1981), pp. 399–433.

Okun, A. M., *Equality and Efficiency: The Big Tradeoff* (Washington, D.C.: 1975).

Patell, J. M., "Corporate Forecasts of Earnings Per Share and Stock Price Behavior: Empirical Tests," *Journal of Accounting Research* (Autumn 1976), pp. 246–276.

Penman, S. H., "An Empirical Investigation of the Voluntary Disclosure of Corporate Earnings Forecasts," *Journal of Accounting Research* (Spring 1980), pp. 132–160.

Rawls, J., *A Theory of Justice* (Cambridge: Harvard University Press, 1971).

Ross, S., "Disclosure Regulation in Financial Markets: Implications of Modern Finance Theory and Signaling Theory," in Edwards, Ed., *Issues in Financial Regulation* (New York: McGraw-Hill, 1979), pp. 177–202.

Rubinstein, M., "A Mean-Variance Synthesis of Corporate Financial Theory," *Journal of Finance* (March 1973), pp. 167–181.

Schwert, G. W., "Public Regulation of National Securities Exchanges: A Test of the Capture Hypothesis," *The Bell Journal of Economics* (Spring 1977), pp. 128–150.

Sen, A. K., *Collective Choice and Social Welfare* (San Francisco: Holden-Day, Inc., 1970).

Stoll, H., "Alternative Views of Market Making," in Y. Amihud, T. Ho, and R. Schwartz, Eds., *Market Making and the Changing Structure of the Securities Industry* (Lexington, MA: Lexington-Heath Co., 1985), pp. 67–91.

———, "Dealer Inventory Behavior: An Empirical Investigation of NASDAQ Stocks," *Journal of Financial and Quantitative Analysis* (September 1976), pp. 359–380.

Svensson, L., "Some Views on a Fair Wage Structure," *Ekonomiska Samfunddets Tidskrift,* 33(3), (1980), pp. 155–166.

Venkatesh, P., and R. Chiang, "Information Asymmetry and the Dealer's Bid-Ask Spread: A Case Study of Earnings and Dividend Announcements," *Journal of Finance* (December 1986), pp. 1089–1102.

Watts, R., and J. Zimmerman, *Positive Accounting Theory* (Englewood Cliffs, NJ: Prentice-Hall, Inc., 1986).
———, and ———, "The Demand for and Supply of Accounting Theories: The Market for Excuses," THE AC-
  COUNTING REVIEW (April 1979), pp. 273–305.
———, "Can Optimal Accounting Information Be Determined by Regulation?" in J. W. Buckley and J. F. Weston,
  Eds., *Regulation and the Accounting Profession* (Belmont, CA: Lifetime Learning Publications (Wadsworth,
  1980), pp. 153–162.
Wilson, R., "Informational Economies of Scale," *Bell Journal of Economics* (Spring 1975), pp. 184–195.

THE RISE OF "ECONOMIC CONSEQUENCES"

Stephen A. Zeff

Since the 1960s, the American accounting profession has been aware of the increasing influence of "outside forces" in the standard-setting process. Two parallel developments have marked this trend. First, individuals and groups that had rarely shown any interest in the setting of accounting standards began to intervene actively and powerfully in the process. Second, these parties began to invoke arguments other than those which have traditionally been employed in accounting discussions. The term "economic consequences" has been used to describe these novel kinds of arguments.

By "economic consequences" is meant the impact of accounting reports on the decision-making behavior of business, government, unions, investors and creditors. It is argued that the resulting behavior of these individuals and groups could be detrimental to the interests of other affected parties. And, the argument goes, accounting standard setters must take into consideration these allegedly detrimental consequences when deciding on accounting questions. The recent debates involving foreign currency translation and the accounting for unsuccessful exploration activity in the petroleum industry have relied heavily on economic consequences arguments, and the Financial Accounting Standards Board and the Securities and Exchange Commission have become extremely sensitive to the issue.[1]

This article is an abridged version of a paper presented on June 9, 1978, at the Stanford Lectures in Accounting, Graduate School of Business, Stanford University.

Stephen A. Zeff, "The Rise of 'Economic Consequences'," *Journal of Accountancy,* December 1978, pp. 56–63. Reprinted with permission from the Journal of Accountancy, Copyright © 1978 by American Institute of Certified Public Accountants, Inc. Opinions of the authors are their own and do not necessarily reflect policies of the AICPA.

[1]Several articles have been written on "economic consequences." See, e.g., Alfred Rappaport, "Economic Impact of Accounting Standards—Implications for the FASB," *Journal of Accountancy,* May 1977, pp. 89–98; Arthur R. Wyatt, "The Economics Impact of Financial Accounting Standards," *Journal of Accountancy,* Oct. 77, pp. 92–94; and Robert J. Swieringa, "Consequences of Financial Accounting Standards," *Accounting Forum,* May 1977, pp. 25–39.

The economic consequences argument represents a veritable revolution in accounting thought. Until recently, accounting policy making was either assumed to be neutral in its effects or, if not neutral, it was not held out to the public as being responsible for those effects. Today, these assumptions are being severely questioned, and the subject of social and economic consequences "has become *the* central contemporary issue in accounting."[2] That the FASB has commissioned research papers on the economic consequences of selected standards and has held a conference devoted entirely to the subject[3] underscores the current importance of this issue.

Accounting policy makers have been aware since at least the 1960s of the third-party intervention issue,[4] while the issue of economic consequences has surfaced only in the 1970s. Indeed, much of the history of the Accounting Principles Board during the 1960s was one of endeavoring to understand and cope with the third-party forces which were intervening in the standard-setting process. In the end, the inability of the APB to deal effectively with these forces led to its demise and the establishment in 1973 of the FASB.

The true preoccupations of the intervening third parties have not always been made clear. When trying to understand the third-party arguments, one must remember that before the 1970s the accounting model employed by the American Institute of CPAs committee on accounting procedure (CAP) and the APB was, formally at least, confined to technical accounting considerations (sometimes called "accounting principles" or "conceptual questions") such as the measurement of assets, liabilities and income and the "fair presentation" of financial position and operations. The policy makers' sole concern was with the communication of financial information to actual and potential investors, for, indeed, their charter had been "granted" by the SEC, which itself had been charged by Congress to assure "full and fair disclosure" in reports to investors. Third-party intervenors, therefore, would have had an obvious incentive to appeal to the accounting model used by policy makers rather than raise the specter of an economic consequences model preferred by the third parties.

When corporate management began intervening in the standard-setting process to an increasing degree, therefore, its true position was probably disguised. An examination of management arguments suggests the following range of tactical rhetoric. Arguments were couched in terms of

1. The traditional accounting model, where management was genuinely concerned about unbiased and "theoretically sound" accounting measurements.

2. The traditional accounting model, where management was really seeking to advance its self-interest in the economic consequences of the contents of published reports.

3. The economic consequences in which management was self-interested.

---

[2] *Report of the Committee on the Social Consequences of Accounting Information* (Sarasota, Fla.: American Accounting Association, 1978), p. 4.

[3] *Conference on the Economic Consequences of Financial Accounting Standards* (Stamford, Conn.: FASB, 1978).

[4] In this article, I am chiefly concerned with third-party intervention in the standard setting for unregulated industries. Accounting policy makers in this country have been alive for several decades to the accounting implications of the rules and regulations of rate-making in the energy, transportation and communication industries. See, e.g., George O. May, *Financial Accounting: A Distillation of Experience* (New York: The Macmillan Company, 1943), chs. 7–8, and William A. Paton, "Accounting Policies of the Federal Power Commission—A Critique," *Journal of Accountancy,* June 44, pp. 432–60.

If one accepts Johnson's dictum that it requires a "lively imagination" to believe that management is genuinely concerned with fair presentation when choosing between accounting alternatives,[5] it could be concluded that the first argument has seldom been employed in third-party interventions. In recent years, particularly since the early 1970s, management has become more candid in its dialogues with the FASB, insistently advancing the third argument and thus bringing economic consequences to the fore.

Two factors tend to explain why economic consequences did not become a substantive issue before the 1970s. First, management and other interested parties predominantly used the second argument cited above, encouraging the standard-setting bodies to confine themselves to the traditional accounting model. Second, the CAP and APB, with few exceptions, were determined to resolve, or appear to resolve, standard-setting controversies in the context of traditional accounting.

EARLY USES OF ECONOMIC CONSEQUENCES ARGUMENTS

Perhaps the first evidence of economic consequences reasoning in the pronouncements of American policy makers occurred as long ago as 1941. In Accounting Research Bulletin no. 11, *Corporate Accounting for Ordinary Stock Dividends,* the CAP, in accordance with "proper accounting and corporate policy," required that fair market value be used to record the issuance of stock dividends where such market value was substantially in excess of book value.[6]

Evidently, both the New York Stock Exchange and a majority of the CAP regarded periodic stock dividends as "objectionable,"[7] and the CAP acted to make it more difficult for corporations to sustain a series of such stock dividends out of their accumulated earnings. As far as this author is aware, the U.S. is still the only country in which an accounting pronouncement requires that stock dividends be capitalized at the fair market value of the issued shares,[8] and this position was originally adopted in this country, at least in part, in order to produce an impact on the stock dividend policies of corporations.

A second evidence of economic consequences entering into the debates surrounding the establishment of accounting standards, this time involving management representations, occurred in 1947–48. It was the height of the postwar inflation, and several corporations had adopted replacement cost depreciation in their published financial statements.[9] Among the arguments employed in the debate involving the CAP were the possible implications for tax reform, the possible impact on wage bargaining and the need to counteract criticisms of profiteering by big business. Despite the pressures for accounting reform, the CAP reaffirmed its

---

[5]Charles E. Johnson, "Management's Role in External Accounting Measurements," in Robert K. Jaedicke, Yuji Ijiri and Oswald Nielsen (editors), *Research in Accounting Measurement* ([n.p.], AAA, 1966), p. 91.

[6]Accounting Research Bulletin no. 11, *Corporate Accounting for Ordinary Stock Dividends* (New York: American Institute of Accountants, 1941), pp. 102–03.

[7]George O. May, letter to J. S. Seidman, dated July 14, 1941 (deposited in the national office library of Price Waterhouse & Co. in New York), p. 1.

[8]Price Waterhouse International, *A Survey in 46 Countries: Accounting Principles and Reporting Practices* ([n.p.], PWI, 1975), table 145.

[9]*Depreciation Policy When Price Levels Change* (New York: Controllership Foundation, Inc., 1948), ch. 14.

support of historical cost accounting for depreciation in ARB no. 33, *Depreciation and High Costs,* and in a letter issued in October 1948.

A clear use of the economic consequences argument occurred in 1958, when three subsidiaries of American Electric Power Company sued in the federal courts to enjoin the AICPA from allowing the CAP to issue a letter saying that the deferred tax credit account, as employed in the then-recently issued ARB no. 44 (Revised), *Declining-Balance Depreciation,* should be classified as a liability.[10] The three public utility companies were concerned that the SEC, under authority granted by the Public Utility Holding Company Act, would not permit them to issue debt securities in view of the unfavorable debt-to-equity ratios which the proposed reclassification would produce. The case reached the U.S. Supreme Court, where certiorari was denied. In the end, the clarifying letter was issued. Nonetheless, the SEC accommodated the public utility companies by consenting to exclude the deferred tax credit from both liabilities and stockholders' equity for purposes of decisions taken under the Public Utility Holding Company Act.[11]

Shortly after the creation of the APB, the accounting treatment of the investment tax credit exploded on the scene. The three confrontations between the APB and the combined forces of industry and the administrations of Presidents Kennedy, Johnson and Nixon have already been amply discussed in the literature.[12] The government's argument was not that the accounting deferral of the investment tax credit was bad accounting but that it diluted the incentive effect of an instrument of fiscal policy.

In 1965, the subject of segmental reporting emerged from a hearing of the Senate Subcommittee on Antitrust and Monopoly on the economic effects of conglomerate mergers. The aim of the senatorial inquiry was not to promote better accounting practices for investor use but to provide the subcommittee and other government policy makers with accounting data that would facilitate their assessment of the economic efficacy of conglomerate mergers. Company managements naturally looked on such disclosures as potentially detrimental to their merger ambitions. Pressure applied by this powerful subcommittee eventually forced the hand of the SEC to call for product-line disclosures in published financial reports. The repercussions of this initiative, which had its origin in a Senate hearing room, are still being felt.[13]

In 1967–69, the APB responded to an anguished objection by the startled Investment Bankers Association of America (today known as the Securities Industry Association) to a provision, once thought to be innocuous, in APB Opinion no. 10, *Omnibus Opinion-1966,* which imputed a debt discount to convertible debt and debt issued with stock warrants. The IBA was concerned about the impact of the accounting procedure on the market for such securities. In

---

[10]*The AICPA Injunction Case—Re: ARB [No.] 44 (Revised),* Cases in Public Accounting Practice [no. 1] (Chicago, Ill.: Arthur Andersen & Co., 1960).

[11]*SEC Administrative Policy Re: Balance-Sheet Treatment of Deferred Income-Tax Credits,* Cases in Public Accounting Practice [nos. 5 and 6] (Chicago, Ill.: Arthur Andersen & Co., 1961), pp. 35–59.

[12]See Maurice Moonitz, "Some Reflections on the Investment Credit Experience," *Journal of Accounting Research,* Spring 1966, pp. 47–61; John L. Carey, *The Rise of the Accounting Profession: To Responsibility and Authority 1937–1969* (New York: AICPA, 1970), pp. 98–104; and Stephen A. Zeff, *Forging Accounting Principles in Five Countries: A History and an Analysis of Trends* (Champaign, Ill.: Stipes Publishing Company, 1972), pp. 178–80, 201–2, 219–21 and 326–27.

[13]Charles W. Plum and Daniel W. Collins, "Business Segment Reporting," in James Don Edwards and Homer A. Black (editors), *The Modern Accountant's Handbook* (Homewood, Ill.: Dow Jones-Irwin, Inc., 1976), pp. 469–511.

Opinion no 14, *Accounting for Convertible Debt and Debt Issued With Stock Purchase Warrants,* the APB rescinded its action in regard to convertible debt while retaining the rest.[14]

From 1968 through 1971, the banking industry opposed the inclusion of bad-debt provisions and losses on the sales of securities in the net income of commercial banks. Bankers believed that the new measure would reflect unfavorably on the performance of banks. Eventually, through a concerted effort by the APB, the SEC and the bank regulatory agencies, generally accepted accounting principles were made applicable to banks.[15]

From 1968 through 1970, the APB struggled with the accounting for business combinations. It was flanked on the one side by the Federal Trade Commission and the Department of Justice, which favored the elimination of pooling-of-interest accounting in order to produce a slowing effect on the merger movement and on the other by merger-minded corporations that were fervent supporters of pooling-of-interests accounting. The APB, appearing almost as a pawn in a game of political chess, disenchanted many of its supporters as it abandoned positions of principle in favor of an embarrassing series of pressure-induced compromises.[16]

In 1971, the APB held public hearings on accounting for marketable equity securities, leases and the exploration and drilling costs of companies in the petroleum industry. In all three areas powerful industry pressures thwarted the board from acting. The insurance industry was intensely concerned about the possible effects on its companies' stock prices of including the unrealized gains and losses on portfolio holdings in their income statements.[17] The leasing initiative was squelched after senators, representatives and even the secretary of transportation responded to a letter-writing campaign by making pointed inquiries of the SEC and APB. The letter writers raised the specter of injury that the board's proposed action would supposedly cause to consumers and to the viability of companies in several key industries.[18] The petroleum industry was unable to unite on a solution to the controversy over full costing versus successful efforts costing, as it was alleged that a general imposition of the latter would adversely affect the fortunes of the small, independent exploration companies.[19] Using its considerable political might, the industry succeeded in persuading the board to postpone consideration of the sensitive subject.[20]

On each of the occasions enumerated above, outside parties intervened in the standard-setting process by an appeal to criteria that transcended the traditional questions of accounting measurement and fair presentation. They were concerned instead with the economic consequences of the accounting pronouncements.

---

[14]Zeff, pp. 202, 211.

[15]Carey, p. 134: Maurice Moonitz, *Obtaining Agreement on Standards in the Accounting Profession,* Studies in Accounting Research no. 8 (Sarasota, Fla.: AAA, 1974), pp. 38–39; Zeff, pp. 210–11.

[16]Robert Chatov, *Corporate Financial Reporting: Public or Private Control?* (New York: The Free Press, 1975), pp. 212–22; and Zeff, pp. 212–16.

[17]Charles T. Horngren, "The Marketing of Accounting Standards," *Journal of Accountancy,* Oct. 73, pp. 63–64.

[18]Leonard M. Savoie, "Accounting Attitudes," in Robert R. Sterling (editor), *Institutional Issues in Public Accounting* (Lawrence, Kan.: Scholars Book Co., 1974), p. 326.

[19]See the testimony and submissions in *APB Public Hearing on Accounting and Reporting Practices in the Petroleum Industry,* Cases in Public Accounting Practice [no.] 10 (Chicago, Ill.: Arthur Andersen & Co., 1972).

[20]Savoie, p. 326.

"Economic consequences" have been invoked with even greater intensity in the short life of the FASB. Such questions as accounting for research and development costs, self-insurance and catastrophe reserves, development stage companies, foreign currency fluctuations, leases, the restructuring of troubled debt,[21] domestic inflation and relative price changes, and the exploration and drilling costs of companies in the petroleum industry have provoked widespread debate over their economic consequences.[22] The list is both extensive and impressive, and accounting academics are busily investigating the empirical validity of claims that these and other accounting standards may be linked with the specified economic consequences.

THE STANDARD-SETTING BODIES RESPOND

What have been the reactions of the standard-setting bodies to the intervention by outside parties and the claim that accounting standards should or should not be changed in order to avoid unhealthy economic or social consequences? In the 1940s and 1950s, the CAP enhanced its liaison with interested third parties through a wider circulation of exposure drafts and subcommittee reports. From 1958 to 1971, through appointments to key committees, joint discussions and symposiums, mass mailings of exposure drafts and formal public hearings, the Institute and the APB acted to bring interested organizations more closely into the standard-setting process. The hope was, one supposes, that these organizations would be satisfied that their views were given full consideration before the final issuance of opinions. These accommodations were, however, of a procedural sort, although it is possible that these outside views did have an impact on the substantive content of some of the resulting opinions. It would appear that the APB was at least somewhat influenced by economic consequences in its prolonged deliberations leading to the issuance of Opinions no. 16, *Business Combinations,* and no. 17, *Intangible Assets.*[23]

---

[21]At the FASB's public hearing, some bankers warned of the dire economic consequences of requiring banks to write down their receivables following restructuring. Walter Wriston, chairman of Citicorp, asserted that the restructuring of New York City's obligations might just not have occurred if the banks would have been required to write down the carrying value of their receivables. Walter B. Wriston, *Transcript of Public Hearing* on FASB discussion memorandum, *Accounting by Debtors and Creditors When Debt Is Restructured* (1977-vol. 1-part 2), pp. 69–70. Yet the FASB, in its lengthy, "Basis for Conclusions" in Statement no. 15, *Accounting by Debtors and Creditors for Troubled Debt Restructurings* (in which the feared write-downs were not required), did not refer to bankers' claims about the economic consequences of requiring significant write-downs. Does that omission imply that the FASB paid no attention to those assertions? Did the FASB conduct any empirical research (as it did concerning the economic consequences claims raised in connection with Statement no. 7, *Accounting and Reporting by Development Stage Enterprises*) to determine whether there was adequate ground to sustain such claims?

[22]See, e.g., Joseph M. Burns, *Accounting Standards and International Finance: With Special Reference to Multinationals* (Washington, D.C.: American Enterprise Institute for Public Policy Research, 1976); Committee on the Social Consequences of Accounting Information, pp. 9–12; Rappaport, pp. 90, 92; FASB, *Conference on the Economic Consequences of Financial Accounting Standards;* U.S. Department of Energy, comments before the Securities and Exchange Commission, "Accounting Practices—Oil and Gas Producers—Financial Accounting Standards," unpublished memorandum, dated April 3, 1978.

Evidence attesting to the attention given by the FASB to economic consequences issues may be found in the "Basis for Conclusions" sections of the applicable statements. In addition to companies and industry groups, government departments (such as the Department of Commerce, in Statement no. 7, and the Departments of Energy and Justice, in Statement no. 19, *Financial Accounting and Reporting by Oil and Gas Producing Companies*) were actively involved in the discussion of economic consequences.

[23]Wyatt, p. 92–93.

During the public hearings in 1971 on marketable equity securities and the accounting practices of companies in the petroleum industry, management representatives on several occasions asserted economic consequences as relevant considerations. Yet members of the APB's subject-area committees neither asked for proof of these assertions nor, indeed, questioned their relevance to the setting of accounting standards.[24]

Since it was the APB's inability to cope with the pressures brought by outside organizations that hastened its demise, it is worth noting that the FASB included the Financial Executives Institute (FEI) among its co-sponsors. In my opinion, the incorporation of the FEI in the formal structure of the Financial Accounting Foundation (FAF, the FASB's parent) is one of the most significant advantages which the FASB possesses in relation to its predecessor.[25]

The procedural machinery established for the FASB is even more elaborate than that which existed in the final years of the APB. The object of these additional procedures has been to expand and intensify the interaction between the board and interested outside parties, notably companies, industry associations and government departments and agencies. A task force drawn from a broad spectrum of interested groups is appointed prior to the preparation of each discussion memorandum. The DM itself is much bulkier than the modest document the APB had issued before its public hearings; it contains a neutral discussion of the entire gamut of policy issues that bear on the resolution of the controversy before the board. A Financial Accounting Standards Advisory Council (FASAC), composed of representatives of a wide array of interested groups, was appointed to be a sounding board for the FASB. The board itself has been composed of members drawn from accounting practice, the universities, companies and government—again, so that it would be responsive, and would appear to be responsive, to the concerns of those "constituencies." In an effort to persuade skeptics of the merit of its recommendations, the board includes in its statements a lengthy explanation of the criteria, arguments and empirical considerations it used to fashion the recommended standards.

Following criticism from within the profession of the board's operations and procedures, the FAF conducted a study in 1977 of the entire FASB operation. Among the FAF's many recommendations were proposals that the board expand its formal and informal contacts with interested groups and that it include an economic impact analysis in important exposure drafts. On this latter point, the FAF's structure committee concluded: "The Board need not be unduly influenced by the possibility of an economic impact, but it should consider both the possible costs and the expected benefits of a proposal."[26] In addition, the structure committee recommended actions that would strengthen the roles of the task forces and the FASAC.[27] In 1978, under pressure from Congress, the board began to conduct virtually all its formal meetings (including those of the FASAC) "in the sunshine."

---

[24]*Proceedings* of Hearing on Accounting for Equity Securities, Accounting Principles Board (New York: AICPA, 1971), section A—Transcript; and *APB Public Hearing on Accounting and Reporting Practices in the Petroleum Industry*.

[25]The inclusion of the FEI could arguably become the undoing of the FASB. If the FEI were to lose confidence in the board, it is possible that many of the companies which now contribute to the Financial Accounting Foundation might decline to continue doing so, provoking a financial crisis that could threaten the board's viability.

[26]Financial Accounting Foundation structure committee, *The Structure of Establishing Financial Accounting Standards* (Stamford, Conn.: FAF, 1977), p. 51.

[27]Ibid., pp. 23–25.

The history of the APB and the FASB is one of a succession of procedural steps taken to bring the board's deliberations into closer proximity to the opinions and concerns of interested third parties. As in the case of the APB, it is possible that an effect of these more elaborate procedures has been a change in the substance of the FASB's conclusions and recommendations.

By the middle 1970's, however, it was decided that the FASB should add economic (and social) consequences to the substantive issues it normally addresses. The inclusion of "probable economic or social impact" among the other "qualities of useful information" in the board's conceptual framework DM,[28] the board's announcement of its interest in empirical studies of economic consequences,[29] and the recommendation of the FAF structure committee that the board inform itself adequately on the "various impacts its pronouncements might have"[30] collectively confirm this new direction. The issue of economic consequences has, therefore, changed from one having only procedural implications for the standard-setting process to one which is not firmly a part of the standard setters' substantive policy framework.

ECONOMIC CONSEQUENCES AS A SUBSTANTIVE ISSUE

Economic consequences have finally become accepted as a valid substantive policy issue for a number of reasons:

- The tenor of the times. The decade of the 1970s is clearly one in which American society is holding its institutions responsible for the social, environmental and economic consequences of their actions, and the crystallized public opinion on this subject eventually became evident (and relevant) to those interested in the accounting standard-setting activity.

- The sheer intractability of the accounting problems being addressed. Since the mid-1960s, the APB and the FASB have been taking up difficult accounting questions on which industry positions have been well entrenched. To some degree, companies that are sensitive to the way their performances are evaluated through the medium of reported earnings have permitted their decision-making behavior to be influenced by their perceptions of how such behavior will be seen through the prism of accounting earnings. Still other such companies have tailored their accounting practices to reflect their economic performances in the best light—and the managers are evidently loathe to change their decision-making behavior in order to accommodate newly imposed accounting standards. This would also be a concern to managers who are being paid under incentive compensation plans.[31]

---

[28]Financial Accounting Standards Board discussion memorandum, *Conceptual Framework for Financial Accounting and Reporting: Elements of Financial Statements and Their Measurement* (Stamford, Conn.: FASB, 1976), par. 367.

[29]Financial Accounting Standards Board, *Status Report,* no. 45, February 7, 1977.

[30]Structure committee, p. 31.

[31]Alfred Rappaport, "Executive Incentives vs. Corporate Growth," *Harvard Business Review,* July–August 1978, pp. 81–88.

- The enormity of the impact. Several of the issues facing the APB and the FASB in recent years have portended such a high degree of impact on either the volatility or level of earnings and other key financial figures and ratios that the FASB can no longer discuss the proposed accounting treatments without encountering incessant arguments over the probable economic consequences. Particularly apt examples are accounting for foreign exchange fluctuations, domestic inflation and relative price changes and the exploration and drilling costs of companies in the petroleum industry.

- The growth in the information economics–social choice, behavioral, income smoothing and decision usefulness literature in accounting. Recent writings in the information economics–social choice literature have provided a broad analytical framework within which the problems or economic consequences may be conceptualized. Beginning with Stedry,[32] the literature on the behavioral implications of accounting numbers has grown significantly, drawing the attention of researchers and policy makers to the importance of considering the effects of accounting information. The literature on income smoothing has suggested the presence of a managerial motive for influencing the measurement of earnings trends. Finally, the decision usefulness literature, although it is confined to the direct users of accounting information, has served to lessen the inclination of accountants to argue over the inherent "truth" of different accounting incomes and, instead, to focus on the use of information by those who receive accounting reports.[33]

- The insufficiency of the procedural reforms adopted by the APB and the FASB. Despite the succession of procedural steps which both boards have taken to provide outside parties with a forum for expressing their views, the claims of economic consequences—and the resulting criticisms of the boards' pronouncements—have continued unabated. The conclusion has evidently been reached that procedural remedies alone will not meet the problem.

- The Moss and Metcalf investigations. By the middle of 1976, it was known that Congressman John E. Moss (D-Calif.) and the late Senator Lee Metcalf (D-Mont.) were conducting investigations of the performance of the accounting profession, including its standard-setting activities, and it could reasonably have been inferred that the responsiveness of the standard-setting bodies to the economic and social effects of their decisions would be an issue.

- The increasing importance to corporate managers of the earnings figure in capital-market transactions. Especially in the 1960s, when capital markets were intensely competitive and the merger movement was fast paced, the earnings figure came to be viewed as an important element of managerial strategy and tactics. This factor is of importance in today's markets, as the pace of merger activity has once again quickened.

- Accounting figures came to be viewed as an instrument of social control. The social control of American enterprise has been well known in the rate-regulated energy,

---

[32]Andrew C. Stedry, *Budget Control and Cost Behavior* (Englewood Cliffs, N.J.: Prentice-Hall, Inc., 1960).

[33]Committee on concepts and standards for external financial reports, *Statement on Accounting Theory and Theory Acceptance* (Sarasota, Fla.: AAA, 1977), pp. 5–29.

transportation and communications fields, but in recent years the earnings figure has, to an increasing degree, been employed as a control device on a broader scale.[34] Examples are fiscal incentives (such as the investment tax credit and redefinitions of taxable income that diverge from accounting income) that have an influence on debates surrounding financial reporting,[35] the price-control mechanism of Phase II in 1972–73[36] and the data base contemplated by the Energy Policy and Conservation Act of 1975.

- The realization that outsiders could influence the outcome of accounting debates. Before the 1960s, accounting controversies were rarely reported in the financial press, and it was widely believed that accounting was a constant, if not a fixed parameter, in the management of business operations. With the publicity given to the accounting for the investment credit in 1962–63, to the fractious dialogue within the AICPA in 1963–64 over the authority of the APB and to other accounting disagreements involving the APB, managers and other outside parties have come to realize that accounting may be a variable after all—that the rules of accounting are not unyielding or even unbending.

- The growing use of the third argument, advanced earlier in the article, in accounting debates. Mostly for the reasons enumerated above, outside parties began to discard the pretense that their objections to proposed changes in accounting standards were solely, or even primarily, a function of differences over the proper interpretation of accounting principles. True reasons came out into the open, and accounting policy makers could not longer ignore their implications.

It is significant that economic consequences have become an important issue at a time when accounting and finance academics have been arguing that the U.S. capital markets are efficient with respect to publicly available information and, moreover, that the market cannot be "fooled" by the use of different accounting methods to reflect the same economic reality.[37]

THE DILEMMA FACING THE FASB

What are the implications of the economic consequences movement for the FASB? It has become clear that political agencies (such as government departments and congressional committees) expect accounting standard setters to take explicitly into consideration the possible adverse consequences of proposed accounting standards. This expectation appears to be strongest where

---

[34]DR Scott, though writing in a different context, nonetheless was prophetic in his prediction that accounting would increasingly be used as a means of social control. DR Scott, *Cultural Significance of Accounts* (New York: Henry Holt and Co., 1931), esp. ch. 14.

[35]The "required tax conformity" issue of the early 1970s (see Zeff, pp. 218–19) is another instance.

[36]Robert F. Lanzillotti, Mary T. Hamilton and R. Blaine Roberts, *Phase II in Review; the Price Commission Experience* (Washington, D.C.: Brookings Institution, 1975), pp. 73–77; and C. Jackson Grayson, Jr., and Louis Neeb, *Confessions of a Price Controller* (Homewood, Ill.: Dow Jones-Irwin, Inc., 1974), pp. 71–76.

[37]See, e.g., William H. Beaver, "What Should Be the FASB's Objectives?" *Journal of Accountancy,* Aug. 73, pp. 49–56.

the consequences are thought to be significant and widespread—and especially where they might impinge on economic and social policies being pursued by the government. In these instances, the FASB must show that is has studied the possible consequences but that the benefits from implementing the standards outweigh the possible adverse consequences. Where the claimed consequences have implications for economic or social policies of national importance, the FASB should not be surprised if a political resolution is imposed by outside forces.

To what degree should the FASB have regard for economic consequences? To say that any significant economic consequences should be studied by the board does not imply that accounting principles and fair presentation should be dismissed as the principal guiding factor in the board's determination. The FASB is respected as a body of accounting experts, and it should focus its attention where its expertise will be acknowledged. While some observers might opt for determining accounting standards only with regard to their consequences for economic and social welfare, the FASB would surely preside over its own demise if it were to adopt this course and make decisions primarily on other than accounting grounds.

The board is thus faced with a dilemma which requires a delicate balancing of accounting and nonaccounting variables. Although its decisions should rest—and be seen to rest—chiefly on accounting considerations, it must also study—and be seen to study—the possible adverse economic and social consequences of its proposed actions. In order to deal adequately with this latter function, the board may find it convenient to develop a staff of competent analysts from allied disciplines, notably economics.

Economic consequences bids fair to be the most challenging accounting issue of the 1970s. What is abundantly clear is that we have entered an era in which economic and social consequences may no longer be ignored as a substantive issue in the setting of accounting standards. The profession must respond to the changing tenor of the times while continuing to perform its essential role in the areas in which it possesses undoubted expertise.

BASIC ISSUES IN ACCOUNTING POLICY

Part II consists of five lettered sections. The sole paper in Section A, "Overview of Issues in Financial Reporting," is by the American Accounting Association Committee on Accounting and Auditing Measurement, 1989–90. This committee was charged to

1. "identify unmet user information needs" in financial reports and audits of such reports;

2. examine measurement issues of extending accounting information; and

3. illustrate extended measurement.

In its report, the committee sees a considerable gap between what financial statements convey and reality. The statements are incomplete and misleading. The committee offers the following principal recommendations:

1. Internally generated goodwill should be reflected in the financial statements.

2. Market values should be reported wherever feasible in the financial statements—in financial instruments, for example.

3. The time value of money should be provided in financial statements, thereby according it greater recognition.

4. A value-added statement should be included in the financial reports.

5. The cost of pollution prevention and correction should be reported, and costs firms impose on society should be disclosed.

6. Forecasts should be provided in financial reports. Auditors should review these forecasts for reasonableness, and management should later comment on variances.

Section 8, "Definitions and Measurement of Income," includes two selections. Barton (1974) demonstrates the importance of *ex ante* and *ex post* income and asset valuation measurements. *Ex ante* and *ex post* data will be unequal except under highly unrealistic conditions; that is, when (1) cost and market values are always equal, (2) the unit of measure is stable, and (3) certainty exists about the future. *Ex ante* data are needed for planning in terms of selecting and evaluating alternatives and budgeting. *Ex post* data, whether in historical costs or current market prices, are needed for operational control, stewardship, and aid in forecasting. Using current market prices (current replacement costs and selling prices) improves operational efficiency and forecast accuracy of future operating circumstances, as well as providing relevant information for decisions. Current market prices, however, should not be viewed as surrogates of present values.

Beaver and Demski (1979) use a fundamental measurement approach to demonstrate that income measurement, reflecting the change in present values of future cash flows during a period, prevails in a world of certainty with complete and perfect markets, but not necessarily in a world of uncertainty with incomplete or imperfect markets. The authors then provide another interpretation of income reporting and accrual accounting as a cost-effective communication tool.

Section C, "Measurement of Assets and Liabilities," contains one paper. Gamble and Cramer (1992) seek to extend the application of present valuation to nonmonetary assets and liabilities. Using progress billings on long-term construction contracts as an example, the authors cite several decision-making advantages to their proposal. They criticize the traditional classification of monetary and nonmonetary items and recommend consideration of various alternative discount rates to use in present valuation: (1) an after-tax debt rate, (2) an unlevered equity rate, (3) a levered equity rate, or (4) a weighted average cost of capital.

Section D, "International Issues in Financial Reporting," features five articles. The first piece examines the "functional currency" choice set forth in FASB *Statement No. 52,* "Foreign Currency Translation" (1981). In his article, Revsine (1984) explains the purpose of the functional currency concept and the factors underlying the choice of functional currency. Statement 52 was issued with the intent of reflecting the economic substance of foreign exchange translation "gains" and "losses." Nevertheless, if the rationale behind the choice of functional currency is not understood, an incorrect decision can be made.

Weetman and Gray (1991) examine differences in income reported under generally accepted accounting principles in the United States, United Kingdom, Sweden, and the Netherlands. Using Form 20-F reports filed by overseas companies reporting to the Securities and

Exchange Commission in the United States, the authors find some support for the belief that Sweden has the most conservative, and the Netherlands the least conservative GAAP of the four countries evaluated. Moreover, U.S. GAAP appears to be significantly more conservative than that of the United Kingdom. They found that the amortization of goodwill is the principal item in reconciling U.S. and U.K. GAAP.

Gray (1988) examines previous research on international differences in financial accounting with a view to developing a framework linking culture to accounting systems. Drawing upon Hofstede's cross-cultural research, Gray sets forth several hypotheses concerning culture and accounting:

> The higher a country ranks in terms of individualism and the lower it ranks in terms of uncertainty avoidance and power distance, the more likely it is to rank highly in terms of professionalism.

> The higher a country ranks in terms of uncertainty avoidance and power distance and the lower it ranks in terms of individualism, the more likely it is to rank highly in terms of uniformity.

> The higher a country ranks in terms of uncertainty avoidance and the lower it ranks in terms of individualism and masculinity, the more likely it is to rank highly in terms of conservatism.

> The higher a country ranks in terms of uncertainty avoidance and power distance and the lower it ranks in terms of individualism and masculinity, the more likely it is to rank highly in terms of secrecy.

Biddle and Saudagaran (1991) delineate the benefits and costs of foreign exchange listings and also discuss the effects of disclosure requirements on foreign investment. Firms seek to have their securities listed on foreign exchanges because they desire to raise foreign capital. Investors wish to have foreign listings in order to expand their investment opportunities. A key problem with foreign listings is the high cost of meeting the accounting and disclosure requirements in the listing country, especially in the United States and United Kingdom. While the SEC adopted the Integrated Disclosure System in 1982 to allow foreign firms to prepare financial statements in their own countries' GAAP (though they must quantify material differences between the two sets of GAAP), U. S. reporting requirements still remain among the most stringent worldwide. The SEC appears to be reluctant to dilute U.S. GAAP for foreign firms seeking to list their securities on American stock exchanges.

Lowe (1990) traces the development and use of consolidated financial statements in Japan. In the United States, consolidated statements reflect legal relationships and majority control. In Japan, these statements reflect neither legal relationships nor control. Japanese business is characterized by stable groups of affiliated corporations, which lack stockholder control but demonstrate economic interdependence; thus Japanese businesses may well have interlocking directors, use the same bank, and sell their products via the same trading company. In the long run, the majority of shares in Japanese corporations remains in stable hands. Japanese consolidated financial statements, required since 1977, are intended to meet the demands of overseas financial reports. Such financial statements are unsuitably focused and downright misleading.

The final section of Part II, "Not-for-Profit Accounting," contains two papers. Falk (1991) provides a conceptual framework in accounting for privately organized not-for-profit organizations, distinguishing between what he terms "clubs" and "nonclubs." Such organizations owe their existence to market failure, government failure, or contract failure. Both clubs and nonclubs raise or receive resources from donors, members, or users, and each generates services which may or may not benefit those who furnished the resources. According to Falk, club members expect benefits in exchange for their dues. Nonclub benefactors do not expect monetary returns, do not own the organization, and do not manage its resources. The nature of the organization and its services dictates its accounting. The author recommends accrual accounting for clubs and a cash or modified-cash basis for nonclubs. At this time, GAAP issued by American and Canadian standard-setting bodies are not mandatory for not-for-profit entities.

Beechy and Zimmerman (1992) observe that GAAP for not-for-profit organizations have evolved in the absence of a conceptual framework. While the standard setters seem to desire an improvement in such accounting along the lines of private-enterprise accounting, as does Robert Anthony, the authors are not sure that this is the approach to follow. The key issues in not-for-profit accounting are: cash or accrual basis, expenses or expenditures, revenue recognition, capitalization or expenditure of fixed assets, valuation of donated goods and services, valuation of volunteer services, consolidation reporting, and supplementary information to the financial statements. Beechy and Zimmerman consider Anthony's framework, which emphasizes a transaction approach and income measurement, and Haim Falk's framework, which focuses on the relationship between resource providers and beneficiaries and whether the goods are private or collective. The authors point out that no single set of accounting methods is appropriate for any not-for-profit entity.

OVERVIEW OF ISSUES IN FINANCIAL REPORTING

REPORT OF THE

AMERICAN ACCOUNTING ASSOCIATION COMMITTEE ON ACCOUNTING AND AUDITING MEASUREMENT, 1989–90

Committee Members:
Michael J. Barrett, William H. Beaver,
William W. Cooper, J. Alex Milburn,
David Solomons, and David P. Tweedie

IN MEMORIAM

The members of the committee express a deep sense of loss at the passing of one of our members, Michael Barrett, who devoted enormous time and energy to the Committee's work and who was responsible for its formation.

Michael J. Barrett, William H. Beaver, William W. Cooper, J. Alex Milburn, David Solomons, and David P. Tweedie, "Report of the American Accounting Association Committee on Accounting and Auditing Measurement, 1989–90," *Accounting Horizons,* Reprinted by permission of the American Accounting Association.

The charge of this committee is as follows:

1. To identify unmet user information needs, either explicit or implicit, as reflected in currently publicized criticisms of externally reported accounting information and the audits of such information.

2. To examine the measurement issues involved in extending accounting information and the audits of such information to fulfill important types of unmet user information needs.

3. To demonstrate what extended measurement entails with guidance and illustration.

When we were appointed, we were told that our report should concentrate on external financial reporting, and that it should be of potential value to the Financial Accounting Standards Board, as well as to standard setters in other countries. We have tried to maintain that focus. However, we do not think that the report that follows fully satisfies the committee's charge. American Accounting Association committees labor under grave disabilities due to the dispersion of their members and their limited budgets. This committee suffered particularly in those respects in that its membership was drawn from the four corners of the United States, as well as from Britain and Canada. The committee's charge is a large and important one, and it deserves deeper study than we have been able to give it. The observations that follow are offered as an initial contribution to that deeper study.

There are two respects in particular in which our report is not fully responsive to our charge. We have not addressed the auditing issues that would arise if present methods of accounting measurement were substantially changed; and we have not considered the special problems of nonprofit organizations. Our discussion is confined essentially to profit-seeking enterprises, although some of our observations may incidentally have relevance to nonprofits.

THE FUTURE OF FINANCIAL REPORTING

Before proceeding further, it is necessary to consider what kind of external financial reporting we shall see in A.D. 2000—we need not try to look further ahead than that. Methods of electronic reporting are already available and are in use to a limited extent. What does that portend for the need for financial statements, and for the SEC and for other regulatory bodies throughout the world? When it is technically feasible for companies to be required to file great amounts of disaggregated data in the central data banks of regulatory agencies, and the public, especially financial analysts, can have ready access to that data electronically, what kind of financial reports shall we have, and what kind of accounting standards, *if any,* shall we need? Will SEC regulations and accounting standards of the kind we now have still be relevant?

We believe that there is a great gap between what is technically feasible and what is politically acceptable. So long as we have a competitive free enterprise system, the participants in it are unlikely to allow unlimited access to every bit of information that is available to management. There will still have to be rules, therefore, regulating what information is to be publicly available. The gap between technical feasibility and political acceptability is well exemplified by the situation in Britain when the first "horseless carriages" appeared on the roads at the beginning of this century. The law required them to be preceded by a man carrying a red flag. The red flag soon became obsolete. But speed limits did not become obsolete. They simply changed their form.

The nature of financial reporting and the role and nature of accounting standards will depend essentially on the level of disaggregation of information at which access is to be permitted. If information were to be accessible by users at the ultimate level of disaggregation, criteria for the recognition of financial statement elements, for example, could be left to be decided by the users themselves.[1] But at any higher level of aggregation, without some rules preparers would have some latitude about what might be included in the aggregates—about what was to be recognized, in other words. Thus, though the form of financial reporting will probably be different from what we have at present, its essential nature might not be so different. The rest of this report is based on that assumption.

Of course that does not mean that we are content to leave financial reports as they now are, nor to rely on evolution to bring progress. We have several suggestions below for improving financial reports without changing their essential character. These suggestions add up to a call for the broadening of their scope with a view to making them more useful to those who seek information about the enterprises they invest in, lend to, are employed by or do business with.

THE ACCOUNTING EXPECTATIONS GAP

Much has been written about an expectations gap in auditing, and the Auditing Standards Board in the US and its counterparts in other countries have been active in recent years in trying to shrink it. Less has been heard about an expectations gap in accounting—specifically, in financial reporting. The FASB's conceptual framework might have been expected to address this matter, especially in its consideration of issues of recognition and measurement; but SFAC No. 5 was virtually silent on the subject. So was the International Accounting Standards Committee's *Framework for the Preparation and Presentation of Financial Statements* (July 1989) and the Canadian Institute of Chartered Accountants' statement, *Financial Statement Concepts* (September 1988).

The same cannot be said of a discussion document prepared by the Research Committee of the Institute of Chartered Accountants of Scotland, *Making Corporate Reports Valuable* (1988). That document at the outset asked what financial reporting achieved, and what it was intended to achieve. The answer the committee gave was: "Surely the intention is to show what is actually happening to an entity, expressing the salient facts as far as practicable in financial terms" (para. 1.2). They then went on to identify "the basic shortcomings of present-day financial reporting,—the adherence to legal form rather than economic substance, the use

---

[1]It may be said that this leaves no room for the use of accounting expertise. The point is that any accounting expertise would be provided by and for the user (or by an expert employed by him), not by the preparer. The user would still call the tune.

of cost rather than value, the concentration on the past rather than the future and the interest in 'profit' rather than wealth" (para. 1.18). These conclusions in part parallel our own, though we set them out here mainly as interesting evidence of concern about an accounting expectations gap in another part of the world.

We believe that concern about this expectations gap is widespread. But before trying to describe it, one must first consider whose expectations are in question. The expectations of a financial analyst will be quite different from those of the person whose only contact with the stock market is through his or her employer's pension fund. In discussing the expectations gap, we shall have in mind the reasonably well-informed investor, one who is able intelligently to read a company's annual report. If general purpose financial reports are primarily addressed to such a person, they will probably be of the greatest value, and other special interests—employees, for example, or financial analysts—can be served, if necessary, by special purpose reports.

It is easy to agree with the Scottish report that financial reports should reflect "economic reality." Unfortunately that leaves much room for disagreement as to where reality is to be found. It is, however, fairly easy to point to some characteristics of financial statements drawn up in accordance with present generally accepted accounting principles—we refer to US GAAP unless otherwise stated—that by no stretch of the imagination can be said to depict reality.

The distinction drawn here between financial reports and financial statements should be noted. The information conveyed by financial reports is certainly not limited to what is contained in the financial statements, and it is easy to excuse deficiencies in the statements by saying that they can be made good by disclosure outside the statements. The ever-increasing volume of information required to be disclosed in notes and supplementary statements is itself in part an indictment of the shortcomings of the financial statements themselves. It is to those shortcomings that we first address ourselves.

The Incompleteness of Financial Statements

The most general criticism to be levelled at financial statements in their present form is that they are seriously *incomplete*. Completeness, in this context, is of course a relative term, for as the FASB pointed out in its Concepts Statement No. 2, using an analogy between financial statements and maps, "a 'general purpose' map that tried to be 'all purpose' would be unintelligible, once information about political boundaries, communications, physical features, geological structure, climate, economic activity, ethnic groupings, and all the other things that mapmakers can map were put on it" (para. 25). A similar limitation in financial statements is inescapable. Nevertheless, just as some gaps in a map would be intolerable, some of the gaps in present-day financial statements are difficult to accept.

One respect in which financial statements are now incomplete is that, because they are substantially transaction-based, they fail to recognize some value changes occurring during a period that are not associated with a transaction. Perhaps the most important consequence of this incompleteness is that it makes "earnings" an unsatisfactory measure of performance, both entity and management performance. The fact is that the concept of "earnings" is one of the most frequently used and one of the most ill-defined concepts in our accounting vocabulary. We shall return to this matter later when we discuss the nature and measurement of "performance" and the bases of measurement to be used in financial statements.

Whether the absence of full information about the uncertainty of the amounts shown in financial statements is an aspect of their incompleteness or whether it constitutes misrepresentation is a moot point. The fact is that the deterministic nature of financial statements does misrepresent the situation depicted therein, because almost all of the items shown as assets and many of the items shown as liabilities or equities have uncertain values. The element of futurity (and therefore of uncertainty) inherent in the concepts of assets and liabilities is clear from their definitions as "probable future economic benefits" and "probable future sacrifices of economic benefits." The very term "probable" implies uncertainty. Yet they are shown in the balance sheet with single values attached to them as if those values alone had any claim to represent them faithfully.

Accrual accounting, by its very nature, involves looking into the future. Depreciation accounting requires an estimate of an asset's life and, ideally, an estimate of its future cash flows. An allowance for uncollectibles is an allowance for losses that cannot be quantified until some future event causes them to crystallize. Accounting for warranty claims, pensions, other post-employment benefits, and deferred taxes all call for estimates of uncertain future amounts. The appendix to SAS 57, *Auditing Accounting Estimates,* gives a long list of examples of accounting estimates.

SFAS No. 5, *Accounting for Contingencies,* states that when a loss contingency exists, the likelihood that a future event will confirm the loss or impairment of an asset or the incurrence of a liability can range from probable to remote. These terms are defined as follows:

(a) Probable. The future event or events are likely to occur.

(b) Reasonably possible. The chance of the future event or events occurring is more than remote but less than likely.

(c) Remote. The chance of the future event or events occurring is slight.

This is one way of classifying uncertainties, but there are many others. The uncertainty of a quantity can be indicated by stating the range within which it might fall. This information might be amplified by stating the most likely value it might take on within the range (i.e. the mode). Better still, all the possible outcomes, with the probabilities attaching to each, can be summed up in an expected value. However, an expected value has a troublesome characteristic in that it may not be one of the possible outcomes. For example, if on the toss of a coin a player may get $200 for a head and nothing for a tail, the expected value of the outcome is $100; yet $100 is not a possible outcome.

Fortunately, uncertainty can be reduced when quantities are aggregated. The life expectancy of the male population is much easier to predict than the life expectancy of any individual man. Thus, the problem of depicting uncertainty in accounting is affected by the level of aggregation of the quantities in question.

The dominant practice at present is to select a single outcome—the most likely outcome, the mode—in quantifying uncertain accounting phenomena, although in some situations conservative accountants choose the lower bound. Since it is rarely feasible to disclose more than one or two possible outcomes, we believe that the mode, the most likely outcome, should be established as standard practice, but that where there is a material difference between the mode and the expected value of possible outcomes, then the expected value should be disclosed as well, with sufficient explanation to make its significance clear to users of the statements.

INTANGIBLES

Another important respect in which financial statements are incomplete results from the treatment accorded intangible items. Goodwill, trademarks, brands and other intangibles are included in the balance sheet when they are acquired by purchase, and consolidation goodwill (under that or some other name) appears when a business is acquired for more than the fair value of its net assets. But these purchased intangibles will be eliminated by gradual amortization through the income statement (or, in some jurisdictions, by immediate write-off to reserves) regardless of whether their value has diminished, has been maintained, or even has increased. Similar intangibles that have been created by the entity itself never enter into the balance sheet at all.

The inclusion of purchased goodwill and the omission of internally generated goodwill is one of accounting's greatest anomalies. It is usually excused on the ground that purchased goodwill is the result of an identifiable transaction that provides evidence of an identifiable cost, whereas nonpurchased goodwill is not. This is a somewhat lame excuse, because nonpurchased goodwill is also the result of transactions—a large number of them—such as the hiring of superior employees, payments for training and research, and so on. Unfortunately it would be difficult to distinguish transactions of this kind that generate goodwill from those that merely maintain it. Accountants have chosen to take the easy road by recognizing identifiable transactions and ignoring the others. Ignoring the others leaves a serious hole in the balance sheet and understates income in the income statement by charging it with expenditures that are in fact creating an asset. Moreover, where the entity has purchased goodwill, which is then amortized, the income statement is burdened with a charge for the diminution in value of an asset that may not be diminishing in value. Indeed, its value may be increasing. If so, the income statement will get no credit for the increase.

Not unrelated to intangibles is the treatment of research and development expenditures. SFAS No. 2 requires that R&D expenditure be written off as incurred. In the UK, SSAP 13 requires that expenditures on pure and applied research (other than that embodied in fixed assets) should be written off as incurred, but development expenditure may, in certain defined circumstances, be deferred to future periods "to the extent that its recovery can reasonably be regarded as assured." The corresponding Canadian standard (section 3450 of the CICA Handbook) goes further and says that development *should* be deferred if certain criteria are satisfied and there is a similar assurance of recovery. The International Accounting Standards Committee is at present in the process of revising its IAS 9 to bring it into line with the Canadian standard as regards the treatment of development expenditures.

Without doubt R&D is an activity that is engaged in with a view to future benefits, though of course those future benefits are not assured when the expenditures are made. But the same thing could be said of many expenditures that are confidently accounted for as assets. Though the uncertainty about the outcome of specific R&D projects may be greater than with most forward-looking expenditures, the same thing is not necessarily true where companies, as in the pharmaceuticals industry, have many projects going at any one time. The probability of total failure of all of them is low. In such a situation, it is likely that a company's assets will be understated in its balance sheet by the immediate expensing of R&D expenditures.

With the decline in smoke-stack industries and the growing importance of service industries and of high-tech industries dependent on research, the gap left in financial statements by the omission of internally generated intangibles is becoming increasingly serious.

The recognition of valuable intangible assets in the balance sheet would without doubt add to that document's relevance. What makes recognition difficult if not impossible is the problem of valuing such assets reliably. But it is worth pausing to consider the meaning of "reliably." The FASB has defined reliability as "the quality of information that assures that information is reasonably free from error and bias and faithfully represents what it purports to represent" (SFAC 2). Another definition says that "accounting information is reliable if the user of it has a reasonable assurance that it faithfully represents what it purports to represent." Both definitions make it clear that faithful representation is an essential ingredient of reliability, and a balance sheet that omits what may be a company's most important assets can hardly be said to be representationally faithful, and hence is not reliable. It is the other ingredient of reliability, verifiability, that is lacking from the numbers put on intangible assets that have been internally generated. Thus, neither including nor excluding nonpurchased intangibles can be said to be reliable—including them because they may lack verifiability, excluding them because that lacks representational faithfulness.

Of course, there is nothing truly reliable about the amount left over after amortizing the cost of purchased goodwill for a year or two. The amount left in the balance sheet will probably have little relationship with the then current value of goodwill. It will be merely the result of an arithmetic computation.

There have been several suggestions for dealing with this problem. The Scottish Institute's committee proposed that a Statement of Assets and Liabilities should show, in addition to the net identifiable assets, the market capitalization of the enterprise. Changes in the difference between the two would be the subject of comment by management. The proposal has some merit. Another suggestion is to have a class of assets, which might be called contingent assets, that would be disclosed but not recognized (in the full accounting sense that they would be recorded in the entity's records and financial statements). There could also be contingent claims. A third suggestion is that the discretionary expenditures, such as research, training, and advertising that result in the formation of goodwill internally should be given special prominence in the financial statements, and summarized for (say) the last five years, to allow users of the statements to form their own judgment about the intangibles that are missing from the balance sheet.

We think this matter needs further research. Our own recommendations will be found at the end of this report.

OFF-BALANCE SHEET ITEMS

There have always been contingent liabilities, such as those for guarantees or the costs of pending litigation, that have been noted on but have not been included in the balance sheet. Thus there is nothing new about off-balance sheet risk. But much attention has been given during the last few years to the proliferation of financial arrangements that have enabled companies to raise money or gain control of assets without increasing their apparent indebtedness on their balance sheets. By this means the entity's financial position is made to look less risky than it otherwise would. This is another respect in which things are not always what they seem in financial statements. However, standard setters and legislators have been closing in on these dubious practices in recent years, and it may in the near future be more difficult to resort to them to avoid disclosing the true facts.

One of the earliest of these devices was the lease. By leasing assets instead of buying them, the need for finance by the lessee was obviated but, depending on the terms of the lease, the risks of ownership as well as the benefits remained with the lessee. In the US, SFAS No. 13 and in the UK SSAP No. 21 have for several years now required lessors to show an asset and a liability in the balance sheet where an asset is held on a finance (generally a long-term) lease. Operating (i.e. nonfinance) leases are exempt from this requirement, and though keeping lease liabilities off the balance sheet is more difficult than it used to be, the standards can still be defeated.

Another device for diminishing apparent risk, by making a loan look like a sale, is the sale and repurchase agreement. The seller/borrower sells an asset (e.g. land) to a purchaser/lender under a contract that binds the seller to repurchase it, or gives him an option to repurchase and/or gives the buyer an option to resell it, at prices that may be fixed in the contract or that may be determinable in some other specified way. The contract may give the seller the right to use the asset (say, to develop the land) during the time that the purchaser has the legal title.

The FASB has already intervened to deal with contracts to sell and repurchase products. SFAS No. 49 (1981) requires that the sponsor (i.e. the "seller") shall record a liability at the time the proceeds are received from the other entity to the extent that the product is covered by the financing arrangement. The sponsor is not to record the transaction as a sale and is not to remove the covered product from the assets in its balance sheet.

The broader question concerning the treatment of other sale and repurchase agreements in financial statements in the US awaits the completion of the FASB's project on financial instruments. The Board has already, in SFAS 105 (March 1990), stipulated certain disclosures of information about financial instruments that have off-balance-sheet risk, but as yet without changing any requirements for recognition, measurement, or classification of such instruments in financial statements.

In the UK, ED 49, "Reflecting the substance of transactions in assets and liabilities," was issued by the Accounting Standards Committee in March 1990 to deal with several situations, including sale and repurchase agreements, involving off-balance-sheet risk. The broad thrust of this document is set out in paragraphs 59 and 60, as follows:

> 59. The substance of an enterprise's transactions should be reflected in its financial statements. In determining the substance of a transaction, all its aspects and implications should be identified and greater weight given to those likely to have a commercial effect in practice. Where a transaction in only one in a connected series, the substance of the series should be viewed as a whole.

> 60. In determining how the substance of a transaction should be reflected in the financial statements, it is necessary to consider the extent to which the transaction has increased or decreased the various assets or liabilities previously recognized in the accounts of the enterprise and the extent to which it has given rise to assets or liabilities not previously recognized.

SUBSIDIARIES AND QUASI SUBSIDIARIES

Another perceived deficiency in the present state of financial reporting, but also one on which the standard setters (or, in the UK, the legislature) have made or are making progress, is the ability of subsidiary companies to escape consolidation. The FASB has narrowed this escape hatch considerably by means of SFAS No. 94 (October 1987), and will have more to say when its reporting entity project is complete. In the UK, the Companies Act 1989 has redefined a subsidiary company.

Representational faithfulness would seem to require that all the companies controlled by a single parent, regardless of their legal relationships, should be regarded as a group and should be included in the consolidated financial statements of the group. The FASB has provided a definition of "control" in SFAS No. 57, Related Party Disclosures, as "the possession, direct or indirect, of the power to direct or cause the direction of the management and policies of a specified party whether through ownership, by contract, or otherwise." Such a definition may give rise to difficulties where a small entity, independently owned, is bound by contract to sell all or a major part of its output to a single customer. Is it "controlled" by the customer and should its affairs be consolidated with the customer's? We think not, though the FASB's answer must be awaited. But in general the idea that control should be the basis of consolidation seems sound. "Significant economic dependence" already has to be reported to the SEC. At the present time, in the US, the general basis of consolidation is still that laid down in Accounting Research Bulletin No. 51 (August 1959). ARB 51, para. 2, states that

> the usual condition for a controlling financial interest is ownership of a majority voting interest, and, therefore, as a general rule ownership by one company, directly or indirectly, of over fifty percent of the outstanding voting shares of another company is a condition pointing toward consolidation.

Of course, control can be exercised in other ways than through holding shares, but without a majority voting interest it need not, under present US GAAP, lead to consolidation. Here are some examples of such situations where consolidation can be avoided.

1. Company X holds 50 percent of the shares in company A and also 50 percent of the shares in company B. The remaining 50 percent of the shares in company B are held by company A, which has another shareholder (frequently a friendly bank) owning the remaining 50 percent of its shares. X is entitled to 75 percent of B's income, yet B is not a subsidiary of X.

2. Company A holds less than 50 percent of the shares in B, the remainder being held by a merchant bank, but A has an option to acquire enough shares to take its holding to over 50 percent of the equity of the investee.

3. A does not hold shares in B but controls it by providing all of its nonequity finance, which could be withdrawn at any time. B's directors therefore obey A's wishes.

We shall content ourselves by drawing attention to these situations, which are presumably receiving the FASB's attention as part of its reporting entity project. In each case, the nonconsolidation of the quasi subsidiary misstates the group's financial ratios and deprives the parent company's shareholders and creditors of relevant information.

ARB 51 had allowed some exceptions from the requirement that a majority shareholding should lead to consolidation, and (the FASB said in 1987) businesses had "increasingly used 'nonhomogeneity' as a basis for excluding from consolidation majority-owned (even wholly owned) subsidiaries considered different in character from the parent and its other affiliates" (SFAS. No. 94, para. 6). This trend was reversed by SFAS No. 94, which requires all majority-owned subsidiaries to be consolidated.

In the UK, the Companies Act 1989, in section 21, now defines a subsidiary as follows:

An undertaking is a "subsidiary" of another undertaking, its parent, if the parent

(a) holds a majority of the voting rights in it, or

(b) is a member of the undertaking and has the right to appoint or remove a majority of its board of directors.

(c) is a member of it and controls alone, pursuant to an agreement with other shareholders or members, a majority of the voting rights in it.

(d) has the right to exercise a dominant influence over the undertaking:
(i) by virtue of provisions contained in the undertaking's memorandum or articles or
(ii) by virtue of a control contract.

(e) has a participating interest (generally 20 percent of the shares in the undertaking), and
(i) actually exercises a dominant influence over it, or
(ii) it and the subsidiary undertakings are managed on a unified basis.

It is too early to say whether this new legislation will prevent the evasion of consolidation that has been widespread hitherto. In case it does not, it will be reinforced by the concept of a "quasi subsidiary," which will be introduced into British accounting standards if ED 49 referred to above is adopted by the new Accounting Standards Board. A quasi subsidiary of a reporting enterprise is defined as "a company, trust or other vehicle which, though not fulfilling the Companies Act definition of a subsidiary undertaking, is directly or indirectly controlled by and a source of benefits or risks for the reporting enterprise or its subsidiaries that are in substance no different from those that would arise were the vehicle a subsidiary." If it looks like a duck and quacks like a duck, then it's a duck.

Debt Disguised as Equity

Another way to minimize the apparent riskiness of an enterprise as judged from its financial statements is to make its debt look like equity. If this can be done while at the same time retaining the tax-deductibility of the interest on the debt, so much the better. Complex schemes have been thought up to secure these ends, and even relatively simple steps may be taken to disguise a liability as equity. For example, shares issued by a subsidiary may be guaranteed by the parent company which, on default by the subsidiary, will pay the due dividend whether or not the parent has any distributable profits. In other words, to the parent company's stockholders the payment is more like interest than a dividend. In addition, the parent may also guarantee redemption of the subsidiary's shares and grant its shareholders the same rights as the parent's creditors over the parent company's assets. Thus the subsidiary shares have all the characteristics of debt rather than equity as far as the parent company is concerned, yet may be treated in the group financial statements as minority interest rather than as a liability on the basis or hope that the balance of probability is that the guarantee will never be called and consequently a liability will never arise.

The issues involved in drawing a line between liabilities and equity are complex, as is evidenced by the publication of the substantial discussion memorandum, *Distinguishing between*

Liability and Equity Instruments and Accounting for Instruments with Characteristics of Both, by the FASB in August 1990. One proposal that the FASB is exploring is to get rid of the distinction altogether. These issues deserve more careful study than we can give them, and we make no recommendations on them.

TWO OTHER GAPS

There are two other defects in financial reports that we shall discuss later. One is their failure, or rather their partial failure, to recognize the time value of money. The other is their failure adequately to reflect the social performance of business. Both of these subjects have a literature of their own, and our discussion will necessarily be brief. But before taking up those topics, we shall consider the nature and measurement of performance more generally.

CRITERIA FOR A MEASUREMENT SYSTEM

Before looking at some of the measurements presently used in financial reports, it is desirable to specify some at least of the criteria by which an accounting measurement system should be judged. Some light was thrown on that matter by the FASB's Concepts Statement No. 2 on Qualitative Characteristics. The criteria seem rather obvious when stated baldly, yet the fact is that our present system of measurement falls far short of them.

The primary criterion must be that the information provided by the reporting system should be relevant to the needs of the user. If it is not relevant, it cannot justify the cost of providing it. The relevance in today's market of the acquisition cost of a building bought 20 years ago is, to say the least, dubious.

Second, the reported amounts of resources and obligations of an enterprise should faithfully represent those resources and obligations at the reporting date. To do this, it will often be necessary to estimate the outcome of future transactions and events. It is debatable as to how faithfully a record of past transactions, except in conditions of unusual stability, can represent resources and obligations at the reporting date.

Third, so far as possible, the information provided should be capable of independent verification, by which we mean more than simply checking the calculations that underlay the accounting entries in the first place. We mean that, so far as possible, information should be based on transactions entered into by the reporting entity or on comparable transactions entered into by other entities at the relevant date. Some important pieces of information in financial statements are not capable of independent verification in the above sense. For example, the cost allocations used in accounting for depreciation are not truly verifiable because they are arbitrary. The allocation of the cost of purchases (and other costs in manufacturing businesses) between the cost of goods sold and the cost of inventory is also substantially arbitrary.

Fourth, the system should be internally consistent. It should make like things look alike, both in periods of stable prices and in periods of changing prices. Our present system fails to do that, both because it treats all units of money as equal, regardless of differences in their purchasing power, and because in some situations it treats present and future amounts as equal without regard to the time value of money.

The Nature and Measurement of Performance

Without much doubt the most widely-used summary indicator of entity performance is earnings per share. Any financially sophisticated person knows that this is a naive measure, but we continue to use it. The fact is that "performance," even in a business context, is too complex and multidimensional a concept to be reduced to any single indicator.

Performance can be viewed from many points of view, because each group involved in an economic entity, whether it be a business enterprise or a nonprofit organization, is looking for different things from it. Thus for each group, performance has a different significance. For stockholders, profitability, in the sense of increasing the value of the enterprise, may have much to commend it. For employees, steady employment and high earnings are what matter. For bondholders, credit rating is a top priority. For environmentalists, performance means concern for the environment. For other sections of the public, fairness in hiring and promotion, product quality, pricing and a hundred other things are matters of prime concern. Thus to capture the many dimensions of entity performance, nothing less than an array of measures will serve. Indeed, each one of the dimensions of performance just mentioned, as well as a multitude of others, calls for an array of measures of its own.

One insuperable difficulty lies in the way of satisfactorily assessing performance, and that is that *past performance can only be judged when the future is known.* An enterprise's sales revenue this year is not simply the result of actions taken this year. Past advertising, past efforts at quality control, past design improvements, past research—these and other past actions are all determinants of this year's revenues and profits. The same is true of past capital expenditures, past hirings, past strategic decisions. And similar actions that are being taken now will only be capable of being judged when their outcomes are known at some time in the future. Nothing that an accountant can do can change this, or make this year's financial statements yield a full assessment of current performance.

Another distinction needs to be drawn before proceeding. That is the distinction between the performance of an entity and the performance of those who run it. This distinction is more important, perhaps, for internal than for external reporting, because the performance of management at each level of authority must be judged by reference to what they can control, abstracting so far as possible from the results of decisions taken at a higher level. But even for external reporting, the distinction is valid because a highly competent CEO may find himself in a no-win situation, due perhaps to a new government regulation or to a sudden and unpredictable change in the supply of an essential raw material. Equally, a mediocre management may appear to be doing well because of conditions that favor them. It would probably be possible, by means of a special investigation, to separate the two kinds of performance in a particular situation. We do not envision it as being possible, at an acceptable cost, as a part of routine financial reporting.

Earnings and Comprehensive Income

We see no evidence that, of all the competing measures of enterprise performance, net income (however defined) or some variant of it is about to lose its primacy, nor do we think it should if it can be defined to provide a better measure of performance than earnings now does. Even then it would need to be supplemented. To achieve these ends, the present reporting system needs to be changed, and we shall discuss why and how those changes should be effected.

The main reason why income, in one or other of its guises, continues to occupy such an important position among measures of enterprise performance is that everything that the entity does has an impact on the "bottom line." There are many partial measures of performance that can be and should be used. To pick a few at random, the marketing function might be judged by the market share of the company's principal products, production and some administrative functions by productivity per head, research by the number of patents obtained, the personnel function by the number of strikes or labor turnover, and so on. All of these have their effect on net income; but only income itself comprehends them all.

We earlier referred to the FASB's failure to define the term "earnings." No other standard setting body has defined it either, so far as we are aware. Probably this lack of definition is due to the fact that it is difficult to encapsulate in a few words our present methods of quantifying assets and liabilities (and therefore revenues and expenses, which are defined in terms of *changes* in assets and liabilities). The difficulty stems from the fact that financial statements are substantially transaction-based, but though most of the values in them are derived from transactions to which the entity itself was a party, they also import values that are not based on any of the entity's transactions, and some that are not transaction-based at all. The simplest example of the use of values determined by outside (market) transactions is when inventory is marked down below cost. For the use of values not based on transactions at all, we need look no further than to the cost allocations used in depreciation accounting or to accruals for pensions. How to sum all of this up in a short phrase?

Perhaps "cost or lower recoverable amount" is as close as we can come to summarizing the present valuation rules in use in the US and Canada, though it implies a fuller recognition of impairment of fixed assets than is common, and it does not cover the asset revaluations that are permissible in Britain.

It is the downward bias of the "cost or lower recoverable amount" rule that is a primary reason for saying that financial statements are incomplete. They are incomplete because they do not recognize upward value changes in assets that may occur between the date of their acquisition and the accounting date. For reasons to be discussed later, it may not be feasible to recognize all such value changes; but at least we should acknowledge that by ignoring them financial statements are incomplete.

The FASB made several statements about the nature of earnings in SFAC No. 5 without arriving at a definition. They said, for example, that "the concept of earnings . . . is similar to net income in present practice . . . However, earnings is not exactly the same as present net income . . ." (para. 33). They said, later, "Earnings is a measure of performance during a period that is concerned primarily with the extent to which asset inflows associated with cash-to-cash cycles substantially completed (or completed) during the period exceed (or are less than) asset outflows associated, directly or indirectly, with the same cycles" (para. 36); and later still, "earnings focuses on what the entity has received or reasonably expects to receive for its output (revenues) and what it sacrifices to produce and distribute that output (expenses). Earnings also includes results of the entity's incidental or peripheral transactions and some effects of other events and circumstances stemming from the environment (gains and losses)" (par. 38).

These statements do not define earnings, because they do not make it clear which asset inflows and outflows enter into earnings and which do not, nor which gains and losses are included and which are not. For instance, inventory write-downs certainly enter into earnings, but do not appear to be covered by the FASB's description (unless it is covered by "reasonably expects to receive"). It is unclear whether gains from "mark-to-market" accounting for investments would be included in the "effects of other events and circumstances" referred to in paragraph 38 of SFAC No. 5. Without question unrealized holding gains would not be included in earnings, nor in the FASB's broader concept of comprehensive income.

It is unfortunate that the FASB has preempted the term "comprehensive income" for a concept that is not comprehensive. SFAC 5 (para. 44) shows the relation between comprehensive income and earnings as follows:

$$\text{Earnings} - \frac{\text{Cumulative}}{\text{accounting adjustments}} + \frac{\text{Other nonowner}}{\text{changes in equity}} = \text{Comprehensive income}$$

The problem lies in the meaning of "other nonowner changes in equity." What the Board means here, it is clear from the rest of the Statement, is "other nonowner changes in equity that are recognized in accordance with present GAAP." But since GAAP do not now recognize unrealized gains in value, comprehensive income as defined by the Board does not correspond to what is usually called Hicksian income, the amount that can be consumed (or, in the case of a corporation, distributed) during a period while remaining as well off at the end of the period as at the beginning.

The partial and biassed recognition of value changes required by GAAP follows from the valuation rule used (with modifications) in accounting, cost or lower recoverable amount. Historical cost is a natural basis for accounting in a double-entry system primarily concerned with the recording of transactions under conditions of price stability. For such a purpose and in such conditions, it is relevant and reliable, in that it is both representationally faithful and verifiable. But when the system is called on to reflect the effects of other events and circumstances besides transactions to which the entity itself is a party, and when it confronts conditions of unstable prices, its virtues fall away.

More specifically, historical cost accounting (HCA) is defective in the following respects:

- HCA introduces a time lag into the matching of costs and revenues. So long as prices, both relative prices and the general level of prices, are stable, this does not matter. But such a situation is quite exceptional. Changes in relative prices are discussed below. If the price-level is rising or falling (as it virtually always is) revenues at one price-level are matched with earlier costs incurred at a different (usually lower) price-level, thus overstating profits when prices are rising and understating them when prices are falling. This is particularly notable in the case of FIFO inventory accounting and in accounting for the depreciation of long-lived assets.

- If relative prices change between the time that resources are acquired and the balance sheet date (assuming that they have not already been sold), the value of resources to the enterprise is misrepresented if they continue to be carried at historical cost. GAAP marks down current assets that have fallen in value, but never marks them up, and generally leaves noncurrent assets at original cost (less depreciation, if any). Unless the time-lag between the date of a transaction and the balance sheet date is minimal, the amount shown in the balance sheet will not reflect current conditions. The problem is exacerbated if the general level of prices is also changing. For these reasons, the balance sheet has little claim to being a statement of financial position at the accounting date. It does not realistically represent the resources employed in the business. Even its name is obsolete.

- By showing only realized gains and ignoring unrealized gains (and some losses), the income statement misrepresents the performance of the enterprise and of its management, period by period. It does this by attributing gains and some losses to the period in which they are realized, not to the period when they accrue. If appreciated assets are held for a long time—land, say—the financial statements may fail to give credit for many years for a good decision to acquire the assets at an earlier time.

- Because of the importance attached to realization in determining gains and losses, management can manipulate profits by judiciously timing the sale of assets or the redemption of liabilities that show gains or losses.

- Since HCA financial statements are kept in nominal units of money, information is lacking about purchasing power gains and losses on monetary assets and liabilities.

- If the assertion made above that a HCA balance sheet does not faithfully represent the resources employed in a business is accepted, it follows that financial ratios such as ROI are distorted.

- Because the purchasing power of money is constantly changing—periods of price stability have been virtually unknown in living memory—and because financial statements are kept in nominal units of money, intertemporal comparisons of accounting results are distorted unless corrected for price level changes.

- HCA can distort comparisons between periods for other reasons. It does not always make like things look alike.

- Because of changes in the value of money, and because financial statements contain a mixture of past costs and current values, they cannot claim to be truly additive.

This is not a comprehensive list of the defects in financial reporting that are attributable to HCA. Additionally, for example, HCA is largely responsible for such anomalies as pooling (merger accounting in the UK), for if book values were close to current values, much of the incentive for pooling would disappear. The retention of outdated book values, with consequent low depreciation expense and low cost inventory in the merged enterprise, would no longer be possible. But leaving such matters aside, the most important problem with HCA is what it does to earnings.

The essential idea behind any concept of income is that it is the surplus left over after capital has been maintained intact. There are many ways of defining "maintaining capital intact," because there are many ways of defining and quantifying capital. Capital may be viewed in financial terms or in physical terms. Maintaining capital in financial terms can mean maintaining the present value of expected net receipts, maintaining the market value of net assets (excluding unrecognized intangibles), or maintaining the market value of owners' equity, and all of these can be measured in nominal or in real terms. "Under a physical concept of capital, such as operating capability," according to the IASC's *Framework for the Preparation and Presentation of Financial Statements* (July 1989), "capital is regarded as the productive capacity of the enterprise based on, for example, units of output per day." Whichever of these meanings is attached to "maintaining capital intact," accounting income, as presently computed, does not do it. It is impossible to say in what sense, if any, capital is maintained by our present methods of income determination.

It is a desirable characteristic of any measure of performance that it should signal promptly and positively when a good decision has been made. By a "good decision" we mean a decision from which the expected net benefits are positive. Earnings cannot be relied on to give a reliable signal. Expenditures for such purposes as research, training, or advertising, made for the purpose of increasing future cash inflows, have to be expensed currently and therefore depress earnings even though they may be having a positive effect on the value of the business. Selling an asset that has appreciated somewhat increases earnings, while holding it for further appreciation (which may be the right thing to do) does not.

Leaving aside the social obligations of business for the present, the objective of those running an enterprise should be to maximize its value. That points to an income number, if one is to be used, that reflects changes in value more readily than earnings now does. If it can do that, it will have gained in relevance. At the same time, it must be reliable; that is, it must be capable of verification and it must be a faithful representation of the value changes it purports to represent. That rules out, for many assets, the theoretically ideal basis of valuation, namely, the present value of their future cash flows. Only in a world of certainty would such a valuation basis be generally acceptable—or, indeed, feasible. In a world of uncertainty, predictions of the kind called for here are, except in certain restricted circumstances and within certain limits, too subjective to provide an acceptable basis of valuation. That points to the use of market values of some kind, where they are available.

In a world of perfect and complete markets, the choice of market values would present no problem. The closer to perfection the market comes, the narrower the spread will be between buying and selling prices and the more uniform will prices be regardless of where and when a transaction is entered into. The more complete the market is, the easier it becomes to find a price that fits any particular situation. In perfect and complete markets, the market price captures all the relevant attributes of an asset or liability, including the time value of money and risk, among other factors. But in the real world, markets are not complete and they are not perfect.

Informational asymmetries are a major difficulty in estimating market prices. The owners of assets may have information that the market does not have, and that may lead to a limitation of the market or even the absence of a market for a particular kind of asset or liability altogether. For example, banks and thrifts may posses information that the market does not possess about default risk on a loan portfolio, and as a result there may be no market for such assets.

In incomplete and imperfect markets, the items being traded may differ in some significant respect from the asset or claim of the firm that is being accounted for. Where there is only a thin market for a particular kind of asset, for example where the time interval between trades is large, there can be disagreement about what the relevant price would have been for a trade that would have occurred during that interval. Thus it may be difficult to establish a price for thinly traded securities that have to be valued at year-end. Moreover, in thin markets, there may be concern as to whether the price at which a small trade takes place can be extrapolated to the price that would result from a larger order at the same point in time, even when control is not an issue in either transaction. Loans to less developed countries (LDCs) are an example of assets for which there is a thin market, if any. Further, again because of information asymmetries and resulting adverse selection, the assets traded by a firm may not be representative of similar (but not identical) assets that it continues to hold. In other words, there may be selective trading.

In imperfect and incomplete markets, then, there are major difficulties in the way of moving from a historical cost based reporting system (albeit with modifications) to a system based to a much greater extent than at present on current market values. But, as Arthur Wyatt once asked, if we had moved to a current value system fifty years ago, does any one suppose that there would now be an outcry for the restoration of historical cost as the basis of financial reporting, or that the past cost of an asset would be thought of as having any relevance in a balance sheet except as evidence of what the market value of the asset was at the time it was acquired? If both relative prices and the price level are stable (as they hardly ever are in practice), and if little time has elapsed since a transaction was entered into, then of course the bargain struck then has evidential value as to the current value of the item acquired. But if those conditions are not satisfied, since bygones are bygones, that past transaction has little or no relevance in determining where the entity stands today.

Caught between the rock of imperfect and incomplete markets and the hard place of the irrelevance of past costs for decision-making and as an indicator of current values, it is not surprising that accountants have argued about their relative merits for decades without reaching agreement. But there is a greater readiness today than formerly to give current values a more prominent position in financial statements, and we think that this trend should be accelerated. We recognize that several empirical studies have failed to find that replacement cost data as required, for example, by SFAS 33 and the SEC's ASB 190 provide incremental explanatory power beyond that provided by historical cost data with respect to the pricing of common shares. But conceptually the superiority of financial reports based on current values is so self-evident, at least on the relevance dimension, that we cannot defend the maintenance of historical cost as the primary basis of measurement. Moreover, current values are already used rather widely in financial reporting. Inventories when marked down below cost, marketable securities, other financial instruments to an increasing extent, allowances for uncollectibles that mark receivables down below the cost of goods sold, the use of current exchange rates for currency translation, and the periodic revaluation of assets in the UK, are all examples of departures from historical cost. Extending this frontier would not be a revolutionary change.

BASES OF MEASUREMENT FOR FINANCIAL STATEMENTS

Our first consideration in seeking valuation bases for use in financial reporting is their relevance. The reliability of the resulting numbers is of course important, but whether irrelevant numbers are reliable need be of no concern to anyone. Of course both relevance and reliability are matters of degree, and the trade-off between the two qualities has constantly to be weighed. We are guided by the thought that it is better to be approximately right than precisely wrong. The question is, in view of the market imperfections and incompleteness referred to above, how much approximation is acceptable as the price of relevance. It is easy to agree that some approximation can be accepted so long as the information resulting from a change in the basis of accounting would be reliable enough to be more useful than the information that we are now producing. But agreement on specifics is not so easy to reach.

Unfortunately, the Committee is not unanimous on how far and how fast we should move away from the present modified historical cost based system. Most of us believe that market values should be used, with or without the retention of historical cost data, where reliably determined market values are available. We are not agreed about the course to be followed where markets are imperfect, as in the case of specialized assets. Our recommendations are set out in the Recommendations section at the end of this report.

The Time Value of Money

We might have noted earlier, when reviewing some respects in which financial reports are now incomplete, that while GAAP recognizes the time value of money in some contexts, it signally fails to do so in others. Fixed term monetary assets and liabilities that are not in risk of default are now carried at their present values (based on the interest rate implicit or explicit in the original contract). Capital leases are carried at present value. Defined benefit pension costs are computed taking full account of the interest factor, and the valuation of oil and gas reserves takes account of discounting. But present value factors are ignored in certain major areas, such as when depreciating fixed assets, and the FASB, in SFAS 96, explicitly forbids discounting of deferred income taxes.

A striking example of where the FASB ignored the time value of money, presumably for political reasons relating to the then shaky position of many US banks, is to be found in SFAS 15, *Accounting by Debtors and Creditors for Troubled Debt Restructuring* (1977). Paragraph 30 of that standard stipulates that:

> A creditor in a troubled debt restructuring involving only modification of terms of a receivable—that is, not involving receipt of assets (including an equity interest in the debtor)—shall account for the effects of the restructuring prospectively and shall not change the recorded investment in the receivable at the time of the restructuring unless that amount exceeds the total future cash receipts specified by the new terms. That is, the effects of changes in the amounts or timing (or both) of future cash receipts designated either as interest or as face amount shall be reflected in future periods.

This means that in determining any loss from the restructuring, the creditor is not to discount any future receipts when comparing them with the face amount of the debt. A full recognition of the time value of money would require that the carrying value of the debt should at all times be equal to the present value of the remaining probable future cash flows discounted either at the rate implicit in the original transaction (under HCA) or at the current rate obtainable in the market for an investment of equivalent term and risk (under CCA).

The FASB has been studying what it calls "interest methods" since the fall of 1988, and it is to be expected that the Board will show more sensitivity to the need for discounting than it has sometimes shown in the past. Deferred taxes are an obvious candidate for discounting, and one interesting result of accounting for the liability for deferred taxes on a present value basis would be to diminish the difference between the US method of full tax allocation and the British method of partial allocation. This would come about because deferred taxes resulting from timing differences that are unlikely to reverse themselves in the near future would have, when discounted, little present value.

Depreciation accounting using a compound interest (CI) method—either the annuity or the sinking fund method—has long had the approval of theorists but has had little acceptance in practice, possibly because its relatively small charges during the early years of the asset's life with increasing charges thereafter seem to make cost recovery more uncertain. If CI depreciation is used for costing and pricing purposes, or in a regulated industry—that is, where prices are cost determined—this fear is not entirely ungrounded. But where prices are determined by the market, cost recovery depends on the amount by which current revenues exceed current outlays. Depreciation policy has little to do with cost recovery in such circumstances, and there is no reason to shun CI depreciation which, as a measurement device, has much to commend it. It is also an appropriate method for use by regulators.

There is fairly general agreement that in discounting the expected cash flows from an asset in order to determine its transaction value (as under APB opinion No. 21) the interest rate to be used should be the current rate obtainable in the market for an investment of equivalent term and risk. But one must be on one's guard against double-counting for risk. If the future cash flows have been budgeted conservatively, something like a default risk-free rate might be appropriate, since the risk premium has already been taken into account in the cash forecast. Similarly, if expected inflation has been built into the cash forecast, a nominal rate of interest is appropriate; but if inflation has not been allowed for, a real rate should be used.

REPORTING TO AND ABOUT LABOR

Our discussion of performance to this point has been conducted from the point of view of those who contribute capital to an enterprise, its investors and creditors. But there are many other stakeholders, notably its employees and, in a wider sense, the community at large. Before coming to the community at large, in this section we discuss briefly how more might be done in corporate reports to address the information needs of labor.

What corporate reports purport to give to those who contribute capital is an answer to the question: how good a company is this to put your money in? The corresponding question for labor would be: how good a company is this to choose as an employer? The answer, of course, may be different for different categories of employee.

As an example of what could be done to provide an answer to this question, we have examined a special report on a British company that gave highly specific information on the following matters:

Pay and fringe benefits: Among other things, the report gave information about payment systems at each of the company's main plants; weekly earnings and hours for each of the last four years, location by location; the distribution of earnings (number of employees at each point on the pay scale) at a typical location; weightings allocated to different factors (by outside consultants) in job evaluation schemes; fringe benefits (holidays, sick pay, pensions, and several other fringes). More information was given about blue-collar workers than about white-collar workers.

Job security: Redundancies and compensation therefor; plant closings.

Participation and alienation: Machinery for consultation; industrial relations (if there had been strikes during the period covered by the report, they would have been reported on); access to information about the company.

Health and safety at work: Frequency of accidents; safety organization; relations with government regulators (including the number of inspections in recent years); noise; chemical hazards.

Training: Number of training days per worker (by category); types of training.

Women—equal pay and opportunity: Numbers of male and female workers (by location); female average earnings and hours worked as percentage of male earnings and hours; number of male and female employees in each earnings bracket.

Race relations: Policy on employment of minorities; employment practices.

Employment of the handicapped: Percentage of handicapped workers at each location.

We offer this report simply as an example of what can be done to expand the coverage of corporate reporting and to correct, in part, its present narrow focus on one constituency, capital providers. We do not suggest that the volume of information given above about labor could all be given on an annual basis without incurring excessive costs. But it would be possible to select one or two aspects of employee welfare each year for discussion (in quantitative terms) in an annual report, so that over a five-year cycle all aspects would be covered.

Corporate Social Performance

Broadening still further our view of performance, one might ask "How good a citizen is this company?" Of course it would be naive to suppose that any easy answer is possible to such a question. To one person, off-shore drilling for oil is a threat to the environment, to another it is a valuable contribution to the national need for energy. The recent argument about the survival of the spotted owl and the protection of the remaining redwoods versus logging jobs in the Pacific northwest is another case in point. The accountant's duty in such matters (qua accountant) is clear. It is to be as neutral as possible, and to provide unbiased information that, together with information from other sources, will help the user to arrive at his/her own judgment. Of course the accountant is also a citizen, and as such is entitled to an opinion like everyone else.

Traditionally, financial reporting focuses on those costs and benefits that are internal to the firm. These alone are recorded in the firm's books, and these alone are reflected in its financial statements. In some quarters, this is regarded as another aspect of the accounting expectations gap. This view was reflected in an article in the January 1990 issue of *Scientific American* that, referring to the 1990 summit meeting of the Group of Seven major industrial democracies, said:

> The summit might well promote specific reforms in national and corporate accounting practices which currently discourage environmental protection by failing to reflect the real costs to society of pollution and thoughtless short-term exploitation of such natural resources as forests.

The costs and benefits internal to the firm of course also have external effects. Amounts disbursed through a firm's payroll have a direct impact on the local economy, and so do the purchases it makes. In fact, any attempt to draw a line between what is internal to the firm and what is external is fraught with difficulty. When looking for the social impact of an enterprise, the first things to look at are its products, which are not externalities in the economist's usual sense of that word. Its products are not merely the source of its revenue; they also satisfy the needs of its customers—essential needs when they are things like electrical power and telephone service, more questionable needs when they are cigarettes and handguns.

There are several measures that the accountant could report on in this connection, such as the quantity of output of principal products, the ratio of returns to sales (reflecting on customer satisfaction), and ratings of product quality by rating services such as Consumers Union. One statistic of general applicability that could easily be reported on to show the firm's con-

EXAMPLE

A Manufacturing Company Statement of Value Added

		Year to 31 Dec £M		Preceding Year £M
Turnover		103.9		102.3
Bought-in materials and services		67.6		72.1
Value added		£36.3		£30.2
Applied the following way:				
To pay employees				
wages, pensions, and fringe benefits		25.9		17.3
To pay providers of capital				
interest on loans	0.8		0.6	
dividends to shareholders	0.9		0.9	
		1.7		1.5
To pay government				
corporation tax payable		3.9		3.1
To provide for maintenance and expansion of assets				
depreciation	2.0		1.8	
retained profits	2.8		6.5	
		4.8		8.3
Value added		£36.3		£30.2

tribution to the gross national product is its value added. A simple example of such a statement, taken from *The Corporate Report* (Accounting Standards Steering Committee, London, 1975), is reproduced on page 401. The Committee's Task Force put it forward as "the simplest and most immediate way of putting profit into proper perspective vis-a-vis the whole enterprise as a collective effort by capital, management and employees . . . Value added is the wealth the reporting entity has been able to create by its own and by its employees' efforts. This statement would show how value added has been used to pay those contributing to its creation" (*The Corporate Report,* paragraph 6.7).

By expressing this statistic on a per capita basis, over a series of years and corrected for inflation, some idea might be given of the trend of productivity. But a word of caution is necessary here. Value added is heavily dependent on the firm's selling prices, which in turn are dependent on changes in product specification, the competitiveness of the market, and other factors. Equating value added per head with productivity is simplistic. If productivity is to be reported on—and it would add useful information for the firm's stakeholders—it needs to be done in a more sophisticated manner.

EXTERNALITIES

It was noted above that the costs borne by a firm (e.g. its payroll) have effects that extend beyond its boundaries. But costs like payroll are internalized by the firm in the first place. Money is exchanged for labor. But there are other costs of doing business that are not internalized, that is to say, they are not borne by the firm at all—or only marginally so, as when its own employees suffer from the air pollution it causes or because of damage suffered from a political backlash. To a much greater extent, these other costs are imposed on others. From society's point of view, they are as much costs of production as those that show up in the firm's books; but they do not appear in any financial statement.

An important allocational effect follows from that fact. Products that do not bear all of their own costs but impose part of them on others are undercosted and therefore, probably, underpriced. More than the optimum amount of society's resources are therefore likely to be attracted to their production.

Many externalities have market effects on others, but those effects are not always discernible, and certainly not always measurable. For example, if an incinerator opens up in a neighborhood, the surrounding land is likely to fall in value, and this effect may well be measurable. The effects of other externalities are more subtle, as when coal-burning power stations in the Middle West produce acid rain in New England. It is unlikely that the market effects of that can be discerned directly.

Where the market effects of externalities can be estimated, the threat of litigation may bring the parties themselves to make and receive payments by way of compensation. Joshua Ronen gave an example of such an arrangement.

> To illustrate, suppose that a machine shop, A, produces noise that brings about an increase in the number of defective devices produced by B, a neighboring manufacturer of highly specialized precision-electronic instruments. B's loss resulting from the noise interfering with the skilled workers' ability to perform is $400 per month, while his profit in the absence of damage amounts to $300 per month. A's profit from operations amounts to $350 per month. A noise stifling device could be installed in the machines to eliminate the damage to B; this would cost A $250 monthly.
>
> Clearly, from a social viewpoint, A should continue its operations, since the value of its production ($350) exceeds the cost of eliminating the damage to B. Given that A and B can get together and bargain, the socially desirable solution (with A continuing its operations) will prevail irrespective of whether A is legally liable to pay damages to B. If A is liable to B, the corrective device will be installed. It would be more profitable for A to incur the $250 monthly cost rather than produce the noise and pay $400. A's actual profit will be reduced from $350 to $100. The $250 are actual costs for A incurred to preclude the adverse effects of its operations on B. ("Accounting for Social Costs and Benefits," *Trueblood Report,* Volume 2, p. 319 (AICPA, New York, 1974).)

Our present accounting methods have no difficulty in handling a situation like that described above. It is where the effects of an externality (which may, incidentally, be positive as well as negative) are more diffused and therefore less measurable that we run into trouble. Progress has been made in recent years, by environmental protection laws, both state and federal, and also through the pressure of public opinion, to force those who impose costs on society to internalize them by paying compensation or clean-up costs. Cleaning up oil spills has cost the oil companies billions of dollars. Accountants could contribute to this process by giving more prominence to these internalized costs in their reports.

The "pure" externality, the noninternalized externality, is more difficult to report on. It may be that the lack of progress in this matter has in part been due to over-ambitious proposals that have been made in the past. The major difficulties arise when we try to evaluate external costs and benefits in dollars. A seemingly naive but perhaps more effective approach is to concentrate on physical quantities except where dollar amounts are easy to come by (e.g. differential earnings in dollars of minority workers and others). Everyone is familiar with miles per gallon of gasoline as a measure of fuel economy for automobiles. Converting that figure to dollars does add to the statistic's informativeness, but few situations are as simple as that.

This seems to be what David Linowes was saying as long ago as 1972:

> Maybe we should begin thinking of adding another dimension to periodic reporting, just as we have added the statement of source and application of funds to the customary profit and loss statement and balance sheet. You might have something in the nature of a separate socio-economic operating statement, a statement that would somehow quantify the positive and negative effects on society of actions taken by the business organization during the period being reported.

> I can't believe it is ever going to be possible to transform social costs into the traditional forms of business reporting where all costs and gains are expressed in monetary terms. (*Social Measurement* (AICPA, New York, 1972), p. 20)

Many suggestions about the kind of information that businesses might make available about their impact on society were brought together in *The Measurement Of Social Performance,* the report of the AICPA's Committee on Social Measurement (Arthur B. Toan, Jr., chairman), published by the Institute in 1977, and there is little point in repeating those suggestions here. Some progress, but not much, has been made in the directions indicated by the committee since that report was published. As with financial reporting in general, it looks as though nothing less than regulatory pressure will cause companies to report hard quantitative data in place of or in addition to the bland words of comfort that, for the most part, investors and the public get now. Much of the information is already being collected, to comply with environmental protection laws, antidiscrimination laws, various health and safety regulations, and the like. The incremental cost of making it more widely known would be relatively small, and the benefits from having better informed financial markets and a better informed public would be considerable.

FORECASTS

Managements are constantly making forecasts of various kinds for use in managing the entity, but few of them have shown any enthusiasm for making them public, even though the SEC provides a "safe harbor" for forecasts made in good faith and with reasonable care. They are made available to those who need to know in private placements and public capital issues; and they are made implicitly by auditors whenever they satisfy themselves that a client entity is a going concern. And, as we noted earlier, forward looking estimates are implicit in every accrual.

It is tempting to say that as forecasts of various kinds are routinely made for management's own use, no extra cost would be incurred if one or more of them were made available to the public. However, internal forecasts are sometimes meant to be incentives rather than predictions; they may represent targets rather than expectations. If they are to be shared with the public, they must represent management's honest expectations.

Financial statements themselves are often said to have predictive power, and are used by extrapolation as the basis of predictions. But as they are in part derived from predictions, as we have noted already, there is surely something circular about looking to them as the source of predictions. They cannot be a substitute for a straightforward forecast.

We think it would be useful, feasible, and not unduly costly, to require companies to publish, with their financial statements for the year just ended, a set of forecast statements for the current year. These would be covered by the SEC's "safe harbor" rule (or by similar rules in other jurisdictions), and they would be subject to audit to the extent that the auditor would determine that the forecast had been made with due care and that it was based on reasonable assumptions. After the end of the forecast year, management would explain any major divergences between the actual and forecast results, and these explanations would also be reported on by the auditor as to their reasonableness.

Conclusions

Based on the discussion above, the Committee makes the following recommendations:

1. Intangibles

The treatment of internally-generated intangibles should be equated with that of acquired intangibles as nearly as possible.

    (a) Acquired intangibles should be written down only if they have lost value. Otherwise they are to be valued as other assets.

    (b) Nonpurchased (i.e. internally generated) intangibles should be recognized in financial statements, if they can be valued with reasonable reliability. If they cannot, their existence should at least be disclosed outside the balance sheet proper. Where a company's stock is publicly quoted, this may be done by comparing the book value of the enterprise with its market value, based on its share price, as proposed in the 1988 Scottish report, *Making Corporate Reports Valuable*. Whether so reported or not, expenditures intended to enhance (as distinct from maintaining) intangibles, such as research and development, training, and advertising promotion of brands, should be highlighted in the financial report.

2. Basis of Measurement

    (a) Given the deficiencies and limited relevance—some would say irrelevance—of historical costs, some version of market value should be used wherever possible. We recommend that market value be initially adopted for those items where the nature of the markets for such items suggests that the relevance and reliability of market value are the greatest and the costs of implementation are the lowest. During a transition period, it may be desirable to continue to report historical costs, at least until sufficient experience is gained regarding the use of market value data.

(b) In particular, financial instruments are a prime candidate for market value based accounting, because the relevance-reliability tradeoff is most likely to favor a non-historical cost based system for such claims. Financial instruments are a natural starting point because of the nature of the markets in which the claims trade and because of the availability of present-value type calculations to estimate market values where direct observation is not possible.

(c) In other cases of well behaved markets, where the current cost (entry price), net recoverable amount (exit price) and value in use are likely to be approximately the same, we recommend the use of the lower of current cost or recoverable amount (adjusted, where recovery is likely to be deferred, to reflect present values).

(d) In imperfect markets, where the current costs, net recoverable amounts, and value in use can depart significantly from one another, the solution is least clear, and there is the least agreement among the Committee members. Specialized assets would be a prime example. Individual members range in their recommendations from retention of historical cost to estimates of value in use. However, the majority of the Committee favors some departure from historical costs even in these more complex cases, with a good deal of support for the use of historical cost indexed by a specific price index where current cost cannot otherwise be determined.

(e) One of the basic reasons for lack of unanimity is that individual Committee members disagree as to the tradeoff between relevance and reliability offered by each of the alternatives in the imperfect markets case. A fundamental source of the disagreement is the lack of empirical data upon which to base an assessment of the tradeoff. As a result, the Committee recommends reporting on a nonhistorical cost basis of accounting with or without the retention of historical cost for comparative purposes, in order to provide some evidence upon which a reasoned judgment can be made.

(f) Members of the Committee who favor a current value system advocate that account should be taken of changes both in relative prices and in the general price level. That requires that real holding gains and losses on nonmonetary items (i.e. nominal gains and losses net of inflation) should be recognized in the income statement. Purchasing power gains and losses on monetary items resulting from changes in the value of money should also be recognized. Recognition of these gains and losses implies that the enterprise's financial capital at the beginning of the period be restated to take account of any change in the purchasing power of money that has occurred during the period.

3. TIME VALUE OF MONEY

Wider recognition of the time value of money should be reflected in the financial statements.

4. VALUE ADDED AND REPORTING ON LABOR

A statement of value added should be included in financial reports, as well as amplified disclosures regarding labor.

5. Social Impact of Business

Reporting entities should report explicitly on the cost to a company of pollution prevention and correction, where ascertainable. Absent improved voluntary disclosure by companies of costs that they impose on society, such disclosure should be required by regulation. Initially, such required disclosure might be limited to environmental damage, measured in terms of cost (if practicable) or in physical terms such as the weight of particulate emissions discharged.

6. Forecasts

A set of forecast financial statements should be provided for the year following that last reported on. The forecast should be reviewed by the auditor to ensure that it had been made with due care and was based on reasonable assumptions. Management should subsequently comment on major divergences from the forecast, and these explanations should also be reviewed by the auditor as to their reasonableness.

7. Specific Restrictions on the Scope of the Report

Many gaps in the coverage of this report could be pointed out, and two were referred to at the outset. We have not addressed the auditing issues that would arise if present methods of accounting measurement were substantially changed; and we have not considered the special problems of nonprofit organizations. Further, in discussing the basis of measurement, we confined our attention to assets. We have not considered the measurement basis of debt, which we think should be the subject of further study.

MINORITY REPORT

by
W. W. Cooper

Although I am in general agreement with the thrust of the [previous] report, I do have differences that I think I need to record as follows:

1. CURRENT VALUES VERSUS HISTORICAL COST:

It seems to me that it is preferable to have both, when they are available, and statements which say that historical costs have no value are much too strong. Witness, for instance, the following excerpt from a news item on page 38 of *Business Week,* August 6, 1990:

> After months of trying, troubled Columbia Savings announced a deal to jettison its huge junk bond portfolio. . . . How did Columbia do? The sales price is some $100 million over the portfolio's market value, but still about $1 billion less than what Columbia paid. . . .

Leaving aside the fact that this was only one part of an elaborate deal, stockholders might have been jubilant over the news that they would be receiving $100 million over current value but the accompanying information that this was $1 billion less than the original cost would almost certainly provide a different perspective, and it would also suggest further questions that might otherwise not be asked. The latter (historical cost) value supplies additional information which is helpful in (a) evaluating management and (b) influencing the conduct of management as part of the stewardship function that accounting is supposed to serve.

My own view is that current value should be supplied alongside historical cost whenever it is available and that a period (indeed, an extended period) of experimentation is in order as we improve our ability to assimilate, evaluate and report current costs. One possibility is suggested by the following adaptation from the June 30, 1990, financial statement of CREF (College Retirement Equities Fund):

		$xxxx
Investment at Cost		
Unrealized Appreciation	$xxxx	
Unrealized Depreciation	(xxxx)	

	Net Unrealized Appreciation or (Depreciation)	xxxx
	Investments at Current Value	$xxxx

To be sure, this is adapted from a report by an insurance company, where the major assets are nearly all in such investment portfolios. Nevertheless, the principle is clear and can provide guidance for use, in single entry fashion (as is the case with CREF), whenever applicable. This applicability, I might add, should extend to liability and net worth accounts, too, whenever such current value information is obtainable.

2. CORPORATE SOCIAL REPORTS:

I am concerned by the almost exclusive emphasis on monetary values in this part of the report. In the first place the recommended "social" evaluations for these kinds of activities are not likely to be easily done, or even easily estimated from the standpoint of the individual companies, where our present auditing and accounting activities are concentrated. This is true even for the example cited in our report, as taken from Joshua Ronen's report to the Trueblood Committee, unless, by chance, this kind of information is being exchanged between two companies or shops. More generally across-company interactions would need to be identified and evaluated if these kinds of broad social costs (and benefits) are to be comprehended in our "individual company" reports. Witness, for instance, the famous (or infamous) case in Donora, Pennsylvania, where the deaths of residents were caused by air pollutants being emitted simultaneously from multiple sources when, as it so happened, an inversion layer was occurring in the weather.

Fortunately there are easier ways to perform this kind of corporate social reporting. One possibility is indicated in Figure 1 which is intended to provide an example of multi-dimensional reporting designed to serve a variety of interests at the individual company level. It uses data which, for the most part, are already required by regulatory bodies. There is a further advantage in that each column uses units of measure that are of interest to particular audiences. This is in contrast to what is recommended in our report where, I am afraid, an orientation toward reporting only in financial units (e.g., $) will fail to supply information in the units that are of concern to others—such as environmentalists or persons interested in what is being accomplished in the way of minority employment and opportunities.

As is the case of moving toward more emphasis on current values, we will need to allow for a period of experimentation in route to any standardization in corporate social reports. Figure 1 is intended to provide an example directed toward an integrated report which attempts to relate different dimensions to each other (at least visually) so that thinking can be directed toward consideration of linkages—such as the effects of environmental improvements on minority employment and these in turn can be related to costs by simple cross comparisons in each row.

I am hopeful that the above will prove to be constructive suggestions that will help to move us in directions where I think that we all want to go.

FIGURE 1

Economic Environment			Physical Environment			Social Environment					
Private		Public	Air	Water	Other	Employment					
Revenues and expenses	Funds flow	Value added to GNP	Particulate emissions	Acid discharge	Soil removal and restoration	Black		Women		Total	
						(% of total)	($)	(% of total)	($)	Man- and woman-years	($)
($)	($)	($)	(tons)	(gal)	(acre feet)						

MINORITY REPORT

by
J. Alex Milburn

I cannot accept certain of the "Basis of Measurement" conclusions and related discussion. While I strongly support market values for financial instruments (conclusion 2 (a) and (b), I believe that assets that are to be used as inputs to revenue-generating processes[1] give rise to unique considerations that have not been recognized in this report. The report fails to acknowledge major problems that would seem to undermine the usefulness of conclusion 2(c) with respect to such assets. Conclusion 2(c) is developed within the conventional wisdom of current cost/value measurement models. This provides an inadequate framework in my view because it does not give adequate recognition to the implications of modern finance theory and market evidence with respect to present values and interest rates.

In order to make progress on measurement issues in financial accounting, I suggest that it is necessary to agree upon the fundamental property of economic resources and obligations that should be the object of measurement. There would seem to be considerable agreement that all assets of a business enterprise derive their value to the enterprise from their perceived capacity to generate future cash flows. Further, there would seem to be reasonably convincing evidence that investment prices under competitive conditions reflect expected future cash flows discounted at current risk-adjusted rates of interest.

This present value interpretation of market value can be applied directly to financial instruments. Conclusion 2(b) recognizes this in observing that "financial instruments are a natural starting point because of the nature of the markets in which the claims trade and because of the availability of present-value type calculations to estimate market values where direct observation is not possible." Certainly there are major issues to be addressed in, for example, valuing contingent cash flows and interest rate risk components. But one may be optimistic that these issues are capable of reasonable resolution. Considerable progress has been made in recent years in developing bases for valuing certain types of contingent flows (options, for example).

The major problem lies in trying to apply this present value concept to assets that are inputs to revenue-generating processes. The concept leads to *value in use* (the estimated present value of future net cash flows to result from the use of an asset by an enterprise). But it is well established that the value in

---

[1]Inputs to a revenue-generating process may be tangible (such as raw materials or plant and equipment), or intangible (such as research, computer software, acquired customer lists or brand names).

use of any individual input to a revenue-generating process is unknowable, even after the fact. The reason for this is the "interaction problem."[2] A typical revenue-generating process involves many inputs which interact over time to produce outputs (goods or services). It is the market value of these *outputs* that is the object of investment in the inputs. The inputs themselves lose their identity in their transformation into outputs for sale, so that it is impossible to determine which revenues are the result of which inputs.

Within this context, what is one to make of conclusion 2(c)? It reads:

> In other cases of well-behaved markets [that is, for assets other than financial instruments], where current costs (entry price), net recoverable amount (exit price) and value in use are likely to be approximately the same, we recommend the use of lower of current cost or recoverable amount. . . .

This recommendation would seem to have little prospect for significant application. Even for those assets for which there are active second-hand markets (automobiles and aeroplanes for example), there is a serious question as to whether such market values can be relied upon to represent the values of outputs to be generated by particular revenue-generating processes.

The report as a whole indicates a preference for current cost (or a specific price-indexed historical cost substitute therefor) even if the condition of 2(c) is not met. Such current costs would seem to have a very dubious claim to reflect the value of the future cash flows (revenues from the sale of outputs) that are the primary objective and expectation of investment in inputs to revenue-generating processes. Put another way, the fact that an input asset has increased in price since it was acquired does not of itself create value and income to the enterprise, except in the rare case that one may be able to establish a cause and effect relationship between future output revenue values and the current cost of inputs. The lack of evident link between the current cost of inputs and value to the enterprise may help to explain why current costs have received such a poor reception in the U.S., the U.K., Canada and other countries.

In my view then, current entry and exit values of individual inputs have very serious flaws which must give pause to endorsing them as the primary, general-purpose measures of financial position and results of operations. This report does not adequately address these issues.

But are there any alternatives that have promise of being better? I suggest that inadequate attention has been paid to reasoning within the "value-in-use" measurement objective. The essential question, in my view, is how far accounting can expect to go in providing reliable measures that are consistent with this objective.

As observed above, we cannot expect to be able to estimate the future revenues to result from a particular input. But we can make reasonable imputations of the expected value-in-use contribution implicit in any input asset investment at the date of its acquisition. The starting point premise for such a determination is that any investment may be assumed to have been made with the rational expectation of achieving future cash-equivalent flows sufficient to recover its cost plus a rate of return commensurate with interest rates available on securities of equivalent risk. Reasoning from this presumption, the stream of future cash-equivalent flows implicit in an input asset investment is determinable given its cost, estimated useful life and residual value, a pattern of benefit assumption, and the interest rate that is consistent with current market and risk conditions.[3]

This implicit value-in-use calculation can then be used as the basis for amortizing the cost of the asset. Such amortization would be on the basis of expecting the rate of return implicit in the investment, and would be determined in the same way that the principal amounts of mortgage payments are determined. This would result in amortization, and balance sheet carrying values, being consistent with the implicit value-in-use expectations at the date of investment.

The question then is to what extent these figures should be adjusted for subsequent changes in conditions. It would clearly be appropriate to adjust these figures to reflect changes in the basic estimate

---

[2]See for example, Arthur L. Thomas, *The Allocation Problem: Part Two.* Studies in Accounting Research No. 9. American Accounting Association, 1974.

[3]This is a thesis that I pursue in some depth in *Incorporating the Time Value of Money Within Financial Accounting.* Canadian Institute of Chartered Accountants, 1988.

parameters (useful life and residual value). As well, input asset carrying values should be written down if there is persuasive evidence that the revenue-generating process cannot be expected to achieve the revenues implicit in the aggregate carrying value of its input assets. This may be about as far as it is possible for accounting to go in reflecting what can be known or capable of estimation that is relevant to the value-in-use measurement objective.

The severe criticisms of historical costs accounting (HCA) expressed in this report envisage the highly arbitrary inter-period allocation conventions of existing generally accepted accounting principles. They do not give consideration to this "value-in-use" based amortization possibility. The report is particularly critical that HCA does not reflect current prices of input assets or the effects of inflation. I propose that this criticism need to be carefully evaluated in terms of both (1) the major problems with current costs cited above, and (2) the interpretability of "value-in-use" amortization values under inflationary conditions.[4]

None of this is to deny the possible value of supplementary information on either (1) current costs of inputs (which may indicate, as an example, the possible advantage to an enterprise that has purchased input assets before a price increase) or (2) current exit values of inputs (which may indicate the alternative value of inputs should they be sold individually rather than used in the business).

In sum, I suggest that the case has not been made for current cost/value measures for input assets, and that a productive direction for future investigation would be to examine the issues from a value-in-use perspective. Within this perspective, those advocating current values for input assets would need to put forward persuasive evidence that such values are representative of value in use—that is, that there is good cause to believe that changes in input values will lead to corresponding changes in output values.

---

[4]Ibid., chapter 13.

DEFINITIONS AND MEASUREMENT OF INCOME

EXPECTATIONS AND ACHIEVEMENTS IN INCOME THEORY

A. D. Barton

A major confusion concerning the relationship between *ex ante* present value and *ex post* concepts of income and asset valuation underlies much of the recent literature in income theory and asset valuation. Many claims have been made in favor of the present value concepts and measurements as providing the ideal accounting system which are not valid, and many criticisms of historical accounting which are based on the supposed merits of present value accounting are not sound. The case for the use of current value or replacement cost accounting is thought by many to rest on the merits of present value accounting whereas it really rests upon other grounds. In this paper, I hope to show that: (i) both *ex ante* and *ex post* concepts of income and asset valuation are required; (ii) they are separate concepts; and (iii) they serve different purposes. The mixing up of the two sets of concepts causes great confusion in the analysis of income theory.

The claims of leading authorities on the virtues of *ex ante* concepts are first noted and the indirect measurement hypothesis of asset valuation is explained. The relationship between current market prices of assets and their present values is examined to test the validity of the

---

This paper was presented at the annual conference of the Association of University Teachers of Accounting of the United Kingdom, held at Edinburgh University, April, 1973. The writer acknowledges some useful comments on the paper by Mr. Deryl H. Street of Macquarie University.

A. D. Barton, "Expectations and Achievements in Income Theory," *The Accounting Review,* January 1974, 664–681. Reprinted by permission of the American Accounting Association.

indirect measurement hypothesis, and it is rejected. Present value concepts of income are then analyzed and compared with *ex post* income and the realization convention is shown not to be the major reason for the difference between them. The necessary conditions for equality of present value and *ex post* magnitudes are examined and found to be highly unrealistic. Finally, the role of each set of concepts is examined and it is shown that both are necessary for the firm operating in conditions of uncertainty because they serve different functions.

THE DOMINANT ROLE CLAIMED FOR PRESENT VALUE CONCEPTS AND THE INDIRECT MEASUREMENT HYPOTHESIS

The case for the dominant position of *ex ante* present value income rests on the needs of investors for information about the future income prospects of the firm.[1] Investors in business enterprises, i.e., owners, are interested in the prospects of future income from investments, and it is differences in these future prospects which determine the allocation of their investment funds.[2] Ideally they require information on the expected income to be earned in each form of investment so that they can select those promising the highest returns. The appropriate measures for this are present value income and its corollary, the present value of assets. They do not invest money in firms just because of past financial performances. However, it is recognized that present value income and assets are subjective and very difficult to measure and hence some substitute measures may have to be adopted for practical reasons. Current market buying prices of assets are used as the substitute values. It is claimed that current market prices reflect the present values of assets and that the measurement of periodic income on the basis of current replacement costs of assets consumed in the period would approximate present value income.[3] The case for current replacement cost accounting is often made to rest on this surrogate relationship.

The following statements from some of the leaders of contemporary accounting thought support this general position.

Professor E. S. Hendriksen, after examining various concepts of income and value in his widely used text, concludes:

> The capital maintenance concepts of income are assumed by many to be the most basic because they derive their support from economic theory. Changes in the capitalized value of expected cash receipts serve as the foundation of this concept; however accruals, amortisation procedures, and current market valuations . . . are

---

[1] It should be noted that there are two separate concepts of *ex ante* income—present value income and budgeted income. The analysis here relates to present value income, except where budgeted income is mentioned.

[2] The origins of the investor point of view (which is completely sound as far as it goes) can be traced back to J. B. Canning, *The Economics of Accountancy* (Ronald Press, 1929), and to the works of many economists. It was taken up in accounting in the A.A.A. report of the Committee of Accounting Concepts and Standards, "Accounting and Reporting Standards for Corporate Financial Statements, 1957 Revision," *The Accounting Review* (October 1957), and has become a popular theme since then.

[3] See L. Revsine, "On the Correspondence Between Replacement Cost Income and Economic Income", *The Accounting Review* (July 1970), for a more detailed explanation of the indirect measurement hypothesis.

frequently justified on the basis that they represent surrogates (reasonably accept-able substitutes) for current value [i.e., present value].[4]

Although Hendriksen acknowledges some difficulties (both practical and conceptual) with the capitalisation approach, he has it as the ideal one. Professor D. Solomons, in his celebrated analysis of the relationship between the economic (or present value) concept of income and the accounting concept, says:

> Since it seems to carry out the function generally ascribed to income. [i.e., to guide investment policy] growth in present value [of the firm] must be what we had better understand income to mean.[5]

The 1957 A.A.A. statement of "Accounting and Reporting Standards for Corporate Financial Statements" states:

> The value of an asset is the money equivalent of its service potentials. Concep-tually, this is the sum of the future market prices of all streams of services to be derived, discounted by probability and interest factors to their present worths. However, this conception of value is an abstraction which yields but limited practical basis for quantification. Consequently, the measurement of assets is commonly made by more feasible methods.[6]

In subsequent reports the feasible methods advocated were generally the use of current re-placement costs.[7] Professor G. J. Staubus, after examining various bases for the valuation of as-sets, concluded:

> . . . the choice of a measurement method to apply to a particular asset for finan-cial reporting purposes should be made on the basis of two criteria: (1) proxim-ity of the measurement method to the ideal of maximum time-adjusted cash po-tential (MATACAP), and (2) availability of a reliable reading of the particular type of evidence chosen.[8]

---

[4]E. S. Hendriksen, *Accounting Theory* (Revised Edition) (Irwin, 1970) p. 156. Note: all words in squared brackets in this and subsequent quotations are not in the original statement.

[5]D. Solomons, "Economic and Accounting Concepts of Income" *The Accounting Review* (July 1961); reprinted in R. H. Parker and G. C. Harcourt (Eds.), *Readings in the Concept and Measurement of Income* (Cambridge University Press, 1969), p. 108.

[6]A.A.A. "Accounting and Reporting Standards for Corporate Financial Statements, 1957 Revision," *The Accounting Review* (October 1957), p. 538.

[7]A.A.A. Committee on Concepts and Standards—Long Lived Assets, "Accounting for Land, Buildings and Equipment—Supplementary Statement No. 1," *The Accounting Review* (July 1964); Committee on Concepts and Standards—Inventory Measurement, "A Discussion of Various Approaches to Inventory Measurement— Supplementary Statement No. 2," *The Accounting Review* (July 1964); Committee to Prepare a Statement of Basic Accounting Theory, *A Statement of Basic Accounting Theory* (Evanston, Illinois, 1966).

[8]G. J. Staubus, "Current Cash Equivalent for Assets: A Dissent," *The Accounting Review* (October 1967), p. 660.

Professor K. W. Lemke had earlier reached a similar conclusion after his review of the problem.

> Where sufficiently definite verifiable evidence is available to permit the value of an asset on one or more bases, the basis to be used is the one considered to yield the closest approximation to the discounted value of an asset's future cash flows.[9]

Professor Corbin states:

> Given a satisfactory degree of competition, the prices of assets in the market place would then be based on estimates of their future income streams made by many independent individuals; market prices would serve as objective, indirect estimates of value. . . . In this manner the values of all assets and liabilities, *except goodwill,* could be determined indirectly each period, in order to calculate net income as the increase in an enterprise's net (present) value during the period.[10]

Even those great advocates of current replacement cost accounting, Professors Edwards and Bell, in arguing for the *conceptual* superiority of their own concepts of business and realizable profits, reject economic income as the ideal for accounting measurement on *practical* grounds. They reject *ex post* economic income because

> . . . (i) it cannot be measured objectively, and (ii) even its subjective measurement normally cannot be accomplished until the firm's plan of operation has been revised.[11]

A measurement problem should not be the reason for rejecting the conceptual merit of economic income.

Several articles which are highly critical of the indirect measurement hypothesis and the use of current replacement cost accounting take a converse point of view on the whole subject. Thus, Professors Dickens and Blackburn state:

> A . . . fundamental question is whether cost of replacing fixed assets, however determined, provides a reasonable measure of economic value of those assets. It is here contended that the question must be answered in the negative. . . .
>
> The failure of replacement cost as a measure of economic value of specific assets, . . . coupled with the impossibility of objective measurement of replacement cost, effectively condemn any concept of income proposed to date that would include holding gains or losses on fixed assets.[12]

[9]K. W. Lemke, "Asset Valuation and Income Theory," *The Accounting Review* (January 1966), p. 40.

[10]D. A. Corbin, "The Revolution in Accounting," *The Accounting Review* (October 1962), p. 630.

[11]E. O. Edwards and P. W. Bell, *The Theory and Measurement of Business Income* (California University Press, 1961), pp. 43–4.

[12]R. L. Dickens and J. O. Blackburn, "Holding Gains on Fixed Assets: An Element of Business Income?" *The Accounting Review* (April 1964), pp. 315–24.

Finally, Professor J. Snavely states:

> The primary purpose of financial statements is to present information that will assist in estimating the value of the firm. . . .
>
> The relevant asset figure for balance sheet purposes is the real value of that asset to the owner. Neither historical cost nor current replacement cost is directly relevant [where real values are defined as present values]. . . .
>
> The current cost of an asset reflects only the amount being paid by other firms . . . at a particular point in time. . . . It does not reflect . . . an asset's real value—the figure which represents the asset's current economic significance.[13]

An interesting methodological attribute of all these sources is that not one of them analyzes the relationships between current market prices of assets and their present values. It is to this analysis that we now turn. The analysis can only be conducted in terms of a very general price determination model, and its results can only be tested at this stage on the basis of general observations of business conduct.

RELATIONSHIP BETWEEN ASSET MARKET PRICES AND PRESENT VALUES

To establish the relationship between the current market prices of assets and their present values from private use, it is necessary to examine the processes by which current market prices and present values are determined.

The determination of fixed asset prices is formally similar to that for single-use consumption goods, in that they result from a compromise between supply and demand factors for the asset. The supply function for a commodity shows the minimum prices at which a firm is willing to supply the market for the commodity. In the long run this supply function must cover all necessary costs of production and selling, including the costs of financing operations, and a reward for undertaking business risks. The costs of financing and risk undertaking are subsumed in the normal profit component in the supply function. The shape of the supply function depends on the form of the physical production function and factor supply prices, and it may exhibit increasing, decreasing, or constant returns over scale, or combinations thereof, according to the characteristics of its two determinants. In the short run the supplier may be prepared to forego part of these costs—unavoidable periodic fixed costs—in order to keep the firm operating, as part of a loss minimization strategy. The market supply function for a non-differentiated product is then the aggregation of the supply functions of each producer. The analysis for both single-use consumer goods and durable-use investment goods, which become fixed assets of other firms, is formally identical.

On the demand side, the analysis differs somewhat between single-use consumer goods and investment goods because the demand for the latter is derived ultimately from the demand for consumer goods; investment goods yield their benefits over a long period of time as compared with the more-or-less instantaneous pleasures afforded by single-use consumer goods; and investment goods are generally used jointly in operations rather than singly. However the

---

[13]H. J. Snaveley, "Current Cost for Long-Lived Assets, A Critical View," *The Accounting Review* (April 1969), pp. 346–50.

fundamental principles on which the demand function are based and its role in price determination are identical for the two types of goods.

The demand function for a particular type of fixed asset is obtained by aggregating the demands at each price of each buyer in the market during a specified period of time. Firms buy fixed assets primarily for use within their own operations rather than for resale at a later date. The demand for fixed assets is governed by the expectations of management for their profitable use over the long run. The only way to evaluate their expected profitability over the long run is through determining their time-and-risk-adjusted present values, or the internal rates of return on the investment outlays. We shall use the present value technique for purposes of explanation. Fixed assets are normally used in groups rather than singly, and we shall refer to the group as an investment project. The fixed assets require a stream of inputs (materials, labor, power, etc.) over time for production to proceed, and they generate a stream of outputs (finished products). Some working capital investment is required to commence production and sustain it, and this is added to investment in fixed assets to determine the total investment outlay. The relevant characteristic of the inputs and outputs for determination of present values of the expected profit stream is the cash outlays and cash receipts to which they give rise in each period. These can be netted out to derive the cash surpluses expected from operations. The cash flows encompass all operating items (sales plus purchases of all outputs and inputs, including plant replacement expenditures, plant sale receipts, taxes, etc., and entire proceeds from the sale of remaining assets at the terminal date) up to the planning horizon; but exclude all financing receipts and payments (i.e., owners' capital and creditors' loans received and repaid, and interest and dividend payments). The present value of each investment project is then determined as:

(i)
$$V_0 = \frac{S_1}{(1 + c)^1} + \frac{S_2}{(1 + c)^2} + \ldots + \frac{S_n}{(1 + c)^n}$$

(ii)
$$= \sum_{t=1}^{n} \frac{S_t}{(1 + c)^t}$$

where

V_0 = gross present value of the expected operating cash surplus stream;

S = the cash surplus generated in each period;

c = the average annual cost of servicing the firm's total pool of finance, measured at current market prices of securities, or the firm's cost of capital; and

$t = 0, \ldots, n$ are the periods during which the assets are used where n is the planning horizon.

Because the cash surplus stream is one projected into the future, there is no guarantee that the forecasts will be fulfilled. There is risk and uncertainty surrounding the firm's future operations, and the cash surplus stream is best viewed as a probabilistic one, with each value of S being interpreted as the (mathematical) expected value. For simplicity it is assumed that all cash flows occur at the end of each period. The cost of capital which is used as the discount rate in evaluating the cash surplus stream is the rate of return which must be paid to investors (both creditors and stockholders) in the long run to attract and retain their funds. Where, as is typical, funds are obtained from a variety of sources, the cost of capital is a weighted average of the costs from each source. The cost of debt finance is the effective interest rate on that finance, whereas the cost of equity finance is the effective dividend-cum-capital gain yield on the shares.[14] These rates of return are determined according to the opportunities of investors for investment in the securities of other firms judged to have the same risk characteristics. The cost of equity capital becomes the normal profit requirement of the firm, i.e., that rate of profit which must be earned on net assets to enable stockholders to be rewarded just sufficiently to maintain share prices.

The net present value (NV_0) of each project is:

(iii)
$$NV_0 = \sum_{t=1}^{n} \frac{S_t}{(1 + c)^t} - I_0$$

i.e., the gross present value less the initial outlay (I_0) on assets (both fixed and current). Prospective projects are then ranked according to their net present values.

The same form of analysis is applied to assessment of individual fixed assets. Most fixed assets bought by a firm during a period are either replacement items or assets acquired to expand the firm's existing productive capacity. They form part of an integrated operation and their marginal productivity depends very much upon the set of complementary assets and upon the lifespan proposed for the asset (where this is finite). The assessment must be done on a marginal basis—the relevant cash flows are those that occur in addition to what is otherwise expected without the asset—and it covers the asset's own lifespan only. Thus, the present value of an asset is the measure of its contribution to the expected gross proceeds resulting from its use by the firm, while its net present value (i.e., after deducting the cost of the asset) is its contribution to the future pure profits of the firm.

The decision rules for asset purchase are:

1. Where $NV_0 > 0$ (i.e., $V_0 > I_0$) the asset is expected to return more than the cost of the investment outlay on it, running and financing it, and this surplus is *pure* profit. A positive net present value shows the present value of expected *pure* profits from purchase of the asset.

2. Where $NV_0 = 0$ (i.e., $V_0 = I_0$), the asset is expected to just pay for itself—the cost is exactly covered by the expected proceeds from its use. All outlays on the asset are recovered, interest charges on borrowed funds can be met and the debts repaid, and the dividend requirements of stockholders can be met and they can be repaid if necessary. Only normal profits are made from the use of such assets.

3. Where $NV_0 < 0$ (i.e., $V_0 < I_0$), the asset is expected to incur a loss and total outlays or financial costs may not be recovered. Such assets should not be purchased by a firm seeking to maximize profits.

---

[14]The effective dividend-cum-capital gains yield is r in the formula:

(x)
$$P_0 = \sum_{t=0}^{n} \frac{Dt}{(1 + r)^n} + \frac{P_n}{(1 + r)^n}$$

where D_t is the expected stream of dividends per share which includes growth in dividends per share and is after adjustment for bonus and rights issues; and P_n is the expected selling price per share at some specified horizon date.

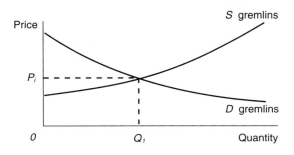

FIGURE 1

Determination of Current Market Prices

The present value of a given asset can vary substantially according to a large number of circumstances. For example, consider the present value of some hypothetical gremlin machine which is typical of fixed assets. Gremlins are used in a wide range of industries, from the manufacture of perambulators through cars to aircraft and ships, and the markets for the products of these industries vary tremendously. The present value of a gremlin will vary according to whether it is the first or tenth machine used by a firm (where there are nonconstant returns to scale), the firm is profitable or otherwise, management is optimistic or pessimistic about the future, the firm has excess capacity, the firm is growing, and so on; and according to the life-span adopted for the gremlin, the complementary equipment available which affects its productivity, and the discount rate (which incorporates the risk characteristics of the firm).

The present values of gremlins, when ranked according to size and aggregated for all firms considering buying them over a specified period, forms the demand function for them—it is an investment demand function. *Every* point on it is an estimate of present values. The interaction of this demand function with the supply function from machinery manufacturers determines the market price of gremlins, as shown in Figure 1.

The demand function must be downward sloping (because the assets are ranked according to profitability), whereas the supply function may be horizontal, upward sloping, or downward sloping (so long as it has a lesser slope than the demand function). The equilibrium price, P_1, is determined by the interaction of the demand and supply factors in the market, and at it Q_1 gremlins are sold. All gremlins bought prior to Q_1 are expected to yield pure profits—their net present values are positive. The gremlin Q_1 should yield normal profits to its buyer, while any gremlins bought for price P_1 beyond Q_1 could not be profitably used, given the present state of expectations and the cost of capital. In equilibrium, the buyer equates his present value to the market price of gremlins. Similarly on the supply side, firms more than cover their costs at outputs below Q_1, i.e., they make pure profits in the long-run case. At Q_1 their costs are just covered and normal profits are made on the last unit; while beyond Q_1 marginal losses would be incurred. This analysis is formally similar to that for a single-use consumer good, only the demand function reads in terms of marginal utility rather than present value, and consumer surplus takes the place of pure profits. The claim that the market prices of assets measure their present values is similar to the claim that the price of an ice-cream *always*

FIGURE 2

Firm's Demand for Assets

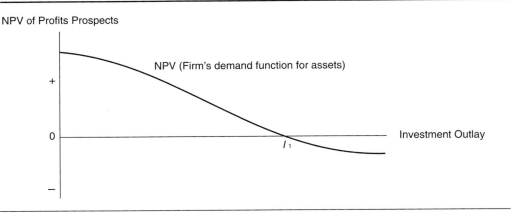

measures its marginal utility to the buyer, no matter how desperate he is for the ice-cream, and that there can be no consumers' surplus.

The analysis can be generalized to cover all the individual firm's investment projects requiring combinations of assets by expressing its investment demand function for all assets for a given capital budgeting period in terms of *net* present values. This can be illustrated as shown in Figure 2. The length of the capital budgeting period varies mainly according to the gestation period required to implement investment plans and the firm's own internal administrative procedures, but 1–3 years may be taken as being fairly typical.

In the absence of a capital rationing situation, the profit maximizing firm will accept all mutually exclusive investment projects with a positive or zero net present value, i.e., expand up to $0I_1$. At this point it is maximizing the net present value of the firm, and its share prices and owners' wealth should likewise be maximized.

The relationship between current market prices of fixed assets and their present values is now evident. *At the time of purchase, the present values of all fixed assets exceed their current market prices* by various amounts, *or just equal the price in the case of the marginal asset.* The purchase decision is based on the *marginal* present values of assets, and the marginal present values of all assets of the one type bought by the firm for the same price need not be equal. *At later dates,* current market prices may change because of various changes in market supply or demand conditions and *there is no necessary relationship between current replacement costs of existing assets and their present values:* current replacement costs may be greater or less than the present values of existing fixed assets. The investment decision facing the firm here is different from the initial decision—it is now whether to keep on operating the fixed asset. For this, the current selling price of the asset is the relevant outlay to match against the present value from continued use. The current selling price measures the opportunity cost of keeping the asset by foregoing the proceeds from its sale. So long as the net present value as calculated on this basis is positive, it pays to retain the asset: if the net present value is negative the asset should be sold.

Hence the use of current replacement costs of assets as surrogates for present values is generally unsound. The equality holds only for those assets purchased at the margin of profitability for firms, and it will continue to hold only in conditions where neither expectations, the discount rate, nor current market prices have changed since the purchase date. It does not hold for the purchase of all premarginal assets, nor for the marginal assets after the date of purchase if any one of the above conditions changes. Thus, except for when the very stringent conditions outlined above apply, current replacement costs of assets in the *market* could not be considered as reliable estimates of their present values in *private* use. The present values of a given fixed asset are likely to vary enormously between firms (according to factors outlined earlier), and it requires a fair stretch of the imagination to believe that all firms owning a particular asset derive exactly the same benefit from it and that there is no possibility of pure profits being earned anywhere. Furthermore, the equality of current replacements costs with present values throughout implies that all assets acquired are equally profitable (at zero net present value), hence there is no optimum composition of assets. It implies there are no increasing returns to scale. It implies there is no complementarity in asset usage notwithstanding the fact that most fixed assets are used jointly in a firm's operations. It implies the absolute size of the firm is indeterminate and therefore that small and mammoth firms can always coexist in the one industry. It implies there is no optimum lifespan for depreciable fixed assets. These are implications about reality which are at variance with observations of it.

The adoption of current replacement cost as surrogates for the present values of assets must therefore be rejected and, with it, the indirect measurement hypothesis. There are, nevertheless, sound reasons for the use of current replacement cost accounting which are not based on this surrogate relationship.

THE RELATIONSHIP BETWEEN PRESENT VALUE AND EX POST INCOME

It is generally agreed that the rational objective of the firm should be to maximize the net present value of its assets as this enhances the wealth of owners by the greatest amount. This maximand is formally identical to stating that the firm should aim to maximize the net present value of its prospective profit stream, subjective income, *ex ante* income, economic income, the growth in present value of net assets, or subjective goodwill. Since this is the objective of owners, it seems to follow that the accountant ought to measure it.[15]

This concept of income is then promoted to the supreme position of being the ideal theoretical concept for use in accounting, and only practical measurement problems appear to prevent it from being adopted.

The notion of present value income has been developed most by Hicks in his influential *Value and Capital.* With appropriate modifications to change the concept from an individual to a firm context, Hicks' definition states that income is the maximum amount a firm can distribute in dividends this year and still *expect* to be able to pay the same dividends in each ensuing year.[16]

---

[15]D. Solomons, "Economic and Accounting Concepts of Income," p. 108, (footnote 5 above).

[16]J. R. Hicks, *Value and Capital (Second Edition)* (Oxford, Clarendon Press, 1946), reprinted in Parker and Harcourt, *Readings in the Concept and Measurement of Income,* p. 77. This is equivalent to Income Number 2 in Hicks. If prices are expected to change, the definition is amended to read "the payment of the same dividends *in real terms* in each ensuring year."

Professor Solomons advances the following reconciliation of economic income with traditional accounting income:

Accounting income + (i) unrealized changes in the values of tangible assets over the period (after deducting depreciation and inventory markdowns)

- (ii) amounts realized in respect of value changes in tangible assets of previous periods not recognized then

+ (iii) changes in the value of intangible assets (goodwill)

= economic income.[17]

Adjustments (i) and (ii) are to adjust accounting income for currently *realizable* holding gains in place of currently *realized* holding gains on assets sold, and adjustment (iii) brings in the change in subjective goodwill. Professor Solomons observes that: "obviously the main difference between the two concepts lies in the accountant's test of realization as to the emergence of income."[18] This is true if by realization is meant everything, both past and future, that has not been evidenced by a market transaction. However, the concept of realization as normally used in accounting is much narrower than this, and the controversy about it normally refers to the recognition of market events that *have occurred* but have not been embodied in a transaction by the firm, e.g., increases in fixed asset prices, and not to hypothetical events of the future. "The essential meaning of realization is that a change in an asset or liability has become sufficiently definite and objective to warrant recognition in the accounts."[19]

Apart from the adjustment for holding gains, the basic difference between accounting income and economic income is that the former relates to actual past events whereas the latter relates to expected future events. *Accounting income* is *ex post;* it measures achievements to date and is based on market transactions and events that have actually occurred in the past. It can be measured by the increase in net *tangible* assets owned by the firm over the period after maintaining capital intact, i.e., by the gain in actual monetary and physical assets. (For the purpose of contrasting it with present value income, it does not matter whether the *ex post* valuation of assets adopted is based on historic cost or current market prices. The relevant point is that the transactions—plus asset market prices in a current value system—have occurred and hence the firm's net *tangible* assets have increased).

Economic income is *ex ante;* it evaluates expectations of future income and refers to transactions that have *not yet occurred*. It relates to the transactions that are expected to occur in the future. It is a case of counting one's chickens before any is hatched. Economic income is measured by the gain in an *intangible asset*—viz., subjective goodwill—and not by the gain in monetary and physical assets on hand. Each concept refers to a *different period of time* and set of transactions. This is the essential difference between the two concepts which appears to have been overlooked in much of the literature. As well, there are various technical differences between the two concepts which result from the above and which complicate the making of direct comparisons.

---

[17]D. Solomons, "Economic and Accounting Concepts of Income," p. 110.

[18]*Ibid.*, p. 110.

[19]A.A.A. *Accounting and Reporting Standards for Corporate Financial Statements,* 1957 Revision, p. 3.

These differences can be seen most clearly by examining the nature of economic income. The remaining adjustments are of no great moment in the reconciliation.[20] First, economic income, defined as the *net* present value of a firm, is essentially a concept of *total income* up to the planning horizon, not *periodic* income. It is the sum of *pure* profits expected by management to be earned in each period up to the planning horizon of the firm, and discounted back to its present value, i.e.,

(iv)
$$NV_0 \equiv Y_A = \sum_{t=0}^{n} \frac{S_t}{(1 + c)^t} - I_0$$

where Y_A is the present value of expected future income from the current time (t_0) to the planning horizon of the firm (t_n).

Second, present value income is recognized at the time of *perception* by management, not at the time of the transaction nor the time of any other actual market event; and consequently it is very sensitive to the state of expectations. Given imperfect knowledge of the future, the state of expectations has a tendency to be rather volatile, and hence economic income tends to be an unstable figure. Every improvement in business confidence, up-turn in expected market conditions, increase in expected selling prices, and so on, boosts it; every wave of pessimism, increase in operating costs, and so on, depresses it. One only has to look at movements in share prices to appreciate how volatile economic income is in the eyes of investors in general. Economic income depends upon the effort and ingenuity put into the search for profitable future business activities. It depends upon the risk-taking attitudes of management. And so the list of subjective factors affecting *ex ante* income can be extended. Furthermore, the measure of economic income depends upon the discount rate. Any reduction in interest rates in the capital market increases economic income, expectations constant; and conversely any increase in interest rates reduces it.

Finally, economic income, as defined, is a measure of pure profit only, and it is based on the stream of earnings before interest, whereas accounting income does not distinguish between pure and normal profit but it does differentiate between profit and interest. The discount factor used in the measure of economic income comprises the charge for normal profits plus interest on borrowed funds, i.e., the weighted average cost of capital. The cash surplus stream evaluated in equation (iv) is taken before interest payments. Any reconciliation between the two concepts must include adjustments for these differing treatments of interest and normal profits and the fact that economic income is a discounted measure (the costs of finance over time are removed from it) whereas *ex post* income is a nondiscounted measure.

Although present value income is conceptually a measure of *total* income expected to be earned up to the planning horizon of the firm, nevertheless allocations to future periods can be made by *averaging* it over them. It must be emphasized that these periodic allocations are based on *assumptions* in much the same way as the measurement of historic periodic income has to be based on some assumptions (and is frequently criticized for this need). Assumptions

---

[20]Accounting income plus the adjustments for realizable holding gains of the period in place of realized holding gains, and plus adjustments to put the cost of goods sold and fixed asset consumption on a current replacement cost basis, yields the "business income" concept of Edwards and Bell. This is a different income concept from that of *ex ante* economic income, and it is an *ex post* concept. Business income differs from accounting income because it extends the realization test beyond market transactions to include sufficiently verifiable market events (changes in current replacement costs of assets) in the measurement of *ex post* periodic income.

are always necessary whenever the cycle of transaction affecting a period's operations are not completed within the confines of the period. Second, the allocations are based on concepts of capital maintenance and depreciation which differ from those used in *ex post* accounting.

Two methods of determining *periodic ex ante* income are available.

1. All perceived pure profits are allocated to the first year and each subsequent year is assumed to earn only a normal rate of return on investment. Periodic income is defined as the growth in present value over the period, i.e.,

(v) $$Y_{A1} = V_1 - I_0, \qquad Y_{A2} = V_2 - V_1, \ldots \qquad Y_{An} = V_n - V_{n-1}$$

where

$V_1 =$ the present value of the firm at the end of year 1, etc.;

$I_0 =$ the initial investment in the firm;

$Y_{A1} =$ the expected income of year 1, etc.;

$n =$ the horizon date.

It is assumed that there are no capital contributions or withdrawals by investors over the period, and that expectations and the discount rate remain constant. Holding investment contributions constant makes it easier to calculate income as growth in (total) present value. Normal profits and interest then do not have to be added back to determine total profit before interest.

Year 1 income can be restated as:

(vi) $$Y_{A1} = (V_1 - V_0) + (V_0 - I_0)$$

and the incomes of year 2 ... n as:

(vii) $$Y_{A2} = cV_1, \qquad Y_{A3} = cV_2, \ldots, \qquad Y_{An} = cV_{n-1}$$

where c is the cost of capital, or rate of return on investment required by investors.

The pure profits (i.e., $V_0 - I_0$) are allocated to year 1, even though the major cash surpluses may be expected to accrue in later years, because they are recognized at the date of perception. All future years are allocated a constant rate of return on investment as this is the growth in present value, notwithstanding fluctuations in the periodic cash surpluses. The total profits over time $c \ldots n$ before interest and net of pure profits are *averaged* over each period at the rate c. It should be noted that the method is a roundabout one in practical terms because determining the income of each year requires estimating the income up to the horizon on each occasion.

Any subsequent changes in expectations or the discount rate cause complications. If, for example, during year 2 the cash surplus expected in year 3 increases so that V_2 as perceived at the start of the year differs from V_2 as perceived at the end of the year, the change in year 3 results is included in year 2 income as pure profit (the so-called "windfall" component). The same type of reallocation is made if the discount rate changes as this alters the values of V at each date.

2. All perceived pure profits are spread so as to even out the rate of return on investment each year. They are allocated to each year at the internal rate of return on investment, so that annual income is:

(viii)
$$Y_{A1} = rV_0, \qquad Y_{A2} = rV_1, \ldots, \qquad Y_{An} = rV_{n-1}$$

where r is the internal rate of return. The internal rate of return is that rate of discount which reduces the net present value of an investment prospect to zero, i.e.,

(ix)
$$\sum_{t=0}^{n} \frac{S_t}{(1+r)^t} - I_0 = 0$$

It is the *average* rate of return earned by the firm up to its horizon, and its expression on an annual basis means that the firm earns the *same* rate of return on investment each year. Again, this occurs notwithstanding substantial fluctuations in the cash surpluses expected each year. As this method spreads the perceived pure profits over each year, the periodic *ex ante* incomes differ from those in method (1) so long as pure profits are expected, i.e., where $r > c$.

Again, the allocations are complicated by any changes in expectations. r must be recalculated if they change and the total expected income up to the horizon reallocated.

The capital maintenance concept on which periodic present value income is based is not the normal type of capital maintenance concept used in accounting. It does not refer to keeping a *stock* of capital resources intact (whether expressed in terms of historic costs, current market prices, real purchasing power of investment, or physical capacity, etc.), *but to keeping intact a stream of expected income earning power.*[21] And how is this stream of income earning power measured?—in terms of its present value, which is present value income again! In other words the process is completely circular and capital has no independent existence as such. Professor Kaldor has observed that:

> In Hicks the source disappears as a separate entity—capital appears only as the capitalized value of a certain future prospect and income as the standard stream equivalent of that prospect. Capital and income are thus two different ways of expressing the same thing, not two different things.[22]

For example, if with a given stock of assets (for which current market prices equal historic cost), expectations of income earning power in year 3 hence improve, existing assets to the extent of present value of the improvement can be distributed now while maintaining expected income earning power intact.

The above methods of determining periodic economic income require a unique concept of depreciation which differs substantially from *ex post* concepts. The depreciation problem is avoided in *total* present value income, but capital consumption must be included in any measure of *periodic* income. *Ex ante* depreciation in fact becomes the residual quantity in the cash flows which enables the rate of return to be kept constant; i.e., rather than income being the residual as in *ex post* measures, depreciation is the residual in periodic present value income.[23] This of course is another arbitrary assumption implicit in the present value measures of periodic

---

[21] Refer to the Hicksian definition.

[22] N. Kaldor, "The Concept of Income in Economic Theory," from his book, *An Expenditure Tax* (Allen and Unwin, 1955); reprinted in Parker and Harcourt, *Readings in the Concept and Measurement of Income*, p. 170.

[23] The two different approaches to depreciation measurement are explained in W. J. Vatter, "Income Models, Book Yield and the Rate of Return," *The Accounting Review* (October 1966); and O. Johnson, "Two General Concepts of Depreciation," *Journal of Accounting Research* (Spring 1968).

income. Thus the reasons for the divergence between *ex ante* and *ex post* periodic income are complex ones in which the realization concept plays only a minor role. Periodic present value income is not normally directly comparable with *ex post* income of the same year because periodic present value income is futuristic—it is an *annual average of total income expected up to the horizon* and it is thereby affected by the events of years 2 . . . *n* as well as year 1, by the accuracy of forecasts and by the discount rate. Periodic *ex post* income refers to the income earned from the *actual* market transactions and events of the *past* year, at least in principle.[24] Furthermore, each measure is based on different concepts of capital maintenance and depreciation.

Periodic present value income would not, therefore, appear to be the ideal income concept for accounting purposes.[25] The argument that the accountant ought to measure it because it shows the extent to which the firm's net present value maximization objective is achieved over the period in fact is not sound. The extent to which the firm's profit objective is achieved is shown by the increase in net *tangible* assets over the period, i.e., by *ex post* periodic income, and not by present value periodic income (which shows the increase in *intangible* assets). *Ex post* income is the measure of the conversion of net present value income (i.e., subjective goodwill) into actual tangible assets of the firm. The relevant *ex ante/ex post* comparisons are between the *budgets* for year 1 (which show the forecasted transactions in terms of cash flows and changes in financial position) and the *ex post* cash, funds, income and financial position statements for year 1. The budgets and the *ex post* statements cover the *same* period and are prepared according to the same accounting principles; hence divergences between the two are due to forecasting errors rather than conceptual differences or events expected to occur beyond year 1. This information is required to assist in operating control and in subsequent planning for the future. Thus not only is periodic present value income not the accounting ideal, but it appears to serve no useful purpose at all. The accounting proponents of the Hicksian concept of periodic present value income do not appear to have heeded Hicks' own warnings about it: "We shall be well advised to eschew income and saving in economic dynamics. They are bad tools, which break in our hands."[26]

The conditions under which the measures of *ex ante* periodic income coincide with *ex post* periodic income are extremely stringent ones which are completely untypical of reality, and it is instructive to consider them. Not only do these conditions result in the equality of *ex ante* and *ex post* periodic income, but in addition there is only the one measure of each income possible. They are the necessary conditions for equilibrium in the stationary state. The stationary state is a theoretical economic model of an economy or industry in perpetual equilibrium and without growth or technical progress, and it is not meant as a description of economic reality. The conditions are:[27]

---

[24]In reality some assumptions about the future may be necessary for the measurement of some items, e.g., depreciation and credit losses.

[25]In addition to the above points concerning the relationship between the two sets of income measures, there are some technical limitations of present value income which are discussed by K. Schwayder, "A Critique of Economic Income as an Accounting Concept," *Abacus* (Aug. 1967). For example, present value income cannot be computed if the growth rate in profits exceeds the discount rate because the answer is infinity.

[26]Hicks, *Value and Capital,* from Parker and Harcourt, *Readings in the Concept and Measurement of Income,* p. 79.

[27]See Edwards and Bell, *The Theory and Measurement of Business Income,* p. 7.

(a) *Identity of cost and market values is maintained throughout.* The cost of anything purchased always equals its current market value, and the sum of production costs, including normal profit, equals its market selling value. The present market prices of assets equal their historic cost. This cost-market value identity ensures that no individual price changes occur. Perfect competition throughout all industry must exist to maintain this identity and to ensure that no pure profits occur. Hence investors earn just their required rate of return and there can be only the one discount rate in the market (i.e., $r = c$) which never changes. This in turn ensures that periodic income never changes and that historically based measures of income, assets, liabilities, and capital always coincide with their valuations on a discounted cash flow basis.

(b) *The unit of monetary measurement is stable;* i.e., the price level remains constant, or the measuring rod of the dollar remains constant over time. Hence all dollars are homogeneous in terms of value. The value of the 1900 dollar equals that of the 1972 dollar, and the two dollars can be added together to give the sum in terms of current dollar values. It is irrelevant therefore whether some land was acquired 40 years ago, and some yesterday, as the dollar values placed on each are comparable. The identity of cost and market values throughout ensures that inflation does not occur.

(c) *Certainty.* Only if the future is known with certainty can the allocation of costs and revenues among past, present, and future periods be accurately done in a continuing firm. Certainty implies perfect knowledge of all future events, the absence of risk in business operations, and the need for only one rate of interest in the economy.

Where any one of these conditions does not hold, periodic accounting reports cannot be unique and be the only true and correct reports possible. For example, if condition (a) does not hold, historic and current market values diverge and several *ex post* balance sheets can be prepared; likewise with several discount rates, several *ex ante* balance sheets are possible. If condition (b) is not fulfilled, dollars of different vintages cannot be summed together without some price level adjustment being made. If condition (c) does not hold, the future is not known with certainty and various assumptions about future events must be made. Periodic reports therefore require some estimates to be made.

It is because these conditions do not hold in reality that various valuations can be placed upon assets and liabilities and consequently that several concepts of periodic historic income and of *ex ante* income can be developed. They are the conditions of full long-run equilibrium in which no changes in any variables are permitted, or the conditions of economic *rigor mortis*. There are no decisions to be made and no control actions are required because everything is fixed by the market. There is only the one measure of income and of financial position possible. However, where these conditions do not hold, it is important for analytical reasons to keep each valuation system separate.

THE NEED FOR BOTH EX ANTE AND EX POST CONCEPTS

To appreciate the need for both *ex ante* and *ex post* measurements of income and financial position, it is necessary to understand the nature of a firm's operations and its need for financial information. Most firms operate in economic environments which are subject to more or less continual change—in factor supply prices, technology, products, prices, competitors' actions, expectations, and so on. They are relatively ignorant of the future course of events; they do not have perfect knowledge of what is going to happen in the future. Yet they are forced to pay substantial attention to the future because they incur commitments which run into the distant future—expenditure on processes and products which cannot be recouped from revenues within a few years, raising of long-term loans which can only be repaid if the firm is profitable, and so on. Their profit objective is generally a long-term one, and for this reason it is better formulated in terms of maximizing present value income rather than maximizing this year's profit without any regard being paid to operations beyond the year. In order to survive so as to have the chance of maximizing profits in the long run, they must keep on adapting their operations to comply with changes in economic conditions, both current and expected. Management must be kept well-informed of current changes so that it can modify operations and plans appropriately.

One of the most basic functions of accounting should be to supply management with necessary information on all the firm's financial affairs so that management can effectively perform its functions. The accounting system should be management's primary source of financial information.

The functions of management may be viewed as planning, controlling, evaluating, and reporting. Planning covers the determination of objectives for the firm, formulating alternative policies which should achieve these objectives, evaluating the alternatives, and selecting the preferred ones. The selected plans must then be broken down into detailed operating requirements for the near future and coordinated through a sequence of budgeted accounting reports. Budgeted accounting reports are *periodic* reports which are prepared on the same principles as periodic *ex post* reports. Planning can relate only to the future; it is too late to plan for the past; and it requires an extensive network of forecasts of possible market conditions for the firm's product, technological change, operating costs, product innovation, and so on. The forecasts of the future may be simply guesses or hunches or they may be the result of careful extrapolations of past history, as adjusted for expected future changes in operating conditions. There are no simple solutions to crystal ball gazing, but the process is helped substantially by having reliable and timely information on what occurred in the past. Planning can only be based on expectations of the future, and the more accurate the forecasts, the more successful the firm will be. Alternative policies for future action should be evaluated and selected on the basis of their contribution to expected profits, and the present value technique is the most scientific one for doing this.

The primary role of present value accounting is to assist in planning the future operations of the firm in the way which best meets the profit objective. Present value calculations are required for the evaluations of alternative policies and their selection. All long-term decisions concerning the firm at the current time involve the interaction of present value data with the firm's current position because the decision involves a movement from an existing position to a proposed future position. *Current market price* data (either replacement cost or selling price, according to the context) show the firm's current position. *Present value* data shows the firm's *future position* if specified actions are taken and the forecasts are correct, but the future position is evaluated as of now to see if it is a preferred one. As the selected plans are put into effect, total assets remain unchanged; however, subjective goodwill is realized and converted into *tangible* assets. Present values are subjective and are in the eye of the decision maker, and he should act according to their comparison with objective, current position data. All operating plans and actions of a firm are based on the interaction of private subjective values with current market values. If the management perceives the present values of some machines in the firm's operations are greater than their market prices, then it is profitable to buy those machines and use them; if it believes that the present value of retaining some existing assets in use is falling below their current selling prices, it sells them; and so on. In this way the firm keeps on adapting its own plans and operations to current market prices of assets. It is perhaps worth recalling that market prices of assets are determined by the interaction of *market* supply and *market* demand conditions. In a similar vein, the firm's own demand for assets (which form part of market demand) is determined by the interaction of the management's subjective asset valuations (which depend upon expectations of the future) with their current market prices (which measure the investment outlay on the asset).[28] It should also be emphasized that the relevant present value concepts for planning purposes are *total* present values and not *periodic* present values; and secondly that the decision rules for the purchase, retention, or sale of an asset require the comparison of *total* present value with current market prices. Information on *both* the current situation and proposed future positions is necessary for rational decision-making by the firm.

The control function involves the implementation of the plans into current operating activity. For effective control of operations, management must be provided with timely and reliable information on how operations are proceeding and where they are diverging from the plans. Regular comparisons of *ex post* data must be made with the budgets for this. The variances might indicate the need for stricter control of operations or for a revision of the plans because hindsight has improved foresight. In either case the variances cause the firm to adapt. It is part of the process of learning from experience in an environment of imperfect knowledge. Control relates to the current time. A basic function of historic cost accounting is to assist the control function of management. Historic data and *ex ante* budgeted data are necessary information for this. It should be noted that the comparison of historic data is with *ex ante budgeted data,* not with the *ex ante* present value data from which the effects of time, financial costs, and risk-taking have been removed.

Evaluation follows on at periodic intervals. Measurements of income earned and financial position must be taken from time to time, both as part of the control function and because management wants to know just how much profit has been earned to date and the firm's current financial position. The firm's net tangible assets are increased by the amount of profits earned. These measurements show the *consequences* of the decisions taken earlier, partly on a present value basis. One can measure progress only to date in terms of *ex post* data. Hence another basic function of historically-based accounting is to measure achievements and the extent to which the plans have been fulfilled. One cannot measure achievements in terms of *ex ante* data, notwithstanding the human failing in some people to confuse their pipe-dreams with their achievements.

These historic measurements are needed as well to provide more recent information to assist in forecasting the future and to assist in planning or revising plans of future operations.

Again in appraising performance and current financial position, the relevant comparisons of historic income and financial position are with budgeted reports for the same periods and with external yardsticks (rates of return earned by competitors, ability to meet financial commitments, and so on), and not with present value data.

---

[28]See Figures 1 and 2, and the rules for asset purchase, retention or sale on p. 669–70.

Finally, it is necessary for companies to report income earned and current financial position to persons outside the business, particularly to stockholders and investors generally. This is part of the stewardship function of management, and it is a necessary requirement for the attraction of capital funds. Historic cost data are relevant for stewardship purposes. In addition, stockholders require information on the achieved performance of the firm in the past and on its current financial position to assist their predictions of its future profit prospects and financial position. While it can be argued that the management's present value assessments provide appropriate predictions for stockholders, it must be appreciated that these are management's own self-evaluations of the future and that it is the stockholders who provide the risk capital to firms. Stockholders gain the financial benefits from risk-taking and suffer the losses from it, and they ought to appraise the firm's prospects and risks for themselves. Investors value the firm on the stock market, not management. Investors buy and sell shares according to their *own* assessments of the present value of the shares in each firm relative to the current market prices of the shares. The present value of a share to the stockholder is the sum of the returns per share expected by him over time, as discounted at the market yield appropriate for the share's risk class.[29] Reliable information on the firm's past profit performance and financial position is relevant, though not sufficient, information for forecasting purposes in an uncertain world and the assessment of risk.

The functions of management analyzed above and their relationships to accounting systems can be summarized in the loop diagram shown in Figure 3. It is now evident that the information requirements of management and of investors are such that *ex ante* and *ex post* data are both required. Future data in present value form are required for the decision-making parts of planning, and in budgeted form for the coordination and implementation of the selected plans. *Ex post* data (in either historic cost or current market price terms) are necessary for the effective control of operations according to plans and for the revision of expectations, for determining income earned and current financial position, for reporting on the stewardship of a professional management, and for assistance in forecasting and planning. Current market prices of assets are always required as part of the information for decision-making.

The time sequence of accounting data runs from present value data through budgeted data to historic data. Thus the attempt to merge *ex ante* with *ex post* data deprives management and investors of necessary information for decision-making, control, and evaluation. The two sets of data are always required for the proper exercise of these functions (unless the unrealistic conditions of the perfect knowledge stationary state are assumed) and they must be kept separate. A decision cannot be made on the basis of present value data alone. The rules for decision-making all require the comparison of personal subjective values arising from proposed future actions with existing market values, i.e., of present values with current market prices. *Two* measurements must be made and the fusion of them into the one measurement deprives the decision-maker of vital information. Control likewise requires the comparison of estimates with actual data. Evaluation of past performance can be made only on the basis of *ex post* data; and the incorporation of present value data into this evaluation confuses future plans and hopes with past achievements. For all functions of accounting data, the fusion of *ex post* and *ex ante* data only can confuse the user of the information. The two sets of data must be kept separate if accounting is to fulfill its role providing relevant information for various purposes. Finally,

---

[29]See footnote 14.

FIGURE 3

Relationship between Management Functions and Accounting Systems

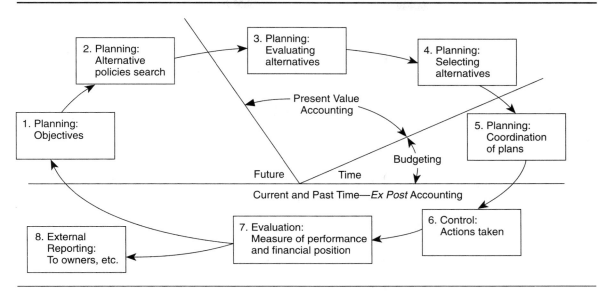

the case for the use of current market price (both replacement cost and selling price) data rather than historic cost data in *ex post* accounting must rest on the advantages which the provision of this data has with respect to measuring performance and financial position according to current market conditions, to improving efficiency of operations by indicating the need for adapting to changing asset prices, to improving the accuracy of forecasts of future operating conditions by the timely reporting of changes in the current market prices of assets, to the provision of relevant current information for decision-making, and to the formulation of sounder financial and dividend policies. It certainly should not be made to rest on the false assumption that current market prices measure the present values of a firm's existing assets.

THE NATURE OF
INCOME MEASUREMENT

William H. Beaver and Joel S. Demski

Financial reporting is heavily concerned with income "measurement." Theorists have, for decades, argued the nature of income and how best to measure it. Practitioners define their task in terms of income measurement. In turn, the FASB's reaffirmation of the importance of income [FASB, 1976] raises renewed interest in the measurement issue and provides a motivation for our paper.

In particular, the purpose of this paper is to explore the nature of income measurement. We offer initially a strict fundamental measurement perspective in which income measurement is viewed as the representation of a preference ordering on a firm's production plans. Such a measure exists and is open to a straightforward present-value interpretation in the usual economic setting of perfect and complete markets. Unfortunately, these market assumptions render the measure superfluous. Movement to a setting of imperfect or incomplete markets is necessary for economic returns to such measurement to exist, but the desired measurement does not necessarily exist in such a setting.

The authors acknowledge the helpful comments of the participants in the Stanford Summer Research Seminar (August, 1977) on an earlier draft of this paper.

This research was sponsored by the Stanford Program in Professional Accounting, major contributors to which are: Arthur Andersen & Co.; Arthur Young & Company; Coopers & Lybrand; Ernst & Ernst; Peat, Marwick, Mitchell & Co.; and Price Waterhouse & Co.

Abandoning the fundamental measurement perspective, we then offer a reinterpretation of income measurement as a noisy communication process that may be more useful than a strictly cash flow measure and more cost effective than a more ambitious disclosure policy. In this communication setting, however, we do not view the reported datum as a measure in the fundamental sense.

The paper consists of four sections. In the first we review the traditional notion of income measurement in a conventional neoclassical setting under subjective certainty. In the second section we extend the discussion to an uncertain setting where complete and perfect markets are retained. Incomplete markets and the possibility of fundamental income measurement in such a setting are discussed in the third section. Finally, our reinterpretation of financial reporting as a noisy communication process in the light of potentially impossible fundamental measurement is presented in the fourth section.

INCOME MEASUREMENT IN A CERTAIN WORLD WITH PERFECT AND COMPLETE MARKETS

Consider a conventional economic setting in which non-satiating households supply various factors of production and consume various commodities that are produced by various firms employing the supplied factors. The market structure is complete in the sense that *all* consumption goods as well as all factors of production are traded in organized markets. And each such market is perfect in the sense that prices are known by all agents, no transactions costs of any form are present, all agents behave as strict price takers, and the transaction technology is convex.[1] Moreover, we presume the economy is at an equilibrium, in which supply and demand offers are equated at the prevailing price.

Initially, we focus on an instantaneous setting in which some firm acquires resources and instantaneously transforms these factors into salable consumption goods. Let the m dimensional vector $q = (q_1,\ldots, q_m)$ denote the list of factor quantities acquired by our firm in question. Also let the n dimensional vector $r = (r_1,\ldots, r_n)$ denote the quantities of consumption goods produced. Finally, let P denote the $m + n$ dimensional price vector. We call the receipts less the expenditures of this firm its *income:*

(1)
$$I = \sum_{j=m+1}^{m+n} P_j r_j - \sum_{j=1}^{m} P_j q_j$$

At a fundamental level we would term this an *income measure.* One of the features of the neoclassical setting is that the heterogeneous individual shareholders are unanimous in their rankings of alternative production plans for the various firms in the economy [Radner, 1974b].

This ranking is represented by the income measure in Equation (1). In particular, one production plan is as good as another if and only if it leads to an income measure that is not lower.[2] Each individual is assumed to be nonsatiating, (*i.e.*, each prefers more consumption to

---

[1] Fractional quantities of all factors and commodities are available.

[2] In more precise terms, we have (with a given set of endowments and prices) a set of production plans that is rank-ordered in a complete and transitive manner. This is then represented by an income measure mapping the production plans into the real numbers and using the $\geq$ relation defined on the real numbers. See Ijrii [1967], Coombs *et al.* [1970], Krantz *et al.* [1971], and Mock [1976].

less). With perfect and complete markets, an increase in the individual's wealth is commensurate with more consumption. And with the firm's income increased, each shareholder's wealth is increased. Thus, the income measure is well-defined here—receipts less expenditures—and the firms are described as behaving as if they maximized the income measure.

Extension to a multiperiod setting retains the income measure description, but in a more familiar present-value format. We merely recognize production factors and consumption goods in each period and decompose the initial period measure in the obvious manner: that is, a period's income is now defined as the change in the present-value of the future receipts during that period. This provides a series of income measures, one for each period, such that their sum equals the firm's net receipts over the horizon and such that vector maximization of the measures is equivalent to present-value maximization.[3]

We conclude this brief summary of income measurement in a conventional neoclassical setting with several additional points. First, the emphasis is on fundamental measurement. We have existence of a mapping from alternative production plans into the real line that (using the $\geq$ relation) represents a complete and transitive ranking of production plans.[4] The measure is by no means unique, but it surely exists and is open to straightforward, conventional interpretation. Second, since plans, possibilities, and market prices are all known, no one would pay an agent to report this measure. Income is already known or is costlessly constructable by each agent. This, of course, follows from the assumptions of certainty and perfect and complete markets.

Third, the distinction between *ex post* and *ex ante* measurement is unimportant. At each intermediate point in time, the market value of the firm's assets (and claims against those assets) is known because complete and perfect markets exist. Moreover, an outcome which results in higher market value and higher net income is preferred. Hence, the net income measure easily and unambiguously performs the role of ranking outcomes as well. Indeed, with subjective certainty assumed, the *ex ante* and *ex post* measures will be identical.

INCOME MEASUREMENT IN AN UNCERTAIN WORLD WITH PERFECT AND COMPLETE MARKETS

Movement to an uncertain world leaves the above argument intact, provided we endow the economy with an appropriately rich set of perfect markets. In such a setting, the precise pro-

---

[3]An interesting feature of this income measure is that none of the usual income measurement conundrums, such as depreciation in the sense of cost allocation, arise in this setting. To be sure, we may interpret the periodic income measure as consisting of periodic cash flow less depreciation. But it is unnecessary to view the depreciation datum as an allocation of some cost. To see this, consider a situation in which factors acquired in one period produce receipts in several future periods. In a completely rich market setting, any factors carried over from one period to the next are marketable with a known price. In that sense no conventional accrual concepts are involved; nor, for that matter, is any conventional depreciation in the sense of interperiod allocation of a purchase price involved. Moreover, the perfect markets assumption ensures the equivalence among present value, replacement cost, and exit value measures.

[4]Somewhat casually, we say a ranking of elements in a set is complete if all elements in the set are ranked. Similarly, the ranking is transitive when one element is ranked ahead of a second and the second is ranked ahead of a third necessarily implies the first is ranked ahead of the third.

ductive outcome is unknown at the time of production. We model this uncertainty in the usual way, by introducing a state variable, denoted $s \in S$, such that any productive outcome is precisely determined by the productive act chosen and which state of nature obtains [Debreu, 1959, especially Chapter 7].

This provides a basis for trading in factors and consumption goods contingent on which state actually obtains. That is, complete insurance arrangements are possible, through the mechanism of event contingent trading. (Note that we assume all agents eventually learn which state does obtain, otherwise their trade arrangements would be constrained to be equal across state occurrences they are unable to distinguish.)

Return now to our instantaneous production setting in (1). With state indexing, $q^s = (q_1^s, \ldots, q_m^s)$ now denotes the quantities of factors acquired if and only if state s obtains. Similarly, $r^s = (r_1^s, \ldots, r_n^s)$ denotes the quantities of consumption goods produced if and only if state s obtains; and P^s denotes the corresponding price vector. Suppose there are l possible states. Then the firm's production plan is an l dimensional list of input-output combinations:

$$((q^1, r^1), \ldots, (q^l, r^l))$$

and the income of such a firm with such a plan is defined as

(2)
$$I = \sum_{s=1}^{l} \left(\sum_{j=m+1}^{m+n} P_j^s r_j^s - \sum_{j=1}^{m} P_j^s q_j^s \right)$$

Note in particular that—with the complete and perfect markets assumption—there is a market valuation of each possible production plan. That is, even acknowledging uncertain returns, the presumed rich set of perfect markets allows for an unambiguous (market) valuation of the firm's production plan. And now repeating the prior argument, we again view this valuation as representing the unanimous preference ordering on the set of possible production plans.

Of course, we have merely expanded the notions of factor and commodity in the original setting. Thus, with such a rich set of markets, all that was said before extends with equal force. In particular, the income measure exists in a fundamental sense, and we would not pay anyone to provide it because the component items are already assumed known. In short, existence of uncertainty in and of itself creates no problems with, or interest in, income measurement.

Further note that the *ex ante* and *ex post* measures are now influenced by the state variable. Before the event, the firm's production plan called for production of r^1 if state 1 obtains, r^2 if state 2 obtains, and so on, using some appropriate state contingent factor schedule and resulting in the contemporaneous income measure in Equation (2). After the fact, state $\hat{s}$ has obtained, $r^{\hat{s}}$ was actually produced, and $q^{\hat{s}}$ was actually used. However, under either perspective, the income measure represents a *unanimous* ranking (of production plans in the *ex ante* perspective and outcomes in the *ex post* perspective). Hence, as in the certainty case, the distinction is a trivial one, because both perspectives can be easily reconciled.

It is clear, however, that such a rich set of markets is incongruent with the existent economic structure. We, therefore, turn to the incomplete markets setting, in which all conceivable state contingent trades are *not* available; rather, only a proper subset are.

INCOME MEASUREMENT IN AN UNCERTAIN
WORLD WITH INCOMPLETE MARKETS

A setting of imperfect and incomplete markets is important because it is more realistic than the setting discussed above. Concentration on the incomplete setting is, however, sufficient for our purpose. In this setting, the firm is still envisioned as specifying a production plan consisting of state-contingent inputs and outputs. The only difference is that some of the inputs and outputs cannot be traded in organized markets. At one level, the firm may not have markets for certain assets and liabilities, such as outcomes from research and development expenditures, petroleum reserves, rights to accelerated depreciation for tax purposes on its assets, used equipment and the like [Arthur Andersen, 1977]. At another level, the non-existence of futures and insurance markets (except in a limited number of cases) provides *prima facie* evidence of the lack of such completeness.

Without marketability of *all* of the factors and commodities, it is possible to lose the unanimous ranking of alternative production plans. Some shareholders may prefer one plan over another based on nonmarketable commodities. And without trading opportunities, there is no way to resolve, via the implicit compensation mechanism of trade, the differences in taste. That is, in a regime of complete and perfect markets, income maximization is unanimously preferred because it is commensurate with increased consumption. But without access to some markets, irreconcilable conflicts may arise. Shareholders may, for example, display heterogeneous tastes in ranking production plans because of non-marketable assets which each possesses.[5]

It is, of course, possible to construct settings in which unanimous agreement on production plans does exist in an incomplete market setting. For example, if a proposed production plan is spanned by existing plans (from an existing equilibrium) unanimity will exist and prices can be used to evaluate the proposed plan. Similarly, unanimity exists in the mean-variance world of modern finance. [Ekern and Wilson, 1974; Radner, 1974b.]

But even when unanimity does occur in this setting, it is not necessarily represented by an income measure *in any traditional sense.* Under monopolistic conditions, the firm's owners, for example, may be unanimous in *not* seeking to maximize the firm's market value. And in such a setting representation of the unanimous tastes amounts to representation of subjective

---

[5]To illustrate, consider a three-commodity world (α, β, and γ) and a firm that must select one of the three production plans listed below (For example, the three commodities could be consumption in three states of the world.):

Net Production	Plan 1	Plan 2	Plan 3
α	45	40	35
β	20	30	34
γ	8	5	10

Three owners equally share in the returns and no market for either commodity exists. Their respective utility functions and evaluations are:

Individual	U_i (α, β, γ)	U_i (45, 20, 8)	U_i (40, 30, 5)	U_i (35, 34, 10)
1	$2\alpha + \beta + \gamma$	118	115	114
2	$\alpha + \beta$	65	70	69
3	γ	8	5	10

Observe that all three disagree on the best plan and that, under majority voting, they will be intransitive.

tastes. The measure, in other words, becomes entirely subjective; and in this sense it does not enjoy the supposed objectivity of the traditional income measure of resting on observed prices.

The important point, though, is that unanimity in the rankings of production plans is not necessarily present here. In such a case, the firm may simply be unable to select between two alternative production plans. (Game theory solution concepts, for example, often result in exasperatingly rich sets of possible solutions and no basis for distinguishing among them.) Thus, some plans are non-comparable. Indeed the ranking may even be intransitive.

Income measurement, on the other hand, is viewed as a mapping from a set of production plans into the real line (with plans ranked by the magnitude of this income). If such a measure represents a ranking of the alternative production plans, then that ranking must be complete and transitive. The income measure, that is, maps from the entire set of plans and it is surely transitive. Hence, whatever it represents must be complete and transitive. But the ranking of production plans is not necessarily complete and transitive in this setting. Thus, fundamental income measurement, in the sense of representing a unanimous ranking of alternative production plans for the firm, is not necessarily possible here.

Financial reporting cannot, therefore, be described in terms of income measurement in this setting of incomplete markets.

A POSSIBLE REINTERPRETATION

What, then, is the nature of income? One possible answer is available if we more closely examine the nature of the economy with incomplete markets. A particular firm offers a complex set of state-contingent production plans, but many individuals (*e.g.*, investors) do not distinguish among the various states to the extent that the firm's management does. This is a major reason for market incompleteness. Hence, the firm now possesses information that is potentially useful to individuals external to its direct operations.

Such information may be useful in the sense of revising beliefs before decisions (*e.g.*, investment decisions) are made (termed pre-decision information). It may also be useful in terms of providing a basis for contracting, as exemplified by cost-plus payment arrangements, dividend restrictions stated in terms of income, managerial incentive arrangements based on income, and so on (termed post-decision information). Of course, these two roles may occur simultaneously in a multiperiod world [Radner, 1974a].

In transmitting this information, for either or both purposes, a number of options become interesting once we recognize costliness of the communication process. The firm might list its specific $(r^{\hat{s}}, q^{\hat{s}})$ realizations, which would be potentially useful because not everyone (or anyone) is presumed to observe $\hat{s}$. But this is a vast undertaking. Alternatively, it might list its ending cash balance, say $q_1^{\hat{s}}$. An intermediate role is to aggregate the $(r^{\hat{s}}, q^{\hat{s}})$ realizations with the introduction of various groupings and allocations (which can be interpreted as use of pseudo prices for non-marketable factors and commodities). Presumably, this notion of accrual accounting is a cost-effective alternative.

However, the crux of the argument on behalf of accrual accounting rests on the premise that (1) reported income under accrual accounting rules conveys more information than a less ambitious cash-flow-oriented accounting system would,[6] (2) accrual accounting is the most

---

[6]Note that with cash also reported we can meaningfully speak of "more" information in this context.

efficient means to convey this additional information, and, as a corollary, (3) the "value" of such additional information system exceeds its "cost."

Income reporting under accrual rules, then, is neither "good" nor "bad" as such. Rather, it may be a desirable middle ground between more and less reporting. But interpreted in this light, it derives its support from the information it conveys (at whatever cost) and *not* from such criteria as "more income is better than less." Indeed, there is no reason to label the bottom line as "income." (Of course, there is no reason not to label it as "income" either.)[7]

This is further discussed below, where we focus more explicitly on the pre- and post-decision settings.

PRE-DECISION INFORMATION

Consider the pre-decision perspective in the AICPA Objectives Study [1973] and the Tentative Conclusions of the FASB's Conceptual Framework Project [1976]. Both studies adopt the view that the primary purpose of financial statements is to provide information to some defined class of users (*e.g.*, investors and creditors in the case of the FASB).[8] At the same time, they also support the usefulness of income reporting as a vehicle for providing the desired information. By implication, they have reached a judgment regarding the three issues noted above.

However, the basis for this judgment is less than clear. As indicated earlier, accounting income rules can be viewed as resulting in aggregations over quantities and prices. If the aggregated number which results is a sufficient statistic, there is no loss of information. In this situation, there is a potential savings in cost of processing, and the income-rule question is resolved on pure efficiency grounds [Feltham, 1977].

In general, of course, there will be a loss of information. In this case, heterogeneity of preferences for income rules may arise because the "value" and "cost" of the information may fall differently across users. A lack of unanimity regarding preferences for income rules obviously characterizes many of our popular controversies. This occurs for the same reasons that we lack unanimity with regard to production plans; indeed, it is a by-product of the basic argument because information is, strictly speaking, a factor of production.

In a world where markets (for information) were perfect and complete, this heterogeneity could be accommodated by some market-based or elaborate contracting mechanism. Gonedes and Dopuch [1974], among others, have alluded to the possibility that accounting information may induce externalities (and in the limit, a type of public good). In such a situation, some form of collective action may appear, either in the form of private sector self-regulation (*e.g.*, FASB) or a public-sector-mandated system (*e.g.*, Securities and Exchange Commission).

---

[7]Though the terminology differs, this is the spirit of Sorter's [1969] "events" approach in which the proper combination of "aggregation" and "valuation" are sought so as to balance information demands and cost. And by extending the argument we may find accrual procedures to be that happy medium.

[8]Although portions of the conceptual framework create ambiguity regarding the extent to which the FASB intends to adopt an informational perspective, recent statements by Sprouse [1977] at an Annual Meeting of the American Accounting Association confirm this informational perspective. In answer to advocates of the "full disclosure" approach to financial reporting, Sprouse responded with a view of income as a cost-effective alternative to a comprehensive disclosure policy.

Contextually, however, there is one important distinction between the measurement and information viewpoints that is worth noting. For certain classes of controversies over "most-preferred" income rules, the major alternatives can be reported via an essentially costless disclosure policy. The measurement approach would still attempt to resolve the issue as to which rule results in the "best" measure of income (within limits imposed by nonuniqueness of the measures). However, from an informational perspective, the issue is not a substantive one. While this constitutes a special case from an analytical point of view, empirically many popular accounting controversies fall into this category. Examples include interperiod tax allocation, accounting for the investment credit, and certain aspects of accounting for business combinations.[9] From an informational perspective, substantive issues occur where disclosure or cost is at least implicitly involved. Examples would be replacement cost accounting, foreign currency translation, segment reporting, and "fair value" aspects of business combinations.

In any event, the jump from a desire to supply information to income reporting as a desirable vehicle for such reporting remains unclear. Appeal to fundamental measurement arguments is inadequate. On the other hand, the income orientation may be rationalized with a costly communication perspective. But the studies in question have not professed such a perspective.

POST-DECISION INFORMATION

Essentially the same observations emerge in the post-decision setting of traditional stewardship reporting in which the *ex post* reported income datum is used for contingent contracting purposes. An employment contract based on a target income goal requires *ex post* income reporting, a cost-plus contract requires *ex post* reporting, a current ratio constraint on a lender requires *ex post* balance sheet reporting, and so on. And in each instance, the motivation for reporting rests on the improved allocations which such reporting provides, and not on such criteria as "more income is better than less." From an informational perspective we analyze this setting just as the pre-decision setting was analyzed.

Accrual-income measures may again be interpreted as a middle ground between extensive reporting of production plans and results and cash basis reporting that can be rationalized on cost-of-information grounds. In special cases resolution of the "proper" aggregation is straight-forward (*e.g.*, when an aggregate datum is a less costly sufficient statistic for the more useful datum). But in general, we expect heterogeneity of preferences for information systems, which are resolved via non-market determination mechanisms. And our basic point remains: choice of an income rule cannot be resolved by applying fundamental measurement arguments.[10]

---

[9]This implicitly assumes that the format of disclosure does not convey information or otherwise affect the firm's production and financing opportunity set.

[10]Recent articles have expressed reservations about various deficiencies in income as a fundamental measure and about present value as a valuation mechanism (Ashton [1977], Bromwich [1977], McIntyre [1977], Peasnell [1977], and Scapens [1978]). The expressed concerns arise because of some assumed incompleteness (or imperfection) in the markets. Hopefully, the framework provided here will serve to synthesize these concerns and to provide some "convergence" on this long-standing debate.

SUMMARY

In a regime of incomplete markets, income measurement in a fundamental sense does not describe what accountants do. A condition for fundamental measurement may be missing in cases where we would commit scarce resources to production of accounting numbers. An informational perspective does, however, describe the accountant's activity. But it raises deep concerns over the role of the income concept. Matching of costs and revenues, for example, is not an underlying notion here. Rather, the case for income rests on the assumption of aggregating more informative but also more costly data such that a cost-effective communication mechanism is obtained. However, this assumption is problematical, and in our view, one challenge to accounting theorists is to address the primitive question of the propriety of the accrual concept of income.

REFERENCES

AICPA Objectives Committee, *Objectives of Financial Statements* (AICPA, 1973).

Arthur Andersen & Co., "Objectives of Financial Statements: The Conceptual Framework for Financial Accounting and Reporting," (June 1977).

Ashton, R., "Objectivity of Accounting Measures: A Multirule-Multimeasurer Approach," *The Accounting Review* (July 1977), pp. 567–575.

Bromwich, M., "The Use of Present Value Valuation Models in Published Accounting Reports," *The Accounting Review* (July 1977), pp. 587–596.

Coombs, C., R. Dawes, and A. Tversky, *Mathematical Psychology: An Elementary Introduction* (Prentice Hall, 1970).

Debreu, G., *Theory of Value* (Yale University Press, 1959).

Demski, J., "Choice Among Financial Reporting Alternatives," *The Accounting Review* (April 1974), pp. 221–232.

Demski, J. and G. Feltham, *Cost Determination: A Conceptual Approach* (Iowa State University Press, 1976).

Ekern, S. and R. Wilson, "On the Theory of the Firm in an Economy with Incomplete Markets," *Bell Journal of Economics and Management Science* (Spring 1974), pp. 171–180.

Feltham, G., "Cost Aggregation: An Information Economic Analysis," *Journal of Accounting Research* (Spring 1977), pp. 42–70.

Financial Accounting Standards Board, *Tentative Conclusions on Objectives of Financial Statements of Business Enterprises* (Stamford, Connecticut, 1976).

Gonedes, N., "Information-Production and Capital Market Equilibrium," *The Journal of Finance* (June 1975), pp. 841–864.

Gonedes, N. and N. Dopuch, "Capital Market Equilibrium, Information Production, and Selecting Accounting Techniques: Theoretical Framework and Review of Empirical Work, *Studies on Financial Accounting Objectives: 1974,* supplement to the *Journal of Accounting Research,* (1974), pp. 49–129.

Ijiri, Y., *The Foundations of Accounting Measurement: A Mathematical, Economic, and Behavioral Inquiry* (Prentice-Hall, 1967).

Krantz, D., R. Luce, P. Suppes, and A. Tversky, *Foundations of Measurement* (Academic Press, 1971).

McIntyre, E., "Present Value Depreciation and the Disaggregation Problem," *The Accounting Review* (January 1977), pp. 162–171.

Mock, T., *Measurement and Accounting Information Criteria* (American Accounting Association, 1976).

Peasnell, K., "A Note on the Discounted Present Value Concept," *The Accounting Review* (January 1977), pp. 186–189.

Radner, R., "Market Equilibrium and Uncertainty: Concepts and Problems," in M. Intriligator and D. Kendrick (eds.), *Frontiers of Quantitative Economics,* Volume 2 (North-Holland, 1974a), pp. 43–105.

———, "A Note on Unanimity of Stockholders' Preferences among Alternative Production Plans: A Reformulation of the Ekern-Wilson Model; *Bell Journal of Economics and Management Science* (Spring 1974b), pp. 181–184.

Scapens, R., "A Neoclassical Measure of Profit," *The Accounting Review* (April 1978), pp. 448–469.

Sorter, G., "An 'Events' Approach to Basic Accounting Theory," *The Accounting Review* (January 1969), pp. 12–19.

Sprouse, R., "Toward a Conceptual Framework for Financial Reporting in the United States," (speech delivered at the Annual Meeting of the American Accounting Association, August, 1977).

Vickrey, D., "Is Accounting a Measurement Discipline?" *The Accounting Review* (October 1970), pp. 731–742.

MEASUREMENT OF
ASSETS AND LIABILITIES

THE ROLE OF PRESENT VALUE
IN THE MEASUREMENT AND
RECORDING OF NONMONETARY
FINANCIAL ASSETS AND
LIABILITIES: AN EXAMINATION

George O. Gamble and Joe J. Cramer, Jr.

In 1990, the Financial Accounting Standards Board (FASB) issued a *Discussion Memorandum* entitled "Present Value-Based Measurements in Accounting."[1] The objective of the *Discussion Memorandum* is to focus on the development of a framework for future issues concerning present value-based measurements. Currently, in financial reporting, the theory of present value is used on a limited basis.[2]

    The objective of this paper is to examine the feasibility of applying the theory of present value to nonmonetary financial assets and liabilities, in general, and progress billings on long-term construction contracts, in particular. Progress billings on long-term construction contracts was selected to represent an application of the discounting process to nonmonetary

---

George O. Gamble and Joe J. Cramer, Jr., "The Role of Present Value in the Measurement and Recording of Nonmonetary Financial Assets and Liabilities: An Examination," *Accounting Horizons*. Reprinted by permission of the American Accounting Association.

[1] Financial Accounting Standards Board, *Present Value-Based Measurements in Accounting—A Discussion Memorandum* (Stamford, Connecticut: Financial Accounting Standards Board, 1990).

[2] For the most part, the present value framework has been used in the valuation of selected lease, real estate, deferred compensation (including pensions), insurance company policy benefits, monetary asset and liabilities and mortgage banking transactions. For a complete list of those transactions requiring discounting by GAAP, the reader should refer to FASB, Ibid., 110–111.

transactions because it typifies a contractual arrangement that, under GAAP, is not measured in terms of present value and it extends the FASB's suggestion of potential applications of the discounting process to include product contracts.[3]

The methodology employed to satisfy the general and particular objectives is normative in nature. This approach was selected because it is useful in those situations where the researchers are concerned with demonstrating that the consequences of using a particular model will lead to a better state, judged from a given set of goals. Thus, the normative approach will allow the researchers to: (1) assess the importance of the discounting process (present value theory) to financial reporting; (2) evaluate the appropriateness of discounting nonmonetary financial assets and liabilities, in general, and progress billings on long-term contracts, in particular; (3) determine the benefits from discounting nonmonetary financial assets and liabilities, in general, and progress billings on long-term contracts, in particular. The benefits derived from the discounting process will be based upon selected objectives; and (4) assess an accounting measurement and reporting problem with the same methodology employed by the FASB in its evaluation of accounting practice.

The first section of the paper includes a discussion of the difference between monetary and nonmonetary assets and liabilities and the importance of the discounting process in their periodic evaluation as determined by present accounting practice. Further, the proper classification of progress billings within the above classification scheme is also presented. The second section advances discussion on the selection of an appropriate discount rate and the methodology used to measure this rate. The third avenue of investigation is based on: (1) the objective of providing earning power and cash flow[4] information to current and potential creditors and investors and (2) maintaining consistency with contemporary accounting practice with respect to the measurement of accounting information. Sample journal entries will be used to illustrate the proposed framework.

THE NATURE OF PRESENT VALUE THEORY

The consideration exchanged in a transaction usually is expressed in terms of monetary units. For some transactions, the total amount of consideration involved is transferred in a single amount on the date of the transaction. In this case, each dollar is not only homogenous with respect to the monetary unit, but each is also equivalent in terms of units of present value. That is, each dollar possesses the equivalent time value of money.

The consideration exchanged in other transactions is, by contrast, distributed over a series of accounting periods. Other factors being equal, the relative value of the flow of consideration to be received or given earlier in the series is greater than the value of the flows to be received or given at a later date. These flows initially may be expressed in terms of a common monetary unit and are thus homogenous in this respect. Because they occur at different points

---

[3]In its *Discussion Memorandum* (114–115), the FASB listed service contracts as a potential application of the discounting process. We will demonstrate in the section entitled "Importance of Monetary-Nonmonetary Distinction to Discounting," that the discounting process is also important to product contracts.

[4]The FASB is of the opinion that it is important to report information on earning power and cash flow. See, for example, Financial Accounting Standards Board, *Statement of Financial Accounting Concepts No. 1,* "Objectives of Financial Reporting by Business Enterprises" (Stamford, Connecticut: FASB, 1978), paras. 37, 43, and 44.

in time, however, the nominal (undiscounted) units of money in which they are stated do not reflect equivalent amounts of present value. The separate amounts are, therefore, nonhomogenous with respect to the time value of money or units of present value. For purposes of clarity, discounting is applied to ensure that each unit of currency employed to express the separate amounts of consideration received and given at different times reflects the equivalent amount of present value on any given balance sheet date.

Concisely stated, the discounting process recognizes the effect of time as one of the determinants of the value of the monetary unit used to express accounting information. Further, because the principle of present value relates exclusively to time, in the strictest sense the process of interest accumulation and discounting is continuous rather than discrete.

IMPORTANCE OF MONETARY-NONMONETARY DISTINCTION TO DISCOUNTING

Monetary-nonmonetary assets and liabilities are defined in the following manner by APB Opinion No. 29 (APBO-29):

> **Monetary assets and liabilities** are assets and liabilities whose amounts are fixed in terms of units of currency by contract or otherwise. Examples are cash, short-or-long-term accounts and notes receivable in cash, and short-or-long-term accounts and notes payable in cash.
> **Nonmonetary assets and liabilities** are assets and liabilities other than monetary ones. Examples are inventories; investments in common stocks; property, plant and equipment; and liabilities for rent collected in advance.[5]

In contemporary accounting practice, the monetary-nonmonetary distinction is important to the discounting process because one classification is determinable and the other characterized by the variability of its parameters. Cash flows associated with monetary assets and liabilities are presumed to be more readily determinable than nonmonetary items since they are expected to be held until maturity. This contrast holds because the amounts to be paid or received, respectively, at maturity and periodic interest revenue and expense are known with certainty. This information about cash flows simplifies the discounting process.

On the other hand, the amounts at which nonmonetary assets and liabilities will be settled are not fixed in terms of units of currency. They can be realized and liquidated, respectively, by the future receipt or disbursement of a presently undetermined amount of cash or by the future receipt or transfer of other forms of consideration, such as economic goods and services, whose prices may fluctuate over time. Thus, their present value is heavily dependent on many variables over which an entity has no control. The amounts at which they will ultimately be settled can be affected by external events such as:

1. Changes in interest and tax rates.
2. Changes in other specific price levels due to changes in supply-demand relationships, technology, and other variables.
3. Changes in the general price level.

---

[5]Accounting Principles Board, *Opinion No. 29,* "Accounting for Nonmonetary Transactions" (New York: AICPA, 1973), para. 3.

Therefore, values assigned to nonmonetary financial items[6] are probabilistic in comparison with the deterministic character of cash flows, interest rates, and values associated with monetary assets and liabilities.

Concisely stated, the issues suggest that the result of discounting may be more precise in the valuation of monetary items because of the greater degree of certainty which characterizes the factors that enter into the determination of their values. Further, because of that precision, the accounting profession has deemed that the discounting of monetary items is compatible with the historical cost model.[7] Because the discounting of nonmonetary items does not produce a value with the same degree of precision as monetary items, present accounting practice places greater reliance on market forces for determining their discounted present value. Thus, for selected nonmonetary items, the determination of discounted present value permits accounting practice to deviate from the historical cost principle.[8]

Monetary-nonmonetary assets and liabilities can be further classified into operating or financial categories. Assets can be classified either as operating or financial while liabilities must be classified as financial.[9] Operating assets are always classed as nonmonetary; financial assets and liabilities are classed as either monetary or nonmonetary. Consequently, in terms of the discounting procedure used in present accounting practice, monetary financial assets and liabilities are treated differently than nonmonetary financial assets. Table 1 contains examples of nonmonetary financial assets and liabilities.

It is our opinion that the conventional classification of financial assets and liabilities as monetary or nonmonetary may be overly subjective and restrictive when used as a guide for determining accounting procedures for nonmonetary financial assets and liabilities. If such classification is disregarded and the interest accruals related to nonmonetary items are determined only by reference to the prevailing rate of interest in effect when the nonmonetary financial assets are acquired or nonmonetary liabilities are incurred, i.e., subsequent changes in interest rates are ignored, then procedures to account for nonmonetary items would be consistent with those used to account for monetary items. Thus, investors and creditors would be able to evaluate accounting information on an equivalent basis that has been measured over a period of time.[10]

---

[6]Financial items will be defined in a later part of this section of the paper.

[7]Joe J. Cramer, Jr., *The Nature and Importance of Discounted Present Value in Financial Accounting and Reporting* (Arthur Andersen & Co., 1980), 6.

[8]For example, note the use of a lower of cost or market rule for valuing inventory and marketable equity securities and under certain conditions debt securities. For an excellent discussion, the reader should refer to Joe J. Cramer, Jr., op. cit., 6–8.

[9]Operating assets are those assets employed by an entity for the primary purpose of providing economic goods and services, e.g., property, plant and equipment. On the other hand, financial assets are those assets employed by an entity to acquire economic resources or assets that are necessary for carrying on operating activities and for fulfilling financial responsibilities. Liabilities can only be classed as financial in nature, for they never enter directly into the production process.

[10]The recommendation that the same accounting procedure is used should not be interpreted that we are proposing the same disclosure policy for monetary and nonmonetary items. On the contrary, it is our opinion that additional disclosures should be made for nonmonetary assets and liabilities for such items as changes in interest and tax rates and specific and general prices because they too are financial in nature and will aid the market in determining their final value.

TABLE 1

Examples of Nonmonetary Financial Assets and Liabilities

Assets	Liabilities
• Marketable securities (stocks and bonds—except bonds that are expected to be held to maturity and redeemed at a fixed number of dollars).	
• Accounts and notes receivable (that represent claims to nonmonetary assets or an unknown amount of cash).	• Accounts and notes payable (that will be settled by transfers of nonmonetary assets or an unknown amount of cash—including the *unearned revenue* category such as advance sale of tickets, tokens, certificates and subscriptions).
• Advance payments for the acquisition of resources and raw materials (including deposits or progress payments on construction contracts and advances to encourage exploration in the extractive industries).	• Advances received on sales contracts.
• Pension, sinking and other funds under an entity's control (to the extent that the asset composition of the fund is not monetary).	• Estimated pension obligations (that are not fixed in terms of numbers of dollars).

APPROPRIATENESS OF PRESENT VALUE THEORY TO PROGRESS BILLINGS

For the contractor, the contemporary accounting methodology for a progress billing on a project requires a debit to an asset account (accounts receivable) and a credit to a liability account (partial billings). When a periodic amount billed less the retained percentage (the agreed upon percentage of the billed amount withheld by the buyer from the payment) is collected during a period, it is recorded as a debit to cash and a credit to accounts receivable. However, in a partially completed project, the periodic amount recorded in the partial billings account will remain in the balance sheet until the project is completed. Once the project has been completed, the dollar amount in the progress billings account related to that project is removed. Thus for a five year contract, it is possible for a periodic billed amount to remain in the partial billings account and a retained percentage in the accounts receivable account up to five years.

It is assumed that the periodic amounts added to accounts receivable and progress billings are homogenous with respect to the same units of *present value* for amounts already recorded in those accounts. Unfortunately, under present accounting practice, the above accounts are nonhomogenous with regard to the same units of *present value*. Homogeneity is wanting in the progress billings account because the periodic amounts recorded are undiscounted. Dollar amounts recorded in accounts receivable also are nonhomogenous because, as previously stated, most construction contracts stipulate that a certain percentage of the periodic billed amount be retained by the buyer until the project has been accepted. Thus, over the life of a project, the accounts receivable balance is comprised of amounts representing different time periods.

The discussion makes it appear that discounting is appropriate for progress billings because it allows amounts recorded in different time periods to become homogenous with regard to units of present value. Further, the discounting procedure recommended would permit the contractor to recognize interest expense on partial billings (a liability), as well as a gain on the forgiveness of the *payment* of interest on partial billings. The gain recognized would equate to the interest expense.

The recommended discounting procedure also requires the recording of interest revenue on the retained amount in accounts receivable as well as a loss on the foregone *receipt* of interest on that same amount. The loss recognized would equate to interest revenue.

For the buyer, the recommended discounting procedure would require the recognition of interest revenue on advances to contractor (an asset) as well as a loss on the foregone *receipt* of interest on that same asset. The loss recognized would be equal to interest revenue. With regard to the retained percentage, the recommended procedure requires the recognition of interest expense on the amount retained in accounts payable as well as a gain on the forgiveness of the *payment* of interest on the retained percentage. The gain recognized would be equal to interest expense.

THE SELECTION OF AN APPROPRIATE DISCOUNT RATE

Because an important part of the proposed framework is interest recognition, the selection of an appropriate discount rate is significant. Several alternative rates are available to the contractor: (1) the after-tax debt rate, (2) the unlevered equity rate, (3) the levered equity rate, and (4) the weighted average cost of capital. The first is an *after-tax debt rate*. The rationale associated with that selection holds that progress billings represent resources that the contractor need not borrow to construct the asset under contract, i.e., foregone interest payment. As such, the appropriate discount rate is the rate (after taxes) that would have been paid on borrowed funds. An after-tax debt rate is selected because it is more representative of the true cost of borrowed funds. Thus, progress billings and interest are more realistically measured using an after-tax debt rate. The major argument against using an after-tax debt rate, however, is that it assumes that debt is the only source of financing for the construction contract(s).

Another plausible discount rate is an *unlevered equity rate*. The rationale for using this rate assumes the contractor only uses equity to finance the construction project(s). That is, the rate represents unlevered risk to the firm. This rate is not appropriate, however, for those contractors who employ both debt and equity to finance their operations.

Another rate that could be used by the contractor is a *levered equity rate*. The rationale for using this rate is that the contractor is levered, but has elected only to use equity to finance the construction of a particular project. Application of this rate assumes that a contractor can differentiate projects financed with all debt from those financed with all equity or a combination of both.

A discount rate that incorporates both debt and equity—*weighted average cost of capital*—has major advantages: (1) it is consistent with the balance sheet equation in the sense that it recognizes the fact that both debt and equity are jointly used by contractors to finance their operations and (2) it eliminates the need for making assumptions about capital mix and the ability of a contractor to decompose its capital structure.[11]

---

[11]For an excellent discussion of these rates the reader is referred to Thomas E. Copeland and J. Fred Weston, *Financial Theory and Corporate Policy* (Reading, Massachusetts; Addison-Wesley, 1988), 437–481.

We feel that, even though all of the above rates are acceptable, the *weighted average cost of capital* should be used because it minimizes the number of assumptions one has to make.[12] Consequently, the use of the weighted average cost of capital should enable entities to calculate a discount rate on a more consistent and comparable basis than the other methods.

The above interest rates are also appropriate for the buyer. The *weighted average cost of capital* is preferred as the appropriate discount rate for the buyer because investors are provided with comparable and consistently measured information needed in their decision making. We are not proposing that for a given contract, the contractor and buyer use the same discount rate. On the contrary, they should have different discount rates if they have entirely different environments with respect to investor expectations, operating and financing risks, etc. Forcing firms to use an identical rate might mislead investors if that particular rate does not mirror those entity specific attributes that might be required by investors in their evaluation of performance and financial status. Thus, we are proposing consistency between the contractor and buyer with regard to the methodology used to determine their respective weighted average cost of capital.

Methodology for Calculating Weighted Average Cost of Capital

Under the weighted average cost of capital (WACC) formula, the Capital Asset Pricing Model (CAPM) can be used to estimate the cost of debt and equity. Under the CAPM, the following WACC formula is used:

$$\text{WACC} = r_b(1 - T_c)\left(\frac{D}{V}\right) + r_s\left(\frac{E}{V}\right)$$

where:

r_b = the firm's current borrowing rate, i.e., cost of debt, which can be estimated under the CAPM by estimating Beta-debt

T_c = the firm's marginal income tax rate

r_s = the expected rate of return on the firm's stock, i.e., the cost of equity, which can be estimated under the CAPM by estimating Beta-equity

D = the market value of currently outstanding debt

E = the market value of currently outstanding debt

$V = D + E$ = the total market value of the firm

The cost of debt is calculated in the following manner:

$$r_b = r_f + \beta\,(r_f - r_m)$$

where:

r_f = the riskless rate which can be measured by the return on 90-day U.S. Treasury Bills

---

[12]In the weighted-average-cost-of-capital formula, all variables in it refer to the entity as a whole. Thus, the formula gives a discount rate for projects that are just like the entity undertaking them. The formula works for the average project and does not take into account individual risk attributes of a particular project.

r_m = the market return which is estimated by the Standard & Poor's Composite Index

β = a firm's beta is estimated by regressing past company bond returns on past market bond returns using a standard ordinary least-squares regression approach.

Returns are derived from bond price changes, as follows[13]:

$$r(t) = \frac{P(t) - P(t-1)}{P(t-1)}$$

Furthermore, the cost of equity is calculated in the following manner:

$$r_s = r_f + \beta\,(r_f - r_m)$$

where:

r_f = the riskless rate which can be measured by the return on 90-day U.S. Treasury Bills

r_m = the market return which is estimated by the Standard & Poor's Composite Index

β = a firm's beta is estimated by regressing past company stock returns on past market stock returns using a standard ordinary least-squares regression approach

Returns are derived from price changes, as follows:

$$r(t) = \frac{P(t) - P(t-1) + \text{Dividends}}{P(t-1)}$$

BENEFITS FROM DISCOUNTING PROGRESS BILLINGS

This recommended discounting procedure has the major benefit of allowing entities to account for progress billings and retained percentages in a manner similar to other receivables and payables with a stated rate of interest different than their market rate, as described in APB Opinion No. 21.[14] The similarities between the proposed procedure and APB Opinion 21 are limited to the imputation of interest and the use of the effective interest method for the determination of interest revenue and interest expense. Thus, creditors and investors are able to evaluate the interest element of receivables and payables in a consistent and equitable manner.

The proposed procedure has the added advantage of allowing entities to account for the elements of gains and losses on financial arrangements on a more consistent and expanded basis.

---

[13]Estimating a Company's beta may be difficult if the appropriate return data are not available. In this case, beta may be estimated by identifying characteristics of a company associated with a high or low beta, e.g., cyclicality (the strength of the relationship between a firm's earnings and the aggregate market earnings on all real assets), operating leverage (the extent to which a firm is committed to fixed production charges), financial leverage (the extent to which a firm's assets are financed with debt) and economic characteristics of a firm's lines of business. Further, progress billings may have a beta that is different than the beta for the firm as a whole. In this case, progress billings should be evaluated using their associated risk factors, e.g., probability of default of payment.

[14]Accounting Principles Board, Opinion No. 21, "Interest on Receivables and Payables" (New York: AICPA, 1971).

For example, the recognition of a purchase discount taken or lost by the purchaser of inventory is no more than a quantitative expression of the gain or loss experienced by taking or not taking advantage of an opportunity created by a financial arrangement.[15] The recognition of the gain on the forgiveness of the payment of interest on progress billings and accounts payable is similar to purchase discount taken in the sense that they both represent gains created by a financial arrangement. On the other hand, the recognition of the loss on the foregone receipt of interest on advances to contractor and accounts receivable is similar to purchase discount lost because they too represent amounts created by a financial arrangement.

The discounting of progress billings and the retained percentage will also provide additional information that should help current and potential creditors and investors to make decisions. Decision makers will be able to:

1. Assess leverage and financing risk of the contractor and the buyer in a more meaningful manner because the dollar effect of additional financing information is estimated and reported in the form of interest expense.[16]

2. Assess the return on assets of the buyer and contractor in a more meaningful manner because the dollar effect of additional information on earnings is estimated and reported in the form of interest revenue.[17]

3. Determine a surrogate for total project cost. For a contractor the surrogate is determined, for a particular contract, by adding the contract price to the total periodic gains recognized on partial billings for the contract. On the other hand, the buyer would determine its surrogate by adding to the contract price the total periodic losses recognized on advances to contractor. Total project cost is important in terms of evaluating intraindustry cost structure(s) and contract profitability.

4. Assess the total impact of progress billings on the cash flows of the contractor and buyer. Additional Cash flow information for the contractor is provided in the form of cash savings on interest payments not made to buyer. Additional cash flow information for the buyer is in the form of foregone cash receipts on interest payments not made by contractor.

5. Assess the impact of the retained percentage on cash flows in terms of amount, timing and related uncertainty.

Finally, the discounting of retained percentages could lead to a more consistent disclosure practice among construction companies. For example, Table 2 contains the reporting and disclosure practices of 29 construction companies for retained percentages in 1990. While all of the sampled firms included retained percentages in accounts receivable, only 59 percent reported in the comparative financial statements actual dollar amounts retained. Furthermore, 34 percent disclosed in the notes to the financial statements a breakdown of retained percentages

---

[15]Other examples of financial arrangements that result in gains or losses are early extinguishment of debt, debt restructuring and in-substance defeasance.

[16]For the contractor, interest expense is calculated on partial billings. On the other hand, the buyer's interest expense is calculated on the retained amount in accounts payable.

[17]For the buyer, interest revenue is calculated on advance payments to contractor. The contractor's interest revenue is calculated on the retained amount in accounts receivable.

TABLE 2

Reporting and Disclosure Practices for Retained Percentage(s)

Company	Retained Percent Included in Accounts Receivable	Discloses Dollar Amount of Retained Percent in Notes	Discloses Retained Percent in Years & Dollar Amount
Abrams Industries, Inc.	yes	no	no
Apogee Enterprises, Inc.	yes	yes	no
American Medical Bldgs.	yes	yes	no
Bank Bldg. & Equip. Corp.	yes	no	no
Blount, Inc.	yes	no	no
Burnup & Sims, Inc.	yes	yes	yes
Centex Corp.	yes	yes	no
Devcon International	yes	yes	yes
Fluor Corp.	yes	no	no
Foster Wheeler	yes	no	no
GBI International Industries	yes	no	no
GMX Communications, Inc.	yes	yes	yes
Goldfield Corp.	yes	no	no
Halliburton Co.	yes	yes	yes
Insituform Gulf South, Inc.	yes	no	no
IREX Corp.	yes	yes	yes
Jacobs Engineering Group, Inc.	yes	yes	no
LVI Group, Inc.	yes	yes	no
Metalclad Corp.	yes	yes	yes
MMR Holding Corp.	yes	yes	yes
Morrison Knudsen Corp.	yes	yes	yes
Oppenheimer Industries	yes	no	no
Perini Corp.	yes	yes	no
TD Industries	yes	no	no
The Mischer Corp.	yes	no	no
Thermo Electron Corp.	yes	yes	no
Turner Corp.	yes	yes	yes
United Building Service	yes	yes	yes
Wheelabrator Technologies	yes	no	no

Source: 1990 Annual Reports

in terms of years and the specific dollar amount associated with each year disclosed. Because of the nature of the discounting process, the above reported percentages should increase to approximately the same level of conformity that is experienced by the reporting of the retained percentage in accounts receivable.

ILLUSTRATION OF PROPOSED FRAMEWORK

Assume that on January 1, 19x1 the CT Construction Co. signs a fixed-price contract with the LLG Co. to construct a $7,500,000 building that is expected to be completed December 31, 19x3 at an estimated cost of $6,300,000. The contract specifies the following with regard to progress billings: $2,250,000-19x1, $2,625,000-19x2 and $2,625,000-19x3. Billings are made at the end of each period and 90 percent of the billed amount in 19x1 and 19x2 will be

EXHIBIT 1

Illustrative Journal Entries for Proposed Framework

Progress billings recorded at present value

(1) Accounts receivable	2,250,000	
Discount on partial billings	390,496	
Future interest accruals on accounts receivable	39,049	
Partial billings		2,250,000
Future interest accruals on partial billings		390,496
Discount on accounts receivable		39,049

Recognition of interest expense and gain on net partial billings and future interest accruals
($1,859,504 + $390,496) × .10

(2) Interest expense	225,000	
Gain on noninterest bearing partial billings		225,000

Recognition of loss and interest revenue on retained percentage in net accounts receivable and future interest accruals
($185,000 + $39,049) × .10

(3) Loss on noninterest bearing accounts receivable	22,500	
Interest revenue		22,500

Recognition of reduction in the future interest accruals on net retained accounts receivable
($225,000 − $39,049) × .10

(4) Discount on accounts receivable	18,595	
Future interest accruals on accounts receivable		18,595

Recognition of reduction in the future interest accruals on net partial billings
($2,250,000 − $390,496) × .10

(5) Future interest accruals on partial billings	185,950	
Discount on partial billings		185,950

collected during 19x3 and 19x4 respectively. The 10 percent retained percentage from 19x1 and 19x2 along with the 19x3 billing will be collected at the beginning of 19x4. Further, computations will be based on the assumption that the appropriate discount rate for the CT Co. is 10 percent. For the purpose of expediency, illustrative journal entries will be limited to those changes proposed in the paper. Further, the illustration will be limited to the 19x1 progress billing and the 19x2 interest expense (revenue) and gain (loss) recognition.

Exhibit 1 contains the illustrative journal entries of the first year. We determined the discount on partial billings for entry one by multiplying the periodic interest amount ($225,000)[18]

---

[18]$2,250,000 × .10 (cost of capital) = $225,000.

times the present value of an annuity factor for two periods at 10 percent. To provide future interest accruals on partial billings we followed the same methodology as with the discount. These accounts are equal because the discount is no more than the present value of future interest accruals on the progress billing amount. The discount and the future interest accruals on accounts receivable were determined by multiplying the retained percentage ($2,250,000 × .10) times the present value of an annuity factor for two periods at 10 percent.

Entries four and five recognize the fact that, with the passage of time, the future interest accruals accounts decrease. Further, the carrying value of accounts receivable and partial billings increase by those decreases. This increase occurs because the recognition of interest causes the present value of net accounts receivable and net partial billings to increase.

Presently, the future interest accruals account is not currently used in accounting practice to account for discounted amounts. We feel that the recording of future interest accruals would improve accounting practice by providing a more informed description of the logic associated with the discounting procedure. That is, the difference between a present and future dollar amount is *interest*. Further, the use of a future interest accruals account would permit the formal recognition of additional elements of a transaction, such as a gain or loss.

CONCLUDING OBSERVATIONS

We believe that the proposed framework, though not an established part of financial accounting methodology, is consistent with conventional methods. Further, the methodology employed to account for progress billings is equally applicable to other nonmonetary financial assets and liabilities, e.g., marketable securities (stocks and bonds—except bonds that are expected to be held to maturity and redeemed at a fixed number of dollars); accounts and notes receivable that represent claims to nonmonetary assets or an unknown amount of cash; accounts and notes payable that will be settled by transfers of nonmonetary assets or an unknown amount of cash—including the unearned revenue category such as advance sale of tickets, tokens, certificates and subscriptions and advances received on sales contracts.

The extension of the present value theory to accommodate the preceding recommendations would augment the information set given to financial statement users having to evaluate progress billings. The cost of implementing the proposed recommendations should be minimal. A number of software packages are currently capable of enormous computations, and accountants are generally familiar with the discounting process. Because of the investment community's interest in market risk, beta estimates of varying quality are regularly published by a number of brokerage and advisory services, e.g., Merrill Lynch's beta book. Thus, it is practical for firms to use the capital asset pricing model for determining their weighted average cost of capital.

INTERNATIONAL ISSUES IN FINANCIAL ACCOUNTING

THE RATIONALE UNDERLYING THE FUNCTIONAL CURRENCY CHOICE

Lawrence Revsine

FASB Statement Number 52 on Foreign Currency Translation was issued in December 1981. This Statement superseded the highly controversial Statement 8. Statement 8 was attacked because of the widespread belief that firms were compelled to report foreign currency gains and losses that bore little correspondence to the economic effects that they were actually experiencing. Under Statement 8, firms might report foreign exchange *gains* when their underlying real foreign exchange position was *deteriorating,* and vice versa. By contrast, Statement 52 is intended to achieve compatibility between firms' reported exchange gains and losses and these firms' underlying real economic changes.

Statement 52 tries to achieve compatibility between the accounting numbers and the underlying economic effects by allowing firms discretion in selecting a foreign subsidiary's *functional currency.* The FASB describes the subsidiary's functional currency as "the currency of the primary economic environment in which the entity operates . . ." To illustrate, if a U.S. parent has a Dutch subsidiary that conducts business in both Holland and France, the functional currency might be the parent's currency (the dollar), or the subsidiary's currency (the guilder), or even the French franc. Individual circumstances must be used to determine which currency should be selected as the functional currency.

Understanding the factors that govern the functional currency choice is crucial for achieving the primary objective of Statement 52—i.e., compatibility between financial numbers and underlying economics. Unfortunately, the underlying goals and objectives for selecting among

The author gratefully acknowledges the helpful comments of Arthur R. Wyatt of Arthur Andersen & Co. and Professor Robert P. Magee of Northwestern University.

Lawrence Revsine, "The Rationale Underlying the Functional Currency Choice," *The Accounting Review,* July 1984, pp. 505–51. Reprinted with the permission of the American Accounting Association.

the possible functional currencies of a subsidiary are complicated. The concepts underlying the procedures are often particularly difficult for students to grasp. To overcome the problem, this paper explains the rationale behind the functional currency choice by using three illustrative case settings.

Case I presents a series of foreign currency transactions and shows their financial statement effects. Case II is identical to Case I in an economic sense except that the foreign transactions are undertaken through a subsidiary that acts as a conduit for transforming foreign currency flows into dollars. The example demonstrates that applying the FASB's functional currency guidelines in Case II leads to financial statements identical to those derived in Case I. This equivalence is not accidental; instead, the FASB guidelines are designed to generate consolidated results for a conduit subsidiary that are identical to the statement results that arise when the foreign transactions are undertaken directly by the parent. Finally, Case III introduces a modification of the Case II assumptions that alters the underlying economics. The example shows how the FASB guidelines lead to the selection of a different functional currency in Case III and why the chosen functional currency captures the altered economic circumstances.

Thus, the objective of this paper is to clarify the rationale underlying the functional currency choice. A thorough understanding of the rationale should enable students (who will soon become managers, auditors, and external statement users) to apply and interpret Statement 52 in an informed manner and thereby achieve the compatibility benefits sought by the FASB.

FOREIGN CURRENCY TRANSACTIONS: CASE I

The need to select a functional currency exists only when the financial statements of a foreign subsidiary are consolidated with those of the parent or when the equity method is used. While the functional currency choice arises only as a prelude to combining intercorporate interests, it is easier to understand the rationale behind the Statement 52 rules if we first consider a simple non-consolidation setting which will be called Case I.

Assume in Case 1 that the Wildcat Corporation, a U.S. company, desires to sell its product in Britain. On January 1, 19x5, when the exchange rate was 1£ = 1.50$, Wildcat purchased a warehouse building in London to facilitate product distribution. The building cost £200,000, which is equivalent to $300,000 at the date of purchase. It also deposited £5,000 (equivalent to $7,500) in a London bank. On July 1, 19x5, it makes credit sales totalling £100,000 when the exchange rate is still 1£ = 1.50$. Wildcat produced these goods in the U.S. at a total cost of $110,000. The receivables are collected on August 1, 19x5, when the exchange rate is 1£ = 1.40$. The proceeds are converted into dollars and remitted to Wildcat's U.S. headquarters. (For simplicity, we ignore all other costs which might be incurred.) Further assume that the exchange rate was 1£ = 1.39$ on December 31, 19x5.

In Case I, there is no foreign subsidiary. The facts simply describe a series of foreign currency transactions encompassing purchase of a foreign nonmonetary asset (a building), a monetary asset (the £ deposit), and the credit sale.

The accounting for these transactions is straightforward and noncontroversial under the assumed conditions. The transactions that would be recorded on Wildcat's books are described below.

PURCHASE OF A FOREIGN NONMONETARY ASSET (LONDON BUILDING)

At the time of purchase, the dollar equivalent cost of the building would be recorded. The entry would be:

DR Building $300,000
    CR Cash $300,000
(To record purchase of building for £200,000 when the exchange rate was 1£ = 1.50$.)

No adjustment to the gross book value is needed at the end of 19x5, despite the fact that the exchange rate is then 1£ = 1.39$. This is a direct consequence of historical cost accounting; original transaction amounts (in this case, the dollar equivalent cost) are entered and not subsequently adjusted. (For simplicity, we ignore depreciation.)

PURCHASE OF A MONETARY ASSET (STERLING DEPOSIT)

When the pound sterling account is opened, the following entry is made:

DR Cash ($ equivalent of £ deposit) $7,500
    CR Cash $7,500
(To record deposit of £5,000 when the exchange rate was 1£ = 1.50$.)

Again for simplicity, we assume that the account balance was maintained intact throughout the year. Since the year-end exchange rate has fallen to 1£ = 1.39$, the dollar equivalent of the sterling deposit is only $6,950; thus, a loss has arisen as a consequence of the foreign currency transaction. In accordance with existing U.S. accounting practice, monetary assets are shown at net expected realizable value and therefore the loss to date must be recognized in the accounts of Wildcat. The entry is:

DR Foreign exchange loss $550
    CR Cash $550
(To reflect the decline in the dollar equivalent of the foreign currency deposit balance; $7,500 − $6,950.)

FOREIGN CURRENCY SALES TRANSACTION

Wildcat Corporation's British sales were denominated in pounds sterling; these are clearly foreign currency transactions. Exchange rate changes between the time of the original transaction and the time of eventual conversion into dollars result in foreign exchange gains or losses. The accounting entries are:

DR Accounts receivable $150,000
    CR Sales revenue $150,000
DR Cost of goods sold $110,000
    CR Inventory $110,000
(To record sterling denominated sales of £100,000 at their dollar equivalent in terms of the then prevailing exchange rate of 1£ = 1.50$ and to record associated cost of goods sold.)

FIGURE 1

Wildcat Corporation Partial Balance Sheet (as of December 31, 19x5) and Income Statement (for the Year Ended December 31, 19x5)

Balance Sheet

Cash
Dollar deposits $140,000
Sterling deposit—
dollar equivalent 6,950

Retained earnings
Building 300,000 ($150,000 − 110,000 − 10,000 − 550) = $29,450

Income Statement

Sales revenues	$150,000
Cost of goods sold	(110,000)
Foreign exchange loss (10,000 + 550)	(10,550)
Net Income	$29,450

Upon collection, the foreign currency receivables are immediately converted to dollars at the exchange rate of $1\pounds = 1.40\$$. The entry on Wildcat's books would be:

DR	Cash	$140,000	
DR	Foreign exchange loss	$ 10,000	
	CR Accounts receivable		$150,000

(To record collection of $\pounds100,000$ receivables and conversion to dollars at a rate of $1\pounds = 1.40\$$.)

To help the reader visualize the overall effect of this accounting treatment, a partial balance sheet and income statement for Wildcat Corporation are presented in Figure 1. These statements include only the foreign assets and results of the foreign operations that are included in the example.

It will be useful to summarize the accounting treatment incorporated in the example. First, foreign currency transactions, whether completed (i.e., the dollar proceeds from sales) or uncompleted (i.e., the sterling deposit), have an immediate or potentially immediate impact on future dollar cash flows. Because of this dollar flow impact, foreign currency gains or losses are recorded as they occur and are included in income. Second, nonmonetary asset acquisitions follow the historical cost convention; therefore, the original dollar cash equivalent of the nonmonetary asset cost is carried forward in the accounts, despite subsequent exchange rate changes.

With this background, we are now able to turn to the central issue—an explanation of the rationale underlying the choice of functional currency.

THE DOLLAR AS THE FUNCTIONAL CURRENCY: CASE II

The theory underlying the selection of a functional currency will be illustrated using a slightly altered version of the Wildcat Corporation example, called Case II. All assumptions in Case I are retained except that we now further assume that Wildcat forms a wholly owned British subsidiary, Proper Kitty, Ltd., which handles British sales. As before, however, all goods are shipped from the U.S., and British sales receipts are converted into dollars and remitted back to the U.S.

When Proper Kitty, Ltd. is formed, Wildcat Corporation would make the following entry:

DR   Investment in subsidiary $307,500
     CR   Cash $307,500

(To record formation of subsidiary which purchases a building for £200,000 and deposits £5,000 in a London bank. The exchange rate at the time of formation is 1£ = 1.50$.)

Immediately after formation, Proper Kitty, Ltd.'s balance sheet would appear as follows:

Proper Kitty Ltd.
Balance Sheet as of January 1, 19x5

Cash	£ 5,000		
Building	200,000	Equity	£205,000
	£205,000		£205,000

Notice that Proper Kitty's equity (£205,000) when translated at the exchange rate of 1£ = 1.50$ is precisely equal to the $307,500 investment in subsidiary account on Wildcat's books.

When Wildcat ships goods to Proper Kitty, we assume that the following entry is made on Wildcat's books:

DR   Receivable due from subsidiary $150,000
DR   Cost of goods sold   110,000
     CR   Inventory $110,000
     CR   Sales revenue   150,000

(To reflect shipment of goods to subsidiary, accounted for at eventual sales value.)

Assuming that Wildcat bills Proper Kitty Ltd. in sterling, when the dollar proceeds from the £100,000 sales are remitted to Wildcat on August 1, 19x5, the following entry would be made on Wildcat's books:

DR   Cash $140,000
DR   Foreign exchange loss   10,000
     CR   Receivable due from subsidiary $150,000

(To reflect receipt of proceeds from £100,000 sales when the exchange rate was 1£ = 1.40$.)

After remitting the cash back to Wildcat, Proper Kitty's balance sheet will be identical to that shown above for January 1, 19x5. Since no further entries take place during 19x5, these balances also reflect balance sheet carrying amounts at December 31, 19x5. The income statement would show:

Property Kitty, Ltd.
Income Statement for the Year Ended
December 31, 19x5

Sales revenues	£100,000
Cost of goods sold	100,000
Net Profit	0

Obviously, forming a subsidiary has complicated Wildcat's accounting entries considerably. Intercompany accounts must now be kept and consolidation adjustments and eliminations must be made. However, the reader should verify that the underlying transactions and basic economic effects in Case II are absolutely identical to those in Case I. Whereas Wildcat itself undertook the transactions in the earlier example, here these same transactions are performed through a subsidiary. But the organizational form does not alter the ultimate economic effects. *The two cases are completely equivalent in an economic sense.*

If the two cases are equivalent, logic suggests that the consolidated numbers that result from a subsidiary's foreign transactions should be identical to those that would have resulted if the parent had undertaken the transactions directly. This is precisely what the FASB's functional currency guidelines accomplish. Let's see how.

Prior to consolidation, Statement 52 requires a company to identify the functional currency of its foreign subsidiaries. In Case II, the question is whether Proper Kitty's functional currency is the pound or the dollar. It is important to understand two characteristics of this choice:

1. The functional currency will not *always* be the currency in which the subsidiary's statements are expressed; and

2. The functional currency choice is intended to trigger a set of accounting mechanisms which result in reported foreign exchange numbers that correspond to the underlying economics.

The FASB presents guidelines for choosing the functional currency. These guidelines are reproduced in Table 1.

The FASB guidelines help determine whether the subsidiary is a free-standing unit or simply an intermediary that exists only as a conduit for transforming foreign currency transactions into dollar cash flows. When the subsidiary is simply a conduit, the consolidation approach treats the foreign currency statements of the subsidiary as artifacts which must be remeasured into dollars.

In Case II, FASB indicators A(2), D(2), and F(2) identify Proper Kitty as simply a conduit for foreign transaction cash flows back into dollars. In other words, the subsidiary is artificial; it is as if Wildcat had engaged in the foreign transactions directly. In such situations, the functional currency is the dollar, not the pound. The reporting goal is to end up with financial statements equivalent to those that would have resulted had Wildcat entered into the foreign transactions directly (i.e., as in Case I), rather than through Proper Kitty. This result is accomplished by using the temporal method [FASB, 1975, Appendix D] to remeasure pounds into dollars and by treating any remeasurement gains or losses as an element of Wildcat's income.

In the temporal method, monetary assets are translated at the current rate of exchange, nonmonetary assets at the historical rate of exchange, and income statement items at the rate that was in effect at the time of the transaction.[1] After using these rates to remeasure Proper Kitty's accounts, the result yields a dollar measure for each account that would have resulted had the original transactions been recorded initially in dollars. This is illustrated in Figure 2, where the temporal method is applied to Proper Kitty Limited and the resulting dollar measures are consolidated with Wildcat Corporation.

---

[1]An exception exists for nonmonetary asset expirations. These expenses on the income statement are usually translated at the historic rate that existed at the time of original asset acquisition. Since our example does not encompass such items, we ignore this issue.

TABLE 1

Statement 52 Guidelines for Functional Currency Choice*

A. Cash Flow Indicators
  (1) Foreign Currency—Cash flows related to the foreign entity's individual assets and liabilities are primarily in the foreign currency and do not directly affect the parent company's cash flows.
  (2) Parent's Currency—Cash flows related to the foreign entity's individual assets and liabilities directly affect the parent's cash flows on a current basis and are readily available for remittance to the parent company.

B. Sales Price Indicators
  (1) Foreign Currency—Sales prices for the foreign entity's products are not primarily responsive on a short-term basis to changes in exchange rates but are determined more by local competition or local government regulation.
  (2) Parent's Currency—Sales prices for the foreign entity's products are primarily responsive on a short-term basis to changes in exchange rates; for example, sales prices are determined more by worldwide competition or by international prices.

C. Sales Market Indicators
  (1) Foreign Currency—There is an active local sales market for the foreign entity's products, although there also might be significant amounts of exports.
  (2) Parent's Currency—The sales market is mostly in the parent's country or sales contracts are denominated in the parent's currency.

D. Expense Indicators
  (1) Foreign Currency—Labor, materials, and other costs for the foreign entity's products or services are primarily local costs, even though there also might be imports from other countries.
  (2) Parent's Currency—Labor, materials, and other costs for the foreign entity's products or services, on a continuing basis, are primarily costs for components obtained from the country in which the parent company is located.

E. Financing Indicators
  (1) Foreign Currency—Financing is primarily denominated in foreign currency, and funds generated by the foreign entity's operations are sufficient to service existing and normally expected debt obligations.
  (2) Parent's Currency—Financing is primarily from the parent or other dollar-denominated obligations, or funds generated by the foreign entity's operations are not sufficient to service existing and normally expected debt obligations without the infusion of additional funds from the parent company. Infusion of additional funds from the parent company for expansion is not a factor, provided funds generated by the foreign entity's expanded operations are expected to be sufficient to service that additional financing.

F. Intercompany Transactions and Arrangements Indicators
  (1) Foreign Currency—There is a low volume of intercompany transactions and there is not an extensive interrelationship between the operations of the foreign entity and the parent company. However, the foreign entity's operations may rely on the parent's or affiliates' competitive advantages, such as patents and trademarks.
  (2) Parent's Currency—There is a high volume of intercompany transactions and there is an extensive interrelationship between the operations of the foreign entity and the parent company. Additionally, the parent's currency generally would be the functional currency if the foreign entity is a device or shell corporation for holding investments, obligations, intangible assets, etc., that could readily be carried on the parent's or an affiliate's books.

*Note: Table 1 is taken directly from FASB [1981], pp. 26–27.

FIGURE 2

**Partial Consolidated Financial Statements
(Includes Only Foreign Assets and Results of Foreign Operations)
Case II**

Account Title	Property Kitty, Ltd. £'s	Exchange Rate (Temporal Method)	Remeasured In $'s	Wildcat Corporation	Consolidation Eliminations (DR) CR	Consolidated $'s
Dollar deposit				$140,000		$140,000
Sterling deposit	£ 5,000	1.39	$ 6,950			6,950
Investment in subsidiary				$307,500	(1) 307,500	
Building	200,000	1.50	300,000			300,000
	£205,000		$306,950	$447,500		$446,950
Original Equity	205,000	1.50	307,500		(1) (307,500)	
				40,000		
Retained Earnings			(550)	(10,000)		29,450
	£205,000		$306,950	$ 30,000		$ 29,450
Sales	£100,000	1.50	$150,000	$150,000	(2) (150,000)	$150,000
Cost of Goods Sold	100,000	1.50	150,000	110,000	(2) 150,000	110,000
				40,000		
Foreign Exchange Loss			(550)	(10,000)		(10,550)*
Net Income				$ 30,000		$ 29,450

*Note: This total is comprised of:

Foreign exchange loss on sale proceeds	$10,000
Foreign exchange loss on sterling deposit	550
	$10,550

   Notice that the consolidated dollar numbers in the right-hand column of Figure 2 are identical to the numbers shown in Figure 1 where Wildcat undertook the foreign transactions directly, rather than through a subsidiary. This equivalence is no accident. Since the economics of the two cases are identical, the FASB has selected an accounting method for the foreign subsidiary which leads to the same dollar result that would have existed had the transactions been undertaken directly by Wildcat.

   To summarize, when the Statement 52 guidelines identify the parent's currency as the functional currency:

1. The subsidiary is treated for accounting purposes as a mere conduit.

2. One implication is that foreign transactions are deemed to have an immediate (or potentially immediate) impact on dollar cash flows of the parent. For this reason, all foreign exchange gains and losses are taken through income.

3. Since the subsidiary is an artifact, all balance sheet numbers are reflected at amounts that would have existed had the subsidiary's account initially been recorded in the functional currency. The temporal method is designed to achieve this result.

THE FOREIGN CURRENCY AS THE FUNCTIONAL CURRENCY: CASE III

We have seen that when the foreign subsidiary is merely a conduit for dollar cash flows, the functional currency is the dollar. By contrast, when the foreign subsidiary's operations "are relatively self-contained and integrated within a particular country or economic environment" [FASB, 1981, para. 80], then the functional currency is the currency of that foreign country.

To illustrate the rationale behind this rule, we introduce a Case III variation on the Wildcat Corporation setting. Consistent with Case II, we assume in Case III that Wildcat Corporation forms a U.K. subsidiary, Proper Kitty, Ltd., by investing $307,500 when the exchange rate was 1£ = 1.50$. Again, as in Case II, the investment proceeds are used to buy a building for £200,000 and to open a £5,000 account in a London bank. Sales totalling £100,000 are again made on July 1, 19x5, and collected on August 1. In contrast to the previous cases, however, we now assume that these goods were not shipped from the U.S.; instead, they were acquired by Proper Kitty from an unaffiliated U.K. supplier at a cost of £73,333 (which is equivalent to $110,000 at the then prevailing exchange rate). The sales proceeds are used to pay the supplier and the remaining cash (£26,667) is retained in the London account to finance Proper Kitty's future operations, expansion, and growth.

Notice that the economics of this case are quite different from the previous ones. In Case III, Proper Kitty does not engage in transactions merely to influence near-term dollar cash flows. Thus, the effect of an exchange rate change on future dollar cash flows is unclear.

In its Conceptual Framework, the FASB [1978] argues that the goal of financial reporting is to provide a forecast base for assessing "the amounts, timing, and uncertainty of prospective net cash inflows." Applying this logic to the circumstances of Case III (where the cash-flow impact of exchange rate changes is unclear), these exchange rate changes are not included in income under FAS 52. Specifically, in Cases I and II the decline in the pound from $1.50 to $1.40 between the time of sale and the time of collection resulted in an unequivocal $10,000 foreign exchange loss, which is deducted from income. No such loss is included in the Case III income number since Proper Kitty is an on-going, self-contained entity that will redeploy the sales proceeds in the U.K. In other words, it is not at all clear that a loss has occurred in Case III. Under such circumstances, the functional currency is designated as the foreign currency, and the decline in the dollar equivalent of the sales proceeds is taken directly to a special owners' equity account, rather than deducted from income. Similar treatment is accorded to the change in the dollar equivalent of the £5000 deposit in the London bank.

Furthermore, when the foreign entity is a self-contained unit, as in Case III, the FASB contends that the balance sheet translation process "should retain the financial results and relationships that were created in the economic environment of the foreign operations" [FASB, 1981, para. 74]. In other words, after translation, the foreign subsidiary's financial statement items should bear the same proportionate relationship to one another in dollars as they did in the foreign currency. This can be accomplished only if all items are translated using the same exchange rate. For this purpose, the FASB mandates the use of the current rate as of the balance sheet date. Using the current rate method on the income statement, all items are translated at the rate of exchange as of the transaction date.

Considering Proper Kitty's functional currency to be the pound and using the current rate method leads to the consolidated result shown in Figure 3. Notice carefully that the consolidated result in Figure 3 is quite different from the Case I result that was derived in Figure 1.

This difference reflects the fact that Case III and Case I are not identical. In Case III, it is not at all clear that the impact of the exchange rate changes on the initial cash balance and subsequent cash collections will necessarily affect future *dollar* flows. Since Proper Kitty is a self-contained entity, these pound balances will be redeployed within the U.K., and the eventual dollar impact of these reinvestment activities may not materialize for years. For this reason, the FASB concludes that the effect of these rate changes should be excluded from the income computation.[2]

Also notice that the dollar equivalent carrying balance for the nonmonetary asset differs from Case I. In Case I, the building was translated at the historic rate of exchange, in accordance with historical cost accounting principles. But in Case III, Proper Kitty is a self-contained entity. The FASB contends that in such circumstances, financial statements are more informative if they maintain proportionate relationships that exist in the functional currency. Thus, the building is also translated at the current rate of exchange and most ratio relationships for Proper Kitty's dollar statements are equal to those contained in the pound statements (i.e., compare ratios based on column 3 data versus column 1 data in Figure 3).

To summarize, when a foreign entity is a self-contained unit:

1. The functional currency is the currency of the foreign economic environment.

2. The impact of rate changes on future dollar flows is uncertain. Thus, translation gains and losses are not run through income; instead, they are accumulated in a separately designated owners' equity account.

3. Subsidiary balance sheets should preserve the proportionate relationships that existed in the functional currency. Therefore, all assets and liabilities are translated at the current rate of exchange. Any gain or loss on translation is put into a special owners' equity account rather than through income.

Will Statement 52 Lead to Compatibility?

The previous analysis demonstrates how the functional currency choice required by Statement 52 is crucial for achieving compatibility between accounting signals and underlying economic consequences. But since choice injects potential for error, it is legitimate to question whether Statement 52 will lead to its intended result.

To some accountants, the latitude inherent in the functional currency choice may be troublesome, since the existence of latitude raises the specter of statement manipulation. However, statement manipulation via the functional currency choice does not appear to be a major threat since firms have a built-in motive to make the "correct" choice. For example, firms would be ill-advised to select the dollar as the functional currency in order to gain some near-

---

[2]The FASB's decision to exclude from income uncompleted foreign transactions with uncertain dollar flow effects is arguable. Although consistent with the dominant treatment of uncompleted transactions in existing practice, the FASB approach ignores the fact that existing rates in foreign exchange markets may be a least biased indicator of dollar flows that will ultimately be realized. In this view, changes in exchange rates signal changes in expected future flows. Since the FASB views income as a potential cash flow predictor, such exchange rate changes might (consistent with FASB [1978]) be includable in income.

FIGURE 3

Partial Consolidated Financial Statements
(Includes Only Foreign Assets and Results of Foreign Operations)
Case III

Account Title	Property Kitty, Ltd. £'s	Exchange Rate	Translated in $'s	Wildcat Corporation	Consolidation Eliminations (DR) CR	Consolidated $'s
Cash	£ 31,667	1.39	$ 44,017			$ 44,017
Investment in subsidiary				307,500	(1) 307,500	
Building	200,000	1.39	278,000			278,000
	£231,667		$322,017			$322,017
Original equity	205,000	1.50	307,500		(1) (307,500)	
Retained earnings	26,667 ⌐	1.50	40,000 ⌐			40,000 ⌐
Cumulative translation adjustment			To balance (25,483)*			(25,483)
	£231,667		£322,017			$ 14,517
Sales	£100,000	1.50	$150,000			$150,000
Cost of goods sold	73,333	1.50	110,000			110,000
	£ 26,667 ⌐		$ 40,000 ⌐			$ 40,000 ⌐

*Note: The cumulative translation adjustment in this simplified example is determined by multiplying the decline in the value of the £(1.50 − 1.39) by the net asset balance of £231,667 just prior to the decline.

term income enhancement (i.e., from foreign exchange gains that are included in income under the temporal method). The reason is that this short-run benefit may backfire if and when the foreign exchange effect reverses in subsequent years. That is, today's income enhancement may lead to tomorrow's income decrement. Thus, the likelihood of statement manipulation arising from the functional currency choice appears slight.

A much more real danger is that firms, their auditors, and outside analysts may not understand the subtle philosophy that underlies the functional currency choice. As a consequence, innocent but incorrect choices and assessments may be made, and compatibility may not be achieved. Unfortunately, the FASB's guidelines for the functional currency choice, reproduced in Table 1, may increase the likelihood of this possibility. That is, unless the theory underlying the selection mechanism is understood, some firms may be tempted to merely count-up the indicators in each direction; the choice would simply depend on which currency (the dollar or the foreign currency) garners more indicators. This simplistic application of Statement 52 is unsatisfactory since, for example, five indicators may point to the foreign currency as the functional currency and only one may point to the dollar. Despite this, the one criterion which points to the dollar may clearly dominate. Unless those making the selection clearly understand the theory underlying the choice, an incorrect selection is very likely using a straightforward tally of the indicators in each direction. It is to forestall precisely this possibility that this paper was written.

REFERENCES

Financial Accounting Standards Board, *Statement of Financial Accounting Standards No. 8*, "Accounting for the Translation of Foreign Currency Transactions and Foreign Currency Financial Statements" (October 1975).

———, *Statement of Financial Accounting Concepts No. 1*, "Objectives of Financial Reporting by Business Enterprises" (November 1978).

———, *Statement of Financial Accounting Standards No. 52*, "Foreign Currency Translation" (December 1981).

A COMPARATIVE INTERNATIONAL ANALYSIS OF THE IMPACT OF ACCOUNTING PRINCIPLES ON PROFITS: THE USA VERSUS THE UK, SWEDEN, AND THE NETHERLANDS

Pauline Weetman and Sidney J. Gray

The purpose of this paper is to explore the extent to which there are significant quantitative differences in profits reported under US generally accepted accounting principles (GAAP) compared to profits reported in accordance with GAAP in three European countries, namely the United Kingdom, Sweden and the Netherlands. This is an important issue because the growing internationalisation of equity markets has highlighted the need to take account of international accounting differences, especially in respect of making comparative analyses of profits in the context of assessments of price/earnings ratios. While there is a growing appreciation of the existence of such differences, there is a lack of evidence about their overall quantitative impact.

The focus here on Sweden and the Netherlands as well as the UK is motivated by the fact that, in classifying financial reporting measurement practices in developed Western countries, Nobes (1989) positions Sweden and the Netherlands at two extremes of a classification structure. The Netherlands is classed as micro-based, influenced by business economics theory, while Sweden is classed as macro-uniform, influenced by government as an economic planner and tax collector. At the same time, UK and USA accounting practices are apparently

Pauline Weetman and Sidney J. Gray, "A Comparative International Analysis of the Impact of Accounting Principles on Profits: The USA versus the UK, Sweden, and the Netherlands," *Accounting and Business Research*. Reprinted by permission of Accounting and Business Research.

closer to the Netherlands than to Sweden in that they are also micro-based, but classed as being influenced by business practice and pragmatism. Qualitatively, differences in practices between these countries are well documented, for example Nobes (1988) on UK/USA, Cooke (1988) on Sweden/UK, and Nobes (1990) on Netherlands/UK. However, in terms of the overall *quantitative* impact of accounting differences on measures of profit, very little empirical work has been carried out to date using published financial statements. Gray (1980) produced a comparison in respect of UK/France/ Germany based on reported total profits only. Choi *et al.* (1983) analysed quantitative differences for USA/Korea/Japan. Weetman and Gray (1990) explored UK/US GAAP differences in greater detail. A case study analysis of a hypothetical company, carried out by Simmonds and Azieres (1989), illustrated the range of profit which could be reported using the GAAP of each of the EC countries, but did not link this to US GAAP or to European countries outside the Community.

DIFFERENCES IN GAAP, AND THE CONSEQUENCES FOR FINANCIAL REPORTING

US GAAP is a useful yardstick for comparison as the USA is one of the world's major capital markets and an important source of finance for foreign companies. It also appears that significant accounting differences exist between the USA and a number of other countries including the UK, Sweden and the Netherlands. Nobes (1988 p. 83), for example, has identified twelve matters of accounting policy for which US financial statements would require adjustment before they could be regarded as comparable to UK practice:

1. Inventories: US use of LIFO compared to UK use of FIFO may lead to lower reported profits.
2. Deferred tax: US use of full provision *and* full deferral (until SFAS 96), then full liability method compared to UK partial provision.
3. Foreign currency translation: UK is more permissive with regard to profit and loss account translation, i.e. permits either closing or average rate.
4. Fixed assets: US does not permit revaluation.
5. Goodwill: US requires amortisation compared to UK majority practice of immediate write-off against reserves.
6. Subsidiaries: US now requires inclusion of all subsidiaries.
7. Pooling: US rules differ from UK rules on merger accounting.
8. Dividends: US companies do not provide for undeclared dividends.
9. Extraordinary items: US is less liberal with regard to the treatment of gains and losses on disposals of businesses, i.e. treated as exceptional items.
10. Capitalisation of interest: US requires capitalisation under specific conditions.
11. Oil and gas: US/UK rules differ in some respects.
12. P & D: US insists on writing off all expenditure.

From the above list there are seven items which could be taken as indicating different attitudes to 'conservatism'. These items are the treatment of inventory (a consequence of US tax rules), deferred taxation, valuation of fixed assets, amortisation of goodwill, extraordinary items, interest capitalisation and research and development. Interestingly, the only US practice which is not relatively more 'conservative' than UK practice in the context of profit measurement is in respect of the capitalisation of interest. Taken overall, UK GAAP seem likely to be less conservative than US GAAP in terms of relative impact on profits.

Cooke (1988) provides a detailed review of accounting disclosure practice in Sweden, including surveys of existing practice at December 1985. He explains and illustrates the impact of the valuation rules where these differ from the UK or USA (e.g. Cooke, p. 129) but does not, however, attempt to quantify the detailed effects of such differences. From the information which Cooke provides, the following list outlines the accounting differences which might be expected in a Sweden/USA comparison:

1. Taxation: Income for tax purposes is based on the published financial statements. Special tax allowances are recorded in the income statement as 'allocations' and in the balance sheet as 'untaxed reserves'. Deferred tax is not recognised in law or in GAAP, although deferred taxes are often provided on the acquisition of a subsidiary.

2. Legal reserves: There must be a transfer of 10% of net income to a legal reserve until it represents 20% of the issued par value of share capital.

3. Fixed assets: Revaluation is permitted, using a revaluation reserve, but may not exceed the assessed value.

4. Goodwill: This should be amortised over a period not exceeding 10 years.

5. Associated companies: Not dealt with in either Swedish company law or accounting law. There is a variety of accounting practices and differences in the levels of disclosure.

6. Foreign currency translation: A variety of approaches to problems of foreign currency translation, both in the method of calculation adopted and in the treatment of translation differences.

Taken overall, the impact on profits of Swedish accounting principles seems likely to be more 'conservative' than US GAAP with particular reference to taxation effects, the amortisation of goodwill and the treatment of associated companies.

A recent comparative analysis of accounting practice in the Netherlands is provided by Nobes (1990) in which he identifies the following specific differences from US or UK practice:

1. Depreciation: For tax purposes may follow accounting depreciation, but it may also differ. Consequently depreciation is a source of timing difference which could lead to a provision for deferred taxation.

2. Deferred tax: Allocation on a full provision basis and changes in corporation tax rates are allowed for.

3. Fixed assets: May be revalued upwards, with a consequent increase in the depreciation charge.

4. Extraordinary items: Profit figures used for earnings per share calculations tend to include extraordinary items.

5. Consolidation: The Seventh EC Directive, implemented in an Act of 1988, came into force in respect of accounting periods beginning on or after 1st January 1990 (i.e. did not apply to the financial statements covered in this exercise).

6. Merger accounting: Permissible, the rules resembling those of the IASC.

7. Goodwill: May be deducted from reserves, amortised against income within one year or amortised over its useful economic life. Most companies choose deduction from reserves.

8. Foreign currency translation: In the individual company's accounts, foreign exchange gains and losses on debtors and creditors would be taken to the income statement. In translating the financial statements of subsidiaries, Dutch companies rarely use the temporal method.

9. Inventories: LIFO is allowed for stock valuation.

In items 1, 2, 4, 8 and 9 the Dutch practice appears to resemble that of the USA, while in items 3, 5, 6 and 7 it is similar to that of the UK. To the extent that Dutch accounting principles are similar to those of the UK, it would seem that the impact on profits is likely to be less conservative than that of US GAAP, although the elements of similarity with US GAAP suggest that overall the Dutch approach might be more conservative than that of the UK, relative to US GAAP.

CRITERIA FOR COMPARISON: A 'CONSERVATISM' INDEX

Using US GAAP as the yardstick, it is possible to make an assessment of the relationship between reported profits of other countries and those same earnings adjusted in accordance with US GAAP. This methodology may be implemented by developing an index for comparative purposes as used by Gray (1980).

Accordingly, an index of 'conservatism' was calculated, using the formula (taking the UK as an example):

$$1 - \left(\frac{\text{Profits USA} - \text{Profits UK}}{|\text{Profits USA}|} \right)$$

An index value *greater than* 1 means that the UK, Sweden or Netherlands profits are *less* 'conservative' than the US measure would have been. An index value *less than* 1 means that the UK, Sweden or Netherlands profits are *more* 'conservative' than the US measure would have been. An index value exactly *equal to* 1 indicates neutrality in comparison to US GAAP with respect to the effect of accounting standards.

The denominator has been taken as US profits to provide a benchmark against which the UK, Sweden or Netherlands profits can be compared.

Having established an overall index of 'conservatism' it is then possible to establish the relative effect of the various individual adjustments by constructing partial indices of adjustment using the formula:

$$\text{Partial index of 'conservatism'} = 1 - \left(\frac{\text{partial adjustment}}{|\text{profits USA}|} \right)$$

For example: £m
   UK earnings   120
   Adjustments for US GAAP:
      Deferred taxation   (15)
      Goodwill amortisation   (5)

Adjusted earnings per US GAAP $\dfrac{100}{}$

Overall index of 'conservatism'   1.2

Partial index for deferred taxation $1 - \left(\dfrac{-15}{100}\right) = 1.15$

Partial index for goodwill amortisation $1 - \left(\dfrac{-5}{100}\right) = 1.05$

THE RESEARCH DATA

An opportunity to compare profits measured under UK, Swedish and Dutch GAAP with profits measured under US GAAP is given by those companies which are obliged to report to the Securities and Exchange Commission (SEC) in the USA. The 'Form 20-F' report to the SEC is typically longer and more complex than the financial sections of the domestic company reports. Form 20-F contains additional disclosures required by the SEC but not by the domestic regulations. In particular, where the reporting company has used its domestic accounting policies, the SEC requires in Form 20-F a reconciliation of home-reported profits with the earnings which would have been reported under US GAAP. The effect of each accounting policy which differs in the two countries under comparison is quantified separately. In addition to the quantified difference, the accounting policies as they affect the company are explained by way of note, which occasionally gives further insight into the differences between domestic and US accounting practice. The reconciliations in Form 20-F may thus be used to test the extent to which profits before extraordinary items in the UK, Sweden and the Netherlands are more or less conservative than they would have been if US GAAP were applied.

The SEC requires a Form 20-F report where the company sponsors an ADR (American Depositary Receipt) which is traded on one of the national stock exchanges such as the New York Stock Exchange (NYSE), the American Stock Exchange (AMEX) or the National Association of Securities Dealers Automated Quotations (NASDAQ). A company search agency was employed to determine the number of UK, Sweden and Netherlands companies which lodged a 20-F form with the SEC in respect of accounting periods ending between 1 July 1988 and 30 June 1989. It was found that there were 41 UK companies, 8 Swedish and 8 Dutch companies in total (see Appendix). This permits statistical analysis of the data on UK companies, with a comparison on a case study basis of Swedish and Dutch accounting practice, using US GAAP as the reference point for comparison.

ANALYSIS AND RESULTS

UNITED KINGDOM

In the case of the UK, the sample of 41 companies is a sub-set of a larger group of companies (162 in 1988 according to information contained in a list provided by Citibank) whose shares are traded in ADR form in the United States but the majority of which are exempt from the 20-F filing requirement. This exemption is available where the ADRs are traded over-the-counter rather than on one of the official US stock exchanges such as NYSE, AMEX or NASDAQ. The majority of these ADRs are sponsored by the companies, meaning that the directors have taken a positive decision to adopt a US presence (as opposed to an unsponsored ADR where investors have taken the initiative, using a US bank as authorised depositary, but where the company has no active involvement beyond supplying a copy of the annual report to the SEC). The companies not reporting on Form 20-F have therefore taken an active interest in being in the US market, the only difference being that they use over-the-counter trading rather than an official stock exchange. The commercial reason for this interest is the development of a US presence because of, or with a view to, commercial activity in the US. This commercial purpose is shared with those 41 companies which do report on Form 20-F.

The published reconciliations were found to be non-uniform in their presentation. The starting point in some cases was earnings before extraordinary items, but in others was earnings after extraordinary items. There are items, chiefly those associated with discontinued operations, which are extraordinary in the UK but are not treated as extraordinary in the USA. Since, in the UK, earnings before extraordinary items is the critical measure of earnings per share and hence is significant for investment performance indicators, it was decided to rebase all data to a starting point of UK profits before extraordinary items and to apply the US GAAP adjustments in such a way as to determine what the profits figure would have been had the US rules been applied. The overall index of conservatism was measured and tested for each of the three years 1986, 1987 and 1988, taking each year separately in order to obtain a view of the impact on reported profit on a year-by-year basis. The label '1986' means a year end on 31 December 1986 or within six months either side. It was found that in each year there were some outlying values which would have distorted the results. The outlying values were removed before calculating a mean value and a t-statistic to establish that the mean was significantly higher than the neutral value of 1.0. Histograms were plotted to confirm that there was a spread about the mean which justified calculation of the t-statistic. A single-tailed test of significance was applied as the direction of the relationship between UK and US profits was hypothesised. More specifically, the statistical analysis was carried out to test the hypothesis that UK profits measured under UK GAAP were significantly less conservative (and therefore higher) than they would have been if measured under US GAAP.

Use of the t-statistic was justified by the sample size being greater than 30 and by inspection of the shape of the distribution of index values. In view of the problem of outlying values potentially distorting the mean, a non-parametric Wilcoxon signed ranks test was also applied, based on departures from a hypothesised neutral median value of 1.0, without adjustment for outliers. For comparison, the Wilcoxon statistic and significance levels are tabulated with the t-statistic results in the relevant tables. Using Minitab, the estimated median is also computed based on the signed ranks. This provides an alternative to the mean as an estimate of the effect of the accounting policy change and is less affected by the outliers.

The results shown in Table 1 may be interpreted as saying that in 1986 the UK reported profit was 12.3% higher than the US GAAP result; in 1987 the UK profit was 19.9% higher; and in 1988 the UK profit was 16.9% higher. The 1987 and 1988 mean index values were significantly greater than the neutral value at the 1% significance level, while the 1986 mean index was significant at the 10% but not at the 5% level. The Wilcoxon test confirms the significance of the 1987 and 1988 results.

Informal discussion with practising accountants, on an earlier draft of this paper, suggested that they perceived greater interest in the outlying values than they did in those which were more representative of the overall picture. Accordingly the index values were grouped

TABLE 1

UK: Income Statements

Mean value and t-statistic for total index of conservatism

Year	N	Mean	St dev	SE mean	t	P value
1986	38	1.1233	0.4528	0.0735	1.68	0.051
1987	36	1.1988	0.4147	0.0691	2.88	0.003
1988	36	1.1694	0.3150	0.0525	3.23	0.001

(See Table 2 for list of outlying values removed)

Actual median, Wilcoxon statistic and estimated median

Year	N for test	Actual median	Wilcoxon statistic	P value	Estimated median
1986	39	1.0466	509.0	0.098	1.094
1987	40	1.1049	675.0	0.000	1.158
1988	39	1.1093	625.0	0.001	1.205

according to measures of accounting 'materiality', taking the levels of 5% and 10% of profit as rule-of-thumb materiality limits. Table 2 shows the grouping of values and also reports the range together with information on extreme outlying values. The distribution is seen to be skewed towards a less conservative UK reported profit, but it also demonstrates that, for particular companies, the effect of a change in accounting policy can have a major impact in either direction on reported profit. The outlying values, which are all such that UK reported profit is greater than US reported profit, illustrate the potentially dramatic effect of different accounting principles in particular circumstances.

To analyse further these total index values, a partial analysis was attempted in order to discover and quantify the principal component policies which differ between UK and US accounting practices. The only adjustments which occurred sufficiently frequently for statistical analysis were those for amortisation of goodwill and provision for deferred taxation. The statistical results for these are discussed below, followed by a brief review of some of the other adjustments reported in the Form 20-F.

1. AMORTISATION OF GOODWILL US GAAP require amortisation of goodwill through the income statement as compared with the write-off against reserves permitted in UK SSAP 22. Thirty-seven of the companies made this adjustment. A single-tailed t-test was applied after removing one outlier for 1986 and two for each of 1987 and 1988. The results are as shown in Table 3.

The t-statistic shows that for all years the mean value is significantly greater than 1.0 at the 1% significance level. The significance is confirmed by the Wilcoxon statistic. The results may be interpreted by saying that in 1986 the profits under UK GAAP were 10.2% higher than under US GAAP because of the effect of not amortising goodwill. In 1987 the UK profits were 16.3% higher on average and in 1988 they were 15.1% higher on average.

Table 4 shows that the distribution of mean index values grouped under categories of accounting 'materiality' confirms the relatively high incidence of index values greater than 1.0.

TABLE 2

UK: Income Statements

Total index of conservatism

Level of Materiality	Index Values	1986	1987	1988
UK profit 10% or more below the US profit	≤0.9000	9	5	6
UK profit 5% or more below the US profit but less than 10% below	0.9001–0.9500	3	3	3
UK profit within ± 5% of US profit	0.9501–1.0499	8	8	6
UK profit 5% or more above the US profit but less than 10% above	1.0500–1.0999	1	4	4
UK profit 10% or more above the US profit	≥1.100	18	20	21
		39	40	40
Range: Lowest value		0.180	0.542	0.664
Highest value		5.779	11.745	40.083

Elimination of outliers

The following outlying index values were eliminated before calculating the t-statistic presented in Table 1:

Name	Index Value Eliminated			Principal Cause
	1986	1987	1988	
Lep Group	5.779	3.757	4.833	Extraordinary items plus US deferral of recognition of profits on real estate sales
United Newspapers		11.745		Amortisation of goodwill including effect of disposal of a subsidiary
Blue Arrow			40.083	Amortisation of goodwill including write-off in respect of discontinued operations
WPP		4.124		Amortisation of goodwill
WCRS			5.454	Amortisation of goodwill
Cambridge Instruments		3.428		Extraordinary item
Jaguar			2.943	US recognition of exchange losses on forward currency contracts

The extreme outlying values listed in Table 4 illustrate the potentially material impact of goodwill amortisation.

The statement of adjustment to UK earnings provides a useful opportunity to gauge the effect of writing off goodwill to reserves as compared with amortisation through the income statement (see, also, Russell *et al.,* 1989 for estimates of the likely effects of a change to amortisation in the UK). All of the companies surveyed which made adjustments did so because they had followed the current UK practice of writing off goodwill against reserves.

There are two main conclusions at this stage of the analysis so far as amortisation of goodwill is concerned. The first conclusion is that amortisation of goodwill is the single *most* material item in the reconciliation of earnings under UK practice with earnings under US GAAP. The second conclusion is that the relative materiality of amortisation increased from 10% of US earnings in 1986 to over 15% of US profit in 1988.

TABLE 3

UK: Income Statements

Mean value and t-statistic for index of amortisation of goodwill

Year	N	Mean	St Dev	SE mean	t	P value
1986	36	1.1022	0.1501	0.0254	4.03	0.0001
1987	35	1.1629	0.2664	0.0450	3.62	0.0005
1988	35	1.1513	0.2238	0.0378	4.00	0.0002

(See Table 4 for list of outlying values removed)

Actual median, Wilcoxon statistic and estimated median

Year	N for test	Actual Median	Wilcoxon Statistic	P value	Estimated Median
1986	33	1.0413	559.0	0.000	1.074
1987	36	1.0806	666.0	0.000	1.100
1988	37	1.0800	703.0	0.000	1.097

UK: Income Statements

Amortisation of goodwill: partial index of conservatism

Level of Materiality	Index Values	1986	1987	1988
UK profit 10% or more below the US profit	≤0.9000	0	0	0
UK profit 5% or more below the US profit but less than 10% below	0.9001–0.9500	0	0	0
UK profit within ±5% of US profit	0.9501–1.0499	19	14	13
UK profit 5% or more above the US profit but less than 10% above	1.0500–1.0999	5	7	8
UK profit 10% or more above the US profit	≥1.1000	12	16	16
		36	37	37
Range: Lowest value		0.994	1.000	1.005
Highest value		2.300	3.693	20.333

Elimination of outliers

The following outlying index values were eliminated before calculating the t-statistic presented in Table 3:

	1986	1987	1988
	2.300	3.693	20.333
		3.415	4.774

TABLE 5

UK: Income Statements

Mean value and t-statistic for index of deferred taxation

Year	N	Mean	St dev	SE mean	t	P value
1986	35	1.0186	0.0688	0.0116	1.59	0.060
1987	38	1.0311	0.1120	0.0182	1.71	0.047
1988	39	1.0494	0.1220	0.0195	2.53	0.008

(See Table 6 for list of outlying values removed)

Actual median, Wilcoxon statistic and estimated median

Year	N for test	Actual median	Wilcoxon statistic	P value	Estimated median
1986	34	1.0049	354.0	0.338	1.006
1987	36	1.0163	442.0	0.088	1.025
1988	36	1.0109	462.0	0.044	1.022

2. DEFERRED TAXATION   A total of 40 companies made the deferred taxation adjustment in at least one year. After removal of outlying values, the mean index numbers are as shown in Table 5. The conclusion is that in 1986 UK profit was higher than US profit by 1.9%; in 1987 the UK profit was higher by 3.1%; and in 1988 UK profit was higher by 4.9%. The 1987 and 1988 results were significantly greater than the neutral value at the 5% significance level. The 1986 result was significant at the 10% level but not at the 5% level. The Wilcoxon test confirms the significance of the 1988 result and of the 1987 result at the 10% level, but shows the 1986 result as inconclusive.

The explanation appears complex but may be analysed under three main headings:

(i) the treatment of timing differences which are not expected to reverse in the foreseeable future;

(ii) the treatment of tax losses and recoverable Advance Corporation Tax (ACT) brought forward; and

(iii) the difference between the liability method and the deferral method.

One factor which is not taken into account is the tax regime. The profit is being adjusted for US GAAP but not for US fiscal regulations.

SSAP 15 in the UK allows partial provision for timing differences while US GAAP require full provision. SSAP 15 allows recoverable losses to be offset against the deferred tax liability to a greater extent than do US GAAP. This reflects a more liberal UK tax regime on time periods for loss recovery, which creates a further complication when the deferred tax liability is increased to comply with US GAAP. The increased liability is used as a basis for an increased set-off of deferred UK tax assets and thus it was not possible in most of the 20-Fs to distinguish these separate effects except in the relatively few cases where the separation was disclosed. Further, the liability method is used in the UK while the deferral method was used in the US in the periods under investigation.

TABLE 6

UK: Income Statements

Deferred taxation: partial index of conservatism

Level of Materiality	Index Values	1986	1987	1988
UK profit 10% or more below the US profit	≤0.9000	2	4	1
UK profit 5% or more below the US profit but less than 10% below	0.9001–0.9500	3	1	3
UK profit within ±5% of US profit	0.9501–1.0499	26	20	23
UK profit 5% or more above the US profit but less than 10% above	1.0500–1.0999	2	7	5
UK profit 10% or more above the US profit	≥1.1000	5	7	7
		38	39	39
Range: Lowest value		0.062	0.619	0.865
Highest value		2.368	1.313	1.427

Elimination of outliers

The following outlying index values were eliminated before calculating the t-statistic presented in Table 5:

	1986	1987	1988
	2.368	0.619	none
	0.371		
	0.062		

(The three index values eliminated which were less than 1.0 were associated, in two cases, with adjustments for different accounting treatments of tax losses, classified by the companies as part of the overall deferred tax adjustment. The third related to a major write-down of assets reducing the tax charge on a full provision basis.)

This is further complicated in some cases by the switch in US practice announced in December 1987 whereby SFAS 96 in the US required full provision based on the liability method. The deadline for implementing SFAS 96 was subsequently postponed to 1990. Consequently there was a lack of consistency, twenty of the companies tested having switched to SFAS 96 in respect of some or all of the periods examined while the other twenty were still considering the effects of the change in policy. In the year of changeover there is a major adjustment which completely outweighs any other effects present.

A distribution of index numbers by category of accounting 'materiality' is presented as Table 6, which shows a heavy concentration of values within the immaterial level of ±5% of US profit but that there are outlying values which have a material effect in specific instances. In the case of deferred tax there were outliers causing the UK reported profit to be lower, either because of losses brought forward or because of an unusually high asset write-off.

Any hypothesis about the relative 'conservatism' or lack of it in UK deferred tax accounting policies cannot be separated from the tax regime operating at the time. If there had been a constant corporation tax rate, the analysis of actual results would have been more informative regarding the effects of partial provision. If the US had not switched from the deferral to the liability method at the end of 1987 there would have been a clearer result from the actual data.

The lack of detail in the 20-F reconciliation of UK and US profits would not have created an insurmountable problem if all the companies had complied fully with the disclosure requirements of SSAP 15 in their UK annual reports, which were also obtained for this study. The revised version of SSAP 15, which applies to accounting periods beginning on or after 1 April 1985, requires (para. 35) disclosure of the amount of any unprovided deferred tax in respect of the period to be disclosed by way of note and analysed into its major components. The UK annual reports rarely made this disclosure in respect of income statement items (although it was disclosed in respect of the full balance sheet provision).

3. OTHER ADJUSTMENTS MADE TO PROFITS BY UK COMPANIES   There were in total approximately 250 adjustments made by the 41 companies analysed, or between 6 and 7 adjustments for the typical company (with a range of between 1 and 12 adjustments per company). A classification of the varied reasons for adjustment may give some further insight into the technical problems facing those who seek to make comparisons between UK and US GAAP in a practical situation. The major reasons for the differences (other than amortisation of goodwill and the deferred tax adjustment) are discussed as follows:

(a) Inventories: No adjustment was observed in respect of FIFO/LIFO comparisons. The companies concerned had all used FIFO but made no reference to the potential effect of using LIFO. It is therefore possible that any results from this paper will underestimate the overall conservatism of US GAAP to the extent that LIFO is widely used by US companies.

(b) Foreign currency translation: Ten companies made an adjustment for foreign currency translation but the reasons were varied. Five had used the closing rate for translating UK income rather than the average rate required by US GAAP, with an impact of within ±5% of US earnings in all cases. The remaining five spanned differences in treatment of long-term debt, disposal of investments, and depreciation charges. They included one instance each of adjustments 15% above and 15% below US earnings. The direction and magnitude of adjustments depended on the nature of the item and the exchange rate movement. It would seem unlikely that external analysts could make any estimate of such an adjustment without provision of full information by the company.

(c) Fixed assets: Fifteen companies made adjustments to depreciation charges by virtue of eliminating revaluations of fixed assets. This had the effect of increasing the profit reported under US GAAP. Four companies also made specific revaluation adjustments in respect of gains or losses calculated on the disposal of assets. Five companies provided property depreciation for US GAAP purposes where none had been provided against the UK earnings. There was one example of an investment valued at directors' valuation in the UK but reduced to historical cost for US GAAP. In two cases of property sale, the US GAAP required greater assurance about the liquidity of the proceeds before allowing recognition of a gain on sale.

(d) Subsidiaries: The US requirement to include all subsidiaries was not applicable to all of the period covered. It was found that twelve companies made adjustments in respect of aspects of business combinations, due to a range of highly technical matters where the US approach to purchase accounting differs from that of the UK. These included costs which are capitalised in the UK but expensed for US

GAAP, tax adjustments to fair value, the method of accounting for interest charged on deferred purchase schemes, and the timing of recognition of a gain on disposal of a subsidiary. In specific cases these adjustments had a material accounting effect but it would have been highly unlikely that an analyst could have made the same adjustment with only the published accounting information available. There was no evidence here of a systematic effect to be analysed.

(e) Pooling: Five of the adjustments mentioned under (d) above were related to the different rules on merger accounting, but it was not found to be a frequently occurring issue of difference.

(f) Dividends: This was not relevant to the exercise carried out here as the profit analysed was that reported before dividend was declared. All companies which had declared, but not paid, a dividend made this adjustment.

(g) Extraordinary items: Thirty companies adjusted the profit in respect of items which had been treated as extraordinary in the UK but non-extraordinary in the US. Many related to disposal of parts of the business. The effect was not unidirectional, involving gains as well as losses. In individual cases the effect could be highly material and is clearly an item to be noted in making adjustments between UK and US GAAP.

(h) Capitalisation of interest: Eight companies adjusted profit for capitalisation of interest. All added back a portion of interest, so that the effect appears to be unidirectional in providing an instance of US profit being less conservative than the UK version. Capitalisation was an adjustment found relatively infrequently in the sample evaluated here, despite being cited in informal discussions with ADR specialists as one of the significant adjustments between UK and US practice.

(i) Oil and gas: Only three oil and gas companies were included in the sample. None made any adjustment specifically related to oil and gas accounting matters.

(j) R & D: Two instances were found of development expenditure being capitalised for UK purposes but expensed under US GAAP.

This list of major categories was found to have covered the most frequently occurring reasons for adjustment, apart from sixteen instances of provision for pension costs. The treatment of pension costs was in a state of transition during the period examined because SFAS 97 was in existence but was not yet mandatory for pension schemes based outside the USA, while SSAP 24 in the UK was also not in full force.

SWEDEN Form 20-F reports were obtained for 8 Swedish companies. All of these contained a reconciliation of income and equity under Swedish GAAP with the amounts derived from US GAAP. Table 7 presents the results of the comparison of reported profits under Swedish and US GAAP. It was found that some of the Swedish companies used the net profit after tax and appropriations as the starting point for reconciliation, on the grounds that this is the traditional 'bottom line' for Swedish reporting purposes, while others preferred to take the approach of using the net profit after tax but before appropriations, on the grounds that it gives a more useful indication of performance. Table 7 therefore uses both approaches.

In preparing Table 7, some further calculations had to be carried out because the published reconciliations of income under Swedish and US GAAP present the allocation to reserves

TABLE 7

Sweden: Income Statements

Total index of conservatism

Under each year:

Column a = Comparison of Swedish net profit after appropriations and tax charge
Column b = Comparison of Swedish net profit before appropriations and after tax charge

Level of Materiality	Index Values	1986 a	1986 b	1987 a	1987 b	1988 a	1988 b
Swedish profit 10% or more below the US profit	≤0.9000	5	2	5	0	5	3
Swedish profit 5% or more below the US profit but less than 10% below	0.9001–0.9500	0	1	0	2	0	1
Swedish profit within ±5% of US profit	0.9501–1.0499	0	4	0	3	1	3
Swedish profit 5% or more above the US profit but less than 10% above	1.0500–1.0999	1	0	0	1	0	0
Swedish profit 10% or more above the US profit	≥1.1000	2	1	3	2	2	1
		8	8	8	8	8	8
Range: Lowest value		−22.25	−12.63	0.58	0.91	0.48	0.00
Highest value		1.61	1.29	2.65	2.91	1.18	1.19

and the total provision for deferred taxation as two separate gross amounts. A more useful comparison may be made if the relevant amount of deferred taxation is matched against the allocation. This matching can be estimated from the published note to the accounts which reconciles the standard rate of tax (52%) with the effective rate of tax, which is generally much lower. The note to the accounts includes a separate figure for the tax effect of allocations to reserves. The estimated adjustment to calculate the allocation net of tax was carried out for each company in the sample.

The effect of the appropriations is clearly demonstrated as making a material difference to the distribution of index values. Swedish profit reporting appears very conservative after the appropriations are deducted but much less so when the appropriations are left out of the comparison.

Although statistical testing of significance is not possible on this small sample, the calculation of a mean value gives some indication of relative magnitudes:

Adjustments to income	1986	1987	1988
Total index for Swedish net profit after appropriations and tax	0.92	1.20	0.85
Appropriation net of deferred tax provision	0.11	0.21	0.12
Total index for Swedish net profit after tax but before appropriations, compared with US GAAP	1.03	1.41	0.97

These averages are, unfortunately, inconclusive because they lie either side of the neutral value of 1.0 and because for 1986 and 1988 one outlier in each case had to be omitted to avoid excessive distortion.

The interpretation of the 1986 data is that the Swedish net profit overall was 8% lower than the profit adjusted for US GAAP. The appropriation was 11% of US reported profit, so that before appropriations the Swedish net profit was 3% higher than that reported under US GAAP. In 1987 the Swedish net profit before appropriations was on average 41% higher than the US profit but in 1988 was 3% lower.

There is insufficient data to carry out any statistical analysis, but Table 8 explains those situations where the overall Swedish profit was more than 10% above or below the comparable US net profit. These extremes have been analysed in some detail in Table 8 because informal discussion with accountants and analysts leaves the impression that they attach considerable weight to these extremes, however infrequently they may occur. The extreme values would also be of interest if they disclosed some consistent pattern which could be of use to analysts.

Taxation differences (loss carryforwards and taxes paid on intercompany transactions) were the most frequent cause for Swedish profit remaining relatively low, even after removing the effects of allocations. Failure to use equity accounting for associated companies was found to be significant in one instance. These are all instances of consistent conservative bias in Swedish accounting practice. Capitalisation of interest as a US requirement was significant in one case.

Other reasons for low Swedish profits are not instances of consistent bias since, depending on circumstances, they could lead to positive or negative adjustments. These were significant in two instances related to accounting for business combinations and in one instance related to currency translation.

Disallowance of some elements of Swedish profits caused income on a US GAAP basis to be lower in other cases. Evidence of a consistent lack of conservatism in Swedish practice, with a potentially significant outcome, was found in the treatment of profits on sale and leaseback transactions, the writing-up of investments to match write-downs elsewhere, and the taking of profit on a pooling of interests which would not qualify as such under US GAAP. The treatment of sale and leaseback would be consistent with an approach which concentrates on legal form rather than economic substance. The investment write-up and less cautious use of pooling of interest do appear to provide some evidence that Swedish accounting practice is not consistently 'conservative'.

Following Cooke's list of Swedish GAAP practices, cited earlier in this paper, the findings are as follows:

1. Special tax allowances and transfers to untaxed reserves
   These were by far the most significant adjustments in the reconciliation of Swedish net profit after appropriations. The magnitude and direction of adjustment in individual cases or in different years is not predictable from the income statement alone, since it also depends on the existing level of the reserve. Out of the 8 companies over the 3 year period (24 data items) there were only 6 instances of transfers from reserves to income statement in any particular year (see Table 9 for summary of the effect of allocations).

2. Increased depreciation through revaluation of fixed assets
   This was found in four out of the six companies. In terms of the effect of the reduced depreciation charge it was material at the 10% level on only two occasions (see Table 9 for the average and range of index values).

3. Deferred taxation
   When the Swedish profit is adjusted for the transfers to untaxed reserves, a provision for deferred taxation is also required in order to satisfy US GAAP. This provision is substantial where the transfer to or from reserves is substantial. As explained

| TABLE 8 |

Sweden: Main Causes for Extreme Differences in Reported Profit (Plus or Minus 10% or More):

Overall index value ≤0.9

1986: Pharmacia: A loss of 117 MSEK under Swedish GAAP is reduced to a loss of 8 MSEK under US GAAP, chiefly by adding back an estimated transfer from deferred taxation provision of 75 MSEK and the capitalisation of interest of 33 MSEK. This example represented by far the most significant difference between US and Swedish GAAP. The transfer from deferred tax provision reflects the use of losses carried forward.

Cellulosa: Amounts added to Swedish net income related principally to the inclusion of a share of profits of associated companies and the capitalisation of interest.

1988: Pharmacia: A loss of 3 MSEK under Swedish GAAP was changed to a profit of 900 MSEK under US GAAP, due to the combined effects of three relatively large items. An amount of 1,156 MSEK was added to Swedish net income because the method of accounting for business combinations did not follow US GAAP (treatments of pooling of interests and extraordinary write-offs). An estimated amount of 363 MSEK was added back as a result of transfers from deferred taxation provisions, while 636 MSEK was deducted from Swedish net income in respect of sale and leaseback profits which would not be recognised under US GAAP.

Volvo: A significant amount (6.6% of US net income) was added to Swedish income in respect of a share of profits of associated companies. A further 5.5% was added in respect of different treatments of business combinations (utilisation of tax carryforwards from purchased subsidiaries) plus a foreign exchange loss included in income under Swedish GAAP but excluded under US GAAP under the rules on gains and losses for hedged transactions.

Ericsson: The most significant addition to Swedish net income related to tax effects on intercompany transactions. Under US GAAP, income taxes paid by the selling company on intercompany profit eliminated in consolidation is eliminated as a prepayment of income tax.

Overall index value ≥1.1

1986: Volvo: There were two significant deductions from Swedish net income. In the first case, a write-down of an investment had been matched with an equal write-up of another investment. US GAAP does not allow the write-up. In the second case there was a foreign exchange gain included in income under Swedish GAAP but excluded under US GAAP under the rules on gains and losses for hedged transactions.

1987: SKF: An amount taken to income as a result of a sale and leaseback transaction was not allowed under US GAAP.

Gambro: A business combination which was treated as a pooling of interests for Swedish GAAP was regarded as an acquisition under US GAAP, principally because the two parties were not independent during the two years prior to acquisition. Consequently for 1987 only a portion of income of the subsidiary could be taken to the income statement for US GAAP purposes.

1988: Gambro: The main cause of difference continued to be the substitution of acquisition accounting methods for pooling of interests.

TABLE 9

Sweden: Summary of Quantified Effect of Appropriations to Reserves and Adjustment of Depreciation

Appropriations to reserves

All eight companies adjusted the Swedish reported profit to eliminate, for US GAAP purposes, appropriations to reserves. The table classifies the magnitude and direction of the appropriation as a percentage of US reported profit.

	1986	1987	1988
Swedish profit more than 50% below US profit	3	—	—
Swedish profit more than 30% but less than 50% below US profit	2	2	1
Swedish profit more than 10% but less than 30% below US profit	1	4	3
Swedish profit less than 10% below US profit	—	1	2
Swedish profit less than 10% above US profit	1	—	—
Swedish profit more than 10% but less than 30% above US profit	1	1	1
Swedish profit more than 50% above US profit	—	—	1
	8	8	8

Note: The percentage appropriation is estimated net of tax.

Reduction of depreciation to historical cost basis

Four companies made this adjustment.

	1986	1987	1988
Average index	0.737	0.959	0.979
Range: Low	0.875	0.895	0.961
High	0.994	0.998	0.999

earlier, an attempt has been made in this research to isolate the tax effect of the allocations to reserves. Other reasons for making provision for deferred tax include the profit sharing tax, different tax rates in other countries, capital gains and losses, and the utilisation of tax loss carryforwards. These are generally not material, with the exception in some instances of the tax loss carryforwards. Deferred tax is not recognised in Swedish law or GAAP.

4. Business combinations

   There was one case where pooling of interests was not allowed under US GAAP, causing significant deductions from the Swedish profit. In six companies there were adjustments because the US rules on calculation of goodwill and the treatment of items such as tax losses brought forward in subsidiaries are different. It would be extremely difficult to formulate any rule-of-thumb adjustments for such matters because they are highly dependent on the circumstances of each case.

5. Amortisation of goodwill

   Under Swedish GAAP, goodwill should be amortised over a period not exceeding 10 years (FAR Accounting Recommendation No 11) and this is done in all cases, so that no further adjustment is made for US GAAP purposes. It does seem likely that

TABLE 10

Netherlands: Income Statements

Total index of conservatism

Level of Materiality	Index Values	1986	1987	1988
Nl profit 10% or more below the US profit	≤0.9000	2	3	0
Nl profit 5% or more below the US profit but less than 10% below	0.9001–0.9500	0	0	0
Nl profit within ±5% of US profit	0.9501–1.0499	3	2	1
Nl profit 5% or more above the US profit but less than 10% above	1.0500–1.0999	0	0	1
Nl profit 10% or more above the US profit	≥1.1000	1	1	4
		6	6	6
Range: Lowest value		0.714	0.581	1.004
Highest value		1.124	1.274	2.416

if the companies were reporting primarily for US purposes, they would probably take a period longer than 10 years, so that the adjusted profit for US purposes which is reported in the 20-F is probably still too low in comparison with what might have been reported under US GAAP.

6. Equity accounting

   Accounting for associated companies is not dealt with in either Swedish company law or accounting law. There is a variety of accounting practices and differences in the levels of disclosure. Three of the companies did not use equity accounting for Swedish purposes and therefore made an adjustment for US GAAP. Two companies changed to equity accounting during the period and adjusted comparative figures accordingly. In the other three cases associated companies appear to have been immaterial.

7. Foreign currency translation

   There is a variety of approaches to problems of foreign currency translation, both in the method of calculation adopted and in the treatment of translation differences. In particular, under Swedish GAAP the gains and losses on translation of long-term loans are taken to the income statement whereas under US GAAP they could be taken to reserves on grounds of hedging. The direction of this effect is not predictable since it depends on relative exchange rate movements.

THE NETHERLANDS   In the case of the Netherlands, Form 20-F reports were obtained for 8 Dutch companies. However, two had to be rejected because they had used US GAAP in the financial statements and therefore did not provide a reconciliation with income under Dutch GAAP. In respect of the six companies examined, Table 10 shows that there was considerable variation in the relative conservatism of Dutch reporting. The distribution of index values for 1988 would lend support to the view that Dutch reporting is at the liberal end of the spectrum (Nobes, 1989), but the distributions for 1986 and 1987 are inconclusive.

Turning to a partial analysis of the components of each total adjustment, Table 11 summarises the main causes for the extremes of differences in profits (plus or minus 10% or more)

TABLE 11

The Netherlands: Main Causes for Extreme Differences in Reported Profit (plus or minus 10% or more):

Overall index value ≤0.9

1986: KLM: An exchange rate difference, favourable at the balance sheet date, is amortised over a time period corresponding to the use of the items giving rise to the difference. Under US GAAP a favourable exchange rate difference would be recognised as income. Hence the 1986 adjusted US profit was materially higher because of the magnitude of the difference arising in that period.

Aegon: In this insurance company, investment gains and losses are taken direct to reserves whereas for US GAAP purposes they must pass through the income statement. In 1986 there was a material investment gain which causes the adjusted US GAAP net income to be higher.

1987: Unilever: The cumulative effect of a change in depreciation policy had to be charged against income for US GAAP purposes.

Aegon: See discussion of investment gains for 1986.

Oce: The company values its fixed assets at the lower of replacement value or value to the business. US GAAP requires valuation at cost and consequently on disposal of a subsidiary there was an additional profit under US GAAP.

Overall index value ≥1.1

1986: Philips: The index value would have been 1.071 after deducting current cost adjustments. This is still relatively high compared with the other Dutch companies, reflecting the full credit to income of government investment subsidies received. Under US GAAP these are spread over 5 years. The index value for 1986 would have been 1.023 if the investment subsidy had been spread as required under US GAAP, this 2.3% excess over US GAAP being accounted for by the non-amortisation of goodwill under Dutch GAAP.

1987: Philips: The index value would have been 1.168 after deducting current cost adjustments. This is high because of the investment subsidy treatment explained above for 1986 (4.3% in 1987), plus a deferred tax adjustment which was 3.4% of US net income and a goodwill amortisation charge which had risen to 7.3% of US income.

1988: Philips: The index value would have been 1.073 after deducting current cost adjustments. The investment subsidy adjustment was now immaterial but the amortisation charge was 7.8% of US income.

Aegon: The total index value of 2.416 was principally due to an investment loss (65.2% of US net income) which had bypassed the Dutch income statement but was included for US GAAP. The high index value is explained further by an amortisation charge (16.1% of US net income) and provision for deferred taxation (12.4% of US net income).

Oce: On disposal of a subsidiary in 1988 there was a substantial translation difference which was taken direct to equity under Dutch GAAP but had to pass through the income statement for US GAAP purposes. Without this material item (53.8% of US net income) the index value for 1988 would have been 0.974, comparable to the value for previous years.

Unilever: There was a translation adjustment of 8.2% of US net income. Without this the index value would have been 1.053, still high due to a goodwill amortisation adjustment amounting to 8.3% of US net income.

between Dutch and US GAAP. The only company which reported higher Dutch income in all three years was Philips, using current cost accounting. The reconciliation provided by Philips disclosed only the net effect of current cost accounting so that, although it would appear that the benefit of the gearing adjustment outweighed additional cost of sales and higher depreciation charges, this supposition cannot be confirmed from the information provided. Even when the current cost adjustments were removed, Philips still reported higher profits under Dutch GAAP due to the lack of amortisation of goodwill and other items, including provision for deferred taxation and the non-spreading of investment subsidies received. Income smoothing, rather than relative conservatism as such, appears to be the main factor in accounting for the extreme differences, so that investment gains and losses for an insurance company, foreign currency translation adjustments and the cumulative effect of a change in depreciation policy could all bypass the Dutch income statement but have to appear under US GAAP. Since all these items could potentially take positive or negative values they could not be classed as arising from a consistent desire for greater conservatism in one country or the other and must be interpreted as being consistent with the 'business income' approach of Dutch accounting which would seek to iron out unpredictable distortions in recurring income.

There were, however, some differences between Dutch and US GAAP which had a consistent effect. Revaluation of fixed assets in the balance sheet results in higher depreciation charges and therefore lower Dutch profits. Lack of amortisation of goodwill through the income statement results in higher Dutch profits but lower net asset values. All six companies chose to write off goodwill directly against reserves, despite the alternative allowed practice of amortising through the income statement for up to five years. The index values for each of these adjustments are summarised in Table 12.

Dutch accounting shows a more conservative approach than US GAAP in not capitalising interest which would have to be capitalised for US purposes, but the adjustment was found in only one company and was immaterial in effect. Deferred tax adjustments were found in the income statements of three companies, but in all cases there were index values above and below the neutral value of 1.0. The net effect was that, after making allowance for the material items which caused the extreme differences in net income, the result of the consistent and recurring adjustments was to leave Dutch income within plus or minus 5% of the US GAAP equivalent.

SUMMARY AND CONCLUSIONS

The comparative international accounting literature suggests that generally accepted accounting principles in the US are likely to be more conservative than those in the UK and the Netherlands in terms of their impact on profits. At the same time, US GAAP are likely to be less conservative compared to GAAP in Sweden.

This study has attempted to assess the quantitative impact of these differences on measurement of profit in practice, so far as companies reporting on Form 20-F to the SEC in the US are concerned. There is no doubt that such an assessment is complex and difficult in view of the fact that some differences in accounting principles are indeterminate in terms of their bias towards increasing or reducing measures of profit. Further, the sample sizes are such that tests of statistical significance are feasible only in the case of the UK data. In the case of Sweden and the Netherlands, a case study approach was necessarily adopted.

TABLE 12

Netherlands Summary of Quantified Effect of Amortisation of Goodwill and Adjustment of Depreciation

Amortisation of goodwill

All six companies reduced the Dutch reported net income to incorporate goodwill amortisation for US GAAP purposes.

	1986	1987	1988
Average index	1.024	1.048	1.078
Range: Low	1.000	1.000	1.009
High	1.029	1.077	1.083

They were generally non-specific about the amortisation period chosen, one quoting the '5–10 years' of Dutch alternative practice, the rest quoting the 'not more than 40 years' US requirement.

Reduction of depreciation to historical cost basis

Three companies made this adjustment but only two could be distinguished separately (the adjustment by Philips being part of a global current cost adjustment).

Range: Low	0.938	0.936	0.904
High	0.996	0.996	0.999

Taken overall, the results of this research support the hypothesis that UK GAAP are significantly less conservative than US GAAP in terms of the impact on profits. Although Swedish GAAP tend to be more conservative, particularly when the transfers to reserves are analysed, there is insufficient evidence to establish a systematically more conservative bias compared to US GAAP when the accounting profit before transfers to reserves is examined. In the Netherlands, on the other hand, there is some evidence that Dutch GAAP are at the less conservative end of the spectrum, in a position similar to that of UK GAAP, but there is insufficient evidence to establish a systematically less conservative bias when compared to US GAAP. Income smoothing may be a stronger motive governing accounting practice. Since Dutch rules are flexible, it is possible that the Dutch companies considered here may have chosen to move towards US GAAP where this was permissible under Dutch GAAP. The same conjecture could be applied to the UK companies investigated here. The extent to which these companies might be atypical would require further investigation. It might be connected to the relative importance which the companies attach to the figures presented to domestic and to foreign readers of the annual report.

This research demonstrates that the overall quantitative impact of differences in accounting principles on profits in the US, UK, Sweden and the Netherlands is often significant and, in individual company cases, may be dramatic. While some general tendencies have been identified, the complexity of the analysis is evident. It is clearly not easy for analysts to develop quantitative 'rules of thumb' for adjustment of accounts from the generally accepted accounting principles of one country to those of another. Further research is now required to explore the impact of international accounting differences for a much larger number of sample companies in a wider variety of countries.

REFERENCES

Choi, F. D. S. *et al.* (1983), 'Analysing Foreign Financial Statements: The Use and Misuse of International Ratio Analysis', *Journal of International Business Studies,* Spring/Summer.

Cooke, T. E. (1988), *European Financial Reporting: Sweden,* Institute of Chartered Accountants in England and Wales.

Gray, S. J. (1980), 'The Impact of International Accounting Differences from a Security-Analysis Perspective; Some European Evidence', *Journal of Accounting Research,* Spring.

Nobes, C. W. (1983), 'A Judgmental International Classification of Financial Reporting Practices', *Journal of Business Finance and Accounting,* Spring.

Nobes, C. W. (1988), *Interpreting US Financial Statements,* Butterworths.

Nobes, C. W. (1989), *Interpreting European Financial Statements: Towards 1992,* Butterworths.

Nobes, C. W. (1990), *Accounting Comparisons: UK/Europe Vol. 1,* Coopers and Lybrand Deloitte.

Russell, A., Grinyer, J., Walker, M. and Malton, P. (1989), *Accounting for Goodwill,* ACCA Research Paper No. 13, Chartered Association of Certified Accountants.

Siegel, S. and Castellan, N. J. (1988), *Nonparametric Statistics for the behavioural sciences,* McGraw Hill.

Simmonds, A. and Azieres, O. (1989), *Accounting for Europe,* Touche Ross Europe.

Weetman, P. and Gray, S. J. (1990), 'International Financial Analysis and Comparative Corporate Performance: The Impact of UK versus US Accounting Principles on Earnings', *Journal of International Financial Management and Accounting,* Vol. 2:2 and 3.

APPENDIX

Classification of UK companies analysed, using FT-Actuaries list and list of alpha/beta/gamma stocks

Attwoods	Miscellaneous	b
Barclays	Banks	a
Beazer	Contracting and construction	a
BET	Conglomerate	a
BOC	Chemicals	a
Blue Arrow	Agencies	a
British Airways	Shipping and transport	a
British Gas	Oil and gas	a
British Petroleum	Oil and gas	a
British Steel	Metals and metal forming	a
British Telecom	Telephone networks	a
Cadbury Schweppes	Food manufacturing	a
Cambridge Instruments	Other industrial materials	b
Carlton Communications	(Television industry products)	b
Dixons	Stores	a
English China Clay	Other industrial materials	a
Glaxo	Health and household products	a
Hanson	Conglomerate	a
Huntingdon International Holdings	(Biological testing services)	g
ICI	Chemicals	a
Jaguar	Motors	a
Lep Group	Transport	a
Lex Service	(Distribution; automotive etc)	b
Midland Bank	Banks	a
National Freight Consortium	(Freight transport)	a
National Westminster Bank	Banks	a
Plessey	Electronics	a
Ratners	Stores	a
Reuters	Agencies	a
Rodime	(Computer disk manufacture)	—
Royal Bank of Scotland	Banks	a
Saatchi and Saatchi	Agencies	a
Shell Transport and Trading	Oil and gas	a
Tomkins	Other industrial materials	a
Unilever	Food manufacturing	a
United Newspapers	Packaging and paper	a
Ward White	Stores	b
Waterford Glass	(Crystal and china)	b
WCRS	Agencies	b
Wellcome	Health and household products	a
WPP Group	Agencies	a

Key: ( ) = not included in FT-Actuaries list; a = alpha stock, b = beta stock, g = gamma stock, "—" = infrequently traded shares

Classification of Netherlands companies

Aegon	Insurance
Akzo	Conglomerate
KLM Royal Dutch Airlines	Airline
Oce-Van der Grinten	Copying equipment
Philips	Electrical products

Unilever NV	Oil
Ausimont*	Chemicals
Advanced Semiconductor Materials*	Semiconductor manufacture

Classification of Swedish companies

AB Electrolux	White goods
Gambro Incorporated	Health care products
LM Ericsson Telephone Company	Telecommunications products
Pharmacia Corporation	Health care products
SKF Incorporated	Bearings, tools and components
The Swedish Cellulose Company	Forest and paper products
Swedish Export Credit Corporation	Export finance
Volvo Corporation	Motor vehicles

---

*Used US GAAP in their 20-F and therefore did not provide a reconciliation with Dutch GAAP.

TOWARDS A THEORY OF CULTURAL INFLUENCE ON THE DEVELOPMENT OF ACCOUNTING SYSTEMS INTERNATIONALLY

S. J. Gray

This paper explores the extent to which international differences in accounting, with specific reference to corporate financial reporting systems, may be explained and predicted by differences in cultural factors.

While prior research has shown that there are different patterns of accounting internationally and that the development of national systems tends to be a function of environmental factors, it is a matter of some controversy as to the identification of the patterns and influential factors involved (Mueller, 1967; Zeff, 1971; Radebaugh, 1975; Nair and Frank, 1980; Nobes, 1983). In this context the significance of culture does not appear to have been fully appreciated and thus the purpose of this paper is to propose a framework which links culture with the development of accounting systems internationally.

The first section of the paper reviews prior research on international classification and the influence of environmental factors. The second section addresses the significance of the cultural dimension and its application to accounting. The third section proposes a framework and develops hypotheses linking culture with the development of accounting attitudes and systems internationally, based on the cross-cultural work of Hofstede (1980, 1983). In the fourth section some culture area classifications are proposed. They have been developed on a judgmental basis,

---

S. J. Gray, "Towards a Theory of Cultural Influence on the Development of Accounting Systems Internationally," *Abacus,* vol. 24, no. 1, April 1988, 1–15.

in the context of combinations of accounting attitudes or 'values' which determine (a) the authority for and enforcement of accounting systems, and (b) the measurement and disclosure characteristics of accounting systems.

INTERNATIONAL CLASSIFICATION AND ENVIRONMENTAL FACTORS

Comparative accounting research has provided an enhanced awareness of the influence of environmental factors on accounting development (e.g., Mueller, 1967; Zeff, 1971; Radebaugh, 1975; Choi and Mueller, 1984; Nobes, 1984; Arpan and Radebaugh, 1985; Nobes and Parker, 1985). This research has contributed to a growing realization that fundamentally different accounting patterns exist as a result of environmental differences and that international classification differences may have significant implications for international harmonization and the promotion of economic integration. In this regard it has also been suggested that the identification of patterns may be useful in permitting a better understanding of the potential for change, given any change in environmental factors; and that policy-makers may be in a better position to predict problems that a country may be likely to face and identify solutions that may be feasible, given the experience of countries with similar development patterns (e.g., Nobes, 1984).

Research efforts in this area have tended to approach the international classification of accounting systems from two major directions. First, there is the deductive approach whereby relevant environmental factors are identified and, by linking these to national accounting practices, international classifications or development patterns are proposed (e.g., Mueller, 1967, 1968; Nobes, 1983, 1984). Second, there is the inductive approach whereby accounting practices are analysed, development patterns identified, and explanations proposed with reference to a variety of economic, social, political, and cultural factors (e.g. Frank, 1979; Nair and Frank 1980).

As regards the deductive approach to accounting classification, the environmental analysis by Mueller (1967) provides a useful starting point. Mueller identified four distinct approaches to accounting development in western nations with market-orientated economic systems. These were:

1. the macroeconomic pattern—where business accounting interrelates closely with national economic policies;

2. the microeconomic pattern—where accounting is viewed as a branch of business economics;

3. the independent discipline approach—where accounting is viewed as a service function and derived from business practice; and

4. the uniform accounting approach—where accounting is viewed as an efficient means of administration and control.

While all of these approaches were perceived to be closely linked to economic or business factors, a wider set of influences, for example, legal system, political system, social climate were recognized as being relevant, though without precise specification, to accounting development (Mueller, 1968; Choi and Mueller, 1984). Cultural factors received no explicit recognition, however, and were presumably subsumed in the set of environmental factors identified.

Mueller's analysis was adapted and extended by Nobes (1983, 1984) who based his classification on an evolutionary approach to the identification of measurement practices in developed Western nations. Nobes adopted a hierarchical scheme of classification in an endeavour to provide more subtlety and discrimination to the assessment of country differences. However, similarly to Mueller, no explicit mention was made of cultural factors. A basic distinction between microeconomic and macroeconomic systems was made together with a disaggregation between business economics and business practice orientations under a micro-based classification, and between Government/tax/legal and Government/economics orientations under a macro-uniform based classification. Further disaggregations were then made between U.K. and U.S. influences under the business practices orientation and between tax-based and law-based systems under the Government/tax/legal orientation. This classification system was then tested by means of a judgmental analysis of national financial reporting systems in fourteen countries.

A structural approach to the identification of accounting practices was adopted whereby major features were assessed, such as, the importance of tax rules, the use of prudent/conservative valuation procedures, the strictness of application of historical cost, the making of replacement cost adjustments, the use of consolidation techniques, the generous use of provisions, and the uniformity between companies in the application of rules. The results of the statistical analysis did not, however, go much beyond providing support for the classification of countries as either micro-based or macro-based. Thus the disaggregated elements of the classification scheme, though plausible, remain hypothetical accounting patterns subject to further empirical analysis.

By way of contrast, the inductive approach to identifying accounting patterns begins with an analysis of accounting practices. Perhaps the most important contribution of this type was by Nair and Frank (1980), who carried out a statistical analysis of accounting practices in forty-four countries. An empirical distinction was made between measurement and disclosure practices as these were seen to have different patterns of development.

The empirical results, using factor analysis applied to individual practices, showed that in respect of the Price Waterhouse (1975) data it was possible to identify five groupings of countries, with Chile as a single-country 'group', in terms of measurement practices. The number of groupings increased to seven when disclosure practices were considered. The measurement groupings were characterized broadly, following the 'spheres-of-influence' classification suggested by Seidler (1967), as the British Commonwealth, Latin America/South European, Northern and Central European, and United States models. The disclosure groupings, on the other hand, could not be described plausibly on a similar 'spheres-of-influence' classification on account of their apparent diversity.

Subsequent to the identification of groupings, Nair and Frank attempted to assess the relationships of these groupings with a number of explanatory variables. While relationships were established in respect of some of the variables which included language (as a proxy for culture), various aspects of economic structure and trading ties, it was clear that there were differences as between the measurement and disclosure groupings. However, the hypotheses that (a) cultural and economic variables might be more closely associated with disclosure practices, and (b) trading variables might be more closely associated with measurement practices were not supported. It is curious to note here that the language variable, as a proxy for culture, was perceived to be a means of capturing similarities in legal systems which were thought to be particularly important in the determination of disclosure patterns. This is questionable in itself, but in any event no justification was given for the use of language as a proxy for culture.

From this brief review of some of the major studies in international classification it seems clear that to date only very broad country groupings or accounting patterns have been identified. At the same time, only very general relationships between environmental factors and accounting patterns have been established.

The significance of culture in the context of prior classification research is far from clear. It may be that cultural influences have been generally subsumed in the predominant concern with economic factors but this has not been made explicit. Accordingly, the influence of culture on accounting would seem to have been largely neglected in the development of ideas about international classifications.

THE CULTURAL DIMENSION

The significance of culture in influencing and explaining behaviour in social systems has been recognized and explored in a wide range of literatures but especially the anthropology, sociology and psychology literatures, (e.g., Parsons and Shils, 1951; Kluckhohn and Strodtbeck, 1961; Inkeles and Levinson, 1969; Douglas, 1977; Hofstede, 1980).

Culture has been defined as 'the collective programming of the mind which distinguishes the members of one human group from another' (Hofstede, 1980, p. 25). The word 'culture' is reserved for societies as a whole, or nations, whereas 'subculture' is used for the level of an organization, profession or family. While the degree of cultural integration varies between societies, most subcultures within a society share common characteristics with other subcultures (Hofstede, 1980, p. 26).

An essential feature of social systems is perceived to be the inclusion of a system of societal norms, consisting of the value systems shared by major groups within a nation. Values have been defined as 'a broad tendency to prefer certain states of affairs over others' (Hofstede, 1980, p. 19). Values at the collective level, as opposed to the individual level, represent culture; thus culture describes a system of societal or collectively held values.

In the accounting literature, however, the importance of culture and its historical roots is only just beginning to be recognized. While there has been a lack of attention to this dimension in the international classification literature, Harrison and McKinnon (1986) and McKinnon (1986) have recently proposed a methodological framework incorporating culture for analysing changes in corporate financial reporting regulation at the nation specific level. The use of this framework to assess the impact of culture on the form and functioning of accounting is demonstrated with reference to the system in Japan. Culture is considered an essential element in the framework for understanding how social systems change because 'culture influences: (1) the norms and values of such systems; and (2) the behaviour of groups in their interactions within and across systems' (Harrison and McKinnon, 1986, p. 239).

Complementing Harrison and McKinnon's approach is the suggestion here that a methodological framework incorporating culture may be used to explain and predict international differences in accounting systems and patterns of accounting development internationally. More specifically, it is proposed here to explore the extent to which cultural differences identified by Hofstede's cross-cultural research (1980, 1983) may explain international differences in accounting systems.

Culture, Societal Values and the Accounting Subculture

Hofstede's (1980, 1983) research was aimed at detecting the structural elements of culture and particularly those which most strongly affect known behaviour in work situations in organizations and institutions. In what is probably one of the most extensive cross-cultural surveys ever conducted, psychologists collected data about 'values' from the employees of a multinational corporation located in more than fifty countries. Subsequent statistical analysis and reasoning revealed four underlying societal value dimensions along which countries could be positioned. These dimensions, with substantial support from prior work in the field, were labelled Individualism, Power Distance, Uncertainty Avoidance, and Masculinity. Such dimensions, which are examined further below, were perceived to represent elements of a common structure in cultural systems. It was also shown how countries could be grouped into culture areas, on the basis of their scores on the four value dimensions, using cluster analysis and taking into account geographical and historical factors. Figure 1 shows the culture areas identified and within each group any identifiable sub-groups.

The point of reviewing Hofstede's research here is that if societal value orientations are related to the development of accounting systems at the subcultural level, given that such values permeate a nation's social system, then it may be hypothesized that there should be a close match between culture areas and patterns of accounting systems internationally.

In order to explore further the relationship between culture and accounting systems in an international context it is necessary to identify the mechanism by which values at the societal level are linked to values at the accounting subcultural level as it is these latter values which are likely to influence directly the development of accounting systems in practice.

A model of this process is proposed in Figure 2. This is an adaptation and extension of the model relating to the formation and stabilizing of societal culture patterns proposed by Hofstede (1980, p. 27). In this model, societal values are determined by ecological influences modified by external factors such as international trade and investment, conquest, and the forces of nature. In turn, societal values have institutional consequences in the form of the legal system, political system, nature of capital markets, pattern of corporate ownership and so on. These institutions reinforce both ecological influences and societal values.

An extension of this model is proposed here whereby societal values are expressed at the level of the accounting subculture. Accordingly, the value systems or attitudes of accountants may be expected to be related to and derived from societal values with special reference to work-related values. Accounting 'values' will, in turn, impact on accounting systems.

If Hofstede has correctly identified Individualism, Power Distance, Uncertainty Avoidance, and Masculinity as significant cultural value dimensions then it should be possible to establish their relationship to accounting values. If such a relationship exists then a link between societal values and accounting systems can be established and the influence of culture assessed.

FIGURE 1

Culture Areas (Hofstede)

More Developed Latin	Less Developed Latin	More Developed Asian
Belgium	Colombia	Japan
France	Ecuador	
	Mexico	
Argentina	Venezuela	
Brazil		
Spain	Costa Rica	
	Chile	
Italy	Guatemala	
	Panama	**African**
	Peru	East Africa
	Portugal	West Africa
	Salvador	
	Uruguay	

Less Developed Asian	Near Eastern	
Indonesia	Arab countries	
Pakistan	Greece	
Taiwan	Iran	
Thailand	Turkey	**Asian-Colonial**
	Yugoslavia	Hong Kong
India		Singapore
Malaysia		
Philippines		

Germanic	Anglo	Nordic
Austria	Australia	Denmark
Israel	Canada	Finland
	Ireland	Netherlands
Germany	New Zealand	Norway
Switzerland	U.K.	Sweden
	U.S.A.	
	South Africa	

Before an attempt can be made to identify significant accounting values which may be related to societal values it is important to understand the meaning of the four value dimensions identified by Hofstede (1980, 1983) and referred to earlier. These dimensions are well expressed in Hofstede (1984, pp. 83–4) as follows:

Individualism versus Collectivism
Individualism stands for a preference for a loosely knit social framework in society wherein individuals are supposed to take care of themselves and their immediate families only. Its opposite, Collectivism, stands for a preference for a tightly knit social framework in which individuals can expect their relatives, clan, or

FIGURE 2

Culture, Societal Values and the Accounting Subculture

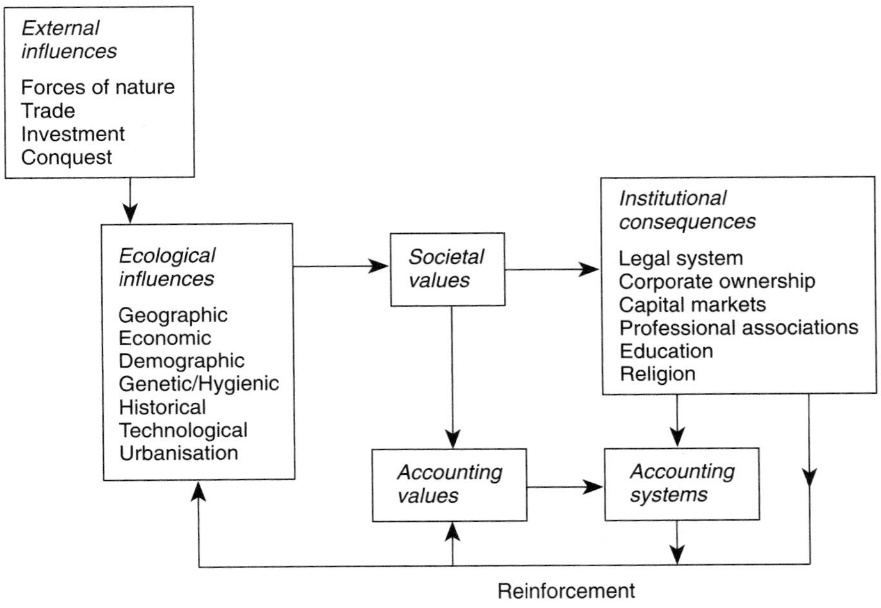

other in-group to look after them in exchange for unquestioning loyalty (it will be clear that the word 'collectivism' is not used here to describe any particular political system). The fundamental issue addressed by this dimension is the degree of interdependence a society maintains among individuals. It relates to people's self-concept: 'I' or 'we'.

Large versus Small Power Distance
Power Distance is the extent to which the members of a society accept that power in institutions and organisations is distributed unequally. This affects the behaviour of the less powerful as well as of the more powerful members of society. People in Large Power Distance societies accept a hierarchical order in which everybody has a place which needs no further justification. People in Small Power Distance societies strive for power equalisation and demand justification for power inequalities. The fundamental issue addressed by this dimension is how a society handles inequalities among people when they occur. This has obvious consequence for the way people build their institutions and organisations.

Strong versus Weak Uncertainty Avoidance
Uncertainty Avoidance is the degree to which the members of a society feel uncomfortable with uncertainty and ambiguity. This feeling leads them to beliefs promising certainty and to maintaining institutions protecting conformity.

Strong Uncertainty Avoidance societies maintain rigid codes of belief and behaviour and are intolerant towards deviant persons and ideas. Weak Uncertainty Avoidance societies maintain a more relaxed atmosphere in which practice counts more than principles and deviance is more easily tolerated. The fundamental issue addressed by this dimension is how a society reacts on the fact that time only runs one way and that the future is unknown: whether it tries to control the future or to let it happen. Like Power Distance, Uncertainty Avoidance has consequences for the way people build their institutions and organizations.

Masculinity versus Femininity
Masculinity stands for a preference in society for achievement, heroism, assertiveness, and material success. Its opposite, Femininity, stands for a preference for relationships, modesty, caring for the weak, and the quality of life. The fundamental issue addressed by this dimension is the way in which a society allocates social (as opposed to biological) roles to the sexes.

Having identified societal values is it possible then to identify significantly related accounting values at the level of the accounting subculture?

The following 'accounting' values, derived from a review of accounting literature and practice, are offered for consideration:

Professionalism versus Statutory Control—a preference for the exercise of individual professional judgment and the maintenance of professional self-regulation as opposed to compliance with prescriptive legal requirements and statutory control.

Uniformity versus Flexibility—a preference for the enforcement of uniform accounting practices between companies and for the consistent use of such practices over time as opposed to flexibility in accordance with the perceived circumstances of individual companies.

Conservatism versus Optimism—a preference for a cautious approach to measurement so as to cope with the uncertainty of future events as opposed to a more optimistic, laissez-faire, risk-taking approach.

Secrecy versus Transparency—a preference for confidentiality and the restriction of disclosure of information about the business only to those who are closely involved with its management and financing as opposed to a more transparent, open and publicly accountable approach.

It should be emphasized that there is no suggestion that these 'values' are necessarily the only values involved. What they do represent, however, is an attempt to identify value dimensions which appear to be widely recognized.

What arguments are there to support these accounting value dimensions? How do they relate to societal values? How are they likely to impact on the development of national accounting systems?

PROFESSIONALISM VERSUS STATUTORY CONTROL

This is proposed as a significant accounting value dimension because accountants are perceived to adopt independent attitudes and to exercise their individual professional judgments to a greater or lesser extent everywhere in the world.

A major controversy in many Western countries, for example, surrounds the issue of the extent to which the accounting profession should be subject to public regulation/statutory control or be permitted to retain control over accounting standards as a matter for private self-regulation (e.g., Taylor and Turley, 1986).

The development of professional associations has a long history but they are much more firmly established in countries such as the U.S.A. and the U.K. than in some of the Continental European countries and in many of the less developed countries (e.g., Holzer, 1984; Nobes and Parker, 1985).

In the U.K., for example, the concept of presenting 'a true and fair view' of a company's financial position and results depends heavily on the judgment of the accountant as an independent professional. This is so to the extent that accounting information disclosures additional to, and sometimes contrary to, what is specifically required by law may be necessary. This may be contrasted with the traditional position in France and Germany where the professional accountant's role has been concerned primarily with the implementation of relatively prescriptive and detailed legal requirements (e.g., Gray and Coenenberg, 1984). With the implementation of the EEC directives this situation is now changing to the extent that there is some movement, if not convergence, along the professionalism spectrum.

To what extent then can professionalism be linked to the societal values of Individualism, Power Distance, Uncertainty Avoidance, and Masculinity? It is argued here that professionalism can be linked most closely with the individualism and uncertainty-avoidance dimensions. A preference for independent professional judgment is consistent with a preference for a loosely knit social framework where there is more emphasis on independence, a belief in individual decisions and respect for individual endeavour. This is also consistent with weak uncertainty avoidance where practice is all important, where there is a belief in fair play and as few rules as possible, and where a variety of professional judgments will tend to be more easily tolerated. There would also seem to be a link, if less strong, between professionalism and power distance in that professionalism is more likely to be accepted in a small power-distance society where there is more concern for equal rights, where people at various power levels feel less threatened and more prepared to trust people, and where there is a belief in the need to justify the imposition of laws and codes. As regards masculinity, however, there does not appear to be any significant link with professionalism.

Following from this analysis it may be hypothesized that:

H1:   The higher a country ranks in terms of individualism and the lower it ranks in terms of uncertainty avoidance and power distance then the more likely it is to rank highly in terms of professionalism.

UNIFORMITY VERSUS FLEXIBILITY

This would seem to be a significant accounting value dimension because attitudes about uniformity, consistency or comparability are incorporated as a fundamental feature of accounting principles world-wide (e.g., Choi and Mueller, 1984; Arpan and Radebaugh, 1985; Nobes and Parker, 1985).

This is a value which is open to different interpretations ranging from a relatively strict inter-company and inter-temporal uniformity, to consistency within companies over time and some concern for comparability between companies, to relative flexibility of accounting practices to suit the circumstances of individual companies.

In countries such as France, for example, a uniform accounting plan has long been in operation, together with the imposition of tax rules for measurement purposes, where there is a concern to facilitate national planning and the pursuit of macroeconomic goals. In contrast, in the U.K. and U.S.A. there is more concern with inter-temporal consistency together with some degree of inter-company comparability subject to a perceived need for flexibility (e.g., Choi and Mueller, 1984; Holzer, 1984; Arpan and Radebaugh, 1985).

To what extent then can uniformity be linked to societal value dimensions? It is argued here that uniformity can be linked most closely with the uncertainty-avoidance and individualism dimensions. A preference for uniformity is consistent with a preference for strong uncertainty avoidance leading to a concern for law and order and rigid codes of behaviour, a need for written rules and regulations, a respect for conformity and the search for ultimate, absolute truths and values. This value dimension is also consistent with a preference for collectivism, as opposed to individualism, with its tightly knit social framework, a belief in organization and order, and respect for group norms. There would also seem to be a link, if less strong, between uniformity and power distance in that uniformity is more easily facilitated in a large power-distance society in that the imposition of laws and codes of a uniform character are more likely to be accepted. As regards masculinity, however, there does not appear to be any significant link with uniformity. Following from this analysis it may be hypothesized that:

> H2: The higher a country ranks in terms of uncertainty avoidance and power distance and the lower it ranks in terms of individualism then the more likely it is to rank highly in terms of uniformity.

CONSERVATISM VERSUS OPTIMISM

This would seem to be a significant accounting value dimension because it is arguably 'the most ancient and probably the most pervasive principle of accounting valuation' (Sterling, 1967, p. 110).

Conservatism or prudence in asset measurement and the reporting of profits is perceived as a fundamental attitude of accountants the world over. Moreover, conservatism varies according to country, ranging from a strongly conservative approach in the Continental European countries, such as France and Germany, to the much less conservative attitudes of accountants in the U.S.A. and U.K. (e.g., Beeny, 1975, 1976; Nobes, 1984; Choi and Mueller, 1984; Arpan and Radebaugh, 1985).

The differential impact of conservatism on accounting measurement practices internationally has also been demonstrated empirically (e.g., Gray, 1980; Choi and Mueller, 1984). Such differences would seem to be reinforced by the relative development of capital markets, the differing pressures of user interests, and the influence of tax laws on accountants in the countries concerned.

To what extent then can conservatism be linked to societal value dimensions? It is argued here that conservatism can be linked most closely with the uncertainty avoidance dimension. A preference for more conservative measures of profits is consistent with strong uncertainty avoidance following from a concern with security and a perceived need to adopt a cautious approach to cope with the uncertainty of future events. There would also seem to be a link, if less strong, between high levels of individualism and masculinity on the one hand, and weak uncertainty avoidance on the other, to the extent that an emphasis on individual achievement and performance is likely to foster a less conservative approach to measurement.

As regards the power distance dimension there does not, however, appear to be any significant link with conservatism.

Following from this analysis it may be hypothesized that:

> H3: The higher a country ranks in terms of uncertainty avoidance and the lower it ranks in terms of individualism and masculinity then the more likely it is to rank highly in terms of conservatism.

Secrecy versus Transparency

This would seem to be a significant accounting value dimension which stems as much from management as it does from the accountant owing to the influence of management on the quantity of information disclosed to outsiders (e.g., Jaggi, 1975). Secrecy, or confidentiality, in business relationships is, nevertheless, a fundamental accounting attitude (Arpan and Radebaugh, 1985).

Secrecy would also seem to be closely related to conservatism in that both values imply a cautious approach to corporate financial reporting in general; but with secrecy relating to the disclosure dimension and conservatism relating to the measurement dimension. The extent of secrecy would seem to vary across countries with lower levels of disclosure, including instances of secret reserves, evident in the Continental European countries, for example, compared to the U.S.A. and U.K. (e.g., Barrett, 1976; Choi and Mueller, 1984; Arpan and Radebaugh, 1985). These differences would also seem to be reinforced by the differential development of capital markets and the nature of share ownership which may provide incentives for the voluntary disclosure of information (e.g., Watts, 1977).

To what extent, then, can secrecy be linked to societal value dimensions? It is argued here that secrecy can be linked most closely with the uncertainty-avoidance, power-distance and individualism dimensions. A preference for secrecy is consistent with strong uncertainty avoidance following from a need to restrict information disclosures so as to avoid conflict and competition and to preserve security. A close relationship with power distance also seems likely in that high power-distance societies are likely to be characterized by the restriction of information to preserve power inequalities. Secrecy is also consistent with a preference for collectivism, as opposed to individualism, with its concern for those closely involved with the firm rather than external parties. A significant but less important link with masculinity also seems likely to the extent that more caring societies where more emphasis is given to the quality of life, people and the environment, will tend to be more open especially as regards socially related information.

Following from this analysis it may be hypothesized that:

> H4: The higher a country ranks in terms of uncertainty avoidance and power distance and the lower it ranks in terms of individualism and masculinity then the more likely it is to rank highly in terms of secrecy.

Accounting Values and Culture Area Classifications

Having formulated hypotheses relating societal values to accounting values internationally, it is evident that the most important societal values at the level of the accounting subculture would seem to be uncertainty avoidance and individualism. While power distance and masculinity are

FIGURE 3

Accounting Systems: Authority and Enforcement

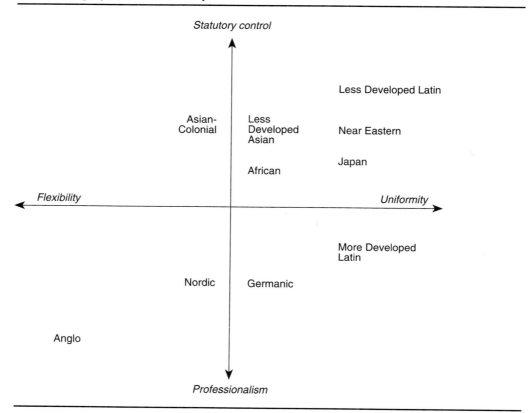

also significant to some extent, masculinity appears to be of somewhat lesser importance in the system of accounting values.

It is now proposed to hypothesize culture area classifications in the context of combinations of accounting values. For this purpose it is argued here that a useful distinction can be made between the authority for accounting systems, that is, the extent to which they are determined and enforced by statutory control or professional means on the one hand, and the measurement and disclosure characteristics of accounting systems on the other.

Accounting values most relevant to the professional or statutory authority for accounting systems and their enforcement would seem to be the professionalism and uniformity dimensions in that they are concerned with regulation and the extent of enforcement or conformity. Accordingly, these can be combined and the classification of culture areas hypothesized on a judgmental basis as shown in Figure 3. In making these judgments reference has been made to the relevant correlations between value dimensions and the resultant clusters of countries identified from the statistical analysis carried out by Hofstede (1980, pp. 223, 316). From this classification

FIGURE 4

Accounting Systems: Measurement and Disclosure

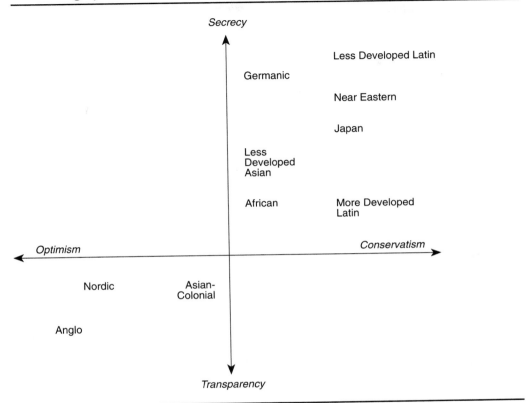

it seems clear that the Anglo and Nordic culture areas may be contrasted with the Germanic and more developed Latin culture areas on the one hand, and the Japanese, Near Eastern, less developed Latin, less developed Asian and African culture areas on the other. The Colonial Asian countries are separately classified, representing a mixture of influences.

Accounting values most relevant to the measurement practices used and the extent of information disclosed are self-evidently the conservatism and secrecy dimensions. Accordingly, these can be combined and the classification of culture areas hypothesized on a judgmental basis as shown in Figure 4. In making judgments in respect of these classifications reference has also been made to the relevant correlations between value dimensions and the resultant clusters of countries identified from the statistical analysis carried out by Hofstede (1980, pp. 316, 324). Here there would appear to be a sharper division of culture area groupings with the Colonial Asian group relating more closely with the Anglo and Nordic groupings in contrast with the Germanic and more developed Latin groupings which appear to relate more closely to the Japanese, less developed Asian, African, less developed Latin, and Near Eastern area groupings.

SUMMARY AND CONCLUSIONS

While prior research has shown that there are different patterns of accounting and that the development of national systems of corporate financial reporting is related to environmental factors, identification of the patterns and the influential factors involved remains controversial. The significance of culture in this context is far from clear and has been a relatively neglected issue in the development of ideas about international classification.

In this paper, a framework for analysing the impact of culture on the development of accounting systems internationally has been proposed. Value dimensions at the accounting subculture level have been identified, that is, professionalism, uniformity, conservatism and secrecy. These have been linked to cultural value dimensions at the societal level and hypotheses have been formulated for testing. Classifications of country groupings by culture area have also been hypothesized as a basis for testing the relationship between culture and accounting systems in the context of systems authority and enforcement characteristics on the one hand, and measurement and disclosure characteristics on the other.

Following this analysis, empirical research now needs to be carried out to assess the extent to which there is in fact a match between (a) societal values and accounting values, and (b) the proposed classification of country groupings, based on cultural influence, and the groupings derived from an analysis of accounting practices related to the value dimensions of the accounting subculture. However, for this to be feasible, further work to operationalize the link between accounting practices and accounting values will be necessary, and the relevant cross-cultural data assembled and organized.

In interpreting the results of empirical research relating to culture, the influence of any change factors will also need to be taken into account, bearing in mind the existence of external influences arising from colonization, war, and foreign investment, including the activities of multinational companies and large international accounting firms.

While much work lies ahead, this paper is offered as a contribution towards a theory of cultural influence on the development of accounting systems internationally. In doing so it is fully recognized that the ideas advanced are exploratory and subject to empirical testing and verification.

REFERENCES

Arpan, J. S., and L. H. Radebaugh, *International Accounting and Multinational Enterprises,* Wiley, 1985.

Barrett, M. E., 'Financial Reporting Practices: Disclosure and Comprehensiveness in an International Setting', *Journal of Accounting Research,* Spring 1976.

Beeny, J. H., *European Financial Reporting—West Germany,* ICAEW, 1975.

————, *European Financial Reporting—France,* ICAEW, 1976.

Choi, F. D. S., and G. G. Mueller, *International Accounting,* Prentice-Hall, 1984.

Douglas, M., *Cosmology: An Enquiry into Cultural Bias,* Royal Anthropological Institute, 1977.

Frank, W. G., 'An Empirical Analysis of International Accounting Principles', *Journal of Accounting Research,* Autumn 1979.

Gray, S. J., 'The Impact of International Accounting Differences from a Security Analysis Perspective: Some European Evidence', *Journal of Accounting Research,* Spring 1980.

Gray, S. J. and A. G. Coenenberg (eds), *EEC Accounting Harmonisation: Implementation and Impact of the Fourth Directive,* North Holland, 1984.

Harrison, G. L., and J. L. McKinnon, 'Cultural and Accounting Change: A New Perspective on Corporate Reporting Regulation and Accounting Policy Formulation', *Accounting, Organizations and Society,* Vol. 11, No. 3, 1986.

Hofstede, G., *Culture's Consequences,* Sage Publications, 1980.

———, 'Dimensions of National Cultures in Fifty Countries and Three Regions', in J. B. Deregowski, S. Dziurawiec and R. Annis (eds), *Expiscations in Cross-Cultural Psychology,* Swets and Zeitlinger, 1983.

———, 'Cultural Dimensions in Management and Planning', *Asia Pacific Journal of Management,* January 1984.

Holzer, H. P. (ed.), *International Accounting,* Harper & Row, 1984.

Inkeles, A., and P. J. Levinson, 'National Character: The Study of Modal Personality and Sociocultural Systems', in G. Lindsey and E. Aronson (eds), *The Handbook of Social Psychology,* (2nd edn), Addison-Wesley, 1969.

Jaggi, B. L., 'The Impact of the Cultural Environment on Financial Disclosures', *International Journal of Accounting,* Spring 1975.

Kluckhohn, F. R., and F. L. Strodtbeck, *Variations in Value Orientations,* Greenwood Press, 1961.

McKinnon, J. L., *The Historical Development and Operational Form of Corporate Reporting Regulation in Japan,* Garland, 1986.

Mueller, G. G., *International Accounting,* Macmillan, 1967.

———, 'Accounting Principles Generally Accepted in the United States Versus those Generally Accepted Elsewhere', *International Journal of Accounting Education and Research,* Spring 1968.

Nair, R. D., and W. G. Frank, 'The Impact of Disclosure and Measurement Practices on International Accounting Classifications', *The Accounting Review,* July 1980.

Nobes, C. W., 'A Judgemental International Classification of Financial Reporting Practices', *Journal of Business Finance and Accounting,* Spring 1983.

———, *International Classification of Financial Reporting,* Croom Helm, 1984.

Nobes, C. W., and R. H. Parker, (eds), *Comparative International Accounting,* Philip Allan, 1985.

Parsons, T., and E. A. Shils, *Toward a General Theory of Action,* Harvard University Press, 1951.

Price Waterhouse International, *International Survey of Accounting Principles and Reporting Practices,* 1975.

Radebaugh, L. H., 'Environmental Factors Influencing the Development of Accounting Objectives, Standards and Practices in Peru', *International Journal of Accounting Education and Research,* Fall, 1975.

Seidler, L. J., 'International Accounting—the Ultimate Theory Course', *The Accounting Review,* October 1967.

Sterling, R. R., 'Conservatism: The Fundamental Principle of Valuation in Traditional Accounting', *Abacus,* December 1967.

Taylor, P., and S. Turley, *The Regulation of Accounting,* Blackwell, 1986.

Watts, R. L., 'Corporate Financial Statements: A Product of the Market and Political Processes', *Australian Journal of Management,* April 1977.

Zeff, S. A., *Forging Accounting Principles in Five Countries: A History and an Analysis of Trends,* Stipes, 1971.

FOREIGN STOCK LISTINGS: BENEFITS, COSTS, AND THE ACCOUNTING POLICY DILEMMA

Gary C. Biddle and Shahrokh M. Saudagaran

INTRODUCTION

The accelerating globalization of the world's capital markets holds profound implications for accounting practice and policy. In just six years between 1982 and 1988, trading in foreign stocks by U.S. investors increased 900 percent, to nearly $150 billion per year. During the same period, foreign trades in U.S. stocks increased to nearly $400 billion per year.[1] By year-end 1988, shares worth $640 billion (6.7 percent of the total) were held by foreign investors.[2] By year-end 1989, foreign stocks accounted for 14 percent of total world stock

We appreciate research support provided by the KPMG Peat Marwick Foundation through the Research Opportunities in International Business Information program. Additional research support was provided by the Accounting Development Funds at the University of Washington and at Santa Clara University. Helpful comments were provided by two anonymous referees.

Gary C. Biddle and Shahrokh M. Saudagaran, "Foreign Stock Listings: Benefits, Costs, and the Accounting Policy Dilemma," *Accounting Horizons,* September 1991, 69–80. Reprinted by permission of the American Accounting Association.

[1]U.S. Government Accounting Office, *International Finance: Regulation of International Securities Markets* (Washington, D.C., GAO, 1989), pp. 9–10.

[2]M. R. Sesit, "Foreign Investing Makes a Comeback," *The Wall Street Journal,* September 1, 1989.

trading volume.[3] One recent survey identified over 500 companies whose shares are actively traded on international markets.[4]

As firms enter foreign markets for customers and capital, accounting practitioners must wrestle with cross-border differences in languages, customs, accounting conventions, and auditing standards. Around the globe accounting policy makers and government officials face difficult choices regarding the appropriate disclosure requirements for foreign versus domestic firms. In the U.S., longstanding policies aimed at providing domestic investors with comparable financial statements conflict with rising demands for increased access to foreign investment opportunities. Stock exchanges in the U.S. claim that they are at a competitive disadvantage because stringent U.S. reporting requirements discourage foreign firms from listing here.

This study presents evidence on three key questions raised by these developments:

1. What are the benefits and costs to listing on a foreign stock exchange?

2. To what extent do accounting disclosure requirements influence foreign listing decisions?

3. What are the accounting policy issues posed by foreign stock exchange listings and how have regulatory authorities responded?

BENEFITS AND COSTS OF LISTING ABROAD

Why list on a foreign stock exchange? Until recently, this question was considered seriously only by large or multinational firms. With increasing opportunities to sell products and services and to obtain capital in foreign markets, large, medium, and even small-sized firms are weighing the benefits and costs of foreign listings. Access to foreign capital is a primary benefit. However, many firms are finding that foreign listings also offer marketing, political, and employee relations advantages.[5] Among the costs to foreign listings, anecdotal and empirical evidence suggest that accounting disclosure requirements are an important consideration.

FINANCIAL BENEFITS

A key financial advantage to listing on a foreign stock exchange is a reduced cost of capital. In countries with small or segmented capital markets, local demand for additional shares may be relatively inelastic. As a result, the issuance of additional shares will have a greater negative impact on share prices, effectively raising capital cost. Market segmentation can result from government tax policies, restrictions on capital transfers, and language, cultural, and legal barriers.

---

[3]M. R. Sesit and B. Donnelly, "Global Stock Trading Develops Own Haves, Have-Nots," *The Wall Street Journal,* May 8, 1991.

[4]"The Corporate List," *Euromoney* (May 1988), pp. 127–143.

[5]For a more detailed examination of benefits to foreign listings, see S. M. Saudagaran, "An Empirical Study of Selected Factors Influencing the Decision to List on Foreign Stock Exchanges," *Journal of International Business Studies,* 19 (Spring 1988), pp. 101–27.

This effect will be more important for firms whose capital demands are large relative to domestic capital supplies.

Nestle, for example, with a market value of $14.2 billion at the end of 1987, accounted for 11.7 percent of the total market value of all domestic firms listed on Swiss stock exchanges whereas Exxon, which is considerably larger (market value of $54.1 billion at year-end 1987), accounted for only 2.4 percent of the market value of U.S. firms listed on the New York Stock Exchange.[6] Nestle's greater relative size would make it more likely to list abroad for financial reasons than Exxon (*ceteris paribus*). Indeed, empirical evidence confirms that relative size is a primary determinant of decisions to seek foreign listings.[7] However, other benefits of a foreign listing (discussed below) might also motivate Exxon to list abroad.

For some firms, foreign capital markets offer lower transactions costs, narrower quotation spreads, and greater market stability than are available domestically. Foreign listings can also reduce capital costs through their effects on investment portfolio risk. Several studies have shown that if economic activity is less than perfectly correlated across countries, adding foreign securities to a domestic investment portfolio can decrease systematic (beta) risk.[8] This implies that the rate of return demanded by investors should be lower on internationally traded securities. The experiences of a Danish pharmaceutical firm, Novo, are documented in a case study that suggests such an effect.[9]

In countries like Germany and Japan where debt is a primary source of capital, lenders may demand a role in managing the companies they finance. By accessing foreign equity capital, managers can obtain increased managerial autonomy. In addition, listing abroad can facilitate foreign acquisitions, mergers, stock swaps, and tender offers by creating supplies of shares which satisfy local regulatory requirements. Funding foreign expansions, debt servicing, and operating requirements with locally-raised capital also reduce currency exchange rate risks.

---

[6]Market values of Nestle and Exxon obtained from the Euromoney Corporate List, *Euromoney* (May 1988). Total market values of stock exchanges obtained from the International Federation of Stock Exchanges' *Activities and Statistics 1988 Report.*

[7]See S. M. Saudagaran (1988), *op cit.*

[8]See, for example, H. G. Grubel, "International Diversified Portfolios: Welfare Gains and Capital Flows," *American Economic Review,* 58 (December 1968), pp. 1299–1314; H. Levy and M. Sarnat, "International Diversification of Investment Portfolios," *American Economic Review,* 60 (September 1970), pp. 668–675; H. G. Grubel and K. Fadner, "The Interdependence of International Equity Markets," *Journal of Finance,* 26 (March 1971), pp. 89–94; T. Agmon, "The Relations Among Equity Markets: A Study of Share Price Co-Movements in the United States, United Kingdom, Germany and Japan," *Journal of Finance,* 27 (September 1972), pp. 839–856; R. A. Cohn and J. J. Pringle, "Imperfections in International Finance Markets: Implications for Risk Premia and the Cost of Capital to Firms," *Journal of Finance,* 28 (March 1973), pp. 59–66; D. R. Lessard, "World, Country, and Industry Relationships in Equity Returns: Implications for Risk Reduction through International Diversification," *Financial Analysts Journal* (January-February 1976), pp. 32–38; H. L. Brewer, "Investor Benefits from Corporate International Diversification," *Journal of Financial and Quantitative Analysis* (March 1981), pp. 113–126; G. Ragazzi, "On the Relation between Ownership Dispersion and the Firm's Market Value," *Journal Banking and Finance,* 5 (1981), pp. 261–276; and R. C. Stapleton and K. B. Dullum, "Market Imperfections, Capital Market Equilibrium, and Corporation Finance," *Journal of Finance,* 32 (May 1977), pp. 307–319.

[9]A. I. Stonehill and K. B. Dullum, *Internationalizing the Cost of Capital: The Novo Experience and National Policy Implications* (Copenhagen, Denmark: John Wiley & Sons, 1982).

MARKETING AND PUBLIC RELATIONS BENEFITS

A foreign listing can boost corporate marketing efforts by enhancing name recognition among investors and consumers in the foreign country. Share ownership by foreign investors creates local demand for information on a firm's products and performance. Resulting reports by local press and news media provide "free" advertising that is especially appealing to producers of industrial and consumer products who would normally spend large sums to obtain such visibility.

The process of listing itself can build ties to the local financial community through meetings with investment bankers, brokers, exchange officials, and regulatory authorities. Many firms also present "road shows" which familiarize financial analysts and journalists with company performance, products, and personnel. If in the process of conducting these activities the company gains credit for adapting to local practices, it makes for excellent financial public relations. Several multinational firms, including Hewlett Packard and Sony, have cited public relations as a major motive for listing abroad.[10] A recent *Forbes* article describes how Apple has garnered publicity in the Japanese investment community by listing on the Tokyo Stock Exchange.[11]

POLITICAL BENEFITS

Many countries impose local ownership requirements on businesses operating within their borders. Although joint ventures can sometimes be arranged, they may require sharing technology with local partners. In some cases, listing on a local exchange will allow the firm to meet local ownership requirements without jeopardizing control of technology. Share ownership by local individual and institutional investors may also engender political support and help blunt potentially hostile nationalistic sentiments.

EMPLOYEE RELATIONS BENEFITS

Employee stock ownership plans have gained notoriety recently in the U.S. as defensive tactics against hostile takeovers. At least as important are the incentive benefits of stock ownership in aligning employee and shareholder incentives. The incentive benefits of stock purchase, bonus, and option plans are likely to be enhanced if employees, including foreign employees, can trade their shares on a local exchange. With foreign employment growing at many companies, improved employee incentives may alone justify the cost of a foreign listing.

COSTS OF A FOREIGN LISTING

What are the costs of a foreign listing? Most stock exchanges levy initial listing and continuing annual registration fees based on numbers of shares listed and traded. However, these costs are

---

[10]Based on comments to second author during interviews with William M. Klein, External Reporting Manager, Hewlett Packard and Yukio Ozawa, Corporate Financial Communications Manager, Sony.

[11]A. Tanzer, "How Apple Stormed Japan," *Forbes* (May 27, 1991), pp. 40–1.

relatively minor. For most firms the largest costs by far associated with foreign listings are due to accounting and disclosure requirements. These costs arise from differences between countries in accounting and auditing practices, financial reporting and registration requirements, and regulatory and legal restrictions. Thus, the costs faced by a given firm would depend on its characteristics, including its domicile, and on the foreign exchange being considered. Table 1 lists accounting and disclosure-related costs identified in the literature on securities listings,[12] articles in the financial press,[13] and from on-site interviews with officials from the SEC, the New York, American and Toronto stock exchanges, investment bankers, securities analysts, legal consultants, public accountants, and managers of multinational corporations.[14]

First, regulatory authorities in most countries require foreign firms to prepare financial disclosures in accordance with local reporting requirements. A firm may have to incur substantial costs to bring its financial reporting systems into compliance. In the U.S., for example, foreign firms are required to provide financial information substantially similar to that provided by domestic firms in accordance with U.S. generally accepted accounting principles (GAAP).[15] Despite ongoing efforts to harmonize accounting standards across countries,

---

[12]See, for example, M. Adler and B. Dumas, "International Portfolio Choice and Corporate Finance: A Synthesis," *Journal of Finance* 38 (June 1983), pp. 925–84; D. K. Eiteman and A. I. Stonehill, *Multinational Business Finance* (Reading, Massachusetts: Addison-Wesley, 1989); J. S. Howe and K. Kelm, "The Stock Price Impacts of Overseas Listings," *Financial Management* 16 (Autumn 1987), pp. 51–56; R. Stapleton and M. Subrahmanyam, "Market Imperfections, Capital Market Equilibrium and Corporation Finance," *Journal of Finance* 32 (May 1977), pp. 307–19; and Stonehill and Dullum, *op cit.*

[13]See, for example, R. Leach, "Who Lists Abroad—And Why," *Euromoney* (October 1973); J. McNish, "Why Toronto-Dominion Went to London," *Euromoney* (May 1984); Q. P. Lim, "Why Wall Street was Shunned," *Euromoney* (May 1984); M. R. Sesit, "More U.S. Concerns Seek to be Listed Overseas," *The Wall Street Journal* (June 10, 1985); M. Cox, "American Express Plans to List, Issue Shares in Tokyo," *The Wall Street Journal* (July 16, 1985); E. S. Browning, "Tokyo Exchange: To Join or Not To Join?" *The Wall Street Journal* (September 27, 1985); A. Freeman, "Montreal Exchange Plans Bid to Attract U.S. Investors by Listing Overseas Stocks," *The Wall Street Journal* (September 30, 1985); M. R. Sesit and A. Monroe, "Small U.S. Companies Go Public in London," *The Wall Street Journal* (October 28, 1985); A. Tanzer, "Listing for Success," *Forbes* (December 15, 1986); W. C. Freund, "Stock Exchange Rivalry Yields Dividends," *The Wall Street Journal* (October 5, 1987); M. Winkler, "Rule on Private Placements Seen Altering Market," *The Wall Street Journal* (January 19, 1989); A. Newman, "New Electronic Bulletin Board Promises to Make Trading Foreign Stocks Easier," *The Wall Street Journal* (June 11, 1990).

[14]The following individuals, all of whom are actively involved in foreign stock listings, were interviewed by the second author: Edmund Lukas, Regional Managing Director, New York Stock Exchange; Bernard H. Maas, Consultant, American Stock Exchange; Robert G. Cook, Director, Original Listings, Toronto Stock Exchange; Mark J. Lerner, V.P. Investment Banking Division, Merrill Lynch Capital Markets; Tetsuo Kadowaki, V.P. Investment Banking, Nomura Securities International; Martin J. Siegel, V.P.-Manager International Arbitrage Department, Salomon Brothers; Albert K. Woo, Sr. V.P. and Controller of International Operations, Shearson Lehman Brothers; Richard Watkins, Managing Director, Phillips & Drew International; Stephen A. Grant, Partner, Sullivan & Cromwell; Morton B. Solomon, Partner, KPMG Peat Marwick; Robert M. Tarola, Partner, Price Waterhouse; Richard P. Miller, Manager, Ernst & Whinney; William M. Klein, External Reporting Manager, Hewlett Packard; Peter Aslet, U.S. Investor Relations Manager, Imperial Chemical Industries; Yoichi Aoki, Manager, Financial Public Relations Office, American Honda Motor Co.; Yuji Ikeo, Manager, New York Financial Liaison Office, Kubota; Yukio Ozawa, Corporate Financial Communications Manager, Sony.

[15]If a foreign firm's financial statements are prepared in compliance with any other body of accounting rules then the firm is required to discuss the nature of the differences from U.S. GAAP. It is also required to quantify material variations and to reconcile the income statement with the earnings as they would appear under U.S. GAAP.

TABLE 1

Major Accounting and Regulatory Costs of a Foreign Listing

1. Adjustment of accounting procedures to meet local requirements.
2. Adjustment of auditing procedures to meet local requirements.
3. Changes in the frequency of financial reporting.
4. Costs resulting from more extensive foreign financial disclosures than are required for domestic competitors.
5. Monetary expense, time, and administrative effort in initial registration.
6. Recurring costs of compliance.
7. Simultaneous offerings at home and abroad could be affected by foreign regulations.
8. Foreign regulatory agency's jurisdiction over worldwide business practices.

significant differences remain.[16] As recently observed by a prominent investment banker, "the cost of converting to U.S. accounting standards is at least $1 million for a major Japanese or British company. Why do that unless there is availability of capital, or a cost of capital, that you can't get anywhere else in the world?"[17] In contrast, the Amsterdam Exchange accepts "home country" financial statements from foreign listers with few modifications.

Audit practices in foreign countries may also differ from those in a firm's home country. For instance, auditing standards in most countries including the U.S. require that the auditors observe physical inventories and obtain direct confirmation of receivables. This would involve additional costs for firms based in countries where audit standards do not require these steps. Obtaining acceptable audit certification following local requirements may also increase the time it takes for the firm to list its securities on a foreign stock exchange. For example, local requirements may specify that certification be obtained from a local auditor. Additional auditing and accounting costs will also be incurred to translate the results of foreign operations into the domestic financial statements.

Greater frequency of financial reporting (e.g., semi-annually or quarterly) required by some stock exchanges and regulatory authorities can impose additional costs on companies not required to report as frequently at home. Managements in certain countries such as Japan strongly oppose quarterly reporting on philosophical grounds, arguing that it adversely affects their ability to take actions that are in the long term interests of their firms.

Costs can also result if a foreign exchange requires disclosures not required at home. For example, segment reporting (i.e., segmentation of financial information of a business by industry and/or geographic area in which the entity operates) is required by FASB Statement No. 14 in the U.S. but not under Japanese accounting principles. Japanese firms complain that

---

[16]For a historical perspective on these attempts, see F. D. S. Choi and G. G. Mueller, *International Accounting* (Englewood Cliffs: Prentice-Hall, 1984). Others have suggested that the increasing internationalization of capital markets will produce increased harmonization of financial disclosures. Self-interest, it is argued, will prove to be a more effective motivator than the dictates of any government or accounting board. As the title of an article in *The Wall Street Journal* suggested "Where Boards and Governments have Failed, the Market Could Internationalize Accounting" (May 8, 1985, p. 38).

[17]John Hennessy, chairman of Credit Suisse First Boston Limited, *Forbes* (March 9, 1987, p. 64).

these disclosures put them at a competitive disadvantage relative to other Japanese companies which are not listed in the U.S.[18] A recent survey revealed that firms based in countries where segmental disclosures are not required tended not to provide that information.[19] Another study concluded that segment disclosure requirements have been a major barrier to listings on U.S. stock exchanges by firms from foreign countries without such requirements.[20]

Countries with extensive accounting disclosure requirements also tend to have extensive pre-registration requirements. The monetary costs of an initial listing in a foreign country typically includes underwriting and lawyers' fees and translation and printing expenses. The exchange may also require accounting disclosures and historical documentation beyond that required by the accounting regulatory bodies. Cumbersome registration and exchange reporting requirements can cause lengthy delays which may be unacceptable to firms for whom quick access to the stock market is a priority. There may also be recurring monetary and nonmonetary costs of complying with periodic re-registration and updating requirements. The experts cited above expressed the view that accounting and regulatory costs are typically considered jointly in exchange listing decisions.

Restrictions imposed by regulatory agencies in foreign countries may affect stock offerings made concurrently at home and abroad. For instance, in the U.S., the Securities Act of 1933 prohibits a publicity campaign advertising a new issue during the period prior to initial filing of the registration statement. These restrictions extend beyond the U.S. and apply even to the firm's home country if such publicity may reasonably be expected to reach the U.S. market. Given the sophistication of modern telecommunications and the wide media coverage present today, this effectively precludes a campaign anywhere in the world prior to SEC registration and may even constrain the nature of an offering in a firm's home country.

Another potential cost of a foreign listing is a foreign regulatory agency's jurisdiction over a firm's business practices, not only in that country, but worldwide. Many foreign firms believe that these regulations adversely affect their global competitiveness and contradict established business practices. Additional anecdotal evidence of the concern of foreign firms regarding U.S. disclosure and regulatory requirements is provided by a study commissioned by the *Keidanren,* Japan's Federation of Economic Organizations. The *Keidanren* engaged Sullivan and Cromwell, a major U.S. law firm, to canvas U.S. regulatory agencies, stock exchange officials and professional organizations concerning a possible relaxation of reporting and regulatory requirements for Japanese firms.[21]

---

[18]See F. D. S. Choi and A. I. Stonehill, "Foreign Access to U.S. Securities Markets: The Theory, Myth and Reality of Regulatory Barriers," *Investment Analyst* (July 1982), pp. 17–26.

[19]D. J. Tonkin, *World Survey of Published Accounts* (London: Lafferty Publications, 1989).

[20]R. Balakrishnan, T. S. Harris, and P. K. Sen, "The Predictive Ability of Geographical Segment Disclosures" (Working Paper, Columbia University, July 1988).

[21]The study concluded that, for the time being, Japanese firms raising capital in the U.S. would be held to virtually the same reporting requirements as U.S.-domiciled firms. Sullivan and Cromwell, Attorneys at Law, "Report to the Keidanren on Segment Reporting by Japanese Companies" (New York, June 7, 1985).

THE EFFECTS OF ACCOUNTING DISCLOSURE LEVELS ON LISTING DECISIONS

Do accounting, disclosure, and regulatory requirements influence foreign exchange listing decisions? Anecdotal and research evidence suggest that they do. Table 2 presents the numbers of foreign firms from each country listed on each of the world's nine largest stock exchanges as of year-end 1981 and year-end 1987. Despite recent growth in foreign listings, it is clear that not all exchanges have had equal success in attracting foreign firms. By year-end 1987, only 121 foreign firms had listed on one of the two major U.S. exchanges. In contrast, 584 foreign firms were listed in London, 320 in Amsterdam, 213 in Zurich, and 172 in tiny Luxembourg (not shown), despite the fact that the U.S. exchanges are far larger in terms of market value and volume of shares traded. Between 1981 and 1987, the U.S. exchanges added only 25 new foreign listings, compared with 107 new listings in London, 63 in Amsterdam, and 45 in Zurich.

Listing choices by domicile in Table 2 are also revealing. As documented in the previous section, Japanese firms often cite U.S. financial reporting requirements and regulatory restrictions as reasons for not listing on a U.S. exchange. Despite actions by U.S. regulatory authorities beginning in 1982 to ease reporting requirements for foreign firms (these actions are described more fully below), only eight Japanese firms were listed on the New York/American stock exchanges as of year-end 1987. In contrast, 58 Japanese firms were listed in Frankfurt, 30 in Amsterdam, and 18 in Paris. It is also noteworthy that only nine Japanese firms were listed in London, despite the fact that London is the exchange with the largest number of total foreign listings. U.S. and British reporting requirements are generally viewed as among the most stringent.[22]

Two recent research studies confirm that foreign listings in cross-section and changes in foreign listings between 1981 and 1987 are correlated with cross-country rankings of disclosure levels.[23] To help mitigate the effects of other factors that may influence foreign listing decisions, additional tests introduced control variables for industry, geographic location, size of export market, and equity capital relative to the firm's domestic exchange. These test results were also consistent with the hypothesis that firms are less likely to list their shares on foreign exchanges with more stringent reporting requirements.

---

[22]A recent survey revealed the following overall ranking of reporting and regulatory requirements in the opinion of 142 managers and professionals actively involved in the foreign listing process (from most to least stringent):

1. United States
2. Canada
3. United Kingdom
4. Netherlands
5. France
6. Japan
7. Germany
8. Switzerland

For details see S. M. Saudagaran and G. C. Biddle, "Financial Disclosure Requirements and Foreign Stock Exchange Listing Decisions" (Working paper, University of Washington, July, 1991).

[23]G. C. Biddle and S. M. Saudagaran, "The Effects of Financial Disclosure Levels on Firms' Choices Among Alternative Foreign Stock Exchange Listings," *Journal of International Financial Management and Accounting,* 1 (Spring 1989), pp. 55–87, and S. M. Saudagaran and G. C. Biddle, "Financial Disclosure Requirements and Foreign Stock Exchange Listing Decisions" (Working paper, University of Washington, July, 1991).

TABLE 2

Foreign Firm Listings on Nine Major Exchanges by Domicile[a]

Domicile	Stock Exchange[b]							
	AMS	FRA	LDN	NYSE/AMEX	PAR	TKY	TOR	ZUR
Panel A: Foreign Listings in 1981								
Netherlands	—	15	16	2	12	1	0	10
Germany	12	—	7	0	11	0	0	23
U.K.	17	14	—	9	16	0	5	9
U.S.A.	164	49	203	—	42	12	58	92
France	4	10	3	0	—	2	0	7
Japan	25	55	8	6	8	—	1	2
Canada	13	2	29	58	13	0	—	6
Switz.	1	4	1	0	2	0	0	—
Other	21	28	210	21	58	0	3	19
Totals	257	177	477	96	162	15	67	168
Percentage Foreign[c]	59%	28%	17%	4%	22%	1%	8%	60%
Panel B: Foreign Listings in 1987								
Netherlands	—	16	16	5	13	1	0	14
Germany	16	—	8	0	13	2	0	33
U.K.	22	14	—	19	17	10	8	11
U.S.A.	141	56	195	—	51	60	49	107
France	10	8	5	0	—	0	0	7
Japan	30	58	9	8	18	—	1	8
Canada	12	2	26	59	13	6	—	6
Switz.	2	11	1	0	2	2	0	—
Other	87	43	324	30	63	7	7	27
Totals	320	208	584	121	190	88	65	213
Percentage Foreign[c]	50%	27%	22%	5%	28%	5%	5%	58%

[a]From fact books of individual stock exchanges.
[b]Exchanges in alphabetical order. Stock Exchange Codes: AMEX American, AMS Amsterdam, FRA Frankfurt, LDN London, NYSE New York, PAR Paris, TKY Tokyo, TOR Toronto, ZUR Zurich.
[c](Number of foreign companies listed/Total companies listed) × 100.

Results of a survey of 52 organizations headquartered in Japan, Switzerland, the United Kingdom, the United States, and Germany and representing institutional investors, corporate issuers, underwriters, and regulators indicate that "accounting differences *are* important and affect the capital market decisions of a significant number of market participants."[24] Another study found that continental European firms listed on the London Stock Exchange disclosed more than the requirements of the exchange and that there were persistent national characteristics in the items voluntarily disclosed. The authors concluded that the competitive pressures

---

[24]F. D. S. Choi and R. M. Levich, *The Capital Market Effects of International Accounting Diversity* (Homewood, Illinois: Dow Jones-Irwin, 1990).

of raising capital in international capital markets significantly influence the level of disclosure provided by companies that participate in these markets.[25]

THE REGULATORY DILEMMA

Recent growth in foreign stock exchange listings poses difficult questions regarding the applicability of domestic reporting requirements to foreign firms. Accounting policy makers and regulatory officials in many countries are grappling with tradeoffs between the comprehensiveness of disclosures and the availability of investment opportunities. In the U.S., the SEC's mandate to protect investors suggests that foreign firms listing securities in the U.S. should provide the same financial information as domestic issuers. However, if the imposition of domestic disclosure requirements on foreign firms makes U.S. listings less attractive, U.S. stock exchanges will be placed at a competitive disadvantage relative to stock exchanges in other countries and, as a result, individual investors will be deprived of desirable investment opportunities.

Over the past decade, stock exchanges in other countries have experienced dramatic growth relative to those in the U.S.[26] One expert has recently expressed a fear held by many that "inadequate savings and a surfeit of regulations will combine to diminish the importance of the U.S. in the burgeoning international capital market."[27] Of particular interest are his observations regarding the role of accounting disclosure and registration requirements:

> There's been this huge movement to simplify the rules and procedures for issuing securities in France, Germany, Britain, even Japan. But the U.S. market during this time runs the risk of becoming, in effect, a regional market. No foreign corporation will go to the U.S. market.

> I think the SEC should greatly simplify the whole process of registration, disclosure and whether companies need to transform their accounts to American standards. These are all very provincial type rules.

> Somehow in the European market we are able to float Japanese companies, Australian companies, Belgian, Finnish, and Swiss companies. Accounting figures, certified by accountants but with different types of national practices, are accepted by the market as legitimate.

> If you just looked at interest rates, European firms or governments could have raised money more cheaply in the U.S. So why are they going to the international

---

[25]G. K. Meek and S. J. Gray, "Globalization of Stock Markets and Foreign Listing Requirements: Voluntary Disclosures by Continental European Companies Listed on the London Stock Exchange," *Journal of International Business Studies* (Summer 1989), pp. 315–336.

[26]In April 1987, the Tokyo stock exchange surpassed the New York stock exchange in size as measured by the total capitalization of listed equity securities ($2.688 versus $2.672 trillion) (*The Wall Street Journal,* April 13, 1987). Measured in U.S. dollars, Japan's capital markets grew at an annual rate 23 percent from 1978 to 1986. The corresponding figure for the U.S. was 14 percent. Between 1984 and 1986, the Japanese markets grew at an annual rate of 68 percent compared to 22 percent for the U.S. Adjusting for the decline of the dollar relative to the yen, the Japanese markets grew by 34 percent over the two years.

[27]John Hennessy, *op cit.*

market? It must be because the price they put on harassment and regulation makes the cheaper cost of the money not worth the effort. That's the only explanation I have.

Accounting policy makers and regulatory authorities in the U.S. are expressing concern that stringent domestic disclosure requirements are discouraging foreign firms from listing in the U.S. For example, a recent *Wall Street Journal* headline read: "NYSE's New Chief Seeks to Make Big Board More International."[28] The accompanying article quotes William H. Donaldson, incoming chairman of the New York Stock Exchange as indicating that he will "tackle the major issue that has impeded the trading of large numbers of foreign stocks on the Big Board—the fact that most big foreign corporations don't meet stringent U.S. financial disclosure and accounting rules." He "wants to greatly expand the number of foreign stocks trading on the Big Board" and to "make shares of top companies around the world easily available to U.S. investors. [. . .] We have to work with the Securities and Exchange Commission and Congress and try and get some rules here that will allow the listing of these securities."

Similar concern was expressed recently by Dennis Beresford, Chairman of the Financial Accounting Standards Board.[29] In a prepared speech on "Financial Reporting, Comparability and Competition," he observed that:

> It is widely reported that many foreign companies are reluctant to offer their securities in U.S. public markets or list them on U.S. exchanges because they are unwilling to comply with the voluminous and detailed U.S. accounting and disclosure requirements or submit to the SEC's jurisdiction. This is said to put the U.S. exchanges and securities industry at a competitive disadvantage.
>
> Comparable national accounting standards are needed by any multinational company as a matter of internal economy and effectiveness. Complying with national securities registration requirements, training foreign national employees, and converting foreign subsidiary books to parent company accounting methods are all complicated by differing national standards.

REGULATORY RESPONSE IN THE U.S.

Under increasing pressure to make foreign securities more accessible to U.S. investors and to enhance the competitiveness of U.S. exchanges, the SEC adopted the Integrated Disclosure System (IDS) in 1982, after more than three years of deliberation.[30] Apart from reducing paperwork by eliminating some of the duplication in registration requirements, these rules also

---

[28]*The Wall Street Journal* (December 21, 1990).

[29]Dennis Beresford, Chairman of the Financial Accounting Standards Board, "Financial Reporting, Comparability and Competition" (Speech presented at the University of Washington in Seattle and at the University of California in Berkeley, October 18–19, 1990).

[30]Securities and Exchange Commission. *SEC Docket,* 24; No. 15 (March 16, 1982), pp. 1262–1349.

modified some of the other disclosure requirements foreign issuers found burdensome.[31] These include the use of the registrant's domestic GAAP in preparing financial statements, segment reporting, timeliness of the financial statements incorporated in the prospectus, and disclosure of top management's compensation.

Foreign firms may now prepare their financial statements using foreign, as opposed to U.S., GAAP when the foreign GAAP is part of a comprehensive set of standards. They are required, however, to quantify material differences, if any, between the amounts determined under the foreign accounting principles and those that would have resulted under SEC Regulation S-X and U.S. GAAP. No concessions, however, were made with regard to auditing standards.

Segment reporting under U.S. GAAP requires the disclosure of assets, revenues, and profits by line of business and geographic area. Under the new rules, firms using foreign GAAP may dispense with segment reporting of profits and assets if they are not required to disclose them under their domestic standards. However, they must provide a narrative explanation if a segment's contribution to total profits is materially different from its share of revenues.

IDS has also relaxed the timeliness requirements for some foreign issuers. Unlike U.S. issuers who must generally provide financial statements no older than 135 days at the date of filing, foreign issuers are now permitted to use financial statements that are up to six months old at the effective date of the registration statement. Foreign companies' financial statements, however, have to include more recent financial statements if issued in compliance with foreign law. In addition, foreign issuers are now allowed to use financial statements up to twelve months old at the effective date of registration statement for rights offerings to shareholders.

The disclosure of individual managers' compensation was perceived as onerous by foreign issuers from countries where disclosure of individual performance and compensation packages is considered inappropriate. The SEC responded to this concern by permitting aggregate disclosure of top managers' and directors' salaries in lieu of individual disclosure, unless information on individual remuneration is routinely disclosed to the shareholders or the public in the issuer's home country.

In February 1985, the SEC issued a concept release[32] soliciting public comment on two approaches—reciprocal and common prospectus, aimed at facilitating multinational securities offerings by non-governmental issuers. The approaches proposed in the release were intended

---

[31]SEC commissioner Barbara Thomas characterized IDS as "the most significant change in foreign issuer registration requirements since the original passage of the Securities Act in 1933" (B. S. Thomas, "Increased Access to United States Capital Markets: A Brief Look at the SEC's New Integrated Disclosure Rules for Foreign Issuers," *Journal of Comparative Business and Capital Market Law,* 5 (June 1983), pp. 129–35).

Under IDS certain foreign private issuers can satisfy the registration requirements of the Securities Act of 1933 (Securities Act) by incorporating by reference or by attachment, information disclosed in Form 20-F already filed with the SEC in accordance with the Securities Exchange Act of 1934 (Exchange Act). These issuers must file a Form 20-F, under the Exchange Act, if they have previously offered securities in the U.S., have securities listed on a U.S. exchange, or have more than 500 shareholders and more than $5 million in total assets. The information to be provided varies depending on the nature of the securities being registered, the market value of the stock being held by non-affiliates ("float") and the length of time that the company has been an SEC registrant. SEC forms for foreign private issuers are different from those used by domestic issuers, ensuring that distinctive foreign disclosure issues receive specific SEC attention. Foreign private issuers using these forms are also immune from the effects of changes in forms used by domestic issuers.

[32]Securities Act of 1933 Release No. 6568.

to harmonize disclosure and distribution practices between the United States, Canada and the United Kingdom.

The reciprocal approach would require agreement that a prospectus of an issuer in its own domicile would be accepted *as is* for offerings in the other participating countries, providing that certain minimum requirements were met. Under the common prospectus approach, agreement would be required on common disclosure standards for a prospectus that could be used in all the participating countries. Under both approaches, a foreign issuer would be subject to the liability provisions of the U.S. securities laws applicable to domestic issuers for false or misleading statements contained in a prospectus.

In October 1990, the SEC commissioners unanimously agreed to repropose the rules for the multijurisdictional system between the United States and Canada, which had originally been issued in July 1989[33] after considering respondents' comments on the February 1985 conceptual release. The system being considered is a hybrid between the reciprocal approach and the common prospectus approach.

The first phase would be limited to prospectuses used in offerings of investment grade non-convertible debt and preferred stock of "substantial issuers" in Canada.[34] The Canadian regulatory authorities would be responsible for applying their disclosure standards for reviewing the prospectus. Unless the SEC staff had reason to believe that there was a problem with the filing or offering, the documents would be assigned a "no review" status by the SEC. Canadian issuers would, however, be liable under U.S. civil liability and antifraud laws. They would also be subject to the SEC's authority to stop the issue if it were considered necessary for the protection of U.S. investors.

Under the proposed rule, periodic reporting under Canadian rules would satisfy the reporting requirements of the Exchange Act in the U.S. In addition, Canadian issuers are exempt from U.S. proxy regulations as well as from insider reporting requirements under Section 16 of the Exchange Act.

The securities commissions of the Canadian provinces of Ontario and Quebec concurrently issued proposals that detail the implementation of the multijurisdictional disclosure system in Canada for U.S. issuers using disclosure documents prepared in accordance with SEC requirements. Currently negotiations are in progress with other countries that are interested in participating in the multijurisdictional disclosure system.

In April 1990, the SEC adopted Rule 144A that provides a safe harbor exemption from the registration requirements of the 1933 Securities Act for resales of restricted securities to "qualified institutional buyers."[35] Rule 144A defines qualified institutional buyers as institutions that own and invest on a discretionary basis at least $100 million in securities of issuers that are not affiliated with that qualified institutional buyer.

Rule 144A is designed to promote liquidity for restricted securities received in private placements. Prior to its passage, traders were unable to resell private-placement securities without registering them with the SEC or holding them for two years. The main implication

---

[33]Securities Act of 1933 Release Nos. 6841 and 6879.

[34]As relates to investment grade debt and preferred stock, a "substantial issuer" is defined as one that has a market value of at least Canadian $180 million.

[35]Securities Act of 1933 Release No. 6862.

of Rule 144A is that it permits traders to resell private-placement securities without registration and without a waiting period thereby creating a new market in which institutions will trade securities among themselves. In response to concerns about the potential development of side-by-side public and private markets for the same class of securities, the SEC announced that Rule 144A is not available for securities that are of the same class as securities listed on a U.S. securities exchange. Certain resale restrictions are also imposed under Rule 144A for securities of nonreporting foreign issuers of private-placement securities which are of the same class as securities traded in the U.S.

The "Rule 144A market" is expected to be competitive with the Euromarkets. Observers believe that it will allow U.S. issuers to raise capital in the U.S. private markets as efficiently, and with lower transactions costs than, in the Euromarkets. Foreign private issuers, often deterred from entering the U.S. public markets by the SEC's reporting and disclosure requirements, are likely to increase their offerings in the newly liquid U.S. private markets. U.S. institutional investors will also benefit from increased access to these securities.[36]

Despite IDS and Rule 144A, there remains significant resistance within the SEC to proposals to relax U.S. GAAP for foreign listers. For example, SEC Chairman Richard Breeden recently rejected a New York Stock Exchange plan to loosen reporting standards for foreign firms.[37] Breeden argued that without adequate protection, U.S. investors "might select a foreign company's stock . . . only to discover later that differences in accounting or auditing standards made the foreign stock look better." He also asserted that allowing foreign firms to use more lenient standards "would seriously disadvantage U.S. firms in their home market."

REGULATORY RESPONSE IN OTHER COUNTRIES

Other countries have also responded to pressures to relax reporting requirements for foreign firms. In December 1983, the Japanese government adopted amendments to the "Enforcement Order of the Securities and Exchange Law" and to the "Ministerial Ordinance on the Audit Certificate of Financial Statements" eliminating the dual audit requirement for foreign companies listed on the Tokyo Stock Exchange. Previously, listed foreign companies whose financial statements had been audited by a public accountant in their home country were required to file a separate audit report provided by Japanese public accountants. Under the revised regulations, the audit report provided by the foreign company's auditor in its home country is sufficient if the Japanese Ministry of Finance considers it to be adequate protection for Japanese investors. The new regulations became effective for fiscal years ending on or after January 1, 1984. Timeliness requirements for foreign issuers were also relaxed in Japan by an amendment of the Securities and Exchange Law in May 1984. The deadline for filing the financial statements has been extended from within three months to within six months after the end of the fiscal year.

These changes were largely due to the efforts of the Tokyo Stock Exchange, which had been urging the Japanese government to relax or eliminate regulatory disclosure burdens on

---

[36]S. Hanks, "SEC Ruling Creates a New Market," *The Wall Street Journal* (May 16, 1990).

[37]K. Salwen, "Breeden Rejects Big Board Plan to Relax Listing Standards for Foreign Concerns," *The Wall Street Journal* (May 3, 1991).

foreign companies. It had argued that this was necessary for it to attract foreign companies to the exchange. In 1983, the Tokyo Stock Exchange had already taken measures within its authority, to reduce the documents to be filed with the exchange by foreign companies. In addition it had also simplified and reduced the frequency with which certain other documents were to be submitted to the exchange by foreign companies. Several reports which were previously required on a quarterly basis (and still are for Japanese companies), are now only required to be filed annually by foreign companies.

Authorities in France and U.K. have also taken steps to increase the competitiveness of the Paris and London stock exchanges, respectively.[38] However, their actions consisted of deregulating securities trading rather than relaxations in disclosure requirements as was the case in the U.S. and Japan. As relates to stock transactions, the French government allowed negotiation of discounts on commissions charged by brokers. Previously, all these commission discounts were fixed. With a view to maintaining orderly markets, the government also introduced a system of using stock jobbers, or specialists, where none had existed before. In 1985, the London Stock Exchange approved plans to open ownership of members to outsiders and usher in deregulated equities trading in London in an effort to make the London market better capitalized and more competitive internationally. The approval allowed foreign banks and stockbrokers, which had been limited to acquiring minority stakes in British brokerage firms, to own 100 percent of such firms. It also did away with fixed commissions. More recently it was revealed that the American Stock Exchange and a British securities firm are seeking approval for the establishment of a U.S.-based stock exchange which would allow institutional investors to buy and sell foreign securities that have not been registered with the SEC.[39]

THE LINGERING DILEMMA

Recent actions by regulatory authorities in the U.S. and other countries make clear how seriously they view the effects of disclosure requirements on stock exchange listing decisions. Available empirical evidence lends credence to their concerns in suggesting that firms avoid listing on exchanges with costly disclosure requirements. Stock exchanges in the U.S. argue that if stringent domestic reporting requirements are applied to foreign firms, it will put them at a competitive disadvantage and deny domestic investors of desirable investment opportunities. This view conflicts directly with longstanding regulatory policies designed to provide domestic investors with comprehensive and comparable financial statements.

Despite recent and major changes in U.S. disclosure requirements for foreign firms listing in the U.S., reporting standards and regulatory restrictions remain more stringent in the U.S. than in most other countries. In part for this reason, many foreign firms continue to shun U.S. stock exchanges in favor of listings in Europe and the Far East. As accounting policy makers, regulators, and stock exchange officials around the world debate the wisdom of allowing different disclosure standards for foreign and domestic firms, others are at work attempting to resolve the

---

[38]"France Announces Steps to Deregulate Financial Markets," *The Wall Street Journal* (April 2, 1985); "London Stock Exchange Members Pass Plans to Deregulate Equities Trading," *The Wall Street Journal* (June 5, 1985).

[39]*The Wall Street Journal* (March 27, 1987), p. 28.

underlying cause, differences across countries in accounting, auditing, and disclosure standards. Dennis Beresford, FASB Chairman, described the process as follows:[40]

> Those who think of accounting as a body of arbitrary conventions see the internationalization process as one of negotiation or horse trading. If I held that view, I would be pessimistic about the future of international accounting. Either it would degenerate into a body of inconsistent and toothless generalities or, probably more likely, a substantial stalemate.

He remains optimistic.

---

[40]Dennis Beresford, *op. cit.*

SHORTCOMINGS OF JAPANESE CONSOLIDATED FINANCIAL STATEMENTS

Howard D. Lowe

INTRODUCTION

The Japanese began to use consolidated financial statements at least half a century later than many of the other industrialized countries of the world. Responding to external pressure they reluctantly adopted the accounting practices applicable to consolidated reporting employed in the United States and have made a determined effort to adapt them to their own business environment. The results, however, have not been entirely satisfactory.

United States GAAP for preparing consolidated financial statements recognizes groups based upon the legal relationships arising from the majority ownership of voting shares. Japanese corporate groups on the other hand tend to form from substantive relationships of a non-legal nature. Consequently, American users of Japanese consolidated statements assume they are analyzing the financial position and results of operations of a group of companies operating as an economic entity. Actually they may be analyzing something quite irrelevant because the

The research for this paper was based upon personal interviews conducted during the summer of 1989. Interviewed were representatives of the Business Accounting Deliberation Council, the Japanese Institute of Certified Public Accountants, senior partners of major Japanese accounting firms, partners in the Tokyo offices of international accounting firms, and accounting professors at Waseda, Chuo, Nihon, Riyyko and Kyushu universities.

Howard D. Lowe, "Shortcomings of Japanese Consolidated Financial Statements," *Accounting Horizons,* September 1990, 1–9. Reprinted by permission of the American Accounting Association.

statements do not represent the substance of the actual business relationships. This obviously impairs the ability of readers to make appropriate judgments from these statements.

This theme is developed by first identifying the major events which brought about the adoption of consolidated reporting in Japan and the current standards for preparing Japanese consolidated statements. Following this is an explanation of the factors responsible for the inferior status of Japanese consolidated statements as currently being prepared. This leads to some suggestions for Japanese reporting requirements and to implications for the challenge facing the International Accounting Standards Committee and other organizations in their efforts to bring about "harmonization" of accounting standards.

THE DEVELOPMENT OF CONSOLIDATED REPORTING IN JAPAN

Consolidated financial statements became a vehicle for corporate reporting in the United States about the turn of the century, and in the United Kingdom in the 1920s. In both countries the introduction of consolidated statements was regarded as an improvement on the use of conventional financial reports and they were rapidly accepted and popularized. By the 1930s consolidated statements were regarded as the customary vehicle for communicating financial information to users of the securities market.

The introduction of consolidated accounting to financial reporting in Japan, however, did not occur until 1976. It is traceable to the entry of Japanese corporations into foreign capital markets which began in the 1960s, to the bankruptcy of Sanyo Special Steel Company in 1965, and to the entry of foreign corporations into Japanese capital markets.[1]

The pioneer corporation into foreign capital markets was Sony Ltd., which issued American Depository Receipts on the New York Stock Exchange in 1961. Raising funds on an international market was an abrupt departure from the traditional custom of depending only on Japanese banks for financing. Following Sony's success many other large corporations including Mitsubishi, Honda, and Matsushita, began to offer securities in foreign markets.

As bonds of Japanese companies began to appear on international capital markets it became clear that Japanese accounting practices were not acceptable overseas. Presentation of consolidated financial statements were required by most foreign exchanges and for international reporting. By 1973, more than sixty Japanese corporations were voluntarily producing consolidated financial statements in order to meet the requirements for offering their securities abroad.[2]

The perception of Japanese regulatory authorities that Japan's parent-only financial statements had relatively low international status was reinforced in 1972. Based upon the information disclosed in their consolidated financial statements several U.S. corporations sought listing on the Tokyo Stock Exchange. In May 1973, the Ministry of Finance and the Tokyo Stock Exchange, resisting foreign influences, announced jointly that the exchange would accept

---

[1]Jill McKinnon, "Application of Anglo-American Principles of Consolidation to Corporate Financial Disclosure in Japan," *Abacus*, Vol. 20, No. 1, 1984, pp. 18–19.

[2]Robert J. Ballon, and Iwao Tomita, *The Financial Behavior of Japanese Corporations*, Kodansha International Ltd., 1988, p. 207.

applications for listing by foreign companies only if the applicants disclosed their financial position and results of operations in the form of parent-only financial statements. However, by the end of 1973, this position had been modified and six of these foreign companies obtained listing on the Tokyo Exchange.

The other major stimuli for consolidated reporting was the publicity surrounding the fraudulent bankruptcy of Sanyo Special Steel Company in 1965. This company, under the direction of an aggressive president had grown to the level of a major steel manufacturer. On March 3, 1965, it applied for reorganization under the bankruptcy law. Investigation revealed that the company had created fictitious earnings over the previous six years of about 7 billion yen and paid dividends of 10 percent to 12 percent annually out of the overstated profits. The inflated earnings had been achieved largely through fabricated intercompany sales to subsidiaries and related companies not subject to the Securities Exchange Law. Consequently, these fictitious sales generally went undetected.[3]

Public outcry was overwhelming. Further investigation disclosed that window dressing through this process was rather widespread. Remedies included revising the Certified Public Accountancy Law, strengthening the Japanese Institute of Certified Public Accountants, creating audit corporations, and amending the commercial code.

In October 1976, Ordinance No. 30 was released by the Ministry of Finance. This Ordinance provided that all corporations subject to the Securities Law prepare consolidated financial statements for accounting periods commencing on or after April 1, 1977. These statements must be prepared in accordance with Ordinance No. 28, which provided for the concurrent introduction of consolidation and the equity method of accounting for investments in a manner almost identical with U.S. accounting standards.

The Japanese attempted to be thorough in their implementation of U.S. consolidation practices. In adapting them to their business environment they made only two modifications of consequence and neither changed the substance of U.S. rules. One modification was a provision intended to minimize the number of firms to be included in the consolidated statements. When (a) the total assets of a subsidiary are less than 10 percent of the total assets of the parent company and the other consolidated subsidiaries, and (b) the total sales of the subsidiary is less than 10 percent of the total sales of the parent company and other consolidated subsidiaries, such subsidiaries are excluded from consolidation. No consideration is given to income in meeting the materiality test.

The form in which the parent company may hold shares is the other adaptive modification. Even though the voting shares of a subsidiary are owned personally by a director, an officer of the parent company, or some other related person, the voting power is considered to be held in substance by the parent if it has any responsibilities toward these parties. In other words such shares are included with the shares held directly by the parent company in determining majority ownership.

Japanese companies whose shares are traded on major securities exchanges have had approximately thirteen years of experience in preparing consolidated statements. It is surprising to Americans and other foreign users that these statements have not yet become fully accepted by the Ministry of Finance, the Japanese business community, and the Japanese accounting profession. Parent company-only statements with the investment in affiliated companies carried at cost

---

[3]*Ibid,* p. 169.

are always considered to be the primary statements. Consolidated statements, using the equity method with the 20 percent to 50 percent provision similar to U.S. practice, serve domestically as supplementary schedules only. The Japanese give two explanations for this. First and foremost, they recognize that consolidated accounting procedures often require them to prepare financial reports for unnatural corporate groups. Secondly, they point out the traditional bias of the accounting standards embodied in their commercial code toward the protection of creditors in contrast to providing information for investors. Following is a more complete explanation of the factors which are responsible for the inferior status of consolidated statements in Japan.

EFFECT OF JAPAN'S UNIQUE CULTURE UPON CORPORATE GROUPINGS

Japan has a tradition of teamwork, conformity, and consensus. This became evident as far back as the 17th Century when business activities were organized around the Ie (house and branch houses of the leading merchant families). The Ie was a separate entity, perpetuated by successive family generations whose activities in conducting the house business was guided by a "House Code."

With entrenched ties of family and tradition a smooth transition occurred as the corporate form of organization was introduced to Japan under the German inspired Commercial Code of 1899. Ten large groups of companies (zaibatsu) were formed which dominated economic activity in Japan until the end of World War II.

The power and control the zaibatsu had on Japan was not consistent with the plans the occupation forces had for Japan's future. On October 31, 1945 the fifteen Japanese zaibatsu then existing were ordered by directive of the military occupation to stop the sale, trade, transfer, or adjustment of their corporate shares, bonds, debentures, voting trusts, or other forms of securities. Immediately following, the four major holding companies: Mitsubishi, Mitsui, Yasuda, and Sumitomo, were directed to transfer all securities and ownership of other firms to a Holding Company Liquidation Commission for public distribution. Days later the other zaibatsu shared the same fate.[4]

Securities were issued first to employees of the respective firms, then sold to inhabitants of the areas in which the firms were located, and finally to the public at large. In short order an Antimonopoly Law (1947) prohibiting holding companies was enacted to prevent the reappearance of monopolistic domination of the economy. The Securities Act followed which virtually adopted American accounting standards and practices and provided for the regulation of security trading. From this the Japanese Institute of Certified Public Accountants emerged as an institution for regulating and policing the accounting profession. "Japanese spirit, American techniques," was the expression coined by the Japanese to explain these events.

Many small companies emerged immediately after the economic restructuring but the vast amounts of capital required for reconstruction put banks in the center of the arena. This occurred, also, because Japanese citizens overwhelmingly put their savings in bank deposits. Consequently, business firms looked to commercial banks for capital creation, and the Japanese government was able to seize the opportunity of steering investments by controlling the banks.

---

[4]*Ibid*, p. 57.

With several large banks, each one serving as a focal point, postwar concentration soon emerged as large corporate groupings were again formed. These were not legal or institutional groupings but groupings based upon dependence on a bank, intercompany loans, mutual shareholdings, preferred business transactions, and multiple personal ties throughout the group. This economic phenomenon is somewhat different from the prewar zaibatsu but has the same characteristics in that it involves basically the same groups and a heavy concentration of power. "Keiretsu" is the Japanese term for the postwar form of corporate grouping. This term indicates a grouping or alignment when stockholder control is formally lacking.

Following are the general characteristics of a keiretsu.[5]

1. Members are all "independent" major firms in their own oligopolistic industries.

2. The keiretsu is a confederation of firms excluding competition but aiming at representing all lines within the confederation.

3. Service firms such as banking, trading, insurance and shipping companies from within the keiretsu perform special functions for industrial member firms to the complete exclusion of outsiders.

4. Between the firms there are many cross ties. Examples are borrowing from the same bank, mutual shareholdings, interlocking directors, using the same trademark, or selling their products through the same trading company.

5. The presidents of each member firm meet together once a month and discuss matters of mutual interest to the member corporations. These are backed up with meetings of directors and of upper level managers.

6. Interfirm business within the group has a high priority.

7. Holding companies at the top are prohibited so the relationship between the firms in these groupings is based on cooperation not control as would be the case in the U.S.

There are currently six major groups in Japan of which the first three are considered to be the "big three."

(a) The Mitsui Group

(b) The Mitsubishi Group

(c) The Sumitomo Group

(d) The Fuyo Group (Fuji Bank)

(e) The Daiichi-Kangyo Group

(f) The Sanwa Group

Each of these groups is centered around a bank and includes a trading company, a real estate company, an insurance company, and numerous other companies each performing a special function useful to the group. For example, the Mitsui Group includes the Mitsui Bank, Mitsui and Co. (Trading Co.), The Mitsui Real Estate Company, Toshiba, The Tashio Marine Insurance Company, The Mitsui Life Insurance Co., the Mitsui Chemical Co., et al. Each of these major companies has from a few to hundreds of affiliated firms many with small and others with large intercompany stockholdings. Each also holds a small fraction of the out-

---

[5] *Ibid*, p. 58.

standing voting shares of the other "parent-like" firms in the group. This is not done for control purposes but to create good relationships and stimulate the feeling of interdependence.

It is difficult to determine the size of these corporate groups. They exist as a matter of fact but not as a matter of record. Sales, net income, or asset information is not published on a group basis. However, judging from the information available regarding members, each of these six is as large as a hypothetical group composed of one of the ten largest banks in the United States and from five to fifteen of the thirty largest manufacturing, construction, retail, insurance, transportation, or public utility companies in America.

There are also many groupings of firms other than the giant groups. Members are often as large as U.S. *Fortune* 500 firms. These operate on a similar basis. Examples are the groups identified as the following:

N.E.C.	Toyota
Panasonic-Matsushita	Mazda
Nissan	Suzuki
Sony	Hitachi
Honda	

Each of these has many affiliates and they are sometimes related with the major groups in utilizing trading and financing facilities.

A keiretsu may also be formed on the basis of sharing a raw material, technological equipment, or a market outlet but this is much less common. However, a rather common type of grouping is illustrated in Figure 1. A Co. assembles parts P, Q, X, Y, and Z, and G Co. sells the

FIGURE 1

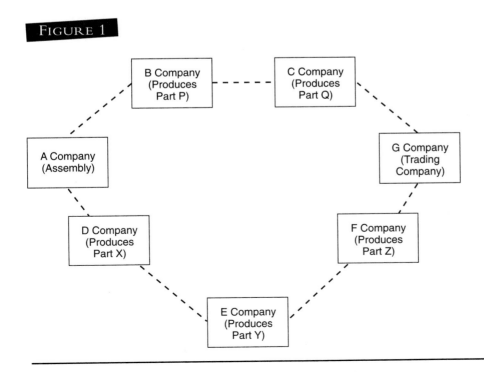

finished product. Each company may own up to 10 percent of each other's voting shares but none has voting control over any of the others. Human ties within the group insure the cohesiveness through intercompany meetings, interlocking directorates, and transfers of personnel.

THE BINDING ELEMENTS WHICH KEEP THE GROUPS TOGETHER

It is difficult for the typical American to understand the forces which bind together on a stable and permanent basis a group of corporations of the type described. If legal control by a parent is not present an American would say a stable group does not exist. However, this is perfectly rational for a person reared in the Japanese culture and tradition. The vital factors in the maintenance of the keiretsu are the generally recognized characteristics of group consciousness (dantai ishiki) and interdependence.

Group consciousness at the personal level is manifested in the tendency of individuals in Japanese society to perceive themselves in terms of their group and to accept and emphasize the interdependence among group members. This is in contrast to individuals in the U.S. who perceive themselves as being separate from one another and of groups as being separate from the individuals comprising them. It is also in contrast to the concept that an individual should be ready to sell his or her personal skills to the highest bidder at any time. In Japan, the orientation is to the group and is reflected in an individual's perception of a permanent and interdependent association with a specific organization.[6]

Similarly, among corporations codes of conduct and standards of behavior associated with interdependent group relationships are based upon mutual loyalty and trust. They are based upon acceptance of internal settlement of disputes and the mutual help and protection of each other's interests. The corporation is perceived as emphasizing the people which it represents not as a legal organization existing in the eyes of the law. Mutual shareholdings, loans, business transactions, and human relationships are the binding forces which hold the keiretsu together.[7]

Power is achieved through group consciousness and the acceptance of interdependence. It provides group members with security through access to finance, raw material supplies, market outlets, insurance, transportation, and above all, group support during periods of adversity. An admitted role of the council of group presidents is the rehabilitation of financially weak or failing corporations within the group. At the same time the obligations to the group and the standards of performance imposed by the interdependent relationships within it are demanding.

The nature of Japan's corporate group associations reflect that nation's cultural and historical interpersonal and intergroup relationships. These corporate related entities deal with each other much in the same manner as we in the United States expect of parent and subsidiary company groups. It is because of this kind of special relationship that we in the U.S. insist upon consolidated reporting. But because Japanese groups are often not connected through legal ownership they are not consolidated. Instead entities with weak relationships are consolidated because they are tied together legally.

---

[6]Frederick D. S. Choi, and Kazuo Hiramatsu, *Accounting and Financial Reporting In Japan,* Van Nostrand Reinhold (UK) Co. Ltd., 1987, p. 20.

[7]McKinnon, *Op. Cit.,* p. 26.

STABLE SHAREHOLDERS

Another feature binding corporate groups is the Japanese practice adopted for protecting corporations from foreign intrusion through stable shareholdings. In order to maintain Japan's unique system of corporate groupings based upon interdependence, the Japanese had to find a way to prevent outside interests from obtaining legal control from time to time by acquiring majority share ownership. This destabilizing threat was averted by systematically swapping shares within the group with a tacit understanding that the shares traded were not to be resold. The objective was to develop a rather permanent cross-holding pattern of share ownership which would exceed 50 percent of the total shares outstanding for each participating corporation.

When the Japanese government liberalized foreign capital entry into Japan, management became concerned about the thin capitalization of many Japanese companies. This seemed to offer too much temptation for takeover by foreign capital. At first, when foreign interests demanded management participation as a condition for transfer of technology, government authorities recommended establishing international joint ventures as the best solution for promoting business cooperation. But vulnerability to take over persisted because of the unrestricted entry of foreign capital compounded by the heavy dependence of Japanese corporations upon debt financing. A better solution was to develop in each firm a large group of stable shareholders who would not allow shares to be acquired by foreign interests planning a takeover.

The announcement in 1969 by General Motors that it intended to buy shares of Isuzu proved to be a strong stimulant for taking action to protect Japanese corporations. An agreement was finally reached to accept up to 35 percent foreign capital participation in Isuzu on the condition that at least 50 percent of Isuzu's shares would be held by stable shareholders. The term, "stable shareholders," was used to indicate Japanese corporate shareholders or individual shareholders of Japanese nationality who could be counted upon to retain their shares regardless of the financial fortunes of the company or offers by foreign interests. The most feasible means of accomplishing the desired objective was for participating companies in each group to protect each other by becoming stable shareholders. If the group was unable to accommodate each individual corporation by holding a sufficient percentage of its shares it became a major duty of financial executives to develop additional relationships and thereby find banks, life insurance companies, suppliers, and other companies also to become stable shareholders.

Consider the Mitsubishi Group as an illustration of the results of this practice.

Each of these companies is a huge parent corporation with numerous subsidiary and affiliated companies. There are also companies other than the twelve giants above which make up the Mitsubishi group. Mitsubishi Bank lists the eleven other companies as being its principal shareholders.[8] Each has a small percentage of the bank corporation's shares but the total number of shares held by these eleven corporations is well over 50 percent of the total shares outstanding. This forms a stable majority in numbers of shares which are not traded and trend to be permanent.

An analysis of the holders of Mitsubishi Co. (trading) voting stock shows the same pattern as does all the other major corporations in the group. Mentally visualize the cross-holding of shares of the Mitsubishi group if eleven more diagrams similar to the one in Figure 2 had been presented. In each diagram a different corporate member of the group would

---

[8]Japan Company Handbook, 1988 (in Japanese).

FIGURE 2

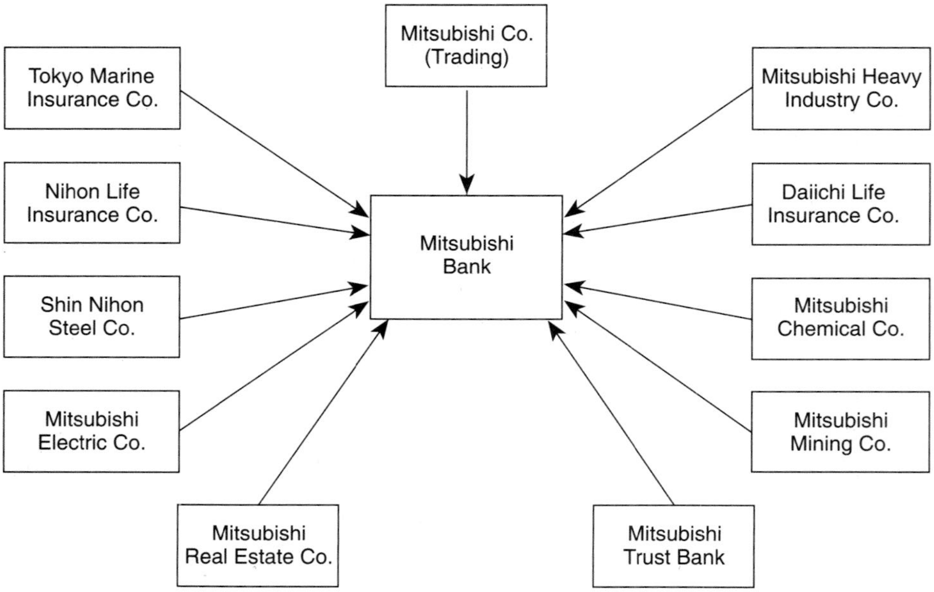

```
                        ┌──────────────┐
                        │ Mitsubishi Co.│
                        │  (Trading)   │
                        └──────────────┘
                               │
                               ▼
┌──────────────┐                              ┌──────────────┐
│ Tokyo Marine │                              │Mitsubishi Heavy│
│Insurance Co. │──────┐              ┌────────│ Industry Co. │
└──────────────┘      ▼              ▼        └──────────────┘
┌──────────────┐   ┌──────────────┐           ┌──────────────┐
│  Nihon Life  │──▶│              │◀──────────│ Daiichi Life │
│Insurance Co. │   │  Mitsubishi  │           │Insurance Co. │
└──────────────┘   │    Bank      │           └──────────────┘
┌──────────────┐   │              │◀──────────┐┌──────────────┐
│  Shin Nihon  │──▶│              │            │ Mitsubishi   │
│  Steel Co.   │   └──────────────┘            │ Chemical Co. │
└──────────────┘                              └──────────────┘
┌──────────────┐                              ┌──────────────┐
│  Mitsubishi  │                              │  Mitsubishi  │
│ Electric Co. │                              │  Mining Co.  │
└──────────────┘                              └──────────────┘
      ┌──────────────┐          ┌──────────────┐
      │  Mitsubishi  │          │  Mitsubishi  │
      │Real Estate Co.│          │ Trust Bank  │
      └──────────────┘          └──────────────┘
```

occupy the center position. Around it would be the other eleven corporations and the percentage shareholdings of each in the featured corporation. In addition many of these companies have similar intercompany stockholding relationships with their subsidiaries and related companies. The stable shareholder concept which now permeates Japanese business practice was brought to light internationally by the press in 1989 when T. Boone Pickens was unable to acquire more than a 26 percent position in Koito Manufacturing Company.

It is estimated that not more than 25 percent to 35 percent of the shares in Japan's large companies are traded regularly on the securities exchanges. The remaining majority are held by stable or semi-permanent shareholders. In contrast, in the U.S. not more than 30 percent of the shares tend to be stable with 70 percent or more regularly traded. This helps to explain why corporate executives in the U.S. must be more concerned with short-term performance of their firms than their counterparts in Japan where a long-term steady earnings growth pattern is the goal.

CONCLUSIONS

Cultural and historical influences provide significant contrasts between corporate group associations and corporate behavior in Japan and the United States. Evidence of these contrasts in Japan are found in the stable ownership of a majority of the shares, the decentralized cross-holding pattern of share ownership, the predominance of small shareholdings, and the importance of non-share ownership criteria as a basis for forming corporate groups. The corporate group associations tend to be maintained by the cultural characteristic of group consciousness with a strong orientation toward interdependence.

The notion of control through direct or indirect majority share ownership and the presence of a holding company or a dominant parent company are foreign concepts to the typical Japanese executive. Share ownership is generally regarded as of minor significance in the forming and maintaining of corporate groups. Consequently, American practices of consolidation tend to group Japanese corporations in a manner contrary to their normal functioning. Such practices tend to break up the complex and dynamic reality of the natural groups into American-type corporate groups attempting to portray an American perspective to something uniquely Japanese.

Consolidated financial statements were introduced in Japan to accommodate the events which intruded upon the perceived adequacy of corporate reporting in Japan during the 1960s and 1970s. Improving the usefulness of corporate disclosure for shareholders, prospective investors, and other users were considerations largely ignored. Instead, the objective was to decrease the opportunity for accounting manipulation among members of corporate groups and to enhance the status of Japanese corporate reporting in the eyes of foreign users. These objectives have been accomplished, but unfortunately, at the expense of creating reporting misfits. Japanese consolidated statements patterned after American standards have survived only because foreign users have been largely unaware of their inappropriate focus and innocent misrepresentation.

Two final conclusions are appropriate from the foregoing. No financial statements yet developed are capable of dealing with the typical Japanese sphere of influence concept of economic interdependence. Parent-company only financial statements do alert readers to the fact that they are seeing only a segment of the financial position and results of operations of the total economic entity. Consolidated statements prepared in such circumstances have the serious weakness of tending to mislead users into believing they are getting a full picture of the group when obviously they are not. Many of the most important firms affecting the future fortunes of the group are not even represented in these statements.

With this in mind, the world's major capital markets might be advised to consider requiring the following in place of or in addition to the consolidated statements presented by Japanese companies:

1. Parent-company only financial statements.

2. Use of the equity method of carrying the investment account for all firms interpreted to be included in a corporate group regardless of the percentage of shares held.

3. A schedule of the amount of income taken up in the income statement from each related company.

4. A listing of all the corporations included in the corporate group both vertical and horizontal, together with the percentage of shares held by each.

5. A listing of all the major shareholders of the company, and the percentage owned by those considered to be stable shareholders.

6. A description of the scope, nature, and extent of interdependence of the group to which the company belongs in its status as a joint-venturer.

7. A description of the scope, nature, and degree of interdependence of the group in which the company is a dominant member, like a parent.

The other conclusion relates to the worldwide efforts to bring about harmonization of accounting practices and reporting. A proliferation of accounting standard setting bodies both private and governmental reacting to different political, economic, social, and cultural factors create diverse, often conflicting, accounting standards throughout the world. This fosters the belief that the information being produced and published by corporations internationally is not capable of being understood by users in countries other than that where it originated.

The IASC has taken a two step approach to overcoming this problem. First, it formulates international accounting standards similar to the manner in which the FASB develops its statements. Then with standards in place it seeks to secure their acceptance on a country by country basis over a period of time. Target dates for compliance in terms of years are advocated.

This study suggests that Japan's experience with consolidated statements pinpoints an unexpected problem associated with the process of harmonizing accounting standards. All nations have their own peculiar cultural features. It is expected that each country will make an effort to harmonize its own financial reporting methods with international reporting standards in order to make its reports more useful to foreign users. But it will do so only as fast as it is able to reconcile these standards with its culture.

In contrast to this, Japan adopted harmonizing consolidated reporting standards without reconciling them with its culture and it attempts to apply these standards meticulously. Consequently, its unique business organizational environment often makes its consolidated financial reports less rather than more useful to readers. The IASC may be advised to give this some attention.

NOT-FOR-PROFIT ACCOUNTING

TOWARDS A FRAMEWORK FOR NOT-FOR-PROFIT ACCOUNTING

Haim Falk

This paper offers a framework for accounting for not-for-profit (NFP) organizations. The framework is tied to theories explaining the NFP phenomenon, the nature of the giving or philanthropic decision, and the type of products or services offered by such organizations. NFPs are clustered into two mutually exclusive categories: club and nonclub organizations; each category may produce public or collective goods or services, private goods or services, or both. Accrual accounting is proposed for clubs, and cash or modified cash systems are proposed for nonclub NFPs.

The paper's purpose is to enhance our understanding of the nature of privately organized NFPs and their related contracts with capital providers. It relates this particular nature

EDITOR'S NOTE: An earlier version of this paper and the discussions by Colin Graham and John Waterhouse were presented at the 1990 CAR Conference, The Role of Information in Organizations and the Economy, held at the University of Waterloo.

This paper was instigated by and builds on Sunder (1987). The author is indebted to Shyam Sunder, George Benston, Alan Macnaughton, Dan Thornton, and Mike Gibbins for extensive guidance and fruitful discussions and to Nick Dopuch, Ramy Elitzur, Paul Dunmore, Khalid Nainar, Jim Heintz, Al Oakie, Bill Scott, and Ron Bossio for useful comments and suggestions. Comments from the participants of accounting research workshops at Indiana University, the University of Alberta, McMaster University, Université Laval, University of Waterloo, and York University also helped to improve previous drafts.

Haim Falk, "Towards a Framework for Not-for-Profit Accounting," *Contemporary Accounting Research,* vol. 8, no. 2, 468–499. Reprinted by permission of Contemporary Accounting Research.

to accounting and reporting consequences. The suggested framework may also lead to a theory to guide NFPs with respect to the choice of their particular accounting and reporting practices. Recent promulgations by the Financial Accounting Standards Board (FASB) in the United States and the Canadian Institute of Chartered Accountants (CICA), prescribe, for NFPs, accounting procedures that fail to recognize the distinct nature of the various privately organized NFP organizations. Since those prescribed procedures are not mandatory for U.S. or Canadian NFPs, the framework in this paper may be helpful to the latter in choosing, and securing adoption of, the accounting and reporting practices that best suit the nature of their contracting setting.

The current state of accounting standards and pronouncements as well as the magnitude of the NFP sector in the U.S. and Canadian economies are discussed in the next section. The third section provides a theoretical analysis explaining the NFP phenomenon. The fourth section discusses the nature of the giving decision as compared with the decision to invest in profit-oriented entities, and the fifth part offers a two-dimensional grouping of NFPs that is consistent with economic theories. The sixth section suggests a framework for accounting by NFPs, and the seventh section discusses the limits and boundaries of that framework. The last section offers concluding remarks.

NFP ACCOUNTING PROMULGATIONS AND MAGNITUDE

STANDARDS AND PRACTICE

In its 1980 Statement of Financial Accounting Concepts, the FASB examined the merit of promulgating accounting standards specifically designed for nonbusiness enterprises (i.e., NFP organizations) and concluded that "it is not necessary to develop an independent conceptual framework for any particular category of entities (e.g., nonbusiness organizations or business enterprises)" (FASB, 1980, par. 1). Although the FASB (1980) statement recognizes some distinguishing characteristics of NFPs when compared to profit-oriented entities,[1] it based its conclusion on the *similarity of transactions* performed by business and NFP organizations (paragraphs 14–17).[2] The statement prescribed, therefore, accrual accounting for NFP organizations (par. 50) and also concluded that "no persuasive evidence [exists] that [accrual accounting is] inappropriate for general purpose external financial reports of governmental units" (par. 66). Consistent with the above conclusion, the FASB requires in its Statement No. 93 (1987) that *all* "not for profit organizations shall recognize the cost of using up the future economic benefits or service potentials of their long-lived tangible assets—depreciation—and shall disclose" the periodic depreciation expense, balance of major asset categories, accumulated de-

---

[1]Those are outlined in par. 6: (a) "significant amount of resources is received from providers who do not expect to receive either repayment or economic benefits proportionate to resources provided," (b) have objectives other than providing goods or services at a profit, (c) absence of defined ownership interest that is transferable or has residual claim.

[2]See also Rose-Ackerman (1986), pp. 8, 9, Table 1.

preciation, and description of the method of depreciation (par. 5), including restatement of prior period financial statements presented on or after the effective date.[3]

Similar to the FASB statement (1980), a CICA study (1980) concluded that both profit and nonprofit organizations have similar financial reporting objectives. Consistent with the recommendations of that study, the CICA issued a 1988 standard requiring that NFP organizations prepare their financial statements "using the accrual basis of accounting" (par. 03). The standard, however, "is not making recommendations for accounting measurement of fixed assets for non-profit organizations" (par. 19) and therefore did not address the issue of whether such assets must be depreciated.

Neither the FASB nor the CICA statements were promulgated in a vacuum with respect to NFP accounting practices. Accounting practices for NFPs have been debated in the U.S. literature since 1912, and various national NFP organizations concerned themselves with reporting by members of their respective industries. Some pronouncements, such as the ones by the American Hospital Association and the United Way of America, recommended accrual accounting, including depreciation for certain assets. Other pronouncements, such as those issued by the Catholic Bishops and the National Committee of the American Council of Higher Education, suggest modified cash accounting and no depreciation. Nevertheless, all pronouncements recommend the application of fund accounting. The nature and description of the various funds, however, differ with the nature of the NFP organization. The Appendix documents the various publications by national NFP organizations.

The American Institute of Certified Public Accountants (AICPA) also developed accounting and audit guides for NFPs that are inconsistent across pronouncements with respect to some accounting policies (e.g., depreciation) and to some extent are also inconsistent with the guides endorsed by the various national NFP organization associations.[4] Further, in 1973 the AICPA's Accounting Standards Division also recommended that universities apply both consolidated financial statements and accrual accounting, including depreciation,[5] neither of which is practiced by most of those institutions (Flesher and Rezaee, 1988).

With respect to accounting practices concerning fixed assets, Harvey and Sorkin (1988, p. 46.11) note:

---

[3] In response to comments on the exposure draft that preceded Statement No. 93, the FASB exempted certain art works or historical treasures from those requirements (par. 6). The original effective date of Statement No. 93 was May 15, 1988. In January 1988, the Governmental Accounting Standard Board issued its Statement No. 8, which states that "no useful purpose will be served by applying the provisions of FASB Statement No. 93 to . . ." government-supported entities (par. 18). This created a jurisdictional dispute that resulted in FASB Statement No. 99 (1988), postponing the effective date to January 1, 1990. On July 20, 1989, the trustees of the Financial Accounting Foundation (which oversees both standard-setting bodies) resolved the FASB—GASB jurisdiction issue by granting the FASB jurisdiction to set the standards for colleges and universities and health care organization but left the option to those organizations supported by the government to elect the GASB as the standard setter for their entities (FASB, 1989a).

[4] AICPA pronouncements include those for hospitals (1972, 1980), universities (1973, 1974, 1974c), health and welfare organizations (1974a), and NFP organizations in general (1979). The latter exempts many assets from depreciation but requires it for others. The inconsistencies among those pronouncements is an issue that was added to the FASB agenda in March 1986 (FASB, 1989a).

[5] The 1973 AICPA guide, *Audits of College and Universities,* however, left the choice of whether to depreciate assets to the reporting entity.

> Accounting for fixed assets has historically been one of the most controversial areas of non-profit accounting. Extensive and conflicting hypotheses have been developed . . . that differ from commercial entities. As a result, every possible combination of accounting techniques is presently in use by one non-profit organization or another.

Similarly, Anthony (1978, ch.2) observed lack of unanimity as to items disclosed by NFPs, and "users' needs and [the items'] relative importance [to them]."

The above description indicates the diversity of accounting procedures and policies in practice by the various types of NFP organizations. It also suggests that NFPs could resort to their national organizations for guidance when necessary. No public cry or demand for FASB pronouncement is documented. It is unclear, therefore, what prompted the FASB to add the accounting by NFPs to its busy agenda. It is also not surprising that the provisions of FASB Statement No. 93 drew much criticism and objection. The FASB received 167 "classifiable letters" in response to its request for comments on the preceding exposure draft; the majority of the letters suggested that "depreciation on substantially all long-lived depreciable assets would not be worthwhile."[6] Further, the FASB received 132 letters in response to the exposure draft that later became FASB Statement No. 99 (which deferred the effective date of FASB Statement No. 93). Some respondents "suggested that the Board use the deferral period as an opportunity to reconsider (and perhaps rescind) Statement 93" (FASB, 1988). The Board, however, refused to do so.

The CICA standard, which may affect *all* Canadian NFPs, is also inconsistent with NFP practice. Beechy (1990) observed that "expensing immediately is the most common method . . . applied to fixed assets" (p. 118), that "some nonprofit organizations use the cash basis of accounting, recording revenues and expenditures only when cash flow occurs" (p. 115), and that "recording and reporting the value of donated goods and services [to NFPs] seems to be the exception rather than the rule" (p. 122). Further, the CICA requirement is also inconsistent with the Canadian Association of University Business Officers (CAUBO) Guide, which Canadian universities followed. The CAUBO Guide states: "Depreciation should not be recorded for plant assets" (par. 100.08).

The adoption of the FASB and CICA requirements by affected NFPs would be costly. Such cost might be justified if the standards were supported by a defensible theory for NFP accounting. Neither of the standards setters offers such a theory, nor is one available in the literature at the present time. Further, as shown below, the magnitude of the NFP phenomenon in the United States and Canada is sufficiently great that an effort towards the establishment of a theoretical framework is justified. This paper is an initial step towards such a framework for privately organized NFPs.

---

[6]Quoted from an October 12, 1989, letter to the Director of Research and Technical Activities of the FASB from John McArthur, Robert Anthony, and 11 professors of the Harvard Business School. See also Mautz (1988) for strong criticism on the FASB's requirements to depreciate assets owned by NFPs. Although Mautz bases his objection on the nature of NFPs versus profit entities, Pallot (1990), using the nature of the asset as criterion, suggests that "community assets" (i.e., public goods) should not be depreciated but that private goods owned by NFPs should be. In response to some of the criticism, the FASB reconsidered its exposure draft and exempted some assets from the depreciation requirement (see footnote 3).

ECONOMIC SIGNIFICANCE

Assessing the number of NFP organizations in the United States or Canada is difficult. Indeed, Hansmann (1980) states: "At present there are no accurate and comprehensive published data on the size and growth of the nonprofit sector." However, Smith, Baldwin, and White (1988) suggest that "there are, in fact, probably 7 to 8 million NFP organizations in the United States today" (p. 1.4) with "approximately 14,000 national voluntary organizations and associations" (p. 1.6). Palmer and Sawhill (quoted by Wing Adler, 1988) assess that "there are more than 300,000 nonprofit organizations in the United States delivering much of this country's education, health care and social services."

Hansmann (1980) assesses that the share of NFP organizations in the national U.S. income "increased by roughly 33 percent in the period 1960–1974" and "The growth of the sector in absolute terms, of course, has been even more dramatic." Further, "Because nonprofits are concentrated in the labor-intensive service industries, the share of total direct employment accounted for by non-profits is even larger than its contribution to [the] GNP" (Hansmann, 1980).

Registration of NFP organizations with the Department of National Revenue in Canada for tax exemption status was initiated in 1966. In 1967 the Department approved 31,373 NFPs. A news article in the *Globe and Mail* (January 8, 1988) reported on 60,000 Canadian-registered charities. Also, "Almost three quarters of all families contribute to some type of charitable organization. On a regional basis, participation ranges from a low of 60% in Quebec to a high of 84% in Atlantic Canada" (Kitchen and Dalton, 1990).

Donation or contribution figures in the form of assets and working hours are not readily available. Turney (1985, p. 193) assesses that in 1980, Canadians volunteered 370 million hours of their time, "a figure equal to 220,000 full time jobs worth at least $1.7 billion to the economy." In addition, local, provincial, and federal governments spent about $16 billion on "humanistic services," much of which was channeled through privately organized NFPs.

This magnitude suggests that reasons for the existence of NFP organizations deserves attention. Gaining understanding in this respect is a necessary step to a theoretical foundation for an accounting framework for NFP organizations.

WHY DO NFPS EXIST?

Three groups of theories or models that attempt to explain collectively the NFP phenomenon are found in the literature. NFPs are said to arise in response to (1) market failure, (2) government failure, or (3) contract failure.

MARKET FAILURE

It is commonly assumed "that markets do arise to allocate all valued goods and services efficiently. In reality, we observe many valued commodities which are not efficiently allocated by markets: . . . basic scientific research, charity and insurance against nuclear attack are examples" (Inman, 1987, p. 653). As demonstrated by Demsetz (1970), efficient allocation of commodities (products and services) depends, inter alia, on the ability of the provider firm to price discriminate between low, middle, and high demanders. With respect to public goods, each consumer has a private incentive to free ride on goods provided; there is no incentive for consumers to reveal their true demand. Inman (1987, pp. 663–672) demonstrates that the free rider problem may also result in noncooperative behavior among providers of public goods. Thus, the inability of a market mechanism to apply price discrimination and enforce cooperative behavior is a major source for its failure to allocate public goods and services efficiently.

Further, as Oakland (1987, p. 486) suggested "A further source of difficulty is encountered if the public good has the property that potential users cannot be costlessly excluded from its services. In the event that exclusion costs are prohibitive, private sellers will be unable to use prices to finance production costs. Instead, the latter will have to be covered by voluntary contributions of users." When public goods are subjected to congestion, and exclusion is not too costly, collective goods and services may be provided by organizations, labeled as clubs, that are NFPs in which utilities of resource providers (patrons) and beneficiaries are interdependent and benefits are restricted to their members (Buchanan, 1965). Clubs, however, are not restricted to public or collective goods. Three additional market failure models, which apply to either private or public-collective goods or both, are advanced in the literature.[7]

The first model suggests that although profit-oriented and NFP organizations are members of similar (or the same) industries, they produce different private goods. For example Ben-Ner (1986) suggests that "when only insufficient information about consumer demand is available" or when for-profit firms "have an incentive to cheat their consumers," the "conflict of interest and its consequences can be eliminated by . . . consumer control of firms as nonprofit organizations." Such an arrangement, it is claimed, "guarantees that consumers will receive the nonprofit organization's surplus—distributed in form of lower prices, larger quantities, or higher qualities . . . and provides incentives for consumer demand revelation and honest treatment of consumers" (p. 109). This type of argument or model applies to clubs that are controlled by consumers of their product(s) and limit the benefits to members (Buchanan, 1965, 1975; McGuire, 1972; Pauly, 1967, 1970). Buchanan (1975) shows that under conditions of producer-customer utility interdependence, a club will be Pareto optimal. Further, a good that is private to some may simultaneously be a public good to others. Certification and or conferring professional designation are examples of such goods. Although a certificate or professional designation is a private good to those who hold it, other members of society can use information about such designation for their own benefit, and no one is excluded from doing so.

The second category of models is best represented by Rose-Ackerman (1981, 1982a, and 1982b), who sees NFPs as a diverse group of firms producing close substitutes to products produced by for-profit firms (e.g., day care, education, health services) but having different markets. Although a for-profit firm will supply the quality/price combination of products that maximizes its profits, NFPs specialize in producing particular predetermined qualities or in serving specific customer groups. An example is NFP hospitals, which have been shown to "provide a broader range of relatively less profitable services, and provide a greater magnitude of uncompensated care than for profit" hospitals, and which provide more services to rural communities than do their profit-oriented counterparts (Fitzgerald and Jacobsen, 1987;

---

[7]For a survey of some of this literature, see Rose-Ackerman (1986).

Coelen, 1986, p. 322; Pattison and Katz, 1983).[8] It is also argued that "in an oligopolistic industry, where individual firms can affect price levels," equilibrium prices might be lower when one or some of the firms are NFP (Rose-Ackerman, 1982b). These types of arguments relate to clubs that work for the benefit of their members. Such arguments are also applicable to more general public-oriented NFPs, such as consumer protection associations and community NFP hospitals, which benefit a large body of persons and do not exclude free riders.

The third category in the market failure models group relates to social contracts and charities. This category differs from those that explain the existence of clubs in that the benefits are not immediately realized and the exclusion of non patrons is not possible. It is argued that the market is incomplete and that NFP organizations fulfill an important role by offering certain social contracts unavailable in the government or profit sectors. For example, "Alumni support their school beyond paying 'their implicit loan,' they take pride in the athletic and scientific accomplishments of their schools, and send their children back to their old schools as a way of continuing an intimate involvement in that community" and of increasing the probability that the school will be available to their children (Krashinsky, 1986).

Whinston (1980, p. 185) discusses charities in the context of social contracts. "People can start from a rich family, yet have their assets dissipated as speculative, risky ventures, ending up in a state that would require transfer payments." He suggests that people contribute to charities when they can to "have it there if we need it." Atkinson (1987) takes the argument further and distinguishes between risk and uncertainty in the context of social contracts. He suggests:

> Fears that there will be widespread recession, or a breakdown of a family support for the aged, are not easily translated into the expected utility calculus. They are sources of uncertainty for which insurance in a narrow sense may be inapplicable. What is required is mutual support of a kind described by the French term "solidarite" or by Beveridge's phrase that "men should stand together with their fellows."

GOVERNMENT FAILURE

In the United States, voluntary NFP agencies predated governmental concern with social problems (Wing Adler, 1988) and voluntary nonprofit organizations provided health care, education, roads and other goods and services "centuries ago before the existence of income taxation" (Weisbrod, 1975). Indeed, as Wing Adler (1988) noted, "It was only natural that [government] turned to the established voluntary agencies" and often subsidized existing agencies

---

[8]See also Weisbrod and Schlesinger (1986) for a model and empirical findings suggesting the NFP organization's product quality, measured in terms of variables indicative of consumers' dissatisfaction, is superior on average to those of profit entities. They concluded that their findings "are consistent with the view that under the conditions of substantial information asymmetry other forms of institutions (i.e., NFP are more 'trustworthy' than is the proprietary form of institution in that they are less likely to take advantage of their informational advantage to the detriment of their customers" (p. 147). Similarly, Hansmann (1980) suggests "that non-profit enterprise is a reasonable response to a particular kind of 'market failure,' specifically the inability to police producers by ordinary contractual devices."

rather than setting up its own.[9] Nevertheless, Kramer (1981, p. 20) observed that until the great depression in the 1930s, government did not play a major role in supporting NFP organizations. Since that time, government welfare expenditures increased but varied extensively over time while private charity contributions and the number of NFP organizations grew significantly.[10]

A similar pattern is observed in Canada. Martin (1975) notes "In the simplistic era of the 1600s and 1700s, education was largely a private matter, greatly assisted by religious organizations" (p. 30), and "many of the earliest [health and welfare services] undertakings were initiated by voluntary organizations" (pp. 31–32). Not until 1914 did the government of Ontario become involved in "the public welfare and social security field" (p. 32), a step followed by the federal government in 1927 (p. 33). Since then, the level of government funding of humanistic services has played a significant role but varies among periods.[11]

Considering that the basic function of government is to establish rule and order,[12] the above evolution is not surprising. Today, however, government is also expected to provide public and some basic private goods (e.g., education) to enhance welfare. Theories concerning government failure relate primarily to the provision of public or collective goods and services. Consequently, although governments may supply private goods and services, the private profit sector could also provide these types of activities. These activities are not considered as pure government activities in this section.

It is argued that government choices reflect the aggregated wishes of individuals and that it is cheaper for government to perform certain activities when compared to individual initiative. However, in a democratic setting, government supplies "a quantity and quality of any commodity that is determined by a political voting process" (Weisbrod, 1975b). Such voting process involves a majority rule that is subject to Hotelling's (1929) median vote theorem, and that may produce intransitive orderings of alternatives that cannot satisfy Arrow's (1963) five

---

[9]Early in the 19th century, the state of California provided subsidies to private institutions that cared for orphans, deaf and blind children, and the mentally handicapped. Similarly, Congress in 1817 granted a piece of land to the American Asylum for the Education and Institution of the Deaf and Dumb, a Hartford, Connecticut, volunteer organization (Kramer, 1981, p. 60). Salamon (1984), who reported on an 1894 study by Amos Warner, suggests that all agencies "serving orphans and the friendless in New York City" received that year "two-thirds of their funding from government sources" (p. 20).

[10]For example, from 1950 to 1970, U.S. federal welfare expenditures increased from $6,181 million (in 1958 dollars) to $17,180 million while private charitable contributions grew from $4,716 million to $10,358 million (Abrams and Schmitz, 1986). In 1980, "The federal government funded projects relevant to NFPs to the level of $150 billion . . . approximately 25 percent of all federal funding" (Salamon, 1984, p. 19). However, by 1985, the Reagan administration reduced government support by 10 to 30 percent using 1980 as a benchmark (Salamon and Abramson, 1985, p. 49).

[11]See Martin (1975), Appendix B.

[12]For a good survey of the related literature, see Ostrom (1984) and Buchanan (1979), who build on Hobbes (1651). In Chapter IX of his book *The Wealth of Nations,* Adam Smith, defines three basic functions for government in a system of natural liberty: (1) protecting society from violence and invasion of other independent societies, (2) protecting every member of society from the injustice or oppression of every other member of it, and (3) erecting and maintaining certain public works and certain public institutions, which can never be for the interest of any individual or small number of individuals, to erect and maintain, because the profit could never repay the expense to any individual or small number of individuals, though it may frequently do much more than repay it to a great society (quoted from Inman, 1987, p. 649).

axioms.[13] The "tendency of majority voting rules to produce dominant outcomes that correspond to the preferences of the median voter" also leads "government or political organizations . . . to 'fail' in certain respects when tested for the satisfaction of idealized criteria for efficiency and equity" (Buchanan, 1979). Thus, "A coercive government with the power to tax and spend is necessary if we are to achieve cooperative allocation. Yet we do not wish our governments to be oppressive" (Inman, 1987). Consequently, if one chooses democracy over efficiency, much of the demand for collective consumption (or public) goods will not be satisfied by governments (Weisbrod, 1975). Further, it has been demonstrated that a majority rule with vote trading may lead to government overspending (Tullock, 1959) and cannot result in Pareto efficiency (Inman, 1987). In contrast, voluntary provisions allow for greater revelation of consumers' preferences, resulting in an outcome that is Pareto superior to the government alone providing public goods (Weisbrod, 1975; Weiss, 1986).

The democratic process does not guarantee that the allocation decisions of government representatives coincide with the preference of those who elected them to office. Politicians are elected to office on the basis of their platform, which addresses a portfolio of issues. Voters support a candidate whose portfolio of issues best reflects their preferences. When such portfolio does not perfectly match these preferences, an NFP organization may emerge to fill the gap. Public sector decision makers also may frequently have personal interests that conflict with either their platform or efficient allocation of public goods, or both. Oakland (1987) observes that:

> Public officials cannot be supposed to ignore their own economic self-interests when formulating policy. They have strong incentives not only to retain their positions but to upgrade them, thereby augmenting their salaries and positions of authority. In part this reflects the quasi-rent characteristics of an occupation— once selected they are difficult to change without the loss of earnings. It also reflects the opportunity . . . to confer rents upon particular constituents.

Further, it is very costly to monitor and difficult to police politicians' votes or behavior. Because elections are held at intervals, politicians cannot be ousted from office on the basis of their voting contrary to their platform or election promises. Allocation of tax money is likely to result in a portfolio of public goods or welfare package, which may not maximize or correspond to individual taxpayers' utilities (Thompson, 1980). One measure open to voters to discipline politicians is to move to another geographical area where their preferences are better satisfied (Tiebout, 1956). Such remedy, however, may be prohibitively costly (Laffont, 1987). It may, therefore, be more efficient for common utility maximizers to combine efforts, by means of a privately organized NFP, to pursue their goals. This, of course, still leaves a role for government in that it may (and does) subsidize NFP organizations whose goals correspond to those of the ruling majority (Niskanen, 1971; Buchanan and Tullock, 1962; Downs, 1957).

Government exercises two major avenues in subsidizing privately organized NFPs: (1) direct subsidy via grants and (2) allocating tax privileges, such as tax exemption status and allowing donors to deduct their donations to preferred NFPs. Both avenues are subject to the above criticism concerning government allocation decisions. However, the tax deduction

---

[13]For a more extensive discussion on these points, see Mueller (1976), Inman (1987), Sen (1970), and Fishburn (1973). The two latter papers survey the median voter theorem literature.

privilege allows donors to make their own choice of public good and are less costly to government when compared to direct subsidy.[14] Research examining whether the tax deduction provision affects the level of donations reports mixed results. Although Toolson (1989), Hood, Marin, and Osberg (1977), Glenday, Gupta, and Pawlok (1986), and Kitchen and Delton (1990), among others, suggest that donors' behavior is responsive to the after-tax price of donation, Broman (1989) and Martin (1975, p. 85) report findings suggesting that giving habits are not correlated with current tax rate or tax deduction status.[15]

Inman (1987) examines the extensive findings related to government efficiency and concludes that "neither the institution of markets, or voluntary trading, nor the institution of government, or collectively decided and enforced trading, stands as *the* unarguable preferred means for allocating societal resources." Government failure gives rise to the formation of clubs, such as community parks or libraries, which may benefit members of particular geographic concentrations and exclude others. It also gives rise to other NFPs, such as charities, in which the utilities of patrons and beneficiaries are not interdependent.

CONTRACT FAILURE

Quantities and qualities of both inputs and outputs of public or common goods are difficult and costly to assess and monitor. Inman (1987), quoting Holstrom (1984), suggests that in situations of incomplete or asymmetric information, when effort or care on the part of the producer "cannot be monitored, the incentive for sellers is to underprovide quality, even though consumers would pay for better product." Consequently, trust plays a major role in such instances. NFP organizations have no distributable surplus and are prevented from engaging in management incentive schemes that call for sharing periodic surpluses. Indeed, management receives a fixed predetermined reward. Such an arrangement, it is argued, leaves management little incentive to conceal truth, misallocate funds, or distort information (Weisbrod, 1980; Easley and O'Hara, 1986; Pauly, 1980). Further, because no dividends can be distributed, controlling parties have no incentive to underspend. NFPs, therefore, are more trustworthy to donors or resource providers (Weisbrod, 1980). Further, if an efficient market for managers of NFPs exists, it will further induce truthful reporting and operational efficiency. Consequently, NFPs are preferred over profit-oriented organizations as producers of public or collective goods. They are also preferred as producers of private goods and services when quality and mixture of goods play a significant role and patrons do not control the organization's operation. Examples of the latter are charities designed to help the poor or the needy, such as soup kitchens or shelters for the homeless.

In sum, although privately organized NFPs predated government involvement in offering social and humanistic services and in providing many types of public or collective goods, it is the failure of governments and markets to efficiently allocate such goods that led to the NFP phenomenon as we know it today. Further, contract failure, where trust plays a major

---

[14]Annual tax deductible donations in Canada increased from $61 million in 1946 to $270 million in 1970. They were first allowed in 1917 and, except for 1920–1929, this practice has been followed ever since (Martin, 1975, p. 40). In the United States the deduction of donations was first allowed in 1917 and has been in effect ever since (Toolson, 1989).

[15]Indeed, NFP organizations, such as Greenpeace, which do not enjoy tax deduction status for their donors, claim to be little affected by such disadvantage.

role in the production and allocation process, and the incompleteness of the market and its failure to allocate some private goods efficiently contributed to the increasing number of NFPs (e.g., charities) and the variety of their activities.

These differences in the allocation mechanism also affect the nature of resource allocation decisions by individuals (and corporations). Specifically, the nature of the decision to pay or not to pay taxes differs from that of the investment decision and both differ from the giving or donating decision. Government has the power to impose tax and make disobedience prohibitively costly. Neither market nor privately organized NFPs can resort to such measure to raise money or resources for their objectives. Although this introduces a commonality between the market-type investment and NFP-type giving decisions, the two decisions also differ in some important respects. Some additional similarities and differences between the two decision types are discussed next.

THE GIVING DECISION

Like profit organizations, NFPs differ one from another with respect to the products and services they offer. NFPs compete for scarce resources with other NFPs and profit organizations. The choice among investment objects (e.g., profit organizations) is left to (potential) investors, and the choice among competing NFPs is left to (potential) donors or members. Both the investment[16] and giving decisions are aimed at maximizing the investor's or donors' utility.[17] Further, like investors who consider alternative uses for their money, "Individuals who derive consumption benefits from enhancing the community or contributing to the well-being of others would . . . still be weighing such consumption benefits against alternative uses of time and money" and "an individual would be expected to join a private voluntary organization as long as the value of perceived benefits exceeded the opportunity costs" (Ulbrich and Wallace, 1989).

The two decisions, however, differ in many respects. All investment options offer pecuniary returns, and the utility for such returns is normally independent of the source or activity that produces it (e.g., oil and gas firms, financial institutions, real estate).[18] Investors can form portfolios and choose desired investment options on the basis of their ex ante risk-return preferences. Exchange prices for residual ownership claims are necessary for the formation of efficient investment sets.

In contrast, ownership in NFPs is not negotiable, nor are there residual claims. Resource providers derive different utilities for the various NFP goals and activities (e.g., soup kitchen for the poor versus cancer research), which are difficult to aggregate[19] and do not have a common denominator. This fact makes it impossible to form a frontier of NFP giving options and

---

[16]The term *investment* in the context of this analysis refers to resources spent on the acquisition of ownership and residual claims.

[17]Throughout the analysis, it is assumed that the donors or club members are utility maximizers.

[18]Some investors may restrict their investments to, say, socially responsible firms or to those that do not contradict their ideological views. This, however, does not detract from the general nature of the difference between the giving and investment decisions. Further, within each subset of firms, the investor is indifferent between the sources of expected risk-adjusted return.

[19]See Harsanyi (1955) for a model for the aggregation of individual utilities. This model is quite weak because no practical way is offered to determine the weight for each utility (Mueller, 1976).

efficient portfolios. It is not surprising, therefore, that although profit-oriented firms may seek diversification, NFPs specialize in activities that are designed to meet a limited number of well-defined goals. We do not, for example, observe NFP conglomerates and, as Smith (1988) suggests, "the greater the focus of a nonprofit organization on the more distinctive and characteristic functions . . . the greater its own chances of surviving and being effective on the long run" (p. 211).[20] The nature of NFP organizations helps donors and patrons match their preferences with corresponding NFPs. However, because of the vast number of NFPs in the economy, it may be prohibitively costly for donors to engage in a one-by-one matching procedure. This might explain the attempt, found in the literature, to cluster NFPs into relatively homogeneous groups. These groupings are discussed next.

NFP GROUPING

The literature offers several definitions of NFP organizations,[21] and various classifications of such organizations are utilized in practice and referred to in the literature. For example, Form 1023 of the U.S. Internal Revenue Service lists 366 NFP activities grouped in 22 categories. Smith et al. (1988) offer a different typology of NFP organizations with 18 "principal categories." The annual *Donor's Guide to Fund Raising Organizations in Canada* lists approximately 4,500 charities classified into eight major categories, each of which is further divided into various subcategories. The latter classification differs from that of the IRS and the Smith et al. (1988) grouping. Smith (1988) offers yet another classification of NFPs based on their positive and negative impacts on society. Other writers such as Hansmann (1980), Martin (1975), Weisbrod (1975b, 1980), Weiss (1981), and Pauly (1980) distinguish between NFP organizations on the basis of the types of service they provide. Although these classifications might be useful in facilitating donation decisions, they are of little help in explaining the observed differences in accounting practices between profit and NFP organizations.

---

[20]Nevertheless, we observe organizations such as the United Way that allocate gifts to charities engaging in a variety of activities and various goals. It is the policy of the United Way, however, to allow donors to restrict their contributions to particular member organizations. When such option is exercised, it may be argued that the United Way is "providing a low 'cost' ideological homogeneous package of charities" (Rose-Ackerman, 1980). Many donors may not use such options. In such cases, a contribution to the United Way may be viewed as a donation portfolio. Three explanations are offered for this phenomenon: (1) The United Way primarily serves geographically defined communities and as such increases the quality of life in the donor's neighbourhood. National corporate donors are willing to contribute to the United Way because of both the national and regional exposure and recognition that comes with such donations (Martin, 1975, p. 127). (2) The United Way performs a monitoring function that is costly for individual donors. The latter are, therefore, willing to compromise their utility preferences in exchange for the high probability that the supported organizations are honest and efficient. (3) The United Way's function reduces collective fund-raising cost. Because increase in fund-raising cost is disliked by donors, they are willing to compromise their ideological preferences in return for higher efficiency in fundraising (Feldstein, 1975; Feldstein and Clotfelter, 1976; and Feldstein and Taylor, 1976).

[21]For example, Smith (1988) suggests that NFP organizations refer "to all those persons, groups, roles, organizations and institutions in society whose goals involve primarily voluntary actions." Similarly, Smith, Baldwin, and White (1988) propose that NFPs "are simply the collective forms of individual voluntary action" and that they are the vehicles used by people to "pursue together goals that are not primarily renumerative and that they are not forced to pursue." In contrast, Hansmann (1980) characterizes NFP organizations as those "barred from distributing [their] net earnings, if any, to individuals who exercise control over [them], such as members, officers, directors or trustees." Other researchers such as Strnad (1986) emphasize the tax exemption status as a major characteristic of NFP organizations.

Indeed, we observe that both profit and NFP organizations provide similar goods and services and coexist in the same industries (see Rose-Ackerman, 1986, Table 1; and Weisbrod and Schlesinger, 1986), but the two types of organizations differ with respect to their accounting practices. Similarly, Anthony (1978, pp. 9–10) and the FASB (1980) suggest a grouping that fails to explain the observed differences in accounting. They distinguish between two groups of NFPs based on the source of their resources: those that "obtain their financial resources . . . from revenues realized from selling goods or rendering services" and those that obtain their resources "from sources other than the sale of goods and services." This dichotomy does not provide for mutually exclusive categories. More importantly, it is possible to group profit organizations in the same manner. Indeed, the FASB (1980) concluded that business (profit) and nonbusiness (NFP) organizations should be subject to the same accounting standards. It failed to address the *differences* in observed practices.

Some economists categorize NFPs by the type of control (ownership) and beneficiaries.[22] NFPs are categorized as those for which the utilities of patrons and beneficiaries are interdependent (clubs)[23] and those for which such utilities are not interdependent (e.g., charities). In addition, distinction is made between NFPs that provide collective goods or services and those that supply private goods and services. This leads to a two-dimensional classification that is consistent with the theories or models explaining the privately organized NFP phenomenon as discussed in the third section. This two-dimensional classification is also helpful in differentiating profit from NFP organizations. The control (ownership) beneficiary criterion will be discussed first, followed by an analysis of product or services criterion.

Figure 1 illustrates the above two-dimensional NFP grouping. Two common characteristics are shared by all NFPs in Figure 1: (1) absence of indicia of ownership that give owners or resource providers a simultaneous share in both profits and control[24] and (2) no intentional surplus from "operation."[25] These characteristics translate into nonnegotiability of ownership and absence of residual claims. Those characteristics also deserve special attention in the context of accounting, monitoring, and control. Karpoff and Rice (1989) provide empirical evidence supporting the claim that "when shares [in profit organizations] can be transferred, the endogenous adjustment of ownership structure and the information summarized in market prices are important in encouraging superior firm performance" (p. 70).[26]

---

[22]For example, Hansmann (1980), Thompson (1980), and Sunder (1987).

[23]There are two aspects to the utility interdependence characteristic: (1) owners–users' utility interdependence and (2) utility interdependence among users. The former determines club membership composition and the latter may affect the club's optimal size. In a club that provides facilities subject to congestion (e.g., swimming pool), the net utility of each user increases to a point because additional membership results in reduction of average cost. However, when the marginal disutility outweighs the marginal reduction in cost due to congestion, the net utility is diminishing. This, in turn, affects the optimal size of the club.

[24]See Hansmann (1980) on this point. Also as Vatter (1979) noted: "The business firm is motivated by the hope of augmenting its capital to produce growth from profits, the typical non-business organizations has no such motivation, because its capital (indeed, practically all its inflows except service charges) is supplied by asking for it . . ." (p. 575).

[25]See Ginzberg, Hiestand, and Ruebens (1965) for extensive discussion of this characteristic.

[26]See also Brickley, Bhagat, and Lease (1985).

FIGURE 1

NFP Organizations

Utilities of patrons and beneficiaries are:	Interdependent (clubs)	Not interdependent (nonclubs)
Producers of collective goods or services	a	b
Producers of private goods or services	c	d

Examples for NFP organizations in cells:

a   community park restricted to neighborhood residents

b   environmental society

c   employee union-owned cafeteria restricted to union members

d   soup kitchen

Further, it has been suggested that "well organized markets for ownership and residual claims are the most important single control mechanism affecting managerial behavior" (Jensen and Meckling, 1979, p. 485) and "the most powerful check on agency costs" (Easterbrook and Fischel, 1981, p. 1196). Karpoff and Rice (1989) also suggest that diffusely held profit-seeking firms whose shareholders are prohibited from transferring their claims are characterized by poor managerial monitoring and economic performance and that the absence of a market mechanism is the most likely cause for this poor performance. In contrast, external monitoring services for traded firms are provided by security analysts, investors, take-over threats, and information production agencies. "Managers' and shareholders' interests could be better aligned through compensation contracts based on market value" (Karpoff and Rice, 1989, p. 100). Such mechanisms are not available for NFP organizations and, as discussed below, this also affects the characteristics of their (optimal) accounting and control systems.

With respect to the ownership/beneficiaries criterion, Figure 1 distinguishes between clubs (cells a and c) and nonclubs (cells b and d). "Voluntary groups form because individuals realize a congruence of interests in a particular activity, but individuals are always free to leave the group at any time" (Inman, 1987). Although this statement applies to both clubs and nonclubs, the former are said to be more efficient in allocating collective goods when their size is relatively small (Mueller, 1976).[27] Other major characteristics of clubs are that (1) the utilities of resource providers (patrons) and beneficiaries are interdependent, (2) benefits are normally restricted to membership and exclusion from benefits of collective goods is possible, (3) clubs are normally controlled by membership through elected representatives (board of directors),

---

[27]See also footnote 23. For further discussion of the relationship between group size and the provision of collective goods, see also Olson (1965) and Chamberlain (1974).

(4) the addition (exit) of a new (present) member lowers (increases) the average cost of a good, and (5) membership has relatively homogeneous tastes.[28] Examples of clubs are faculty clubs and professional organizations.

The NFP organizations in cells b and d in Figure 1 are those in which the utilities of patrons and beneficiaries are not necessarily interdependent.[29] They also are similar to Hansmann's (1980) "entrepreneurial" NFPs, which "are largely free from exercise of formal control by their patrons" and are usually controlled by a self-perpetuating board of directors. Such organizations provide their products or services for free (or below cost), resulting in an unreciprocated outflow that is balanced by resources received via unreciprocated contributions (Sunder, 1987). Examples are soup kitchens or food banks for the poor and environmental societies (such as Greenpeace).

Clubs and nonclubs are distinguished in Figure 1 with respect to whether they provide public or collective goods or services (cells a and b) or private goods and services (cells c and d). The nature of the former is discussed in the third section above. As Sunder (1987) notes, "Some goods are public to small groups (e.g., a golf partnership or a family) while others are public to larger groups such as a state or a country." Consequently, I prefer the term *collective goods or services,* indicating that benefits are designed for certain defined groups such as club members, the poor, or residents of certain geographical areas.

Both profit and NFP organizations produce and allocate private goods and services. The preceding discussion of market failure suggests that the two types of organizations differ with respect to the quality and price at which the private goods are produced and distributed, and the markets in which they are allocated. Further, club and nonclub NFPs also allocate their private goods in different markets. However, the major characteristics of a private good or service are that it has an identifiable unit cost and quality mix and that exclusion of others from benefiting from it is possible.

The grouping in Figure 1 and the related characteristics of the respective NFP organizations serve as the basis for the development of a framework for NFP accounting as discussed in the next section.

ACCOUNTING FRAMEWORK

Figure 1 treats the four types of NFP organizations as if they were mutually exclusive. In reality, NFP organizations seldom fall exclusively into one cell or another. A church or synagogue that conducts services and offers sermons only is an example for a cell b organization; a religious facility that specializes exclusively in wedding or funeral services is an example of a cell d organization. However, we normally observe religious organizations that specialize in both types of services and therefore may be viewed as two combined entities. Similarly, a professional organization that provides seminars (cell a) and educational material (cell c) can be viewed as an entity with two distinct units. The same logic is applied to a cell c organization

---

[28]See McPherson and Smith-Lovin (1987) and Ulbrich and Wallace (1989) for empirical findings related to social and economic factors associated with homogeneity of various type club membership.

[29]Hochman and Rodgers (1969) suggest, for example, that transfer of income from rich to poor may increase the utility of both. Such utility interdependence, however, is not a necessary characteristic for cells b and d organizations.

that provides certification services to its members. Such certification information, as discussed above, is also a public good (cell b) in that it may be useful to others in making their hiring selection decisions.

Indeed, as Stigler (1971) demonstrates, certification results in the increase of income to certified individuals. Atkinson (1987) concluded that, in the context of charity giving, the income to some contributors is a collective good to others (see also Arrow, 1981, p. 287). Similarly, a community park (cell a) that is a collective good may affect the (private) value of neighboring dwellings or the quality of its inhabitants' lives. Further, when entry to a community or public park is subject to an entry fee, the good supplied is a combination of collective and private good, which then can be rationed by imposing differential user rates (e.g., adults versus minors). In effect, there are very few pure public goods or services. Most goods can be arranged on a continuum between pure public and pure private, and many NFPs can be placed on a continuum between pure clubs and pure nonclubs (charities). For the purpose of this paper, however, it is convenient to examine the properties and their related accounting implications of each cell in Figure 1 separately. An organization that falls into two cells or more or that may be placed on a continuum between them may be viewed as a combination of entities that share some common accounting practices but differ with respect to others.

Sunder (1987) analyzes the characteristics that distinguish public from private goods and services and lists the unique characteristics that are associated with each goods category. Those characteristics can be attributed to the NFP organizations in the various cells. Properties of organizations in cells a and c (clubs) are discussed first.

Cell a:

1   Services are restricted to members of the club for a periodic fee.
2   The club is governed by members via a representative board.
3   It has no per unit production cost.
4   Production input and output are difficult to monitor and control and, therefore, activities and related expenditures are determined by the board.
5   No member is excluded from benefits.

Cell c: Characteristics (1) and (2) of cell a organizations also apply to NFPs in cell c. Entities in this cell, however, differ from cell a organizations in that:

3   They produce goods with identifiable per unit production cost.
4   The production mix, cost, and quality are less difficult to control, and, therefore, are determined by the manager under the board's guidelines.
5   Individual members exercise control on the product, can monitor its quality, and may exclude others.

Membership in both a and c NFPs is restricted to those who contribute resources. A member who is not satisfied may withhold dues by not renewing membership. Others who wish and who are qualified may join and contribute dues. Such an arrangement amounts to transfer of ownership.[30] A member who chooses to renew membership for an additional period or a new member buys ownership for the paid period and, during *this* period, is respon-

---

[30]In some clubs, members' entry and exit are also associated with initiation fees from new members or payments to the exiting member. Such an arrangement is similar to trade in ownership shares.

sible with other members for the club's liabilities and asset maintenance. Accrual accounting can play a role in matching expenditure with periodic benefits and obligations. A depreciation procedure that determines the proportion of assets consumed and the proportion available for future periods and a method that determines the assets and liabilities that have been accumulated in each period seem appropriate under such circumstances.

Another similarity between the organizations in cells a and c is that both are governed by membership via a representative board. This is an important characteristic that increases the probability that utilities shared by all members will be satisfied. Consequently, it is desirable that the board design policies to ensure that the shared utility of members be maximized. Further, as observed by Weisbrod (1980), Easley and O'Hara (1986), and Pauly (1970), managers of NFPs receive a fixed predetermined reward. Such arrangements are also a condition for the organization being granted a tax exempt status.[31] Because no incentive risk/surplus sharing scheme for management is possible, the probability exists that, in the absence of board supervision and control, managers will opt for greater than optimal level of production when such action enhances their power or importance. In contrast, if greater production means only more work for management, it may opt to reduce production below the optimal level. Consequently, tight control by the board is desirable. The optimal extent of such desired control, however, differs between type a and type c organizations.

In both type a and type c organizations, the mix of products and their quality must satisfy the members. Therefore, the representative board must exercise an overseeing function over management. Tighter control must be exercised in type a organizations than in type c because no per unit cost is identifiable. Further, because the detailed production input is not observable by membership, tight monitoring measures by the board are necessary to enhance compliance with members' wishes and preferences. Such monitoring devices may include itemized budgets and the requirement of preexpenditure authorization. By having management (or the board) report on each type of collective good or service individually (fund accounting), patrons' giving decisions are better facilitated since patrons are able to rank the collective good or service the organization produces and compare it with their own preference scale. The better the match, the higher the probability that patrons will continue their support.

Thus, detailed fund accounting in such organizations may enhance patrons' giving and increase the probability of the organization's long-term survival. Because NFP organizations compete for funds (patrons), it is in the best interest of NFPs to provide a cost-efficient, detailed report to patrons. Patrons are likely to select those organizations that demonstrate the highest probability of maximizing their specific utility or utilities (see Martin, 1975, pp. 50, 55, and 67 for survey results supporting this argument). Such a detailed reporting system is necessary because of the absence of a market price mechanism and the scarcity of information produced by agencies other than the particular NFP organization.

Indeed, detailed fund accounting systems are observed in economies that do not enjoy efficient markets for ownership and residual claims, such as the People's Republic of China and the former Soviet Union.[32] Most enterprises in such countries are state owned and are subject

---

[31]In Canada, however, it is possible for tax-exempt noncharities to design incentive plans for management. Such plans normally relate to efficiency in fund-raising and increase in membership, such as automobile clubs.

[32]For a detailed description of the accounting systems in the People's Republic of China, see Coopers and Lybrand (1987).

to uniform detailed prespecified fund accounting with preauthorization requirements for certain expenditures and interfund balance transfers. Further, enterprises are required to report certain nonfinancial information in their periodic statements to allow for monitoring their activities and to ensure that the enterprise indeed fulfills the objectives (e.g., ideology) of the state sponsor. Such detailed reporting applies also to NFPs.

Note that consolidated funds reporting does not serve a purpose in this context. Nevertheless, a consolidated financial statement may reflect the magnitude of the organization's activities and assets. Such a statement may be useful for lending decisions in which collateral plays a role. Thus, it may be useful for organizations that borrow heavily to provide statements that consolidate unrestricted assets and activities.

In contrast to type a organizations, entities in cell c have identifiable per unit costs. It is sufficient, therefore, that the board of such organizations determine the production mix, quality, and cost per unit and that no itemized budgets and preexpenditure authorization are necessary. Product quality of type c organizations is more readily observable than that of type a by members and users. Consequently, in clubs where members are charged a price for each private good, they can vote with their dollars by refraining from buying an unsuitable product, to discipline management.[33]

However, since patrons may have different uses for different goods, products, or services, and because the production of such goods depends on common cost (and possible subsidy from a general membership fee), it would be advisable to report the cost of each good (relevant allocated common cost, product-specific cost, subsidy, inventory, etc.) individually and to segregate the various products by identifiable fund accounts. This increases patrons' monitoring ability and helps to facilitate use-related choices.

As is the case with type a organizations, in the context of the giving or membership decision, little can be gained by combining the individual product-type costs. Nevertheless, the aggregate of such costs and activities may serve as a surrogate for size and activity level. Such surrogate measure may be of interest to lenders when they consider credit decisions.

As discussed above, we rarely observe clubs that fall exclusively into cells a or c. Further, we may observe type c components of NFP clubs that are not restricted to membership and that charge a per product price to members and nonmembers (e.g., a faculty club restaurant that sells meals to nonmembers). Because such private goods are sold at cost or above, and since increase in production reduces average cost per product, selling such goods to nonmembers results in either a subsidy of type a operations or a reduction of membership fees.

Such combined operations are similar to profit organizations in that club members have a residual claim—profits (losses) that reduce (increase) their fees—and affect the magnitude of their periodic contributions to the club. In essence, members must contribute only the difference between the total cost of the operation and the revenues from selling products to outsiders. Because this arrangement is similar to a profit organization with unlimited liability, combined a and c NFPs should also be subject to accounting rules that govern profit-oriented entities.

In sum, both types a and c organizations are designed to serve their members. However, membership composition may vary from period to period. New members (and renewing members) buy *periodic* benefits and share the related costs and risks. This calls for accrual

---

[33]To use this as a sole control device, however, may be costly because any deficit must be covered by membership.

accounting to match costs and changes in assets and liabilities with periods and, in type c organizations, with products. Depreciation is part of the periodic cost that must be attributed to membership in current and future periods.[34]

Type a associations must exercise tight control on management in the form of itemized budgets and fund accounting with preexpenditure authorization; type c associations itemize budgets but do not require preexpenditure authorization. Detailed fund accounting is necessary in both types to enhance membership's giving, joining, or existing decision. Although consolidated fund statements are unlikely to play a role in members' considerations, clubs that rely heavily on borrowing may benefit by providing lenders with such statements.

NONCLUBS

Nonclub NFP organizations are those in cells b and d in Figure 1. NFP organizations in cells b and a share two related characteristics: they have no per unit production cost and their production inputs are not mutually observable by management and patrons. Therefore, their activities and related expenditure levels must be predetermined by the board. Those activities must match donor's utilities if the organization is to survive. These characteristics call for itemized budgetary control by the board, preexpenditure authorization, and fund accounting. The need for fund accounting in type b organizations may be even more pronounced when compared to type a clubs because donors commonly specify particular restrictions or purposes for the use of their donations. Each such donor may expect a detailed report specifying how funds were spent. This also applies to fund-raising campaigns for specific purposes (e.g., Christmas parties for sick children). Further, donors may utilize detailed fund accounting information when making their giving decisions.

Type b organizations differ from those of type a in that resource providers' (donors') and beneficiaries' (donees') utilities are not necessarily interdependent. There is no formal membership in the organization and benefits are offered to all eligible beneficiaries with no exclusion. Further, there are no reciprocal contributions, and most patrons (donors) do not exercise formal control over the operation. No economic return is expected by patrons either in monetary terms or in the form of goods or services. Donors share neither assets nor surpluses nor deficits and are not responsible for liabilities. Consequently, accrual accounting has no role to play in this context; a cash accounting system suffices.

Accrual accounting, depreciation included, might be useful in the assessment of risk by lenders or suppliers (FASB, 1980). However, because nonclub NFP organizations are not expected to have an intentional surplus or ownership capital, risk assessment is largely based on expected cash inflows from donations versus the entity's obligations. Expected donations, even those pledged, are normally not enforceable. Indeed Adams, Bossio, and Rohan (1989) report that most NFPs or charities do not record them. Other receivables are minimal in type b operations because no price (or only minimal *cash* price such as for entry tickets to parks) is attached to the use of, or benefit from, the goods or services. Thus, the risk to suppliers (accounts payable) and other creditors is largely affected by the value of salable assets and cash reserves. The latter is reflected in cash accounting; the former can be assessed independently.

---

[34]However, historical cost-based depreciation does not necessarily indicate assets' value. Indeed, McArthur et al. in their October 12, 1989, letter to the FASB research director (see footnote 6) suggested that "the leading bond rating agencies have stated that they will pay no attention to the depreciation number."

Type d NFPs are similar to those in cell c in that their products have an identifiable cost per unit and beneficiaries have control of the product as well as the ability to exclude others. Although the mix of products and their quality must match contributors' tastes, it is not necessary to impose tight preexpenditure authorization or control because the cost is determined by the mix of products and quality. Further, when beneficiaries' needs can be satisfied by competing or alternative arrangements or sources, or when beneficiaries are expected to pay for a good or service, they can refrain from using or buying those goods or services. For example, some homeless people may prefer to seek shelter on the streets rather than move into a house shelter. If donors are displeased with this choice, they may discipline management by witholding resources from the organization. Thus, it is not necessary to have a budget that itemizes each ingredient of a specific good or activity. A budget for specific activities or of production goods and board supervision by determining the mix of production and its quality will suffice.

As is the case with type b NFPs, detailed unconsolidated fund accounting and expenditure reports specific to each product type and group of beneficiaries are necessary for type d entities. Such reporting systems should be useful for enhancing patrons' giving decisions. Further, as the organizations in cells b and d share the same patrons-management-beneficiaries relationship, a cash accounting system is appropriate. However, because the production or provision of private goods may be associated with a large number of accounts payable, a modified cash system may be justifiable in type d organizations for control purposes.

As is the case with clubs, we also rarely observe nonclub NFPs specializing in either collective *or* private goods or services. Further, it is possible that type d units are also operated to produce profits (e.g., a gift shop in a NFP hospital). By definition of NFP, such profits must be used to subsidize other activities, the costs of which are ultimately balanced by donations. That is, an NFP profit-making unit (b) can operate only in conjunction with a money-absorbing unit (b). Otherwise, the organization will produce intended profit and become disqualified as an NFP. No residual or ownership claims exist on such profits or profitable production units and, in contrast to clubs, membership dues or fees do not exist and are not affected. Consequently, accrual accounting is not useful for type b and d combined organizations.

In sum, cash accounting is appropriate for nonclub NFP organizations. For units engaged in extensive production or provision of private goods, a modified cash accounting system may be justified for control purposes. Because most patrons are not involved directly or indirectly in the governance of such organizations, and because the long-run survival of such NFPs depends on their ability to maximize patrons' utilities, it is imperative that they apply detailed fund accounting and reporting. This is especially so because donors depend almost solely on the organization for information. Because no market price mechanism is available to assess the monetary value of the products or services and practically no known private agency produces information about the organizations' performance, detailed nonconsolidated fund accounting and reporting play a major role in the giving decision. Consolidated funds statements might, however, be useful for NFP organizations that rely heavily on lenders or creditors.

The framework suggested above is summarized in Table 1. Accrual accounting is relevant to clubs; other NFPs are better served with cash or modified cash accounting. Fund accounting is recommended for all four types of NFP organizations. Itemized budgets and preauthorization of expenditures are appropriate for those units that produce collective goods or services. Predetermined product mix and quality are sufficient control devices for units that produce private goods or services.

TABLE 1

Accounting Framework

Product	Organization	
	Clubs	Nonclubs
Collective	(a) fund accounting itemized line budget preauthorized expenditure	(b) fund accounting itemized line budget preauthorized expenditure
Private	(c) fund accounting predetermined mix and quality	(c) fund accounting predetermined mix and quality
Financial accounting	accrual	cash or modified cash

As is the case with Figure 1, the cells in Table 1 represent the extreme locations on two continuums. NFPs can be arranged on a horizontal continuum by the degree to which the utilities of patrons and beneficiaries are interdependent. Similarly, NFP organizations can be arranged on a vertical continuum according to the degree to which their products or services are pure public, impure public, or pure private. An example of an NFP that is at an interior point on both continuums is an art gallery with open-ended membership that charges an entrance fee for nonmembers. The accounting and control system must correspond to the nature of the NFP and its location on the continuums. The closer the NFP is to the left (right)-hand extreme of the horizontal continuum, the more complete (pure) its accrual (cash)-based accounting system.[35] The closer the products or services to being pure private, the lesser the control in terms of itemized line budgets and preauthorized expenditure procedures.

LIMITATIONS AND BOUNDARIES

The framework proposed above focuses on information items that are monetary in nature. A financial accounting framework cannot satisfy all information requirements. Nonmonetary and supplementary information indicative of the efficiency and effectiveness of NFP operations in enhancing their proclaimed goals and objectives must accompany the periodic reports. Such information may include efficiency measures, statistics about type and number of beneficiaries, and other information of the organization's activities. In a recent Governmental Accounting Standards Board-sponsored research report, Hatry, Alexander and Fountain, Jr. (1989) recommend a host of nonmonetary performance measures for reporting by education institutions. Although the supply of such information is relevant to NFP reporting, it is also organization specific and cannot be covered by a general framework.

NFPs enjoy donated services and goods. Such donations are especially common in type b and d organizations and play a significant role in their operations. Complex measurement problems are associated with such noncash donations, and many (if not the vast majority) of NFPs do not recognize the monetary value of such items. The cash or modified cash system suggested for organization types b and d does not recognize such noncash donations. There is

---

[35]For a range of accounting methods, on the continuum, used in practice by NFPs, see Beechy (1990), pp. 115–122.

nothing, however, to prevent organizations from providing information in this regard (e.g., volunteer hours) in periodic reports. Indeed, since 1986 Canadian tax authorities have provided space in the annual tax return form for reporting volunteer hours, and many organizations voluntarily report this information. Detailed discussion of this matter is beyond the scope of the present paper. It is possible, however, to extend the framework to include, within the accounting scheme, such measures as shadow prices for goods and services and the allocation of activities and related costs that are common to all funds. Examples are administrative costs, fund-raising costs, and management compensation packages including perks. The latter are private goods that can be controlled by the means suggested for cells c and d, thereby reducing moral hazard problems arising from nonincentive compensation schemes.

In the context of economic contracting, accounting reporting should be designed to satisfy contracting parties and to facilitate efficient contracts. Accounting standards (GAAP), when agreed upon by the contracting parties, play a positive role in the contracting environment. In the absence of external intervention (e.g., regulation or legislation), the reporting scheme by management to contracting parties must be left for them to decide. NFP organizations are no exception. There is nothing to prevent contracting parties from setting their own rules for reporting. Indeed, we observe restricted donated endowed funds with specific reporting requirements (see also FASB, 1985, for discussion on restricted assets) and fund-raising campaigns for specific projects, which constitute a contract. Such arrangements are beyond the scope of the proposed framework.

Local, state, provincial, or federal governments support NFP organizations via tax exemptions or direct contributions and may require specific information for their purposes. For example, in some states (e.g., Indiana) salaries of employees in supported universities are made public. Recently, the state of Florida announced that students' tuition fees paid to a specific university must cover at least 25 percent of their education costs. In Canada both the Federal Department of Revenue and the Office of the Public Trustee in Ontario announced that they intend to increase reporting requirements concerning political activities and related cost by charities. The definition of such activities and costs (e.g., whether it includes accruals or depreciation) is a matter to be decided by the relevant parties. The framework in this paper is designed for NFP operations that are not subject to specific contractual or regulated reporting requirements, although it may be useful in determining what such requirements should be.

Finally, this paper made no attempt to assess the desired extent or degree of detail in reports by NFP organizations. Such discussion is beyond the scope of a general framework. However, Fama and Jensen (1983) argue that large donors fulfill a function in monitoring NFP management's performance similar to that fulfilled by major shareholders in profit corporations. This is so because large donors are likely to require a (nonmonetary) return from providing capital to NFPs. Since there is probably little return from being associated with an inefficient or wasteful organization, large donors are motivated to monitor NFP management. Williamson (1983), who builds on Fama and Jensen (1983), suggests that because NFP "ownership" is not negotiable and there are no market prices to assess periodic "added value" produced by NFPs, a relatively cheap way to monitor management is for donors to participate in such organizations' governing bodies. Thus, one may infer the relative efficiency and effectiveness of the organization from the degree of major donors' involvement in the NFP organization's decision-making process. Whether this conjecture is indeed correct is a question that must be answered based on empirical findings. If it is correct, then it may be argued that NFPs with boards that have high proportions of large donor directors to inside (employees) directors may report in less detail than others.

CONCLUSION

The population of privately organized NFPs is clustered on two dimensions: (1) resource-providers'/beneficiaries' utility interdependence and (2) type of products or services provided. This results in a framework suggesting different accounting treatments for different types of NFPs. This framework does not correspond to either the latest FASB requirements that *all* NFPs apply depreciation accounting or the CICA requirement that *all* NFPs apply accrual accounting. This paper suggests that the nature of the organization and its products, not the type of transaction, governs the accounting and control system.

In neither the United States nor Canada are the pronouncements by the respective standard-setting bodies enforceable by law or regulations on privately organized NFPs. Although in Canada "most federal and provincial corporations acts governing incorporated nonprofit organizations require that annual audited financial statements be prepared, . . . they do not require that these statements adhere to GAAP or the CICA Handbook" (Ernst and Young, 1990, p. 5). Thus, NFPs may choose their own accounting and reporting systems. The framework in this paper may be useful for those organizations that do so.

Indeed, many pronouncements by national NFP organizations or associations conflict with the standard-setting bodies' requirements, as do their accounting practices. Some correspondence between the accounting pronouncements of nationally organized NFP organizations and the suggested framework are observed.[36] Empirical examination of the suggested framework may further advance a theory for accounting for nonprofit organizations.

APPENDIX: ACCOUNTING PRONOUNCEMENTS

Flesher and Rezaee (1988) document the historical development of college and university accounting practices and related procedures for auditing such institutions from 1912 to 1986. They summarize recommendations by the Carnegie Foundation (1910, 1912), Arnett (1922), and the National Committee on Standard Reports for Institutions of Higher Education (1930, 1935), all advocating fund accounting. Flesher and Rezaee (1988) also describe a debate on whether depreciation is a proper accounting procedure for universities. Morey (1930, 1950) and McGladrey (1949) supported depreciation accounting (and fund accounting), but Baldassare (1949) and Washburn (1925) opposed the depreciation of universities' fixed assets. Guy (1971) surveyed college and university accounting practices and found them to be quite uniform. He concluded that the matching of revenue and expense, depreciation included, is not applicable to, nor applied by, colleges and universities. Similar practices to those observed by Guy (1971) were also recommended by the National Committee of the American Council of Higher Education (1968).

The National Assembly of National Voluntary Health and Social Welfare Organizations issued its original comprehensive guide, *Standards of Accounting and Financial Reporting for Voluntary Health and Welfare Organizations,* in 1964 and revised it in 1974 and 1988. The *Standards* recommend fund accounting, accrual accounting, including depreciation for certain assets, and

---

[36]The author examined the financial statements of 72 Canadian charities listed in the "Specific Health Focus Organizations" section of the *1988 Donor's Guide to Fund Raising Organizations in Canada. All* statements are based on fund accounting, to various extents, and with the exception of three organizations, none used depreciation accounting.

consolidated statements for nonrestricted funds.[37] The American Hospital Association issued several guidelines in 1960 and 1983.[38] Other publications include those by the National Conference of Catholic Bishops (1971), the Club Managers Association of America (1967), the National Association of Independent Schools (1969, 1977), the Association of Science-Technology Centers (1976), and the United Way of America (1989). All those guides suggest the application of fund accounting for most activities but differ with respect to the applicability of accrual accounting and the matching principle, depreciation included.

REFERENCES

Abrams, B.A. and M.D. Schmitz, "The Crowding-Out Effect of Governmental Transfers on Private Charitable Contributions" in S. Rose-Ackerman (ed.), *The Economics of Nonprofit Institutions* (New York: Oxford University Press, 1986) pp. 303–312.

Adams, J.B., R.J. Bossio, and P. Rohan, *Accounting for Contributed Services: Survey of Preparers and Users of Financial Statements of Non-for-Profit Organizations* (Norwalk, Conn.: FASB, April 1989).

American Hospital Association, *Chart of Accounts for Hospitals* (Chicago: AHA, 1983).

———, *Accounting Manual for Long-Term Care Institutions* (Chicago: AHA, 1968).

———, *Uniform Hospital Definitions* (Chicago: AHA, 1960).

American Institute of Certified Public Accountants, *Hospital Audit Guide* (New York: AICPA, 1980).

———, *Statement of Position 78-10 on Accounting Principles and Reporting Practices for Certain Nonprofit Organizations* (New York: AICPA, 1979).

———, *Audits of Voluntary Health and Welfare Organizations* (New York: AICPA, 1974a).

———, *Statement of Position 74-8 on Financial Accounting and Reporting by Colleges and Universities* (New York: AICPA, 1974b).

———, *Accounting Standards Division. Accounting Reporting by Colleges* (New York: AICPA, 1974c).

———, *Audits of Colleges and Universities* (New York: AICPA, 1973).

———, *Hospital Audit Guide* (New York: AICPA, 1972).

Anthony, R.N., *Financial Accounting in Nonbusiness Organizations: An Exploratory Study of Conceptual Issues* (Stanford, Conn.: Financial Accounting Standards Board, 1978).

Arnett, T., *College and University Finance* (New York: General Education Board, 1922).

Arrow, K.J., "Optimal and Voluntary Income Distribution," in S. Rosefielde (ed.), *Economic Welfare and the Economics of Soviet Socialism* (Cambridge, U.K.: Cambridge University Press, 1981).

———, *Social Choice and Individual Values,* rev. ed. (New Haven: Yale University Press, 1963).

Association of Science-Technology Centers, *Museum Accounting Guidelines* (Washington, D.C.: ASTC, 1976).

Atkinson, A.B., "Income Maintenance and Social Insurance" in A.J. Auerbach and M. Feldstein (eds.), *Handbook of Public Economics,* vol. 2 (Amsterdam: North-Holland, 1987) pp. 485–535.

Baldassare, E.W., "Reasons Why University Accounting Must Differ from Conventional Commercial Accounting," *Journal of Accountancy* (August 1949) pp. 111–120.

Beechy, T.H., *Canadian Advanced Financial Accounting,* 2nd ed. (Toronto: Holt, Rinehart and Winston of Canada, 1990).

Ben-Ner, A., "Nonprofit Organizations: Why Do They Exist in Market Economies?" in S. Rose-Ackerman (ed.), *The Economics of Nonprofit Institutions* (New York: Oxford University Press, 1986) pp. 94–113.

Beveridge, L., *Social Insurance and Allied Services* (London: HMSO, 1942).

Brickley, J.A., S. Bhagat and R.C. Lease, "The Impact of Long-Range Managerial Compensation Plans on Shareholder Wealth, "*Journal of Accounting Economics* (April 1985) pp. 53–71.

Broman, A.J., "Statutory Tax Rate Reform and Charitable Contributions: Evidence from a Recent Period of Reform," *The Journal of the American Taxation Association* (Fall 1989) pp. 7–21.

Buchanan, J.M., "Politics without Romance: A Sketch of Positive Public Choice Theory and Its Normative Implications, "*IHS Journal 3* (1979) pp. B1–B17. Reprinted in I.M. Buchanan and R.D. Tollison (eds.), *The Theory of Public Choice II* (Ann Arbor: University of Michigan Press, 1984) pp. 11–22.

---

[37]For more detail, see National Health Council et al. (1988).

[38]See American Hospital Association (1960, 1968, 1983). Similar guidelines are normally followed by Canadian hospitals (all NFP) as specified in CHA (1968, 1974).

————, "The Political Economy of the Welfare State" in R.T. Selden (ed.), *Capitalism and Freedom: Problems and Prospects* (Charlottesville, Va.: University of Virginia Press, 1975) pp. 52–77.

————, "An Economic Theory of Clubs," *Econometrica* (February 1965), pp. 1–14.

————, and G. Tullock, *The Calculus of Consent* (Ann Arbor: University of Michigan Press, 1962).

Canadian Association of University Business Officers, *Task Force Report—Implementation of CICA Handbook Recommendations* (Toronto: CAUBO, undated).

Canadian Hospital Association, *Canadian Hospital Accounting Methods* (Ottawa: CHA, 1968, revised 1974).

Canadian Institute of Chartered Accountants, *CICA Handbook,* Section 4230, "Non-Profit Organizations" (Toronto: CICA, 1988).

————, *Financial Reporting for Non-Profit Organizations* (Toronto: CICA, 1980). Carnegie Foundation for the Advancement of Teaching, *Seventh Annual Report of the President and the Treasurer* (New York: The Foundation, 1912).

————, *Fifth Annual Report of the President and Treasurer* (New York: The Foundation, 1910).

Chamberlain, J., "Provision of Collective Goods as a Function of Group Size," *American Political Science Review 68* (1974) pp. 707–716.

Club Managers Association of America, *Uniform System of Accounts for Clubs,* 2nd ed. (Washington, D.C.: CMAA, 1967).

Coelen, C.G., "Hospital Ownership and Cooperative Hospital Costs," *For Profit Enterprise in Health Care* (Washington, D.C.: Institute of Medicine, National Academy Press, 1986).

Coopers and Lybrand, *Accounting and Auditing in the People's Republic of China* (Dallas: Center for International Accounting Development, The University of Texas at Dallas, 1987).

Demsetz, H., "The Private Provision of Public Goods," *Journal of Law and Economics 13* (1970) pp. 292–306.

Downs, A., *An Economic Theory of Democracy* (New York: Harper and Row, 1957).

Easley, D. and M. O'Hara, "Optimal Nonprofit Firms," in S. Rose-Ackerman (ed.), *The Economics of Nonprofit Institutions* (New York: Oxford University Press, 1986) pp. 85–93.

Easterbrook, F.H. and D.R. Fischel, "The Proper Role of a Target's Management in Responding to a Tender Offer," *Harvard Law Review* (April 1981) pp. 1161–1204.

Ernst and Young, *Financial Accounting Issues for Non-Profit Organizations* (Toronto: Ernst and Young, February 1990).

Fama, E.F. and M.C. Jensen, "Separation of Ownership and Control," *Journal of Law and Economics 26* (1983) pp. 301–325.

Feldstein, M.S., "The Income Tax and Charitable Contributions: Part I—Aggregate and Distributional Effects," *National Tax Journal* (March 1975), pp. 81–100.

———— and C. Clotfelter, "Tax Incentives and Charitable Contributions in the United States," *Journal of Public Economics* (January/February 1976) pp. 1–26.

Feldstein, M.S. and A. Taylor, "The Income Tax and Charitable Contributions," *Econometrica* (November 1976) pp. 1201–1222.

Financial Accounting Standards Board, "FASB Plan for Technical Projects, Research, and Other Technical Activities," *Financial Accounting Series, Status Report #200* (April 7, 1989a).

————, "FAF Trustees Give Tentative Approval to Compromise on Boards' Jurisdiction," *Financial Accounting Series, Status Report No. 204* (Norwalk, Conn.: FASB, 1989b).

————, *Statement of Financial Accounting Standards No. 99,* "Deferral of the Effective Date of Recognition of Depreciation by Not-for-Profit Organizations—An Amendment of FASB Statement No. 93" (Norwalk, Conn.: FASB, 1988).

————, *Statement of Financial Accounting No. 93,* "Recognition of Depreciation by Not-for-Profit Organizations" (Stamford, Conn.: FASB, 1987).

————, *Statement of Financial Accounting Concepts No. 6.* "Elements of Financial Statements—Revised" (Stamford, Conn.: FASB, 1985).

————, *Statement of Financial Accounting Concepts No. 4,* "Objectives of Financial Reporting by Nonbusiness Organizations" (Stamford, Conn.: FASB, 1980).

Fishburn, D.C., The Theory of Social Choice (Princeton: Princeton University Press, 1973).

Fitzgerald, J. and B. Jacobsen, "Study Fails to Prove For-Profits' Superiority," *Health Progress* (April 1987) pp. 32–37.

Flesher, D.L. and Z. Rezaee, "History of College and University Accounting and Auditing" in R.H. Tondkar and E.D. Coffman (eds.), *Working Paper Series 4,* Working Papers 61–80 (The American Academy of Historians, 1989) pp. 195–197.

Ginzberg, E., D.L. Hiestand, and B.J. Reubens, *The Pluralistic Economy* (New York: McGraw Hill, 1965).

Glenday, G., A.K. Gupta, and H. Pawlok, "Tax Incentives for Personal Charitable Contributions," *The Review of Economics and Statistics* (1986), pp. 688–693.

Globe and Mail staff, "Ottawa to Review Charities Reporting," *Globe and Mail* (8 January 1988) A4.

Governmental Accounting Standards Board, *Statement No. 8—Applicability of FASB Statement No. 93.* "Recognition of Depreciation by Not-for-Profit Organizations to Certain State and Local Government Entities" (Stamford, Conn.: GASB, January 1988).

Guy, J., "An Inquiry into the Applicability of Accountancy for Profit Making Enterprises to Colleges and Universities," Ph.D. Dissertation, University of Illinois at Urbana-Champaign (1971).

Hansmann, H.B., "The Role of Nonprofit Enterprise," *The Yale Law Journal* (April 1980) pp. 835–898.

Harsanyi, J.C., "Cardinal Welfare, Individualistic Ethics, and Interpersonal Comparison of Utility." *Journal of Political Economy* (August 1955) pp. 309–321.

Harvey, B.H. and H.L. Sorkin, "Nonprofit Accounting and Financial Reporting," in T.D. Connors (ed.), *The Nonprofit Organization Handbook* (New York: McGraw Hill, 1988).

Hatry, H.P., M. Alexander and J.R. Fountain, Jr., *Service Efforts and Accomplishment Reporting: Its Time Has Come— Elementary and Secondary Education* (Norwalk, Conn.: Governmental Accounting Standards Board, 1989).

Hobbes, T., *Leviathan,* Michael Oakshott Edition. (Oxford, England: Basil Blackwell, 1960). Original published in 1651.

Hochman, H.M. and J.D. Rodgers, "Pareto Optimal Redistribution," *The American Economic Review* (September 1969) pp. 542–557.

Holstrom, B., "The Provision of Services in a Market Economy," in R.P. Inman (ed.), *Managing the Service Economy: Problems and Prospects* (Cambridge, U.K.: Cambridge University Press, 1984).

Hood, R.D., S.A. Martin, and L.S. Osberg, "Economic Determinants of Individual Charitable Donations in Canada," *Canadian Journal of Economics* (November 1977) pp. 653–669.

Hotelling, H., "Stability in Competition," *Economic Journal* (March 1929) pp. 41–57.

Inman, R.P., "Markets, Governments, and the 'New' Political Economy" in A.J. Auerbach and M. Feldstein (eds.), *Handbook of Public Economics 2* (Amsterdam: North-Holland, 1987) pp. 647–777.

Jensen, M.C. and W.H. Meckling, "Rights and Productions Functions: An Application to Labor-Managed Firms and Codetermination," *Journal of Business 52,* no. 4 (1979) pp. 469–506.

Kalt, J.P. and M.A. Zupan, "Capture and Ideology in the Economic Theory of Politics," *American Economic Review* (July 1984) pp. 279–300.

Karpoff, J.M. and E.M. Rice, "Organizational Form, Short Transferability, and Firm Performance," *Journal of Financial Economics* (September 1989) pp. 69–105.

Kitchen, H. and R. Delton, "Determinants of Charitable Donations by Families in Canada: A Regional Analysis," *Applied Economics* (March 1990) pp. 285–293.

Kramer, R.M., *Voluntary Agencies in the Welfare State* (Berkeley: University of California Press, 1981).

Krashinsky, M., "Transaction Costs and a Theory of the Nonprofit Organization," in S. Rose-Ackerman (ed.), *The Economics of Nonprofit Organizations* (New York: Oxford University Press, 1986) pp. 114–132.

Laffont, J.J., "Incentives and the Allocation of Public Goods," in A.J. Auerbach and M. Feldstein (eds.), *Handbook of Public Economics 2* (Amsterdam: North-Holland, 1987) pp. 537–569.

Martin, S.A., *Financing Humanistic Service* (Toronto: McClelland and Stewart, 1975).

Mautz, R.K., "Monuments, Mistakes, and Opportunities," *Accounting Horizons* (June 1988) pp. 123–128.

McGladrey, I.B., "Something Is Wrong with College Financial Reports," *Journal of Accountancy* (August 1949) pp. 103–110.

McGuire, M.C., "Private Good Clubs and Public Good Clubs: Economic Models of Group Formation," *Swedish Journal of Economics* (March 1972) pp. 84–99, cited in D.C. Mueller, "Public Choice: A Survey," *Journal of Economic Literature* (June 1976).

McPherson, J.M. and L. Smith-Lovin, "Homophily in Voluntary Organizations: Status Distance and Composition of Face-to-Face Groups," *American Sociological Review 52,* no. 3 (1987) pp. 370–379.

Morey, L., "Better Application of Recognized Principles Would Improve University Accounting," *Journal of Accountancy* (September 1950) pp. 201–205.

———, *University and College Accounting* (New York: John Wiley, N.Y., 1930).

Mueller, D.C., "Public Choice: A Survey," *Journal of Economic Literature* (June 1976) pp. 395–433.

National Association of Independent Schools, *Accounting for Independent Schools,* 2nd ed. (Boston: N.A.I.S., 1977).

———, *Accounting for Independent Schools* (Boston: N.A.I.S., 1969).

———, *Financial Reports for Colleges and Universities* (Chicago: The University of Chicago Press, 1935).

———, *A Study of Financial Reports of Colleges and Universities in the United States* (Urbana, Ill.: American Council of Education, 1930).

American Council of Higher Education, National Committee to Revise Volumes I and II, *College and University Business Administration,* rev. ed. (Washington, D.C.: A.C.E., 1968).

National Conference of Catholic Bishops, *Diocesan Accounting and Financial Reporting* (Washington, D.C.: N.C.C.B., 1971).

National Health Council, Inc., National Assembly of National Voluntary Health and Social Welfare Organizations Inc., and United Way of America, *Standards of Accounting and Financial Reporting for Voluntary Health and Welfare Organizations* (New York: National Health Council Inc., 1988).

Niskanen, W.A., *Bureaucracy and Representative Government* (Chicago: Aldine, 1971).

Oakland, W.H., "Theory of Public Goods," in A.J. Auerbach and M. Feldstein (eds.), *Handbook of Public Economics 2* (Amsterdam: North-Holland, 1987) pp. 485–535.

Olson, M., *The Logic of Collective Action* (Cambridge, Mass.: Harvard University Press, 1965).

Ostrom, V., "Why Governments Fail: An Inquiry into the Use of Instruments of Evil to Do Good" in J.M. Buchanan and R.D. Tollison (eds.), *The Theory of Public Choice II* (Ann Arbor: University of Michigan Press, 1984) pp. 422–435.

Pallot, J., "The Nature of Public Assets: A Response to Mautz," *Accounting Horizons* (June 1990) pp. 79–85.

Palmer, J. and I. Sawhill, *The Reagan Experiment* (Washington, D.C.: The Urban Institute Press, 1982).

Pattison, R.V. and H.M. Katz, "Investor-Owned and Not-for-Profit Hospitals," *New England Journal of Medicine* (August 11, 1983).

Pauly, M.V., "Delivered Comments," *Research in Law and Economics*. Supplement 1, *Economics of Nonpropietary Organizations* (1980) pp. 170–175.

———, "Cores and Clubs," *Public Choice* (Fall 1970) pp. 53–65.

———, "Clubs, Commonality, and the Core: An Integration of Game Theory and the Theory of Public Goods," *Econometrica* (August 1967) pp. 314–324.

Rose-Ackerman, S., "Introduction," in S. Rose-Ackerman (ed.), *The Economics of Nonprofit Institutions* (New York: Oxford University Press, 1986).

———, "Charitable Giving and 'Excessive' Fundraising," *The Quarterly Journal of Economics* (May 1982a), pp. 195–212.

———, "Unfair Competition and Corporate Income Taxation." *Stanford Law Review* (May 1982b) pp. 1017–1039.

———, "Do Government Grants to Charity Reduce Private Donations?" in M. White (ed.), *Nonprofit Firms in a Three Sector Economy* (Washington, D.C.: Urban Institute, 1981) pp. 95–114.

———, "United Charities: An Economic Analysis," *Public Policy* (Summer 1980) pp. 323–350.

Rubinfeld, D.L., "The Economics of the Local Public Sector," in A.J. Auerbach and M. Feldstein (eds.), *Handbook of Public Economics 2* (Amsterdam: North-Holland, 1987) pp. 571–645.

Salamon, L.M., "The Results Are Coming In," *Foundation News* (July–August 1984).

———, L.M. and A.J. Abramson, "Nonprofits and the Federal Budget: Deeper Cuts Ahead," *Foundation News* (March–April, 1985).

Sen, A.K., *Collective Choice and Social Welfare* (San Francisco: Holden Day, 1970).

Shibata, H., "A Theory of Group Consumption and Group Formation," *Public Finance 34*, no. 3 (1979) pp. 395–412.

Smith, D.H., "The Impact of the Nonprofit Voluntary Sector on Society" in T.D. Connors (ed.), *The Nonprofit Organization Handbook* (New York: McGraw Hill, 1988) pp. 2.1–2.12.

———, B.R. Baldwin and E.D. White, "The Nonprofit Sector," in T.D. Connors (ed.), *The Nonprofit Organization Handbook* (New York: McGraw Hill, 1988) pp. 1.3–1.15.

Stigler, G.J., "The Theory of Economic Regulation," *Bell Journal of Economics and Management Science* (Spring 1971) pp. 3–21.

Strnad, J., "The Charitable Contribution Deduction: A Politico-Economic Analysis" in S. Rose-Ackerman, *The Economics of Nonprofit Institutions* (New York: Oxford University Press, 1986) pp. 265–296.

Sunder, S., "Structure of Organizations for Production of Public and Private Goods," Working Paper, University of Minnesota (November 1987).

Thompson, E.A., "Charity and Nonprofit Organizations," *Research in Law and Economics,* Supplement 1, *Economics of Nonproprietary Organizations* (1980), pp. 125–138.

Tiebout, C.M., "A Pure Theory of Local Expenditures," *Journal of Political Economy 64* (1956) pp. 416–424.

Toolson, R.B., "The Charitable Contribution Deduction: New Evidence of Tax Incentive Effect," *Advances in Taxation 2* (1989) pp. 107–129.

Tullock, G., "Problems of Majority Voting," *Journal of Political Economy* (December 1959) pp. 571–579.

Turney, B., "Volunteerism Seminar Attracts 60 Delegates," *The Daily Gleaner* (March 4, 1985) p. 14, cited in E. Abraham and C. Loughrey, "CAs and Charities: The Value of Volunteering," *CA Magazine* (October 1985) pp. 22–24.

Ulbrich, H.H. and M.S. Wallace, "Determinants of Club Membership: An Economic Approach," *Atlantic Economic Journal* (March 1989) pp. 8–15.

United Way of America, *Accounting and Financial Reporting—A Guide for United Ways and Not-for-Profit Human Services Organizations* (Alexandria, Va.: U.W.A., 1974 and 1989).

Vatter, W.J., "State of the Art—Non-Business Accounting," *The Accounting Review* (July 1979) pp. 574–584.

Washburn, E.T., *Accounting for Universities* (New York: Romelot Press, 1925).

Weisbrod, B.A., "Private Goods, Collective Goods: The Role of the Nonprofit Sector," *Research in Law and Economics,* Supplement 1, *The Economics of Nonproprietary Organizations* (1980) pp. 139–177.

———, "Toward a Theory of Voluntary Nonprofit Sector in a Three Sector Economy" in B.A. Weisbrod (ed.), *Altruism, Morality and Economic Theory* (New York: Russell Sage Foundation, 1975) pp. 171–195.

——— and M. Schlesinger, "Public, Private, Nonprofit Ownership and the Response to Asymmetric Information: The Case of Nursing Homes," in S. Rose-Ackerman (ed.), *The Economics of Nonprofit Institutions* (New York: Oxford University Press, 1986) pp. 131–151.

Weiss, J.H., "Donations: Can They Reduce a Donor's Welfare?" in S. Rose-Ackerman (ed.), *The Economics of Nonprofit Institutions* (New York: Oxford University Press, 1986) pp. 45–54.

————, "The Ambivalent Value of Voluntary Provision of Public Goods in Political Economy," Ph.D. dissertation, University of Wisconsin, Madison (1981); cited in J.H. Weiss, "Donations: Can They Reduce a Donor's Welfare?" in S. Rose-Ackerman (ed.), *The Economics of Nonprofit Institutions* (New York: Oxford University Press, 1986) pp. 45–54.

Whinston, A., "Discussion," *Research in Law and Economics,* Supplement 1, *The Economics of Nonproprietary Organizations* (1980) pp. 184–185.

Williamson, O.E., "Organization Form, Residual Claimants and Corporate Control," *Journal Law and Economics 26* (1983) pp. 351–366.

Wing Alder, M., "Relations between Government and Nonprofit Organizations" in T.D. Connors (ed.), *The Nonprofit Organization Handbook* (New York: McGraw Hill, 1988) pp. 9.1–9.9.

Wood, C., "Securing Tax Exemption for Exempt Organizations" in T.D. Connors (ed.), *The Nonprofit Organization Handbook* (New York: McGraw Hill, 1988) pp. 4.1–4.25.

COSTS AND THE COLLECTIVE GOOD

Thomas H. Beechy and Brenda J. Zimmerman

In recent years, financial reporting for nonprofit organizations has received much attention in Canada and the United States. Traditionally, accounting for Canadian NPOs has been based on the terms of their contractual relationships with granting agencies, especially provincial government ministries, whose reporting guidelines differ little from one jurisdiction to another. Most of the accounting literature on NPOs is descriptive, and, in North America, the profession has issued specialized guides in the past several decades. Some have been issued by accounting organizations,[1] others by the equivalent of trade associations for NPOs.[2] The guides have described existing accounting practices, drawing on the experience and expertise of the NPOs and their accountants, both public and private. Significant similarities among NPOs have emerged in areas like depreciation accounting and expenditure reporting. Because generally accepted accounting principles (GAAP) are influenced significantly by historical precedent and practice, it can be said that GAAP for NPOs do exist, but that they have evolved without the benefit of a coherent conceptual framework.

Although there appears to be no compelling demand by the users of NPO financial statements for CICA or FASB involvement, the accounting profession (or parts thereof) seems bent

---

Thomas H. Beechy and Brenda J. Zimmerman, "Costs and the Collective Good," *CAmagazine,* November 1992, 44–49. Reprinted with permission from CAmagazine, (November, 1992), published by the Canadian Institute of Chartered Accountants, Toronto.

[1]R. M. Skinner, *Canadian University Accounting.* CICA, 1969; *Hospital Audit Guide,* AICPA, 1972, and *Audits of Voluntary Health and Welfare Organizations,* AICPA, 1974.

[2]*Canadian Hospital Accounting Methods,* Canadian Hospital Association, 1968; *Standards of Accounting and Financial Reporting for Voluntary Health and Welfare Organizations,* National Health Council, Inc., 1988.

on improving NPO accounting in order to bring it closer to business-oriented GAAP. Without a conceptual framework for NPO accounting, however, it's difficult to assess the merits of this intention.

Only two conceptual frameworks have been proposed to date. Harvard Business School professor Robert Anthony says NPO accounting should be based on the nature of the NPO's transactions.[3] McMaster University professor Haim Falk says accounting for NPOs should be built on a conceptual foundation that includes both the constitution of the organizations and the character of their products and services.[4]

Earlier studies of accounting for NPOs generalized the issues by including all nonbusiness organizations—both nonprofit ones (such as symphonies) and public sector organizations (such as governments and school boards).[5] The CICA apparently disagreed with this approach when, in 1980, it released separate research studies pertaining to NPOs and governments.[6] Soon after, the Public Sector Accounting and Auditing Committee was established, and it removed governmental reporting from the *CICA Handbook* altogether. In contrast, the CICA is now attempting to incorporate explicit NPO accounting guidelines into the *Handbook,* evidently assuming that NPOs are more like businesses than like governments. But governments are currently shifting certain social services (such as child care) and health services (such as in-home care and visiting nurse programs) away from government agencies to volunteer NPOs. Should such programs be accounted for differently after the shifts? Let's look at the accounting decisions that need to be made for any NPO, then see whether the two conceptual frameworks can help us to tailor the accounting to particular organizations and their programs.

Canadian and US studies have repeatedly identified eight basic accounting issues for NPOs:

1. Cash versus accrual. Should NPOs recognize assets and liabilities on their balance sheets? In practice, this question is usually resolved by accruing receivables and payables. Fixed assets, however, are often treated differently and are therefore discussed separately.

2. Expenditure versus expense. Under expenditure accounting, costs are recognized on the statement of operations when they are incurred; under expense accounting, recognition occurs only when the goods and services represented by the costs are used. This boils down to an issue of interperiod allocation, affecting items of cost such as inventories, startups, pensions and capital leases.

3. Revenue recognition. Should donation pledges be recognized as revenue when they are pledged, or when they are received? Should capital grants and the proceeds

[3]Robert Anthony, *Should Business and Nonbusiness Accounting Be Different?* Harvard Business School Press, 1989, and *Financial Accounting in Nonbusiness Organizations: An Exploratory Study of Conceptual Issues,* FASB, 1978.

[4]Haim Falk, "Towards a framework for not for profit accounting," *Contemporary Accounting Research,* Spring 1992, pp. 468–499.

[5]American Accounting Association, "Report of the committee on accounting for not-for-profit organizations," Supplement to the *Accounting Review,* vol. XLVI, 1971.

[6]*Financial Reporting for Non-Profit Organizations,* CICA, 1980, and *Financial Reporting by Governments,* CICA, 1980.

of capital fund-raising campaigns be recognized as revenue? Both the CICA and the FASB have proposed recognizing capital grants as revenue.

4. Fixed assets. Should they be capitalized? Should they be depreciated? Depreciation accounting is consistent with the expense basis of reporting, but not the expenditure basis. Even under expenditure accounting, however, fixed assets can be capitalized without charging depreciation to the operating programs. The two questions are separable.

5. Donated goods and services. Should NPOs recognize the value of goods and services that are donated to them? The trend seems to be toward recognizing donated goods and services if the organization would have to pay for them if they were not donated.

6. Volunteer services. For some NPOs, volunteer effort is incidental to the main activities of the organization; for others, it is essential. At the moment, NPOs generally don't recognize such services' value on their financial statements.

7. Consolidation. Should reporting be standardized, with a new emphasis on combined or consolidated reporting? Currently, some NPOs practise consolidated reporting, wherein all activities are combined and related organizations are consolidated. Others base their reporting on major funds or programs.

8. Supplementary information. It is not the principal goal of NPOs to generate a financial return, so they often report nonfinancial information to help readers understand how their resources are being used to accomplish the organization's objectives. What kinds of supplementary information should they publish?

These issues cannot be resolved without a conceptual framework. To be useful for evaluating alternative accounting policies, such a framework should address the fundamental characteristics of NPOs, and it should not be based on the assumption that all NPOs must be similar to either public sector organizations or businesses. We think the recent proposal by Falk, together with some of the ideas advocated by Anthony, provide the best basis for the framework's development.

TRANSACTIONS APPROACH

Anthony argues that transactions should get the same accounting treatment whether they are undertaken by a business entity or a nonbusiness entity.[7] He acknowledges that the receipt of capital contributions by NPOs distinguishes them from business organizations, but rejects the nonprofit objective as a basis for differential accounting treatment. Instead of a profit motive, Anthony substitutes a "no profit" or break-even objective: "The primary focus of accounting in both business and nonbusiness organizations," he says, "is on the measurement of net income so as to report the organization's success in maintaining its financial capital during an accounting period."[8] By continuing the emphasis on income measurement, Anthony pushes

---

[7]Anthony, 1989, p. 21.

[8]Anthony, 1989, p. 3.

NPO accounting toward normal business accounting. Both the CICA and FASB have added momentum to this push.

Another important characteristic of the transactions approach is that it emphasizes reporting for the organizational entity as a whole. "It is essential that the operating statement report on the operating performance of the whole organization," Anthony says, "with a single column of numbers, starting with revenues and ending with net income."[9] This emphasis on entity reporting is based on the assumption that NPOs, like businesses, can shift resources from one program to another. Often, they can't.

An indication that the transactions approach isn't completely satisfactory is that it doesn't explain how and why GAAP developed for NPOs in the first place, as positive accounting theory would require (see "Practice in a positive light," July 1992, p. 37).[10] Although parts of the transactions-based analysis are helpful, we think it generally diverges too far from the realities of NPO accounting. Also, adopting the transactions approach would mean changing the bulk of NPO financial reporting.

We do, however, see considerable value in one aspect of Anthony's approach: his categorization of NPOs on the basis of their source of revenue. His Type-A NPOs derive their financial resources mainly from the sale of goods and services. Type-B NPOs obtain significant amounts from sources other than the sale of goods and services. We will apply this useful distinction later.

THE FALK FRAMEWORK

Falk suggests that NPOs can be distinguished on the basis of two characteristics: first, the relationship between the providers of the organization's resources and the beneficiaries of its goods and services (which we call "products"); and second, whether the goods are private or collective. He identifies two types of organizations, clubs and nonclubs. In a club, such as a golf facility, members pay dues and benefit directly in return. In nonclubs, this interdependence between resource providers and beneficiaries does not exist. Rather, resources are provided by donors, who can be governments, businesses or individuals. The benefits of the nonclub NPO's activities are enjoyed by others. Most arts organizations and social service agencies belong in this category. Private goods are provided to individuals, collective goods are provided to groups of beneficiaries.

An NPO can provide both private and collective goods. Consider, for example, the CICA. It offers professional development courses to its members. These private goods benefit its members directly. It publishes *CAmagazine* as well as various books and materials for its members and others. These private goods are offered to everyone. It promotes the value and importance of CAs in business and society. This is a collective good that benefits its members. And it engages in research and development of accounting standards. This is a collective good that benefits society as a whole. In form, the CICA is a club, because the members provide the financial resources by paying their dues and by volunteering their time, and they benefit from the activities of the club. They benefit directly, as consumers of the private goods. They also

---

[9]Anthony, 1989, p. 87.

[10]Irene Gordon and Lawrence Boland, "Practice in a positive light," *CAmagazine,* July 1992, pp. 37–41.

Types of NPO Programs

benefit indirectly, as beneficiaries of the collective goods. For instance, if the CICA's accounting standards make capital markets more efficient, everyone benefits.

An example of a nonclub NPO that offers both private and collective goods is an urban community centre. It is a nonclub because the resource providers aren't the beneficiaries of its activities. Resources are provided by local and provincial governments, by individual donors, and by other social service agencies such as the United Way, while the beneficiaries are residents of the local community that the centre serves. Private goods that might be provided by a community centre include child care, meals on wheels and low-cost housing. Collective goods may include addiction education programs, teen activity programs or environmental responsibility campaigns, as long as they are free and open to all.

ORGANIZATION MATRIX

The identifying characteristics of each type of organization can be used to construct a 2 × 2 matrix, as shown in Exhibit 1. Cells A and B represent private goods, cells C and D represent collective goods. Vertically, cells A and C contain clubs, while cells B and D contain nonclubs. Although Falk discusses placement within the matrix in terms of organizations, it may be even more useful to examine the matrix in terms of the programs the organizations administer, because an individual NPO may operate in more than one cell. This is particularly true for the vertical dimension. A private golf course that lets the public pay to play crosses the horizontal division; however, we think horizontal crossing is much less common than vertical crossing.

Nonclubs may offer private goods on either a cost-recovery basis or a "free" (or heavily subsidized) basis. For example, a community centre may offer meals on wheels on either basis. If the program is offered on a cost-recovery basis, the quantity of the service provided is not constrained by revenue, but, if the program is free to the beneficiaries, the activity level is circumscribed by the level of funding provided to support it. This distinction, based on revenue sources, is similar to the Type-A/Type-B distinction made by Anthony, and it leads us to subdivide cell B into B1 and B2. Identifying the organizational, product and revenue characteristics of NPOs and their programs gives us a conceptual framework for NPO accounting. We will look first at the private-versus-collective dimension of activity, then at the organizational type.

Private goods have an identifiable unit cost. The costs of providing private goods can be traced to the product in NPOs just as well as they can in private sector organizations. The costs of providing child care, producing magazines and books, delivering professional development programs, and running a soup kitchen are all traceable to the product. The unit costs can be used to help set prices. Because these services may also be provided by private sector organizations, the discipline of the marketplace comes into play and efficiency measures are appropriate. Conversely, collective goods often do not have identifiable unit costs because there is no way to measure the organization's outputs. How can one determine a unit cost relating to environmental monitoring, to the development of accounting standards, or to substance-abuse education? Instead of unit costs and other efficiency measures, program evaluation must rely on effectiveness measures. As University of Calgary professor Dean Neu's article in this department (November 1991) pointed out, these measures cannot be provided by an accounting system because they depend on socio-economic measurements that are external to the organization and subject to many intervening variables.[11]

The resource providers for NPOs that produce collective goods (and for those that produce heavily subsidized private goods) provide fixed amounts of money each year through grants and donations. The amount of resources provided does not normally depend on the level of the services provided, even though the anticipated demand for the product may be taken into consideration when the funding level is set. When external, nonbeneficiary resource providers fund a specific product, whether it is collective or private, they generally expect that the funds provided will be matched by funds expended on that activity in a particular year. This expectation is directly tied to budget estimates provided by the NPO, so noncash items (for example, depreciation or nonfunded pension expense) are normally irrelevant. Although the NPO providing the product may be expected to continue, program funds are provided strictly on a year-by-year expenditure basis.

Whereas the production of private as opposed to collective goods has a major impact on an NPO's management control system, the club/nonclub distinction has implications for financial accounting policies. Falk says club members will be concerned that they receive the benefits due to them in return for the dues or fees paid. Individuals can opt in and out of a club. Only during the period of membership in the club do people enjoy their shares of ownership of the club's activities and net assets. Therefore, they will want program startup costs and asset costs to be allocated so that one particular year does not bear the burden of providing assets that will be used in future years. For those reasons, allocation or expense accounting is appropriate for clubs.

Clubs generally exhibit transferability of resources and need to report expenses and allocations to their members on an entity basis. Nonclubs, however, tend to exhibit accounting policies that differ not only from those of clubs, but also from one nonclub to another, de-

---

[11]Dean Neu, "Let's get critical," *CAmagazine*, November 1994, pp. 37–41.

pending on the nature of their programs. Entity reporting is generally of little interest because funders require reporting by program, not by entity.

In nonclubs, there is no implicit ownership interest. Falk points out that a nonclub's resource providers do not expect any economic return on their contribution, do not share in the NPO's assets and liabilities, and do not manage the organization or its resources. The donors' expectations and the organization's long-term viability depend on effective expenditure control; therefore, expenditure accounting is more appropriate than expense accounting for those entities.

For nonclub, private goods programs, there is an additional variable in determining the appropriate accounting policies: Are the funds provided by the beneficiaries through sales or by external donors? This corresponds to Anthony's distinction between Type-A and Type-B NPOs. The upshot of the analysis is that no single set of accounting policies can be appropriate for all NPOs or their programs. The current variance in reporting practices between NPOs (and even within NPOs), which has developed over decades of practice, can be largely explained and justified by the Falk framework.

ACCOUNTING POLICIES

Our matrix can now be filled in with the accounting policy choices that are most appropriate for each type of cell (see Exhibit 2). The two most dissimilar cells are A and D. Cell A consists of club-type organizations delivering private goods. The NPOs in this cell are almost indistinguishable from their private sector counterparts. Unit costs are identifiable, and the relationship between inputs and outputs is clear and measurable. Because members have opted into the club and are interested in its financial performance as a whole, and because the club's resources can usually be shifted between activities, financial reporting should emphasize the organizational entity. Cell D consists of nonclubs delivering collective goods. Many social service agencies and arts organizations fall into this cell. The organizations use fixed budgets and pre-authorized expenditure controls, often including encumbrance systems, because the funding available for the programs generally doesn't correspond to changes in demand. The programs are revenue-driven rather than cost-driven. Their viability depends on donor constancy, not on revenue generated by incurring costs. The efficiency and effectiveness of programs in cell D are not easily measured; therefore, nonfinancial activity and supplementary reporting of performance information are more important than they are for cell A.

An organization in cell D is a nonclub, so members won't be asking for financial statements based on allocation accounting to see that they have received their money's worth. Because the organizations offer collective goods with funds provided in fixed amounts by granting agencies, expenditure accounting gives more useful information to both the donors and managers. Professor Anthony invited us to "demonstrate how the needs of other users are sufficiently different from the needs of users of financial statements of businesses to justify different standards for nonbusiness organizations."[12] Picking up that gauntlet, we note that NPOs in cell D do indeed have users with different needs the granting agencies who want to see programmatic reports, who want to examine expenditures and not expenses, and who have little or no interest in consolidated entity statements.

---

[12]Anthony, 1989, p. 26.

Financial and Management Accounting by NPO Program Type

	Club	Nonclub
Private goods	**A** Financial reporting (Type F1): –Expense/allocation basis –Capitalize assets –Depreciate assets –Recognize capital inflows as revenue –Recognize value of volunteer services –Entity reporting Managerial controls (Type M1): –Flexible budget –Unit cost control –Break-even expectations	**B1 Cost-recovery** Financial reporting (Type F1): –Same as A Managerial controls (Type M1): –Same as A **B2 Subsidized** Financial reporting (Type F2): –Same as D Managerial controls (Type M2): –Same as D
Collective goods	**C** Financial reporting (Type F1): –Same as A Managerial controls (Type M2): –Same as D	**D** Financial reporting (Type F2): –Expenditure basis –Expense assets* –No depreciation –Nonrecognition of capital inflows as revenues –Nonrecognition of volunteer services –Programmatic reporting Managerial controls (Type M2): –Fixed budget –Predetermined expenditures –Encumbrances accounting

*Assets are charged as expenditures when they are accrued.

The programs that fall into cell B are those characterized by private services offered by nonclubs. These can be self-sustaining or cost-recovery programs (cell B1), or they can be subsidized programs (cell B2). Some examples are child care, low-cost housing and visiting-nurse services. The programs have much in common with those in which clubs provide private goods. Resources can be shifted from one program to another because the resource providers do not dictate how their fees will be used. The fees that are generated often have to be used to recover a portion of the costs of long-term assets or obligations. The standard efficiency tests and cost-volume-profit analyses that are used by many business organizations are also useful for monitoring the programs. The business style of financial accounting and management controls outlined for cell A organizations are also appropriate for cell B1.

Nonclubs that provide private goods on a subsidized basis (cell B2) have more in common with nonclubs that provide collective goods. Resource providers can restrict the use of funds to a certain program and normally require programmatic reporting. Capital assets are usually funded through a separate grant or fundraising drive, and therefore the NPO's operations are not expected to contribute toward their acquisition. Entity reporting and interperiod allocations may actually distort the picture for users of the financial statements of such an entity. Although costs can be accumulated on a per-unit basis, the revenues are not volume-driven. The expenditures need to be controlled so that they do not exceed the donations or grants received. The financial accounting and managerial controls appropriate for cell D organizations are also relevant for organizations or programs that fall into cell B2.

Cell C programs are characterized by collective services provided by clubs. Pure examples of such programs include those offered by condominium associations, restricted neighbourhood swimming pools, and local hockey associations. Organizations that otherwise belong in cell A also may conduct programs that fall into this cell (see, for example, the discussion of the CICA earlier). The collective services are intended to benefit the club's members, either directly or indirectly. As discussed earlier, members need allocation accounting in order to see whether the club has provided good value for the membership year. For example, suppose a rifle association that wants to change gun legislation sponsors a two-year publicity program. The startup costs should not be charged fully in the startup year because club members will not receive the full benefit in that year; instead, the costs should be allocated to the years in which the program is placed before the public. Entity accounting continues to be appropriate for the programs in this cell, because the club controls the allocation of funds between the provision of private goods and collective goods. An exception arises when a club is given a lot of money for restricted purposes by an external donor; for such purposes, programmatic reporting is appropriate.

Recently, those who set accounting standards have tended to focus on the similarities between NPO and business transactions, to assume the pre-eminence of net income determination, and to assume that an entity approach to reporting is essential. Businesses, however, do not initiate the production of collective goods—only governments and NPOs do. Requiring NPOs to adopt reporting practices that have evolved for business is like trying to bash a square peg into a round hole, forcing collective goods into a framework intended for private goods. We believe this accounts for the reluctance of users to support the proposals. For example, the FASB has had to defer repeatedly the introduction of its Statement No. 93, which would require all NPOs to use depreciation accounting.[13] To gain general acceptance of NPO accounting standards, we need a conceptual framework that both explains the evolution of GAAP for NPOs and provides a prescription for accounting practice in specific situations. Falk provides such a framework. We have elaborated on his basic approach and have melded it with some ideas suggested by Anthony. We think this framework will be helpful, but we'll have to wait to see whether standard-setters agree.

---

[13]Statement of Financial Accounting Standards No. 93: "Recognition of depreciation by not-for-profit organizations," FASB, 1987.